THE · URBAN · WORLD

THIRD EDITION

THE · URBAN · WORLD

J. JOHN PALEN
Virginia Commonwealth University

McGraw-Hill Book Company
New York   St. Louis   San Francisco   Auckland   Bogotá   Hamburg
London   Madrid   Mexico   Milan   Montreal   New Delhi
Panama   Paris   São Paulo   Singapore   Sydney   Tokyo   Toronto

THE URBAN WORLD

3 4 5 6 7 8 9 0 DOCDOC 8 9 4 3 2 1 0 9

ISBN 0-07-048111-3

Library of Congress Cataloging-in-Publication Data

Palen, J. John.
  The urban world.

  Bibliography: p.
  Includes indexes.
  1. Cities and towns.   2. Cities and towns—United States.   3. Urbanization—Developing countries.
I. Title.
HT151.P283   1987   307.7′6   86-12804
ISBN 0-07-048111-3

Credits for Part Opening Photographs

Part I: Joan Menschenfreund/Taurus Photos
Part II: Tom Ebenhoh/Black Star
Part III: Bernard Pierre Wolff/Photo Researchers
Part IV: Michal Heron/Woodfin Camp & Assoc.
Part V: Richard Kalvar/Magnum
Part VI: Art Seitz/Black Star

The cover photograph is from Chris Morris, Black Star.

This book was set in Times Roman by Monotype Composition Company, Inc.
The editor was Barbara L. Raab; the cover was designed by Tana Klughertz;
the production supervisor was Leroy A. Young.
Project supervision was done by The Total Book.
The photo editor was Inge King.
R. R. Donnelley & Sons Company was printer and binder.

ABOUT THE AUTHOR

J. John Palen is Professor of Sociology and Chairperson at Virginia Common-wealth University. His primary research interests are patterns of neighborhood revitalization and gentrification in the United States, and comparative urbanization in Southeast Asia. Urban focused publications by Professor Palen include *Gentrification Displacement and Revitalization* (co-editor with Bruce London, State University of New York Press, 1984), and *City Scenes* (Little Brown, 1981). Palen enjoys hiking in Virginia's Blue Ridge Mountains, canoeing, and observing the street life in any large city.

For Joseph, Beth and Ellen,
who are growing up in an urban world

CONTENTS

Part One: Focus and Development

Part Two: American Urbanization

Part Three: Urban Life

Part Four: Urban Problems and Planning

Part Five: Worldwide Urbanization

Part Six: Conclusion

LIST
OF SPECIAL SECTIONS

PREFACE

Urbanism has become the American way of life; residence in an urban area being the norm. The overwhelming majority of those reading this book have been life-long residents of either central cities or surrounding suburbs and are now in college studying for urban professions and occupations. We can thus predict with reasonable certainty that their future lives will be spent in, and intimately bound up with, urban areas. Both intellectual and practical concerns thus demand that we know as much as possible about the nature of our cities and how urban areas have changed and can be expected to change over time.

The third edition reflects the range and depth of these changes since 1981. While keeping the same basic organization, every chapter has been revised and new chapters added. The goal is to give the student having little formal exposure to urban sociology and related urban studies a coherent overview of the changing urban scene by providing the most up-to-date information on urbanization and the nature of urban life. Of course selectivity is both inevitable and necessary. The topics included and the emphasis they receive reflect in part the state of social science knowledge, in part my own interests, and in part a conscious effort to provide for the needs of students with different backgrounds and interests.

There has also been a conscious attempt to explore emerging developments. A textbook need not rehash the tired issues of decades past. It should reflect contemporary debates. A new chapter discussing the social environment of the city has been added. The third edition also includes thorough discussion of develoments such as the comeback of downtown areas, gentrification, non-metropolitan growth, Sunbelt cities, northern revival, and black suburbanization.

Finally, the third edition retains its cross cultural emphasis looking beyond the confines of the United States. There is increased emphasis on urbanization and urban planning in socialist countries and an updated chapter on Asian developments.

The book consists of eighteen chapters divided into six parts. Part One "Focus and Development" consists of two chapters. Chapter 1, "The Urban World" provides an introduction to the urban explosion and sets the scene for the chapters to follow. Chapter 2, "Emergence of Cities" provides a framework for describing and analyzing the early growth and development of urban places. The emphasis is on providing a perspective for understanding the changes in our contemporary society. The influence of technology, population growth, and environmental considerations are stressed.

Part Two, "American Urbanization" is substantially revised. It contains three chapters on the development and contemporary changes in American urbanization. Chapter 3, "The Rise of Urban America" provides the students with knowledge of the historical patterns of North American urbanization. Chapter 4 "Ecology and Structure of American Cities" concentrates on current patterns of urbanization and theories developed to account for changes in urban structure. Traditional ecological models as well as social area analysis and factoral analysis are discussed. The chapter stresses how physical patterns reflect social organization. Chapter 5, "Metropolitan Nonmetropolitan, and Sunbelt Growth" discusses metropolitan trends in the United States.

Part Three, "Urban Life" includes three chapters on the social, social psychological, ethnic, and racial aspects of differing urban ways of life. Chapter 6, "City Life-Styles," discusses theories regarding the consequences of urban living and the varying lifestyles of different urban communities. Chapter 7, "Social Environment of the City: Strangers, Neighbors, Crowding, and Crime," is new and deals with how urban dwellers cope with suposed urban problems. Chapter 8, "Patterns of Suburbanization" examines suburban lifestyles and has material on growing black suburbanization and community attempts at managing integration. Chapter 9, "Ethnic Diversity: Ethnics, Blacks, Hispanics, Indians, and Asians" is largely revised and contains material on our newest urban immigrants from Southeast Asia.

Part Four, "Urban Problems and Planning" discusses changes in American cities and ways of planning for the future. Chapter 10, "Urban Crisis or Urban Rebirth" is substantially new and takes a fresh look at the question of urban crisis. Considerable discussion of neighborhood revitalization and gentrification is also provided. Chapter 11, "Housing Programs and Urban Change" provides new material on the status of housing in the 1980s including federal programs, abandonment, urban homesteading and tax credits. Chapter 12, "Planning in Europe: With Discussion of New Towns" includes considerable new material on Holland, Germany, and Scandinavia. An updated discussion of urban policies and housing in the Soviet Union as well as material on changes in New Towns in England, Holland, and Scandinavia is included. Chapter 13, "Planning in the United States" reviews this country's planning experience and evaluates American New Town efforts.

Part Five, "Worldwide Urbanization" consists of four chapters discussing the urban explosion in the third world, and the different regional responses to resulting urban problems. In spite of the fact that developing countries will account for 90 percent of all urban growth between now and the turn of the century most urban texts still largely ignore developing nations or at most lump them all together in a single chapter.

Chapter 14, "Less Developed Countries: Overview and Common Problems" looks at the effects of the urban explosion, squatter settlements, primacy, and overurbanization. Modernization and dependency theories are contrasted. Chapter 15, "Asian Urban Patterns" includes new material on Bombay, Calcutta and Beijing. The effect of China's "responsibility system" on cities is extensively discussed. Chapter 16, "African and Middle Eastern Urbanization" looks at the effects of the 1980s population growth on city life. The impact of colonial patterns and history on contemporary urbanization is stressed. Chapter 17, "Urbanization in Latin America" discusses the impact of the continent's colonial past both on urban design and city life. Life in squatter settlements and the effect of immigrants on the city and the city on immigrants is detailed.

The conclusion, "Toward the Urban Future" is largely new. After briefly recapitulating some of the century's major urban trends it discusses the role of technology in producing a wired society. Changes in housing trends, population distribution and government policies are discussed. The conclusion also includes discussion of several plans and speculations about what the city will or might be like in the future.

Reviewers play an important role in the development of a manuscript and I would like to thank a number of colleagues for their careful and critical reading of the third edition—specifically Gary Crester, William Cross, Tom Drabek, William Engelman, Christen Jonassen, Michael Lang, Alex Muntean, John Stahura, and Ralph Thomlinson. Contributions to earlier editions were made by Ed Borgatta, Harvey Choldin, Scott Greer, George Hesslink, Ephraim Mizruchi, and Leo Schnore. Special thanks go to Barbara Raab as editor, Annette Bodzin as project supervisor, and Inge King as photo editor. It was a pleasure to work with such professionals. All errors of omission and commission are solely my responsibility.

J. John Palen

THE · URBAN · WORLD

PART ONE

FOCUS
AND
DEVELOPMENT

CHAPTER

1

THE URBAN WORLD

A city is a collective body of persons sufficient in themselves for all purposes of life.

Aristotle, Politics

INTRODUCTION: THE PROCESS OF URBANIZATION

The human species has been on this globe for perhaps a couple of million years, according to archeologists, but for the overwhelming number of these millennia humans have lived in a world without cities. Cities and urban places, in spite of our acceptance of them as an inevitable consequence of human life, are in the eyes of history a comparatively recent social invention, having existing a scant 7,000 to 9,000 years. Their period of social, economic, and cultural dominance is even shorter. Nonetheless, the era of cities encompasses the totality of the period we label "civilization." The saga of wars, architecture, and art—almost the whole of what we know of human triumphs and tragedies— is encompassed within that period. The story of human social and cultural development—and regression—is in major part the tale of the cities that have been built and the lives that have been lived within them. The very terms "civilization" and "civilized" come from the Latin *civis,* which means a person living in a city.

The vital and occasionally magnificent cities of the past, however, existed as islands in an overwhelmingly rural sea. Less than 200 years ago, in the year 1800, the population of the world was still 97 percent rural.[1] By the beginning of the twentieth century, the world was still 86 percent rural. The proportion of the world's population in cities of 100,000 or more had increased to 5.5 percent, and 13.6 percent lived in places of 5,000 or more. While cities were growing very rapidly, most people still lived in the countryside or small villages. England was the first country to undergo the urban transformation. A century ago it was the world's only predominately urban country.[2] Not until 1920 did the United States have half its population residing in urban places.

By the 1980s this had changed radically. Today we are on the threshold of living in a world that for the first time will be numerically more urban than rural. Currently, some 45 percent of the world's population is urban. This will increase to over half by the year 2000 (Table 1-1).[3]

The rapidity of the change from rural to urban life is as important as the degree of urbanization. As of 1850, not a single country was as urban as the world is today. The highly urban United States did not even reach the present level of world urbanization until around World War I. Between 1920 and 1980 alone, the world's urban population quadrupled.

Because we live in an urban world where the mega-metropolis Tokyo-Yokohoma already has a population of over 20 million and greater New York has over 16 million, and because almost all of us have spent at least part of our lives in central cities or their surrounding suburbs, it is difficult for us to conceive of a world without numerous large cities. The rapidity and extent of the urban revolution can perhaps be understood if one reflects that if metro-

---

[1]As of 1800, only 1.7 percent of the world's population resided in places of 100,000 or more, 2.4 percent in places of 20,000 or more, and 3 percent in communities of 5,000 or larger. Philip Hauser and Leo Schnore (eds.), *The Study of Urbanization,* Wiley, New York, 1965, p. 7.

[2]Adna Ferrin Weber, *The Growth of Cities in the Nineteenth Century,* Cornell University Press, Ithaca, N.Y., 1899, table 3.

[3]Philip Hauser and Robert Gardner, "Urban Future: Trends and Prospects," in Philip Hauser et al., *Population and the Urban Future,* U.N. Fund for Population Activities, SUNY Press, Albany, N.Y., 1982, pp. 10–11.

TABLE 1-1
Percent of Urbanization by World Regions, 1920, 1950, 1980, 1990, 2000

Region	1920	1950	1980	1990	2000
World	19.4	28.4	41.3	45.9	51.3
More developed countries	38.7	51.8	70.7	75.9	80.3
Less developed countries	8.4	16.2	30.5	36.3	42.5
Africa	7.0	14.4	28.9	35.7	42.5
Latin America	22.4	40.6	64.8	70.7	75.2
North America	51.9	63.8	73.7	77.2	80.8
Asia	8.8	15.7	27.4	32.3	38.9
East Asia	9.0	16.0	33.1	38.6	45.4
South Asia	8.5	15.5	23.1	28.1	34.9
Europe	46.2	55.2	75.9	82.4	88.4
Oceania	47.1	60.6	75.7	80.4	82.9
Australia-New Zealand	60.6	74.3	81.5	82.8	83.7
Soviet Union	16.1	39.3	64.8	71.3	76.1

Source: United Nations, Dept. of Economic and Social Affairs, *Patterns of Urban and Rural Population Growth.* No. 68, 1980.

politan Indianapolis, Indiana (1980 population, 1.2 million), had had the same population two centuries ago, it would have been the largest urban agglomeration that had ever existed in the world at any time.[4]

According to the United Nations, as of 1980 there were 235 cities worldwide of one million or more inhabitants. Most spectacular have been the changes in the cities of economically less developed countries. It is difficult for us to keep up either intellectually or emotionally with these changes. Already there are some 118 cities of over one million in population in less developed nations, and the United Nations projects that there will be 284 such cities by the year 2000. Few of us could name more than a handful of such places. Since 1950 there has been a tenfold increase in the population living in such cities. By the year 2000, the United Nations projects a population of 26.3 million for Mexico City (over three times its present size), 24 million for São Paulo, Brazil, 16.6 million for Calcutta, and 16.3 million for greater Cairo.

Living as we do in such an urban world, it is easy for us to forget two important facts: (1) Over half the world's population is still rural-based, and (2) even in the industrialized west, massive urbanization is a recent phenomenon. Some of our difficulty in understanding or coping with urban patterns and problems can be attributed to the recency of the emergence of our contemporary urban world. As noted earlier, urbanization has accelerated until today, for the first time, we are on the threshold of living in a world that is numerically more urban than rural. Barely over a decade from now the majority of the world's population will be living in urban rather than rural places. This rapid transformation from a basically rural to a heavily urbanized

[4]The best source of data for cities in earlier eras is Tertius Chandler and Gerald Fox, *3000 Years of Urban Growth*, Academic Press, New York, 1974.

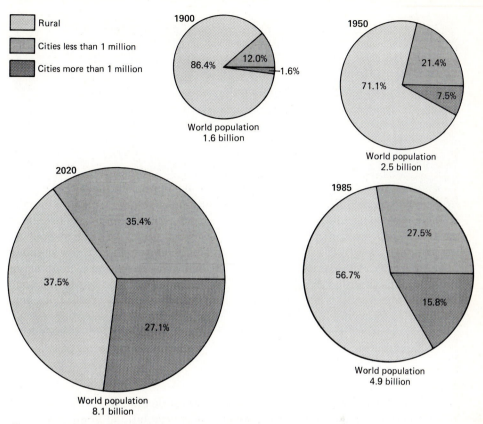

Figure 1-1. Patterns of Urbanization, 1900–2020. (*From Kingsley Davis*, International Technical Cooperation Centre Review (7172); World Facts and Figures (1985); *United Nations Population Division; and Population Reference Bureau.*)

world and the development of urbanism as a way of life have been far more dramatic and spectacular than the much better known population explosion.

THE HISTORY OF URBAN EXPLOSION

Urban growth, which began to explode during the latter part of the eighteenth century, accelerated cumulatively during the nineteenth and twentieth centuries. By 1800 the population of London had reached almost 1 million, Paris exceeded 500,000, and Vienna and St. Petersburg had each reached 200,000. As this century began, ten cities had reached or exceeded 1 million: London, Paris, Vienna, Moscow, St. Petersburg, Calcutta, Tokyo, New York, Chicago, and Philadelphia. Today, the number of people living in cities outnumbers the entire population of the world 150 years ago. This urban explosion, which will be discussed in greater detail later, occurred for a number of reasons. Among

Tokyo is one of the world's great cities, with all the clamor, confusion, and opportunities that suggests. (James Holland/Stock, Boston)

the more important reasons were (1) declining death rates, (2) scientific
management of agriculture, (3) improved transportation and communication
systems, (4) stable political governments, and (5) the development of the
industrial revolution. While details differ from country to country, the pattern
for western nations is similar. Agriculture raised the surplus above previous
subsistence levels. Then, in rather short order, this extra margin was transferred
by entrepreneurs, and later by governments, into the manufacturing sector.[5]
The result was urban expansion and growth fed by a demand by the burgeoning
manufacturing, commercial, and service sectors for a concentrated labor force.

Whichever stereotypes we embrace, whether we are delighted by the
variety and excitement of urban life or horrified by the cities' anonymity and
occasional brutality, population concentration—that is, urbanization—is
increasingly becoming the way of life in developing as well as developed
nations. Attempts to return to a supposedly simpler rural past must be
considered futile escapism. Images of a pastoral utopia where all exist in rural
bliss have no chance of becoming reality. We live in an urban world; and for
all our complaints about it, few would reverse the clock.

[5]*Urbanization in the Second United Nations Development Decade*, United Nations, New York, 1970, p. 6.

DEFINING URBAN AREAS

Before proceeding further, it is necessary to define some of the terms we will be using.

This is not altogether as simple as it might seem, since countries differ in what they mean when they call a place "urban." About thirty definitions of "urban population" are currently in use, none of them totally satisfactory.[6]

Urban settlements have been defined on the basis of an urban culture (a cultural definition), administrative functions (a political definition), the percentage of people in nonagricultural occupations (an economic definition), and the size of the population (a demographic definition). In the United States, we define places as "urban" by using population criteria along with some geographic and political elements.

Let us look briefly at some of the criteria that can be used. In terms of cultural criteria, a city is "a state of mind, a body of customs and traditions."[7] The city thus is the place, as sociologists put it, where relations are "gesellschaft" ("society" or formal role relationships) rather than "gemeinschaft" ("community" or primary relationships) and forms of social organization are organic rather than mechanical. In short, the city is large, culturally heterogeneous, and socially diverse. It is the antithesis of "folk society." The problem with the cultural definitions of an urban place is the difficulty of measurement; for example, if a city is a state of mind, who can ever say where the boundaries of the urban area lie?

Economic standards have also been used in defining what is urban. In terms of economic criteria, a country has sometimes been described as urban if less than half its workers are engaged in agriculture. Here "urban" and "nonagricultural" are taken to be synonymous. This distinction, of course, tells us nothing about the degree of urbanization or its pattern of spatial distribution within the country. A distinction has also been made between the town as the center for processing and service functions and the countryside as the area for producing raw materials.[8] However, it is becoming increasingly difficult to distinguish among areas by means of such criteria. How far out do the producing and service functions of a New York or a Los Angeles extend?

Politically, a national government may define its urban areas as such in terms of administrative functions. The difficulty is that there is no agreement internationally on what the political or administrative criteria shall be. In many countries small administrative centers are recognized as urban regardless of their population or economic significance. Kenya, for example, has a number of "urban" administrative centers with populations well under 2,000, and the same is true of a number of other countries.

[6]Milos Macura, "The Influence of the Definition of Urban Place on the Size of Urban Population," in Jack Gibbs (ed.), *Urban Research Methods,* Van Nostrand, New York, 1961, pp. 21–31.
[7]Robert E. Park, "The City: Suggestions for the Investigation of Human Behavior in the Urban Environment," in Robert E. Park, E. W. Burgess, and Roderick D. McKenzie (eds.), *The City,* University of Chicago Press, Chicago, 1925.
[8]Amos H. Hawley, *Human Ecology: A Theory of Community Structure,* Ronald Press, New York, 1950, p. 245.

Finally, size of population is used frequently as a criterion in deciding what is urban and what is not. Demographically, a place is defined as being urban because a certain number of people live in it. Measurement and comparison of rural and urban populations within a country are relatively simple when demographic criteria are used, although the problem of making comparisons among nations still remains. Only 250 persons are necessary to qualify an area as urban in Denmark, while 10,000 are needed in Greece.

According to the definition adopted by the United States Bureau of the Census for the 1980 census, the urban population of the United States comprises all persons living in urbanized areas and all persons outside of urbanized areas who live in places of 2,500 or more. For practical purposes the urban population of the United States therefore includes anyone in a place having 2,500 or more inhabitants. By this definition, three-quarters of the United States population is urban.

The United Nations has attempted to bring some order out of the various national definitions by setting up its own classifications scheme, which it uses for publishing its international data. The definitions of the United Nations are as follows:

A *"big city"* is a locality with 500,000 or more inhabitants.
A *"city"* is a locality with 100,000 or more inhabitants.
An *"urban locality"* is a locality with 20,000 or more inhabitants.
A *"rural locality"* is a locality with less than 20,000 inhabitants.[9]

This is a reasonable classification scheme for less developed countries since it is rare that places under 20,000 have urban characteristics. The major limitation of the United Nations definition is not logical but practical: most of the more urbanized countries, such as the United States, simply do not use them, preferring to keep their own national definitions.[10] To make a complicated situation as simple as possible, this book will use the definitions established by the United States when presenting data for the United States and the definitions established by the United Nations when presenting international data. The reader can thus assume that outside the United States, "urban" refers to the population in places of 20,000 or more.

According to the United Nations, the percentage of the population living in urban places varies from 2 percent in Burundi to 100 percent in the city-state of Singapore. Table 1-1 shows degrees of urbanization by world regions.

[9]*Demographic Handbook for Africa.* United Nations Economic Commission for Africa, Addis Ababa, 1968, p. 38.
[10]A team working under Kingsley Davis during the 1950s defined "metropolitan areas" for 720 of the then 1,046 areas in the world having at least 100,000 persons in their metropolitan areas and at least 50,000 in the central city (International Urban Research, *The World's Metropolitan Areas,* University of California Press, Berkeley, 1959). This system will be used in this text, since the United Nations system is far more widely accepted and provides more current data.

URBANIZATION AND URBANISM

As we will see in Part Five, Worldwide Urbanization, cities in the developing world are among the largest and the fastest growing in the world. Nevertheless, it must be kept in mind that the growth of cities and a high level of urbanization are not the same thing. In the western world the two things happened at the same time, but it is quite possible to find extremely large cities in overwhelmingly rural countries. Some of the world's largest cities—for example, Shanghai, Bombay, and Cairo—exist in nations that are still largely rural. A number of extremely large cities does not necessarily indicate an urban nation.

"Urbanization" refers to the changes in the proportion of the population of a nation living in urban places—that is, the process of people moving to cities or other densely settled areas. The term "urbanization" is also used to describe the changes in social organization that occur as a consequence of population concentration. Urbanization is thus a process—the process by which rural areas become transformed into urban areas. In demographic terms, urbanization is an increase in population concentration; organizationally, it is an alteration in structure and functions. Demographically, urbanization involves two elements: the multiplication of points of concentration, and the increase in the size of individual concentrations.[11]

"Urbanization," described demographically as the percentage of a nation's total population living in urban areas, is a process that clearly has a beginning and an end. For instance, three-quarters of the United States population of 240 million is now urban; the maximum level of urbanization is probably somewhere around 90 percent. (Places that comprise only city, such as Singapore, can be 100 percent urban.) However, even after a nation achieves a high level of urbanization, its cities and metropolitan areas can continue to grow. This is clearly the case in North America and western Europe. While there is a limit to the percentage of urbanization possible, it is not yet known what the practical limit is on the size of cities or metropolitan areas.

While "urbanization" has to do with metropolitan growth, "urbanism" refers to the conditions of life associated with living in cities.[12] Urbanism, with its changes in the values, mores, customs, and behaviors of a population, is often seen as one of the consequences of urbanization.[13]

Under the conceptual label "urbanism" is found research concerning the social psychological aspects of urban life, urban personality patterns, and the behavioral adaptations required by city life. Urbanism as a way of life receives detailed treatment in Chapters 6, 7, and 8, City Life-styles, Social Environment of the City, and Patterns of Suburbanization, as well as in later chapters, particularly those on developing areas.

---

[11]Hope Tisdale Eldridge, "The Process of Urbanization," in J. J. Spengler and O. D. Duncan (eds.), *Demographic Analysis,* Free Press, Glencoe, Ill., 1956, pp. 338–343.
[12]Paul Meadows and Ephraim Mizruchi (eds.), *Urbanism, Urbanization, and Change: Comparative Perspectives,* Addison-Wesley, Reading, Mass., 1969, p. 4.
[13]Leo Schnore, "Urbanization and Economic Development, The Demographic Contribution," *American Journal of Economics and Sociology,* **23**:37–48, 1964.

Gridlock is common in Cairo during rush hours. (B. P. Wolff/United Nations)

It should be noted, though, that it is possible for an area to have a high degree of urbanization and a low level of urbanism or—less commonly—a low level of urbanization and a high level of urbanism. Examples of the former can be found in the large cities of the developing world, where the city is filled with immigrants who now reside in an urban place but remain basically rural in outlook. Cairo is typical of developing cities in that over one-third of its residents were born outside the city. Many of these newcomers are urban in residence but remain rural in outlook and behavior.[14] On the other hand, if the urbanization process in the United States is now one of population decentralization, the United States might in the future have some decline in urbanization while urban life-styles become even more universal.[15]

The explicit belief in most older sociological writings—and an implicit premise in much of what is written about cities today—is that cities produce a characteristic way of life known as "urbanism." Moreover, urbanism as a way of life, while often successful economically, is said to produce personal alienation, social disorganization, and the whole range of ills falling under the cliché "the crisis of the cities."

A classic statement of the effects of urbanization on urban behavior

[14]See, for example, Janet Abu-Lughod, "Migrant Adjustment to City Life: The Egyptian Case," *American Journal of Sociology,* **67**:22–32, July, 1961.
[15]Brian J. L. Berry, "The Counterurbanization Process: Urban America since 1970," in *Urbanization and Counterurbanization,* Vol. II: *Urban Affairs Annual Reviews,* Sage Publications, Beverly Hills, Calif., 1976, pp. 17–39.

Cairo, like other exploding third world cities, combines traditional as well as modern elements. (B. P. Wolff/United Nations)

patterns is Louis Wirth's article "Urbanism as a Way of Life."[16] According to Wirth, "For sociological purposes a city may be defined as a relatively large, dense, permanent settlement of socially heterogeneous individuals."[17]

Wirth further suggested that these components of urbanization—size, density, and heterogeneity—are the independent variables that create a distinct way of life called "urbanism." Urbanism, with its emphasis on competition, achievement, specialization, superficiality, anonymity, independence, and tangential relationships, is often compared—at least implicity—with a simpler and less competitive idealized rural past. (The adequacy of this approach is addressed in detail in Chapter 6, City Life-styles.)

Today urbanism as a way of life is virtually universal in highly urbanized nations such as the United States, with their elaborate media and communi-

---

[16]Louis Wirth, "Urbanism as a Way of Life," *American Journal of Sociology*, **44**:1–24, July, 1938.
[17]Ibid, p. 8.

cations networks. The attitudes, behaviors, and cultural patterns of rural areas in the United States are dominated by urban values and life-styles. Rural wheat farmers, cattle ranchers, and dairy farmers—with their accountants, professional lobbies, and government subsidies—are all part of a complete and highly integrated agribusiness enterprise. They are hardly innocent country bumpkins being preyed upon by city slickers. By comparison, urban consumers often appear naive.

The degree to which urbanism has permeated every aspect of American culture was documented in Vidich and Bensman's study of an upstate New York hamlet with a population of 1,700. Their book, which they titled *Small Town in Mass Society,* presents a detailed and careful picture of how industrialization and bureaucratization have totally permeated the rural village.[18] Everything—from 4H clubs and Boy Scout and Girl Scout troops, through the American Legion and national churches, to university agriculture agents, the Social Security Administration, and marketing organizations to raise the price supports for milk—influenced how the village residents thought, acted, and lived. The town was totally dependent on outside political and economic institutions for its survival.

The small-towners, though, had an entirely different conception of themselves and their hamlet. They saw themselves as rugged individualists living in a town that, in contrast to outside city life, prided itself on friendliness, neighborliness, grass roots democracy, and independence. Their town was small, self-reliant, and friendly, while the city was large, coldly impersonal, and filled with welfare loafers. In spite of the absence of a viable local culture, and the clear division of the town by socioeconomic class differences, the myth of a unique rural life-style and social equality persisted. Small-town America is totally enmeshed in an urban economic and social system despite its pride in its independence of the city and cosmopolitan ways. The small town even relies on the mass media to help reaffirm its own fading self-image.[19] Today kids in both rural and urban areas follow the same TV and rock concert stars. There is no unique rural culture.

APPROACHES TO THE STUDY OF URBAN LIFE

Over the years cities have been studied by scholars in many different ways. Academics and others have concerned themselves with a wide variety of questions such as: why cities are located at particular places and not others; what the growth patterns of cities are; who lives in cities; how different ethnic and racial groups arrange themselves therein; how living in cities affects social relationships; and whether city living produces social problems.

If these, and numerous other questions addressed in this book, are to

[18]Arthur J. Vidich and Joseph Bensman, *Small Town in Mass Society,* Princeton University Press, Princeton, N.J., 1958.
[19]Maurice R. Stein, *The Eclipse of Community,* Princeton University Press, Princeton, N.J., 1961.

have meaning for the student, the questions have to be more than an ad hoc list of interesting topics. The material has to be related and organized in some general fashion in order to provide a common understanding and body of knowledge.

The material that follows can be categorized—with an occasional bit of squeezing—into two generalized approaches. The first approach is that of *urbanization*. Under urbanization are included those questions and issues dealing with the city as a spatial, economic, and political entity. This is often referred to by sociologists as the *human ecological* approach since it is broadly concerned with the interrelationship and interdependence of organisms and their environment. This urbanization or ecological approach has a long and proud history in sociology and is heavily utilized in Part One, Focus and Developments, and Part Two, American Urbanization. The urbanization or ecological focus is generally on the big picture. It tends strongly to be on the macro level, using cities—or, at its most micro level, neighborhoods—as its unit of analysis. A human ecologist, for example, might research the possibility of a predictable pattern of neighborhood change over time.

The second generalized approach of *urbanism* as a way of life, on the other hand, is far more micro level oriented. It focuses on small groups or individuals. This *sociocultural, social psychological,* or *psychosocial* approach focuses on how the experience of living in cities affects people's social relationships and personalities. The concern of this approach is primarily with the psychological, cultural, and social ramifications of city life. For example, one of the questions regarding the social psychological impact of city life that we will examine in some detail is whether living in a city, suburb, or rural area produces differences in personalities, socialization patterns, or even levels of pathology. To put it in oversimplified form, are city dwellers different?

Historically, urban ecologists and urban social psychologists have gone their own way, while largely ignoring their opposite numbers. Textbooks also sometimes perpetuate the division by all but ignoring the alternative approach. This is unfortunate, for the perspectives complement each other in the same way that the social science disciplines of political science, economics, and sociology provide alternative focuses and approaches. This book, while written by one trained in the urban ecology tradition, makes a conscious effort to understand better the patterns of metropolitan areas and of the lives of those of us living within them. For this it is necessary to have some understanding both of urbanization and of urbanism as a way of life, or if you prefer the alternate terminology, urban ecology and social psychology.

CONCEPTS OF THE CITY

Urban Change and Confusion

The scientific study of urbanism and urbanization is a relative newcomer to the academic scene. Systematic empirical examination of cities and city life only began somewhat over half a century ago during a period in which American cities were experiencing considerable transformation in terms of both industrialization and a massive influx of immigrants from the rural areas of Europe and the American south. To many observers of the time, the city, with its emphasis on efficiency, technology, and division of labor, was undermining simpler rural forms of social organization. The social consequences were disorganization, depersonalization, and the breakdown of traditional norms and values. An anonymous poem of 1916, called "While the City Sleeps," mirrors this typical view of urban life:

> Stand in your window and scan the sights,
> On Broadway with its bright white lights.
> Its dashing cabs and cabarets,
> Its painted women and fast cafes.
> That's when you really see New York.
> Vulgar of manner, overfed,
> Overdressed and underbred.
> Heartless and Godless, Hell's delight,
> Rude by day and lewd by night.

Rural Simplicity versus Urban Complexity

In the usual description of the transition from simple to complex forms of social organization, there is, at least implicitly, a time frame in which rural areas represent the past and traditional values, and the city represents the future with its emphasis on technology, division of labor, and emergence of new values. Such a picture of a fast-paced, alienating, stimulating, and anonymous city life along with the contrasting romanticized picture of the warm, personal, and well-adjusted rural life is, of course, a stereotype. There are some indications that the actual case may even be the opposite. With the exception of the largest cities, Fischer found, for example, that on a worldwide scale there is greater evidence of rural as opposed to urban dissatisfaction, unhappiness, despair, and melancholy.[20]

Research by Palen and Johnson on the relationship between urbanization and health status in nineteenth- and twentieth-century American cities found that inhabitants of large cities were rather consistently healthier than inhabitants of rural areas or small towns.[21] Contrary to the stereotype, mental health is also probably superior in the city, and possibly is improving in Manhattan.[22]

Social Theory and Urban Change

The cleavage between the city and the countryside is, of course, not a uniquely American idea. The great European social theorists of the nineteenth century

---

[20]Claude S. Fischer, "Urban Malaise," *Social Forces*, **52**(2):221, December, 1973.
[21]J. John Palen and Daniel Johnson, "Urbanization and Health Status," in Ann and Scott Greer (eds.), *Cities and Sickness*, Sage Publications, Beverly Hills, 1983, pp. 25–54.
[22]Leo Srole, "Mental Health in New York," *The Sciences*, **20**:16–29, 1980.

Physical changes and social changes often proceed at different paces. In La Paz, Bolivia Indian women still dress in traditional fashion. (Beryl Goldberg)

described the social changes that were then taking place in terms of a shift from a warm, supportive community based on kinship in which common aims are shared to a larger, more impersonal society in which ties are based not on kinship but on interlocking economic, political, and other interests. These views had, and continue to have, profound impact on sociological thought.

European Theorists. Many of the core ideas of the classical Chicago school writings of the 1920s and 1930s were based implicitly on the thoughts of late nineteenth- and early twentieth-century European social theorists. Of these, the most influential were the Germans Ferdinand Tönnies (1855–1936), Karl Marx (1818–1883), Max Weber (1864–1920), and Georg Simmel (1858–1918) and the Frenchman Emile Durkheim (1858–1917).

These theorists sought to explain the twin changes of industrialization and urbanization that were undermining the small-scale, traditional, rural-based communities of Europe. All about, they saw the crumbling of old economic patterns, social customs, and family organization. The growth of urbanization was bringing in its wake new urban ways of life.

The changes were presented by the theorists in terms of dichotomous typologies of logical constructs which sociologists refer to as "ideal types." One of these ideal types was a model of rural society; its opposite number was urban society. For Marx, the shift was from a feudal society to the new, urban, property-owning bourgeoisie. (Since a bourg is a town, a bourgeois is by definition a town dweller.) According to Marx:

> The greatest division of material and mental labour is the separation of town and country. The antagonism between town and country begins with the transition from barbarism to civilization, from tribe to State, from locality to nation, and runs through the whole history of civilization to the present day. . ... Here first became the division of the population into two great classes, which is directly based on the division of labour and on the instruments of production.[23]

In early urban sociology Tönnies had perhaps the greatest impact with his elaborate discussions of the shift from "gemeinschaft"—a community based on ties of blood or kinship—to "gesellschaft"—a society or association based on economic, political, or other interests.[24] In rural gemeinschaft people were bound together by common values and by family and kinship ties, and they worked together for the common goal. At the gesellschaft pole of the typology, on the other hand, personal relationships count for little, with money and contract replacing sentiment. For Tönnies this change arose as a consequence of the growth of money-based capitalism. Further, he saw this evolutionary change as inevitable, but not desirable. Tönnies mourned the increasing loss of community.

Others were more positive regarding urban life. The great French sociologist Emile Durkheim similarly saw societies moving from a commonality of tasks and outlook to a complex division of labor. Societies based on shared sentiments and tasks were said to possess "mechanical solidarity," while those based on integrating different but complementary economic and social functions were said to possess "organic solidarity."[25] In Durkheim's view, the collective conscience of rural society is replaced by a complex division of labor in urban society. Some of the same concepts can be found in the distinction made by the German sociologist Max Weber. Weber's distinction was between "traditional society" based upon ascription and "rational society" based on the "technical superiority" of formalized and impersonal bureaucracy.[26]

More psychologically oriented than these theorists was Georg Simmel, whose famous essay "The Metropolis and Mental Life" concentrated on how urbanization increases individuals' alienation and mental isolation.[27] Simmel saw the city as a place of intense stimuli that stimulated freedom but forced the city dweller to become blasé and calculating in order to survive. Simmel's ideas are discussed further in Part Three, Urban Life.

[23]Karl Marx and Friedrich Engels, *The German Ideology*, R. Pascal (trans.), International Publishers, New York, 1947, pp. 68–69.
[24]Ferdinand Tönnies, *Community and Society*, Charles P. Loomis (trans.), Harper and Row, New York, 1963.
[25]Emile Durkheim, *The Division of Labor in Society*, George Simpson (trans.), Free Press, Glencove, Ill., 1960.
[26]H. H. Gerth and C. Wright Mills (trans. and ed.), *Max Weber, Essays in Sociology*, Oxford University Press, New York, 1966.
[27]Georg Simmel, "The Metropolis and Mental Life," in Kurt Wolff (trans.), *The Sociology of Georg Simmel*, Free Press, New York, 1964.

Finally, a twentieth-century version of the dichotomy between rural and urban places is the distinction made by the anthropologist Robert Redfield between what he characterized as "folk" and "urban" societies. Folk peasant societies were described as being:

> . . . small, isolated, non-literate, and homogeneous, with a strong sense of group solidarity. The ways of living are conventionalized into that coherent system which we call "a culture." Behavior is traditional, spontaneous, uncritical, and personal; there is no legislation, or habit of experiment and reflection for intellectual ends. Kinship, its relationships and institutions, are the type categories of experience and the familial group is the unit of action. The sacred prevails over the secular; the economy is one of status rather than market.[28]

Interestingly, Redfield never did fully define "urban life," simply saying that it was the opposite of folk society.

Assumptions. The theoretical frameworks described above contain three general assumptions: (1) The evolutionary movement from simple rural to complex urban is unilinear, (2) modern urban life stresses achievement over ascription, and (3) the characteristics of the city apply to urban areas as a whole. As you read through this text, note whether these assumptions are supported or rejected. These models have at least an implicit evolutionary framework: Societies follow a unilinear path of development from simple rural to complex urban. Rural areas and ways of life typify the past, while the city is the mirror to the future. This change is assumed to be both inevitable and irreversible.

A subset of the belief that the city fosters secondary- rather than primary-group relationships is the unspoken but often implicit value judgment that the old ways were better, or at least more humane. The city is presented as more efficient, but the inevitable price of efficiency is the breakdown of meaningful social relationships. The countryside exemplifies stable rules, roles, and relationships, while the city is characterized by innovation, experimentation, flexibility, and disorganization. In cultural terms the small town represents continuity, conformity, and stability, while the big city stands for heterogeneity, variety, and originality. In terms of personality, country folk are supposed to be neighborly people who help one another—they lack the sophistication of city slickers but also lack the city dweller's guile. In short, country folk are "real," while city people are artificial and impersonal.

Fortunately, the newly emerging discipline of urban sociology did not calcify into explaining differences between the rural and the urban, but rather began to examine the urban scene empirically and systematically. Eventually the original dichotomy was abandoned, and hypotheses began to be developed on the basis of empirical research.

---

[28]Robert Redfield, "The Folk Society," *American Journal of Sociology,* **52:**53–73, 1947.

Robert Ezra Park (1864–1944), chairman of the University of Chicago's Sociology Department, guided scores of early urban students and developed the idea of using the city as a natural laboratory. (Courtesy American Sociological Association.)

The Chicago School. Early urban research is largely associated with a remarkable group of scholars connected with the University of Chicago during the 1920s and 1930s. The "Chicago school" found sociology a loose collection of untested theories, interesting facts, social work, and social reform. It converted sociology into an established academic discipline and an emerging science.[29]

Foremost among the Chicago school pioneers was Robert Park (1864–1944), who emphasized not moral preachments about the sins of the city, but detailed empirical observation. Park, who had been a newspaper reporter among other things, remained constantly fascinated by the city, and passed his enthusiasm on to several generations of graduate students. He was also most interested in how the supposed chaos of the city actually was underlaid by a pattern of systematic social and spatial organization.[30]

Early empirical sociologists, studying under Park, described the effects of urbanization on immigrant and rural newcomers to the city, and the emergence of "urbanization as a way of life." Works such as *The Polish Peasant in Europe and America, The Ghetto, The Jack Roller,* and *The Gold Coast and the Slum* are minor classics describing the effects of urbanization.[31]

---

[29]For an evaluation of the Chicago legacy, see Lyn H. Lofland, "Understanding Urban Life: The Chicago Legacy," *Urban Life,* **11**:491–511, 1983.

[30]Robert E. Park, "The City: Suggestions for the Investigation of Human Behaviour in the Urban Environment," in Robert Park, E. W. Burgers, and Roderick McKenzie (eds.), *The City,* University of Chicago Press, Chicago, 1925.

[31]William I. Thomas and Florian Zhaniecki, *The Polish Peasant in Europe and America,* 5 vols., University of Chicago Press, Chicago, 1918–1920; Louis Wirth, *The Ghetto,* University of Chicago Press, Chicago, 1928; Clifford R. Shaw, *The Jack Roller,* University of Chicago Press, Chicago, 1930; and Harvey W. Zorbaugh, *The Gold Coast and the Slum,* University of Chicago Press, Chicago, 1929.

However, it remained for Louis Wirth (1897–1952), a student of Park's, to consolidate and expressly formulate how the size, density, and heterogeneous nature of cities produce a unique urban way of life. Wirth's essay "Urbanism as a Way of Life" remains the most influential essay in urban studies.[32] Wirth suggested that large cities inevitably produce a host of changes that, although economically productive, are destructive of family life and close social interaction. Wirth's ideas are examined in detail in Chapter 6, City Life-styles.

For now, however, let us temporarily put aside the questions of the social psychology of city living and focus our primary attention on the spatial and social ecology of urban places. We will begin our discussion of the urbanization process by examining how and why cities have come into existence.

[32]Louis Wirth, "Urbanism as a Way of Life," *American Journal of Sociology*, **44**:1–24, July, 1938.

CHAPTER

2

EMERGENCE OF CITIES

Men come together in cities for security; they stay together for the good life.

Aristotle

INTRODUCTION

This chapter outlines the growth of urban life from the first tentative agricultural villages to the industrial cities of the nineteenth century. Our goal is not to memorize a series of dates and places, but rather to develop some understanding of the process of urban development. Archeological, anthropological, and historical material is included, not because there is anything sacred about beginnings as such, but because having some understanding of the origin and function of cities helps us to better understand contemporary cities and how and why they got to be what they are today.

THE ECOLOGICAL COMPLEX

In this and the following chapters we shall be implicitly using an ecosystem framework, particularly the conceptual scheme of the ecological complex. An "ecosystem" can be defined as a natural unit in which there is an interaction of an environmental and a biotic system—that is, a community together with its habitat. At the upper extreme, the whole earth is a world ecosystem.[1]

Urban ecologists study urban growth patterns in terms of changes in the system, using a set of categories known as the "ecological complex." In basic terms, the ecological complex identifies the relationship between four concepts or classes of variables: population, organization, environment, and technology. These variables are frequently referred to by the acronym "POET."

"Population" refers not only to the number of people but also to growth or contraction through either migration or natural increase. An example of the first is the growth of Houston from 1975 to 1985 through immigration from frost belt cities. "Population" also refers to the composition of the population by variables such as age, sex, and race.

"Organization" or social structure is the way urban populations are organized according to social stratification, the political system, and the economic system. For example, one might want to examine the effect of Houston's political system and related tax system in encouraging population growth through immigration.

"Environment" refers to the natural environment (e.g., Houston's absence of snow) and the built environment. This latter includes streets and parks as well as buildings. "Technology" refers to tools, inventions, and techniques that directly impact on urban growth and form. Examples in Houston's case are the private automobile and air conditioning. Without these recent technological innovations, Houston would never have grown so rapidly.

The ecological complex thus reminds one of the interrelated properties of life in urban settings, and how each class of variables is related to and has implications for the others. Each of the four variables is causally interdependent; depending on the way a problem is stated, each may serve either as an

[1]See Lee R. Rice, *Man's Nature and Nature's Man: The Ecology of Human Communities,* University of Michigan Press, Ann Arbor, 1955, pp. 2–3.

independent (or thing-explaining) or a dependent (thing-to-be-explained) variable. In sociological research, "organization" is commonly viewed as the "dependent variable" to be influenced by the other three "independent variables," but a more sophisticated view of "organization" sees it as reciprocally related to the other elements of the ecological complex. In Otis Dudley Duncan's words: "These categories: population, organization, environment, and technology (P.O.E.T.), provide a somewhat arbitrary simplified way of identifying systems of relationships in a preliminary description of ecosystem process."[2]

Strengths

A major advantage of the ecological complex as a conceptual scheme is its simplicity, since economy of explanation is a basic scientific goal. If our interest is in social organization as the dependent variable—the thing to be explained—our focus is on how population, technology, and environment operate singly and jointly in the modification of urban social organization. For example, Otis Dudley Duncan, using the example of smog in Los Angeles, suggests that as transportation technology changed, the environment, organization, and population of the city also changed.[3] In Los Angeles a favorable natural environment led to large-scale increases in population, which resulted in organizational problems (civic and governmental) and technological changes (freeways and factories). These in turn led to environmental changes (smog), which resulted in organizational changes (new pollution laws), which in turn resulted in technological changes (antipollution devices on automobiles).[4]

This example illustrates how sociologists can use the conceptual scheme of the ecological complex to clarify significant sets of variables when studying urban growth patterns. Note, for example, the dominant importance of environmental factors in the first cities and how this in time is modified by technological and social inventions.

Limitations

A problem with the ecological complex is that the categories themselves are somewhat arbitrary, and so the boundaries between them are not always precise. The ecological complex, however, is simply a tool to help us better understand the interaction patterns within urban systems. It is not intended to be a fully developed theory of urbanization. Perhaps the greatest limitation of the original ecological complex is that it subsumes cultural values under the variable of organization, while a very strong case can be made that "culture" should be a separate reference variable in its own right. Another limitation is that the ecological complex as such does not explain how, when, to what degree, and under what circumstances the categories of variables interact.

[2]Otis Dudley Duncan, "From Social System to Ecosystem," *Sociological Inquiry*, **31**:145, 1961.
[3]Duncan, op. cit., pp. 140–149.
[4]Ibid.

Finally, it has been criticized, particularly by Marxists, for its lack of theoretical object.[5] It doesn't explain why the variables interact in the particular fashion they do. Nonetheless, the ecological complex remains an extremely useful explanatory tool.

FIRST SETTLEMENTS

Our knowledge of the origin and development of the first human settlements and our understanding of the goals, hopes, and fears of those who lived within them must forever remain tentative. Because the first towns emerged before the invention of writing about 3,500 B.C., we must depend for our knowledge on the research of archeologists. Understandably, historians, sociologists, and other scholars sometimes differ in their interpretations of the limited archeological and historical data. Lewis Mumford has stated the problem aptly:

> Five thousand years of urban history and perhaps as many of proto-urban history are spread over a few score of only partly exposed sites. The great urban landmarks Ur, Nippur, Uruk, Thebes, Helopolis, Assur, Nineveh, Babylon, cover a span of three thousand years whose vast emptiness we cannot hope to fill with a handful of monuments and a few hundred pages of written records.[6]

This chapter, which outlines the growth of urban settlements, must necessarily be based in part on scholarly speculation as to what happened before the historical era. Fortunately, though, our interest is not so much in an exact chronology of historical events as in the patterns and process of development.

Agricultural Revolution

It is generally believed that before the urban revolution could take place, an agricultural revolution was necessary.[7] Before the invention of the city, nomadic hunting-and-gathering bands could not accumulate, store, and transport more goods than could be carried with them. All that was to change.

Only when the agricultural system became capable of producing a surplus was it possible to withdraw labor from food production and apply it to the production of other goods.[8] The size of the urban population was thus directly related to the efficiency of agricultural workers, and agriculture remained primitive for millennia.

[5]Manuel Castells, *The Urban Question,* Alan Sheridan (trans.), M.I.T. Press, Cambridge, Mass., 1977.

[6]Lewis Mumford, *The City in History, Its Origins, Its Transformations and Its Prospects,* Harcourt, Brace, and World, New York, 1961, p. 55.

[7]Not everyone agrees with an implicit evolutionary typology such as the one used in this chapter. Bruce Trigger, for instance, strongly argues against an evolutionary approach in explaining the emergence and growth of cities, and states that "what seems to be required is a more piecemeal and institutional approach to complex societies." [Bruce Trigger, "Determinants of Urban Growth in Pre-Industrial Societies," in Peter Ucko, Ruth Tringham, and G. W. Dimbleby (eds.), *Man, Settlement, and Urbanism,* Schenkman, Cambridge, Mass., 1972, p. 576.]

[8]Jane Jacobs reverses the order presented here, suggesting that intensive agriculture was the result rather than the cause of cities. This theory, however, has received little support from scholars. See Jane Jacobs, *The Economy of Cities,* Random House, New York, 1969.

However, while a food surplus was essential to the emergence of towns, it was not essential that the surplus come from agriculture. Perhaps as early as 15,000 years ago, during the Mesolithic period, there were hamlets from India to the Baltic area that based their culture on the use of shellfish and fish.[9] Within these Mesolithic hamlets possibly were seen the earliest domestic animals, such as pigs, ducks, geese, and our oldest companion, the dog. Mumford suggests that the practice of reproducing food plants through plant cuttings—as with the date palm, the olive, the fig, and the grape—probably derives from Mesolithic culture. Small towns and villages could manage by food gathering if their ecological site was especially bountiful. Services and natural resources could also be exchanged for food.

Nor did the absence of settled agriculture necessarily mean the absence of rudimentary division of labor and hierarchical social order. Jericho—which some argue was the first "city," with some 600 people around 8000 B.C.—had a fairly complex architectural construction.[10] The inhabitants, for example, had sufficient civic organization and division of labor to build massive defensive walls and towers in a period when they had barely begun to domesticate grains.

Eventually, some groups gained enough knowledge of the relationship between the seasons and the cycle of growth to forsake constant nomadism in favor of permanent settlement in one location. The Neolithic period is characterized by this change from gathering food to producing it. There is fairly clear evidence that about 8,000 B.C. in the middle east there was a transformation from a specialized food-collecting culture to a culture where grains were cultivated.

Herd animals such as oxen, sheep, donkeys, and finally horses were first used during this period, allowing the available supply of food to be substantially increased and the first solid steps toward permanent settlement of a single site to be made. Animals such as the horse and the donkey could also serve, in addition to humans, as beasts of burden and a source of pulling power. In all likelihood there were decreases in the very high mortality rates, and increases in population, at this same time.

Population Expansion

This first population explosion, by increasing a tribe to the point where hunting and gathering could no longer provide adequate food, further encouraged fixed settlements. This was most likely to occur in fertile locations where land, water, and climate favored intensive cultivation of food. Archaeologists suggest that population growth in fact forced the invention of agriculture.[11] Hunting, gathering, and primitive horticulture simply could not support the growing population.

Since the plow didn't yet exist—it was not invented until sometime in the

[9]Mumford, op. cit., p. 10.
[10]Kathleen Kenyon, *Archeology in the Holy Land*, Praeger, New York, 1970.
[11]Kent J. Flannery, "The Origins of Agriculture," *Annual Review of Anthropology*, 2:271–310, 1973.

fourth century B.C.—farmers of this period used a form of "slash-and-burn" agriculture.[12] This meant cutting down what you could and burning off the rest before planting—an inefficient form of farming but one with a long history. It was even used by the American pioneers who first crossed the Appalachian Mountains into the new lands of Kentucky and Ohio. The first horticulturalists in ancient times soon discovered that slash-and-burn farming quickly depleted the soil, and so they were forced to migrate—thus probably spreading their knowledge by means of cultural diffusion.

The consequences of these developments were momentous; with cultivation a surplus could be accumulated, and people could plan for the future. One of the earliest permanent neolithic farming communities so far excavated, Jarmo, in the Kurdistan area of Iraq, was inhabited between 7,000 and 6,500 B.C. It has been calculated that approximately 150 people lived in Jarmo, and archeological evidence indicates a population density of twenty-seven people per square mile (this is about the same as the population density today in that area).[13] Soil erosion, deforestation, and 10,000 years of human habitation have offset the technological advantages enjoyed by the area's present inhabitants.

The inhabitants of Jarmo had learned to domesticate dogs, goats, and possibly sheep. The farmers living in Jarmo raised an early form of domesticated barley and wheat, but still had to hunt and collect much of their food. Since the earliest farmers lacked plows to break the tight grassland sod, they worked the hillsides where grass was scarce and trees broke the earth. Similarly, America's tightly packed western prairie soil remained untamed until the steel plow was invented in the nineteenth century.

Village farming communities like Jarmo had stabilized by about 5,500 B.C., and over the next 1,500 years such settlements gradually spread from the flanks of hills into the alluvial plains of river valleys like that of the Tigris-Euphrates. A similar process took place in the great river valleys of the Nile, the Indus, and the Hwang Ho. The invention of agriculture was quite possibly an independent development in China and was certainly independent in the new world.[14] The civilizations of Mesomerica were physically isolated from those of the middle east and Asia and thus had to invent independently, since they were unable to borrow.

Particularly environmentally blessed were those settlements of Mesopotamia and the Nile River valley which could exploit the rich soil of the alluvial river beds. Egypt was among the first to adopt sedimentary agriculture. By the middle of the fourth millennium B.C. the economy of the Nile valley in Egypt had shifted once and for all from a combination of farming and food gathering to a major reliance on agriculture.[15] In the great river valley two and sometimes three crops a year were possibly because the annual floods brought rich silt to replace the soil which was exhausted. To the dependable crops of

[12]E. Cecil Curwin and Gudmund Hart, *Plough and Pasture,* Collier Books, New York, 1961, p. 64.
[13]Robert Braidwood, "The Agricultural Revolution," *Scientific American,* September, 1960, p. 7.
[14]Ibid., p. 3.
[15]Robert W. July, *A History of the African People,* Scribner, New York, 1970, p. 14.

Women doing laundry with Bombay high-rises in background. Modern and traditional often merge in third world cities. (Peter Menzel/Stock, Boston)

wheat and barley was added the cultivation of the date palm. This was a great improvement. In Mesopotamia the palm provided more than simple food; from it were obtained wood, roofing, matting, wine, and fiber for rope.

INTERACTIONS OF POPULATION, ORGANIZATION, ENVIRONMENT, AND TECHNOLOGY (POET)

The relationships between population, organization, environment, and technology are clearer in their consequences than in their timing. The immediate result of the agricultural revolution was a spurt in population size, since a larger population could be maintained on a permanent basis. Stable yields meant that larger numbers of people could be sustained in a relatively compact space. The creation of an agricultural surplus made permanent settlements possible. Agricultural villages could support up to twenty-five persons per square mile; this was a dramatic improvement over the maximum of three to ten persons per square mile found in hunting-and-gathering societies.[16] Technology had spurred population growth.

The establishment of sedentary agricultural villages with growing populations increased the pressure for more intensive agriculture and more complex

[16]Gerhard Lenski, *Human Society,* McGraw-Hill, New York, 1970, p. 164.

patterns of organization. Agriculture in the river valleys required at least small-scale irrigation systems, something not necessary in the highlands. Rudimentary social organization and specialization began to develop; the periodic flooding made it necessary for the village farmers to band together to create a system of irrigation canals and repair the damage done by the floods. The existence of irrigation systems also led to the development of systems of control and the emergence of more detailed social stratification within the permanent settlements.

Relatively permanent settlements in one place also allowed the structure of the family itself to change. In a hunting-and-gathering society, the only legacy parents could pass on to their progeny was their physical strength and knowledge of rudimentary skills. Agriculturalists, though, can also pass land on to their children, and all land is not equal. Over generations social stratification emerged, with some children born into prosperity and others into poverty.

Extended family forms can also more easily emerge under sedentary conditions. For example, imagine a male-dominated society where polygyny is practiced. Having more than one wife can have major economic as well as sexual advantages, since extra wives mean extra hands to tend the animals and cultivate the fields. More important, many wives mean many sons—sons to work the fields, help protect what one has from the raiding of others, provide for one in old age, make offerings to the gods at one's grave, and carry one's lineage forward. The last was particularly important in many societies. For example, in the Old Testament the greatest gift God could bestow on Abraham was not wealth or fame or everlasting life, but that his descendants would number more than the stars in the sky.

Environmentally, those located on rivers had advantages not only in terms of soil fertility but also for transportation and trade. The city served as a "central place" where goods and services could be exchanged. The use of rivers for transportation further encouraged the aggregation of population, for now it was relatively easy to gather food at a few centers. Thus in the valleys of the Nile, the Tigris-Euphrates, and the Indus there first developed a population surplus, which in turn permitted the rise of the first cities. By the third century B.C. Egyptian peasants from the fertile river flood plain could produce approximately three times the food they needed.[17] The result was the first cities.

CITY POPULATIONS

By contemporary standards, the largest cities were little more than villages or small towns. However, in their own day they must have been looked upon with the same awe with which nineteenth-century immigrants viewed New York, for these first cities were ten times the size of the Neolithic villages

[17]July, op. cit., p. 14.

which had previously been the largest settlements. Babylon, with its hanging gardens, one of the wonders of the ancient world, embraced a physical area of only roughly 3.2 square miles.[18] The city of Ur, located at the confluence of the Tigris and Euphrates rivers, was the largest city in Mesopotamia. With all its canals, temples, and harbors, it occupied only 220 acres.[19] Ur was estimated to have contained 24,000 persons; other towns ranged in population from 2,000 to 20,000 inhabitants.[20] Such cities remained urban islands in the midst of rural seas.

Hawley estimates that although these cities were large for their time, they probably represented no more than 3 or 4 percent of all the people within the various localities.[21] Even Athens at its peak had only 612 acres within its walls—an area less than 1 square mile. Ancient Antioch was roughly half this size; Carthage at its peak was 712 acres. Of all the ancient cities, only imperial Rome exceeded an area of 5 square miles. Kingsley Davis estimates that even the biggest places before the Roman period could scarcely have exceeded 200,000 inhabitants, since from fifty to ninety farmers were required to support one person in a city.[22] In an agricultural world, the size of cities was limited by how much surplus could be produced and what technology was available to transport it.

EVOLUTION IN SOCIAL ORGANIZATION

These cities were important not because of their size but because they frequently not only tolerated but actively encouraged innovations in social organization. Even though small in number, the urban elite was the principal carrier of the all-important cultural and intellectual values of the civilization. Needless to say, the city also held economic and political sway over the more numerous country dwellers. The philosopher-sociologist Ibn Khaldun, writing in the fourteenth century, pointed out that the concentration of economic power and the proceeds of taxation in the cities led to a profound difference between the economic pattern of the city and that of the country. The concentration of governmental and educational functions in the city also stimulated new demands which affected the patterns of production and supply.

Division of Labor

The city's greater population density, along with its sedentary way of life, made possible the development of an urban culture emphasizing trade, manufacturing, and services. The earliest cities began to evolve a social organization immensely more complex than that found in the Neolithic village.

---

[18]Kingsley Davis, "The Origin and Growth of Urbanization in the World," *American Journal of Sociology,* **60**:430, March, 1955.
[19]V. Gordon Childe, *What Happened in History,* Penguin Books, London, 1946, p. 87.
[20]Ibid., p. 86.
[21]Amos H. Hawley, *Urban Society,* Ronald Press, New York, 1971, p. 22.
[22]Davis, loc. cit.

The slight surplus of food permitted the emergence of a rudimentary division of labor. No longer did each person have to do everything for himself or herself. The city thus differed from a large village not only in numbers, but because it had a larger and more extensive division of labor. The consequence was hierarchy and stratification.

Archeological records indicate that the earliest public buildings were temples, suggesting that specialized priests were the first to be released from direct subsistence functions. That the priests also assumed the role of economic administrators is indicated by ration or wage lists found in places where temples were located.[23] In Egypt the temples were also used as granaries for the community surplus. This surplus could be used to carry a community through a period of famine. The technology of food storage was a major achievement of the city. The biblical story of Joseph, who was sold by his jealous brothers into slavery in Egypt, only to become advisor to the Pharaoh and predict seven good years of harvest followed by seven lean years of famine, points out the vulnerability of the nomadic Israelites to their physical environment, and the relative control of the more advanced Egyptians over their environment. Even if the nomadic Jews had received Joseph's warning, they would have been unable to profit from it. They lacked the transportation and storage technology of the more urban Egyptians. Long-term planning— whether to avoid famines, build pyramids, or construct temples—was possible only where a surplus was assured and storage was available.

Kingship and Social Class

For a long time the temples were the largest and most complex institutions that existed; kingship and dynastic political regimes developed later. Apparently, warrior-leaders were originally selected by all other males and served only during times of external threat. Eventually, those chosen as short-term leaders during periods of war came to be retained even during those periods of peace. As H. G. Creel describes the process in China in the fifth century B.C.:

> Perhaps whole settlements sometimes found it was easier to set up as warriors, and let the people around them work for them, than to labor in the fields. The chiefs and their groups of warriors, no doubt, provided the farmers with "protection" whether they wanted it or not, and in return for that service they took a share of the peasant's crop.[24]

It is hardly necessary to add that the size of the warrior's share of the peasant's crop was fixed by the warrior, not the peasant. The growth of military establishments did contribute, though, to technological innovations—metallurgy for weapons, chariots for battle, and more efficient ships.

It was but a step from a warrior class to kingship and the founding of

---

[23]Robert M. Adams, "The Origins of Cities," *Scientific American,* September, 1960, p. 7.
[24]H. G. Creel, *The Birth of China,* Reynal and Hitchcock, New York, 1937, p. 279.

dynasties with permanent hereditary royalty. The gradual shifting of the central focus from temple to palace was accompanied by the growth of social and economic stratification. Artists working in precious metals became a regular attachment of palace life. Records of sales of land indicate that even among the agriculturalists there were considerable inequalities in the ownership of productive land. As a result, social differences grew. Some few members of each new generation were born with marked hereditary social and economic advantages over the others. If they couldn't afford the luxuries of palace life, they nonetheless lived in considerable comfort. Archeologically, the emergence of social classes can be seen clearly in the increasing disparity in the richness of grave offerings.[25] The tombs of royalty are richly furnished with ornaments and weapons of gold and precious metals; those of others, with copper vessels; while the majority have only pottery vessels or nothing at all. The building of burial pyramids was the ultimate case of monumental graves.

TECHNOLOGICAL AND SOCIAL EVOLUTION

Technology was spurred on by the existence of the palace. The military required armor, weapons, and chariots, and the court demanded ever more ornaments and other luxuries. A constant market was created for nonagricultural commodities, and the result was the establishment of a class of full-time artisans and craft workers. The near-isolation of earlier periods was now replaced with trade over long distances, which brought not only new goods but also new ideas.

The first city was far more than an enlarged village—it was a clear break with the past, a whole new social system. It was a social revolution involving the evolution of a whole new set of social institutions. Unlike the agricultural revolution that preceded it, this urban revolution was far more than a basic change in subsistence. It was "pre-eminently a social process, an expression more of change in man's interaction with his fellows than in his interaction with his environment."[26]

Once begun, the urban revolution created its own environment. Inventions that have made large settlements possible have been due to the city itself—for example, writing, accounting, bronze, the solar calendar, bureaucracy, and the beginning of science. Ever since Mesopotamia, the city as a social institution has been shaping human life.[27]

URBAN REVOLUTION

V. Gordon Childe lists ten features which, he says, define the "urban revolution," that is, features which set cities apart from earlier forms of human settlement. The features are:

[25]Adams, op. cit., p. 9.
[26]H. G. Creel, op. cit., p. 279.
[27]Adams, op. cit., p. 9.

1. Permanent settlement in dense aggregations
2. Nonagriculturalists engaging in specialized functions
3. Taxation and capital accumulation
4. Monumental public buildings
5. A ruling class
6. The technique of writing
7. The acquisition of predictive sciences—arithmetic, geometry, and astronomy
8. Artistic expression
9. Trade for vital materials
10. The replacement of kinship by residence as the basis for membership in the community.[28]

Whether all ten are necessary is debatable. For example, monumental urban places did not develop in Mesoamerica until the first century B.C., but even at that comparatively late date, these cities lacked some of the technical advances found in cities of the middle east, the Indus River area, and China at that time. Central American cities existed without the wheel, the raising of animals, the plow, the use of metals, or a writing system other than the rudimentary use of hieroglyphic symbols. They did, however, have compensatory advantages; the most significant probably was the knowledge of how to cultivate large surpluses of domesticated maize (corn). The Mayans also had made major advances in mathematics, including the invention of the concept of zero. They were accurate astronomers and had an exact calendar. Both of the latter were for religious purposes, but had secular consequences. Social organizations, culture, and technology were interrelated.

Childe's list is perhaps most useful in helping us define what we have come to accept as the general characteristics of cities. What is important for our purposes is that cities possessing these characteristics did emerge in Mesopotamia and the Nile valley.

SURVIVAL OF THE CITY

Finally, it should be noted that the stable location of the city was not an unmixed blessing. It was not simply for the sake of convenience that gardens and pasturelands were found within the city walls. Cities had to be equipped to withstand a siege, since the earliest cities were vulnerable not only to conquest by other peoples but also to periodic attacks by nomadic raiders.

Mesopotamian cities were perpetually under attack by nomadic tribes.[29] The Bible, for instance, devotes considerable attention to the successes of the nomadic Israelites in taking and pillaging the cities of their more advanced

---

[28]V. Gordon Childe, "The Urban Revolution," *Town Planning Review*, **21**:4–7, 1950.
[29]Sturat Piggot, "The Role of the City in Ancient Civilization," in E. M. Fisher (ed.), *The Metropolis in Modern Life*, Doubleday, Garden City, New York, 1955.

enemies. The description of the fall of the Canaanite city of Jericho tells us that

> the People went out into the city, every man straight before him, and they took the city. And they utterly destroyed all that was in the city, both man and woman, young and old, and ox and sheep and ass, with the edge of the sword—and they burnt the city with fire and all that was therein (Joshua 2:20–24).

That "Joshua fit the battle of Jericho . . . and the walls came tumbling down" is known to all those who have heard the stirring spiritual, even if they have not read the Old Testament. While the walls Joshua is believed to have miraculously brought down with trumpet blasts about 1,500 B.C. have not been located with certainty, the remains of other walls dating back to 8,000 B.C. have been excavated. As with some other long-inhabited ancient sites, the walls had been breached many times—sometimes by invaders, sometimes by earthquakes.

Within the city walls there also were threats to the inhabitants, the most dangerous being fires and epidemic diseases. City life was more exciting, but it was not necessarily more secure than the countryside.

THE HELLENIC CITY

As we have noted, environmental factors played a decisive role in early cities. The history of the city can be considered the story of human attempts, through the use of technology and social organization, to lessen the impact of environmental factors. An example is Athens, widely regarded as the apex of ancient western urbanism. Not only was the Greek soil thin and rocky and of marginal fertility, but the mountainous hinterland made inland transportation and communication almost impossible. Aside from the sacred ways to Delphi and Eleusis, the roads were mere paths, suitable only for pack animals or porters. It is estimated that the cost of transporting goods 10 miles from Athens was more than 40 percent of the value of the goods.[30]

But Greece was blessed with fine harbors. Consequently, Athens turned to the sea. A Greek ship could carry 7,000 pounds of grain 65 nautical miles a day, and do it at one-tenth the cost of land transportation. (Storms at sea and pirates, however, often made this an ideal rather than a reality.) There were also technological contributions to Greek prosperity: the use of the lodestone as a basic nautical compass and the development of more seaworthy ships.

Social Invention

The greatest achievement of the Greeks was not in the area of technology but in that of social organization. The social invention of the "polis," or "city-state," enabled families, phratries (groups of clans), and tribes to organize for

---

[30]Gustave Glotz, *Ancient Greece at Work,* Norton, New York, 1967, pp. 291–293.

mutual aid and protection as citizens of a common state. Because they acknowledged a common mythical ancestry among the gods, different families were able to come together in larger bodies. Gradually the principle of common worship was extended to the entire community. Citizenship within the state and the right to worship at civic shrines were two sides of the same coin.

Citizens were those who could trace their ancestry back to the god or gods responsible for the city and thus could participate in public religious worship. An Athenian citizen was one who had the right to worship at the temple of Athena, the protector of the city-state of Athens. The ancient city was a religious community, and citizenship was at its basis a religious status.[31] Socrates's questioning the existence of the gods was considered a grave offense because, by threatening established religion, he was undermining the very basis of citizenship in the city-state. As punishment for such a subversive act he was forced to take poison hemlock. Unfortunately, the Greeks never devised a system for extending citizenship to political units larger than the city-state. That was to be the great achievement of the Romans.

Being a citizen of the city was of supreme importance to the Greeks. When Aristotle wished to characterize humans as social animals, he said that "man is by nature a citizen of the city." To the Greeks, being ostracized, or forbidden to enter into the city walls, was a severe punishment. To be placed beyond the walls was to be cast out of civilized life. The terms "pagan" and "heathen" originally referred to those beyond the city walls; our adjective "urban" and our nouns "citizen" and "politics" are derived from the Latin terms for the city. The English terms "city" and "civilization" are both derived from the Latin "civis."

Physical Design and Planning

Physically, the Greek cities were of fairly similar design, a fact which is not surprising given the amount of social borrowing that took place among the various city-states and the fact that the cities were built with military defense in mind. The major city walls were built around a fortified hill called an "acropolis." Major temples were also placed upon the acropolis. The nearby "agora" served both as a meeting place, and in time, a marketplace. All major buildings were located within the city walls. Housing, except for the most privileged, was outside the walls but huddled as close to their protective shelter as was possible.

In describing the Greek polis, there is a strong tendency to focus on the image of the Athenian Acropolis harmoniously crowned by the perfectly proportioned Parthenon. Separated by seas and centuries, it is perhaps natural for us to accept Pericles's own praise of his fellow Athenians as "lovers of beauty without extravagance and lovers of wisdom without unmanliness."

Yet below the inner order and harmony of the Parthenon was a sprawling

---

[31]Numa Denis Fustel de Coulanges, *The Ancient City*, Doubleday, Garden City, New York, 1956 (first published 1865), p. 134.

The Agora or marketplace of Athens was where the council of citizens met, and thus was the civic center of the state. (Culver Pictures)

jumbled town in which streets were no more than dirty, winding, narrow lanes and unburied refuse rotted in the sun. Housing for the masses was squalid and cramped. Today it is easy to forget that the while stone of the Parthenon was once painted garish colors. While Hippodamus designed a grid street pattern for Piraeus, the port city of Athens, Athens itself had no such ordered arrangement. Athens was the center of an empire, but little of its genius was given to urban design or municipal management.

Population

Athens had considerable population problems—partially due to the scarcity of productive land in Greece, which resulted in heavy migration from rural areas to the cities. During its peak the city achieved a population of only between 120,000 and 180,000. The major limit on population growth was the limited technological base. The city was still dependent on the surplus of agricultural activities. Much of the land within Athens itself was given over to gardening. The great sociologist Max Weber put the Greek city-states in perspective when he wrote, "The full urbanite of antiquity was a semi-peasant."[32]

Expansion of Greek cities was also limited by preference and policy. The ancient Greek preferred fairly small cities. Both Plato and Aristotle firmly

[32]Max Weber, *The City* (trans. D. Martendale and G. Neuwirth), Free Press, New York, 1958.

believed that good government was directly related to the size of the city. Plato specified that in the ideal Republic there should be exactly 5,040 citizens, since that number had fifty-nine divisors and would "furnish numbers for war and peace, and for all contracts and dealings, including taxes and divisions of the land."[33] Why Plato chose the number 5,040 isn't known, since his totalitarian state would be governed not by citizen vote but by a small group of guardians presided over by a philosopher-king. Lewis Mumford suggests two possible reasons for the limited size: A larger population would be more difficult to control strictly; and there may have been a desire to keep the population low enough to live off the local food supply.[34] He also notes that when noncitizens such as children, slaves, and foreigners are added into the calculation, the total population of the city-state is approximately 30,000, or about the size chosen later by Leonardo da Vinci and Ebenezer Howard for their ideal cities. (Slaves constituted perhaps a third of the population.)

Aristotle informs us that the town planner Hippodamus envisioned a city of 10,000 citizens divided into three parts: one of artisans, one of farmers, and one of warriors. The land was likewise to be divided in three parts: one to support the gods, one public to support the warriors defending the state, and one private to support the farm owners.[35] This illustrates the classic Greek interest in balance.

Aristotle's views on the ideal size of the city are less specific, although he recognized that increasing the number of inhabitants beyond a certain point changes the character of a city. In his view, the city-state had to be large enough to defend itself and to be economically self-sufficient, but not so large as to prevent the citizens from knowing each other's character. As he stated it:

> A state then only begins to exist when it has attained a population sufficient for a good life in the political community; it may somewhat exceed this number, but as I was saying there must be a limit. What should be the limit will be easily ascertained by experience.—If the citizens of a state are to judge and distribute offices according to merit, then they must know each other's characters: where they do not possess this knowledge, both the election to offices and the decisions of lawsuits will go wrong—Clearly then the best limit of the population of a state is the largest number which suffices for the purposes of life and can be taken at a single view.[36]

City-states were also restrained from growing overly large by the Greek policy of creating colonies. This policy reinforced the social preference for small cities. Between 479 and 431 B.C., over 10,000 families migrated from established cities to newer Greek colonial settlements. Colonization both met the needs of empire and provided a safety valve for a chronic population problem. This diffusion of population led in turn to a diffusion of Greek culture and ideas of government far beyond the Peloponnesus.

[33]Plato, *The Laws, Book V* 437 (trans. B. Jowett), 1926 ed.
[34]Lewis Mumford, op. cit., p. 180.
[35]Aristotle, *Politics,* Book VII, ii, p. 8 (trans.B. Jowett), 1932 ed.
[36]Aristotle, *Politics,* Book VII, iv, 7–8.

ROME

The city as a physical entity reached a high point under the Roman Caesars. Not until the nineteenth century was Europe again to see cities as large as those found within the Roman Empire. Rome itself may have contained 1 million inhabitants at its peak, although an analysis of density figures would make an estimate two-thirds that number seem more reasonable; scholarly estimates vary from a low of 250,000 to a high of 1.6 million. These wide variations are a result of different interpretations of inadequate data. The number given in the total Roman census, for example, jumped from 900,000 in 69 B.C. to over 4 million in 28 B.C. No one is quite sure what this increase indicates—perhaps an extension of citizenship, perhaps the counting of women and children, perhaps something else.[37]

Readers should remind themselves that all figures on the size of cities before the nineteenth century should be taken as estimates rather than empirical census counts. At their most accurate, such figures are formed by multiplying the supposed number of dwelling units at a given period by the estimated average family size.

Size and Number of Cities

Expertise in the areas of technology and social organization enabled the Romans to organize, administer, and govern an empire containing several cities of more than 200,000 inhabitants. The population of the Roman Empire exceeded that of all but the largest twentieth-century superpowers. According to the historian Edward Gibbon, "We are informed that when the emperor Claudius [reigned A.D. 41–54] exercised the office of censor, he took account of six million nine hundred and forty-five thousand Roman citizens, who with women and children, must have amounted to about twenty million souls." He concludes that there were "about twice as many provincials as there were citizens, of either sex and of every age; and that the slaves were at least equal in number to the free inhabitants of the Roman world. The total amount of this imperfect calculation would rise to about one hundred and twenty millions."[38] The total world population at this time was roughly 250 million.

Gibbon further states that ancient Italy was said to contain 1,197 cities—however defined—and Spain, according to Pliny, had 360 cities.[39] North Africa had hundreds of cities, and north of the Alps major cities rose from Vienna to Bordeaux. Even in far-off Britain there were major cities at York, Bath, and London. What made all this possible for hundreds of years was a technology of considerable sophistication and—most important—Roman social organization. Wherever the legions conquered, they also brought Roman law and Roman concepts of government.

---

[37]William Petersen, *Population,* Macmillan, New York, 1969, p. 369.
[38]Edward Gibbon, *The Decline and Fall of the Roman Empire,* Dell, New York, 1879 (first published 1776), p. 53.
[39]Ibid., pp. 54–55.

Housing and Planning

"Rome, Goddess of the earth and of its people, without a peer or a second" remains the wonder of the ancient world. Yet despite the emperor Augustus's proud claim that he found a city of brick and left one of marble, much of the city centuries later was still composed of buildings with wood frames and roofs on narrow crowded alleys. Fire was a constant worry, and the disastrous fires of A.D. 64 that some say Nero started left only four of the city's fourteen districts intact.

Wealthy Romans lived on the Palatine Hill, where, the imperial palaces overlooked the Forum with its temples and public buildings, and the Colosseum. However, as was the case in Athens, Roman municipal planning was definitely limited in scope. Magnificent though it was, it did not extend beyond the center of the municipality. Once one branched off the main thoroughfare leading to the city gates, there was only a maze of narrow, crooked lanes winding through the squalid tenements that housed the great bulk of the population. The masses crowded in the poor quarters were offered periodic "bread and circuses" to keep their minds off revolt. Magnificent public squares and public baths were built with public taxes for the more affluent Romans, not for the masses. As the city grew, the old city walls were torn down and rebuilt to include buildings that had been constructed on the outer fringe. In time even the Forum became crowded and congested, as the ruins still standing amply testify.

The city was supplied with fresh water through an extensive system of aqueducts. The most important of these, which brought water from the Sabine Hills, was completed in 144 B.C. Parts of aqueducts still stand—testament to the excellence of their engineering and the skill of their builders. Rome even had an elaborate sewer system—at least in the better residential areas. It is an unfortunate comment on progress to note that present-day Rome still dumps untreated sewage in the Tiber River.

In many ways provincial Roman cities such as Paris, Vienna, Cologne, Mainz, and London exhibited greater civic planning than Rome itself. These cities grew out of semipermanent military encampments and thus took the shape of the standard Roman camp. The encampments and later the cities were laid out on a rectangular grid pattern with a gate on each side. The center was reserved for the forum, the coliseum, and municipal buildings such as public baths. Markets were also generally found in the forum. The common origins of European provincial Roman cities meant that they were all remarkably similar in design.

Elsewhere in the empire, the major distinction was between preexisting cities and new provincial towns and cities. In the east there were Hellenic and other cities which the Romans simply took over and expanded under Roman jurisdiction. In the west (western Europe and Britain), on the other hand, there was no preexisting system of cities; here the Romans created a wholly new system of Roman rather than Hellenic cities. The differences between the older eastern and newer western segments of the empire were never fully resolved, with the empire eventually splitting into eastern and western sections. Eastern cities differed from each other physically as well as politically; because of their commonality of origin, the western European provincial Roman cities were all remarkably similar in design (for more detail on Hellenic and Roman planning, see Chapter 12, Planning in Europe: with Discussion of New Towns).

Transportation

Rome was an exporter of ideas—such as Roman law, government, and engineering—which enabled it to control the hinterland. It was an importer of necessary goods and therefore depended on the hinterland not only for tribute and slaves but for its very life. The city of Rome could feed its population and also import vast quantities of goods other than food because of an unrivaled road network and peaceful routes of sea trade. (The roads were built and the galleys powered largely by slaves.) Some 52,000 miles of well-maintained roads facilitated rapid movement of goods and people. Parts of some of the original roads are still in use today, and the quality of their construction surpasses that of even the most rigorous contemporary federal standards.

With the elimination of Carthage as a rival, the Mediterranean truly became "*Mare Nostrum*" or a Roman lake. Foodstuffs for both the civilian population and the legions could be transported easily and inexpensively from the commercial farming areas of Iberia and north Africa. When the African grain-producing areas were lost to the Vandals, and the barbarians in Germany, Gaul, and England pressed the empire, disrupting vital transportation routes, the decline of Rome was inevitable. Rome lived off its hinterland.

Life and Leisure

The prosperity of the Roman Empire during its peak and the leisure it afforded the residents of the capital were imperial indeed. By the second century after Christ, between a third and a half of the population was on the dole, and even those who worked (including the third of the population who were slaves) rarely spent more than six hours at their jobs. Moreover, by that period, religious and other holidays had been multiplied by the emperors until the ratio of holidays to workdays was one to one.[40]

To amuse the population and keep their mind off uprisings against the emperor, chariot races and gladiatorial combats were staged. The scene of the races was the colossal Circus Maximus, which seated 260,000 persons, and gladiatorial fights were staged at the Colosseum. When the emperor Titus inaugurated the Colosseum in A.D. 80 he imported 5,000 lions, elephants, deer, and other animals to be slaughtered in a single day to excite the spectators. The role Christians came to play in these amusements is well known.

[40]Jerome Carcopino, *Daily Life in Ancient Rome,* Yale University Press, New Haven, Conn., 1940.

EUROPEAN URBANIZATION UNTIL THE INDUSTRIAL CITY

The preceding pages discussed the development of the city through the Roman period. Here particular emphasis is placed on the reemergence of European urban places after the decline of Rome and on how such cities laid the basis for the western industrial city with which we are all so familiar.

The dissolution of the Roman Empire in the fifth century after Christ marked the effective decay of cities in western Europe for a period of 600 years. This is not the place to detail why Rome fell; it is sufficient to note that under the combined impact of the barbarian invasion and internal decay, the empire disintegrated and commerce shrank to a bare minimum. Once-proud Roman provincial centers disappeared or declined to the point of insignificance. By the end of the sixth century, war, devastation, plague, and starvation had destroyed the glory that was Rome. From the status of megalopolis, the city was reduced to its early medieval character of a collection of separate villages whose population had taken shelter in the ruins of ancient grandeur and had dug wells to replace the aqueducts. The people were supported by the pope, rather than by the emperor, from the produce of the papal territory.[41]

Nonetheless, while the social and physical city withered and decayed into poverty and ruins, the idea and myth of Rome and a Roman Empire remained alive even in the darkest medieval periods, and led eventually in the Renaissance to a new burst of urban activity. The throttling of Mediterranean trade by the advance of Islam in the seventh century, and the pillaging raids of the Norsemen in the ninth century, did further damage to what remained of European commercial life. In the east, however, cities continued to prosper. Constantinople, created by the emperor Constantine between 324 and 330, survived as the capital of the Byzantine Empire until its conquest by the Turks in 1453.

The Medieval Feudal System

The fall of Rome meant that each locality was isolated from every other and thus had to become self-sufficient in order to survive. Local lords offered peasants in the region protection from outside raiders in return for the virtual slavery—called "serfdom"—of the peasants. Removed from outside influences, local social structures congealed into hereditary hierarchies, with the local lord at the top of the pyramid of social stratification and the serfs at the bottom.[42]

It is important to note that the economic and political base of the feudal system, unlike that of the Roman period, was *rural,* not urban. Its center was not a city but the rural manor or castle from which the local peasantry could be controlled. The economy was a subsistence agriculture based solely on what was produced in the local area; transportation of goods from one area to another was extremely difficult. Lack of communication, the virtual absence

---

[41]Mason Hammond, *The City in the Ancient World,* Harvard University Press, Cambridge, Mass., 1972, p. 324.
[42]Henri Pirenne, *Medieval Cities,* Princeton University Press, Princeton, N.J., 1939, particularly pp. 84–85.

of a commonly accepted currency, and the land-tenure system that bound serfs to the soil all contributed to a narrow inward-looking localism.

However, not all former provincial cities were totally abandoned; a few managed to survive with greatly reduced populations. These were generally under the secular control of the residing bishop. The Catholic church had based its diocesan boundaries on those of the old Roman cities, and as the empire faded and then collapsed, the bishops sometimes came to exercise secular as well as religious power. By the ninth century, "civitas" had come to be synonymous with these "episcopal cities."[43]

According to Henri Pirenne, the "episcopal cities" were cities in name only, for they more clearly resembled medieval fortresses than true cities. They had a maximum of 2,000 or 3,000 persons and were frequently even smaller. But they were to play a crucial historical role as "stepping stones."[44] By the time of Charlemagne (ninth century) the cities—or towns—had lost most of their urban functions:

> The Carolingians used the ancient cities as places of habitation, as fortified settlements from which to dominate the surrounding countryside. The surviving physical apparatus of the old town, the walls, and buildings, served because it already existed, a convenient legacy of an earlier age.[45]

Town Revival

Cities began to revive, very slowly, in the eleventh century. According to Pirenne, most of these new towns were not continuations of ancient cities but new social entities. Originally they were formed as a byproduct of the merchant caravans that stopped to trade outside the walls of the medieval "episcopal cities" such as Amiens, Tours, and Cologne. Under the influence of trade the old Roman cities took on a new life and became repopulated, while new towns were also being established. Mercantile groups formed around the military burgs, along seacoasts, on riverbanks, and at the confluences and junctions of the natural routes of trade and communication.[46]

Over time the seasonal fairs that were held outside the town gates came to take on a more or less permanent year-round character. Since at this time the merchants were not allowed inside the town walls, they settled in the outside shadow of the walls and in some cases built their own walls, which attached to those of the town. These *faubourgs,* or medieval suburbs, came to be incorporated into the town proper, and by the thirteenth century merchants had an accepted and important role in the growing medieval towns. Revitalized city life was most prominent in Italy when city-states such as Venice established extensive commercial ties with the Byzantine and even the Arab empires. Trade with Constantinople enabled the Venetians to prosper and in time create

[43]Max Weber, op. cit., p. 49.
[44]Pirenne, op. cit., p. 76.
[45]Howard Saalman, *Medieval Cities,* Braziller, New York, 1968, p. 15.
[46]Fritz Rörig, *The Medieval Town,* University of California Press, Berkeley, 1967, p. 15.

a mini-empire of their own based upon the skills of their sea captains and the size of their fleets.

Two external factors during the Middle Ages also greatly contributed to the growth of towns elsewhere in Europe: the Crusaders and the overall population growth. A great impetus for the revival of trade came from the medieval religious crusades. The Crusaders returned from urban Byzantine Empire with newly developed tastes for the consumer goods and luxuries of the east. The crusading movement provided an excellent opportunity for the town entrepreneurs to put their commercial instincts into practice.[47]

Trading activities greatly accelerated despite the pillaging which traders suffered from highwaymen and the endless feudal taxes and dues the traders were forced to pay to local lords as they transported goods through their territories. Still, the social system was definitely more stable than that of the early Middle Ages, with their marauding raiders and internal warfare. The increasing stability led to a more constant food supply, which in turn resulted in lower death rates and improvement in the rate of natural increase of the population.

Technological innovations also contributed to population growth. The moldboard plow, which had been used in Roman times, was rediscovered. This heavier plow could turn the tight soils of northern Europe, and it came to be commonly used during the tenth century. The substitution of three-field rotation for the old two-field system also brought substantial gains in agriculture. In practice it permitted three plantings a year rather than two, while at the same time raising the productivity of each planting by 16 percent. The effect was to double production and permit stable growth.

England in the time of William the Conqueror had a population of approximately 1.8 million. Three hundred years later the population had increased to roughly 2.7 million. Some of this increased population migrated to the small but growing towns. Without such increases, the growth of towns would hardly have been possible.

It should be noted that while the feudal order was basically rural, certain elements of the medieval legal and social system indirectly encouraged the growth of towns. Feudal lords were forbidden by custom to sell their lands, but lords badly in need of new funds could sell charters for new towns within their lands. Also, by encouraging the growth of older towns such lords could increase their annual rents. Towns were frequently able to purchase or bargain for various rights, such as the right to hold a regular market, the right to coin money and establish weights and measures, the right of citizens to be tried in their own courts, and—most important—the right to bear arms.[48] Over time cities became more or less autonomous and self-governing. City charters, in fact, bestowed the right of citizenship upon those living within the urban walls.

[47]For a superb analysis of the importance of trade to the development of Europe, see: Fernand Braudel, *The Mediterranean and the Mediterranean World in the Age of Philip II,* Sian Reynolds (trans.), Harper and Row, New York, 1972.
[48]Mumford, op. cit., p. 263.

TABLE 2-1
Estimated Populations and Areas of Selected Medieval Cities

City	Date	Population	Land area, acres
Venice	1363	77,700	810
Paris	1192	59,200	945
Florence	1381	54,747	268
Milan	1300	52,000	415
Genoa	1500	37,788	732
Rome	1198	35,000	3,450
London	1377	34,971	720
Bologna	1371	32,000	507
Barcelona	1359	27,056	650
Naples	1278	22,000	300
Hamburg	1250	22,000	510
Brussels	1496	19,058	650
Sienna	1385	16,700	412
Antwerp	1437	13,760	880
Pisa	1228	13,000	285
Frankfort	1410	9,844	320
Liège	1470	8,000	200
Amsterdam	1470	7,476	195
Zurich	1357	7,399	175
Berlin	1450	6,000	218
Geneva	1404	4,204	75
Vienna	1391	3,836	90
Dresden	1396	3,745	140
Leipzig	1474	2,076	106

Source: J. C. Russell, *Late Ancient and Medieval Population*, American Philosophical Society, Philadelphia, 1958, pp. 60–62.

As a result, medieval cities attracted the more skilled and the more ambitious of the rural population.

Characteristics of Towns

Medieval cities were quite small by contemporary standards, having hardly more inhabitants than present-day towns or villages (Table 2-1). Even during the Renaissance, cities of considerable prominence often had only 10,000 to 30,000 inhabitants.[49] Only Paris, Florence, Venice, and Milan are thought to have possibly reached populations of 100,000.[50] These figures are of course scholarly estimates of past size, rather than counts taken at the time. (For a discussion of the larger and more socially developed Arab cities of this period, see Chapter 16.)

Thick walls enclosed the medieval city; watchtowners and sometimes even external moats added to its military defense. The internal spatial

[49]Frederick Hiorns, *Town Building in History*, Harrap, London, 1956, p. 110.
[50]Henri Pirenne, *Economic and Social History of Medieval Europe*, Harcourt, New York, 1936, p. 173.

arrangement of the medieval town reflected its primary function either as an "episcopal city" functioning as an administrative center for church officials or as a military, and later a commercial, center. The main thoroughfares led directly from the outer gates to the source of protection and power—the cathedral or the feudal castle.[51] Outside the medieval bourgs, land was reserved for expansion, so that when the population increased, the older fortifications could be torn down and new city walls built farther out. The magnificent ringlike boulevards of Vienna and Paris are reminders of the medieval origins of these cities. When the walls were finallly demolished in the latter part of the nineteenth century, the resulting open space was used to construct the now-famous boulevards.

Within the medieval bourgs could be found a new social class of artisans, weavers, innkeepers, money changers, and metalsmiths known as the "bourgeoisie." This new class of merchants was in many ways the antithesis of the feudal nobility. They were organized into guilds, and their way of life was characterized by trade and functionally specialized production, not by the ownership of land. The rise of the medieval bourgeoisie undermined the traditional system and prepared the way for further changes, for, as a German phrase put it, "*Stadtluft macht frei*" ("City air makes one free").[52]

What eventually developed was a distinct form, a full urban community. Such communities, as defined by the German sociologist Max Weber, were economically based on trading and commercial relations. They exhibited the following features: (1) a fortification, (2) a market, a court of its own, and at least partial autonomous law, (3) a related form of association, and (4) at least partial political autonomy and self-governance.[53] Weber argues convincingly that such a totally self-governing urban community could emerge only in the west, where cities had political autonomy and urban residents shared common patterns of association and social statuses.

Medieval towns sometimes became organized around a particular craft or product, but the majority of the towns developed their greatest economic strength because of their performance of trade, commercial, and financial functions. Examples of cities that grew and prospered because of trade and banking are Venice, Milan, and Marseilles in the Mediterranean area, and Bremen, Hamburg, Cologne, and later Antwerp in the north.[54] In the later Middle Ages great financial families came to dominate many of these cities both economically and politically.

By the fourteenth century it was clear that the growth of town-based commerce was turning Europe away from the earlier manorial self-sufficiency toward an urban-centered, profit-oriented economy. The more ambitious cities were starting to flex their economic muscles. The Italian port cities grew

[51]Rose Hum Lee, *The City*, Lippincott, Chicago, 1955, p. 27.

[52]In its precise sense, the phrase refers to the medieval practice of recognizing the freedom of any serf who could manage to remain within the walls of the city for a year and a day.

[53]Weber, op. cit., p. 81.

[54]Bert Hoselitz, "The Role of Cities in the Economic Growth of Underdeveloped Countries," *Journal of Political Economy*, **61**:195–208, 1953.

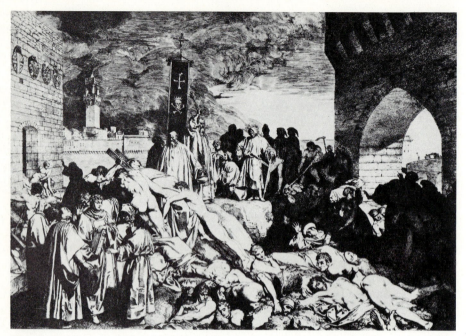

The Great Plague of 1348–1350 claimed as victims at least one-third of all European city dwellers. The engraving is of Florence. (Bettmann Archive)

wealthy on trade and began to expand their influence over the surrounding hinterland. Economic competition among the Italian city-states was augmented by warfare. Florence eliminated the competition of Pisa and Siena by conquering them militarily. The cities to the north were equally active in carving out a hinterland under their economic domination. Rouen was the economic center for 35 villages, Metz controlled 168, and Lübeck claimed 240 dependent villages within its territory.[55]

Plague

Urban development, however, was checked in the fourteenth century by the outbreak of plague. But even the devastation of the plague could not reverse the long-term growth of cities, although it certainly wrought havoc to a degree that is difficult to exaggerate. In its first three years, from 1348 through 1350, the plague, or "black death," wiped out at least a fourth of the population of Europe. One scholar of the plague simply says that "it undoubtedly was the worst disaster that has ever befallen mankind."[56] Before the year 1400, mortality

---

[55]John H. Mundy and Peter Reisenberg, *The Medieval Town,* Van Nostrand, New York, 1958, p. 35.
[56]William L. Langer, "The Black Death," in Scientific American's *Cities, Their Origin, Growth, and Human Impact,* Freeman, San Francisco, 1973, p. 106.

due to the plague rose to more than a third of the population of Europe. Over half the population of most cities was wiped out; few cities escaped with losses of less than a third. Florence went from 90,000 to 45,000 inhabitants and Siena from 42,000 to 15,000, and Hamburg lost almost two-thirds of its inhabitants.[57]

The path of the black death, which began in India and spread to the middle east and then Europe, followed the major trade routes. Thus, the effects were most pronounced in seaports and caravan centers.[58] The greatest losses occurred at the emerging centers of development and change. While the blow to the cities was severe, the effect of the plague on the rural manorial system was fatal. The feudal social structure never really recovered. Those peasants who were not killed by the plague fled to the towns, thus depriving the manors of their essential labor force. Serfs fleeing the plague often found that labor shortages had turned them into contract laborers or even town artisans.

The structure of basic social institutions such as the Catholic church was also dramatically altered by the black death. Many of the senior and most learned clergy perished; those who survived were likely to be more concerned with taking care of themselves than their flocks. New priests were trained hastily, if at all. Their desertions of their parishes when plague threatened, and their participation in the general loose living and immortality of the time, contributed to the religious upheavals that swept Europe for the next two centuries and culminated in the Protestant Reformation.

Since the plagues were considered to be a consequence of the wrath and vengeance of God, some people became fanatically religious, while the majority embraced the philosophy of "live, drink, and be merry, for tomorrow we may die." In the words of one scholar, "Charity grew cold, workers grew arrogant, revenues of Church and State dropped, people everywhere were more self-indulgent and frivolous than ever."[59] Chroniclers stress the lawlessness, depravity, and dissolute behavior of the time. In London, "In one house you might hear them roaring under the pangs of death, in the next tippling, whoring and belching out blasphemies against God."[60]

Various plagues, generally of decreasing severity, occurred in Europe until the late seventeenth century, but by the fifteenth century the cities were beginning to grow again. The plague had given the rural-based feudal system a blow from which it did not recover. From this point onward the history of western civilization was again to be the history of cities and city inhabitants.

Renaissance Cities

By the sixteenth century numerous cities, and particularly the Italian city-states, had developed a wealthy patrician class which had the interest, resources, and time to devote to the development and beautification of their

[57]Ibid., pp. 106–107.
[58]Andre Siegfried, *Routes of Contagion,* Harcourt, Brace and World, New York, 1965.
[59]George Deauz, *The Black Death,* Weybright and Talley, New York, 1969, p. 145.
[60]Langer, op. cit., p. 109.

Preindustrial and Industrial Cities: A Comparison

A comparison of the social structures of preindustrial and industrial cities helps us understand how the cities we live in differ from preindustrial cities and from the cities of the developing nations of the "third world." The industrial and preindustrial cities here described are "ideal types"—that is, they do not exist in reality but are rather abstractions or constructs obtained by carrying certain characteristics of each type of city to their logical extremes. Such "ideal types" can never exist in reality, but they are most useful in accentuating characteristics for the purposes of comparative historical research.

In his much-quoted article "Urbanism as a Way of Life," Louis Wirth gives a number of characteristics that he suggests are common to cities, and in particular to industrial cities.* For Wirth, a city is a permanent settlement possessing the following characteristics: (1) size, (2) density, (3) heterogeneity. The city is the place where large numbers of persons are crowded together in a limited space—persons who have different skills, interests, and cultural backgrounds. The result is the independence, anonymity, and cultural heterogeneity of city dwellers.

Industrial cities, he says, are characterized by (1) an extensive division of labor, (2) emphasis on innovation and achievement, (3) lack of primary ties to a localized neighborhood, (4) breakdown of primary groups, leading to social disorganization, (5) reliance on secondary forms of social control, such as the police, (6) interaction with others as players of specific roles rather than as total personalities, (7) destruction of close family life and a transfer of its functions to specialized agencies outside the home, (8) a diversity permitted in values and religious beliefs, (9) encouragement of social mobility and working one's way up, and (10) universal rules applicable to all, such as the same legal system, standardized weights and measures, and common prices. The industrial city thus is achievement-oriented and prizes a rationally oriented economic system. It is predominantly a middle-class city. In brief, urbanism as a way of life prizes rationality, secularism, diversity, innovation, and progress. It is change-oriented. According to Wirth, "The larger, the more densely populated,

---

*Louis Wirth, "Urbanism as a Way of Life," *American Journal of Sociology*, **44**:1–24, July, 1938.

the more heterogeneous the community, the more accentuated the characteristics associated with urbanism wil be."† (Wirth's views are discussed in detail in Chapter 6, City Life-styles.)

Gideon Sjoberg paints a different picture for preindustrial cities.‡ He suggests that a number of factors we associate with cities are probably generic only to industrial cities. In contrast to Wirth he suggests that preindustrial cities serve primarily as governmental or religious centers and only secondarily as commercial hubs. Specialization of work is limited, and the production of goods depends on animate (human or animal) power. There is little division of labor; the artisan participates in every phase of manufacture. Home and workplace are not separate as in the industrial city; an artisan or merchant lives in back of or above the workplace. Justice is based not on what you do but on who you are. Standardization is not of major importance. Different people pay different prices for the same goods, and there is no universal system of weights and measures. In brief, the preindustrial city stresses particularism over universalism. Class and kinship systems are relatively inflexible; education is the prerogative of the rich. A small elite maintains a privileged status over the disadvantaged masses.

The continuity with rural values is obvious. Emphasis is on traditional ways of doing things; the guild system discourages innovation. Ascription rather than achievement is the norm; a worker is expected to do the job he or she was born into. A person lives and works in a particular quarter of the city and rarely moves beyond this area. Social control is the responsibility of the primary group rather than secondary groups; persons are known to one another and are subject to strict kinship control. Formal police forces are unnecessary. Family influence is strong, with the traditional extended family accepted as the ideal. Within all classes, children, and especially sons, are valued. There is great similarity in values, and little diversity in religion is tolerated. Opportunity for social mobility is severely restricted by a caste system or rigid class system. There is little or no middle class, which is the backbone of the industrial city; one is either rich or poor.

The preindustrial city lacks what the great French sociologist Emile Durkheim called "moral density" or what we today call "social integration." By contemporary standards the preindustrial city is neither socially nor economically integrated. The walled quarters of the preindustrial city are largely independent units; their physical proximity to one

†Ibid, p. 9.
‡Gideon Sjoberg, *The Preindustrial City: Past and Present*, Free Press, Glencoe, Ill., 1960.

47

another does not lead to social interaction. The city as a whole may possess hetereogeneity, but actual social contacts rarely extend beyond one's own group.

No real city of course conforms exactly either to the industrial model or to the preindustrial model. (Note in Chapter 3, The Rise of Urban America, that the preindustrial model does not appear to fit American colonial cities, although these were clearly preindustrial.) Models are best used as aids that sharpen our comparative understanding of differences; they should never be mistaken for actual places.

cities. Renaissance cities such as Florence embarked on major building programs. The revival of interest in the classical style, and in classical symmetry, perspective, and proportion, had a profound effect on the design of both public and private structures. The artistic talents even of artists such as Michelangelo and Leonardo da Vinci were used to beautify the cities; Leonardo also developed proposals for urban planning. Rather than simply building at random, the more prosperous city-states hired architects to make planned changes. The classical effect can be seen in the use of straight streets and regular squares, and particularly in the use of perspective. The early medieval city with its semirural nature had aptly symbolized that age. The sixteenth- and seventeenth-century Renaissance city symbolized the humanistic ideology of its age and proudly proclaimed its secular urban culture.

The sixteenth-century city gained ever-greater economic and cultural domination over rural aeas, but it also marked the beginning of the end of the city as a self-governing unit independent of the larger nation-state. During the medieval period, kings and city dwellers had been natural allies, since both wished to subdue the power of the local nobility. In order to cast off the last fetters of feudal restraint, the city burghers supplied the monarch with men and—most important—money to fight wars; the monarch in turn granted ever larger charter powers to the towns. Once the monarchs had subdued the rural lords, however, they turned their attention to the prosperous towns. Gradually the independent powers of the cities were reduced as they became part of nations in fact as well as in name. The structure of social organization in Europe was changing to the larger geographical unit: the nation-state. The loss of political independence, however, was compensated for by the economic advantages of being part of a nation-state rather than a collection of semi-independent feudal states and chartered cities. National government usually meant better and safer roads and therefore easier and cheaper transport of goods, and a larger potential market area. Merchants also had the advantages of reasonably unified laws, a common coinage, and standardized measures of weight and volume—all things which today we take for granted. Emergent business classes prospered from the certainty and stability provided by the king's national government. The capitalist city was coming into existence.

Influences of Technology. The technological development of gunpowder and the cannon also contributed to changing the nature of the walled city. The traditional defenses of rampart, bastion, and moat were of limited utility in stopping cannon fire. Cities that hoped to resist the armies of a king had to shift their attention from interior architecture and urban planning to the engineering of fortifications. Only elaborate defensive outworks could stop cannon fire, and so the city unwittingly became the captive of its own horizontal defenses. While one can question Lewis Mumford's view that the decline of the city began with the end of the Middle Ages, it is certainly true that the city of the seventeenth century was changing.

Unable to grow outward, cities began to expand vertically and fill in open

This Hogarth print of Beer Street in London shows how streets
served as far more than transportation arteries. (Bettmann Archive)

spaces within the city walls. The increased crowding which resulted had a bad
effect on both the quality and the length of life. Filthy living conditions,
combined with minimal sanitation and an absence of any knowledge of public
health practices, resulted in the rapid spread of contageous diseases and
consequently high death rates. As John Graut's pioneer research in the
seventeenth century on the London Bills of Mortality demonstrated, London
actually recorded more deaths than births. Only heavy migration from the
countryside allowed the city to grow in population rather than decline as would

otherwise have been the case with such a high mortality rate. As late as 1790 the city of London had three deaths for every two births.[61] A century later mortality rates in the city still exceeded those in rural districts.[62] The possibilities of jobs and excitement in the city continued to attract ruralites.

Large-scale urban growth was closely tied to the growth of the population as a whole. Unit about the middle of the seventeenth century, the population of the world had been growing at a very slow rate: 0.4 percent a year. As a result, by the beginning of the eighteenth century the world population was roughly 500 million, or double that at the time of Christ. Then momentous changes occurred that resulted in what we call the "demographic transition" or the "demographic revolution." Population growth suddenly spurted in the latter part of the eighteenth century, not through increases in the birthrate— it was already high—but through declines in the death rate. Population increases continued to the nineteenth and twentieth centuries. The term "demographic transition" refers to this transition from a time of high birthrates matched by almost equally high death rates, through a period of declining death rates, to a period where birthrates also begin to decline, and eventually to a period where population stability is reestablished—this time through low birthrates matched by equally low death rates.

Changes in Agriculture. Much of the decline in the death rates can be attributed to technological changes in agriculture that assured both a better and a more reliable food supply. Without such increases in food supply, cities could not grow and expand. As late as the beginning of the nineteenth century, the produce of nine farms was still required to support one urban family. (Today each American farmer supports approximately seventy-five other persons.)

At the beginning of the eighteenth century English agriculture was still primitive. One-quarter of the farmland was left fallow and thus unproductive each year. Pasturelands and water rights were held in common, as were the woods which provided hunting and firewood. Then, within the period of half a century, English agriculture was revolutionized. Jethro Tull published the results of thirty years of research on his estates, and the new ideas were quickly adopted by much of the landed aristocracy. Tull advocated planting certain crops on fallow land to restore nutrients to the earth, thus radically increasing the usable acreage. He also recommended deep plowing and a system for foddering animals through the winter.

At the same time it was being discovered that selective breeding of animals was far superior to letting nature take its course. Striking changes can be seen by comparing the weight of animals at the Smithfield Fair in 1710 and 1795; the average weight of oxen went from 370 pounds to 800 pounds, that of calves from 50 to 150 pounds, and that of sheep from 38 to 80 pounds.

[61]Dorothy George, *London Life in the Eighteenth Century*, Harper Torchbooks, New York, 1964, p. 25.
[62]Eric Lampara, "The Urbanizing World," in H. J. Dyds and Michael Wolfe (eds.), *The Victorian World*, Routledge & Kegan Paul, London, 1976.

Accompanying these agricultural improvements in England were the notorious Enclosure Acts, which took the village commons from joint ownership and gave them to the lord enjoying ancient title to the land. While disastrous for the local yeoman, the larger enclosures could be worked more efficiently by the lords who were using the new agricultural knowledge. The result was an increase in both the quality and the quantity of the food supply. While it is extremely hazardous to generalize about living conditions, there apparently was an improvement over earlier centuries. Death rates began to go down, and populations expanded rapidly.

The abandonment of traditional subsistence agriculture and the orientation to a market economy meant that rationality was replacing tradition, and contract was taking the place of custom. The calculation implicit in the land-enclosure acts destroyed small peasant landholders but made it possible for London and other cities to be assured of foodstuffs and thus to grow as manufacturing and commercial centers.

INDUSTRIAL CITIES

Technological Improvements and the Industrial Revolution

The movement of agriculture surpluses was facilitated greatly by the construction of new toll roads, which were built in great numbers after 1745. The building of canals also greatly stimulated urban development. By 1800 the city of London was the second-largest in the world, with a population of 861,000.[63] This was roughly 11 percent of the total British population. Without the technological breakthroughs in agriculture and transportation, this type of urban concentration would have been impossible.

Roughly at the same time that agricultural improvements were both increasing yields and releasing workers, inventions were being made that would allow for the growth of whole new industries. Eighteenth-century inventions in the manufacture of cloth, such as the flying shuttle and the spinning jenny, were capped in 1767 by Watt's invention of a usable steam engine. The steam engine provided a new and bountiful inanimate source of energy. The cotton industry boomed, and it was soon followed by other industries. The machines, rather than eliminating the need for workers, rapidly increased the demand for an urban work force. A factory system began to emerge based on specialization and mechanization. As a consequence, new forms of occupational structure and a more complex stratification system began to develop. In the mechanized, capital-intensive industries urban bondage replaced rural bondage for poor laborers.

The Second Urban Revolution

Without population growth and the release of workers from the land, it is hard to see how the early industrial cities could have grown at all, for as noted

[63]Tertius Chandler and Gerald Fox, *3000 Years of Urban Growth*, Academic Press, New York, 1974, p. 323.

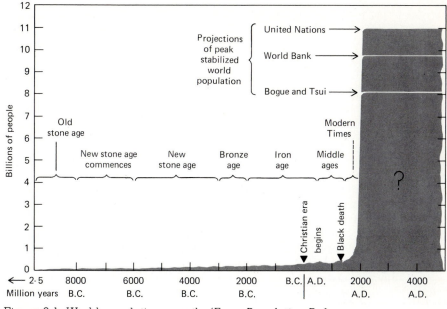

Figure 2-1. World population growth. (*From Population Reference Bureau.*)

earlier, unhealthful living conditions in cities meant that they were not able to maintain, much less increase, their population without in-migration from rural areas.

Thus the second urban revolution was not the emergence of cities but rather the changes that for the first time made it possible for more than 10 percent of the population to live in urban places. This new urban revolution started in Europe. Rapid expansion of population (Figure 2-1) and national economic expansion did not, however, translate into healthful living conditions in the bulging European towns that were turning into cities. Eighteenth-century London was a model of filth, crowding, and disease. The early stages of industrialism hardly did much to improve the situation. While rural mortality decreased, urban mortality was kept high by unbelievably poor sanitary conditions. The novels of Charles Dickens give an accurate portrayal of life in such cities. Cholera and other epidemics were common until the middle of the nineteenth century, and until the 1840s many of London's sewers emptied into the Thames just a few feet above the ducts that drew drinking water from the river. It was fortunate that the fascination and opportunities of the city continued to attract rural migrants, since without migration the cities would not have grown but died. Until the latter part of the nineteenth century, the old English observation, "The city is the graveyard of countrymen" was all too accurate.

Engels on Industrial Slums

Fredrich Engels (1820–1895), Karl Marx's close associate and collaborator, was an acute observer of the social horrors of nineteenth-century urban industrialization. He likewise was a fine writer with a mastery of detail and mood rivaling Dickens's. Note his description of life in the industrial slums of Manchester.*

The view from this bridge—mercifully concealed from smaller mortals by a parapet as high as a man—is quite characteristic of the entire district. At the bottom the Irk flows, or rather stagnates. It is a narrow, coal-black stinking river full of filth and garbage which it deposits on the lower-lying bank. In dry weather, an extended series of the most revolting blackish green pools of slime remain standing on this bank, out of whose depths bubbles of miasmatic gases constantly rise and give forth a stench that is unbearable even on the bridge forty or fifty feet above the level of the water. . . . Above Ducie Bridge there are tall tannery buildings, and further up are dye-works, bone mills, and gasworks. The total entirety of the liquid wastes and solid offscourings of these works finds its way into the River Irk, which receives as well the contents of the adjacent sewers and privies. One can therefore imagine what kind of residues the stream deposits. Below Ducie Bridge, on the left, one looks into piles of rubbish, the refuse, filth and decaying matter of the courts on the steep left bank of the river. Here one house is packed very closely upon another, and because of the steep pitch of the bank a part of every house is visible. All of them are blackened with smoke, crumbling, old, with broken window panes and window frames. The background is formed by old factory buildings, which resemble barracks. On the right, low-lying bank stands a long row of houses and factories. The second house is a roofless ruin, filled with rubble, and the third stands in such a low situation that the ground floor is uninhabitable and is as a result without windows and doors. The background here is formed by the paupers' cemetery and the stations of the railways to Liverpool and Leeds. Behind these is the workhouse, Manchester's "Poor Law Bastille." It is built on a hill, like a citadel, and from behind its high walls and battlements looks down threateningly upon the working-class quarter that lies below. . . .

Passing along a rough path on the river bank, in between posts and washing lines, one penetrates into this chaos of little one-storied, one-roomed huts. Most of them have earth floors, cooking, living and sleeping all take place in one room. In such a hole, barely six feet long and five feet wide, I saw two beds—and what beds and bedding—that filled the room, except for the doorstep and fireplace in several others I found absolutely nothing, although the door was wide open and the inhabitants were leaning against it. Everywhere in front of the doors were rubbish and refuse, it was impossible to see whether any sort of

*Friedrich Engels, *The Condition of the Working Class in England in 1844*, (first published in 1845), Progress Publishers, Moscow, 1973.

pavement lay under this, but here and there I felt it out with my feet. This whole pile of cattle-sheds inhabited by human beings was surrounded on two sides by houses and a factory and on a third side by the river. . . . [A] narrow gateway led out of it into an almost equally miserably-built and miserably-kept labyrinth of dwellings.

PART TWO

AMERICAN URBANIZATION

CHAPTER

3

THE RISE OF URBAN AMERICA

Cities force growth and make men talkative and entertaining, but they also make them artificial.

Ralph Waldo Emerson

INTRODUCTION

In this chapter we cross the ocean to the wilderness of North America and trace the coming of age of the American city. As you read through the following pages, note the major role played by environmental factors during the colonial period. (All the major early cities were seaports.) During the nineteenth century, by contrast, changing technology, particularly advances in transportation such as the railroad, came to have a far more important—if not dominant—impact. Dramatic population growth through immigration and changes in urban governance and organization also came to play a major role in the growth and development of cities. This chapter, then, takes us from Jamestown up to the contemporary era following World War II.

COLONISTS AS TOWN BUILDERS

We are rather new at being an urban continent. The first European colonists to arrive in North America found a land without indigenous cities, although the Indians of the northwest coast, with their reliable food supply from the sea, had established well-built settled villages with an elaborate social structure. Also at Mesa Verde in southwest Colorado the "ancient ones" had built cliff dwellings. By and large though, the North American Indian population was nomadic or lived in agricultural villages such as Taos in the southwest. Cahokia, located in the Mississippi River valley of southern Illinois, was the most populous pre-Columbian settlement north of Mexico, thriving from about A.D. 900 to A.D. 1400 as a farming and trade center. The Native American population of North America may have numbered less than 1 million at the time of the Jamestown settlement (1607).[1]

From the first, the town-building orientation of the colonists contrasted with Indian ways. The North American Indians lived in nature rather than building upon it. They viewed themselves as part of the ecology, part of the physical world. Their goal was not to master nature but to identify their niche and their relationship with the world around them. The Europeans came, on the contrary, not to adjust to the environment but to dominate and reshape it. The Puritans, for example, believed themselves to be God's chosen people.

The colonists' emphasis was on conquering nature, and unfortunately for the Indians, the colonists tended to view them as a part of the environment. The Indians were treated as just another environmental problem that had to be encountered and mastered before civilization could be introduced. The implication for the future was clear. There was no niche for the Indian in the town-oriented civilization of the colonists.

What has just been said is, of course, an overgeneralization, but from our urban perspective the important point is that the concept of the city, and all the good and evil it represents, came to the new world with the first European

---

[1]Some estimates range as high as 10 million Indians, but in any case, malaria and other European-introduced diseases destroyed most of the indigenous population.

59

colonist. This concept, with all the special technology, social organizations, and attitudes it entailed, was an importation from post-Renaissance Europe. This meant, among other things, that North American cities had no feudal period.[2]

The plans of the various companies that settled the English colonies in North America called for the establishment of tight little villages and commercial centers. The first successful settlements at Jamestown and Plymouth Colony were in fact small towns. Thus, early English settlers were not primarily agriculturists but rather town dwellers coming with town expectations. In fact, the initially limited number of farmers was a problem. Jamestown nearly perished from an excess of adventurers and a dearth of skilled artisans and farmers. As John Smith wrote back to the English sponsors of the Jamestown colony,

> When you send againe I intreat you rather send but thirty Carpenters, husbandmen, gardners, fisher men, blacksmiths, masons, and diggers up of trees, roots, well provided; then a tousand of such as we haus: for except we be able both to loge them, and feed them the most will consume with what of necessaries before they can be made good for anything.[3]

The wilderness of the new world appeared strange and hostile, and the early colonists sorely missed their towns. William Bradford movingly describes the world of the Pilgrims of 1620:

> They had now no friends to wellcome them nor inns to entertaine or refresh their weatherbeaten bodys, no houses or much less townes to repaire too, to seeke for succoure. . .. Besids, what could they see but a hidious and desolate wilderness, full of wild beasts and wild men? and what multituds ther might be of them they knew not.[4]

MAJOR SETTLEMENTS

Five communities spearheaded the urbanization of the seventeenth-century English colonies. The northernmost was Boston on New England's "stern and rockbound coast"; the southernmost was the newer and much smaller settlement of Charles Town in South Carolina.[5] Barely making an indentation in the 1,100 miles of wilderness separating these two were Newport, in the Providence Plantations of Rhode Island; New Amsterdam, which in 1664 became New York; and William Penn's Philadelphia on the Delaware River at the mouth of the Schuylkill.

---

[2]Lewis Mumford would not agree with this statement. Mumford sees the New England villages and towns as the last flickering of the medieval order. See, for example, Lewis Mumford, *Sticks and Stones,* Liveright, New York, 1924.
[3]John Smith, *The General Historie of Virginia, New England, and the Summer Isles,* University Microfilms, Ann Arbor, Mich., 1966 (first published in London, 1624), p. 72.
[4]*Bradford's History of Plymouth Plantation* (William T. Davis, ed.), Scribner, New York, 1908, p. 96.
[5]Constance McLaughlin Green, *The Rise of Urban America,* Harper and Row, New York, 1965, p. 2.

Environment played a heavy role in the early development of these first five cities. All five were seaports, either on the Atlantic or—as in the case of Philadelphia—with access to the sea. Later towns such as Baltimore had similar environmental advantages. As seaports they became commercial centers funneling trade between Europe and the colonies. In terms of social structure all were Protestant, and against the established church, except for the ruling class of Charleston and (partially) New York. As Bridenbaugh points out, the social structure of these towns was fashioned by a background of relatively common political institutions; and the economic and cultural roots, whether English or Dutch, lay for the most part in the rising middle class of the old world.[6]

The five important urban settlements had certain similar characteristics. First, all had favorable sites. As noted above, all were seaports, or, like Philadelphia, were on a navigable river. Second, all were commercial cities emphasizing trade and commerce. Third, all had hinterlands or back country to develop, although Newport would find its hinterland increasingly cut off by Boston in the eighteenth century. Finally, all these cities were fundamentally British. Even New York, which was more cosmopolitan than many European cities, was controlled by a British upper stratum.

New England

The story of early New England is the story of its towns, for New England from the very beginning was town-oriented. The Puritan religious dissenters who originally settled New England came heavily from the more populous centers of old England. They numbered in their midst many tradespeople, mechanics, and artisans. In the new world these religious dissenters sought to create tight urban communal utopias rather than spreading themselves widely over the landscape. Massachusetts Bay, according to John Winthrop, was to be "as a City upon a Hill." In that colony there existed a social system of a nature unknown outside New England. The cordial union between the clergy, the bench, the bar, and respectable society formed a tight, self-reinforcing social elite.

Boston early outstripped its rivals in both population size and economic influence and kept its lead for a century in spite of Indian wars that twice threatened its existence. Boston had barely 300 residents in the 1630s, but by 1650 there were over 2,000 residents, and a visitor could report—with some exaggeration, perhaps—that it was a sumptuous "city" and "Center Towne and Metropolis of this Wildernesse."[7]

By 1742, Boston had a population of 16,000. The barrenness of Boston's hinterland inclined Bostonians to look to the sea, and the town grew to prosperity on trade and shipbuilding. Before Boston was a generation old it

[6]Carl Bridenbaugh, *Cities in the Wilderness*, Capricorn Books, New York, 1964.
[7]Quoted in Kenneth T. Jackson and Stanley K. Schutty (eds.), *Cities in American History*, Knopf, New York, 1972.

had "begun to extend its control into the back country, and to develop a metropolitan form of economy that was essentially modern."[8]

Newport, the second New England city down the coast, was founded in 1639 by victims of religious bigotry in Massachusetts. Newport's growth was steady but far from spectacular; in a hundred years the population grew from 96 to 6,200. However, although Newport remained small, its growing commerce and well-ordered community life gave it a significant place in emerging urban America. In Newport, as in Boston, education was encouraged; in addition, Newport had religious toleration.

The Middle Colonies

Manhattan was from the beginning the most cosmopolitan of the colonial cities, a fact reflected in the diversity of languages spoken there. Father Isaac Jogues recorded that as early as 1643 there were already "men of 18 different languages." Partially because of this mixture of national and religious backgrounds (Dutch Calvinists, Anglicans, Quakers, Baptists, Huguenots, Lutherans, Presbyterians, and even a sprinkling of Jews, Congregation Shearith Israel being organized in 1706), New York was by far the liveliest of towns, a position many people maintain it still holds. Interestingly enough, as of 1720 a third of New York's population was black.[9] With the abandonment of slavery in the north—largely for economic reasons—the proportion of blacks declined substantially. New York was already an American melting pot, although the stew would still be a bit lumpy three centuries later.

New York also had decisive environmental advantages that contributed heavily to eventual emergence as "*the* American city." First, Manhattan had a magnificent deepwater natural harbor. Second, New York was blessed with a fertile soil. Third, the city had easy access to the interior hinterland by way of the Hudson River. The New England towns, by contrast, found their economic growth greatly hindered by the lack of an accessible, fertile hinterland.

Philadelphia, William Penn's "City of Brotherly Love," laid out in 1692, was the youngest of the colonial cities. This was in many ways an advantage, for by the time the city was organized, the Indians had departed and the land was already being settled. A policy of religious toleration and an extremely rich and fertile hinterland allowed rapid growth. By the time Philadelphia was six years old it had 4,000 inhabitants; by 1720 the number had risen to 10,000.[10] Accounts of the day noted the regularity of the town's gridiron pattern with its central square, and most frequently the substantial nature of its buildings.

> A City, and Towns were raised then,
> Wherein we might abide,
> Planters also, and Husband-men,

---

[8]Carl Bridenbaugh, quoted in Charles N. Glaab and A. Theodore Brown, *A History of Urban America,* Macmillan, New York, 1967, pp. 25–26.
[9]Green, op. cit., p. 22.
[10]Ibid., p. 27.

Had Land enough beside.
The best of Houses then was known,
   To be of Wood and Clay,
But now we build of Brick and Stone,
   Which is a better way.[11]

The South

The southernmost of the colonial cities was Charles Town (Charleston), founded in 1680 on a spit of land between the mouths of the Ashley and Cooper rivers. The town grew slowly; two decades after its founding it had only 1,100 inhabitants and had "not yet produced any Commodities fit for ye markett or Europe, but a few skins—and a little cedar."[12] For decades rice, indigo, and skins formed the basis of its commerce.

Charleston's social structure was unique among the major cities. The major difference was that by the 1740s over half of Charleston's inhabitants were slaves. The middle-class artisans and shopkeepers who were the backbone of the northern cities were caught in Charleston between the aristocratic pretensions of the large landowners and the increasing skills of the trained slaves. The result was civic atrophy, the major local event being the opening of the horse-racing season. Charleston had few municipal services and could not claim even a single tax-supported school.

COLONIAL URBAN INFLUENCE

The relatively small populations by contemporary standards of the cities and towns of colonial America should not distract us from their seminal importance. Politically, economically, and socially these five towns dominated early colonial life. Because of their access to the sea they served as entrepôts, exchanging the produce of the hinterland for the finished products of Europe. In addition to their commercial function they also served as the places where new ideas and forms of social organization could be developed.

Because the colonial cities had to meet uniquely urban problems, such as paving streets, removing garbage, and caring for the poor, collective efforts developed. In the words of one historian:

> In these problems of town living which affected the entire community lay one of the vast differences between town and country society, and out of the collective efforts to solve these urban problems arose a sense of community responsibility and power that was to further differentiate the two ways of life.[13]

---

[11]Richard Frame, "A Short Description of Pennsylvania in 1692," in Albert Cook Myers (ed.), *Narratives of Early Pennsylvania, West New Jersey, and Delaware*, Scribner, New York, 1912; reprinted in Ruth E. Sutter, *The Next Place You Come To*, Prentice-Hall, Englewood Cliffs, N.J., 1973, p. 90.
[12]Green, op. cit., p. 21.
[13]Charles N. Glaab, *The American City*, Dorsey, Homewood, Ill., 1963, p. 3.

New York's Wall Street in 1790. The two men in the foreground are Governor Phillip Schuyler and Alexander Hamilton. Walking toward them are Aaron Burr and his daughter, Theodosia. (Museum of the City of New York)

As a result of the town-based settlement pattern, by 1690 almost 10 percent of the colonial population was urban, a higher percentage than that found in England itself at the same time. With the subduing of the Indians and the opening up of the hinterland for cultivation, the percentage (not, of course, the actual number) of urban dwellers decreased between 1690 and 1790. The opening up of frontier hinterlands permitted greater population dispersal than had previously been possible. Not until 1830 was the urban percentage of the total population as high as it had been at the close of the seventeenth century.[14]

Politically, the cities were dominant. With the exception of Virginia, where the landed aristocracy did not live in cities but nonetheless followed the latest London fashions and maintained a strong commerce with Europe, the cities set the political as well as the social tone. And the merchant classes became increasingly dissatisfied with British policy. The Crown's tax measures had a bad effect on business. Boston was called "the metropolis of sedition"; and as Lord Howe, commander of the British forces at the time of the Revolution, noted, "Almost all of the People of Parts and Spirit were in the Rebellion."[15] This was not surprising, since Britain's revenue policy had struck deep at

[14]Charles N. Glaab and A. Theodore Brown, *A History of Urban America,* 2d. ed., Macmillan, New York, 1976, p. 21.
[15]Green, op. cit., p. 51.

TABLE 3-1
Great Cities of America, 1790, 1870, 1980

1790	1870	1980
New York, N.Y.	New York, N.Y.	New York, N.Y.
Philadelphia, Pa.	Philadelphia, Pa.	Chicago, Ill.
Boston, Mass.	Brooklyn, N.Y.	Los Angeles, Cal.
Charleston, S.C.	St. Louis, Mo.	Philadelphia. Pa.
Baltimore, Md.	Chicago, Ill.	Houston, Texas
Salem, Mass.	Baltimore, Md.	Detroit, Mich.
Newport, R.I.	Boston, Mass.	Dallas, Texas
Providence, R.I.	Cincinnati, Ohio	Baltimore, Md.
Gloucester, Mass.	New Orleans, La.	San Diego, Cal.
Newburyport, Mass.	San Francisco, Cal.	San Antonio, Texas

Source: U.S. Bureau of the Census and author.

urban prosperity. Business and commercial leaders were determined to resist the Crown rather than suffer financial reverses. This helps to explain the middle-class and upper-class nature of much of the support for the American Revolution.

THE GROWING NEW REPUBLIC: 1790–1860

After the Revolutionary War the cities continued their growth, although the first United States Census, taken in 1790, revealed that only 5 percent of the new nation's 4 million people lived in places of 2,500 or more. Numerically America was overwhelmingly rural, but this demographic dominance was not reflected in the distribution of power or the composition of the leadership groups. The urban population had an influence on government, finance, and society as a whole far out of proportion to its size. The Federalist Party, which elected John Adams as the second President, was largely an urban-based party representing commercial and banking rather than agrarian interests.

Although three-quarters of the national population still lived within 50 miles of the Atlantic Ocean, there were already clear and widening differences between townspeople and rural dwellers. The farmers' orientation was toward the expanding western frontier, while the townspeople were still oriented toward Europe. Because of their status as ocean ports, the American coastal cities frequently had more in common with the old world, and certainly better communication with it, than with their own hinterlands.

The census of 1790 showed that the largest city in the young nation was New York, with 33,000 inhabitants. Philadelphia was the second-largest city, with a population of 28,000 (see Table 3-1). Twenty years later New York had over 100,000 persons.

Such rapid growth of the cities after the Revolutionary War was not only the result of foreign and rural immigration; an exceptionally high rate of natural replacement also played a large part. Precise data are lacking, but the birthrate

TABLE 3-2
Percent of Population Urban, United States,
1790–1980

1790	5.1	1900	39.7
1800	6.1	1910	45.7
1810	7.3	1920	51.2
1820	7.2	1930	56.2
1830	8.8	1940	56.5
1840	10.8	1950 (old def.)	59.0
1850	15.3	1950 (new def.)	64.0
1860	19.8	1960	69.9
1870	25.7	1970	73.5
1880	28.2	1980	73.7
1890	35.1		

Source: U.S. Bureau of the Census.

is estimated to have been at least 55 per 1,000, or near the physiological upper limit. Each married woman in 1790 bore an average of almost eight children. One result of the high birthrate and the immigration from Europe of young adults was a national median age of only sixteen years. (By comparison, the median age for the white population today is thirty-two years.) Between 1790 and 1860 the population would increase dramatically, doubling every twenty-three years—a rate equivalent to that in some developing countries today.

The sheer abundance of land and the almost unlimited possibilities for fee-simple tenure meant freedom from Europe's lingering feudal constraints.[16] As put by a European visitor: "It does not seem difficult to find out the reasons why people multiply faster here than in Europe. . .. There is such an amount of good land yet uncultivated that a newly married man can get a spot of ground where he may comfortably subsist with his wife and children."[17]

As Table 3-2 indicates, the percentage of the population that is urban has grown every decade except 1810–1820. The decline in that decade was chiefly due to the destruction of American commerce resulting from the Embargo Acts and the War of 1812. That war came close to destroying the coastal cities; and, partially as a result of isolation from English manufactures and products, the American cities began developing manufacturing interests. Even Thomas Jefferson, an ardent opponent of cities, was forced to concede:

> He, therefore, who is now against domestic manufacture, must be for reducing us either to dependence on that foreign nation or to be clothed in skins and to live like wild beasts in dens and caverns. I am not one of them; experience has taught me that manufacturers are now as necessary to our independence as to our comfort.[18]

[16]Sam Bass Warner, Jr., *The Urban Wilderness*, Harper and Row, New York, 1972, p. 16.
[17]Quoted in James H. Cassedy, *Demography in Early America*, Harvard University Press, Cambridge, Mass., 1969, pp. 154–155.
[18]P. L. Ford, *The Works of Thomas Jefferson*, Putnam, New York, 1904, pp. 503–504.

Founding and Expansion of Cities

The period before the Civil War saw a rapid expansion of existing cities and the founding of many new ones. The invention of the railroad played a major role in this growth. During the period from 1820 to 1860, cities grew at a more rapid rate than at any other time before or since in American history.[19] It is noteworthy that of the fifty largest cities in America, only seven were incorporated before 1816, thirty-nine were incorporated between 1816 and 1876, and only four have been incorporated since 1876. Cincinnati, Pittsburgh, Memphis, Louisville, Detroit, Chicago, Denver, Portland, and Seattle are all early and mid-nineteenth-century cities. In the far west, the discovery of gold and then silver did much to spur town building. Some later became ghost towns, but San Francisco prospered as *the* major city of the west.

The influence of environmental factors on the growth of nineteenth-century cities can be seen from the fact that of the nine cities which by 1860 had passed the 100,000 mark, eight were ports. The one exception really wasn't an exception; it was the then independent city of Brooklyn, which shared the benefits of the country's greatest harbor.[20] (As of 1980 only one of the nation's 30 largest cities—Atlanta—was not located on a waterway.)

By the eve of the Civil War the first city of the nation was clearly New York. It had both a magnificent harbor and a large hinterland to sustain growth, and relatively flat terrain westward from the Hudson River. Nonetheless, what assured New York its dominance was the willingness to speculate on the technologies of first the Erie Canal and then the railroad. Mayor DeWitt Clinton prophesied that the canal would "create the greatest inland trade ever witnessed" and allow New York to "become the granary of the world, the emporium of commerce, the seat of manufactures, the focus of moneyed operations." He was right.

The completion of the canal in 1825 greatly stimulated New York City's trade and gave it an economic supremacy which has yet to be surpassed. Thus, the original environmental advantage stimulated a technological advance—the Erie Canal—which in turn led to population growth and changes in the social organization of business and government. New York's quick acceptance of railroads as a technological breakthrough, and the possibilities thus presented, further solidified the city's dominant position. Not only was New York the most important American city, it also had become a major world metropolis by the time of the Civil War. New York grew from just over 60,000 in 1800 to over 1 million in 1860 (1,174,774, to be exact, including Brooklyn, which was then an independent municipality). Of the world's cities only London and Paris were larger. By 1860, in addition to serving as the nation's financial center, New York also handled a third of the country's exports and a full two-thirds of the imports. New York's increase in size was matched by the

[19]Glaab, op. cit., p. 65.
[20]Blake McKelveg, *The Urbanization of America, 1860–1915*, Rutgers University Press, New Brunswick, N.J., 1963, p. 4. See Howard P. Chudacoff, *The Evolution of American Urban Society*, Prentice-Hall, Englewood Cliffs, N.J., 1975, chap. 9.

increasing heterogeneity of its inhabitants, with their different tastes, aspirations, and needs—all of which could be best satisfied only in the large city.

Land speculation spurred the growth of cities. Fueled by a stream of immigrants and a greed for profits, cities went through periods of wild land speculation and building—only to be followed eventually by economic collapse and depression. Cincinnati, the "Queen City of the West," for example, experienced a boom during the 1820s, and during that decade its population expanded rapidly as a result of the development and use of steamboats. In other cities the technology of the railroad played a similar role in spurring growth.

Only in the deep south, where cotton was king, did the building of cities languish. In the plantation owners' view, cotton fields came before manufacturing and commerce. The dominance of agriculture can be seen in the development—or, more correctly, the lack of development—of Charleston. At the beginning of the nineteenth century Charleston was the fifth-largest American city; by 1860 it had slipped to twenty-sixth place.[21] (As a consequence of the war, a devastating earthquake, and economic stagnation, Charleston was not numbered among even the fifty largest cities in 1900.) The post-Civil War stagnation of Charleston is reflected in the saying that Charleston was "too poor to paint and too proud to whitewash."

Marketplace Centers

Before the Civil War, American cities, while undergoing tremendous growth, retained many preindustrial characteristics. The urban economy was still in a commercial rather than an industrial stage. Businesspeople were primarily merchants who intermittently took on subsidiary functions such as manufacturing, banking, and speculating. In 1850, 85 percent of the population was still classified as rural; 64 percent was engaged in agriculture.

Physically, the city was a walking city with a radius extending over 3 miles. The separation of workplace and residence so common in contemporary American cities was limited. Residences, businesses, and public buildings were intermixed with little specialization by area: "The first floor was given over to commerce, the second and third reserved for the family and clerks, and the fourth perhaps for storage. People lived and worked in the same house or at least in the same neighborhood."[22]

The separation that did occur was the obverse of the pattern of wealthy in the suburbs and poor in the city that we have come to accept as the American norm. (See Chapters 4 and 5 for discussion of theories of contemporary urban growth.) In early American cities, the well-to-do tended to live not on the periphery but near the center. In an era of slow, uncomfortable, and inadequate

---

[21]Nelson M. Blake, *A History of American Life and Thought*, McGraw-Hill, New York, 1963, p. 156.
[22]Christopher Tunnard and Henry Hope Reed, *American Skyline: The Growth and Form of Our Cities and Towns*, New American Library, New York, 1956, p. 59.

TABLE 3-3
Number of Urban Places by Population Size: Selected Years, 1850–1980

Size of place	1850	1900	1950	1980
Total—2,500 and over	236	1,737	4,284	7,749
1,000,000 or more	—	3	5	6
500,000 to 1,000,000	1	3	13	16
250,000 to 500,000	—	9	23	34
100,000 to 250,000	5	23	65	117
50,000 to 100,000	4	40	126	290
25,000 to 50,000	16	82	252	675
10,000 to 25,000	36	280	778	1,765
5,000 to 10,000	85	465	1,176	2,181
2,500 to 5,000	89	832	1,846	2,665

Source: U.S. Bureau of the Census, U.S. Census of Population 1950 vol II; and 1980, vol. 1, table 23.

transportation, the poor were more often relegated to the less accessible areas on the periphery.[23]

THE INDUSTRIAL CITY: 1860–1950

The Civil War accelerated the shift from a mercantile or trade to an industrial economy. Aided by the new protective tariffs and the inflated profits, stimulated by the war, northern industrialists began producing steel, coal, and woolen goods, most of which had previously been imported. The closing of the Mississippi was a boon to Chicago and the east-west railroads.

A century after its founding (1896), the American nation had grown to 50 million and stretched from coast to coast. The lands of the Louisiana Purchase and the Northwest Cession were already settled, while the western prairie was being peopled and plowed. However, in retrospect, this was the end, not the beginning of the age of agriculture. The census of 1880 for the first time indicated that less than half the employable population worked in agriculture. Meanwhile, foreign in-migration was swelling the cities, and urban areas held 28 percent of the population. By 1880 the nation already boasted four cities of over half a million inhabitants.[24]

During the last quarter of the nineteenth century, urbanism for the first time became a controlling factor in national life. This was a period of economic expansion for the nation. Capital-intensive industrialism was changing the nature of the economic system, rapidly changing America from a rural to an urban continent. The extent of this change can be seen in Table 3-3.

While the frontier captured the attention of writers and the imagination

[23]Sam Bass Warner, Jr., *The Private City: Philadelphia in Three Periods of Its Growth*, University of Pennsylvania Press, Philadelphia, 1968, p. 13.
[24]U.S. Bureau of the Census, *Historical Statistics of the United States, Colonial Times to 1957*, Washington, D.C., 1960, p. 14.

of the populace, the bulk of the nation's growth during the nineteenth century took place in cities. (The classic statement on the significance of the west was Frederick J. Turner's famous 1893 paper, "The Frontier in American History." A major urban response did not come until almost half a century later, with Arthur M. Schlesinger's "The City in American History."[25]) By the turn of the twentieth century, fifty cities had populations of over 100,000; the most notable of these new cities was the prairie metropolis of Chicago, which had bet heavily on the technology of the railroad. Chicago mushroomed from 4,100 at the time of its incorporation in 1833 to 1 million in 1890. Between 1850 and 1890 Chicago doubled its population every decade; in 1910 it passed 2 million. Nationally, in 100 years beween 1790 and 1890 the total population grew sixteenfold, while the urban population grew 139-fold.

Technological Developments

As Richard Wade aptly phrased it, "The towns were the spearhead of the frontier." This was particularly true west of the Mississippi, where the technological breakthrough of the railroad had reversed earlier patterns of settlement. Josiah Strong, writing in 1885, noted:

> In the Middle States the farms were the first taken, then the town sprang up to supply its wants, and at length the railway connected it with the world, but in the West the order is reversed—first the railroad, then the towns, then the farms. Settlement is, consequently, much more rapid, and the city stamps the country, instead of the country stamping the city. It is the cities and towns which will frame state constitutions, make laws, create public opinion, establish social usages, and fix standards of morals in the West.[26]

Strong may have exaggerated his case somewhat, but the railroad was crucial in the development of the west. During the second half of the nineteeenth century, the railroads expanded from 9,000 to 193,000 miles—much of it built with federal loans and land grants.[27] The railroads literally opened the west.

At the same time, changes in farming technology were converting the yeoman into an entrepreneur raising cash crops for market. Horse-drawn mechanical reapers, steel plows, and threshers heralded the shift from self-sufficient to commercial farming.

Spatial Concentration

The great cities of the east and midwest, with their hordes of immigrants, frantic pace, municipal corruption, and industrial productivity, built much of their present physical plant in the era of steam stretching from the 1880s to the depression of the 1930s. The late-nineteenth-century city was a city of

---

[25]Arthur M. Schlesinger, "The City in American History," *Mississippi Valley Historical Review,* 27:43–66, June, 1940.

[26]Josiah Strong, *Our Country: Its Possible Future and Its Present Crisis,* Baker and Taylor, New York, 1885, p. 206.

[27]William Petersen, *Population,* Macmillan, New York, 1961, p. 34.

Twelve immigrants slept in this room for "5¢ a spot." The photo was taken by the slum reformer, Jacob Riis. (Museum of the City of New York)

concentration and centralization accentuated by industrialization. Initial industrialization encouraged centripetal rather than centrifugal forces; since steam is most cheaply generated in large quantities and must be used close to where it is produced, steam power thus fostered a compact city. Steam power encouraged the proximity of factory and power supply. It fostered the concentration of manufacturing processes in a core area that surrounded the central business district and had access to rail and often water transportation. This in turn tended to concentrate managerial and wholesale distributing activities and, above all, population near the factory.

The limited transportation technology meant that workers had to live near the factories; this in turn gave rise to row upon row of densely packed tenements. The distant separation of residence and place of work was a luxury only the very wealthy in commuting suburbs could afford. Surrounding the factories, slumlords built jaw-to-jaw tenements on every available open space. These tenements were then packed to unbelievable densities with immigrant workers—first Irish, then German, Jewish, Italian, and Polish—who could afford no other housing on the pitiful wages they made working twelve hours a day, six days a week. Slums provided the immigrant laborers with housing

A Note on Environmental Pollution

It is revealing, if depressing, to recognize that the problems of pollution and environmental destruction did not begin in the twentieth century. Until late in the nineteenth century most American cities, such as Baltimore and New Orleans, still relied on open trenches for sewage. The only municipal garbage collection provided by most cities until after the Civil War was that provided by scavenging hogs and dogs and other carrion-eaters. Colonial Charleston even passed an ordinance protecting vultures because they performed a public service by cleaning the carcasses of dead animals.* In 1666 a Boston municipal ordinance ordered the inhabitants to bury all filth, while "all garbage, beasts, entralls &c," were to be thrown from the drawbridge into Mill Creek.† Colonial Boston's system of burying what you can and throwing the rest into the nearest river was used by many cities well into the modern era.

A description of Pittsburgh dating from the late nineteenth-century details its air pollution in these terms:

> Pittsburgh is a smoky, dismal city, at her best. At her worst, nothing darker, dingier or more dispiriting can be imagined. The city is in the heart of the soft coal region; and the smoke from her dwellings, stores, factories, foundries, and steamboats, uniting settles in a cloud over the narrow valley in which she is built, until the very sun looks coppery through the sooty haze. According to a circular of the Pittsburgh Board of Trade, about twenty per cent, or one-fifth of all the coal used in the factories and dwellings of the city escapes into the air in the form of smoke. . . . But her inhabitants do not seem to mind it; and the doctors hold that this smoke from the carbon sulphur, and iodine contained in it, is highly favorable to the lung and cutaneous diseases, and is the sure death of malaria and its attendant fevers.‡

Public waterworks were luxuries found in few communities until well after the Civil War. Some medium-size cities such as Providence, Rochester, and Milwaukee relied entirely on private wells and water carriers. Sanitation fared little better. Boston, which had attained a level few communities could equal, had under 10,000 water closets for its residents.§ Until the twentieth century, facilities were all but nonexistent in the congested tenements of the slums.

*Charles N. Glaab (ed.), *The American City*, Dorsey, Homewood, Ill., 1963, p. 115.
†Carl Bridenbaugh, *Cities In the Wilderness*, Capricorn Books, New York, 1964, p. 18.
‡William Glazier, *Peculiarities of American Cities*, Hubbard, Philadelphia, 1884, pp. 322–333.
§Blake McKelveg, *The Urbanization of America, 1860–1915*, Rutgers University Press, New Brunswick, N.J., 1963, p. 13.

Congestion was a serious problem in the densely packed city of the turn of the century. Pictured in downtown Chicago ca. 1910. (Chicago Historical Society)

close to the factories, but at a horrendous price in terms of health and quality of life.

The compact trade and commerce-oriented central business districts of northern industrial and commercial cities reflected the needs of the nineteenth century. Before the widespread use of the automobile and telephone, it was necessary that business offices be close to one another so that information could be transmitted by means of messengers. High central-city land values were an inevitable result of the common business demand for a central location. Nineteenth-century inventions such as a practical steam elevator and steel-girdered buildings further enabled the core aera to become even more densely inhabited. Buildings no longer had to be supported by massive outer walls, and offices and businesses could be stacked vertically upon one another as high as foundations, local ordinances, and economics would allow.

The fact that New York, Chicago, Philadelphia, and St. Louis, to name only a few, are essentially cities built before the twentieth century and before the automobile is a problem we have to cope with today. Any attempt to deal with present-day transportation or pollution problems has to take into account the fact that most American cities were planned and built in the nineteenth century. We still live largely in cities designed for the age of steam and the horse-drawn streetcar.

As a side note, a quick way of determining the boundaries of an early city is to note the location of cemeteries. Since cemeteries were traditionally placed on the outskirts, large cemeteries within present city boundaries effectively show earllier high-water marks of urban growth.

Twentieth-Century Dispersion

Contemporary metropolitan areas reflect dispersion rather than concentration. Three inventions contributed to this change: the telephone, the electric streetcar, and, most important, the automobile. The telephone meant that city business could be conducted other than by face-to-face contact or messenger. It enabled businesses to locate their factories separate from their offices.

Before the electric streetcar, separation of places of living from place of work was a luxury restricted to the affluent or well-to-do. Nineteenth-century suburbs developed along commuter railroad lines and were the private preserves of those who had both the time and the money to commute. The North Shore suburbs of Chicago are an example. Common people, however, walked or rode the horse streetcars to work. At the beginning of the twentieth century, the average New Yorker lived a quarter of a mile, or roughly two blocks, from his or her place of work. Chicago at that time contained 1,690,000 inhabitants, half of them living within 3.2 miles of the city center.[28]

The electric streetcar changed all this. Perfected in 1888 in Richmond, Virginia, the streetcar moved twice as fast as the horse-drawn car and had over three times the carrying capacity. The new system of urban transportation was almost immediately adopted everywhere. By the turn of the century horsecar lines, which had accounted for two-thirds of all street railways a decade earlier, had all but vanished. Electric trolleys accounted for 97 percent of all mileage in 1902, with 2 percent still operated by cable car lines, and only 1 percent by horse cars.[29]

The result was the rapid development of outer areas of the city, and proliferation of middle-class streetcar suburbs.[30] With one's home somewhere along the streetcar line, it was possible to live as far as 12 miles from the central business district and commute relatively rapidly and inexpensively. This led to an outward expansion of the city and the establishment of residential suburbs in strips along the right-of-way of the streetcar line. Those high in the electric traction industry and corrupt politicians with influence made fortunes when streetcar lines were built to outlying areas where they just happened to own all the vacant lots.

Land lying between the "spokes" formed by the streetcar lines remained undeveloped. The cities thus came to have a rather pronounced star-shaped configuration, with the points of the star being the linear rail lines.[31] This is a shape cities would hold until the era of the automobile.

[28]Paul F. Cressey, "Population Succession in Chicago: 1898–1930," *American Journal of Sociology,* **44**:59, 1938.
[29]Glaab and Brown, op. cit., 2d ed., p. 144.
[30]For an excellent account of this phenomenon, see Sam Bass Warner, Jr., *Streetcar Suburbs,* Harvard and M.I.T. Presses, Cambridge, Mass., 1962.
[31]Richard Hurd, *Principles of City Land Values,* The Record and Guide, New York, 1903.

Where street rail lines intersected, natural breaks in transit took place and secondary business and commercial districts began to develop. These regional shopping areas were the equivalent of the peripheral shopping centers of today. With the coming of the automobile, the city areas between the streetcar lines filled in, and by the 1920s most of our major cities had completed the bulk of their building. The depression of the 1930s effectively stopped downtown building; thus, many central business districts remained basically unchanged until building resumed again in the early 1960s.[32] Outlying areas similarly saw little change until the post–World War II suburbanization boom discussed in Chapter 7.

POLITICAL LIFE

Corruption and Service

In 1853 New York was described in *Putnam's Monthly* as possessing "Filthy streets, the farce of a half-fledged and inefficient police, and the miserably bad government, generally, of an unprincipled common council, in the composition of which ignorance, selfishness, impudence and greediness seem to have an equal share." Over the following score of years the situation deteriorated. Virtually everywhere venality and urban politics became synonymous. As Arthur Schlesinger charitably put it, "This lusty urban growth created problems that taxed human resourcefulness to the utmost."[33] A particularly high price was paid in the area of municipal governance. Political institutions that were adequate under simplified rural conditions but inadequate to the task of governing a complicated system of ever-expanding public services and utilities presented an acute problem. The contemporary observer Andrew White was more direct, "With very few exceptions the city governments of the United States are the worst in Christendom . . . the most expensive, the most inefficient, and the most corrupt."[34] Or as the noted British scholar James A. Bryce put it, "There is no denying that the government of cities is the one conspicuous failure of the United States."[35]

Boss Tweed of New York, who plundered the city of between $60 million and $200 million, was even more explicit: "The population is too helplessly split into races and factions to govern it under universal suffrage, except by bribery or patronage or corruption."[36] The political machines were renowned for graft and voting fraud. Immigrants were encouraged to "vote early and often" for the machine candidates.

On the other hand, although the political bosses emptied the public treasury, they also provided the poorer citizens with urban services, jobs, and

---

[32]For more on central business districts, see Chapter 10, Urban Crisis or Urban Rebirth.
[33]Arthur M. Schlesinger, op. cit., pp. 43–66.
[34]James Bryce, *Forum*, vol. X, 1890, p. 25.
[35]James Bryce, *The American Commonwealth*, vol. 1, Macmillan, London, 1891, p. 608. Reprinted by Putnam, New York, 1959.
[36]Arthur M. Schlesinger, *Paths to the Present*, Macmillan, New York, 1949, p. 60.

Boss William Tweed, head of the Tammany Hall political machine, as portrayed by the cartoonist Thomas Nast. Tweed plundered the New York City treasury of between $60 million and $200 million. He was convicted in 1872. (Culver Pictures)

help in solving problems. The bosses were buffers between slum dwellers and the often hostile official bureaucracy. In return for the immigrants' vote, the boss provided not abstract ideals but practical services and benefits. The boss was the one to see when you needed a job, when your child was picked up for delinquency, or when you drank a bit too much and were arrested for drunkenness. The boss would arrange something with the police at the stationhouse or even ''go your bail'' if the offense was serious. The boss was certain to attend every wedding and wake in the neighborhood, and often provided cash to get the newlyweds going or cover funeral expenses for a widow. The boss produced. As a Boston ward heeler, Martin Lomasney, straightforwardly expressed it, ''There's got to be in every ward somebody that any bloke can come to—no matter what he's done—to get help. Help, you understand; none of your law and justice, but help."[37]

In managing the city the bosses distinguished between dishonest graft and honest graft, or "boodie." The former would include shakedowns, payoffs, and protection money for illegal gambling, liquor, and prostitution. "Boodie," on the other hand, involved using your control over contracts for municipal services and tax assessments to maximize your advantage. The boss George Washington Plunkitt in a famous passage explained how it worked.

> Just let me explain by examples. My party's in power in the city, and it's going to undertake a lot of public improvements. Well, I'm tipped off, say, that they're going to lay out a new park at a certain place. I see my opportunity and I take it. I go to that place and I buy up all the land I can in the neighborhood. Then the board of this or that makes its plan public, and there is a rush to get my land, which nobody cared particular for before. Ain't it perfectly honest to charge a good price and make a profit on my investment and foresight? Of course it is. Well, that's honest graft.[38]

In an urban environment committed to the principle of free enterprise, politicians saw no reason for all the profits to go to businesspeople rather than politicians.

While the "better classes" viewed all machine bosses as rogues and thieves, the bosses were apparently far more personable and friendly than the elite captains of industry in the business community. A study of twenty city bosses described them as warm and often sentimental men who had come from poor immigrant families. All were naive urbanites, and most were noted for loyalty to their families.[39] The political machine provided a route for social mobility for bright and alert young immigrants. Police departments were also an avenue of upward mobility for first- and second-generation European immigrants. Without the aid of the ward bosses, the new immigrants would have had an even rougher time than they did. For the immigrants, boss rule was clearly functional. As expressed by the sociologist Robert Merton, "The functional deficiencies of the official structure generate an alternative (unofficial) structure to fulfill existing needs somewhat more effectively."[40]

Immigrants' Problems

The role of immigrants is treated in detail in Chapter 9, Ethnic Diversity: Ethnics, Blacks, Hispanics, Indians, and Asians. Suffice it to say here that the dimensions of the immigrant flood are hard to overemphasize—perhaps some 40 million persons between 1800 and 1925. From the 1840s onward, waves of immigrants landed in the major northeastern ports. The first of the mass ethnic immigrations was that of the Irish, who were driven from home

[37]Quoted in Lincoln Steffens, *The Autobiography of Lincoln Steffens,* Harcourt, 1931, p. 618.
[38]Howard P. Chudacoff, op. cit., pp. 131–132.
[39]Harold Zink, *City Bosses in the United States,* Duke University Press, Durham, N.C., 1930, p. 350.
[40]Robert K. Merton, *Social Theory and Social Structure,* Free Press, Glencoe, Ill., 1957, p. 73.

in the late 1840s by the ravages of the potato blight. Later, Germans and Scandinavians poured into the middle west, particularly after the development of steamships and the opening of the railroads to Chicago.

Immigration accelerated after the Civil War, spurred on by the need for industrialization. This was a period of industrial and continental expansion. Between 1860 and 1870, twenty-five of the thirty-eight states took official action to stimulate immigration, offering not only voting rights but also sometimes land and bonuses.[41]

By 1890 New York had half as many Italians as Naples, as many Germans as Hamburg, twice as many Irish as Dublin, and two and half times the number of Jews in Warsaw.[42] The traditions, customs, religion, and sheer numbers of these immigrants made fast assimilation impossible. Between 1901 and 1910 alone, over 9 million immigrants were counted by immigration officials. These newcomers came largely from peasant backgrounds. They were packed into teeming slums and delegated to the lowest-paying and most menial jobs. Native-born Protestant Americans suddenly became aware of the fact that 40 percent of the 1910 population was of foreign stock—that is, immigrants or the offspring of immigrants.[43] The percentage was considerably higher in the large northern industrial cities, where over half the population was invariably of foreign stock.

To WASP (white Anglo-Saxon Protestant) writers around the turn of the century, the sins of the city were frequently translated into the sins of the new immigrant groups pouring into the ghettos of the central core. Slum housing, poor health conditions, and high crime rates were all blamed on the newcomers. Those on the city's periphery and in the emerging upper-class and upper-middle-class suburbs associated political corruption with the central city. Native-born Americans tended to view city problems as being the fault of the frequently Catholic, or Jewish, immigrants who inhabited the central-city ghettos.

Even sympathetic reformers such as Jacob Riis portrayed central-city slums as anthills teeming with illiterate immigrants. The masses in the ghettos were a threat to democracy.[44]

Reform Movements

The writing of "muckrakers" like Lincoln Steffens, who in his articles on "The Shame of the Cities" exposed municipal corruption, gave considerable publicity to the grosser excesses of municipal corruption, such as the deals with utility franchises. To destroy the power of the bosses and their immigrant supporters, reforms were pushed in city after city. Reformers of the period had a distinctly middle-class orientation. As today, the problems of the city were viewed as problems of and by the poor in the central core. While the

[41]Harold Zink, op. cit., p. 350. For an excellent study of the role of a twentieth-century boss, see A. Theodore Brown and Lyle W. Dorset: *K.C. A History of Kansas City, Missouri,* Pruett Publishing, Boulder, Col., 1978.
[42]Glaab and Brown, op. cit., p. 125.
[43]Donald J. Bogue, *The Population of the United States,* Free Press, Glencoe, Ill., 1969, p. 178.
[44]Jacob A. Riis, *How the Other Half Lives,* Scribner, New York, 1890.

bosses represented personalized politics, reform represented abstract WASP goals such as efficient administration and good accounting. The Progressive Movement at the turn of the century, at least in its urban manifestation, was an attempt by the upper middle class to reform the inner city. This, of course, meant regaining political power. Businesspeople organized in groups such as the National Municipal League.

The National Municipal League provided model charters and moral impetus. By 1912 some 210 communities had dropped the mayor and city-council system and adopted the commission form of government. In 1913 Dayton adopted the first city-manager system, and during the following year forty-four other cities followed suit. Under the city-manager system, a non-political manager is appointed to run the city in a businesslike manner. However, in the largest cities the political machines, while they lost a few battles, managed to weather the storm. The coming of World War I directed crusading energies into new channels, and the Roaring Twenties was not a decade noted for municipal reform. While there were exceptions, such as William Hoan, the socialist mayor of Milwaukee, the city during the 1920s was more likely to have a colorful and corrupt mayor like James ("Gentleman Jimmy") Walker in New York or Big Bill ("The Builder") Thompson in Chicago.

URBAN IMAGERY

Ambivalence

America has never been neutral regarding its great cities; they have been either exalted as the centers of vitality, enterprise, and excitement or denounced as sinks of crime, pollution, and depravity. Our present ambivalence toward our cities is nothing new; even the founding fathers had great reservations about the moral worth of cities. The city was frequently equated by writers such as Thomas Jefferson with all the evils and corruption of the old world, while an idealized picture of the yeoman farmer represented the virtue of the new world. Thomas Jefferson expressed the sentiments of many of his fellow citizens when he stated in 1787 in a letter to James Madison,

> I think our governments will remain virtuous as long as they are chiefly agricultural; and this will be as long as there shall be vacant land in any part of America. When they get piled upon one another in large cities, as in Europe, they will become corrupt as in Europe.[45]

In a famous letter to Benjamin Rush, written in 1800, Jefferson even saw some virtue in the yellow fever epidemics that periodically ravaged seaboard cities. Philadelphia, for example, lost over 4,000 persons, almost 10 percent of its population, in the epidemic of 1793. Jefferson wrote to Rush:

[45]Quoted in Glaab, op. cit., p. 38.

> When great evils happen I am in the habit of looking out for what good may arise from them as consolations to us, and Providence has in fact, so established the order of things, as that most evils are the means of producing some good. The yellow fever will discourage the growth of great cities in our nation, and I view great cities as pestilential to the morals, the health, and the liberties of man.[46]

This, however, is not the entire picture, for in spite of these sentiments Jefferson proposed a model town plan for Washington, D.C., and after the War of 1812 came to support urban manufacturing. Also, although in his writings Jefferson advised against sending Americans to Europe for education lest they be contaminated by urban customs, he himself enjoyed visiting Paris and was a social success there. Other Americans were similarly inconsistent.

Benjamin Franklin, never one to be far from the stimulation, pleasures, and excitement of the city, went so far as to say that agriculture was "the only honest way to acquire wealth . . . as a reward for innocent life and virtuous industry." Ben Franklin was many things during his long, productive life, but never a farmer; and his own way of life indicates that he never considered an innocent life or conventional virtue to be much of a reward. Writers as diverse as de Tocqueville, Emerson, Melville, Hawthorne, and Poe all had strong reservations about the city.[47] According to de Tocqueville:

> I look upon the size of certain American cities, and especially on the nature of their population, as a real danger which threatens the future security of the democratic republics of the New World; and I venture to predict they will perish from this circumstance, unless the Government succeeds in creating an armed force which while it remains under the control of the majority of the nation, will be independent of town population, and able to repress its excess.[48]

Cowley's line "God the first garden made, and the first city Cain" expressed an attitude toward cities shared by many Americans. Thoreau, sitting in rural solitude watching a sunset, is an acceptable image. Thoreau, sitting on a front stoop in Boston watching the evening rush hour, creates an entirely different image.

Americans, even while pouring into the cities, have traditionally idealized the country. A 1985 Gallup poll indicates that, given the choice, almost half of American adults would move to towns with less than 10,000 inhabitants or rural areas.[49] The clearing of the wilderness by the pioneers, and the taming (eradication) of savages—human and animal—was considered a highly laudable enterprise. By contrast, the building of cities by the sweat and muscle of immigrants was ignored. It is as if we consider the history of the immigrants somewhat discreditable and thus best forgotten.

Vigorous attacks on the city came from writers such as Josiah Strong,

---

[46]Andrew A. Lipscomb and Albert E. Bergh (eds.), *The Writings of Thomas Jefferson,* vol. X., The Thomas Jefferson Memorial Association, Washington, D.C., 1904, p. 173.

[47]Morton White and Lucia White, *The Intellectual versus the City,* Harvard and M.I.T. Presses, Cambridge, Mass., 1962.

[48]Alexis de Tocqueville, *Democracy in America,* Henry Reeve (trans.), New York, 1839, p. 289.

[49]Gallup poll, *Los Angeles Times,* March 24, 1985.

who condemned it as the source of the evils of rum, Romanism, and rebellion. Strong's book *Our Country* sold a phenomenal—for that date—175,000 copies. He effectively mirrored the fears of small-town Protestant America that urban technology and the growth of foreign immigrant groups were in the process of undermining the existing social order and introducing undesirable changes such as political machines, slums, and low church attendance. Several excerpts give the general tone of his argument:

> The city has become a serious menace to our civilization. . . . It has a particular fascination for the immigrant. Our principal cities in 1880 contained 39.3 percent of our entire German population, and 45.8 percent of the Irish. Our ten larger cities at that time contained only nine percent of the entire population, but 23 percent of the foreign. . . .
>
> Because our cities are so largely foreign, Romanism finds in them its chief strength. For the same reason the saloon together with the intemperance and liquor power which it represents, is multiplied. . . .
>
> Socialism centers in the city, and the materials of its growth are multiplied with the growth of the city. Here is heaped the social dynamite; here roughs, gamblers, thieves, robbers, lawless and desperate men of all sorts congregate; men who are ready on any pretext to raise riots for the purpose of disruption and plunder; here gather the foreigners and wage-workers who are especially susceptible to socialistic arguments; here skepticism and irreligion abound; here unequality is the greatest and most obvious, and the contrast between opulence and penury the most striking; there the suffering is the sorest.[50]

An extremely influential lecture by Frederick Jackson Turner at the turn of the century, "The Winning of the West," struck a responsive chord: it glorified the pioneer and the virtues of the west. Needless to say, such homage was not paid to tenement dwellers working under oppressive conditions, who were simply trying to raise decent families. Today, television perpetuates the same myth when it gives us drama after drama concerning life in the nineteenth-century American west, but nothing about the nineteenth-century American city dweller. The cowboy, not the factory hand, is the American hero.

Criticism of the city contained some contradictory premises, although these were generally not noticed: while it was being castigated for not exhibiting rural or agrarian values, it was also being taken to task for failing to be truly urban and reach the highest ideals of an urban society. In short, the city was at the same time supposed to be both more rural and more urban.

Distrust and dislike of the city simmered during the latter part of the nineteenth century and finally crystallized around the issue of the free coinage of silver, with silver representing the agrarian west and gold the commercial and industrial east. William Jennings Bryan's campaign for the presidency in 1896 was a major attempt by the agricultural antiurbanites to gain national political power. As Bryan put it in his famous "cross of gold" speech: "Burn down your cities and leave our farms, and your cities will spring up again as

---

[50]Strong, op. cit., Chap. 11.

Carl Sandburg's Chicago

Probably the most quoted image of the raw vitality, strength, and brutality of the early twentieth century American city is Sandburg's poem "Chicago."* An excerpt follows:

Hog Butcher for the World,
Tool Maker, Stacker of Wheat,
Player with Railroads and the Nation's Freight Handler;
Stormy, husky, brawling,
City of the Big Shoulders:

They tell me you are wicked and I believe them, for I have seen your
    painted women under the gas lamps luring the farm boys.
And they tell me you are crooked and I answer: Yes, it is true I have
    seen the gunman kill and go free to kill again.
And they tell me you are brutal and my reply is: On the faces of women
    and children I have seen the marks of wanton hunger.
And having answered so I turn once more to those who sneer at this my
    city, and I give them back the sneer and say to them:
Come and show me another city with lifted head singing so proud to be
    alive and coarse and strong and cunning.
Flinging magnetic curses amid the toil of piling job on job, here is a tall
    bold slugger set vivid against the little soft cities;
Fierce as a dog with tongue lapping for action, cunning as a savage
    pitted against the wilderness,
      Bareheaded,
      Shoveling,
      Wrecking,
      Planning,
      Building, breaking, rebuilding,
Under the smoke, dust all over his mouth, laughing with white teeth,
Under the terrible burden of destiny laughing as a young man laughs,
Laughing even as an ignorant fighter laughs who has never lost a battle.

Bragging and laughing that under his wrist is the pulse, and under his
    ribs the heart of the people,
      Laughing!
Laughing the stormy, husky, brawling laughter of Youth, half-naked,
    sweating, proud to be Hog Butcher, Tool Maker, Stacker of Wheat,
    Player with Railroads and Freight Handler to the Nation.

*Carl Sandburg, *Chicago Poems*, Holt, New York, 1916.

if by magic; but destroy our farms, and the grass will grow in the streets of every city in the country.''[51] But by the end of the nineteenth century Bryan's day had passed, and although agricultural fundamentalism still had some strength, it was no longer a commanding ideology. The city, not the farm, represented the future.

Myth of Rural Virtue

The myth of agrarian virtue nonetheless continued to outline the reality. As Hofstadter has amusingly noted, one of President Calvin Coolidge's campaign photographs in 1924 showed him posing as a simple farmer haying in Vermont. However, the photograph said more than was intended, for the President's overalls are obviously fresh, his shoes are highly polished, and if one looks carefully, one can see his expensive Pierce Arrow, with Secret Service men waiting to rush him back to the city once the picture-taking was completed.[52] One of the lighter moments of the Watergate hearings was seeing Senator Sam Ervin, one of the sharpest constitutional lawyers in the nation, affecting country ways and referring to himself as a ''simple country boy.'' Nor was President Carter averse to having himself pictured as a small-town ''good ole boy.'' President Reagan similarly posed for publicity photos of himself cutting wood on his ''ranch.''

Numerically, for two-thirds of a century America has been a nation of urban dwellers, and with every census the percentage of urban dwellers climbs higher. Even the quarter of the population that does not live in urban places is clearly tied to an urban way of life. As noted in Chapter 1, the profits of wheat farmers, cattle ranchers, dairy farmers, and other agribusiness people are tied more to government price-support systems than to weather or other natural factors.

Today our picture of how rural life is lived and the nature of the basic rural virtues is the creation of mass media based in and directed from cities. Television shows written in New York and produced in Hollywood try to create an image of small towns, filled with friendly folk, with ''down home'' wisdom, rather like a Norman Rockwell painting. Urban advertising also hits hard at the same bogus theme—commercials often depend heavily on nostalgia, with old cars, fields of wheat, the old farmhouse, and the front porch swing.

What all this reflects is a deep ambivalence regarding cities and city life. As a people, we chose to glorify rural life but to live in urban areas. North America is the most urbanized of the continents (excluding Australia) but our attitude toward cities is frequently unrealistic. Ours is an urban continent, but we treat our major cities as though we don't fully trust them and wish they would fade away and stop causing problems.

---

[51]Glaab and Brown, op. cit., 1st ed., p. 59.
[52]Richard Hofstadter, *The Age of Reform*, Knopf, New York, 1955, p. 31.

CHAPTER

4

ECOLOGY AND STRUCTURE OF AMERICAN CITIES

We shape our buildings, and afterwards our buildings shape us.

Winston Churchill

CITY STRUCTURE

Much has been written of the American city: its internal structure, its forms of social organization, its peoples and life-styles, and its problems. The sociologist Louis Wirth suggested that these various topics could be viewed empirically from three interrelated perspectives: (1) as a physical structure comprising a population base, a technology, and an ecological order, (2) as a system of social organization involving a characteristic social structure, series of social institutions, and a typical pattern of social relationships, and (3) as a set of attitudes and ideas, and a constellation of personalities engaging in typical forms of collective behavior, and subject to characteristic mechanisms of social control.[1] In this chapter we shall be concerned with the first two of these perspectives: the spatial and social ecology of the city and how it affects and is affected by the city as a system of social organization. Urbanism as a system of life-styles and values is discussed in Chapter 6, City Life-styles.

The ecological approach is concerned with the development of the form and structure of the community. "Ecology" in its broadest sense is the study of the relationships among organisms within an environment. It is the study not of the creatures and objects themselves but rather of the relationships among them. The sum total of these many relationships among organisms in a habitat is called a "biotic community," and the community together with its physical habitat forms an "ecosystem."

The ecological school and the term "human ecology" originated with the sociologists Park and Burgess in 1921, and represented an attempt to systematically apply the basic theoretical scheme of plant and animal ecology to the study of human communities. Ecological reasoning, which traces its theoretical underpinnings to Charles Darwin's research on evolution, was first applied to the study of plants in the latter part of the nineteenth century. Animal ecology emerged in the early twentieth century, and human ecology soon followed.

Contemporary human ecology is concerned with examing the independence and interdependence of specialized roles and functions (recurrent patterns of behavior) within the society. In examining the relationship between people and their environment and people within their environment, the level of analysis focuses on the aggregate level. The issue is the properties of populations rather than the properties of the individuals who constitute them. Thus, it is based on the study of groups rather than individuals—and this focus on the group or aggregate is basic to sociology, as opposed to disciplines such as psychology in which the focus is on the individual. The focus here is on the structure of organized activity. Human ecology does not—and cannot—explain the beliefs, values, and attitudes of individuals while they are performing certain activities.

EARLY HUMAN ECOLOGY

Classical human ecology came into its own during the 1920s at the University of Chicago. Led by researchers such as Robert Park and Ernest Burgess, the

[1]Louis Wirth, "Urbanism as a Way of Life," *American Journal of Sociology," *44:18–19, July, 1938.

so-called "Chicago school" of sociology produced a prodigious number of studies focused on the spatial-social environment of the city. The interest of the Chicago sociologists was not simply in mapping where groups and institutions were located, but rather in discovering how the sociological, psychological, and moral experiences of city life were reflected in spatial relationships. One member of the Chicago school said that human ecology "deals with the spatial aspects of symbiotic relationships of human beings and human institutions."[2]

Park was interested in how changes in the physical and spatial structure shaped social behavior. He felt that "most if not all cultural changes in society will be correlated with changes in its territorial organization, and every change in the territorial and occupational distribution of the population will effect changes in the existing culture."[3] This postulate of "an intimate congruity between the social order and physical space, between social and physical distance, and between social equality and residential proximity is the crucial hypothetical framework supporting urban ecological theories."[4]

Classical ecological theories of the human community were analogous to evolutionary theories explaining plant and animal development. A person driving from the desert into the mountains finds that different soil, water, and temperature affect the bands of growth of the plants; by analogy, in a drive from a city's business district to its outlying suburbs, there are differing zones of development. In all these theories, competition—the Darwinian struggle for existence—played a core role. In the city, as a consequence of economic competition for prime space, there emerged distinct spatial and social zones. The internal structure of the city thus evolved not as a consequence of direct planning but through competition, which changed areas through the ecological processes of invasion, succession, and segregation of new groups (e.g., immigrants) and land uses (e.g., commercial use displacing residential use).

Park and Burgess, however, were careful to stress the social as well as the economic aspects of competition. For example, in their study of ethnic and racial neighborhoods they examined the relationship between residential proximity and social equality. They found that in the large city, where one's social position would not be widely known to everyone, spatial distance was often substituted for social distance—thus the importance of a fashionable address in the "right" neighborhood.

Invasion and Succession

Change in the city and in community areas comes about through intrusion of a new land use into an area of another land use.

The history of the American city is the story of the invasion of one land use by another. The end result when one group or function finally takes the

---

[2]Roderick McKenzie, *The Metropolitan Community*, McGraw-Hill, New York and London, 1933.
[3]Robert Park, *Human Communities*, Free Press, New York, 1952, p. 14.
[4]Ralph Thomlinson, *Urban Structure*, Random House, New York, 1969, p. 9.

place of another is called "succession."[5] None of the patterns of land use within a city are permanently fixed, although some zoning laws attempt to fix them. As cities have grown, areas that were once characterized by single-family houses have been converted to apartment, commercial, or industrial use—this is succession. All to frequently such ecological processes are given overlays of values or morals. But the city, if it is viable, is always in the process of changing. Ecological patterns are dynamic rather than static. Cities that do not change become historical tourist attractions or stagnant backwaters.

Today the most spectacular instance of invasion and eventual succession is found in the racial changes taking place in the central city. In spite of the evidence that blacks do not bring dilapidation and that the quality of a neighborhood is determined more by the age and condition of the housing and the incomes of the residents than by race, the inaccurate belief that the coming of blacks means the end of a neighborhood still persists. Another instance of population invasion is the flow of limited numbers of affluent young whites to sections of the central city. The in-migration is not to areas of new housing, but rather to older neighborhoods in a state of some decline. This rehabilitation, or "gentrification," of the central-city neighborhoods is discussed in Chapter 10, Urban Crisis or Urban Rebirth.

The process of economic succession, while less dramatic than population changes, can be of equally great long-term importance. Examples are the moving out of industry, the transition within neighborhoods from single-family to multiple-family dwelling units, and the change from residential to commercial land use. Students will note that the last two of these invasion-succession patterns can commonly be found in residential areas abutting growing colleges and universities. Such changes are frequently viewed in moral terms—for example, as the decline of family neighborhoods. Remember though, that a city, if it is viable, is always in a process of change.

The early sociologists of the Chicago school were particularly interested in the segregated areas resulting from the process of selective competition. The Chicago sociologists called these areas "natural areas." They were natural in that they were supposedly the results of ecological processes rather than of planning or conscious creation by any government unit. When zoning laws were established, they generally recognized such natural areas of apartment houses, single-family neighborhoods, commercial areas, warehouse districts, etc., so as to maintain existing land-use patterns. A number of minor sociological classics, such as Wirth's book *The Ghetto* and Zorbaugh's book *The Gold Coast and the Slum,* deal with so-called natural areas.[6] Today, only a few urban neighborhoods possess sufficient social solidarity and identification to be considered natural communities. (The so-called "defended neighborhoods"

---

[5]The term "function," as used by ecologists—not by most other sociologists—means recurrent patterns of activities which depend on other activities. "Structure," to the ecologist, is the orderly arrangements of the parts that make up the whole; the loci within which the functions or activities are performed.
[6]Louis Wirth, *The Ghetto,* University of Chicago Press, 1928; and Harvey W. Zorbaugh, *The Gold Coast and the Slum,* University of Chicago Press, 1929.

discussed in Chapter 6, City Life-styles, might be considerd a contemporary version of natural areas.)

Criticisms

The heavy emphasis on competition in traditional human ecology, plus the nonsocial nature of some of the variables, increasingly disturbed critics during the late 1930s and the 1940s. The human ecologists' emphasis on urban systems and how people organize themselves socially to adapt to their habitat, particularly to the habitat of cities and their environs, was felt by some not to be sufficiently sociological.

Because of its emphasis on the role of human beings in a physical environment, human ecology for years was considered by many sociologists to be only marginal to the discipline of sociology. Analogies to plant and animal life particularly disturbed the critics. The fact that early human ecology was heavily dependent on biology for both concepts and terminology was viewed as a damning fault by some sociologists. As one critic put it, "As the ecologists have admitted, practically all their basic hypotheses have been derived from natural science sources—and the influence of certain geographers and economists is apparent."[7] To such critics the multidisciplinary base of human ecology was a weakness rather than a source of strength. Not the ideas, but where they came from, was considered the more important factor. Fortunately such academic provincialism has few adherents today. Ecological analysis is now recognized as integral to sociology, for, as expressed by Leo Schnore, "the central role given to organization—both as dependent or independent variable—places ecology clearly within the sphere of activities in which sociologists claim distinctive competence, i.e., analysis of social organization."[8]

Some other criticisms of traditional ecological theory had more validity. During the late 1930s a "sociocultural" school emerged which placed renewed emphasis on cultural and motivational factors in explaining urban land-use patterns. Scholars of the sociocultural school tend to feel that early human ecology overemphasized economic factors while ignoring social-psychological variables. Milla Alihan, in a broadly based critique of ecological studies, attacked both the theory and the application of early human ecology.[9] Another critic, Walter Firey, demonstrated in a study of land use in central Boston that many acres of valuable land in the central business district had been allowed to remain in uneconomic use, such as for example, parks and cemeteries.[10] He suggested that "sentiment" and "symbolism" play an important part in determining spatial distributions, pointing out that the 48-

[7]Warner E. Gettys, "Human Ecology and Social Theory," in George A. Theodorson (ed.), *Studies in Human Ecology,* Row, Peterson, Evanston, Ill., 1961, p. 99.

[8]Leo Schnore, "The Myth of Human Ecology," *Sociological Inquiry,* **31**:139, 1961.

[9]Milla A. Alihan, *Social Ecology,* Columbia University Press, New York, 1938.

[10]Walter Firey, "Sentiment and Symbolism as Ecological Variables," *American Sociological Review,* **10**:140–148, 1945.

acre common in the heart of downtown Boston had never been developed commercially and that Beacon Hill had largely remained an upper-class residential area in spite of its proximity to the central business district. Unfortunately, mass data such as census data fail to deal with such social-psychological variables.

A more recent school of ecologists, the "neo-orthodox," see limitations in the early classical studies but also see much of value. While recognizing the importance of social-psychological variables, the members of the neo-orthodox school are more inclined toward the use of nonattitudinal data. They most frequently use mass data such as censuses, and favor interpretation on the macrosociological level. Sociologists such as Amos Hawley, Otis Dudley Duncan, and Leo Schnore are members of this school. Unlike traditional human ecology, which emphasized competition, the neo-orthodox school emphasizes interdependence, as, for example, in their use of the ecological complex (POET).

Finally, in a reversal of the social-cultural criticisms, William Michelson has taken human ecology to task for giving too much attention to social variables and not enough to the effect of the physical environment on behavior.[11] According to Michelson, "space has been utilized as a *medium* in most human ecology rather than as a *variable* with a potential effect of its own."[12] The wheel has thus come close to full turn since the 1920s. Just as cities change, so do social theories. What is taken as truth in one decade may be recast in those that follow to produce new syntheses.

BURGESS'S GROWTH HYPOTHESIS

The most famous early product of the spatial-organizational concerns of the Chicago school was Burgess's concentric-zone hypothesis, first presented in 1924. This was an attempt to explain why cities grow the way they do.[13] Generations of sociology students have been exposed to the concentric-zone hypothesis—all too frequently in a form that makes it a static picture of city structure. This is unfortunate, for what Burgess was positing was the reorganization of spatial patterns that results from urban *growth,* in contrast to Gideon Sjoberg's picture of a static preindustrial city. Burgess was concerned with how industrial cities change over time from the preindustrial model, in which most of the central land is occupied by a residential elite and there is no clear segregation of city land for specific functional purposes (e.g., no central business district in the sense that is characteristic of the western industrial city). His hypothesis is a model, and only a model, of how cities develop spatially as a result of competition.

Burgess noted that in industrial cities factories, homes, and retail shops

[11]William H. Michelson, *Man and His Urban Environment,* Addison-Wesley, Reading, Mass., 1970, pp. 3–32.
[12]Ibid., p. 17.
[13]Ernest W. Burgess, "The Growth of the City: An Introduction to a Research Project," *Publications of the American Sociological Society,* **18:**85–97, 1924.

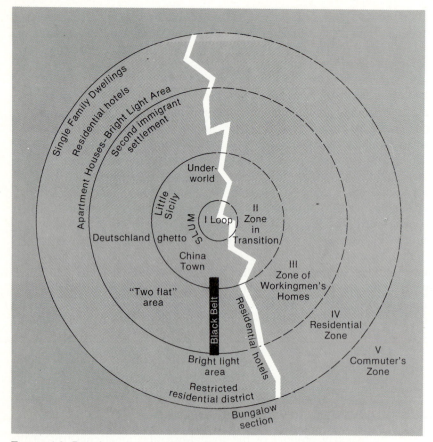

Figure 4-1. Developed in the 1920s, Burgess's zonal hypothesis provided a model of how cities grow. (From *Ernest W. Burgess, "The Growth of the City: An Introduction to a Research Project,"* 1925.)

were not randomly distributed within the urban area. Rather, there was a process of sorting by economic and social factors that resulted in concentration of similar populations and land uses. Competition for space meant that persons, organizations, and institutions were distributed within urban space in a nonrandom fashion. The result is the ecological pattern of American cities. That all this may seem obvious to us today is in part a reflection of the acceptance of the Chicago school's work.

Within the urban area, competition for land means that the most valuable property—usually centrally located—goes to those functions which can use space intensively and are willing to pay the costs. An economic model of land use developed by William Alonso points out that only those who can pay the most can occupy central business district (CBD) land.[14] Costs include not only

[14]William Alonso, "A Theory of Urban Land Market," in Larry Bourne (ed.), *Internal Structure of the City*, Oxford University Press, New York, 1971, pp. 154–159.

purchase price but also taxes and nuisance (congestion, noise, pollution, etc.) from other nearby land users. Centrally located land was thus in the past taken up by those economic units, such as department stores, which could effectively use space and required heavy pedestrian traffic. Consumption-oriented commercial activities still tend to be the most centrally located; production-oriented activities are in the next ring out; and residences are the least centralized. Residential users tend to be pushed out of areas desired for commercial purposes, since residential users cannot pay the high cost of central location and do not want the pollution, noise, and congestion of trucks rumbling down the street and a factory next door.

The result is that land values are highest near the center of the city and tend to decrease as one moves toward the periphery. This means that if housing is to be centrally located, it must use the land intensively. As a result, the two types of housing one finds in central areas are high-income, high-rise luxury apartments, and tenement and slum properties. High-rise apartments escape the pollution and noise of the city not by moving outward but by moving upward. A twentieth-floor apartment not only is quiet and convenient but also has a beautiful view. Slums are likewise intensive users of space. Even when the rent per room is low (and often is not), the rent *per acre* is high.

Consequently, there is a tendency toward an inverse relationship between the value of land and the economic status of those who occupy it. Where people live spatially reflects their position socially. Inner-city slum land is more expensive than land in the suburbs. In inner areas higher land costs are compensated for by density of use. Through crowding, a slumlord can get a great number of rents from a relatively small piece of land. Since land in outer areas is less valuable, less intensive use, such as single-family houses on large lots, is economically feasible. Thus, as you move out from the center of the city toward the periphery, land values and rental per acre tend to grade downward, while the rental per housing unit grades upward.

Burgess suggested that cities grow radially in a series of concentric zones or rings. Through a competitive struggle—expressed in ability to pay the cost of land and to tolerate nuisances such as noise and congestion—the most strategic or valuable land goes to the user who can afford to pay for it because of intensive use. Thus the ecologist would expect that the land located at the center of the transportation network, called the "central business district" (CBD), would be occupied by intensive users such as department stores, major business headquarters, and financial institutions. Near such dominant land users, one would also expect to find small establishments catering to their needs. Restaurants and coffee shops, quick printing firms, business supply houses, messenger services, and parking lots would be some of the related enterprises one would expect to find in the CBD. One would not expect to find used-car lots or industrial plants occupying the most costly central land.

The "combat zone" in Boston. American cities have long had sleazy areas specializing in commercial "vice" located near the downtown center. (Frank Siteman/The Picture Cube)

Concentric Zones

The most familiar version of Burgess's theory divided the urban area into five zones. They are presented here essentially as they existed during the 1920s, and so they can serve as a baseline from which to examine patterns of change.

Zone 1 was the central business district: the economic and (usually) the geographic center of the city. The heart of the zone was the retail shopping district, with its major department stores, theaters, hotels, banks, and central offices of economic, political, legal, and civic leaders. Consumption-oriented commercial activities tended to locate at the very core of the CBD, while the outer fringes, with lower rents, contained the wholesale business district; markets, warehouses, and storage buildings. Here also were found the wholesale markets for fresh fruits and vegetables, the markets often looking as if they had been in disrepair for a century—as they sometimes had.

Today commercial and retail functions in CBDs are losing importance, while the function of providing office space and convention centers is increasing. (The changing functions of the CBD is discussed in some detail later in this chapter.) Specialized retailing of nonstandardized goods is still found in the CBD, but with the emergence of large, convenient suburban shopping centers sales of general merchandise in central business districts have declined.

American cities have poured millions of dollars into CBDs during the past

Red-Light Districts and Combat Zones

In Burgess's day, at one edge of the CBD was located a sleazy but highly profitable area specializing in those activities and enterprises of a disreputable nature which needed accessibility but could not for social reasons be located in the heart of the downtown area. Here were found cheap bars specializing in girls hustling drinks, pornographic movie houses, strip joints, pinball arcades, and bookshops that sold magazines you couldn't buy in the suburbs. Today these areas are dying, partially because of expressways and urban renewal, and partially because they no longer perform an exclusive function. It is no longer necessary to sit in a dirty movie house to see pornographic movies; they can be seen on home videos.

Until the period before World War I, every major city in the United States also had a clearly marked "red-light district" just off the central business district that devoted itself to servicing needs which were not met elsewhere. Among the most famous were Storyville in New Orleans, the Tenderloin in San Francisco, and the Levee in Chicago. A turn-of-the-century social reform tract, *If Christ Came to Chicago*, provided a detailed map of every brothel, gambling place, and saloon in the downtown area of that city. The intent was to document the amount of vice, but the map also probably proved a useful guide to many visitors.

The term "red-light district" comes from the red lights which prostitutes put in their front windows to indicate that they were open for business. Numerous European cities such as Amsterdam and Hamburg still have clearly defined red-light districts—lights and all. These areas become quite congested during the evening and during lunch hours. American red-light districts were shut down by local societies for the suppression of vice, and as a result, displaced prostitutes set up business in apartments throughout the city. The call girl replaced the brothel. With service only a telephone call away, public visibility was a disadvantage rather than an asset.

During the 1970s, a number of cities reintroduced a section of the city devoted to commercial vice, known officially as "adult entertainment districts" but commonly called "combat zones." Combat zones were established in response to citizens' outcries over adult bookstores, pornographic movie houses, massage parlors, and gay pickup bars in residential areas.

The Supreme Court has ruled that it is legal to restrict certain activities to a specialized zone. Contemporary combat zones are if anything more tawdry than the old red-light districts.

As the term "combat zone" indicates, the contemporary "sporting life" areas are far from free of violence. Boston's combat zone has become notorious for its homosexual violence, and female prostitutes have been involved in attacks on "johns." A Harvard football player on the town with his buddies was stabbed and died as the result of an on-the-street attack by a prostitute. Contemporary combat zones have all the sleaziness but little of the life and color of a Storyville.

twenty years with the hope of maintaining them or changing them back into what they once were. Not everyone agrees that this makes sense. As one national authority on planning said, "Many activities are downtown just because they are there or in response to linkages which disappeared years ago. Many could be served better elsewhere."[15]

Zone 2—the zone in transition—contained both older factory complexes, many from the last century, and an outer ring of deteriorating neighborhoods of tenements. The zone in transition was known as an area of high crime rates and social disorganization.

The zone in transition was where immigrants received their first view of the city. It was the point of entry. Immigrants settled here in the cheap housing near the factories because they could not compete economically for more desirable residential locations. As they moved up in socioeconomic status, they moved out spatially and were in turn replaced by newer immigrants. Thus, a nonrandom spatial structure or pattern emerged, with groups of lower socioeconomic status most centrally located. In Burgess's day, land in the zone of transition was being held for speculation by landlords who provided only minimum maintenance in the expectation that the CBD would eventually expand into the area. It didn't happen that way, and half a century later many of the same slums remain—others having only recently been destroyed by urban renewal. Chapter 6, City Life-styles, discusses patterns of life in zones 2 and 3 in greater detail.

Zone 3 was the zone of working people's homes. This was the area settled by second-generation families, the children of the immigrants; it was the place where one moved when one could get out of the inner core. Physically it was (at least in Chicago, Burgess's model) a neighborhood of two-family houses rather than tenements, apartments, or single-family houses. Typically, the father of the family had a blue-collar job in the city. The children, however, planned to marry and move out of the old neighborhood, perhaps to live in the suburbs (see Chapter 8, Patterns of Suburbanization).

Zone 4 was called the "zone of the better residences." The ring included the area beyond the neighborhood of the second-generation immigrants. This was the zone of the great middle class—small businesspeople, professional people, sales workers, and those holding white-collar jobs. However, even in the 1920s this zone was in the process of changing from a community of single-family houses to one of apartment buildings and residential hotels (that is, there was an invasion of new land-use patterns).

The final zone, zone 5, was the commuter zone. In the early 1920s zone 5, thanks to the commuter railroads and the private automobile, comprised the upper-middle-class and upper-class dormitory suburbs. Here were found the classic suburban life patterns—the husband leaving in the morning for the city and returning in the evening, the wife left to raise the children, maintain

[15]Edward Ullman, "Presidential Address: The Nature of Cities Reconsidered," *The Regional Science Association Papers and Proceedings* **9**:21, 1962.

the house, and participate in civic affairs. Chapter 8 deals further with this outer zone, which today we call "suburbia."

We study the Burgess hypothesis today because it provided a long-accepted model of how American cities, and by implication, cities elsewhere, would change. This hypothesis has held real policy implications. For example, belief in the filter-down housing model based on the Burgess hypothesis dominated American real estate for decades. The filter-down model suggested that housing and neighborhoods would inevitably filter from higher to lower status populations. Thus, inner-city neighborhoods were seen as going from middle to lower class (or from white to black) but never the reverse. As Chapter 10 details, this led to policies of disinvestment in the central city. Urban gentrification during the 1980s is turning Burgess's pattern inside out. Central-city commercial property and warehouses are now sometimes being converted to residential usages (see Chapter 10).

The Zonal Hypothesis: Criticism and Support

Over the years there has been considerable debate about the adequacy of the zonal hypothesis in analyzing community spatial organization and growth. In the decades since its formation, Burgess's hypothesis has come under severe criticism on both theoretical and empirical grounds. As Alihan pointed out, Burgess's zonal boundaries "do not serve as demarcations in respect to the ecological or social phenomena they circumscribe, but are arbitrary divisions."[16] This is an overstatement, but it is clear that Burgess's zones are not toally homogeneous units. When evaluating Burgess's hypothesis, we have to keep in mind that he was proposing a "model" or "ideal type" of what American cities would look like if other factors did not intervene—but of course other factors do intervene. Burgess's own statements make it clear that he recognized the effects of distorting factors. He said:

> If radial extension were the only factor affecting the growth of American cities, every city in this country would exhibit a perfect exemplifiction of these five urban zones. But since other factors affect urban development (including) situation, site, natural and artificial barriers, survival of an earlier use of a district, prevailing city plan and its system of transportation, many distortions and modifications of this pattern are actually found. Nevertheless, so universal and powerful is the force of expansion outward from the city's core that in every city these zones can be more or less clearly delimited.[17]

The question, then, is not whether the zonal pattern is an exact description, for it obviously is not. The question is whether the growth patterns of American cities are best described by Burgess's or other models.

To date, empirical tests have both supported and failed to support Burgess's

---

[16]Alihan, op. cit., p. 225.
[17]Ernest W. Burgess, "Residential Segregation in American Cities," *Annals of the American Academy of Political and Social Science,* **140**:108, November, 1928.

hypothesis.[18] Haggerty, for example, looked at changes in educational levels from 1940 to 1960 in census tracts in eight large cities, using the statistical technique of Markov analysis. He reported that there was a definite trend through time toward a direct association between an area's social status and its distance from the city center. This tendency toward higher status on the periphery held even in cities whose original or present pattern was for higher-status groups to be more centrally located. Thus, whatever the original pattern, over time there appears to be a movement toward a concentric-zone system.[19]

Schwirian and Matre, on the other hand, found a more mixed pattern in their study of Canada's eleven largest cities.[20] Major research carried out by Schnore for 200 urbanized areas in the United States supports the position that for the oldest and largest cities, there is the predicted pattern of higher socioeconomic status being found in peripheral suburban rather than central-city locations. However, newer and younger cities tend to have populations of higher socioeconomic status in the central city (the preindustrial model).[21] A follow-up study by Palen and Schnore found that for the black population, Burgess's pattern holds in the north and west but not the south.[22]

The internal spatial structure of black city neighborhoods is also related to socioeconomic status. There is a fairly regular progression upward in socioeconomic status as one moves outward from the city center. Schnore's study of social-class segregation within the black communities of twenty-four large cities confirms that the higher social classes disproportionately occupy the more peripheral locations.[23] Marston, however, suggests that his research on variation by socioeconomic status in sixteen American cities shows that in addition to decentralization or distance from the city's center, the age and prestige of the area being entered are of crucial importance. Simply put, black groups of higher socioeconomic status move toward newer areas and areas of higher prestige, even if they are located close to the city center.[24]

Thus, research shows that a rough version of Burgess's model does appear to hold, at least for larger and older American cities. As Schnore suggested, "An area might show a certain pattern of city-suburban status differences when it is relatively small and young but evolve toward another, predictable pattern of differences as it grows and ages."

[18]Leo F. Schnore and Joy K. O. Jones, "The Evolution of City-Suburban Types in the Course of a Decade," *Urban Affairs Quarterly*, 4:421–422, June, 1969; Joel Smith, "Another Look at Socioeconomic Status Distributions in Urbanized Areas," *Urban Affairs Quarterly*, 5:423–453, June, 1970; and Lee J. Haggerty, "Another Look at the Burgess Hypothesis: Time as an Important Variable," *American Journal of Sociology*, 76:1084–1093, May, 1971.

[19]Haggerty, op. cit., pp. 1084–1093.

[20]Kent P. Schwirian and Marc D. Matre, "The Ecological Structure of Canadian Cities," in Kent P. Schwirian (ed.), *Comparative Urban Structure*, Heath, Lexington, Mass., 1974.

[21]Leo F. Schnore, "The Socioeconomic Status of Cities and Suburbs," *American Sociological Review*, 28:76–85, February, 1963.

[22]J. John Palen and Leo F. Schnore, "Color Composition and City-Suburban Status Differences," *Land Economics*, 41:87–91, February, 1965.

[23]Leo F. Schnore, *The Urban Scene*, Free Press, New York, 1965, chap. 16.

[24]Wilfred G. Marston, "Socioeconomic Differentiation within Negro Areas of American Cities," *Social Factors*, 48:165–176, December, 1969.

More specifically . . . (1) smaller and younger central cities in the United States tend to be occupied by the local elite, while their peripheral, suburban areas contain the lower strata; (2) with growth and the passage of time, the central city comes to be the main residential area for both the highest and lowest strata, at least temporarily, while the broad middle classes are overrepresented in the suburbs; and (3) a subsequent stage in this evolutionary process is achieved when the suburbs have become the semiprivate preserve of both the upper and middle strata, while the central city is largely given over to the lowest stratum. In a very rough fashion, of course, this last stage corresponds to the way in which the various social classes are arrayed in space according to the original Burgess (1924) zonal hypothesis.[25]

There is some evidence to support this view.

In a longitudinal study of 198 metropolitan areas, James Pinkerton suggested that the patterns that were true of larger metropolitan areas are increasingly being found in smaller areas as well. As Pinkerton puts it:

I propose that a new stage is approaching in which the city-ring distribution of classes will no longer vary according to size and age of the metropolis; instead, all areas will house their lower status groups in the city.[26]

URBAN GROWTH OUTSIDE NORTH AMERICA

The concentric-zone pattern of urban growth, which says that there is an increasing status gradient as one goes from city core to periphery, is far less useful in describing patterns of ecological growth outside North America. The zonal pattern has not been the typical pattern of growth in the nonindustrial cities of Asia, Africa, and Latin America.

In contemporary cities with a preindustrial heritage, there appears to be an inverse zonal hypothesis. That is, instead of the poor in the inner core and the elite farther out, the central core is occupied by the elite whereas the disadvantaged fan out toward the periphery.[27] In such cities, it is common to find a pattern in which upper-class and upper-middle-class groups occupy the city proper and poor in-migrants settle on the "suburban" periphery in squatter shantytowns. These *favelas, barriadas, gecekondulas,* or *bustees* can be found on the periphery of almost every major city in Latin America, Africa, and Asia. Several decades of research on Indian, Latin America, and some European cities generally indicate an inverse zonal hypothesis.[28]

[25]Leo F. Schnore, *Class and Race in Cities and Suburbs,* Markham, Chicago, 1972, p. 72.
[26]James R. Pinkerton, "The Changing Class Composition of Cities and Suburbs," *Land Economics,* **49:**469, November, 1973.
[27]Gideon Sjoberg, *The Preindustrial City,* Free Press, New York, 1960, pp. 97–98.
[28]See, for example: Noel Gist, "The Ecology of Bangalore India," *Social Forces,* **35:**356–365, May, 1957; Surinder Mehta, "Patterns of Residence in Poona by Name, Education, and Income," *American Journal of Sociology,* **73:**496–508, March, 1968; Normal Haynes, "Mexico City—Its Growth and Configuration," *American Journal of Sociology,* **50:**295–304, January, 1945; and Theodore Caplow, "The Social Ecology of Guatemala City," *Social Forces,* **28:**113–135, 1949.

As Part Five, Worldwide Urbanization, details, cities in the third world differ from North American cities in a number of respects. First, American cities have a commercial industrial base not found in cities that grew primarily as administrative centers. Second, the American city is based upon a highly developed transportation technology which allows relatively rapid movement between central-city offices and suburban residences. Where inexpensive easy transportation is lacking, central-city location is more desirable. (Higher transportation costs are now contributing toward some return of upper-status groups to the city. Finally, there is the inertia to change created by preexisting locational patterns and preferences. Without draconian measures, cities cannot rapidly change their physical characteristics.

Cultural differences also have to be taken into account. As Caplow has stated:

> The literature of urban geography and urban sociology has a tendency to project as universals those characteristics of urbanism with which European and American students are most familiar. Thus, since a large proportion of all urban research has concerned itself with Chicago, there was until recently a tendency to ascribe to all cities characteristics which now appear to be specific to Chicago and other communities closely resembling it in history and economic function. . . .
>
> In the United States, almost all urban growth has been characterized by the rapid and uncontrolled expansion of the community and by unregulated competition for land. To a lesser degree this has been true also of modern Europe.[29]

There is also reason to question just how applicable Burgess's theory is to European cities. Certainly the major cities of Europe that were established before the industrial revolution have an internal distribution of social and economic classes that does not easily fit Burgess's model.[30] In the older cities the elites preempted the prestigious central locations and the poor were forced to live in more peripheral locations. Manufacturing and commerce, when located within the city, were restricted to specific areas. Thus, the East End of London was, before the bombing of World War II, composed of small factories, workshops, and poor homes surrounding the dock area. On the other hand, the central and western districts of Westminster, Marylebone, and Kensington have continued to retain their upper-class airs for two centuries in spite of their central location. Moscow, before the Russian Revolution, clearly had the urban structure of a preindustrial city with its inverse zonal pattern.[31]

Within European cities with central land already filled, heavy industry was confined to "suburban" areas where there was sufficient land for the growing factories. Thus, Paris has a concentration of automobile and aircraft factories to the south and east of the city, and the population of such suburban

[29]Caplow, op. cit., p. 132.
[30]Francis L. Hauser, "Ecological Patterns of European Cities," in Sylvia F. Fava (ed.), *Urbanism in World Perspective*, Crowell, New York, 1968.
[31]Walter F. Abbott, "Moscow in 1897 as a Preindustrial City: A Test of the Inverse Burgess Zonal Hypothesis," *American Sociological Review*, **39**:542–550, August, 1974.

areas is heavily working-class. The continuation of a preindustrial ecological pattern results in social-class distribution and political voting patterns that are quite different from those found in American cities. Some suburban areas of Paris, the so-called "red ring," provide major political support for the Communist Party, while the inner-city middle-class districts vote for the more conservative candidates—exactly the opposite of the American stereotype. For major political protests, protesters are bused in from the suburbs.

Gideon Sjoberg sees this pattern of identification of high-status groups with central-city location as a persistence of a "feudal tradition" that is not present in American cities. In his view, "In many European cities, including those in the U.S.S.R., the persistence of the feudal tradition has inhibited suburbanization because high status has attached to residence in the central city."[32]

One can question whether a preference for central-city locations is today "feudalistic" or part of a "feudal tradition." Manhattan doesn't have a feudal tradition, but it still has a pattern of the well-to-do locating in certain areas of the central city. Cosmopolites, whether in London, Paris, or New York, simply prefer to live where they can easily get to work and easily get a drink or a sandwich at 2:00 A.M. It can be argued that, particularly in Europe, upper-status urban populations live in the city because they feel it is an exciting and attractive place to live.

It is possible that the differences in land use between North American industrialized cities and nonindustrial cities elsewhere, particularly in the developing world, may be part of an evolutionary pattern. Leo Schnore suggests that Burgess's concentric-zone scheme as well as preindustrial land-use patterns can be subsumed under a more general theory of residential land uses in urban areas.[33] However, such a theory has yet to be fully developed.

ALTERNATIVE THEORIES

Sector Theory

There are two major alternatives to Burgess's hypothesis. Homer Hoyt suggested an alternative to the concentric-zone pattern which became known as the "sector theory."[34] Hoyt suggested that rather than in rings, growth took place in homogeneous pie-shaped sectors which extended radially from the center toward the periphery of the city. His research indicated that residential areas extended rapidly along established lines of travel where economic resistance was least. A pattern of land use was said to develop in which each

---

[32]Gideon Sjoberg, "Cities in Developing and in Industrial Societies: A Cross-Cultural Analysis," in Philip M. Hauser and Leo F. Schnore, *The Study of Urbanization,* Wiley, New York, 1965, p. 230.
[33]Schnore, *Class and Race in Cities and Suburbs,* p. 21.
[34]Homer Hoyt, "The Structure and Growth of Residential Neighborhoods in American Cities," U.S. Federal Housing Administration, Washington, D.C., 1939.

use—industrial, commercial, high-income residential, or low-income residential—tended to push out from the city core in specific sectors or wedges that cut across concentric zones.

Thus, high-income housing could radiate from the core in one wedge, a racial ghetto in a second, industrial firms in a third, and work-class residences in a fourth. Hoyt's theory was based on the movement of high-rent districts in 142 American cities between 1900, 1915, and 1936. Since Hoyt did not attempt to locate social influences on phenomena within the metropolitan area, some sociologists seeking a compromise have used Hoyt's theory to explain residential movement and Burgess's theory to explain social-spatial phenomena.

Multiple-Nuclei Theory

Another theory of spatial growth rejects the idea of a unicentered city altogether and instead holds that differing land uses have different centers. This "multiple-nuclei" theory was suggested by Chauncy Harris and Edward Ullman.[35] They argued that land-use patterns developed around what were originally independent nuclei. Four factors were said to account for the rise of the different nuclei:

1. Certain activities require specialized facilities. Retailing, for example, require a high degree of accessibility, while manufacturing needs ample land and railroad service.
2. Like activities group together for mutual advantages, as in the case of the central business district.
3. Some unlike activities are mutually detrimental or incompatible with one another. For example, it is unlikely that high-income or high-status residential areas will locate close to heavy industry.
4. Some users, such as storage and warehousing facilities, which have a relatively lower competitive capacity to purchase good locations, are able to afford only low-rental areas.[36]

In many respects the multiple-nuclei hypothesis better describes the entire metrpolitan area than the central city. The multiple-nuclei theory, unlike the zonal and sector theories, holds that there can be no predictable pattern of common spatial growth. Maurice Davie took this further and argued that "there is no universal pattern, not even an ideal type."[37] Davie suggested that rather than propping up inadequate hypotheses, sociologists should use their own powers of observation and analysis. He suggested that topographical features such as rivers, lakes, and hills interfere with or take precedence over social or geometrical patterns of growth. He maintained that level land attracts

---

[35]Chauncy Harris and Edward Ullman, "The Nature of Cities," *The Annals of the American Academy of Political and Social Science,* **252:**7–17, 1945.
[36]Harris and Ullman, loc. cit.
[37]Maurice R. Davie, "The Pattern of Urban Growth," in George Murdock (ed.), *Studies in the Science of Society,* Yale University Press, New Haven, Conn., 1937, pp. 131–162.

business; higher land and hills attract private residences; low land near water attracts industry; erratic street arrangement encourages central growth; and expressways expedite radial expansion. As Thomlinson points out, the difficulty with these statements is that they are a list of ad hoc descriptions, lacking any theory to bind them together into a compact system of generalizations.[38] Analysis without theory contributes little to knowledge, since it simply states what is. While such statements have a surface appeal, particularly when the shortcomings of other theories are considered, they provide no hypothesis to be tested and thus cannot be proven right or wrong.

CONTEMPORARY ECOLOGY

Ecologists, by and large, collect their data in the same manner as other sociologists. What distinguishes them is their preference for operating on the systems level rather than the individual level. Ecologists, concerned as they are with the behavior of groups, rely heavily on mass data and are most comfortable with so-called "hard data." Probably the most-used source of data is the United States Census, which provides a wealth of information on the social and economic characteristics of groups, their housing patterns, and their business activities. In the United States the decennial census is supplemented by the monthly Current Population Survey of households across the nation, which yields far more detailed information. The Current Population Survey provides up-to-date information on social and economic questions— detailed information no single researcher or group of researchers could afford to gather. The use of computers enables researchers to obtain previously unavailable information on the characteristics of neighborhoods or groups (e.g., blacks) within urban areas while still protecting the anonymity of the respondents.

The human ecologist's interest is in the characteristics and behavior of groups rather than the attitudes, motivations, and personalities of the individual members of groups. As a result, ecologists usually use quantitative rather than qualitative data. Also, their use of nonsocial variables such as distance, transportation, and physical environment means that ecologists sometimes have more in common with economists than with sociologists doing behavioral studies in the social psychology of small groups.

For example, in a study of occupational stratification and residential location, the Duncans empirically demonstrated the relationship between what one does and where one lives. Spatial distances between occupational groups are closely related to their social distances, whether measured in terms of the conventional indicators of socioeconomic status (income, education, occupation) or in terms of differences in occupational origins. In accordance with accepted ecological theory, they found that the occupational groups most segregated physically were those at the very botton and very top of the

---

[38]Thomlinson, op. cit., p. 151.

occupational scale. Likewise, residence in low-rent areas and residence near the center of the city were inversely related to socioeconomic status. However, near the middle of the socioeconomic scale, where blue-collar and white-collar clerical occupations meet, the pattern is less clear. Although white-collar clerical workers on the average have considerably lower income than blue-collar craftworkers and line supervisors, they have a pattern of residential distribution more in common with other white-collar groups. It appears that social status, or prestige, is more important to clerical groups, although their relatively lower income level vis à vis other white-collar groups does set up cross-pressures, as is indicated by a high rent-to-income ratio for clerical workers.[39] A recent replication by Albert Simkus indicates that occupational segregation remains high.[40] Nonwhites in the highest occupational categories are becoming slightly less segregated from whites, while those in the lowest occupational categories are becoming slightly more segregated.

Social-Area Analysis

In an attempt to move beyond what they consider the somewhat simplistic models already presented, several researchers have turned to a technique or approach known as "social-areas analysis." The goal is to refocus attention on social forces: how changes in the organization of society affect the spatial or physical arrangement of various groups. Social-area analysis seeks to classify urban phenomena systematically. In some respects social-area analysis can be viewed as an attempt to empirically define "natural areas."

The originators of social-area analysis, Eshref Shevky and Wendell Bell, differentiate the structure of urban subareas according to three variables originally named "social rank," "urbanization," and "segregation."[41] These variables were chosen because they were believed to measure crucial factors distinguishing types of urban populations. The social rank index is derived from census-tract measures of occupation and education. When a population in an area shares similar characteristics, the area is called a "social area." The urbanization index, now called "familism" or "family form," is derived from measures of the ratio of children to women, the proportion of working women, and the percentage of single-family dwellings. The segregation index is now labeled "ethnicity," and is derived from the measurement of spatial isolation of ethnic groups. The assumption is that a larger number of variables can be reduced to the three factors of social rank (socioeconomic status), family status, and ethnic status and three scores produced. It was also originally assumed that in an industrialized society, these factors would be relatively independent of one another.

The objective is to classify small sections of the city on the basis of their

[39]Otis Dudley Duncan and Beverly Duncan, "Residential Distribution and Occupational Stratification," *American Journal of Sociology,* **60:**493–503, March, 1955.
[40]Albert A. Simkus, "Residential Segregation by Occupation and Race in Ten Urbanized Areas, 1950–1970,"*American Sociological Review,* **43:**81–93, February, 1978.
[41]Eshref Shevky and Wendell Bell, *Social Area Analysis,* Stanford University Press, Palo Alto, Calif., 1955.

social attributes. Thus, the areas are not determined by spatial criteria, but rather are established on the basis of the social characteristics of the residents, although the basic unit for analysis still remains the spatially defined census tract of roughly 4,000 persons. The technique is designed to get finer detail and a more accurate map of social space by giving social values to the various census tracts and to create a picture of the city's pattern from the social areas. It differs from the more conventional ecological position, which first hypothesizes a given spatial social pattern and then examines the data to discover the degree of fit. The nature of the clustering of variables and the relationships among them are taken as measuring "societal scale," or the degree of the division of labor and social integration. Proponents of the technique argue that it has proved itself valuable in directing attention to social rather than spatial concerns, more adequately delineating subcommunities within the urban area and facilitating comparative and longitudinal study of cities.[42]

Studies have generally tended to confirm that social status, family status, and ethnic status are reasonable factors on which to differentiate subareas of American cities. There is far less agreement on whether these factors are separate from one another.[43] Janet Abu-Lughod has also noted that while social rank was a good cross-cultural measure, family form was far too culture bound to be useful.[44]

Social-area analysis has not had an uncritical reception. It has been strongly criticized by some ecologists as lacking both a theoretical rationale and empirical utility. A major criticism is that abstract variables of social rank, urbanization, and ethnicity are said to be an arbitrary grouping of several census measures into another type of index, where the index gives less detail than the component parts from which it was created. Duncan also argues that the discussion of theoretical reasons for choosing particular index variables does not lead to a unique selection of variables or even to a useful criterion for selection, and that there is no clear theoretical relationship between the basic concepts and the variables used in the index.[45]

Bell and Greer in turn suggest that critics of social-area analysis have applied unreasonable standards, have been uncautious in making conclusions unsupported by data, and have reached different evaluations because of basic differences in intellectual approach.[46] Today, the disagreement between those who favor social-area analysis and those who do not remains an uneasy truce.

---

[42]For a number of social area studies, see Kent P. Schwirian, *Comparative Urban Structures: Studies in the Ecology of Cities,* Heath, Lexington, Mass., 1974.

[43]Maurice Van Arsdol, Jr., Santo F. Camileri, and Calvin F. Schmid, "The Generality of Urban Social Area Indexes," *American Sociological Review,* **23:**277–284, 1958; and Theodore R. Anderson and Lee I. Bean, "The Shevky-Bell Social Areas: Confirmation of Results and a Reinterpretation," *Social Forces,* **40:**119–124, December, 1961.

[44]Janet Abu-Lughod, "Testing the Theory of Social Area Analysis: The Ecology of Cairo," *American Sociological Review,* **34:**198–212, 1969; see also, Janet Abu-Lughod, *Urban Apartheid in Morocco,* Princeton University Press, Princeton, 1980.

[45]Otis Dudley Duncan, Review of "Social Area Analysis," *American Journal of Sociology,* **61:**84–85, July, 1955; and Amos Hawley and Otis Dudley Duncan, "Social Area Analysis: A Critical Appraisal," *Land Economics,* **33:**337–345, November, 1957.

[46]Wendell Bell and Scott Greer, "Social Area Analysis and Its Critiques," *Pacific Sociological Review,* **5:**3–9, 1962.

Factor Analysis

Factorial ecology attempts to use the computer to overcome the criticism that social-area analysis uses too few preselected variables. Thus, factorial ecology differs from social-area analysis in that it does not preselect variables but rather allows them to emerge from the data. This is done through the use of the statistical technique of factor analysis, in which all variables are correlated with one another and are then clustered with other variables that statistically appear to be clustered with and measure the same common factor. A separate factor is said to underlie each cluster of variables.

There is some evidence that factor analysis empirically comes up with the same socioeconomic rank, family status, and ethnicity variables found in social-area analysis.[47]

Factor analysis is a strong statistical tool for reducing a large number of variables to a few factors. Scores of variables may be reduced to half a dozen or so. Factorial ecology is limited more by logical problems of interpretation than by technical problems.[48] Once one identifies a cluster of variables it requires a logical leap to give the factor a label and interpretation. Factorial studies in social ecology have made both methodological and substantive contributions to our understanding of urban ecology.[49]

[47]R. J. Johnston, "Residential Characteristics in Cities," in D. T. Herbert and R. J. Johnston (eds.), *Social Areas in Cities,* Wiley, New York, 1976, pp. 193–235.

[48]Alfred E. Hunter, "Factorial Ecology: A Critique and Some Suggestions," *Demography,* **9:**107–117, February, 1972.

[49]Carl-Gunnar Janson, "Factorial Social Ecology," in Alex Inkeles (ed.), *Annual Review of Sociology,* **6:**433–456, 1980; and F. L. Sweetser, "Neighborhood Typologies and Social Ecological Theory," paper presented at ninth World Congress of Sociology, Uppsala, Sweden, August, 1978.

A Note on Urbanization and Environment

Our discussion of the ecology of the city would be incomplete without mention of the effect of cities on the physical environment and vice versa. The actual physical shape of cities has been modified by human design. Much of contemporary Boston, for instance, was under water at the time of the Revolution. One of the former underwater zones is known today as Back Bay. Chicago in similar fashion created an Outer Drive and lakefront park system out of filled land, as did New Orleans. In other cases the pumping out of subsurface groundwater and other fluids has led, as in parts of Houston and in Long Beach, California, to subsidence. In the latter case, from 1937 through 1962 some 913 million barrels of oil, 482 million barrels of water, and 832 billion cubic feet of gas were extracted, causing parts of this heavily urbanized area to sink as much as 27 feet.*

Cities, of course, are notorious for their effect on air pollution. London in 1952 had a disastrous temperature inversion which kept a deadly smog over the city for a week. The smog was so dense that after landing, an airliner was unable to find the terminal, and a vehicle sent out to lead it in also became lost. More serious was the effect on persons with lung conditions; some 4,000 Londoners died of smog-related causes before the smog lifted. (Today London has strict air pollution controls; the air is actually getting cleaner, and the city has more days of sunshine.)

In the United States, Los Angeles is perhaps most notorious for its polluted air. Its smog is a consequence of an environmental location that encourages thermal inversions that trap pollutants, a population that has been increasing, and a transportation technololgy based on automobiles.

Denver, Colorado's pollution problems are, if anything, growing even more serious. In order to stave off federal regulation, Denver in 1984–1985 implemented a voluntary program of a weekly carless day based on the first number of the license plate. Whether this social organizational response will be adequate without further enforcement is doubtful.

Cities also create atmospheric changes. Buildings and paved streets retain heat, and urban areas become heat

*Donald Eschman and Melvin Marcus, "The Geologic and Topographic Setting of Cities," in Thomas Detwyler and Melvin Marcus (eds.), *Urbanization and Environment*, Buxbury Press, Belmont, Calif., 1972, p. 46.

islands, as anyone who has spent a hot summer day in the central city knows. What is less well-known is that the condensation nuclei produced by activity in cities increase cloudiness and precipitation over cities.[†]

By covering the ground with buildings, paved roads, and parking lots, urban development in effect waterproofs the land surface. Rainfall cannot be normally absorbed into the soil; instead, storm runoff must be handled by massive systems of storm sewers. The paving over of city and suburban areas, by preventing water absorption, actually increases the risk of severe flooding.[‡] The relationship between urban residents and their physical environment is much closer than most city dwellers or suburbanites recognize.

[†]Reid Bryson and John Ross, in Detwyler and Marcus, op. cit., p. 63.
[‡]Robert Kates, Ian Burton, and Gilbert F. White, *The Environment as Hazard*, Oxford University Press, New York, 1976; and Stanley A. Changon, et al., *Summary of Metromex, Volume 1: Weather Anomalies and Impacts*, Illinois State Water Survey, Urbana, Ill., 1977.

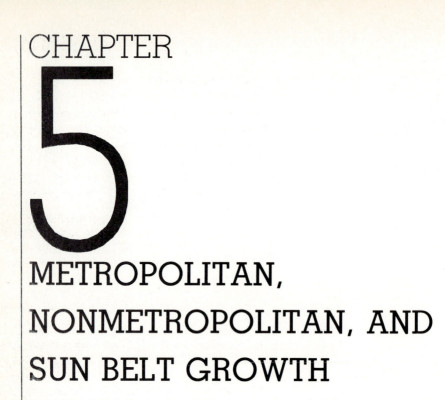

CHAPTER 5

METROPOLITAN, NONMETROPOLITAN, AND SUN BELT GROWTH

By the blessing of the upright a city is built up . . .
Proverbs 11:11

INTRODUCTION

Urbanization patterns in the United States have undergone several profound changes in recent decades. In this chapter three major transformations are emphasized. The first is the replacement of the city by the larger metropolitan area as the major urban unit. The second is the slowing of urbanization during the 1970s and the 1980s revival of metro area population growth. The third is the shifting pattern of interregional movement from frost belt to sun belt.

METROPOLITAN URBAN GROWTH

Let us begin by looking at the metropolitan area. The first eighty-five years of this century was a period of dramatic metropolitan development and ascendancy. By the turn of the century, the era of the frontier was closed, and it was clear that future national growth would have an urban nexus. The ecological and demographic pattern was one of population shifting into ever-larger metropolitan areas. Rural counties were being depopulated, while population in the central cities was becoming denser. The census of 1910 recognized this centripetal population movement by establishing forty-four ad hoc "metropolitan districts" whose boundaries extended beyond those of the central city. At that time, roughly one-third of the nation's population resided in metropolitan areas.

If changes in the definition of "metropolitan areas" are taken into account, *all* population growth in the contiguous United States from the turn of the century to 1970 occurred in metropolitan areas.[1] Metropolitan areas gained population at a rate far in excess of the rate for nonmetropolitan areas during this period.[2] As a result of this centripetal movement, three-quarters of the population now resides within metropolitan areas.[3] Moreover, beyond the metropolitan area there exists a commuting field that further extends metropolitan influence to virtually the entire population. Today the dominance of metropolitan areas is demographic as well as economic and social. Nearly half of all Americans live in the thirty-six largest Metropolitan Statistical Areas with a population of one million or more.

Predictions of such metropolitan dominance had been foreseen by scholars as far back as the 1920s. The awareness that cities had become part of a larger urban complex was reflected in the pioneering works of perceptive writers such as Gras and McKenzie.[4] They foresaw that the city per se was yielding its influence to a larger unit: the metropolitan area.

Movement of population toward the largest urban concentrations (city

---

[1]Amos H. Hawley, *Urban Society: An Ecological Approach,* Ronald Press, New York, 1971.
[2]Amos H. Hawley and Vincent P. Rock (eds.), *Metropolitan America in Contemporary Perspective.* Holsted Press, New York, 1975, pp. 153–154.
[3]R. C. Forstall, "Trends in Metropolitan and Nonmetropolitan Population Growth Since 1970," U.S. Bureau of the Census, Washington, D.C., 1975.
[4]N. B. S. Gras, *Introduction to Economic History,* Harper, New York, 1922; and Roderick McKenzie, *The Metropolitan Community,* McGraw-Hill, New York, 1933.

TABLE 5-1
Metropolitan and Nonmetropolitan Population: 1950–1980
(Excludes Puerto Rico. Reflects areas as defined at each census except as noted)

Area	1950[1]	1960	1970[2]	1980 1981 definitions	1980 1983 definitions
Populations (millions)					
United States	151.3	179.3	203.3	226.5	226.5
Inside PMSAs and MSAs	84.9	112.9	139.5	169.4	171.8
Inside central cities	49.7	58.0	63.8	67.9	72.4
Outside central cities	35.2	54.9	75.6	101.5	99.3
Outside PMSAs and MSAs	66.5	66.4	63.8	57.1	54.8
Percent of United States					
United States	100.0	100.0	100.0	100.0	100.0
Inside MSAs	56.1	63.0	68.6	74.8	75.8
Inside central cities	32.8	32.3	31.4	30.0	32.0
Outside central cities	23.3	30.6	37.2	44.8	43.3
Outside MSAs	43.9	37.0	31.4	25.2	24.2

[1] Including Alaska and Hawaii.
[2] 1970 data include revisions made since publication of 1970 census reports.
PMSA = primary metropolitan statistical area.
Source: Bureau of the Census.

and suburb) both depopulated rural counties and magnified urban problems.[5] The magnitude of the rural out-migration is reflected in Bureau of Census figures (see Tables 5-1 and 5-2). In 1920, 30 percent of the American population still lived on farms; by 1981 this figure had shrunk to only 2.6 percent.[6] In the half century from 1920 to 1970, the net out-migration from farms to cities was 29 million.[7] Only one person in thirty-eight lives on a farm today.

For the first half of this century, while the central city increasingly found its *physical* expansion contained by surrounding suburbs, the *influence* of the central city expanded. Once independent, outlying towns, villages, and cross-road markets found themselves engulfed in an urban network. The local bank became a branch of a large city bank; local papers were replaced by metropolitan dailies; and local dairies and breweries went under, unable to compete with metropolitan-based firms. Where once such places were moderately self-sufficient, they now either declined in significance or began to perform specialized functions for the larger metropolitan area. Some previously independent communities became satellite towns, while others specialized as

[5]Amos H. Hawley, "Urbanization as Process," in David Street (ed.), *Handbook of Contemporary Urban Life,* Jossey-Bass, San Francisco, 1978, p. 7.
[6]U.S. Bureau of the Census, U.S. Department of Commerce and Agriculture, "Farm Population of the United States: 1977," *Current Population Reports,* series P-27, no. 51, Washington, D.C., November, 1978.
[7]U.S. Bureau of the Census, U.S. Department of Commerce, "Population Profile of the United States: 1981," *Current Population Reports,* series P-20, no. 394, Washington, D.C., September, 1982, p. 7.

TABLE 5-2
Percent Change in Metropolitan and Nonmetropolitan Population: 1950–1980
(Reflects areas as defined at end of each decade except as noted)

Area	1950–1960	1960–1970[1]	1970–1980	
			1981 definitions	1983 definitions
United States	18.5	13.3	11.4	11.4
Inside metropolitan areas	26.4	16.6	10.2	10.5
Inside central cities[2]	10.7	6.4	0.1	0.7
Outside central cities[2]	48.6	26.8	18.2	19.0
Outside metropolitan areas	7.1	6.8	15.1	14.4

[1] Based on 1970 tabulated population excluding subsequent corrections.
[2] Data for inside central cities and outside central cities do not include any revisions for annexations or other city boundary changes during the decade.
Source: Bureau of the Census.

bedroom suburbs.[8] The consequence was the emergence of the era of the metropolitan unit.

DECENTRALIZATION OF POPULATION WITHIN METROPOLITAN AREAS

The twentieth century thus has witnessed a massive population implosion or ingathering of population into urban concentrations. However, within metropolitan areas the movement has been from the center toward the periphery. Throughout the twentieth century, again with annexation taken into account, the population of outer "suburban" areas has grown faster than that of central cities.[9] Almost all metropolitan growth during this period occurred in the suburban ring beyond the central city. The redistribution of population began in the larger and older metropolitan areas and then became general for cities of all sizes except the very newest. (This suburban decentralization is treated in Chapter 8, Patterns of Suburbanization.) Moreover, the highest rate of growth in nonmetropolitan counties until the 1970s occurred in counties having metropolitan characteristics, experiencing overspill, or both. The areas of overspill, commonly referred to as "exurbs," simply confirmed the patterns of metropolitan dominance.

Over time the edges of metropolitan areas were increasingly converted from less intensive to more intensive uses, such as housing and manufacturing. Less intensive land uses such as grain production and cattle grazing have been pushed outward; near the city even agriculture is intensive—truck farms, greenhouses, chicken farms, etc. Fertility of the soil is less important than the

[8]Leo F. Schnore, "Satellites and Suburbs," *Social Forces,* **36:**121–127, December, 1957.
[9]Basil Zimmer, "Suburbanization and Changing Political Structures," in Barry Schwartz (ed.), *The Changing Forces of the Suburbs,* University of Chicago Press, Chicago, 1975.

Defining Metropolitan Areas

The term "metropolitan area" is a popular term rather than one defined by the Bureau of the Census. It commonly refers to a large concentration of 100,000 or more inhabitants that contains as its core a legal city with 50,000 or more inhabitants and is surrounded by suburban areas. The Bureau of the Census has two ways of defining metropolitan areas: as urbanized areas and as Metropollitan Statistical Areas.

Urbanized Areas. According to the Bureau of the Census definition an urbanized area consists of a central city, or cities, of 50,000 or more and their surrounding closely settled territory, whether incorporated or unincorporated. The term, thus, refers to the actual urban population of an area regardless of political boundaries such as county or state lines. All those in the urbanized area are considered urban, but the population is also divided into those in the "central city" and those in the remainder of the area, or "urban fringe."

Because it is based on *density* (at least 1,000 persons per square mile), the urbanized area has no fixed boundaries, and thus changes from census to census to reflect actual population changes. This potential strength can, however, become a weakness when one is doing longitudinal research, since the urbanized area of any city covered different land areas in the 1950, 1960, 1970, and 1980 censuses. The proportion of a state's population living in urbanized areas in 1980 varied from 85 percent in New Jersey to 15 percent in Vermont.

Metropolitan Statistical Area. Metropolitan Statistical Areas (MSAs) are officially designated by the U.S. Office of Management and Budget, and are based on territory rather than population. A Metropolitan Statistical Area is a *county or group of counties* having a central city of 50,000 or more, or twin cities with a combined population of 50,000 or more. The MSA includes the county in which the central city is located plus any adjacent counties that are judged by the Bureau of the Census to be metropolitan in character and socially and economically integrated with the central city. In New England, where there are no counties, MSAs consist of townships and cities instead. As of 1985 there were 257 freestanding areas designated as MSAs. Prior to 1983 MSAs were known as SMSAs (Standard Metropolitan Statistical Areas).

Primary Metropolitan Statistical Areas. In addition to the 257 MSAs there are 78 large metropolitan complexes the Bureau of the Census now defines as "Primary Metropolitan Statistical Areas" (PMSAs). Although the 1983 definitions are complicated, PMSAs are basically the larger metropolitan complexes.

Consolidated Metropolitan Statistical Areas.
metropolitan complexes.

Consolidated Metropolitan Statistical Areas. In order to distinguish the very largest concentrations of metropolitan populations, Consolidated Metropolitan Statistical Areas (CMSAs) have been designated. CMSAs are basically conglomerations of PMSAs. As of 1985 there were twenty-three Consolidated Metropolitan Statistical Areas.*

Basically, then, we now have a three-tiered system of metropolitan areas: 257 freestanding MSAs; 78 larger PMSAs; and 23 very large CMSAs (this last group being made up by combining PMSAs).

Megalopolis. Finally, the term "megalopolis" is sometimes used to refer to an agglomeration of closely bound metropolitan areas. Megalopolis, thus, refers not to one metropolitan area but to a string of metropolitan areas. Megalopolis is a popular rather than Bureau of Census term. Originally, the term referred to the so-called BosWash megalopolis, stretching some 500 miles along the Atlantic coast from Boston to Washington and containing some 60 million people. However, there is no evidence that this megalopolis is becoming economically integrated and interdependent, as should be the case if a truly organized super community is being formed. Megalopolis, to date, is more a name than an actual occurrence.**

*U.S. Bureau of the Census, 1980 Census of Population, *Metropolitan Statistical Areas*, PC80-S1-18, Washington, D.C., January, 1985.
**Robert Weller, "An Empirical Examination of Metropolitan Structure," in J. John Palen and Karl Flaming (eds.), *Urban America*, Holt, Rinehart and Winston, New York, 1972, pp. 105–113.

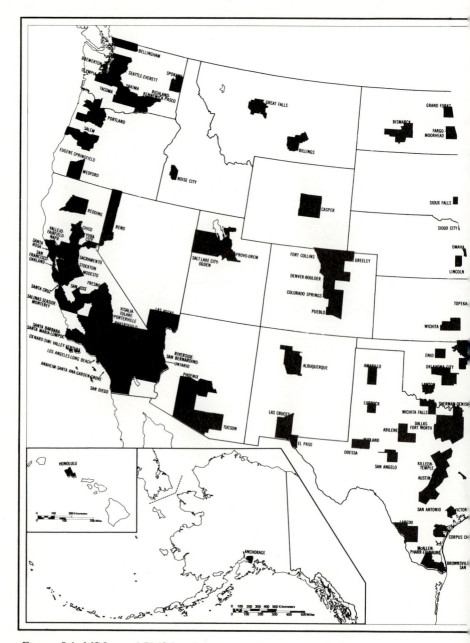

Figure 5-1. MSAs and PMSAs. As the map indicates, urbanism has become the American way of life. (*From Bureau of the Census.*)

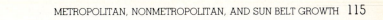

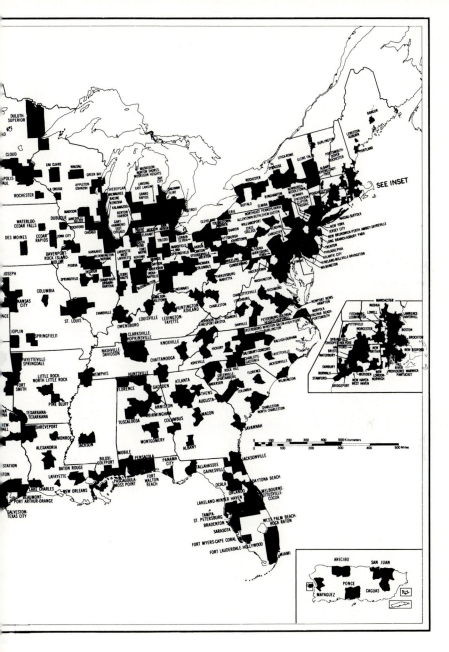

nearness of the city: consider, for example, the intensive use of relatively poor farmland near New England cities.

Outmovement of Industry: 1950 to the Present

After World War II, retail trade, service establishments, and manufacturing firms increasingly followed the population to suburban areas. For example, suburban shopping malls—virtually nonexistent 30 years ago—now number over 15,000 and account for more than half the nation's retail sales. With over three-quarters of employed suburbanites working in suburbs, old commutation patterns (residents of suburbs commuting to the central city), have also broken down. (The major role of the federal government in subsidizing suburbanization is discussed in Chapter 8 and Chapter 11, Housing Programs and Urban Change.)

In the American city of fifty years ago, industry was concentrated in an inner belt located between the central business district (CBD) and the better residential areas. As the factories prospered, the original space became more and more crowded. But expansion was both difficult and expensive. Internally, assembly lines or other factory operations had to be fitted into the existing building, and even moving goods from floor to floor became a serious problem. At the same time, external expansion was limited by the cost, both in land and taxes, of growing horizontally. Surrounding land was already occupied, which meant that whatever was already on the land had to be bought and torn down before the factory could expand. Transportation also became an increasing problem. Trucks had to move down busy city streets before lining up to wait to get into inadequate loading docks. Parking space for workers' cars developed into another major headache.

The move of manufacturing and industry out of the central city was greatly accelerated by the building of interstate superhighways. The building of the interstate expressway system in the 1950s, 1960s, and 1970s gave industry genuine alternatives to central-city locations. Suburban land was cheap, and suburban taxes were low. Most important, the plant could be designed from the inside out. The assembly line, for example, could be laid out all on one level and then walls simply built around the work space. The size and shape of the building could be determined by the needs of the factory rather than by the size and shape of a lot or an existing plant. Suburban plants were also closer to the homes of executives who lived in the suburbs, and this was another factor encouraging the move of management to the suburbs.

Increasingly, industry has leapfrogged over intermediate city residential areas and moved directly from the inner city to suburban industrial parks. When a firm was serving only local markets, a central-city location, with its ease of access to all parts of a city, made sense. Such a location was reasonable even if the major transport between cities was done by rail. Today, however, firms with national markets usually seek a location on or near an interstate expressway, which is far more valuable than one which gives rapid access to all parts of any single city.

Shopping malls have become ubiquitous as symbols of the American way of life. (© Tim Davis 1983/Photo Researchers)

The location of factories in suburbs in turn encouraged workers to move to new suburban tract-type housing developments that were sprouting in the cornfields near the factories. Before long, shopping centers followed; and more and more mixed industrial-residential suburbs were born.

Advances in Transportation and Communication

What made the widespread outward flow of urban population possible was technological breakthroughs in the areas of transportation and communication. The city based on steam power was transformed into one dependent on petroleum and electricity. Widespread use of automobiles, trucks, and telephones increased the movement of persons, goods, and ideas.

Research shows that the factor most closely related to a city's growth was its transportation network with other cities.[10] Within metropolitan areas, transportation was also critical to growth. The automobile provided mobility to the average urban dweller and allowed—and even encouraged—rapid settlement of previously inaccessible areas on the periphery of the central city. Henry Ford's Model T changed the automobile from a toy of the rich to a middle-class necessity. Automobile registration in the United States increased from 2.5 million in 1915 to 9 million in 1920 and 26 million in 1930. Currently, there is one auto for every two persons in the United States.

With the coming of the automobile, the maximum distance workers could live from their place of employment and commute within an hour increased from a dozen miles to perhaps 25 miles or so. (Theoretically, the automobile doubled the commuting radius, but the practicalities of poor roads and traffic congestion set lower limits.) As of 1920 a Chicago study indicated that the average distance from home to workplace was 1.5 miles.[11] By 1960 the distance had increased to 4.7 miles.[12] Just at the time when Burgess was expounding his theory of growth from the center through intermediate zones (detailed in Chapter 4, Ecology and Structure of American Cities), the automobile and the truck were partially outdating his work.

What the automobile did for people, the truck did for goods. Trucks were incomparably more flexible than railroads for short hauls. Trucks were free of fixed routes and fixed schedules, needed no elaborate terminal facilities on expensive inner-city land, and could make door-to-door pick-ups and deliveries. No longer was it necessary for the factory to be on the rail line. For all but the longest hauls, the speed of motor trucks was also superior. However, during the 1920s and 1930s, the major advantage of motor transport was its lower cost per mile within the first 250 miles of the city.[13] Not only were equipment and maintenance costs far lower, but in truck cartage the cost per mile was lowest for the shortest distances. In train transport, on the other hand, the lowest cost per mile was for the longest trips. The motor truck, then, was by far the superior competitor for the short haul—an advantage that was increased considerably by the public building of new roads. The interstate expressway system, began during the late 1950s, extended the trucks' longer-haul advantage, although this advantage is now being modified by fuel costs.

What the motor vehicle did for transportation, the telephone did for communication. Not until 1920 did over half of all residences have telephones. By the 1920s the telephone had become a common adjunct of local business, and long-distance telephone communication was a practical—if expensive— reality. A consequence was the liberation of first residences and then factories

[10]Mark LaGory and James Nelson, "An Ecological Analysis of Growth between 1900 and 1940, "Sociological Quarterly, **19:** 590–603, 1978.

[11]Beverly Duncan, "Factors in Work-Residence Separation: Wages and Salary Workers, 1951," *American Sociological Review,* **21:**48–56, 1956.

[12]Amos H. Hawley, *Urban Society,* p. 191.

[13]National Resources Committee, *Technological Trends and National Policy,* U.S. Government Printing Office, Washington, D.C., 1937.

and offices from central-city locations. More recently air transportation and the use of computers for data transfer have further weakened the need for a central city business location.

Changing Central Cities

The changes noted above have radically altered the relationship between central cities and their suburbs. Between 1970 and 1980, for example, the population of central cities remained about the same. Huge losses in northern cities were offset by growth and annexations in southern and western cities. But during that same period, suburbs grew to 103 million people, so that by 1980 there were three suburbanites for every two central-city residents. More important, the cities have been losing blue-collar jobs, through which poor city dwellers traditionally entered the labor market. During the decade the number of persons holding blue-collar jobs decreased five percent for city dwellers while increasing 20 percent for suburban residents. By 1980 almost twice as many persons were employed in manufacturing in the suburbs (10.9 million) as in the cities (5.9 million).

Moreover, research by Guterbock indicates that the density pattern of cities throughout the country has changed.[14] Although older metropolitan areas have seen sharp decreases in density in their central cores, newer post–World War II cities never had high-density neighborhoods of apartments in their central cities. The result is a national pattern of moderate- to low-level density throughout the metropolitan area—in effect, the suburbanization of the central cities.

Within metropolitan areas decentralization has been specific rather than general, though, as regards both industrial movement and population movement. The greatest decentralization has occurred in the larger, older cities of the northeast and middle west.[15] Decentralization of business and industry to fringe locations has also been selective. Operations which require large plants and large amounts of ground space per worker, have a high "nuisance factor" (that is, create noise, pollution, odor, and waste), and need little contact with local buyers tend to be drawn increasingly toward the periphery. Obsolete central-city plants cannot compete economically with new, specifically designed single-story facilities. Automobile plants, chemical firms, steel mills, and petroleum refineries also require large areas of fringe land for their newer operations. Nissan's new American auto plant was built not in Detroit but in rural Tennessee. Generally, production and distribution have decentralized; and as markets have decentralized, wholesaling has also, since it needs space as well as access to markets. The use of trucks rather than railroads for transportation also argues for the more flexible outer locations. By locating businesses outside the congested city core and near the interstate expressways,

[14]Thomas A. Guterbock, "Suburbanization of American Cities of the Twentieth Century: A New Index and Another Look," paper presented at meeting of the American Sociological Association, Toronto, 1982.
[15]Brian J. L. Berry and John D. Kasarda, *Contemporary Urban Ecology,* Macmillan, New York, 1977, p. 234.

owners could reduce transportation costs. Rapid transportation provides a form of storage en route. Over 2,000 suburban industrial parks have been formed since 1960.

On the other hand, finance, management, educational institutions, medical centers, and government have shown far less inclination to decentralize. Central business districts are experiencing considerable new business construction. From the mid-1960s to 1970s, there was over a 50 percent *increase* in office space in older cities such as New York and Chicago, while Houston doubled its office space.[16] This growth continued into the 1980s. Management, finance, government, and law still remain at the center of the city because they do not require great amounts of space per worker or need access to one another; a downtown location makes far more sense when services are oriented not to individuals but to other organizations. In the CBD, communications are easy and informal—business may be conducted over lunch, for example—and there are many services and economies available outside the firm itself. Outside specialists are readily accessible to cover areas such as advertising, legal services, accounting, tax information, and mailing. Firms located on the periphery must provide all sorts of services often not required of those in the center, such as parking lots, cafeterias, and medical services. Top management may also remain in the city so that it does not become isolated from the informal information networks about competitors, government policy, and buying patterns that are always found when a number of firms in the same sort of business are located in the same spatial area. Even in an era of computer-based information systems, face-to-face contact remains important.

Overall, however, the growth of office white-collar employment has not been able to compensate fully for blue-collar and retail trade losses. New York, for example, lost 600,000 jobs during the 1970s, and this alone resulted in a tax loss to the city of almost $500 million.[17] Census data indicate this employment shrinkage ceased between 1980 and 1985.[18] As of the late 1980s central cities are holding their own in terms of employment.

For thirty years retail trade has followed the population to the suburbs. Central business districts now account for less than half of all sales in personal and household items. The nation's 15,000 shopping malls have sometimes almost become cities unto themselves. San Jose has an enclosed air-conditioned center which includes 130 stores, 27 restaurants, and 9,000 parking spaces. Houston's "Galeria," which is modeled after a nineteenth-century gallery in Milan, Italy, has three levels which in addition to the usual department stores, restaurants, and shops also includes an athletic club with ten air-conditioned tennis courts and a jogging track. (Many college athletic departments would gladly exchange their facilities for those of this shopping mall.) It is connected

---

[16]Gerald Manners, "The Office in the Metropolis: An Opportunity for Shaping Metropolitan America," *Ecomonic Geography*, **50**: 1974, pp. 93–110.
[17]John D. Kasarda, "The Implication of Contemporary Redistribution Trends for National Urban Policy," *Social Science Quarterly*, **61**:389, December, 1980.
[18]*Washington Post*, June 5, 1985.

to two high-rise office buildings and a 404-room hotel. Shopping plazas, with their fountains, film festivals, and wine-tasting contests, have come a long way from the mercantile stores of the last century. The shopping mall is replacing Main Street as the core of the community. Increasingly, the malls serve social as well as commercial functions. (Suburbia and its life-styles are discussed fully in Chapter 8, Patterns of Suburbanization.)

However, the lineal decline of retail sales in recent decades may not be an accurate harbinger of the city to come. Downtown stores may never again have the dominance of retail trade they exercised during the centralizing era of the streetcar and subway, but so long as the downtown is a major white-collar employment center, the CBD will be a solidly profitable location for retail sales, particularly of more expensive and fashionable goods.

NONMETROPOLITAN GROWTH

Historically, metropolitan areas in the United States have grown faster than nonmetropolitan areas. The classical ecological model assumed centripetal movement of population from rural hinterland to metropolitan area. This was the case for the first seventy years of this century, when the metropolitan sector—core or fringe—was growing while rural areas consistently lost population. But some say this pattern of increasing population concentration in metropolitan areas has come to a close.[19] The pattern of metropolitan dominance is said to be challenged by an emerging pattern of increased dispersion and deconcentration. During the 1970s, for the first time, rural counties not only stopped declining, but increased in population.

During the last census period nonmetropolitan growth rates were 15 percent, or higher than the 11 percent for the country as a whole.[20] Moreover, much of this growth took place in truly rural counties which were not adjacent to metropolitan areas and did not have any settlements as large as 2,500.[21]

The fastest growing counties from 1970 to 1980 were those which were rural in character. Whether this was a long-term change is uncertain since as of 1985 metropolitan areas were again growing faster than nonmetropolitan areas. Particularly in the south, metropolitan area growth was outpacing nonmetropolitan growth. Rural areas are again losing population.

Rural Renaissance?

What caused the 1970s nonmetropolitan turnabout? Was the growth of non-metropolitan population a sign of a return to older and simpler rural ways? Is there indeed a "rural renaissance"?

---

[19]Calvin L. Beale and Glen V. Fuguitt, "The New Pattern of Non-Metropolitan Population Change," Center for Demography and Ecology, University of Wisconsin, Madison, Center Paper 75–22, 1975, and James Zuiches, "Residential Preference and Rural Population Growth," paper prepared for Farmers Home Administration, U.S. Department of Agriculture, Washington, D.C., 1980.

[20]U.S. Bureau of the Census, *Population Profile of the United States*, op. cit., p. 7.

[21]Larry H. Long, "Population Redistribution in the U.S.: Issues for the 1980s," Population Reference Bureau, Washington, D.C., 1983, p. 3.

No. We are experiencing a transformation in spatial settlement patterns, but this does not represent a rebirth of rural ways of life. Catchy phrases like "rural renaissance" tend to trap us in our own rhetoric. As previously noted, both the proportion and the absolute number of persons engaged in agriculture continue to decrease. Farm population dropped about a quarter during the last decade. Clearly, any rural renaissance does not mean a renaissance of the family farm or a return to agricultural pursuits.

What does it signify? The whys and wherefores of nonmetropolitan growth are not fully understood, but several factors seem to be significant. First, population growth signified some growth of rural manufacturing. The transportation technology of limited-access and expressway systems that caused suburbs to boom in the 1960s permitted an even more dispersed pattern of economic as well as residential development in the 1970s. Truck-based transportation systems allowed decentralized growth along the interstate highway system rather than concentration in a handful of hub cities, as under a rail-based system. Transportation access, coupled with lower wage rates, land costs, and taxes, has attracted some firms to localities that even a score of years ago would have been considered beyond the pale. Small communities located near major highways are particularly fortunate.[22] This is real economic growth, not simply marginal firms locating in marginal locations. As noted earlier, Nissan built its new Datsun plant not in Detroit, but in semi-rural Tennessee. General Motors Saturn is doing the same. However, the importance of new or transplanted rural manufacturing can be overstressed. The greatest growth of new jobs has been in the service sector,[23] where nearly two-thirds of all nonmetropolitan workers are employed.[24]

Rural growth also signifies the emergence of new growth-producing activities that have a diffused spatial pattern. Foremost among these have been the specialized areas of recreation and retirement. States with much natural beauty and extensive wilderness areas, and locations attractive for recreation and leisure activities, are drawing population; and this is occurring on a year-round as well as a seasonal basis. This process in turn promotes employment, particularly in service industries, which, however, have lower pay levels than manufacturing.

Retirement patterns also increasingly involve transfer of residence. The elderly now number over a tenth of the population, and by the year 2030 there will be a minimum of 46 million elderly—double the present number. If present trends continue, those retiring will be moving in increasing numbers out of large northern metropolitan areas. Already two out of three military retirees reside in sun belt states, drawing billions of dollars in federal funds into both the metropolitan and nonmetropolitan sectors of that region. Retirement activities also create new employment opportunities—again, generally in the service sector.

[22]Craig Humphrey and Ralph Sell, "The Impact of Controlled Access Highways on Population Growth in Pennsylvania and Non-Metropolitan Communities, 1940–1970, *Rural Sociology,* **40:** Fall, 1975.
[23]Long, op. cit., p. 7.
[24]Kasarda, op. cit., p. 381.

A Land Shortage?

The phrase "They aren't making land any more" is often often used to promote land investment or explain the high cost of property. The impression created is that the United States has a shortage of unbuilt land. Clearly, this is not the case. Figures compiled by the Bureau of the Census indicate that three-quarters of the population is concentrated on a mere 1.5 percent of the nation's land area.* Moreover, out of a total 3,536,855 square miles in the country, the amount of urban land in use totals only 54,103 square miles, or a land area roughly equal to the state of Florida. Only 2.6 percent of the nation's land area is characterized as urban or built-up.

Levels of population density vary dramatically from nation to nation. The overall population density of the United States is 51 persons per square mile, compared with 970 persons per square mile in the Netherlands, which is densely settled and heavily urbanized. (The extremes range from Hong Kong with 10,066 persons per square mile to Australia and New Zealand with 5 persons.) Obviously, the United States with 10 acres per person is not suffering from an overall land shortage.

The problem is that we do not have open land in the right places—that is, in or near the cities, where it is needed. Where there is a land shosrtage is in the more desirable city and suburban areas. There are only a fixed, limited number of lots with views, noise-free lots, smog-free lots, and low-crime lots. Because of this, land values are being forced ever higher in desirable urban areas. Open lands in Montana or Nevada are really not relevant.

However, while the amount of desirable urban land may be fixed, land use is not. England and Wales, approximately only the size of North Carolina, house nine times the population of that state while maintaining a feeling of openness.†

Comprehensive land-use policies can create a more livable urban environment. Chapter 12, Planning in Europe: with Discussion of New Towns, discusses some of the European alternatives to American patterns of land use.

*United States Department of Commerce News, Social and Economic Statistics Administration, Washington, D.C., April 21, 1972. p. 1.
†The Use of Land, Rockefeller Brothers Fund, Crowell, New York, 1973, p. 103.

The growing need for energy has greatly affected selected nonmetropolitan areas. The revival of mining after the energy crisis created booms in rural areas from southern Appalachia to Wyoming. However, this energy-related rural revival is highly urban in character and can hardly be considered a "back to the land" movement. Much of the Rocky Mountains area growth, based on energy, has characteristics of boom or bust.

Finally, nonmetropolitan growth reflects change in American life-styles. Migration theory has long held that people move toward economic opportunity. Regardless of residential preference, and while many people do claim a preference for living in smaller towns, most people have resided in urban areas where employment opportunities have been concentrated.[25] Today, many families have enough money, and sufficient flexible work schedules, to afford nonmetropolitan living. Additionally, noneconomic values such as open spaces and clean air are increasingly important factors in determining spatial location. Such considerations can be expected to increasingly influence residential patterns, even if such patterns do not reflect better employment opportunities. Another most important factor is the impact of computers on allowing greater residential choice. At this point we can only speculate about the long-term implications.

It should also be kept in mind that relatively inexpensive energy made residence in the rimland possible; any change to somewhat higher energy costs would radically alter the equation. It is still speculative whether if energy costs soared those having freedom of residential choice would choose to bite the bullet and pay a higher price for transportation, or whether they would instead return to inner urban areas in large numbers. Either way, the remaining years of this century may exhibit a shift from the accepted conventional wisdom regarding urban ecological patterns—which until recently was all but universally accepted.

Until the extent and permanence of new patterns becomes clear, it is perhaps best to view nonmetropolitan growth as an extension of the metropolitan area's influence beyond the commuting range. Over forty years ago, Louis Wirth noted that urbanism—that is, urban behavior patterns—had become the American way of life. Now, urbanization, or living in urban-defined places, has also become ubiquitous. As we continue to expand into a national metropolitan society, distinctions between metropolitan and nonmetropolitan will become even more blurred. With the number of MSAs over 300 and the boundaries of existing metropolitan areas progressively expanding, it becomes increasingly difficult to distinguish between metropolitan and developing nonmetropolitan counties.

A National Society?

We are moving toward a national urban system where old differences cease to make a difference. The pattern of metropolitan dominance is being challenged

---

[25]Zuiches, op. cit.

by an emerging pattern of increased dispersion and deconcentration. Metropolitan areas are no longer even semi-independent. Communication and transportation advances such as WATS lines and commuter air shuttles have further reduced the friction of space. While at the turn of the century the commuter railroad line made it possible for a vanguard of businesspeople to move their residences from the city, commuter air travel now puts a premium on accessibility to an airport. In an era of air travel, the significant factor is no longer distance. Distance is increasingly measured not in miles or kilometers, but by time. Even with terrestrial travel, the question, "How far is it?" commonly anticipates a temporal rather than spatial response: how long it takes to get there. Increased mobility of goods, persons, and ideas suggests that a new urban phase—a national urban unit—is in a formative stage.

Weather reports in Washington, D.C., commonly also give the weather in the "commuter cities," which include not only New York and Boston (one hour by air) but with increasing frequency also Chicago. Numerous air shuttles tie all these cities together: a commuter between New York and Chicago or Los Angeles and San Francisco is able to catch a flight in either direction almost every half hour from dawn to dusk. Shuttle flights linking San Diego, Los Angeles, and San Francisco make it easier to move between these cities than around Los Angeles. It is one of the peculiarities of modern life that the air shuttles from city to city offer better, more frequent, and even faster transportation than that available between some parts of a single metropolitan area.

The emerging pattern of a national urban society forces us to rethink traditional assumptions. In the 1950s, Otis Dudley Duncan suggested that the concept of a "rural-urban continuum," while perhaps having heuristic value, has little empirical validity.[26] Emerging nonmetropolitan growth patterns strongly suggest that the concept of a rural-urban continuum has now lost even heuristic utility. The demographic and economic growth of counties several counties removed from MSAs increasingly suggests that any rural-urban division has lost the shards of meaning it may still have possessed even a score of years ago. New patterns also contradict the theory that the social and economic conditions of urbanization are a consequence of the distance from the point of population concentration. This change has yet to be fully reflected in policy or research.[27] As rural-urban divisions have lost meaning, so contemporary distinctions between metropolitan and nonmetropolitan are losing utility and becoming more blurred with each passing decade. In many respects the rural-urban differences are differences that have ceased to make a difference. Whether we live in a metropolitan area or not, we are all part of a metropolitan society.

---

[26]Otis Dudley Duncan, "Community Size and the Rural-Urban Continuum," in Paul K. Hatt and Albert J. Reiss (eds.), *Cities and Society*,. Free Press, New York, 1957, pp. 35–45.

[27]The Department of Agriculture, for example, still divides nonmetropolitan counties into six types, which "describe a dimension of urban influence in which each succeeding group is affected to a lesser degree by the social and economic conditions of urban areas. This includes the influence of urban areas at a distance as well as within counties themselves," U.S. Department of Agriculture, PA-1, U.S. Government Printing Office, Washington, D.C., 1974.

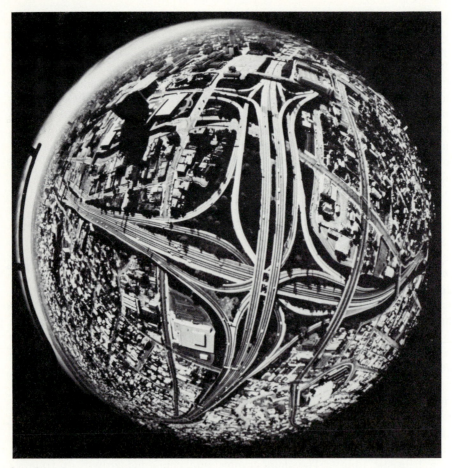

Los Angeles, a city designed with the assumption of automobile ownership, is dominated by its freeways. (J. Eyerman/Black Star)

THE RISE OF THE SUN BELT

Population Shifts

The most dramatic urban change since 1975—at least in terms of attention paid by the media—has been the historic shift of population and power from the old industrial heartland of the northeast and north central regions to the booming metropolises of the southwest. The rise of Houston from a steamy Texas town of little interest to the booming, expanding oil capital of the world "typifies the pattern." Houston is now the nation's fourth largest city, exceeded in size only by New York, Los Angeles, and Chicago. The sun belt, long a virtual dependent colony of the industrial northeast, has undergone an

TABLE 5-3
Changing U.S. Population by Major Regions

	1976	1980	1984
Northeast			
Population (millions)	49.3	49.1	49.2
Percent living in			
cities	35.2%	33.8%	33.0%
suburbs	53.2%	54.3%	55.7%
outside metropolitan areas	11.6%	11.9%	12.1%
Median household income	$13,074	$18,191	$21,818*
Percent unemployed**	9.4%	7.1%	6.4%
Percent in poverty	10.2%	11.1%	13.4%
Midwest			
Population (millions)	57.8	58.9	58.4
Percent living in			
cities	31.8%	30.3%	29.3%
suburbs	38.9%	40.1%	41.1%
outside metropolitan areas	29.3%	29.5%	29.5%
Median household income	$13,683	$18,313	$21,068*
Percent unemployed**	6.6%	8.2%	7.5%
Percent in poverty	9.9%	11.4%	14.6%
South			
Population (millions)	68.9	75.4	78.7
Percent living in			
cities	31.2%	30.1%	29.4%
suburbs	36.6%	38.1%	39.4%
outside metropolitan areas	32.2%	31.8%	31.2%
Median household income	$11,461	$16,298	$19,386*
Percent unemployed**	6.7%	6.4%	7.0%
Percent in poverty	15.2%	16.5%	17.2%
West			
Population (millions)	38.6	43.2	45.7
Percent living in			
cities	36.4%	35.6%	35.0%
suburbs	46.6%	47.2%	47.8%
outside metropolitan areas	16.4%	17.1%	17.2%
Median household income	$13,038	$19,008	$22,217*
Percent unemployed**	8.6%	6.8%	7.2%
Percent in poverty	10.5%	11.4%	14.7%

* 1983 household income
** Percent of labor force unemployed
Source: Based on Bureau of the Census data.

economic transformation.[28] The regional landscape has been transformed by the opening of a new urban frontier. Older northern frost belt cities have seen population and industry depart for the "boom" areas of the south and southwest. Businesses are supposedly attracted to such areas by a "good business climate consisting of lower wages, lower taxes, a lower rate of unionization and higher-productive efficiency."

The result of interregional population shifts has been dramatic. The south, which historically always had migratory outflows of population, now is the fastest growing region in the nation. Since the mid-1960s the south has also replaced the west as the major locus of new employment growth. During this same period, some once economically powerful industrial cities of the north have experienced decline in both population and economic influence.

After several decades of central-city population losses, St. Louis now has only as many people as it did in 1890; Cleveland now has as many as during World War I; and Detroit now has no more than in 1920.[29] In large frost belt metropolitan areas such as Pittsburgh, Philadelphia, Chicago, Boston, and New York, inner suburbs have also been losing population albeit at a rate somewhat slower than their central cities. The sun belt as an energy-producing area also enjoys a cost advantage, particularly when oil costs are high. Also, the milder climate requires less energy for heat (this is only partially offset by higher air-conditioning costs). The racial climate has also improved.

Thus population, reversing the old trend, is now flowing southward and west, attracted by new jobs, the mild climate, a lower cost of living, and a life-style stressing outdoor living, year-round golf and tennis, and informal entertaining. Since 1970, urban areas in the industrial north have generally either lost population or made only marginal gains. On the other hand, more than half the national population growth between 1980 and 1982 occurred in three sun belt states: California, Florida, and Texas.[30] By the year 2000, the sun belt is projected to have 112 million inhabitants, 43 percent of the nation's total population.[31]

Economic Shifts

The impression is sometimes given that most sun belt growth is a consequence of runaway smokestack industries that are abandoning the industrial heartland to build low-wage nonunion plants in the south. This view is largely inaccurate.[32] Steel mills and other heavy industry are not moving south when they close down in older industrial areas. Rather than attracting smokestack industries,

---

[28]For details on the change and its meaning, see David D. Perry and Alfred J. Watkins (eds.), *The Rise of the Sunbelt Cities*, Sage Publications, Beverly Hills, Calif., 1977; and Larry Sawers and William K. Tabb (eds.), *Sunbelt/Snowbelt*, Oxford University Press, New York, 1984.
[29]Long, op. cit., p. 10.
[30]U.S. Bureau of the Census, "Population Profile," op. cit., p. 5.
[31]Jeanne Biggar, "The Sunning of America: Migration to the Sunbelt," *Population Bulletin*, **34**:22, March, 1979; and Sawers and Tabb, op. cit.
[32]Perry and Watkins, op. cit.

TABLE 5-4
Ten Fastest Growing Metropolitan Areas: 1950 to 1960, 1960 to 1970, and 1970 to 1980

Rank	SMSA	Percent increase	Rank	SMSA	Percent increase	Rank	MSA and CMSA	Percent increase
	1950 to 1960*			1960 to 1970*			1970 to 1980**	
1	Fort Lauderdale-Hollywood, FL	297.9	1	Las Vegas, NV	115.2	1	Fort Myers, FL	95.1
2	Las Vegas, NV	163.0	2	Anaheim-Santa Ana-Garden Grove, CA	101.8	2	Fort Pierce, FL	91.7
3	Midland, TX	162.6	3	Oxnard-Ventura, CA	89.0	3	Ocala, FL	77.4
4	Orlando, FL	124.6	4	Fort Lauderdale-Hollywood, FL	85.7	4	Las Vegas, NV	69.5
5	San Diego, CA	121.1	5	San Jose, CA	65.8	5	Sarasota, FL	68.0
6	Odessa, TX	116.1	6	Colorado Springs, CO	64.2	6	Fort Collins-Loveland, CO	65.9
7	Phoenix, AZ	100.0	7	Santa Barbara, CA	56.4	7	West Palm Beach-Boca Raton-Delray Beach, FL	65.3
8	West Palm Beach, FL	98.9	8	West Palm Beach, FL	52.9	8	Olympia, WA	61.6
9	Colorado Springs, CO	92.9	9	Huntsville, AL	48.3	9	Bryan-College Station, TX	61.4
10	Miami, FL	88.9	10	Nashua, NH	47.8	10	Reno, NV	59.9

* Definitions as of later census.
** 1983 definitions.
Source: Bureau of the Census.

the sun belt states are developing new economic activities. As summed up by Kirkpatrick Sale, the writer who first focused national attention on the changing nature of the southern rim:

> In broad terms there has been a shift from the traditional heavy manufacturing long associated with the industrial belt of the Northeast to the new technological industries that have grown up in the Southern Rim—aerospace, defense, electronics.[33]

The fastest growing sun belt industries are service industries such as real estate and tourism plus the newer, highly skilled industries such as electronics, energy, and aircraft. These often have a preference for a location in the southwest, particularly suburbs of major cities. Federal-level political decisions, such as locating the space agency in Houston and the national center for silicon research in Austin, have strongly reinforced growth trends. The Reagan administration's expanding military budget has also disproportionately directed monies and employment to areas with substantial military basing, i.e., the south.

Some even suggest that the advantage of the sun belt is largely political in origin. Mollenkopt argues that the advantage comes not from lower wages or nonunionized work forces but from the comparative political advantages of sun belt cities' being able to push business-oriented growth policies: these cities' governments have little need to placate the poor or nonwhite groups, who wield less influence there than they do in northern cities.[34]

Although the population shift to the south and southwest was long in coming, the consequences and implications for urban areas of the old industrial heartland have been recognized only recently. The northeast was long accustomed to viewing the south as an economic backwater and a cultural desert. Now expansion in the sun belt is recognized as more than crude boosterism. For several years, California, Florida, and Texas have led the nation in building construction. Not only people but the tax base as well has been flowing southward. As a consequence of regional shifts, northern urban areas that have been the nation's centers of population and power for a century or more are finding themselves on the defensive.

Traditionally, federal funds have flowed southward. Those representing northern constituencies have been introducing congressional legislation that would rework federal distribution to favor older—i.e., northern—cities. There already have been several skirmishes in what some have dubbed the "second war between the states." At stake are billions of dollars in federal spending, which means jobs and economic development. Northern and eastern members of Congress have, for example, changed housing and urban development formulas. Instead of allocating money on the basis of population and poverty, weight is now given to the percentage of old housing in the city and whether

---

[33]Kirkpatrick Sale, *Power Shift: The Rise of the Southern Rim and Its Challenge to the Eastern Establishment*, Random House, New York, 1975, p. 5.
[34]John H. Mollenkopt, *The Congested City*, Princeton University Press, Princeton, New Jersey, 1983.

the city is losing population. Northern victories are less certain in the future since members of Congress from the sun belt have now organized to protect their interests.

Sun Belt Problems

However, the sun belt is not all sunshine. The rise of the sun belt has also produced problems for the expanding population. The depletion of groundwater reserves in the southwest is already producing serious problems. Breakneck growth has brought massive urban sprawl, overtaxed water and sewer systems, rising air pollution, environmental degradation, and traffic congestion.

Sun belt cities such as Miami, Houston, Dallas, San Antonio, Albuquerque, Phoenix, and San Diego have all had to cope with phenomenal growth, and the responses have not all been similar.[35] Sun belt cities are being pressured to expand educational opportunities, housing stock, and social services. At the same time, citizen groups are lobbying for limits on taxes like Proposition 13 in California. City officials are caught by contradictory expectations of northern-level services and southern-level taxes. There are those who even question whether all the attention given to southern ascendancy isn't largely a myth in the making.[36]

Sunbelt cities are also discovering that they are not immune to economic slowdowns. Houston, for example, is very vulnerable to any decline in the production or cost of oil. Also the south still has a higher poverty rate than the nation as a whole (see Table 5-3). The economic sun has also shone unevenly on sun belt states. The boom in Florida has not affected Mississippi's status as the nation's poorest state.

It should also be remembered that sun belt cities are not necessarily immune to the population declines that affected frost belt cities. While during the last decade population was lost by cities, 86 percent of the U.S. central cities in the northeast and 66 percent of those in the industrial north central region, this was also true of 26 percent of the south's cities and 12 percent of the west's. A sun belt location does not prevent people from moving out.

Some economists believe that there is less to the sun belt phenomenon than meets the eye. There are those who see industrial growth in the south as a "very transitory surge."[37] Innovative northern high-technology companies, such as those found in Massachusetts, have growth rates exceeding those of southern states.

In the application of high-technology economy, the south still has a major liability: its generally poorer academic system. In competition for the expanding high-technology and service-sector jobs, there is a developing mismatch

---

[35]For a comparison of what has occurred in various cities, see Richard M. Bernard and Bradley R. Rice (eds.), *Sunbelt Cities: Politics and Growth since World War II,* University of Texas Press, Austin, 1983.

[36]C. L. Jusenius and L. C. Ledebur, *A Myth in the Making: The Southern Economic Challenge and Northern Economic Decline,* Economic Development Administration, Department of Commerce, November, 1976.

[37]David Birch of MIT, quoted in "Education Eclipse May Fool Economic Climate of South," *Richmond Times-Dispatch,* October 11, 1984.

between the available jobs and the skill level required for these jobs. As a region, the south has not been as willing to invest the necessary tax money in developing its human capital. Unless it does so, the south may again see itself outshone by the north and particularly by the west, with its much better educational systems at the primary and secondary levels. The northeast, with its strong educational infrastructure, was again booming by the mid-1980s.

With the initial southern advantages of lower wage scales, a nonunion industrial climate, and cheaper energy beginning to lose force, there is nothing permanent about the sun belt boom. The north may rise again.

New Regional Variations

In a book titled *The Nine Nations of North America*, Joel Garreau argues that the sun belt–frost belt dichotomy does not capture the reality of American regional variation much better than the division by states.* He suggests that North America is in reality nine distinct regions, each with its distinctive economy and social outlook. Thus, "The Foundry," the declining industrial region of the northeast, still tends to see itself as the "real" center of power and dominance it once was. The region of Dixie on the other hand sees the Foundry as a series of mistakes to be avoided if Dixie is not to become another New Jersey. The west coast region of Ectopia, with its twenty-first-century industries based on microchips and new technologies views the Foundry as simply irrelevant to its future. Garreau suggests that, rather than North America's becoming more homogenized, regional values on matters such as energy development and environmental concerns are becoming more pronounced.

*Joel Garreau, *The Nine Nations of North America*, Houghton Mifflin, Boston, 1961.

PART THREE

URBAN LIFE

CHAPTER

6

CITY LIFE-STYLES

What is the city but the people?

Shakespeare
Coriolanus

INTRODUCTION

Now we turn from the spatial and ecological construction of the city to a consideration of the city as a unique social organizational form and social psychological milieu. Here we ask questions such as: What are the characteristics of urban dwellers? Do urbanites differ from ruralites or small-town residents? Do cities produce a unique way of life or psychological outlook?

Certainly life in the city is different. Cities differ from towns and rural areas not only in their size and patterns of economic activities, but also in their tone, texture, and pace. Heterogeneity, variety, and change are assumed, as is a potpourri of different occupations, social classes, cultural backgrounds, and interests. As William Munro expressed it half a century ago:

> The city has more wealth than the country, more skill, more erudition within its bounds, more initiative, more philanthropy, more science, more divorces, more aliens, more births and deaths, more accidents, more rich, more poor, more wise men and more fools.[1]

As noted in Chapter 3, The Rise of Urban America, Americans have a history of ambivalence in how they view cities and city life. On one hand the city is the height of civilization—the new Athens—and the center of progress, energy, and enterprise. But more frequently the city is characterized as the source of crime, corruption, and social disorganization—the repository of all the problems of the society. Kenneth Boulding dramatically contrasts these views in western society:

> The city is not only Zion, the city of God; it is Babylon, the scarlet woman. On the one hand, we have the opposition of urbane splendor and culture with rural cloddishness and savagery; on the other hand, we have the opposition of urban vice, corruption and cruelty, as against rural virtue and purity. The Bible, to take but one instance, furnishes us with innumerable examples of this deep ambivalence towards the city. It is at once the house of God and the house of inequity. Amos, the herdsman, denounces it; Jeremiah weeps over it; Christ is crucified for it. One of the great threads through the Bible is the destruction and rebuilding of the city—a pattern which is wholly characteristic of the age of civilization.[2]

The contrast between urban and rural ways of life was very much a part of urban studies and writings before World War II. The terms used to define the dichotomy sometimes differed, but the underlying content remained remarkably similar; the country represented simplicity; the city complexity. Rural areas were typified by stable rules, roles, and relationships, while the city was characterized by innovation, change, and disorganization. The city was the center of variety, heterogeneity, and social novelty, while the countryside or small town represented tradition, social continuity, and cultural conformity. The stereotype also included a view of city people as possessing greater sophistication but less real warmth and feeling.

[1]William B. Munro, "City," in *Encyclopedia of the Social Sciences,* Macmillan, New York, 1930, p. 474.
[2]Kenneth E. Boulding, "The Death of the City: A Frightened Look at Postcivilization," in Gino Germani (ed.), *Modernization, Urbanization, and the Urban Crisis,* Little, Brown, Boston, 1973, p. 265.

Implicit and sometimes explicit in this viewpoint was that modern mass society was destroying close attachments to kin and community. In their place were being substituted uprooted, isolated, and alienated individuals who were free of traditional bonds but alone in the big city. The best statement of this view is perhaps Charlie Chaplin's classic film *Modern Times,* in which the helpless worker is literally chewed up and spit out by the faceless factory.

Here we won't debate the inherent biases that occur when emotionally loaded terms such as "warmth," "friendliness," and "community" are associated with small places, while terms such as "anonymity," "alienation," and "isolation" appear to be reserved for large cities. What is important for our purposes is to understand the influence such beliefs have had on traditional and contemporary views of urban life.

CHARACTERISTICS OF URBAN POULATIONS

Age

Everywhere urban populations are younger than their rural counterparts. This is particularly true of cities in less developed countries (LDCs), but it is also true of North America. (This subject is discussed further in Chapter 15, Asian Urban Patterns; Chapter 16, African and Middle Eastern Urbanization, and Chapter 17, Urbanization in Latin America.) City populations are younger not because they have higher birthrates and thus more children; that is not the case. Rather, cities attract immigrants, and such immigrants tend to be young adults. This in turn means that cities have a smaller proportion of youths and elderly. For example, in 1980 in U.S. metropolitan areas for every 100 persons aged eighteen through sixty-four there were 63 persons younger than eighteen and older than sixty-four. That is, there were 63 dependents per every 100 persons of working age. In rural areas, however, there were some 74 persons in the pre- and postworking ages.[3] A consequence is that cities have both more young adults and more of the activities in which young adults engage. This means more bars (single and otherwise), more places of entertainment (even movies are an activity primarily of the young), more crime (young people commit most crime), and more social change (younger populations are less bound by tradition).

Gender

The pattern of urban-rural sex ratios differs for developed and LDCs. Less developed countries have a higher proportion of urban males because young men come to the city and leave the women behind to care for the farms. In African cities, for instance, there are often three males for every two females.

---

[3]I. Taeuber "The Changing Distribution of the Population of the United States," in S. M. Mazie (ed.), *Population, Distribution and Policy,* Vol. 5, U.S. Commission on Population Growth and the American Future, Government Printing Office, Washington, D.C., 1972, pp. 31–108.

This pattern of women staying at home to care for the farm while men migrate to the cities is particularly prevalent where women marry early. Unmarried men tend to be less socially integrated than are husbands, and to have weaker social commitments to the community. Young males also engage in higher rates of socially disruptive behavior such as drunkenness, gambling, prostitution, and crime.

In developed countries there is a greater likelihood that single women will leave rural areas for city jobs. There is less need in the city for raw labor, and greater need for clerical and office workers. The result is greater numbers of women, with the sex ratio being particularly unbalanced in heavily administration-oriented cities, such as state capitals. Family life also follows less traditional patterns in the city, with more women heading households with children and more unrelated people sharing the same residence.

Race, Ethnicity, and Religion

Cities are more racially, ethnically, and religiously heterogeneous than the countryside. Small villages may be all one race or ethnic group, but cities are far more mixed. Even groups that are proportionately only a small part of the urban population can band with enough similar groups to constitute a minority group. This ethnic, racial, and religious mosaic led Louis Wirth to describe heterogeneity (along with size and density) as one of the basic characteristics of the city.[4]

For example (as was noted in Chapter 3, The Rise of Urban America), New York was from the first a mixture of peoples. This has not changed. As of the 1980s blacks, Hispanics, and Asians made up almost half (47 percent) of that city's population. Moreover, as of the last census one of every four New Yorkers was foreign born—and this does not include an estimated three-quarters of a million undocumented aliens.[5]

Ethnic and racial heterogeneity also raises the potential of intergroup cleavages, competition, and conflict. Greater religious and ethnic heterogeneity can lead to greater tolerance, but it does not have to do so. Tolerance is greater when race, ethnicity, and religion lose force as the primary way of identifying persons. Intermarriage can also contribute to greater tolerance. Problems are most likely to occur when racial, ethnic, and religious boundaries also represent socioeconomic status boundaries.

Socioeconomic Status

As the discussion at the opening of this chapter indicates, the city is a place of extremes, a site of both extreme wealth and poverty. Occupation and education show a similar spread. There are also clear variations inside metropolitan areas. Over the last decade, for instance, suburbs have become richer while

[4]Louis Wirth, "Urbanism as a Way of Life," *American Journal of Sociology,* **44**(10):8, July, 1938.
[5]*New York Times,* February 27, 1983, p. 28.

Isolation in the modern city is a recurrent (and probably over-worked) theme in contemporary literature. (Charles Gatewood/Magnum)

central cities as a whole have fallen farther behind. However, overall city averages tend to hide sharp individual and neighborhood variations in socio-economic status. What is clear is that, in urban areas, socioeconomic status criteria such as income, education, and occupation tend to supplant family, ethnicity, religion, and the other more traditional ways of ordering people used in rural areas and small towns. This matter is explored further later in this chapter and in Chapter 9, Ethnic Diversity.

SOCIAL PSYCHOLOGY OF URBAN LIFE

Earlier Formulations

As noted in Chapter 1, The Urban World, the specter of the city as the source of isolation and alienation for the individual, and social problems and collapse for the society, is far from new. It is not a consequence of the urban riots of the 1960s or the urban financial crisis of the 1970s. Classical social theorists such as Ferdinand Tönnies, Karl Marx, Emile Durkheim, Max Weber, and Georg Simmel all discussed the decline of local attachments and the rise of mass urban society. The changes were frequently presented in terms of logical constructs, which sociologists refer to as "ideal types." Among the most noteworthy of these dichotomies, in terms of its impact upon later urban research, was Tönnies elaborate description of the shift from *gemeinschaft*— a community where ties were based upon kinship—to *gesellschaft*—a society based on common economic, political, and other interests.

The German social theorist Max Weber made similar distinctions between "traditional society" and "rational society"—that is, the substitution of formal rules and procedures for earlier, more spontaneous methods. The prime ideal type of rational behavior was institutionalized bureaucracy. In turn, the French theorist Emile Durkheim distinguished between societies based on "mechanical solidarity" and those based on "organic solidarity." For Durkheim, the old mechanical social order was one in which all had similar interests and carried out similar tasks. Organic solidarity of urban places was by contrast based on the division of labor. Karl Marx also discussed the dichotomy between the urban and the rural. For Marx, the emergence of urban-based capitalism meant destruction of the older agrarian-based social order. Market-based relations replaced feudal relationships, and industrial capitalism encouraged the exploitation and alienation of urban workers. Eventually this would result in the workers' developing a class consciousness and uniting to overthrow their capitalist oppressors. The workers' new unity was based, though, on common interest rather than being a commonality based on residing in similar areas.

All these comparisons had an implicit time frame in which rural areas represented the past—sometimes in a glorified form (the "good old days")— and the city represented the future, with its technology and division of labor.

The Chicago School

American urban scholars were influenced at least implicitly by the previously mentioned European theorists, as well as by the changes they saw occurring in the cities where they lived. Members of the so-called Chicago school of sociology assembled during the 1920s at the University of Chicago and were concerned with change induced by urbanization. They focused particularly on the way urban life disrupted traditional ties to kin and community. Some of their writings on such diverse phenomena as juvenile delinquency, organized vice, ethnic community ghettos, and the nature of the city's ecological growth have become sociological classics. Writings such as *The Ghetto* (Wirth), *The Gold Coast and the Slum* (Zorbaugh), and *The Polish Peasant in Europe and America* (Thomas and Znaniecki) are descriptive gems giving insights into this unique period in the urbanization of the United States.[6]

[6]Louis Wirth, *The Ghetto,* University of Chicago Press, Chicago, 1928; Harvey W. Zorbaugh, *The Gold Coast and the Slum,* University of Chicago Press, Chicago, 1929; William I. Thomas and Florian Znaniecki, *The Polish Peasant in Europe and America,* 5 vols., University of Chicago Press, Chicago, 1918–1920.

Writers of the Chicago school such as Wirth were especially influenced by Georg Simmel's earlier vision of the social-psychological consequences of city life—a life-style where calculated sophistication would replace close and meaningful relationships.[7] Simmel suggested that the pace of the city life and the overwhelming number of stimuli in the city result in a state of mental overstimulation and excitement.

Simmel said that there is a constant nervous stimulation produced by shifting internal and external situations and that city dwellers have difficulty in maintaining an integrated personality in a social situation where the reference points are constantly changing: as a result they seek to protect themselves by anonymity and sophistication. Calculating expediency takes the place of affective feelings and personal relationships. One is forced to become blasé in the urban environment in order to protect his or her psyche from overstimulation.

> If so many inner reactions were responses to the continuous external contacts with innumerable people as are those in the small town, where one knows almost everybody one meets and where one has a positive relation to almost everyone, one would be completely atomized internally and come to an unimaginable psychic state.[8]

Contemporary reformulations of Simmel's belief that the city produces "nervous stimulation" among its inhabitants, and of the socially disorganizing and disruptive effects of urbanism as a way of life, can be found in Alvin Toffler's popular and much overrated book, *Future Shock* and in Stanley Milgram's use of the concept of "psychic overload."[9] The term "overload" comes from systems analysis, where an overload is said to occur when a system cannot process inputs because they are coming too fast or because there are too many of them. Under such circumstances, adaptations are said to occur. This is essentially Simmel's argument of seventy years earlier, restated using a contemporary analogy.

"Urbanism as a Way of Life"

The classic formulation of how urbanization fosters innovation, specialization, diversity, and anonymity is Louis Wirth's essay "Urbanism as a Way of Life."[10] Wirth, using Simmel's ideas as a foundation, argued that the city created a distinct way of life—called "urbanism"—which is reflected in how people dress and speak, what they believe about the social world, what they consider worth achieving, what they do for a living, where they live, whom they associate with, and why they interact with other people.

---

[7]Georg Simmel, "The Metropolis and Mental Life," *The Sociology of Georg Simmel*, Kurt H. Wolff (trans.). Free Press, Glencoe, Ill., 1950.
[8]Ibid., p. 415.
[9]Alvin Toffler, *Future Shock*, Random House, New York, 1970; Stanley Milgram, "The Experience of Living in Cities," *Science*, **167**:1461–1468, March 13, 1970.
[10]Wirth, "Urbanism as a Way of Life," op. cit.

Wirth further suggested that urbanization and its components—size, density, and heterogeneity—are the independent variables which determine urbanism, that is, urban life-styles. Moreover, the relationship is linear: the larger, denser, and more heterogeneous the city, the more prevalent is urbanism as a way of life.

As a way of life, urbanism was viewed by Wirth (and others) as economically successful but socially destructive:

> The distinctive features of the urban mode of life have often been described sociologically as consisting of the substitution of secondary for primary contacts, the weakening of bonds of kinship, the declining social significance of the family, the disappearance of the neighborhood, and the undermining of the traditional basis of social solidarity. All of these phenomena can be substantially verified through objective indices.[11]

Some characteristics of the urban way of life as described by Wirth are:

1. An extensive and complex division of labor replacing the artisan who participated in every phase of manufacture.
2. Emphasis on success, achievement, and social mobility as morally praiseworthy. Behavior becomes more rational, utilitarian, and goal-oriented.
3. Decline of the family (increased divorce) and weakening bonds of kinship, with previous family functions transferred to specialized outside agencies (schools, health and welfare agencies, commercial recreation).
4. Breakdown of primary groups and ties (neighborhood) and substitution of large formal secondary group-control mechanisms (police, courts). Traditional bases of social solidarity and organization are undermined, leading to social disorganization.
5. Relation to others as players of segmented roles (bus driver, shop clerk) rather than as whole persons; i.e., there is a high degree of role specialization. Utilitarian rather than affective relationships with others. Superficial sophistication as a substitute for meaningful relationships leading to alienation.
6. Decline of cultural homogeneity, and diversity of values, views, and opinions. The emergence of subcultures (ethnic, criminal, sexual) that are at variance with the larger society. Greater freedom and tolerance, but also decline in sense of common community.
7. Spatial segregation into disparate sections on the basis of income, status, race, ethnicity, religion, and so on.[12]

Not surprisingly, many of these read like a catalog of contemporary social changes.

---

[11]Ibid., p. 21.
[12]For a discussion of Wirth's and others' views on community, see Dennis E. Poplin, *Communities,* 2d. ed., Macmillan, New York, 1979, pp. 27–47.

REEVALUATION OF URBANISM AND SOCIAL DISORGANIZATION

Given the momentous changes taking place in the growing, immigrant-crowded industrializing cities of the first part of this century, it is not surprising that writers on the city tended to emphasize the negative rather than the positive aspects of urban change. The alienation, atomization, and social isolation of the city were stressed in studies dealing with juvenile delinquency, suicide, mental illness, and divorce; and a whole subfield was developed in sociology under the value-loaded title "social disorganization."

We now know that the sociologists of Wirth's day (the 1930s), in their fascination with the socially disorganizing aspects of urban life, underplayed the role of the city as a social integrator and underestimated the strength of traditional ways of life. William F. Whyte's excellent study of street life in an Italian slum of Boston just before World War II was one of the few to stress the sociocultural continuity and the vitality of traditional culture.[13] Almost fifty years later, we are still predicting the imminent disappearance of these same traditional life-styles. For example, the ethnic affiliations that were supposed to have vanished long ago, and are continually being pronounced dead, seem somehow to be constantly reviving. Ethnic identification is currently undergoing a revival.

Wirth's essay "Urbanism as a Way of Life" has influenced both professional and popular thought about cities for half a century. Today, however, it is easier to see how the essay suffers from not fully recognizing the degree to which Wirth's generalizations were limited both by historical time and by the differing composition and variety of urban areas. Herbert Gans questions Wirth's diagnosis of the city as producing anomic, goal-oriented, segmented role relationships on three grounds. First, Gans says, "Since the theory argues that all of society is now urban, *his analysis does not distinguish ways of life in the city from those in other settlements within modern society.*"[14] He suggests that Wirth's "urbanite" is a depersonalized and atomized member of a mass society, a representative of urban-industrial society rather than of the city itself. Second, there isn't enough evidence either to prove or to deny the posited relationship between size, density, heterogeneity, and social disorganization. Third, even if the causal relationship exists, many city dwellers are effectively isolated from it. For example, research done in San Francisco by Wendell Bell found that, for many city-dwellers, family and kinship bonds were far from dead, and relatives continued to be a significant source of socializing and support.[15] Mental health also appears to be better in urban than

[13]William F. Whyte, *Street Corner Society,* University of Chicago Press, Chicago, 1943.

[14]Herbert J. Gans, "Urbanism and Suburbanism as Ways of Life: A Re-evaluation of Definitions," in J. John Palen and Karl Flaming (eds.), *Urban America,* Holt, Rinehart and Winston, New York, 1972, p. 185.

[15]Wendell Bell, "The City, the Suburb, and a Theory of Social Choice," in Scott Greer et al. (eds.), *The New Urbanization,* St. Martin's Press, New York, 1968; pp. 137–143; Thomas Drabek, et al., "The Impact of Disaster on Kin Relationships," *Journal of Marriage and Family,* 37(3):481–484, August, 1975; and Thomas Drabek and William Key, *Conquering Disaster: Family Recovery and Long Term Consequences,* Irvington Publishers, New York, 1984.

Street fairs have become a common scene in American cities.
(Beryl Goldberg)

in rural areas.[16] The claim that urbanism impairs mental health is unfounded.[17] Moreover, urban residents have relations with others that are as full and meaningful as the relationships of those in small towns.[18] The conventional wisdom is simply wrong in painting city people as being more alienated and isolated.

Wirth's characterization of urban life applies only to some inner-city residents, while other city dwellers—such as cosmopolites and suburbanites—pursue a different way of life. Residents of the outer city, Gans suggests, have a life-style that resembles the life-style of suburbanites far more than the behavior patterns of inner-city residents. These outer-city neighborhoods, and even most inner-city populations, consist "mainly of relatively homogeneous groups, with social and cultural moorings that shield [them] fairly effectively from the suggested consequences of number, density, and heterogeneity."[19] In other words, there is not just one urban way of life but many urban life-styles.

Gans thus argues that urbanism itself does *not* cause a particular way of

[16]See Leo Srole's comments in Tim Hacker, "The Big City Has No Corner on Mental Illness," *New York Times Magazine,* December 16, 1979, p. 136.
[17]Claude Fischer, *To Dwell Among Friends: Personal Networks in Town and City,* University of Chicago Press, Chicago, 1982, p. 52.
[18]Ibid., pp. 59–60.
[19]Gans, op. cit., p. 186.

life to emerge. More important to the individual than the size, density, or heterogeneity of the larger population is the nature of his or her local community and primary groups. Rather than living in the city per se, people actually live in what the early Chicago school called a "mosaic of social worlds." Some of these local social worlds, far from producing alienation, act to protect their members from negative outside influences.

A third perspective, known as "subculture theory," suggests that urbanism does shape social life.[20] Fischer suggests that urbanism does not destroy social groups, as posited by Wirth, but rather strengthens and intensifies subcultural groups. Large cities contain enough people to allow subcultures to emerge. Conflict can arise between what are considered by the mainstream to be deviant cultures (e.g., delinquents and homosexuals) and the mainstream culture itself. However, adherents of subculture theory say this occurs not because social worlds are being broken down, but because subcultures remain strong.

DIVERSE LIFE-STYLES

While cities generally have the highest rates of social problems, this clearly is not the same as saying that all central-city populations or areas have high rates of alienation and disorganization. Some groups thrive in central-city locations. Inner-city working-class ethnic groups, for instance, live lives that, far from being disorganized, are probably more organized and integrated than those of other city dwellers. Characteristics of depersonalization, isolation, and social disorganization simply do not fit. Gans suggests that inner-city populations can be grouped in five classifications:[21]

1. "Cosmopolites"
2. Unmarried or childless people (singles)
3. "Ethnic villagers"
4. The "deprived"
5. The "trapped" and downwardly mobile

As you read the following pages, keep in mind that these classifications or categories are not descriptions of any particular person but rather "ideal types" or logical constructs useful for purposes of comparison. Also remember that we are speaking of the inner city rather than the city as a whole; in the city as a whole, the middle class is the largest population group. For our purposes the last two categories—the "deprived" and the "trapped"—can be combined into one: "outcasts."

[20]Claude Fischer, "Toward a Subcultural Theory of Urbanism," *American Journal of Sociology*, **80**:1319–1341, 1975.
[21]Gans, op. cit., p. 186.

Cosmopolites

Cosmopolitan urbanites in larger cities often choose to remain in the city because of its convenience and cultural benefits. They include artistically inclined persons such as writers and artists, as well as intellectuals and professionals, who are attracted to the center of the city. They tend to be single or, if married, childless. The numbers in this group were augmented during the 1970s and 1980s by young and reasonably affluent whites returning to revitalized central-city neighborhoods. Demographically, such newcomers tended to be young married adults, childless or with preschool children, white, employed in managerial-level positions, and making middle- or upper-middle-class incomes. Cosmopolites or those choosing to return to the city hardly fit the stereotype of the anomic and isolated central-city dweller. (For a discussion of the revitalization of central-city neighborhoods, see Chapter 11, Housing Programs and Urban Change.)

Singles

Another population group that is in the central city voluntarily is young singles, or Yuppies (this group may overlap with cosmopolites). The unmarried and childless between the ages of roughly twenty and thirty remain in the city because it is convenient to their jobs and, most important, is where other Yuppies are found. Community roots and local ties of kinship are relatively rare among singles. Their stay in the city does not usually represent a decision to settle permanently in a neighborhood, but rather is a reflection of a stage in the life cycle. According to the Bureau of the Census there were just under 2 million unmarried-couple households in 1983.[22] The unanswered question today is what percentage of young singles will choose to remain in revitalized city neighborhoods rather than move to the suburbs.

In addition to younger singles, those somewhat older who are divorced or who choose not to marry are attracted to central-city locations. Subcommunities of gays also almost invariably choose central-city locations.

The singles scene is supposedly composed of endless numbers of Yuppies who nightly crowd the city's single bars looking for one-night stands without any emotional commitments or hangups. But the realities of single life in the city are more humdrum. Each year colleges turn out large numbers of more or less similar young graduates who are more or less committed to a career. The marriage market removes some, who settle in apartment areas or move directly to the suburbs. Others follow the available job opportunities to the city. Singles in cities are trying to cope with the everyday problems of making friends, getting some satisfaction from their jobs, finding a decent place to live, and at the same time finding social partners and eventually a mate. They are far from being social or economic radicals. They are trying to achieve

[22]U.S. Bureau of the Census, "Marital Status and Living Arrangements: March, 1983," *Current Population Reports,* series P–20, No. 389, 1984.

The disappearance of ethnic neighborhoods has been predicted for over half a century, yet they continue to show vitality. (Beryl Goldberg)

essentially middle-class happiness and essentially middle-class material goals without being able to rely on many of the older institutional supports for their activities.

Chicago data indicate that housing and neighborhood are not significant in establishing meaningful social interaction, either friendships or dating relationships. Neighbors do not get to know one another; the idea of "turf" or territory, while it is crucial to the understanding of some urban minorities, "is not a useful concept in understanding the lifestyles of this large and growing urban subpopulation."[23] An exception appears to be housing complexes built particularly for singles. Research at Chicago's Carl Sandburg Village indicated that in an age-segregated environment where people also share a similar social class and life-style, residents did come to get acquainted and interact with each other.[24]

Singles bars, according to some reports, serve as substitutes for a community. Available data, however, indicate that interest in and attendance at singles bars evidently decreases with the time one spends in the city.[25]

[23]Joyce R. Starr and Donald E. Carns, "Singles and the City: Notes on Urban Adaptation," in John Walton and Donald E. Carns (eds.), *Cities in Change,* Allyn and Bacon, Boston, 1973, pp. 280–292.
[24]Gerda R. Wekerle, "Vertical Village: Social Contacts in a Singles High-Rise Complex," paper presented at a 1975 meeting of the American Sociological Association, San Francisco.
[25]Starr and Carns, op. cit., p. 288.

Most singles have few community roots. They do not belong to organizations, and view membership in organizations as a poor way of meeting possible mates, since most of the organization's members are likely to be married. The workplace provides the most frequent institutional setting for meeting friends and possible mates. One's work takes up most of the day; it is the place where one is most likely to meet others of similar background and interests in a setting that facilitates easy familiarity.

Ethnic Villagers

Among the various inner-city residents, the working-class ethnic populations probably lead the most highly organized lives. Far from being characterized by depersonalization, isolation, and social disorganization, working-class neighborhoods, particularly when they are dominated by a single ethnic group, often exhibit a high degree of social interaction among residents. Those living in such organized inner-city neighborhoods have been referred to as "urban villagers" or "urban provincials."[26] Such names are used to suggest that they are in, but not of, the city; they are urban in their residential patterns but not in their thought processes. These inner-city neighborhoods, whatever their predominant group, embody more of the family and peer-oriented provincialism of a tight, homogeneous small town than the attitudes of an impersonal large city.

Ethnic villagers, although they live in the city, try to isolate themselves from what they consider to be the harmful effects of urban life, preferring to live in their own tight-knit ethnic neighborhoods. Whether they are Irish in South Boston, Italian in South Philadelphia, or Mexican in East Los Angeles, they resist the encroachment of other ethnic or racial groups. Such primarily working-class neighborhoods place heavy emphasis on kinship and primary-group relationships and resent the secondary formal control mechanisms of the larger city. Some of these Italian, Puerto Rican, Mexican, or eastern European enclaves are no larger than a census tract, but some are quite extensive. Chicago and Detroit both claim the largest Polish population outside Warsaw; Cleveland's Hungarian population is said to be second only to that of Budapest. Los Angeles's Mexican population is second only to that of Mexico City.

An unresolved question is whether these tight ethnic urban neighborhoods are only anachronistic survivals from earlier times or are representative of contemporary urban life. To some people, urban villagers represent only "bypassed preindustrial locals" who have been left behind by modern society. As put by Melvin Webber: "Here in the Harlems and South Sides of the nation are some of the last viable remnants of preindustrial societies where village styles are nearly intact."[27]

---

[26]See Herbert J. Gans, *The Urban Villagers*, Free Press, Glencoe, Ill., 1962.
[27]Melvin M. Webber: "The Post-City Age," in J. John Palen (ed.), *City Scenes*, Little, Brown, Boston, 1977, p. 314.

Outsiders sometimes mislabel such areas as "slums" because the buildings are old and may not appear from the exterior to be in good condition. Often the area is in better condition than it appears when viewed from the window of a passing automobile on the suburban-bound expressway, but even when an area is physically deteriorated, its social fabric may still be strong.[28] Urban villagers remain in older neighborhoods in spite of the obvious physical limitations and conditions of the housing because moving to the suburbs would mean leaving the tight-knit social neighborhood. If they could take neighbors and social atmosphere with them, they would happily become suburbanites.

The mother of six children living in the Near West Side of Chicago clearly expressed the affection working-class urban villagers have for their neighborhoods:

I got everybody on this block that would do something for me. If one of my children were sick, I wouldn't feel any compunction of waking up the man across the street to take me to the hospital. He expects this. He would expect me to do this for him.

One night I took my daughter to the hospital at eleven o'clock at night. Next morning, at least eight people on my way to work asked me how my daughter was. When I got home it was worse than that. It took me an hour to get home. Because everybody wanted to know about Christine. Did the doctors do anything? Did I need anything? I get a cheery hello from everybody. Old ladies, when I get dressed to go out or to work: "Oh, how nice you look." Old and young blend together here. I have friends who live in the suburbs, they wouldn't dare be out in the dark.

I know friends of ours, who've moved away from here, who bitterly lament their predicament now. They've got beautiful homes—I guess the city planners would say they've done better for themselves. Their plumbing works, their electricity is good, their environment is better—supposedly. If you're a type of person who considers a mink stole and a fountain in your living room and big bay windows, front lawn beautifully kept, all these things mean something to you, well . . . to me, we're more concerned about people.[29]

The next pages will spend some time on working-class neighborhoods and norms. Use this material to compare the type of neighborhood described with neighborhoods with which you are personally familiar.

Neighborhood Characteristics. *Territorality.* Inner-city neighborhoods generally have a strong sense of territory. Studies of inner-city working-class areas often find that the residents, although living near the center of a large metropolis, still manage to remain physically, socially, and psychologically isolated from the rest of the urban area.[30] The city outside the neighborhood is viewed as a foreign land—and a potentially hostile one—into which one

---

[28]See, for example, William F. Whyte, op. cit.; and Gerald D. Suttles, *The Social Order of the Slum,* University of Chicago Press, Chicago, 1968.

[29]Quoted in Studs Terkel, *Division Street: America,* Pantheon Books (Avon ed.), New York, 1967, p. 198.

[30]For an explanation of how urban workers view their own lives and achievements, see Richard Sennett and Jonathan Cobb, *The Hidden Injuries of Class,* Vintage Books, New York, 1973.

ventures only when necessary. Even in cosmopolitan New York there are people living in Brooklyn who have never been to Manhattan and have no real desire ever to go there.

Ecologically settled ethnic areas are usually characterized by *ordered segmentation*. That is, each ethnic group carefully and specifically defines its territory. Boundaries between different ethnic groups, while invisible to the outsider, are well known and respected by the local residents. Gerald Suttles, in his study of the Taylor Street area of Chicago, points out that the Italian, Mexican, Puerto Rican, and black groups living in the area have their own provincial enclaves and conduct their daily lives within these known borders.[31] Within these territorial units, one is safe and comfortable. Outsiders are made to feel unwelcome unless they are there as guests. The use of community facilities such as churches and parks is exclusively for one group. The movement of one ethnic or racial group into what is known as the social area of another is likely to lead to violence or the threat of violence.

Awareness and concern over territory are not limited to public or semipublic facilities. Business establishments—particularly bars, but even grocery stores—are viewed by local inhabitants as being the exclusive property of a single minority group. In the words of Suttles:

> When someone from outside the area or from another ethnic group enters, the proprietor and regular customers view them with great suspicion and, in some cases, use *ad hoc* measures to insure their safety. Sometimes they will simply wait for the intruder to get his bearings and leave. If that fails the proprietor may eventually get around to asking what he wants. In the meantime, everyone in the store stops and stares. The treatment of regular customers, of course, is exactly the opposite. Commercial relations with these people are intimate and all economic transactions are buried in the guise of friendship and sentiment. In large part this is the reason they cannot tolerate the presence of strangers from another ethnic group. Among themselves the customers set aside their public face and disclose much of their private life to one another.[32]

Private information is too intimate to be revealed to potentially hostile strangers. In establishments such as small snack shops that may be near the boundary line between different ethnic groups, the problem of privacy may be solved by taking turns. One group of teenagers will not enter while another is inside. Rather, they will wait until the other ethnic group leaves.

Peer-Group Orientation. The primary integrative mechanism of stable inner-city ethnic neighborhoods is the peer group—that is, a group made up of members of the same age and sex who are at the same stage of the life cycle. As Gans says, "The peer group society continues long past adolescence, and, indeed, dominates the life of the West Ender [Boston] from birth to death."[33] The peer group, be it a gang of adolescents or a clique of married friends and

---

[31]Suttles, op. cit.
[32]Ibid., pp. 48–49.
[33]Herbert J. Gans, *The Urban Villagers*, p. 37.

relatives of the same sex, provides a vital buffer between the individual and the larger society.

Gans has described the relationship of the peer-group society to the larger world as follows:

> . . . The life of the West Ender takes place within three interrelated sectors: the primary group refers to that combination of family and peer relationships which I shall call the *peer group society*. The secondary group refers to the small array of Italian institutions, voluntary organizations, and other social bodies which function to support the workings of the peer group society. This I shall call the *community*. . . . The outgroup, which I shall describe as the *outside world,* covers a variety of non-Italian institutions in the West End, in Boston, and in America that impinge on his life—often unhappily to the West Ender's way of thinking.[34]

The peer group sets standards for behavior and acts as a filter through which one can obtain information. It provides psychological support in that it serves as a sounding board against which one can bounce ideas and receive confirmation of values. It reduces anonymity and tells the individual that he or she belongs. Frequently, in-group membership is signified by a distinctive way of dressing and locally distinctive speech patterns.[35] Whyte's classic treatment of a peer-group society, *Street Corner Society,*[36] deals extensively with the conflict in values between locally oriented "corner boys" and neighborhoood adolescents who were success and object-oriented, the so-called "college boys." Peer groups of "corner boys" discouraged striving and emphasized personal relationships. If someone got a job and made some money (this was during the late depression), he was expected to share his good fortune with his friends. Being a good guy was socially rewarded, while putting on airs of social striving was negatively sanctioned. On the other hand, the college boys were oriented toward the achievement values of the outside world, saved rather than shared their money, and constantly sought to "better themselves." The more recent studies of Boston's West End and the Addams area indicate that little has changed over the years: the priority of personal relationships over goal-oriented relationships remains. The absence of material wealth and luxurious consumer goods is rationalized: these goods are associated with the outside world and a cold, impersonal, friendless way of life.

Family Norms. Family life in settled ethnic working-class areas is generally adult-oriented. Once out of infancy, children are expected to accommodate and adjust themselves to a world run by adults. The child is not the center of the family as in many middle-class and upper-middle-class families, where everything is adjusted to avoid conflict with the child's needs, schedule, and general "development." The role of children is to stay out of the way and behave, at least around the home, like miniature adults. When girls reach eight

---

[34]Ibid., pp. 36–37.
[35]Suttles, op. cit., chap. 4.
[36]Whyte, op. cit.

or nine, they are expected to start helping their mothers around the home, frequently by caring for younger siblings. Boys are given a great deal more freedom to roam the streets. Children soon pick up the notion that the home is the preserve of the mother. Leisure activities for males often focus on the local tavern, which is the major neighborhood institution for many blue-collar workers.[37]

Sociability for married adults does not revolve around occupation or involve a search for new or different friends. The basis for gathering with others is kinship or long-standing friendship and association. Parties in the middle-class sense—gatherings for which specific invitations are issued and at which you expect to meet some people you do not know—are not part of the local life-style. As one West Ender put it: "I don't want to meet any new people. I get out quite a bit all over Boston to see my brothers and sisters, and when they come over, we have others in, like neighbors. You can't do that in the suburbs."[38] Usually the same people come the same days of the week. There are no formal invitations; these are used only for major family events such as a christening, graduation, or wedding. Husband and wife are not expected to be as close or to communicate as extensively as in the middle-class family model. Bott's description of this phenomenon among English families applies equally well to American cities:

> Husband and wife have a clear differentiation of tasks and a considerable number of separate interests and activities. They have a clearly defined division of labor into male tasks and female tasks. They expect to have different leisure pursuits, and the husband has his friends . . . the wife hers.[39]

To date the women's movement has not seriously altered this pattern.

One difference between American and English studies is that in the United States interaction is primarily with relatives of the same generation. In the East End of London, the interaction may focus on the family matriarch, "Mum." Mum is the one who settles family quarrels, lends money, and looks after the grandchildren. It is at her house that the family gathers, and if a married daughter does not live in the same building, she will be within a short distance.[40] The cartoon "Andy Capp" typifies the British lower-working-class model. Family ties in the United States are more likely to be horizontal as well as vertical, with greater importance given to cousins and other relatives of the same age.

Housing. Housing often does not have the same meaning in established ethnic working-class neighborhoods that it has in suburban middle-class areas. For the middle class, how one decorates one's home is viewed as an extension of

---

[37]E. E. LeMasters, *Blue Collar Aristocrats,* University of Wisconsin Press, Madison, 1975; and William Kornblum, *Blue Collar Community,* University of Chicago Press, Chicago, 1974, p. 80.

[38]Gans, *The Urban Villagers,* p. 75.

[39]Elizabeth Bott, *Family and Social Network,* Tavistock Publications, London, 1957, p. 53.

[40]Michael Young and Peter Willmott, *Family and Kinship in East London,* rev. ed., Penguin Books, Baltimore, 1962.

one's personality. The home is a reflection of one's tastes and style of life. The working-class home, on the other hand, is not primarily viewed as a status symbol. Homes are old but quite comfortable. Rents are usually well below the average for the city.

Exteriors of buildings are not always in the best repair. However, inside the apartments everything is clean and in good order. To emphasize consumer goods is perceived as trying to be "better than you are," "snooty," or "stuck-up." Social closeness among neighbors is encouraged by the tendency of local landlords to rent apartments to their married children, relatives, and friends. The goal is a "respectable" neighborhood in which neighbors are of the same general ethnic, religious, and economic background. For the upwardly mobile working-class hopeful of moving into the middle class, the home frequently is a symbol of one's respectability. Cleanliness and order are emphasized, with the furniture carefully protected by plastic seat covers and the carpeting by plastic runners.

Imagery and Vulnerability. Blue-collar ethnic neighborhoods, although physically a central part of the city, manage to maintain a psychological distance between themselves and other areas. Their negative images of major urban institutions are remarkably similar to those of small-town dwellers, who also feel powerless in face of the large urban institutions and organizations that control much of their lives. The urban provincials may be city dwellers, but they think of the city as something removed from themselves and their neighborhood. Their area is perceived as being different from the big city outside. Thus the neighborhood is considered friendly, but the city is cold and hostile.

The peer-group orientation of working-class urban neighborhoods leaves them vulnerable to change induced from the outside. The emphasis within the community on personal relations makes residents ill-equipped to participate in large-scale formal organizations or community-wide activities. One learns from the peer group how to get along with others, but not how to deal effectively with an outside bureaucracy.

This means that the community as a whole is rarely able to respond effectively as a unit to threats to its existence, such as urban renewal or an urban expressway that cuts it apart. A traditional distrust of politicians and a lack of knowledge about how to lobby on the level of city government further handicap the working-class neighborhood. Suburban upper-middle-class groups are by training and inclination well equipped to organize ad hoc committees for any purpose under the sun. Working-class people are used to working within an environment of limited size, oriented toward persons more than organizations. Except in cases where a powerful community-wide ethnic church exists, there is no large-scale organization that has the power both to organize and to speak for the neighborhood in its dealings with the larger city. A peer-group society based on ethnicity, age-grading, dominance of a single sex, and limited territoriality is at a considerable disadvantage when it necessarily comes into contact and confrontation with large-scale, complex, bureaucratic, middle-class society.

Urban provincials do not turn to outside bureaucratic structures in time of trouble. They distrust the city hall bureaucracy and that of the courts. They don't understand the system and feel that whatever happens they are going to lose. They are right, and their lack of knowledge of how to fight the system makes it all the easier for city hall and other outside interests to have their way. They lack the organization to be part of the conventional political pressure-group system.

The Outcasts

Our final urban population group is the "outcasts." Descriptions of the negative consequences of urban ways of life best fit life in unstable inner-city slums. For the 15 to 20 percent of the overall population who are the bottom in terms of social status (unskilled manual workers, people with unstable and erratic work histories, and people on welfare, particularly if they are members of minority groups), the slum has the character more of an urban jungle than an urban village. Such areas have high rates of residential instability, with the transient population sharing little but the physical area. They are there because they have no alternative.

Unstable slums house the outcasts of society—the very poor, the old, and the unadjusted. This group, below the manual blue-collar workers, is not simply poorer, although that is also the case—it is in many ways cut off from the social system that includes both the rich and the manual workers. Unstable slums are the slums of despair, for their residents are for all practical purposes excluded from the economic and social life of the larger society. Working-class parents can sacrifice to raise the level of their children, but for those of the urban underclass there is little realistic hope of moving from the slum to something better. Life in such an environment is not an attempt to maximize advantages but rather an attempt, frequently unsuccessful, to minimize the harsh negative realities of everyday life.

Those on the bottom, sometimes called the "disreputable poor" by the larger society, have been left behind by that society. They are people who are downwardly mobile, frequently because of drugs, alcoholism, or mental problems. The "disreputable poor" also includes newer in-migrants to the city who arrive lacking marketable skills or knowledge of urban ways and who, because of this lack and sometimes because of their educational and emotional liabilities, are virtually excluded from modern economic life.[41] They are in many respects America's "untouchable" caste. Additionally, some old people and handicapped people drift into unstable slums because they are not wanted elsewhere and are powerless to prevent the downward slide.

Slum dwellers are never able to find enough money to have a style of life

---

[41]David Matza, "The Disreputable Poor," in Neil J. Smelser and Seymour M. Lipset (eds.), *Social Structure and Mobility in Economic Development*, Aldine, Chicago, 1966, pp. 310–339.

which both they and society would define as reasonable. They are also surrounded by others who are out to exploit them whenever possible. They are considered fair game by everyone from landlords to hustlers.

Survival Strategies. For those locked into lower-class status, it is often unrealistic to have long-range goals. Success is measured in terms of developing strategies for day-to-day survival, not in terms of long-range goals. Even those with jobs usually are not on a track that will lead to a better job. For example, a dishwasher in a restaurant who works hard isn't going to become a chef or restaurant manager.[42] The job leads nowhere, and so long-range planning is meaningless. For a welfare mother with children living in a high-rise public housing project, the problem is not whether there will be enough money in ten years to send a child to college, but whether the family can scrape together enough money to pay current bills and expenses. There is also a constant threat of violence. The extremely high rates of assault, mugging, robbery, and rape in unstable slums further isolates people. Their situation does not encourage openness and easy interaction with others in the area. Rather, it fosters wariness, anonymity, noninvolvement, and impersonality. Protection from hostile others has to take first priority. Lower-class individuals try, with only slight success, to isolate themselves from the violence of their world. And as youths reach "crime-causing" ages, the cycle repeats.

Housing Problems. Housing for the poor living in unstable slums is not a matter of self-realization or self-expression; it is a matter of providing a place of security from the physical and emotional dangers of the outside. The middle class may view housing as an extension of one's personality, and the working class may see the house as a place of comfort, but for the urban underclass the house is a place of refuge.

Urban poor, particularly those stored in public housing projects, have to be constantly on guard against violence against themselves and their possessions. Assaults, robberies, and muggings are a constant danger in stairwells, corridors, laundry rooms, and even apartments. In addition to physical violence, symbolic violence on the part of building supervisors, social workers, and others who perform caretaker services for the lower classes is also endemic in slums and public housing. Lower-class persons protect themselves from such symbolic violence and shaming by avoidance, sullenness, and feigned stupidity when contact cannot be avoided.[43]

To the extent that the world is seen as consisting of dangerous others, the very act of making friends involves risks for the lower-class person. A friend could turn out to be an enemy and might report one to the housing

---

[42]Elliot Liebow, *Talley's Corner*, Little, Brown, Boston, 1967.
[43]Lee Rainwater, "Fear and the House-as-Haven in the Lower Class," in J. John Palen and Karl H. Flaming (eds.), *Urban America*, Holt, Rinehart, and Winston, New York, 1972, pp. 311–321.

authorities or cause other problems. Lower-class persons are constantly being exploited, and thus it is not surprising that they view the world as threatening. In the words of Lee Rainwater, "To lower class people the major causes stem from the nature of their own peers. Thus a great deal of blaming goes on and reinforces the process of isolation, suspiciousness, and touchiness both blaming and shaming."[44] Such patterns of distrust and recrimination make it difficult to establish any type of organization for cooperation in solving problems.

For the outcast poor, life is not getting better. Two decades after the War on Poverty, one out of every seven Americans remains below the poverty level.[45] Nor is poverty evenly distributed. Thirty-four percent of all blacks are below the poverty level compared to 11 percent of whites. Forty percent of those in poverty are children younger than eighteen. Fully half of all poor families are headed by women,[46] and seven out of ten poor black families are headed by women.

With those having economic strength or potential fleeing unstable slums, the isolation of those who are left behind locked into poverty increases. Decreases in discrimination *heighten* the isolation between the very poor and other strata of blacks. Poverty and economic instability lock the urban underclass at the bottom as effectively as discrimination once did. Certainly the feeling of being ignored and bypassed while all around others rise can lead to explosions of frustration—or worse, despair—not only for oneself but also for one's children. The bondage of unstable slums is made doubly oppressive by the relative prosperity of those outside their boundaries.

It is not unreasonable to foresee certain areas of cities, or even entire cities, serving essentially as ghetto reservations for the deprived underclass. A few once-viable cities such as Newark already exhibit major characteristics of urban reservations for the welfare poor.[47]

URBAN LIFE-STYLES

Urbanism as a way of life thus is remarkably diverse. It includes gentrifying communities of yuppies, tightly organized ethnic neighborhoods, and disorganized slums. There is no single urban lifestyle per se.

[44]Ibid., p. 319.
[45]U.S. Bureau of the Census, "Consumer Income," Characteristics of the Population below the Poverty Level: 1981, P–60, No. 138, March, 1983, p. 1.
[46]Ibid.
[47]For more on this, see George Sternlieb, "The City as Sandbox," in J. John Palen (ed.), *City Scenes,* op. cit.; and Joseph M. Conforti, "Newark: Ghetto or City," *Society,* **9**:20–32, September–October, 1972.

CHAPTER

7

SOCIAL ENVIRONMENT OF THE CITY:

Strangers, Neighbors, Crowding, and Crime

Where you find both good and evil, there you find a city.
Hindu Proverb

DEALING WITH STRANGERS

In the last chapter we saw how Simmel, Wirth, and the classical Chicago school emphasized the disruptive and socially disorganizing aspects of cities' size, density, and heterogeneity. Although we saw that this was an overstatement, a question still remains: How do people outside their own defended neighborhood or turf cope with large numbers of other people whom they do not know? How do we learn to operate in what Lyn Lofland refers to as "a world of strangers."[1]

Lofland suggests that we cope by identifying strangers on the basis of their appearance and their spatial location in the city. Type, material, and style of clothing; jewelry; and hair styles are all external symbols of who we are and our position. In earlier eras legal codes and custom often decreed what one could or could not wear. Velvet gowns, for example, were reserved for those of rank, while commoners were restricted to common cloth. In ancient Rome the white toga was a sign of Roman citizenship.[2] Colors also were used to signify position. Royalty in eighteenth-century Europe wore the royal purple; in China the emperor wore yellow. Professions also had their unique garb such as the robes of the professor.

Today professorial robes are worn only on ceremonial occasions such as convocations, but that does not mean we no longer wear distinctive clothing. We still wear a "uniform," but the signs may be more subtle, such as a designer's symbol on one's shirt. Not only priests, nurses, bus drivers, and soldiers wear uniforms or have dress codes. Business executives wear dark blue Brooks Brothers suits, professors wear tweed jackets with a loose or absent tie, and students wear Levis or designer jeans. There are preppy uniforms, punk uniforms, and subculture uniforms. These dress codes help us identify strangers as being similar to or dissimilar from ourselves. Clothing still indicate one's social rank. In China—even during the Cultural Revolution— when everyone wore Mao jackets, some were made of finer material and were better cut than others. Persons of importance also wore jackets having four front pockets, while office workers or peasants had only two pockets.

Where we see people in the city also helps us identify strangers. Young people on a college campus are assumed to be students, and conservatively dressed middle-aged persons in an office district are assumed to be business people. Passengers in airports are assumed to be of higher status than passengers in the city bus station; suburbanites are assumed to be of higher status than those living in slum neighborhoods.

Of course, errors are made because location and dress are not certain signs of a stranger's position. Initial conversation with a stranger is often an attempt to identify socioeconomic status further. One asks a social-class question, "What do you do for a living?" or "What's your line of work?" The college-age student's version of this is, "Where do you go to school?"

---

[1]Lyn Lofland, *A World of Strangers,* Basic Books, New York, 1973.
[2]Ibid., p. 45.

In London social custom dictates that people formally queue up
while waiting for the bus. In the United States, it is done informally.
(Jim Cron/Monkmeyer)

CODES OF BEHAVIOR

The late Erving Goffman pointed out that activity in the city is not without a
system. Even such urban activity as walking down a street has a whole set of
social rules.[3] People do not just walk down the street at random; rather, there
is an intricate code of pedestrian behavior. For example, pedestrian traffic
sorts itself into two clear streams. In North America, pedestrians as well as
drivers, keep to the right, and they "watch their step" by avoiding obstacles
such as lightposts and other people on the sidewalk. Pedestrians also adjust
their speed to avoid collisions; faster traffic moves to the outside lane.
Pedestrians expect others to follow the "rules of the road" and sanction those
who break the rules by bumping into someone (a nasty look or a "Why don't
you watch where you're going"), and apologize for their own infractions ("Oh,
sorry").

   Rules differ by culture. Where auto traffic stays to the left (e.g., England,
Japan), pedestrian traffic does likewise. In Great Britain one queues up for a
bus; in the United States one waits in an informal line. Those pushing ahead

[3]Erving Goffman, *Relations in Public*, Basic Books, New York, 1971.

get a dirty look or comment. A man is also expected not to push ahead of a woman. In Israel, Singapore, or China, on the other hand, there is no queueing of any sort. In Great Britain those on escalators leave the left lane open for those who are in a hurry and wish to pass. Not to do so is considered rude. In North America, on the other hand, people stand side by side on escalators and to push past is considered rude. Thus, even pedestrian behavior follows generally internalized rules. Coping in the city is made easier by whole series of informal rules of which we are not normally conscious.

Neighboring

We have seen that city life per se does not automatically destroy close personal relationships. However, neighboring studies do suggest that, on the whole, large-city dwellers know fewer of their neighbors than do residents of smaller places.[4] Most of us, after all, do not live in ethnic urban enclaves. Studies of vital urban neighborhoods raise two questions: First, what characteristics distinguish the city dweller who is likely to neighbor? Second, what social conditions tend to turn people who live near each other into real neighbors?

Claude Fischer suggests several hypotheses on both these questions.[5] He suggests that persons who neighbor are, first, likely to be raising a family. Children engage parents in neighboring activities (e.g., PTA, Girl Scouts), children meeting other neighborhood children also facilitate their parents' meeting, and having children increases the likelihood that a parent will be home during the day to neighbor. Second, and related to this, neighborly people are likely to be home during the day, perhaps retired or caring for children. Third, they tend to be older and more settled. Fourth, neighboring folk tend to be homogeneous, to share common ethnicity, occupations, interests, and life-styles. Working-class persons tend to rely more on neighbors than do members of the middle class.

Finally, research by Kasarda and Janowitz indicates that the longer one has been a neighborhood resident, the greater likelihood of neighborhood involvement.[6] Since urbanites are more mobile than those living in other places, and are more likely to be working during the day and living in heterogeneous neighborhoods, it is understandable that city dwellers on the whole are less likely to be involved with their neighbors.

Neighbors and Just Neighbors

Fischer, drawing on the existing research, suggests that the social, as opposed to personal, conditions that turn "just neighbors" into "real neighbors" tend to be found less commonly in cities. Three conditions encourage "real"

[4]Claude S. Fischer, *The Urban Experience,* 2d ed., Harcourt Brace Jovanovich, New York, 1984.
[5]Ibid., pp. 130–131.
[6]John D. Kasarda and Morris Janowitz, "Community Attachment in Mass Society," *American Sociological Review,* **39**:328–339, June, 1974.

Neighborhood sidewalks are used for talking as well as for movement. (Barbara Alpert/Stock, Boston)

neighboring.[7] The first is functional interdependence. In rural America this involved mutual help with barn raising, harvesting, or meeting joint local needs. A suburban activity that generates social cooperation today is a neighborhood crime watch patrol. A second condition encouraging involvement is the preexistence of other relationships and bonds. Relatives and people who work together, who share the same ethnicity, and who worship together have already existing bonds that being neighbors simply strengthens. Third, Fischer suggests some people neighbor because they have fewer other alternatives. The elderly, or mothers with small children may have reduced mobility, and thus form close relationships with those nearby. Since large-city dwellers are less likely to have such functional interdependence and do have other alternatives available to them, old fashioned neighboring is less common for them.

DEFINING COMMUNITY

The term "community" has been used but not really defined. Unfortunately, there is no single or even most common usage.[8] Anthropologists dealing with

---

[7]Fischer, op. cit., p. 132.
[8]Some ninety definitions of community are listed by G. A. Hillery, "Definitions of Community: Areas of Agreement," *Rural Sociology*, **20**:111–123, 1955. See also Joseph R. Gusfield, *Community a Critical Response*, Harper and Row, New York, 1975.

localized semi-isolated populations generally find the concept of community more useful than do sociologists researching contemporary urban areas, where the boundaries between distinct groups or patterns of activities become blurred. Today the term community has lost much of its descriptive preciseness and efficiency. It is applied arbitrarily to everything from one block in a neighborhood to the international community.

Contemporary urbanites can, in Weber's terms, have "community without propinquity" (nearness). On the other hand, community, as used by ecologists, can be defined as a territorially localized population which is interdependent with regard to daily needs. Thus, this usage implies a territorial unit, as opposed to other uses of the term such as "community of scholars" or "religious community."

In the writings of the Chicago school, the term community was often a synonym for urban neighborhood. However, two of the most important pre-World War II community studies focused on small cities as the unit of analysis. Robert and Helen Lynd's *Middletown* and *Middletown in Transition* focused on the transformation of life in Middletown (Muncie, Indiana) as a result of absorption into an industrially oriented community.[9] The Lynds documented the decline of control by the community over its own destiny. However, in spite of the economic shocks of the depression, Middletown residents did not become radicalized, but retained complacency and belief in traditional values. A major restudy of Middletown in the late 1970s indicates that while the city is no longer economically in control of its destiny and is heavily beholden to the federal government, the traditional values and normative structure still persist. To a remarkable degree, Middletown still thinks of itself as it did half a century ago.[10]

The second major study, W. Lloyd Warner's *Yankee City* (Newburyport, Massachusetts), dealt with the degree to which the movement from craft work by individuals to mass industrial production led to a breakdown of a sense of community.[11] Local power and control, Warner suggested, had gone from ownership and control by local family-owned firms to large outside corporations. Accompanying this, he also suggested the rigidification of the social structure and decreased social mobility among workers. The historical accuracy of the latter points, however, has been strongly challenged by Stephen Thernstrom.[12]

There is currently no consensus on the significance of community in modern social life. Some, such as Suzanne Keller and Claude Fischer, suggest that urbanites engage in activities on the basis of interests rather than propinquity, and that the neighborhood serves only minimal functions.[13] One

[9]Robert S. Lynd and Helen Merrell Lynd, *Middletown*,Harcourt, Brace, New York, 1929; and *Middletown in Transition*, Harcourt Brace, New York, 1937.
[10]Theodore Caplow, Howard Bahr, Bruce Chadwick, Reuben Hill, and Margaret Holmes Williamson, *Middletown Families: Fifty Years of Change and Continuity*, University of Minnesota Press, Minneapolis, 1982.
[11]W. Lloyd Warner, *Yankee City*, Yale University Press, New Haven, Conn., 1963.
[12]Stephen Thernstrom, "Yankee City Revisited: The Perils of Historical Naivete," *American Sociological Review*, 30:234–242, April, 1965.
[13]Suzanne Keller, *The Urban Neighborhood*, Random House, New York, 1968; and Claude S. Fischer, *The Urban Experience*, Harcourt, Brace, Jovanovich, New York, 1976.

might borrow eggs or a cup of sugar from neighbors or call on them in an emergency, but for everyday life, local attachments are seen as being quite limited. Those taking this view would agree with Roland Warren that the strengthening ties of community units to extracommunity systems orient them in important and clearly definable ways toward larger systems outside the community, making the model of a somehat delineated, relatively independent, and self-sufficient comunity less and less relevant to the modern scene.[14] Larger networks for some have made the spatial unit of the neighborhood no longer important.[15] Others, such as Albert Hunter, see urban neighborhoods continuing to play a sometimes significant if changing role.[16]

CATEGORIES OF LOCAL COMMUNITIES

A number of types of local communities have been defined in the professional literature, among which are:

1. The defended neighborhood
2. The community of limited liability
3. The expanded community of limited liability
4. The contrived or conscious community[17]

The Defended Neighborhood is an area in which local residents feel threatened by external change—be it an invasion of another ethnic or racial group or an attempt to prevent destruction by external forces, such as urban renewal or an expressway through the neighborhood.[18] "Functionally, the defended neighborhood can be conceived of as the smallest spatial unit within which co-residents assume a relative degree of security on the streets as compared to adjacent areas."[19] The defended neighorhood thus is the place where people feel safe and secure. As such, it may or may not have a name or be recognized by government. Those within the defended neighborhood assume a common residential identification and identity.

The Community of Limited Liability   was first described by Morris Janowitz and later elaborated on by Scott Greer.[20] The concept of the community of limited liability emphasizes the voluntary and limited involvement of residents

---

[14]Roland L. Warren, *Perspectives on the American Community,* Chicago, Rand McNally, 1972, p. vi.
[15]Barry Wellman, "The Community Question: The Intimate Networks of East Yorkers," *American Sociological Review,* **84:**1201–1231, March, 1979.
[16]Albert J. Hunter, *Symbolic Communities: Persistence and Change in Chicago's Local Communities,* University of Chicago Press, Chicago, 1974.
[17]For information and discussion of types of communities, see Dennis E. Poplin, *Communities,* 2d. ed., Macmillan, New York, 1979.
[18]For an example of how a Boston neighborhood fought off such destruction, see Alan Lupo. Frank Colcord,and Edmund P. Fowler, *Rites of Way,* Little, Brown, Boston, 1971.
[19]Gerald Suttles, *The Social Construction of Communities,* University of Chicago Press, Chicago, 1972, p. 57.
[20]Morris Janowitz, *The Community Press in an Urban Setting,* University of Chicago, Chicago, 1952; and Scot Greer, *The Emerging City,* Free Press, New York, 1962.

in the local community. The amount of emotional investment in the area, or investment of time or resources, is dependent on the degree to which the community meets the needs of individuals. If the needs are not met, the individual might withdraw psychologically and socially, if not physically. Communities of limited liability usually have names and boundaries which are recognized by local planning agencies and government. Local organizations and particularly the local community press have a vested interest in maintaining the identity and boundaries of the area. The community of limited liability thus is defined by commercial interests and government agencies rather than by internal community awareness, as with the defended neighborhood.

The Expanded Community of Limited Liability is more fragmented and diffuse than the community of limited liability. The expanded community may take in whole sections of the city such as the east side or the north side. As such, it has little real cohesion as an actual unit.

Contrived or Conscious Communities are areas—new or developing—in which builders, financers, public agencies, and residents alike set out consciously to create a community image. Boundaries are clearly laid out, and the housing in the area may even be identical—e.g., all apartments or all townhouses or all public housing. The name of the area is usually given by the builder rather than emerging from the community. Conscious communities tend to be more homogeneous than other communities. Residents in the development may all be young singles, family types, or elderly. Ethnic and racial conformity or similarity of social class is also common in both urban and suburban conscious communities.

DENSITY AND CROWDING

The Chicago school saw high urban rates of density as a social problem. In fact, urban crowding and high density have long been seen as the cause of social pathology. Historically, high density (the number of people per acre, block, or other geographical unit) and crowding (the number of people per room, usually in housing) have been cited as a cause of epidemics, contagion, crime, and moral degradation.[21] The engravings of Hogarth, the novels of Dickens, and primitive health statistics all tell the same unfortunate tale—high density means disorganization and disease. As graphically expressed by Charles Dickens:

> They walked on, for some time, through the most crowded and densely inhabited part of the town; and then, striking down a narrow street more dirty and miserable than any they had yet passed through, paused to look for the house which was the object of their search. The houses on either side were high and large, but very

[21]See A. D. Biderman, M. Louria and J. Bacchus, *Historical Incidents of Extreme Overcrowding*, Bureau of Social Science Research, Washington, D.C., 1963.

old, and tenanted by people of the poorest class: as their neglected appearance would have sufficiently denoted, without the concurrent testimony afforded by the squalid looks of the men and women who, with folded arms and bodies half doubled, occasionally skulked along. A great many of the tenements had shop-fronts; but these were fast closed, and mouldering away; only the upper rooms being inhabited. Some houses which had become insecure from age and decay, were prevented from falling into the street, by huge beams of wood reared against the walls, and firmly planted in the road; but even these crazy dens seemed to have been selected as the nightly haunts of some houseless wretches, for many of the rough boards which supplied the place of door and window, were wrenched from their positions, to afford an aperture wide enough for the passage of a human body. The kennel was stagnant and filthy. The very rats, which here and there lay putrefying in its rottenness, were hideous with famine.[22]

More recently almost every social evil—air pollution, the loss of community, the lack of response of neighbors to cries for help—has been attributed to urban density and overcrowding.[23]

Experimental animal studies tend to support the view that high density and crowding produce a long list of physical and behavioral pathologies. At present we probably know more about the behavior of rats under conditions of crowding than we do about that of city dwellers. John Calhoun's now-famous article "Population Density and Social Pathology" indicates that in experiments with Norway rats, pathological states develop under conditions of crowding even when there is an abundance of food and freedom from disease and predators.[24] In Calhoun's experiment, a behavioral sink developed in which infant mortality increased, females didn't build proper nests or carry infants to term, and homosexuality and even cannibalism occurred. When the experiment was terminated, the rat population was well on the way to extinction.

Unfortunately, there is a tendency to try to transfer findings from animal studies, where they apply, to human populations, where they do not. Sometimes there is even an assumption that what holds for Norway rats automatically applies to humans. For example, one writer suggests:

The implications of animal and human studies are clearcut. Just as the offspring of frustrated mother rats, part of whose pregnancy was spent trapped in problem boxes with no exits, carried an emotional disturbance throughout their own lives, so too many children of frustrated human mothers, trapped by urban slums, show behavioral manifestations of emotional disturbance.[25]

[22]Excerpt from Charles Dickens, *The Adventures of Oliver Twist,* Chapman & Hall, Ltd., London, pp. 42–43.
[23]See James Q. Wilson, "The Urban Unease," *The Public Interest,* **12:**25–39, 1968; James A. Swan, "Public Responses to Air Pollution," in Joachim F. Wohlwill and Daniel H. Carson, *Environment and the Social Sciences,* American Psychological Association, Washington, D.C., 1972, pp. 66–74; Robert Buckout, "Pollution and the Psychologist: A Call to Action," in Joachim F. Wohlwill and Daniel H. Carson, *Environment and the Social Sciences,* pp. 75–81; and B. Latane and J. M. Darley, *The Unresponsive Bystander: Why Doesn't He Help?* Appleton-Century-Crofts, New York, 1970.
[24]John B. Calhoun, "Population Density and Social Pathology," *Scientific American,* **206:**139–148, February, 1960.
[25]Shirley Foster Hartley, *Population Quantity vs. Quality,* Prentice-Hall, Englewood Cliffs, N.J., 1972, p. 76.

This analogy repeats the "commonsense" view of the effects of density and crowding.

The problem is that the commonsense view is both simplistic and inaccurate. A considerable body of sociological and psychological research on density indicates that it does *not* have any clear and definite association with human pathology.[26] Density research is a classic case: What everyone "knows to be true" is simply not being supported by the data.

What is clear is that one's social background and experiences play a major role in how "high-density" is defined. Upper-middle-class populations, for example, have been socialized to view crowding as a problem, and space and separation as natural and necessary. Community studies of working-class populations indicate, on the other hand, that residents of city neighborhoods often view high density as a positive sign of community vitality rather than an indication of social disorganization.[27] Contact with others is viewed positively, as a sign of belonging, rather than negatively, as a sign of crowding. Inner-city youngsters from such areas are more comfortable being with others than being alone. Gans reports how social workers in the West End of Boston were forced to abandon a summer program that gave inner-city boys a chance to spend a vacation exploring nature at Cape Cod.[28] The boys could not understand why anyone would want to visit, much less live in, such a lonely spot. They were accustomed to, and thrived on, crowded and noisy street life. The boys wanted to be where the action was, and were emotionally unprepared for wide vistas and open, unused space.

Similarly, much of the population of crowded and noisy Hong Kong and Singapore, while desiring larger apartments, does not want to be isolateed or set apart from the crowd. In North America, some people choose a camping vacation of backpacking into the wilderness, miles from anyone, while others prefer to settle for weeks in commercial campgrounds where the density is higher than in the city. Middle-class and working-class populations may also vary in orienting themselves to a common spatial feature, such as streets. For working-class and lower-class urban groups, much daily activity takes place in the streets; streets are seen as living space, a place to congregate and gather with others in the neighborhood. Streets serve a vital social function. Upper-middle-class groups, on the other hand, are far less likely to see the streets as performing a social function. In their view streets are corridors to be used to travel from place to place, and they think people should be kept off the streets, lest they interfere with rapid movement.

---

[26]For an overview of available research, see Claude Fischer, Mark Baldassare, and Richard Ofshe, "Crowding Studies and Urban Life: A Critical Review," *Journal of the American Institute of Planners,* **41**:406–418, November, 1975; and Jonathan Freedman, *Crowding and Behavior,* Viking, New York, 1975. Also see Harvey M. Choldin and Dennis Roncek, "Density, Population Potential, and Pathology: A Block Level Analysis," *Public Data Use,* **4**:19–30, July, 1976.

[27]Herbert J. Gans, *The Urban Villagers,* Free Press, Glencoe, Ill., 1962; Gerald Suttles, *The Social Order of the Slum,* University of Chicago Press, Chicago, 1968; and Michael Young and Peter Willmott, *Family and Kinship in East London,* Penguin Books, Baltimore, 1962.

[28]Gans, op. cit.

Urban congestion is taken as a normal part of everyday life in
Hong Kong. (© Jan Lukas/Photo Researchers)

The effects of household crowding on social relationships and mental
health are limited.[29] Since household crowding has been sharply decreasing in
recent years—according to the 1980 census, 97 percent of all housing units

[29]O. R. Galle and Walter R. Grove, ''Crowding and Behavior in Chicago, 1940–1970,'' in J. R. Aiello and A.
Blaum (eds.), *Residential Crowding and Design,* Plenum, New York, 1979, pp. 23–40.

had less than one person per room—this should considerably lessen the causal effect of housing crowding as a variable.

Thus, contrary to the common assumption, density or crowding does not necessarily have either a negative or positive impact on urban life. It all depends on how the level of crowding is socially defined. Urban densities, for example, have been decreasing for seventy-five years, but there has been no corresponding decrease in urban social problems. Freedman suggests that the effect of density and crowding is to "intensity the individual's typical reactions to the situation."[30] Thus, being crowded with friends may produce positive reactions, although the same degree of crowding with those one dislikes may produce negative reactions. People do not respond to density or crowding in a uniform way.

URBAN CRIME

Increases or Decreases?

It is impossible to discuss the contemporary urban environment without some discussion of crime. Crime remains perhaps the most serious problem for urban residents in general and inner-city residents in particular. A 1981 Gallup poll indicated that six out of ten (roughly 58 percent) of those interviewed felt there was more crime in their areas than there had been a year earlier, and half (53 percent) were afraid to walk alone in their neighborhoods at night.[31] An earlier poll indicated that three-quarters (77 percent) of women reported being afraid to go out at night in their own neighborhoods.[32]

The Uniform Crime Reports (UCR) indicate that after a decade of increases there has been a decreasing level of city crime since 1980.[33] However, this decrease is not perceived by many citizens. In part, this is due to the limitations of the way crime data are collected. The Uniform Crime Reports are far from uniform since only crimes known to the police are reported—which means that almost all homicides are reported, but many burglaries and larcenies are not. Central-city residents, in particular, may feel that it is futile to fill out the reports. At best only half of actual crime is reported.

What is worse is that the UCR-reported crime statistics do not include narcotics offenses, while drug offenses continue to skyrocket.[34] The police chief of Washington, D.C. notes that drugs constitute the biggest single source of complaints to his office, and that despite the decline in reported crime, illegal drugs are "eroding the quality of life in the city."[35] The chief added that "somewhere between 50 and 60 percent of all burglaries, larcenies and

[30]Freedman, op. cit., p. 90.
[31]*Newsweek,* March 23, 1981, p. 47.
[32]Gallup poll, Field Enterprises, July 28, 1975.
[33]Uniform Crime Reports (1983), Table 2, F.B.I., Department of Justice, Washington, D.C., 1984.
[34]Ibid.
[35]*Washington Post,* November 15, 1984, p. C7.

robberies in the city are drug related.''[36] Under such circumstances it is not surprising that in some cities there is a paralysing fear and siege mentality, particularly among vulnerable groups such as the aged.

Crime and Youth

Crime is an activity of the young. Forty-five percent of all crimes except murder are committed by people under eighteen, and three-quarters are committed by those under twenty-five. The most likely age for being arrested is sixteen; fifteen, seventeen, and eighteen are the next most likely ages. (White-collar crimes and crimes which require trining or skill such as embezzlement, fraud, and counterfeiting are most likely to be committed by older persons.) Crime is also still largely a male activity, with about 80 percent of all arrests and 90 percent of arrests for violent crimes being of males.

As the proportion of teenagers in high-crime ages within the population decreases, so should the incidence of crime. Between the mid-1960s and the mid-1970s the proportion of males aged fifteen to twenty-five grew 32 percent (30 percent for white and 55 percent for blacks). Now that is reversed. There were three million fewer fourteen- to twenty-four-year-olds in 1985 than in 1975. Even without improved police efficiency, better rehabilitation programs, or an improved moral climate, street crimes committed by the young should decrease or remain stable for the next few years.

Black-on-Black Crime

The question of urban crime is frequently overlayed by racial fears. The undisputed fact is that urban crime rates are much higher for blacks than for whites. Most urban street crime in large cities is black-on-black crime. An attempt discreetly to ignore the number of black perpetrators of crime also ignores the fact that a disproportionate number of victims are black. Blacks are over five times as likely to be homicide victims as are whites. The National Commission on the Causes and Prevention of Violence reports that arrests of blacks are ten to eleven times higher than for whites for assault and rape, and sixteen to seventeen times higher for robbery and homicide. Some of this difference occurs because blacks are more likely to be arrested on suspicion.[37]

The result is that middle-class whites often see crime as a matter of black against white, as a question of race rather than crime. In actuality, blacks are more fearful of crime than are whites. According to the Gallup poll, blacks feel less secure than whites, both walking the streets and in their homes. This is understandable since blacks are more likely to be the victims of crime. In St. Louis 85 percent of all homocide victims are black; in Chicago and Oakland the figure is 70 percent, and in Dallas it is 64 percent. Moreover, in 1980 94

[36]Ibid.

[37]Donald J. Black, ''Production of Crime Rates,'' *American Sociological Review,* **35**:753, August, 1970; and Edward Green, ''Race, Social Status and Criminal Arrest,'' *American Sociological Review,* **35**:476–490, June, 1970.

percent of these black victims were killed by other blacks. Over 85 percent of crimes committed by blacks are against black victims. Robbery is the only largely interracial crime, with 45 percent involving a black offender (almost always a young male) and a white victim (usually an older white male). Given their high victimization rate, it is not surprising that middle-class blacks are more "hard line" against street crime than are middle-class whites.

Blacks have low arrest rates for white-collar crime such as tax evasion, fraud, and embezzlement. This reflects occupational discrimination, which has kept blacks out of policy-making white-collar jobs. A reasonable hypothesis would be that as blacks' incomes improve and their occupational levels rise, street crime by blacks will decline and white-collar crime will increase.

Variations within the City

Not only do crime rates show more crime in larger cities, but crime rates within urban areas generally reflect Burgess's hypothesis, which says that crime rates are highest in inner-city neighborhoods and decrease as one moves toward the periphery. White-collar crime, on the other hand, is more concentrated in suburban populations. Research done half a century ago by Shaw and McKay demonstrated this high concentration in the central city—a phenomenon they attributed to the "social disorganization" of such areas, as typified by high poverty and welfare rates, low levels of education, broken homes, and other social ills.[38] Since that time the concept of social disorganization has largely been superseded by other explanations, but the pattern of decreasing crime rates as one moves toward the urban periphery has been confirmed.

Interestingly, the pattern has held while the occupants, and even the physical characteristics, of the area have changed completely. This consistency does not mean that these neighborhoods or their locations somehow create crime. Rather, it suggests that the inhabitants of these areas—whether European immigrants at the turn of the century, blacks after World War II, or Mexicans and Puerto Ricans today—have been subject to the same pressures.

As Chapter 6, City Life-styles, pointed out, not all central-city neighborhoods have gone through the cycle of invasion and reinvasion by new groups—a process which hinders the development of social control by family, peers, and neighbors. Inner-city areas that have not been successively invaded by disadvantaged newcomers are often among the most stable areas in the city.

Suburban Crime

As newspaper stories document, crime rates in the suburbs are increasing faster than those in the central cities. This can be misleading, though, because the suburban increase is applied to a much smaller base. The amount of

[38]Clifford R. Shaw and Henry D. McKay, *Juvenile Delinquency in Urban Areas,* University of Chicago Press, Chicago, 1942.

The Passing of a Unique Neighborhood: Skid Row

Contemporary concern with "street people" and "bag ladies," either homeless or living in central-city flophouses or missions, refocuses attention on skid row as a distinct neighborhood to meet the needs of the down-and-outers.* In the United States there are more than 150 skid rows, but the number and size of such enclaves are decreasing. One authority estimates that yearly declines may be as high as 7 percent.† The record of the past decade suggests that the inhabitants of skid row are a dying breed, and skid row itself faces extinction.‡ There are two principal reasons. First, the economic system no longer requires large masses of unskilled migratory workers; second, the land occupied by skid rows is being converted by speculators for office buildings and other uses. For example, the beginning of the end of Chicago's skid row on West Madison Street came two decades ago, when across the street from the cheap bars, pawnshops, and flophouses a new Holiday Inn was erected. Similar processes are occurring from New York to San Francisco.

Down-and-Outers. In his study of Chicago's skid row, Donald Bogue found that the three characteristics which distinguish skid row occupants from other urbantes are their homelessness (living outside a private household), poverty, and acute personal problems. Not everyone on skid row had all these characteristics, but skid row had the highest concentration in the city of people with such problems.§ Poverty is a major determinant of almost all aspects of life on skid row, but not all the people on skid row are bums. At any given time, between one-third and one-half are employed, usually at day labor. The amount of employment is linked to the health of the economy; during recessions unemployment increases.

New Inhabitants: The Homeless. As old skid rows die out, newer skid rows appear, inhabited not by old winos but by

*The term "skid row" comes from the skid road the lumberjacks used in Seattle to transport logs. The lodging houses where the lumberjacks lived and the bars they got drunk in were near the "skid road."

†Howard M. Bahr, *Skid Row*, Oxford University Press, New York, 1973.

‡For a history of skid row, see Leonard Blumberg,. Thomas Shipley, and Stephan Barskey, *Liquor and Poverty: Skid Row as a Human Condition*, Rutgers Center of Alcohol Studies, New Brunswick, New Jersey, 1978.

§Donald J. Bogue, *Skid Row in American Cities*, University of Chicago, Community and Family Study Center, Chicago, 1963, p. 2.

Bag ladies unfortunately have become part of our city street scene.
(© Eugene Gordon 1982/Photo Researchers)

large numbers of persons of both sexes released from mental institutions during the "reforms" of the 1970s. Deinstitutionalization was well intended, but it has meant in some cases the virtual abandonment of persons who cannot fully cope with modern urban life. Social service agencies estimate, for example, that some 27,000 men and 9,000 women live on the streets of New York. They are people without homes, dependent upon churches and private and public emergency shelters.

Many of those who previously would have been committed to institutions are now homeless street people. They are not physically dangerous, but rather are disturbed or marginally competent individuals without supportive families. They are the man panhandling along the downtown streets and the old lady mumbling to herself while picking through the refuse can. In addition to such bag ladies, winos, young addicts, and derelicts can be found among the street people.

The Reagan Administration in a 1984 report estimated that there are 250,000 to 350,000 people in the United States who live on the streets without a home of any sort.* Independent studies estimate the true figure is upwards of 2 million persons.† Nationwide, emergency shelters can house, at most, 91,000.

Currently, we deal with such marginal persons by ignoring their existence. We have no system for looking after those who are neither dangerous nor capable of caring for themselves. We pretend they don't exist except when someone freezes to death during the winter. There is a major controversy about whether authoriies are violating individual civil rights when they remove homeless persons from the street without their consent during periods of extreme cold. For example, during a period of arctic cold in New York in 1985, the police were ordered to remove homeless people from the streets, against their will if necessary.‡ Such an action was contrary to state statutes, but it saved lives.

The humanitarian versus civil rights issues of providing involuntary assistance remain controversial, as does the question of building more shelters. Meanwhile, America's urban population without any home or shelter continues to grow.

There are also the young street people, numbering over a million, made up of migratory dropouts and young addicts. In terms of job qualifications and histories, street people resemble older skid row inhabitants. A survey of 305 street people in Berkeley found that one-third had not finished high school.§ Eighty-six percent were unemployed, and those who worked generally had only menial, part-time jobs as dishwashers, gardeners, or domestics.

In terms of mental health, street people also have characteristics of skid row inhabitants. Twenty-two percent of the Berkeley respondents had been hospitalized at least once for psychiatric reasons. The actual figure is higher, since the most disturbed could not fill out questionnaires, and others probably were reluctant to reveal such information about their past.

In other ways, young street people differ from the traditional skid row inhabitants. Unlike the older skid row derelicts, they didn't drift down over a period of years. They are already misfits and down-and-outers before reaching middle age. Second, street people include both sexes. Nineteen percent of

*United Press International, June 16, 1984.
†Ibid.
‡*New York Times*, Feb. 3, 1985.
§Celeste MacLeod, "Street People: The New Migrants," *The Nation*, **217**:395–397, October 22, 1973.

those in the Berkeley study were female. Exploitation of the females is commonplace. One-third of the female street people report being raped at least once. Young runaway girls are particularly vulnerable. Trading sex for room and board is a common form of semiprostitution.

Finally, the most important common denominator of street people is not alcohol but drugs. In the Berkeley sample, virtually all used marijuana, 87 percent had taken LSD, and 37 percent used heroin. One-fifth admitted to past or present addiction, usually to heroin or barbiturates.* To outsiders the drug-oriented street people represent at worst moral deprivation, and at best local color. Stripped of external trappings, what remains is a skid row for society's young rejects.

*Ibid.

suburban crime thus remains smaller. As of 1983, for example, the rate for cities over 250,000 was 15.5 arrests per 1,000 population, while for suburbs the rate was only 8.8 per 1,000. Rural areas had an even lower 5.2 per 1,000.[39]

Suburban crime also tends to be much less violent than city crime. Someone living in the city of Chicago, for instance, is six times more likely to be murdered and seven times more likely to be robbed than a suburban resident.[40] The most frequently reported single crime in suburbs is bicycle theft—a problem if it's your expensive ten-speed that is stolen, but not equivalent to being mugged or shot.

Moreover, within suburbs, crime is not randomly distributed, but rather concentrated in those low-income suburbs whose character most closely approximates the central city. Older inner-ring suburbs generally have higher rates than outlying areas. Around Chicago ten suburbs accounting for 15 percent of the suburban population account for 40 percent of the murder and a majority of the armed robberies, assaults, and rapes. These suburbs have burglary rates three times as high as the richest ten suburbs of Chicago, indicating that "them that hasn't gets taken." High-crime suburbs tend to have low-income or minority residents. Suburbs with large shopping centers and industrial parks also have more crime, particularly automobile theft.

[39]*Uniform Crime Reports*, op. cit., Table 24.
[40]*Chicago Tribune*, January 6, 1975, p. 37.

CHAPTER

8

PATTERNS OF

SUBURBANIZATION

The country life is to be preferred, for there we see the works of God, but in the cities little else but the works of men.

William Penn, *Reflections and Maxims*

SUBURBAN GROWTH

Writing at the end of the nineteenth century, Adna Weber concluded that the most hopeful sign in American urbanization was the "tendency . . . toward the development of suburban towns," for "such a new distribution of population combines at once the open air and spaciousness of the country with the sanitary improvements, comforts, and associated life of the city."[1]

This expresses what is in many ways still a dominant theme in American urbanization. The image of the suburb as a green or pleasant oasis with its single-family homes, neighbors, children, dogs, and ten-speed bikes—all within commuting range of the city—is one that still has force. Intellectuals may scorn "suburbia," but scorned or not, suburbs have transformed the landscape demographically, organizationally, and in life-style. Survey research clearly indicates that Americans prefer to live in smaller places near, but not in, the central city.[2]

We have been a nation of suburbanites since 1970 when the census showed that for the first time suburban areas of Metropolitan Statistical Areas (MSAs) exceeded their central cities in population size and growth rate.

By the 1980s, suburban influence had become overwhelming. The census in 1980 showed 68 million central-city residents and 102 million suburbanites.[3] Thus, the United States is now technically a nation of suburbs rather than a nation of cities. There are now three suburbanites for every two city dwellers.

Suburbs actually have been growing faster than central cities since the 1900s.[4] (Remember, though, that "suburban" as defined by the Bureau of the Census means that territory inside the MSA which is outside the central city. Some of this area and its population would not ordinarily be considered suburban.) Virtually the entire metropolitan area increase of 15.7 million between 1970 and 1980 occurred in suburbs.[5] Central-city population increase was less than 100,000 for all the nation's central cities put together. Population growth in metropolitan areas is now all but synonymous with suburban growth. For the last fifty years virtually all population growth in metropolitan areas has occurred in the suburban rings.

The data document the recency and magnitude of the exodus to the suburbs. In 1920 only 15 percent of all Americans were suburbanites. The percentage was only 19 percent by 1930 and only 20 percent by 1940. The percentage increased to 24 in 1950, and then shot up to 33 percent in 1960, 37 percent in 1970, and 40 percent today. These figures are based on a strict

---

[1]Adna Ferrin Weber, *The Growth of Cities in the Nineteenth Century*, Macmillan, New York, 1899, pp. 458–459.
[2]Conrad Taeuber, "Population Trends in the 1960's," *Science*, **176:**774, May 19, 1972.
[3]U.S. Bureau of the Census, Dept. of Commerce, "Population Profile of the United States: 1981," *Current Population Reports*, series, P–20, No. 374, Washington, D.C., September, 1982, Table 3–6.
[4]John D. Kasarda and George Redfearn, "Differential Patterns of Urban and Suburban Growth in the United States," *Journal of Urban History*, **2:**43–66, November, 1975.
[5]U.S. Bureau of the Census, op. cit., p. 17.

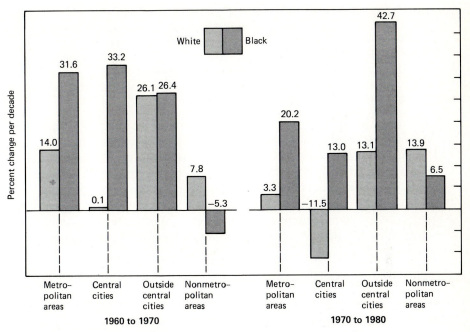

Figure 8-1. Population change in metropolitan and nonmetropolitan areas by race: 1960 to 1970 and 1970 to 1980. (*From Bureau of the Census.*)

density definition of a suburb; using the area inside the metropolitan area but outside the central city, a full 45 percent of Americans are suburbanites.[6]

This chapter begins by discussing the emergence of suburbs, then discusses their organizational and demographic aspects, and finally, spends some pages on the question of suburbia as a way of life.

EMERGENCE OF SUBURBS

The Nineteenth Century

Serious suburbanization was not possible prior to the transportation advances of the latter nineteenth century that permitted population dispersal. The first to move out were the wealthy, who built "suburban" communities out along the railroad lines from the city. These expensive commuter suburbs were to provide a rural refuge from the clamor of the city. As advertised by a promotional piece of a century ago:

> The controversy which is sometimes brought, as to which offers the greater advantage, the country or the city, finds a happy answer in the suburban idea

[6]Ibid., p. 23.

which says, both—the combination of the two—the city brought to the country. The city has its advantages and conveniences, the country has its charm and health; the union of the two (a modern result of the railway), gives to man all he could ask in this respect. The great cities that are building now, all have their suburban windows at which nature may be seen in her main expressions—and these spots attract to them cultured people, with their elaborate and costly adornments.[7]

As this quotation suggests, the first suburbs were generally upper-class villages of substantial country homes. The quotation also notes the importance of the railroad. In the absence of a reliable transportation technology, one could venture no farther from the railway station than one could conveniently walk, or at least be taken by one's driver. Suburbs were thus strung out along the rail lines like beads on a string. Philadelphia's Main Line and Chicago's North Shore are two examples of this pattern. Only those who could afford the costs in both time and money could combine an urban occupation with a rural residence.

Electric Streetcar Era: 1890–1920

As discussed in Chapter Three, The Rise of Urban America, the rapid adoption of the electric streetcar during the 1890s allowed the middle class to move out to the new suburban developments springing up along the streetcar corridors. Boston, for example, as of 1850 was a walking city extending out a maximum of 2.5 miles from city hall. The coming of the electric streetcar at the close of the last century changed the spatial configuration of Boston and other American urban areas from that of a compact city to that of a star-shaped urban area. The compact American walking city of the mid-nineteenth century was replaced by 1900 by a streetcar city in which one could live as far as twelve miles from the central business district. Development, both residential and commercial, occurred along the fingers of the electric streetcar tracks, while the interstices remained empty and undeveloped. The influence of early street railways on Dorchester, Roxbury, and West Roxbury as early streetcar suburbs of Boston has been detailed by Sam Bass Warner.[8]

New housing developments on the edges of the cities, such as Hyde Park and Kenwood in Chicago, began as separate legal areas but were later annexed to the central city. Before the twentieth century, areas on the periphery of central cities often fought to get into the central city rather than stay out of it. Suburbs sought to be annexed by the city in order to benefit from its superior fire protection, schools, and roads; gain access to its water supply; and pay its lower taxes.

By the turn of the century the pattern had generally reversed: suburbs increasingly actively sought "home rule" and opposed annexation. In the twenty-five metropolitan districts defined by the census of 1910, the pattern

---

[7]North Chicago: Its Advantages, Resources, and Probable Future," reprinted in Charles N. Glaab, *The American City,* Dorsey, Homewood, Ill., 1963, pp. 233–234.
[8]Sam B. Warner, Jr., *Streetcar Suburbs,* Harvard and M.I.T. Presses, Cambridge, Mass., 1962.

for the future was emerging. A full quarter of the metropolitan population already lived outside the core city. In some cases, the desire for suburban autonomy was directly linked to the desire to remain free of the graft, corruption, and the control by ethics of the central city. The desire to keep control over land use and particularly taxes was also important, as was influence over the local schools. The fragmentation of governmental units within the metropolitan area thus became part of the American system. Also set by the time of World War I was the pattern of ethnic working-class populations residing in the central city near employing industries, while the more affluent commuted.

Impact of the Automobile: 1920–1950

The widespread adoption of the automobile greatly accelerated the pattern of suburbanization. Car registrations, which had been 2.5 million in 1915, took a jump to 9 million in 1920, and then skyrocketed to 26.5 million in 1930. Registration is over 140 million today. The car was no longer a plaything of the rich. Henry Ford's assembly lines were doing more than producing cars; they were bringing a revolution that was changing the face of the nation. The automobile meant that previously inaccessible land was open for suburban

A turn-of-the-century New York holiday group bound for Coney Island. (Culver Pictures)

development. No longer was it necessary to be located along a railroad line; commuters who were willing to pay the costs in money and time could drive their own cars to work and live where they pleased. The result was an upper-middle-class suburban housing boom.

Suburbs built during the 1920s were sharply distinguished according to income, occupation, religion, and ethnicity. Zoning laws, which had come to be widely used following the pioneering New York City Zoning Resolution of 1916, were often used by the developing suburbs to exclude inexpensive homes on small lots. Certainly the suburban homes of this era were well built.

Popular upper-middle-class suburbs of this era—the Grosse Pointes, Shaker Heights, and Winnetkas—established an image of suburbs as places of substantial single-family houses surrounded by lawns free of crabgrass, populated mainly by white Anglo-Saxon Protestants of upper-middle-class income and educational levels. Voting Republican was frequently included in this image.

These pre-World War II suburbs had the advantage of appealing to the long-standing antiurbanism of Americans—suburbs were supposedly closer to nature and thus better places to live, while at the same time close enough to the city to have all the advantages of the urban life that the suburbanite didn't really want to abandon. Many suburban houses built during this period reflect the romanticism of their owners. Styles were widely eclectic; houses half-timbered in the grand English Tudor style were built next to pillared Georgian colonial houses and Spanish-Moorish villas. To their owners, these homes were far more than mere housing; they represented the romantic idealization of an earlier nonurban era. "A man's home was his castle," where he could live, if not as a lord, at least as a latter-day country gentlemen—and all without being isolated from the advantages of twentieth-century city life such as electricity, indoor plumbing, and central heating.

To real estate developers, the adoption of automobiles was a boon for it meant that unbuilt land lying between the rail and streetcar axes was now open for residential devlopment. The mostly middle- or upper-middle-class character of this development meant that American cities were assuming a spatial configuration in which movement out was increasingly being associated with movement up. By the depression, the social distinction between cities and suburbs was set.[9]

Mass Suburbanization: 1950–1980s

The pent-up demand for housing that had been frustrated first by the depression of the 1930s and then by World War II gained momentum during the 1950s— a momentum that has carried to the present day. Some 60 percent of suburban housing units have been constructed since 1950, compared with 37 percent of city units, most of which have been public housing projects.[10] After World

---

[9]The existence of another type of suburb—the industrial suburb—was conveniently overlooked.
[10]Peter O. Muller, "The Evolution of American Suburbs: A Geographical Interpretation," *Urbanism Past and Present*, 4:8, Summer, 1977.

War II, the exodus from the city included not only the rich and well-to-do but also large numbers of middle-class families and even blue-collar families.

This was made possible by liberalized lending policies of the Federal Housing Authority (FHA) and the new Veterans Administration (VA) loans. Often no down payment was required for purchasing a new home in a suburban subdivision. The consequence, as is discussed later in this chapter, was a de facto national housing policy of subsidizing movement to suburbia.

As noted in Chapter 5, Metropolitan, Nonmetropolitan, and Sun Belt Growth, suburbanizing families were rapidly followed by retailers who discovered that retail shopping centers were more lucrative in suburban locations than in the declining central business districts. Industry was similarly leapfrogging to the suburbs in order to benefit from newer plants, increased space, lower taxes, and access to freeways.

The rapidity with which farmers' fields were converted to single-family housing developments is well known. Using mass production techniques, builders of tract developments of the Levittown type transformed huge areas of rural land into instant suburbia. Homes in the original Levittown on Long Island, New York, cost $6,900 in 1948, which even then was a real bargain. Levitt adopted assembly line techniques to mass produce houses. One of the largest of the mass-produced developments, Lakewood Village, south of Los Angeles, housed over 100,000 persons in 16 square miles. Most developments were, of course, far smaller.

The esthetic vapidness of many of these tracts of "little boxes" has been justly condemned. On the other hand, it should be kept in mind that the city neighborhoods from which many middle-class and lower-middle-class people migrated were far from being architectural gems and that look-alike uniformity was not a suburban invention.

The titles of many suburban subdevelopments built after World War II—Rolling Meadows, Apple Orchard Valley, Oak Forest Estates—are really epitaphs for what was destroyed by the housing developments that carry on the names. I once lived for two years in a suburban apartment complex of several hundred units named Seven Oaks Farm. The farm had been plowed under by the housing project, and there were only three oaks—mere saplings hardly 3 feet tall. Country names are used to suggest an openness and rural nature which—if they ever existed—vanish as soon as the subdivision is built. But, of course, suburban developments called Congested Acres Estates or Flood Plains Hollow, while perhaps more accurately named, wouldn't have the same sales appeal.

CONTEMPORARY SUBURBIA

Suburbia today is remarkably diverse. Affluent commuter suburbs have been joined by working-class suburbs, suburbs of condominiums, and industrial-park suburbs. Historically, suburbs were considered "sub" because they were not economically self-supporting but rather were appendages of the central city, serving as dormitories. Suburban residents had to commute to the central city in order to earn their livelihood. That no longer holds; suburbs are increasingly becoming major centers of employment. Already a decade and a half ago in the fifteen largest metropolitan areas a full 72 percent of workers who lived in the suburbs also worked in suburban areas. This meant that only 28 percent still commuted from the suburbs to the central city. Even in the New York area, the legendary citadel of the commuter, only 22 percent of the suburban workers actually commuted into New York City. Our image of the suburbs, obviously, has not caught up with reality. Today's suburban commuter is more likely to commute to another suburb than to the central city. Two-thirds (68 percent) of all suburbanites who work now work in the suburbs.

There are now more large corporate headquarters in areas surrounding New York City than in the city itself. In terms of number of "*Fortune* 500" corporations, Fairfield County, Connecticut, alone is second nationally only to New York City itself. As a result of suburban employment opportunities, reverse commuting is becoming more common. One may now live in Dallas, Los Angeles, New York, or Chicago while working beyond the city limits. Moreover, suburbs are increasing their lead as places of employment. Between 1970 and 1980 central cities lost 5 percent of their employed blue-collar workers, while suburbs gained 20 percent. Cities gained 18 percent in jobs for service and white-collar workers, but this was considerably outdistanced by the suburban gain of 53 percent.[11]

Although figures such as these don't necessarily signal the "death of the city," they definitely do indicate the increasingly diversified notion of suburbia. The image of the suburb as an exclusive area of single-family homes has to undergo revision. Even putting aside the questions of commercial and industrial construction and examining only residential building, it is clear that suburbs are building up as well as out. High-rises and apartment units—whether rental or condominiums—for young singles and the elderly have become increasingly commonplace. Suburban apartment complexes are now accepted as a part of suburbia.

CAUSES OF SUBURBANIZATION

The "cause" of expansion of the suburbs is frequently equated in the popular press with the decline of cities. Elements in this decline are claimed to be the deterioration of central-city services, poorer-quality schools, higher crime rates, and, of course, the influx of minorities, especially blacks, into city neighborhoods. Whatever the force of such factors today—and they tend to be overrated—it is clear that they are inadequate to explain the massive suburbanization that occurred before the 1960s, when these explanations first became fashionable. Suburban growth represents more a movement *toward* values associated with suburbanization—privacy, space, cleanliness, and other

[11]*New York Times*, February 27, 1983, p. 28.

amenities—than a movement *from* perceived central urban ills.[12] The massive postwar suburban exodus has more to do with government subsidies for suburban housing and postwar fertility than with a simple "flight" from the city.

Five factors largely account for the postwar suburban boom. First, in the eastern and northern sections of the country, all of almost all the land within the legal boundaries of the city had already been developed by the 1950s. Without annexation, additional growth of the urban area would, by definition, *have* to be suburban growth. The depression years of the 1930s saw little building, and during the 1940s there was a war. Thus by the 1950s there was a tremendous pent-up demand for new metropolitan housing, and the available open land was, by definition, suburban.

Second, government policies—whether by intent or not—acted to directly subsidize suburban growth. After World War II, programs of the FHA and the VA provided government-guaranteed housing loans for new homes in the suburbs. Young veterans could purchase a suburban home with nothing or perhaps $500 down and with interest rates below those for conventional mortgages. As a consequence, young families moved to suburbs not just for "togetherness" or safety, but because houses in suburban subdevelopments were frequently cheaper than housing in the city. FHA and VA mortgages with low down payments could be obtained easily on new suburban homes; to buy older homes in the city required larger down payments. To new families just becoming economically established, this was a major consideration. (The FHA program is discussed in some detail in Chapter 11, Housing Programs and Urban Changes.) The new federally financed expressways also encouraged out-movement.

Third, overall suburban costs were initially lower than costs in central cities. Suburban developers often did not include "extras" such as sewers, sidewalks, street lighting, parks, and, of course, schools. Thus, in the early years at least, taxes in the suburbs were generally lower than in the central city. The initial costs of housing were frequently lower and easier to finance in the newer "package" suburbs than in the central city.

Fourth, prosperity and the return of veterans created a "marriage boom" that was quickly followed by a "baby boom." In the decade after the war, some 10 million new households were created. Housing in cities was simply not adequate to absorb large numbers of additional families and children. New city housing had not been built since before the war, existing housing was badly overcrowded, and landlords were not inclined to be tolerant of young children. Young couples with children were, to a degree, forced toward the suburbs, since they were not welcome as renters in city apartments and could not afford to purchase city houses. The suburban "baby boom" children (born between 1947 and 1959, the "baby boom" years) created a need for new and larger houses—a need that suburban developers delighted to fill.

[12]Amos H. Hawley and Basil Zimmer, *The Metropolitan Community: Its People and Government,* Sage Publications, Beverly Hills, Calif., 1970, pp, 31–33.

The Rancher in Levittown
$59 A MONTH
No Down Payment for Veterans!

▶ The famous Rancher of Levittown is now being built in two more sections of Levittown. When these are sold there will be no more Ranchers; we haven't any more room for them.

▶ It's a beauty of a house that's priced unbelievably low at $8990. Carrying charges are only $59 monthly, and veterans need absolutely no down payment. Non-veterans need only a total of $450 down. Can you think of anything much easier than that?

▶ The house at $8990 comes with two bedrooms, but you can have a third bedroom for only $250 more. If you're a veteran you still don't need any money down, and a non-veteran needs only $100 more. We think that's a bargain, don't you?

▶ Of course, you're not buying just a house. You own the ground—60 x 100—beautifully landscaped. You have ac-cess to the community-owned swimming pools, recreational areas, etc.

▶ Your house itself is charming, cheerful, and convenient. Such things as a four-foot medicine chest completely mirrored, picture windows from floor to ceiling, an outside garden storage room, a Bendix washer, an oil-fired radiant heating system, complete rock-wool insulation—all add to your comfort and enjoyment.

▶ Get your application in as soon as possible. Occupancy may be any time from January thru May. You pick the month. You'll need a good-faith deposit of $100, but you'll get it back at settlement if you're a veteran; credited against your down payment if you're a non-veteran.

▶ O, yes, we almost forgot! Total settlement charges are just $10! See you soon, folks!

Furnished Exhibit Homes open every day until 9 P. M.

TO LEVITTOWN
By car from Philadelphia: Drive out Roosevelt Boulevard continuing on Route 1 for about 5 miles. Turn right at Levittown sign to Route 13. Turn left on Route 13 about 4 miles to the Exhibit Center.
By bus from Philadelphia: Take Levittown Express Bus at Bridge Street station of Elevated direct to Exhibit Center.
By car from Camden: Drive out Route 130 - Burlington Pike - to Burlington. Turn left and cross bridge to Bristol. Turn right on Route 13 four miles to Exhibit Center.
By car from Trenton: Cross the bridge into Pennsylvania, turn left to Route 13 - Bristol Pike. Continue on Route 13 four miles past Morrisville.

Levitt and Sons
INCORPORATED
U. S. ROUTE 13 • LEVITTOWN, PA. • Telephone WINDSOR 6-1100

·virt F P 11-9-54

Philadelphia Inquirer—November 14, 1954	Camden Courier-Post—November 12, 1954
Philadelphia Bulletin—November 12, 1954	Trenton Times—November 12, 1954

Note the no money down and small monthly payments in this 1954 Levittown, New Jersey advertisement. (Levitt Homes)

Finally, survey data show decisively that most Americans prefer the type of newer single-family house on its own lot that is most commonly found in the suburbs. Planners and architects may feel that such housing defiles the landscape, but despite such views, most people overwhelmingly prefer suburban sprawl to high-rise luxury apartments or even townhouses. This is true even of those without children. Given a choice, North Americans would rather live in single-family housing outside the city. Most families residing in apartment buildings view their tenancy as a temporary step before moving to a single-family house.[13]

Among other things, this means that people are getting pretty much what they want in housing design. Suburban tract developments succeed while urban developments seek tenants because even when alternatives are open, most people prefer suburban locations. The fact that many professional urbanologists and architects deplore the "little boxes all in a row" has had little impact on the mass of the population. Residents perceive individuality and differences even in large subdevelopments.[14]

The distinction between city and suburbs is, of course, basically legal rather than sociological. While local municipal boundaries are significant in many ways—including financing, taxing, and provision of public services and schools—other social, organizational, ecological, and demographic criteria could be used, such as population density, the proportion of single-family dwellings, and distance from the center of the city. However, none of these alternative schemes have gained anywhere near the acceptance of the traditional city-suburb division. The city line is commonly viewed as a social, economic, and racial boundary.

CATEGORIES OF SUBURBS

Suburbs can be differentiated in many ways: old versus new, rich versus poor, incorporated versus unincorporated, ethnic versus WASP (white Anglo-Saxon Protestant), growing versus stagnant. Suburban settlements are so diverse that no single typology can adequately encompass them all.

Suburbs also differ systematically with regard to housing characteristics. Residential suburbs have the highest proportion of new housing, the highest percentage of owner-occupied units, and the highest percentage of single-family units; the employment suburbs are lowest on these measures.

Probably the most useful typology is the distinction between those suburbs which function essentially as dormitories—"residential" suburbs—and those which are basically manufacturing or industrial areas—"employment" suburbs. A third type—which combines characteristics of the other two—can also be delineated. Leo Schnore has empirically demonstrated the differences among

[13]William Michelson, *Environmental Choice, Human Behavior, and Residential Satisfaction*, Oxford University Press, New York, 1977.
[14]Herbert J. Gans, *The Levittowners*, Vintage Books, New York, 1967.

these types of suburbs in terms of their social and economic characteristics.[15] Schnore used one sample of 74 suburbs surrounding New York City and a second sample of 300 suburbs found within the nation's twenty-five largest urbanized areas. He discovered that there were systematic differences in age and ethnic composition, fertility and dependency, socioeconomic status, population growth, and housing characteristics in residential, mixed, and employing suburbs. Employing suburbs contain higher proportions of both foreign-born inhabitants and nonwhites than residential suburbs, with "mixed" suburbs in the middle.

Socioeconomic status was highest in the residential suburb, as were the percentage having completed high school, the percentage employed in white-collar occupations, and at the median income level. The intermediate type of suburb was in the middle. Residential suburbs were also likely to outstrip the industrial suburbs in growth. Older residential suburbs as of the 1980s are also losing population as birthrates and family size declines.

Robert Lineberry suggests that suburbs be distinguished on the basis of life-style, separately from legal definition as a suburb.[16] Old industrial suburbs, all-black suburbs, and ethnic suburbs, for example, don't fit the conventional image of suburban life-style, yet they are legally suburbs. On the other hand, a place such as River Oaks, inside Houston, is very suburban in life-style, but is legally within the city.

The pollster Louis Harris, using the criteria of income level and rate of growth, classified suburbs into four categories:

1. *Affluent bedroom:* Affluent bedroom communities—e.g., New Canaan, Connecticut; Leawood, Kansas; and Sausalito, California—come closest to the traditional stereotype of suburbia. They rank at the top in income, home ownership, and proportion of professionals and managers.
2. *Affluent settled:* Affluent settled communities—e.g., Oak Park, Illinois; Fairfield, Connecticut; and Arlington, Virginia—today may even be losing population. Since this land is developed, there cannot be a building boom as in more distant suburbs with vacant land. Declining birthrates, plus a pattern of young adults and the elderly living in separate households, also result in fewer people living in each household. Affluent settled communities are more self-sufficient and less likely to be dormitories than are affluent bedroom suburbs.
3. *Low-income growing:* Low-income growing communities are often the home of upwardly mobile blue-collar workers. These communities—e.g., El Monte, California; Sylvania, Ohio; and Millerica, Massachusetts—are far less likely to resemble stereotypical suburbia.
4. *Low-income stagnant:* Low-income stagnant suburbs—e.g., East Orange,

[15]Leo F. Schnore, "The Social and Economic Characteristics of American Suburbs," *Sociological Quarterly,* **4**:122–134, 1963.
[16]Robert L. Lineberry, "Suburbia and Metropolitan Turf," *The Annals of the American Academy of Political Reports,* **442**:1–9, November, 1975.

New Jersey; McKeesport, Pennsylvania; and Joliet, Illinois—are suburban in name but not in life-style. Such places resemble satellite cities, and in fact are likely to have the full range of problems associated with central cities.[17]

Suburban growth, then, is not as chaotic as it might seem. Typologies such as Harris's indicate that while suburbs may vary in many respects, there is a predictable pattern to the variation. There are persistent systematic differences which contribute to predicting the evolutionary development of suburban areas.

Persistence of Characteristics?

Since the 1920s most neighborhoods within central cities have undergone profound changes in terms of the characteristics of the residents and often even the physical structures. A one-time prosperous neighborhood may have declined and then been razed and rebuilt as an upper-income area or perhaps as public housing. Yet research done by Reynolds Farley and by Avery Guest indicates that there is considerable persistence in characteristics over time in the suburbs.[18] Farley's research on 137 suburbs of twenty-four central cities suggests that although we tend to see the suburbs as experiencing a rapid rate of change, there is considerable consistency at least among older established suburbs. The socioeconomic status of individual suburbs was generally the same as it had been twenty or forty years earlier. In fact, a sound prediction of the educational level of a suburb can be made if one knows the school-attendance rate of the high-school-age population of forty years earlier. Guest's later research indicates that suburban persistence was most pronounced in the more recent 1950–1970 period. Population growth of high-status suburbs enhanced their high position.

Individual suburbs thus were said to have changed far less than the central cities. For example, Wilmette, north of Chicago, and Chevy Chase, just outside Washington, occupy positions of social status remarkably similar to the positions they occupied in 1920. Farley suggests that suburban persistency may result because a suburb originally establishes a distinct composition, so that the people who tend to move to it have socioeconomic characteristics similar to those of people already there.

This view of suburban persistence has been challenged by research by Choldin, Hanson, and Bohrer, who found that suburbs do have a neighborhood life cycle, generally moving downward in status over time.[19] Logan and Schneider, on the other hand, found that suburban employment improved the relative income level of poorer suburbs, and that there were wide regional

[17]Louis Harris, as described in *Time*, March 15, 1971, p. 15.
[18]Reynolds Farley, "Suburban Persistence," *American Sociological Review* 29:38–47, 1964; and Avery M. Guest, "Suburban Social Status: Persistence or Evolution," *American Sociological Review* 43:251–264, 1978.
[19]Harvey Choldin, Claudine Hanson, and Robert Bohrer, "Suburban Status Instability," *American Sociological Review*, 45:972–983, 1980.

variations in suburban persistence.[20] For the moment, the question of whether suburbs persist in characteristics over considerable time remains a point of dispute.

It does, however, appear that wealthy suburbs are relatively immune to downward changes in status. Such suburbs are able to employ their considerable resources as well as zoning regulations—such as a minimum lot size—to restrict the nonwealthy. Such suburbs are also able to employ their social prestige of being exclusive areas to attract prestigious residents. Thus, an elite suburb such as Lake Forest, north of Chicago, has maintained its position for a century.

SUBURBANITES

It has become an article of popular faith that cities house the poor, the elderly, minorities, and the dispossessed while suburbia is the home of the affluent middle-class, families and, of course, whites.

Physically, the central city—again according to the popular wisdom—is in a state of deterioration, barely able to stave off economic catastrophe. Suburbs, on the contrary, are said to be experiencing growth, rapid appreciation of real estate values, and an expanding tax base.

Who, then, are the suburbanites, and does the popular image of suburbanites as white, middle-class home owners with children fit the facts? To a degree it does. In terms of income the 1980 census gave a median (half above–half below) suburban household figure of $20,158, while the central-city median was $14,967. Looked at another way, roughly one out of every three city households was below the poverty level income of $10,000, compared with one in five for the suburbs. For incomes $25,000 to $50,000 the figures were reversed: one in three in the suburbs, one in five in the city. In newer and younger sun belt cities city-suburban differences were less, while in older frost belt cities they were greater. New York's median income, for example, was almost $10,000 below its suburbs.[21]

In 1970 there was a difference in household size between cities (2.99 persons) and suburbs (3.36 persons), but by 1980 the size of both had declined to 2.90 in suburbs and 2.66 in cities. More people live alone in the city. One-person households made up 35 percent of city households but 23 percent of suburban households. Over the decade suburbs showed a sharp drop in the number of children. As the "baby boom" generation grew up and left home, the number of children 17 and under declined 5 percent. This was in spite of total suburban population growth of 18 million. In cities the higher birthrate of urban black and Hispanic populations kept the number of city children from declining as rapidly.

---

[20]John R. Logan and Mark Schneider, "Stratification of Metropolitan Suburbs, 1960–1970," *American Sociological Review,* **46**:175–186, 1981.
[21]*New York Times,* February 27, 1983, p. 28.

The big difference, however, was not in the numbers of suburban and city children, but in the fact that suburban children were much more likely to live in two-parent families. Twice as many city children (27 percent) as suburban children (14 percent) live in families headed by an unmarried, divorced, or widowed mother. This is in large part the reflection of the racial composition of cities since almost half (47 percent) of all central-city black families are headed by women.

Suburbanites also tend to be homeowners. Seventy-one percent of suburban housing units are owner-occupied, as compared with half (49 percent) of those in the cities. Home ownership, of course, provides greater economic security, not to mention tax benefits.

However, the most pronounced difference between cities and suburbs is their racial composition. In spite of considerable black suburbanization during the 1970–1980 census period, the percentage of blacks in suburbs was only 6.1. This is half of what would be expected given random distribution. (Black suburbanization trends are discussed later in this chapter.)

THE MYTH OF SUBURBIA

Over the years the suburbs have become more than mere places of residence. Suburbia has become endowed with a long list of physical and even psychological attributes: ranch-style houses, neat lawns, station wagons and car pools, uptight parents, and togetherness. It is the place where one supposedly finds

> . . . a home of one's own, a small piece of real estate on which to practice yeoman's skills, good schools, plenty of land for recreation, clean and traffic free neighborhoods, a small town atmosphere, Christmas lights, a Fourth of July parade, a homogeneous community without social tensions. . . .[22]

This caricature has been called by some sociologists the "myth of suburbia," the myth being the belief that there is, in fact, a uniquely suburban way of life.[23] According to the myth of suburbia, people living in suburbs are, or become, somehow different from those who remain in the city. They are supposedly middle- and upper-class nonethnic whites who have fled the central city. Stereotypes of suburbia are frequently less than complimentary. The suburban way of life is one of wide lawns and narrow minds in which family life is child-oriented rather than adult-oriented. Critics described the suburban family as surrendering all individuality and creativity.[24] The late Margaret Mead characterized suburban life as consisting of "a living room or recreation

[22]Robert Lineberry and Ira Sharkansky, *Urban Politics and Public Policy,* Harper and Row, New York, 1971, p. 34.
[23]Bennet M. Berger, "The Myth of Suburbia," *Journal of Social Issues,* **17**:38–49, 1971; Herbert J. Gans, "Urbanism and Suburbanism as Ways of Life: A Re-Evaluation of Definitions," in Arnold Rose (ed.), *Human Behavior,* Houghton Mifflin, Boston, 1962.
[24]David Riesman, "The Suburban Sadness: in Wm. Dobriner (ed.), *The Suburban Community,* G. P. Putnam's Sons, New York, 1958, pp. 375–408.

room which often resembles a giant playpen into which the parents have somewhat reluctantly climbed.''

In terms of life-style, suburbanites—particularly those in the newer suburbs—are said to be gregarious. Numerous cocktail parties are interspersed with extensive informal visiting or neighboring. Togetherness is a way of life. Organizationally, suburbanites are said to be hyperactive joiners, with hobby groups, bridge clubs, neighborhood associations, and church-related social activities taking several nights a week. On top of this, there is a proliferation of women's groups, scout troops, and kaffeeklatsches. Husbands are said to spend their weekends cutting grass, watching football games, picking up the kids, going to parties, going to church, and watching more football games.

Suburbanites are also charged with being highly status-conscious. Even the home is said to be a status symbol rather than a place to relax—as much a showcase for family goods as a place to unwind.

While the "myth of suburbia" is something of a straw man, it is unfortunately true that suburbs have not received enough study. For all the talk, the study of suburbs has not been a popular topic during the last decade. During the 1960s, "urban research" came to mean the study of inner-city poverty or minority groups. The vacuum left by the absence of hard research on suburban life-styles was filled with a plethora of popular books and articles dealing with suburban conformity, adultery, alcoholism, divorce, and plain boredom. Even the best of the popular writing on suburban life (e.g., *Bullet Park* and *The Man in the Grey Flannel Suit*) painted a highly selective, if not downright inaccurate, picture. The best known of the early works was William H. Whyte's influential book, *The Organization Man*.[25] Unfortunately, many of his imitators were not as careful.

Three problems with the early suburban studies can be cited. First, the problem with most of the postwar suburban studies was not so much that they were inaccurate but that they were selective of one type of suburb. Attention was focused on the large tract developments for young families, while little attention was given to industrial suburbs, working-class suburbs, or even older established suburbs. The end result was that the image of suburbia was loaded by emphasizing middle-class tract suburbs with their culture of backyard barbecues, picture windows, and station wagons. Generalizing from these studies, which presented a loaded sample, to all suburbanites is not scientifically valid, but it was nonetheless done by many writers of the period. Some of the studies are also an example of the ecological fallacy of generalizing from characteristics of an area to characteristics of individuals.

Second, it is possible that some of the communities chosen for study were selected precisely because they were in some respects atypical and thus presumably more interesting. Third, many of the observations were based on a single look at a suburb immediately after the first wave of settlement. It is

---

[25]William H. Whyte, *The Organization Man*, Doubleday (Anchor), Garden City, New York, 1956.

highly likely that another look five or ten years later, after the community had "matured," would show changes in the pace of life.[26]

Differences—Real or Not?

Do suburbanites differ from city dwellers in their behavior and attitudes? The overall answer appears to be no. Differences that do emerge tend to be minor, with high social-class level appearing to be more important than suburban location per se.[27] Suburbanization does not, for example, promote "hypersociability," or mass joining of organizations, as suggested by the myth of suburbia.[28] Suburbanization is usually associated with greater involvement with neighbors, although there is no agreement among researchers on why this is so.[29] Perhaps it is simply a reflection of the fact that greater congeniality is likely in an area where people have similar incomes, education, and occupational backgrounds.

Research done by Scott Greer on the metropolitan St. Louis area suggests that suburbs do foster somewhat greater political participation:

> In general, it seemed that the familistic neighborhoods, with their dense networks of neighboring and voluntary organizations, did produce more involvement and informed political action. However, the size of the municipality made a difference: the kind of people who were local political actors in the suburbs were much less likely to be so in the City of St. Louis. So, organizational type of neighborhood and political unit had independent effects. In general, the type of sub-area (urbanism-familism) predicted the proportion of local actors, but their *political* activity was affected by the organization of the polity.[30]

It has also been suggested that persons who opt to live in a suburban setting have deliberately chosen a life-style that emphasizes "familism" and deemphasizes alternative life-styles such as "careerism" and "consumership."[31] Data supporting this view, however, are lacking. If it were the case, it would mean that suburbanites put family values above achievement in their careers and the accumulation of consumer goods. David Riesman, for instance, has suggested that suburbanism is a form of escapism whereby men devote their time to family roles when they could be—and should be—participating in the public affairs of the city.[32] Riesman's emphasis on the role of men as achievers, by the way, was obviously the product of an era when attention had not yet been given to the value of women as leaders in public life. He also shows an antifamily bias, suggesting family matters are less important.

---

[26]On this point, see S. D. Clark, *The Suburban Society*, University of Toronto Press, Toronto, 1966.

[27]Claude S.Fischer and Robert Max Jackson, "Suburbs, Networks and Attitudes," in Barry Schwartz, *The Changing Face of the Suburbs*, University of Chicago Press, Chicago, 1976, pp. 279–307.

[28]S. Donaldson, *The Suburban Myth*, Columbia University Press, New York, 1969.

[29]Fischer and Jackson, op. cit.

[30]Scott Greer, *The Urbane View*, Oxford University Press, New York, 1972, p. 97.

[31]Wendell Bell, "The City, the Suburb, and a Theory of Social Choice," in Scott Greer, Dennis L. McElrath, David W. Minar, and Peter Orleans (eds.), *The New Urbanization*, St. Martin's Press, New York, 1968, pp. 132–168.

[32]David Riesman, op. cit., pp. 375–408.

A typical suburban scene, in this case a Raleigh, North Carolina suburb. (© Michal Heron 1983/Woodfin Camp & Assoc.)

The belief that suburbanites have different personalities or are more prone to depression than city dwellers is not supported by research. Those who live in suburbs have minor differences in tastes, e.g., preferring gardening over cultural affairs.[33] There is no evidence, however, that suburbanites as individuals make less use of city museums, art galleries, theaters, and concerts than city residents. In many cities suburbanites provide the major support for cultural activities. Thanks to expressways, suburbanites can reach downtown facilities and events such as concerts and plays in little more time than a city resident living in one of the outer neighborhoods. Suburbs also frequently have their own community playhouses, theater groups, and festivals, which indicate interest in the arts. Popular culture (dinner theaters and first-run movies) are increasingly located *outside* the central city. New sports stadiums are more often than not built outside the central city. New York's football Giants and basketball Nets actually have their stadiums in Meadowlands, New Jersey.

Some suburbs are indeed cultural wastelands, but so again are many city neighborhoods. Manhattan may be the center of the nation's theater, ballet, and opera, but only little of it seems to have rubbed off on the Bronx or Queens. Many suburbanites do not make use of the central city's cultural facilities, but

[33]Joseph Zelan, "Does Suburbia Make a Difference?" in Sylvia Fleis Fava (ed.), *Urbanism in World Perspective*, Thomas Crowell, New York, 1968, pp. 401–408.

there is no evidence to suggest that they supported or attended cultural activities even when they were city residents. It remains to be proven that suburbanites differ from city dwellers of similar socioeconomic status in their interest in, and support of, cultural activities.

Also, it should be recalled that middle-class city residents in outlying city neighborhoods lead lives essentially similar to those of suburbanites. Commenting on his study of Levittown (discussed presently), Gans states:

> The findings or changes and their sources suggest that the distinction between urban and suburban ways of living postulated by the critics (and by some sociologists as well) is more imaginary than real. Few changes can be traced to the suburban qualities of Levittown, and the source that did cause change, like the house, the population mix, and newness, are not distinctively suburban. Moreover, when one looks at similar populations in city and suburb, their ways of life are remarkably alike. . . .[34]

Less Affluent Suburbs

In predominately blue-collar suburbs the supposed suburban "involvement syndrome" may not occur at all. Bennett Berger looked at the working-class suburb of Milpitas, California, into which many automobile workers moved when the Ford Motor Company closed its plant in Richmond, California.[35] Two and a half years after the move, 70 percent did not belong to a single club, organization, or association other than their union. Visiting was rare unless relatives lived nearby. There had been none of the supposed suburban "return to religion"; half went to church rarely or not at all. Nor had the move to the suburbs affected their political affiliations; they still voted 81 percent Democratic. Finally, they had no expectations or illusions regarding their social mobility; they had no great hopes of getting ahead in their jobs. They overwhelmingly viewed the suburb not as a transitional stop on the career ladder but rather as a permanent place of settlement. The move from the city to the suburb did not affect the life-style of these workers. Although it definitely improved the quality of their homes, it did not change their behavior patterns. No magical transformation in social customs took place. Working-place norms, attitudes, and behavior persisted with little modification.

Differences between blue-collar urbanites and blue-collar suburbanites were explored further in a study of approximately 2,600 male family heads living in the San Francisco Bay area. The researchers found no significant differences between urban and suburban blue-collar workers in areas such as self-concept, concern over status, familial loyalty, and sex norms.[36] Furthermore, there do not appear to be any changes in involvement with unions,

[34]Gans, *The Levittowners,* p. 288.
[35]Bennett M. Berger, *Working Class Suburbs,* University of California Press, Berkeley, 1960.
[36]Albert Cohen and Harold M. Hodges, Jr., "Characteristics of the Lower Blue-Collar Class," *Social Problems,* **10:**307, Spring, 1963.

according to a study of forty-six urban and suburban dwellers in New Jersey.[37] There were some differences, but these were not great or systematic.

CASE STUDY: LEVITTOWN

Probably the most thorough case study of a suburban community is Herbert Gans's study of the social organization of Levittown, New Jersey, during the first two years of its existence.[38] The various Levittowns were prototypes of the postwar "package suburbs" that can now be found near all of the country's larger cities. Levitt and Sons, Inc., originally built for a lower-middle-class market, but over the years the size of their houses and their prices have increased considerably. The New Jersey Levittown later changed its name to Willingboro to escape the Levittown stereotype.

Gans's findings were based on interviews with two sets of Levittowners and on his own observations, made while he lived in Levittown for two years. Gans suggests that the sociability found within the community is a direct result of the compatibility or homogeneity of the backgrounds of the residents. Homogeneity was most evident in terms of age and income. But diversity in regional backgrounds, membership in ethnic groups, and religious beliefs provided variety for the community. Even the similarity in income did not indicate as much homogeneity as the statistics indicated, for one family might be headed by a skilled worker at the peak of earning power, another by a white-collar worker with some hope of advancement, and a third by a young executive or professional just at the start of a career. Active sociability emerged only when neighboring residents shared common tastes and values, were similar with regard to race and class, and shared similar beliefs regarding child-raising practices.[39] Family togetherness was seen by the residents as a positive attribute of the community. Parents and children all felt that they spent more time together as a family. Even commuting did not have the often-alleged negative effect on family activities. Most Levittowners did not really mind commuting unless it involved a trip of over forty minutes.

Gans's research indicated that residents of the mass look-alike suburb were generally content with their housing, life-style, and general environment. Although the popular literature is rather heavy with criticism of suburban anomie (normlessness) and malaise, boredom was not a serious problem in Levittown. Depression and loneliness appeared if anything to be less common than in the city. Almost all the emotional difficulties were concentrated among working-class women who were for the first time cut off from their parents, and wives with husbands whose jobs kept them on the road and away from the family. Those most likely to find the community lacking were upper-middle-class people who had tried Levittown's organizational life and found it wanting.

---

[37]William Spinrad, "Blue-Collar Workers as City and Suburban Residents—Effect of Union Membership," in A. Shostak and W. Gomberg (eds.), *Blue-Collar World,* Prentice-Hall, Englewood Cliffs, N.J., 1964, pp. 215–224.
[38]Gans, *The Levittowners,* Vintage Books, New York, 1967.
[39]Ibid.

Adolescents also had a hard time. The community was particularly deadly for teenagers owing to the lack of recreational facilities and even places to go. It was designed for families with young children, not adolescents. Thus, bedrooms were small and lacked the privacy or soundproofing necessary to allow teenagers to have their friends visit. Shopping centers were designed for adults who owned cars, and discouraged adolescents who hung around and made only marginal purchases. Even the high school discouraged its students from using its facilities after school hours because of the school administrator's fear of increasing maintenance costs.

Overall, Gans's description of Levittown shows a community that was not overly exciting but that generally met the needs of its residents. The worst thing that can be said about the community is that for anyone with cosmopolitan tastes, it is rather dull. But then, Levittowns weren't built for cosmopolites.

More recently Popenoe, examing another Levittown across the Delaware River from Philadelphia, came to similar conclusions.[40] Residents spend their leisure time in locally based informal activities with friends and in watching television, rarely going into downtown Philadelphia. Life is comfortable, family-based, and not overly exciting. As in Gans's study, Popenoe suggests that teenagers found the residential environment most wanting. While Levittown does have recreational facilities such as pools and parks, it, like many similar suburbs in the United States, has few places just to hang out and see and be seen.

SUBURBAN WOMEN

Life in package suburbs can also pose problems for mothers tied to the home caring for young children. This is particularly true for college-educated women, who may want more variety and stimulation than the community can provide. On the other hand, the contemporary suburban woman, whether she works outside the home or not, is not anywhere near as physically isolated as suggested by some writers of the 1960s. Today, two- and even three-car families are the norm.

Those suburban women whose life-style and problems deserve far more attention than they have received are women who head their households. What happens to a woman's life after divorce? Are female householders in suburbs such as Levittown particularly subject to problems of isolation and economics? Do female heads of households remain in such family-oriented suburbs or do they sell their homes and relocate elsewhere? Impressionistic information would suggest that places such as Levittown are not ideal for unmarried women, but studies of the type provided by Gans and Popenoe remain to be published.

---

[40]David Popenoe, *The Suburban Environment: Sweden and the U.S.,* University of Chicago, Chicago, 1977.

EXURBANITES

Beyond the built-up suburbs surrounding the very largest cities there is a special class of suburbanites who have become known as "exurbanites." These are the people who have achieved success in their professions— frequently the communications industry, advertising, and publishing—and have moved farther out. Their work may allow them to use their own offices at home several days a week and avoid daily commuting. Thus, if their base is New York, they can live as far out as Fairfield County, Connecticut, Bucks County, Pennsylvania, and Marin County, California.

Unfortunately, the best-known study of exurbia, *The Exurbanites,* is a caricature of hyperactive, upwardly mobile, creative people all living in their trilevel houses.[41] The picture is of people desperately trying to find meaning in their lives, people who find that moving out of the city doesn't reduce the anxiety of working in extremely competitive industries where the standards for judging performance are highly subjective and fickle. Since living in the country is a strain on the budget, there is also often the pressure of having to maintain a standard of living that one can't afford. Living in exurbia supposedly also puts considerable pressures on wives, who find themselves locked into a schedule of maintaining a house and providing a station-wagon shuttle service for children and commuting husbands while they attempt to maintain their own careers and interests.

This general outline has, of course, served as the framework for dozens of novels, television dramas, and movies. Unfortunately, it is sometimes taken to be a scientifically valid reflection of reality, rather than inventive fiction. Although research is scarce, there does not appear to be evidence that exurbanites are significantly different from affluent suburbanites. In fact, exurbs have a way of turning into suburbs as more and more people with the same backround move into the same area—all seeking to get away from it all.

BLACK SUBURBANIZATION

Suburbs after World War II lost some of their social class exclusiveness, but not their racial exclusiveness. Blacks in suburbs were noticeable by their absence. The general conclusion of researchers was that black suburbanization was increasing, but only marginally.[42] Census figures for 1960 indicated that suburbs were 4.7 percent black; for 1970 the rate was 4.8 percent. This reflected a long-standing pattern of blacks increasing as a proportion of central-city residents, while whites suburbanized.

[41]A. C. Spectorsky, *The Exurbanites,* Berkeley, New York, 1958.

[42]George Sternlieb and Robert W. Lake, "Aging Suburbs and Black Home-Ownership," *The Annals of the American Academy of Political and Social Science,* **422:**105–117, 1975; Karl E. Taeuber, "Racial Segregation: The Persisting Dilemma," *The Annals of the American Academy of Political and Social Science,* **422:**87–96, 1975; and Leo F. Schnore, Carolyn D. Andre, and Harry Sharp, "Black Suburbanization 1930–1970," in Schwartz, op. cit., pp. 69–94.

Middle-class blacks are suburbanizing in increasing numbers.
(Karin Rosenthal/Stock, Boston)

Changes

Substantial black suburbanization has changed the pattern. For the first time in decades the proportion of blacks living in the central city is declining, and black suburbanization is on the increase.[43] Using the 1970 metropolitan area boundaries, between 1970 and 1982 the black suburban population grew by 2.3 million. Suburban blacks now represent one-fifth (21 percent) of the nation's black population. Blacks, who represent 12 percent of the national population, now represent 6.1 percent of all suburbanites. While the white population is increasingly dispersing to exurbia, small towns, and even rural areas, a growing proportion of the black population is living in suburbs.

A second major transition is that a decreasing proportion of the black population is living in the central city: 55 percent as of 1982, compared with 59 percent in 1970. This transition has continued into the late 1980s. Some large cities have even begun to show declines in black population. Table 8-1 indicates that, of the fourteen cities having a black population over 200,000, four major cities—Philadelphia, Washington, D.C., Cleveland, and St. Louis—

---

[43]Larry Long and Diana DeAre, "The Suburbanization of Blacks," *American Demographics*, **3:**16–21, 44, September, 1981.

TABLE 8-1
Black Population Change in 14 Central Cities and Their Suburbs, 1960–1980

Central cities	Black population 1980	Percent change in black pop. 1960–70	Percent change in black pop. 1970–80	Percent black in central city 1960	Percent black in central city 1970	Percent black in central city 1980
New York City	1,784,000	53.3%	7.0%	14.0%	21.1%	25.2%
Chicago	1,197,000	35.7	8.6	22.9	32.7	39.8
Detroit	759,000	37.0	14.9	28.9	43.7	63.1
Philadelphia	639,000	23.5	− 2.3	26.4	33.6	37.8
Los Angeles	505,000	50.4	0.3	13.5	17.9	17.0
Washington, D.C.	448,000	30.6	− 16.6	53.9	71.1	70.3
Houston	440,000	47.2	39.1	22.9	25.7	27.6
Baltimore	431,000	29.1	2.6	34.7	46.4	54.8
New Orleans	308,000	14.5	15.3	37.2	45.0	55.3
Memphis	308,000	31.6	26.9	37.0	38.9	47.6
Atlanta	283,000	36.8	12.1	38.3	51.3	66.6
Dallas	266,000	62.7	26.3	19.0	24.9	29.4
Cleveland	251,000	14.8	− 12.7	28.6	38.3	43.8
St. Louis	206,000	18.6	− 18.8	28.6	40.9	47.4

Suburbs (1970 definition)	Black population 1980	Percent change in black pop. 1960–70	Percent change in black pop. 1970–80	Percent black in suburbs 1960	Percent black in suburbs 1970	Percent black in suburbs 1980
New York City	285,000	55.5%	31.4%	4.8%	5.9%	7.6%
Chicago	231,000	65.5	79.9	2.9	3.6	5.6
Detroit	128,000	26.1	32.5	3.7	3.6	4.5
Philadelphia	245,000	34.1	28.9	6.1	6.6	8.1
Los Angeles	398,000	105.0	65.7	3.6	6.2	9.6
Washington, D.C.	390,000	98.3	134.9	6.4	7.9	16.6
Houston	80,000	6.2	21.4	12.9	8.8	6.2
Baltimore	126,000	25.6	54.9	7.0	7.0	9.1
New Orleans	79,000	26.9	40.4	15.9	12.5	12.6
Memphis	37,000	− 34.8	− 18.4	40.2	31.7	21.0
Atlanta	179,000	23.5	222.4	8.5	6.2	14.2
Dallas	50,000	1.1	35.4	8.3	5.2	4.7
Cleveland	94,000	452.8	110.6	0.8	3.4	7.1
St. Louis	201,000	65.0	50.4	6.0	7.7	10.9

Source: Long and DeAre, "The Suburbanization of Blacks," *American Demographics*, **3**: September, 1981.

actually had declines in their number of black residents. In Washington, D.C. for example, there was a drastic reversal of the pattern of previous decades.

Blacks left Washington, D.C. during the 1970–1980 decade at twice the rate of whites. Moreover, many of the departing blacks were people in their twenties and thirties with young children.[44] However, this change was not unique to Washington. Betwen 1970 and 1980, black suburban growth exceeded white rates in all regions of the country.[45] Central cities have a higher proportion

[44]*Washington Post*, August 28, 1981, p. C1.
[45]John R. Logan and Mark Schneider, "Racial Change and Racial Segregation in American Suburbs, 1970–1980," *American Journal of Sociology*, **89**:874–888, 1984.

of blacks only because of higher black birthrates and because whites continue to leave the cities.

Who Moves Where?

The crucial questions regarding black suburbanization are: Who moves to the suburbs, and to what areas do they move? An analysis of Bureau of the Census Annual Housing Survey data by Spain and Long indicates four clear patterns.[46] First, most suburbanizing blacks are moving to predominantly white residential areas. (Among whites 99 percent of suburbanizing is done into another area that is at least 90 percent white.) Thus blacks are not simply moving into black suburbs. This is a change from the past, when black suburbanization actually was nothing more than the black ghetto flowing across city boundaries. In the past, "black only" suburbs were found surrounding the largest industrial cities.

Second, the higher the education and income of the blacks, the more likely they are to move into predominantly white neighborhoods. Third, while recent black in-movers have higher socioeconomic status than the total black suburban population, blacks are more likely to move into lower-income and less prestigious neighborhoods than are whites. Finally, both black and white suburban residents are more likely to rate predominantly white neighborhoods as excellent than they are to rate racially mixed neighborhoods as excellent. This may reflect better amenities and services available in predominantly white neighborhoods.

The data thus indicate that black suburbanization is gradually increasing. However, it is also clear that blacks have not suburbanized at the rate one would expect on the basis of economics alone. Decades of racial segregation insure that suburbs still remain white. Blacks, even after the large increases of the last decade, make up only 6 percent of the suburban population because whites have continued to flood to the suburbs. Between 1970 and 1980 alone some 11 million whites became suburban residents. As long as the white exodus to the suburbs continues, suburban areas will retain their white status, regardless of how many blacks suburbanize.

In the future, white suburbanization may be at a less hectic pace. Most upper- and middle-class whites who want to move to suburbs have already done so. Increasingly, the remaining central-city whites, whether there by choice or economics, will remain city folk.

MAINTAINING RACIAL DIVERSITY

Attempts by some suburbs to maintain racial diversity have raised a debate that will probably be settled only by the Supreme Court. The eventual outcome will have profound effects on the racial makeup of metropolitan areas for decades to come.

[46]U.S. Bureau of the Census, Dept. of Commerce, "Black Movers to the Suburbs: Are They Moving to White Neighborhoods," Special Demographic Analyses, CDS–80.4, Washington, D.C., December, 1981, p. 21.

An Example: Park Forest South

Park Forest South, a suburb carved in the early 1970s out of cornfields 30 miles south of Chicago, is a case in point. Park Forest South made every attempt to follow the spirit as well as the letter of open housing laws; as a consequence, the proportion of blacks grew rapidly while neighboring Home-wood and Flossmore remained, respectively, 1 percent and 2 percent black. Park Forest South, concerned that real estate practices were resulting in resegregation, in 1977 passed a so-called affirmative marketing ordinance to prohibit real estate solicitation that acted against attracting whites.

The real estate industry challenged this as reverse steering and argued that the village's counseling of blacks to move into white rather than already black areas was preventing blacks from living where they wanted. The ordinance was later withdrawn, but the controversy over whether communities can or should take action to remain integrated rather than turning all-black is still hotly debated. The issues are complex, with differences even among civil rights groups. The Chicago chapter of the NAACP and the Southern Christian Leadership Conference have joined with their old enemy, the real estate industry, in denouncing as racist both efforts to keep the suburb integrated by controlling realtors and attempts to attract whites. On the other hand, local open-housing groups and the national NAACP support efforts to attract whites. The director of housing programs for the national NAACP calls the efforts of Park Forest South and other integrated communities ''legitimate'' and says that it is ''tragic'' that the town rescinded its affirmative market ordinance.[47]

Further complicating the local picture was the fact that the head of the Chicago NAACP and most members of its board were also real estate brokers. Members of the board interviewed on the television show ''60 Minutes'' denied any conflict of interest, but others have noted that the black real estate firms they own profit directly from racial turnover. Still to be resolved by the Supreme Court is whether integration per se is important enough to justify attempts by communities to attract whites and discourage black resegregation. With the local and national NAACP split on the issue, it is obvious that opinion differs.

Managed Integration: Oak Park

Given the economic and social pressures, is it possible for racially integrated neighborhoods to survive? Or is integration simply the interval between the arrival of the first black family and the departure of the last white family? Racial residential turnover can occur without white flight. All that is necessary is that an area attract more black than white newcomers. To keep an area integrated, it is necessary to maintain an influx of whites.

The suburban Chicago community of Oak Park is a working example of

---

[47]Robert Reinhold, ''Nation Watching Outcome of Racial Puzzle in Illinois,'' *New York Times Service,* April 15, 1979.

how older neighborhoods can be integrated and preserved. Once the home of Frank Lloyd Wright, and with many architecturally interesting homes, Oak Park by the late 1960s was a prime candidate for disinvestment and change. It is an old suburb of 60,000 with half its population in rental units. More important, it directly abuts Chicago's lower-class West Side Ghetto. The adjacent Austin section of Chicago, a prime residential area a score of years ago, has experienced rapid deterioration. Austin is now 98 percent black.

What makes Oak Park unique is that most of its residents, instead of picking up and fleeing, decided to face integration head on. Their efforts have been so successful that Oak Park is currently a desirable housing area, particularly for young white home buyers. The reason for Oak Park's success is a tightly managed community. The community both quickly intervenes to halt building deterioration and encourages racial diversity. The community enforces housing codes, and virtually controls all the activities of realtors.

Ten percent of every apartment building's flats are inspected every year, and every apartment must be inspected and the building brought up to code before selling. A new shopping mall and village hall brighten up the community, while local lending institutions have been persuaded to keep open funds for mortgages and remodeling. Several million dollars has also gone into low-interest loans for upgrading of apartments. House-to-house solicitation by real estate companies and the posting of "For Sale" or "For Rent" signs are banned to prevent panic selling. After some pressure, all real estate companies now report all sales or rentals twice a week to the Oak Park Community Relations Department. To further discourage panic selling, the community in 1978 initiated "moral homeowners' insurance." Homeowners who sign up for the insurance and stay in the community at least five years are guaranteed that they can sell their homes for 80 percent of the difference between the appraisal value and the selling price. The major reason for the homeowners' equity insurance is psychological rather than economic. It is meant to forestall any fears of declining housing values. Actually, the program, which went into operation in 1978, has had few takers, since property values in the suburb have been appreciating.

Currently Oak Park is 12 percent minority. Emphasizing diversity, the community actively welcomes minority residents, and actively discourages all-white or all-black apartment buildings. To do this, Oak Park in 1985 began a unique plan to pay landlords to integrate their apartment buildings.[48] On a voluntary basis the landlord can enter into a five-year agreement to let the Oak Park Housing Center act as the landlord's rental agent. In return the landlord will be eligible for matching grants of up to $1,000 per unit to improve apartment interiors and larger grants for exterior renovations. The Housing Center will then actively seek black tenants for buildings that are now predominantly white, and white tenants for buildings that are now predominantly black. If a suitable tenant cannot be found immediately, the apartment

[48]"Chicago Suburb to Pay Landlords to Integrate," *New York Times,* November 11, 1984, p. 24.

The Chicago suburb of Oak Park provides an example of how older housing areas can both integrate and upgrade. (Ovie Carter, courtesy of the Oak Park Housing Center)

will stay off the market for up to ninety days, while the landlord receives 80 percent of the last rent received in the unit. The goal is to improve racial diversity and prevent resegregation while improving the basic housing stock and protecting landlords against vacant units. In spite of a small tax increase, the plan is supported by most local residents and real estate agents. It has to be kept in mind, though, that Oak Park, with its middle-class to upper-middle-class residents, is not typical of many urban areas faced with blockbusting. Nor do many communities exhibit such a strong sense of community involvement. There is no question that Oak Park manages its housing and rental market to an extent not found elsewhere. The community is integrated racially but not economically. Poor families are not desired.

Still, Oak Park's prosperity indicates that older areas—even when abutting a lower-class ghetto—can both integrate racially and upgrade physically. Outside observers are sometimes critical of the extent of housing controls in the community, but for Oak Park, managed integration works.

CHAPTER

9

ETHNIC DIVERSITY:
Ethnics, Blacks, Hispanics, Indians, and Asians

The rich man in his castle,
The poor man at his gate,
God made them, high or lowly,
And order'd their estate.

From a Church of England hymn,
"All Things Bright and Beautiful"

INTRODUCTION: URBAN MINORITIES

In this chapter attention is concentrated on ethnic and racial minorities whose futures are closely bound to the urban scene: white ethnics, black Americans, Mexican Americans, Puerto Ricans, and Native Americans. These groups differ from one another in numerous respects; what they have in common is that, compared with other Americans, they are relatively recent newcomers to the urban scene and, most important, they are to various degrees deprived minorities encountering problems of acceptance and adjustment. White ethnics, blacks, hispanics, and Native Americans have different histories and cultures, but, until very recently, all have been dismissed as unimportant or marginal to the mainsteam of urban America.

Examination of contemporary trends in urbanization reveals a strong association between ethnicity and race and the patterns of urban residential segregation, patterns that are reinforced by socioeconomic differences. In the classic North American pattern of urban settlement described in Chapter 3, The Rise of Urban America, the point of entry for poor immigrants was the tenement district surrounding the core of the city. As their economic condition improved, the more established immigrants moved outward, leaving their tenements to be occupied by a wave of more recent immigrants such as blacks and Hispanics. Americans tend to assume that this is the natural pattern of urban settlement, but it is not. For instance, in the preindustrial cities discussed in Chapter 2, Emergence of Cities, and in cities of the developing world as seen in Part 5, Worldwide Urbanization, newcomers first settle on the periphery of the urban area. Whether immigrants settle in the decaying core, as in North American cities, or on the least developed periphery, as in the third world, there is one constant: the poor live in the least desirable location.

WHITE ETHNICS

Immigration

There is a story (possibly apocryphal) that President Franklin Roosevelt enraged the Daughters of the American Revolution (DAR) during the 1930s by addressing them as "Fellow Immigrants." If so, he was only stating what is frequently forgotten. That is, all groups—including Indians—were once newcomers. The only difference is in time of arrival. Indians came perhaps 15,000 to 20,000 years ago, while Europeans first came in significant numbers less than 400 years ago. Substantial numbers of blacks have been here for three centuries, while many of the most recent arrivals have been Hispanics, many of whom are first- or second-generation newcomers. Thus, it is impossible to discuss American urban patterns and life without discussing the role played historically—and in the present day—by the newcomer to the American city.

It is a cliché to state that America is a nation of immigrants, but it is sometimes forgotten that the American immigration was the largest mass migration in the history of the world. Precise data are lacking, but some 30 to 45 million immigrants have arrived in the United States since 1820; we will never know the exact number or distribution. In some cases overworked immigration officials automatically listed all newcomers on a ship as being of the same nationality. Thus, those on a ship from Hamburg were automatically German. First-class passengers usually were not even included in the immigration figures until this century.

Generally there is a loose pattern of association between higher social status of an ethnic group and the early arrival of ancestors on these shores. (The exception is the black population, who in spite of their early arrival remained a separate caste excluded from mobility in American society.) So having colonial or Revolutionary War ancestors is considered preferable to being the son or daughter of recent immigrants. At the time of the Revolutionary War some nine-tenths of the new nation's white population traced their ancestry to the British Isles: English, Scotch, or Northern Irish (called Scotch-Irish to distinguish them from Catholic Irish).[1] Even cosmopolitan New York was dominated by English customs, laws, values, and mores. Protestantism in various forms was in effect the national religion.

The founding fathers strongly supported free and open migration. New immigrants were not welcomed, though, without reservations. George Washington's views were that

> The bosom of America is open to receive not only the Opulent and Respectable Stranger, but the oppressed and persecuted of all Nations and Religions, whom we shall welcome to participation of all our rights and privileges, if by decency and propriety of conduct they appear to merit the enjoyment.[2]

Washington was more liberal in his admission criteria than many of his contemporaries (his Federalist successor, John Adams, lengthened the waiting period for citizenship), but even Washington's statement has a final clause that says in effect, "if we think they behave themselves."

Old Immigrants

Major ethnic migrations began in the mid-1840s with the Irish fleeing the potato famine in Ireland. The famine caused over a million deaths by starvation in Ireland, and another million or so impoverished Irish peasants immigrated to America. The Irish were closely followed by the Germans, and somewhat later the Scandinavians. These groups are collectively called the "old immigrants" to distinguish them from the early settlers—overwhelmingly of British origin—who were here first.

The Germans, in spite of the fact that they played cards and insisted on drinking beer on Sunday—shocking some bluenoses—fared rather well. They

[1]David Ellis et al., *A Short History of New York State,* Cornell University Press, Ithaca, N.Y., 1957, p. 64.
[2]Quoted in the President's Commission on Immigration and Naturalization, *Who Shall We Welcome?,* U.S. Government Printing Office, Washington, D.C., 1953.

TABLE 9-1
Ancestry of U.S. Population

Reported ancestry	Percent of population*
German	28.8
Irish	24.4
English	22.3
African	9.0
Scottish	7.9
French	7.8
Spanish	7.0
Italian	6.6
American Indian	5.3
Polish	4.7
Dutch	4.5
Swedish	2.7
Norwegian	2.3
Russian	1.9
Welsh	1.4

* Groups comprising over one percent of population.
Source: Bureau of the Census, Current Population Survey of November 1979, "Ancestry and Language in the United States," Current Population Reports, Series, P-23, no. 116, Washington, D.C., March, 1982.

earned a reputation for industriousness, thrift, and orderly living—although they rioted in Chicago in 1855 when the mayor banned the sale of beer on Sunday. Easing assimilation was the fact that the majority of Germans were Protestant.

The Irish had greater problems, for not only were they viewed as recalcitrant, papist rowdies, but they voted Democratic and were the poorest of the poor. Irish, rather than slaves, were used in hard or hazardous work. As it was explained by a riverboat captain to a famous visitor, "The niggers are worth too much to be risked here; if the Paddies are knocked overboard or get their backs broke, nobody loses anything."[3] Irish labor built many of the nation's railroads, and a saying of the time was, "An Irishman is buried under every tie." Confronted by discrimination—"No Irish Need Apply" was common in help-wanted ads—the Irish organized themselves. For the immigrant Irish, the route to social mobility was said to be through becoming one of the three P's, "priest, politician, or policeman"; and by the latter part of the nineteenth century, the Irish controlled the city halls in cities where they lived in significant numbers. Stereotypes also softened as more and more of the Irish became skilled workers. By the 1880s it was a common saying that "a good worker does as much as an Irishman."[4]

[3]Frederick Law Olmstead, *The Cotton Kingdom*, Modern Library, New York, 1969, p. 215.
[4]John Higham, *Strangers in the Land*, Atheneum, New York, 1977, p. 26.

New Immigrant Groups

While the ethnic groups of the "old immigration" came from northern and western Europe, those of the "new immigration" came largely from southern and eastern Europe (Figure 9-1). After 1880, increasing numbers of immigrants had a Slavic, Polish, Jewish, Italian, or Greek heritage.[5] During the 1860s less than 2 percent of all immigrants came from southern or eastern Europe; by the 1890s southern and eastern Europe were a majority (52 percent) of all immigrants; and by the first decade of this century seven out of ten immigrants came from southern or eastern Europe. Today all European migration is much reduced; major immigration is by Asians and undocumented aliens from Mexico.

To ethnocentric WASP (White Anglo-Saxon Protestant) Americans, the new immigrants were alien races about to overwhelm American institutions and cities. First, they were coming from what were considered the most backward areas of Europe—regions that did not have self-government and thus by implication were incapable of self-government. Second, their customs and even food habits differed greatly from the Anglo-Saxon-Teutonic norm of earlier settlers. Third, their religion was different. They were more likely to be Catholic, Orthodox, or Jewish than Protestant. Finally, they were concentrated in the cities and thus were highly visible.

By the time the new immigrants arrived, the frontier had closed and the good farmlands were taken. Of necessity the new immigrants became industrial factory workers. Easy assimilation of the immigrants was retarded not only by their overwhelming numbers but also by their concentration in ethnic ghettos—in the inner-city zone of transition. Residence in central-city tenements reflected an economic necessity, but it also reflected the desires of the immigrants to have their own communities where they could follow traditional customs free from Anglo-Saxon hostility. The consequence was the development of ethnic neighborhoods which were isolated as far as possible from the larger city. The social organization of one such neighborhood, with its strong peer-group relationships, is described in William F. Whyte's *Street Corner Society*.[6]

Well into the twentieth century, the majority of the urban population was foreign-born or first-generation American. As of 1900, only half (51 percent) the country's population was native white and of native parentage. In eastern seaboard cities such as New York and Boston, over three-quarters of the population was of foreign stock (foreign-born or second-generation).

The negative reaction of WASP rural and small-town America to the nation's cities was closely linked to the perceived "foreignness" of the cities. Cities were considered cesspools of "rum, Romanism, and rebellion." Nine-

---

[5]For an excellent account of the life of the newcomers, see Irving Howe, *World of Our Fathers,* Touchstone, New York, 1976.

[6]William F. Whyte, *Street Corner Society,* University of Chicago Press, Chicago, 1943. See Chapter 6, City Life-styles, for a review of material on inner-city communities.

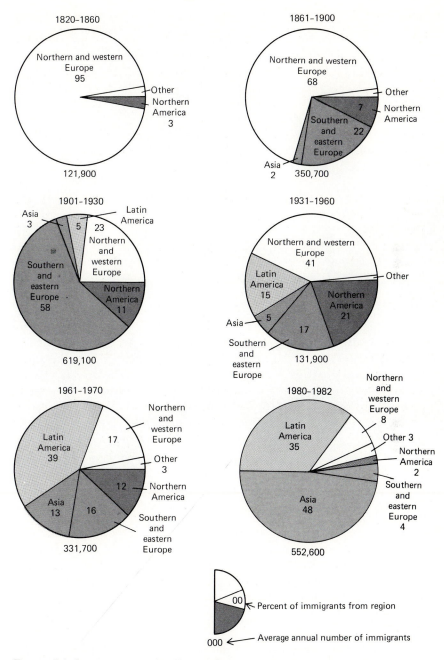

Figure 9-1. Immigrants to the United States by region of origin: 1820 through 1982. (*From Population Reference Bureau, 1984 Statistical Yearbook of the Immigration and Naturalization Service, and author.*)

Immigrants traveling steerage had to undergo complete physical examination on Ellis Island. There were no such requirements imposed on first-class passengers. (Library of Congress)

teenth century writers and preachers such as Josiah Strong raised the clarion call against the menace of cities teeming with foreigners:

> The City has become a serious menace to our civilization. . . . It has a peculiar attraction for the immigrant. . . .
>
> While a little less than one-third of the population of the United States was foreign by birth or parentage, sixty-two percent of the population of Cincinnati was foreign, eighty-three percent of Cleveland, sixty-three percent of Boston, eighty percent of New York and ninety-one percent of Chicago. . . . Because our cities are so largely foreign, Romanism finds in them its chief strength. For the

same reason the saloon, together with the intemperance and the liquor power which it represents, is multiplied in the city.[7]

As noted in Chapter 3, The Rise of Urban America, middle-class attempts to remove the bosses and reform the city generally meant removing power from the central-city immigrants. Then, as today, newcomers were seen as inferior.

"Racial Inferiority" and Immigration

Before the turn of the century, arguments to restrict immigration were largely based upon (1) the ethnocentric assumption of the superiority of American ways and (2) the assumption that American industrial society represented a higher evolutionary form than the backward regions of Europe. Nonetheless, "the wretched refuse of your teeming shore" were felt to be convertible into the American mainstream. As the *Philadelphia Press* commented in 1888: "The strong stomach of American civilization may, and doubtless will, digest and assimilate ultimately this unsavory and repellent throng. . . . In time they catch the spirit of the country and form an element of decided worth."[8]

However, around the turn of the century a new argument, that of racial inferiority, was added to the argument for exclusion. (The term "race" meant ethnicity or nationality rather than color, so that such terms as the "Polish race" and the "Italian race" were used. Various "experts" of the time agreed that the new immigrants were genetically inferior to the Anglo-Saxons who, combined with Germans, Scandinavians, and other "old immigrants," had formed the "American race." Discovering genetics, they jumped to the conclusion that not only hair color, size, and bone structure were genetically transferable, but also disposition, creativity, criminality, poverty, illiteracy, and all social behavior. Blood would tell—and what they believed it told was that Anglo-Saxon America was genetically committing suicide by allowing in unrestricted numbers of inferior races such as Poles, Italians, Slavs, and other eastern and southern Europeans. The conclusion seemed clear to opponents of immigration. "To admit the unchangeable differentation of race in its modern scientific meaning is to admit inevitably the existence of superiority in one race and of inferiority in another."[9]

Even the appearance of the American population was likely to deteriorate: "It is unthinkable that so many persons with crooked faces, coarse mouths, bad noses, heavy jaws, and low foreheads can mingle their heredity with ours without making personal beauty yet more rare among us than it actually is."[10] While this sounds absurd today, the importance of the genetic argument cannot be overstressed. These genetic beliefs were held not by a lunatic fringe but by major scholars with national influence.

---

[7]Josiah Strong, *Our Country,* rev. ed., Baker and Taylor, New York, 1891, chap. 11.
[8]Quoted in Higham, op. cit., p. 63.
[9]Madison Grant, *The Passing of the Great Race,* Scribner, New York, 1921, p. XXVIII.
[10]E. A. Ross, *The Old World in the New,* Century, New York, 1914, p. 287.

In the United States, the effect of the genetic argument was seen in the restrictive immigration laws of 1921 and 1924, the National Origins Act of 1929, and the McCarran-Walter Act of 1952. (President Truman vetoed the latter as discriminatory, but Congress passed it over his veto.) Southern and eastern Europeans were reduced from 45 percent of all immigrants under the already restrictive law of 1921 to 12 percent under the law of 1924. Northern and western Europeans were welcome—particularly if they were Protestant. About 85 percent of the quota went to northwest Europe, and roughly half the total quota went to three countries: England, Germany, and Ireland. Eastern and southern Europeans were given minimal quotas. Not until 1968 were the "racial" quotas eliminated.

The days of mass European migration are past, but we still have a substantial foreign-born population, and that population is overwhelmingly urban. Cities such as Boston, New York, Chicago, Detroit, San Francisco, and Los Angeles still have substantial ethnic colonies; "Little Italys," "Greek-towns," "New Polands," and "Chinatowns" remind us of the heterogeneity of the metropolis. The majority of the white ethnic population has been dispersed outward from segregated ethnic neighborhoods.[11] Today, ethnic neighborhoods, as described in Chapter 6, City Life-styles, are viewed by some as simply historical remnants of bypassed ways of life.[12] New ethnic areas, though, continue to be formed, particularly among Hispanic groups.

Melting Pot or Cultural Pluralism?

There is still debate about the accuracy of the view of America as a melting pot blending diverse groups. Instead of a melting pot, cultural pluralists suggest that there is continued separation of national-origin groups, so that the nation is really a mosaic of ethnic blocks. For instance, Glazer and Moynihan, in *Beyond the Melting Pot,* a study of ethnicity in New York City, found continuing cultural pluralism: "The point about the melting pot is that it did not happen. At least not in New York, and, mutatis mutandis, in those parts of America which resemble New York."[13] On the other hand, the sociologist Scott Greer maintains that the melting pot was effective, and that the result is a common American culture.[14]

In discussing the question of assimilation, it helps to remember Milton Gordon's often-quoted distinctions between "cultural assimilation" and "structural assimilation." Cultural assimilation is said to occur when the newcomers adopt the dress, food habits, and cultural habits of the dominant group. Partially

[11]Stanley Lieberson, *Ethnic Patterns in American Cities,* Free Press, New York, 1963; and Avery M. Gireot and James A. Weed, "Ethnic Residential Segregation: Patterns of Change," *American Journal of Sociology,* **81**:1088–1111, March, 1976.

[12]Melvin M. Webber, "The Post-City Age," in J. John Palen (ed.), *City Scenes,* Little, Brown, Boston, 1977, pp. 307–319.

[13]Nathan Glazer and Daniel Patrick Moynihan, *Beyond the Melting Pot,* M.I.T. Press, Cambridge, Mass., 1963, p. v.

[14]Scott Greer, "The Faces of Ethnicity," in Palen, op. cit., pp. 147, 157.

because of exposure through public schools and common media, cultural assimilation of new groups has been reliatively rapid in America.

Structural assimilation is far more comprehensive, since it involves acceptance into the primary groups, cliques, and institutions of the dominant group. Structural assimilation is thus a more gradual process; ultimately it means intermarriage. "Once structural assimilation has occurred . . . all other types of assimilation will necessarily follow."[15] Richard Alba's research, using a random sample of the national Catholic population, found that one measure of structural assimilation—intermarriage—had proceeded farther than had been commonly acknowledged.[16] Excepting the Hispanic and French Canadian populations, intermarriage was extensive, particularly in the English, Irish, and German populations. Scott Greer goes further in suggesting that ethnicity has lost real meaning when increasing proportions of the population have mixed ancestry and thus can choose whether to identify themselves as, for example, Italian, Irish, or Polish. He believes that "The romantic idealization of the ethnic bond persists, despite the difficulty many Americans have in deciding which ethnic background is the right one."[17]

No one challenges the upsurge in interest in ethnicity and family heritage. What continues to be debated is the strength and depth of the ethnic revival. Is the ethnic interest simply a romantic revival, or does it have deeper significance? Does it extend deeper than a "Polish Power" button, drinking green beer on St. Patrick's Day, or occasionally visiting Little Italy to purchase ethnic food? Does ethnicity make a difference in the attitudes, values, or life-style of second-and later-generation whites now living in the suburbs? For most social scientists, knowing one's social class is far more useful than knowing one's ethnicity.

BLACK AMERICANS

The following pages review the past and present status of black Americans. While reading this material, keep the following points in mind.

First, Afro-Americans did not come to American shores voluntarily, seeking a new way of life. Almost all were brought here in bondage, as slaves, and this has left a profound social-psychological imprint that both blacks and whites must overcome.

Second, major white immigration to the industrializing cities occurred during the nineteenth century, when the number of unskilled jobs was expanding. Black immigration to urban areas, on the other hand, occurred mostly in the twentieth century, a period during which long-term industrial opportunities for the unskilled and poorly educated have been contracting.

---

[15]Milton M. Gordon, *Assimilation in American Life,* Oxford University Press, New York, 1964, p. 81.
[16]Richard D. Alba, "Social Assimilation among American Catholic National-Origin Groups," *American Sociological Review,* **41**:1030–1046, December 1976.
[17]Greer, op. cit., p. 156.

TABLE 9-2
Black Population in the United States by Number and Percent, 1790 to 1980

Year	Number	Percent of total population
1790	757,000	19.3
1800	1,002,000	18.9
1850	3,639,000	15.7
1900	8,834,000	11.6
1930	11,891,000	9.7
1940	12,866,000	9.8
1950	15,042,000	10.0
1960	18,860,000	10.6
1970	22,672,570	11.2
1980	25,969,000	11.8

Source: U.S. Bureau of the Census: Fifteenth Census Reports, *Population* vol. II: Sixteenth Census Reports, *Population* vol. 11 part 1: *U.S. Census of Population: 1950*, vol. II part 1: *U.S. Census of Population: 1950;* vol. 1; U.S. Bureau of the Census, *Current Population Reports*, series P-25, nos. 367, 416, 441 and 460.

Third, and most important, those who are visibly nonwhite are immediately subject to racist classification. White ethnics who suffered from discrimination or the imposition of quotas could, and often did, change their names as well as their life-styles, adopting the attitudes and customs of WASP America. But this choice is not open to most blacks and other nonwhites. Unlike ethnicity, color is a difference that cannot be denied. Table 9-2 shows the black population of the United States from 1790 to 1980. Blacks in the United States now number some 30 million—more than the total population of Canada.

Historical Patterns

The first blacks in the American colonies were not slaves but indentured servants. That meant that they had to serve for a given time—usually seven years—in bondage or indentureship before they became legally entitled to own property. However, this system—particularly in the south, where plantations required large labor forces—rapidly evolved into one of perpetual servitude. In 1661 Virginia passed a law allowing perpetual slavery, and two years later the Maryland colony declared that "all Negroes or other slaves within the province, to be hereafter imported, shall serve during life."

The fundamental conflict between America's social and political philosophy of freedom and equality on the one hand and the practice of social inequality on the other was aptly characerized by Gunnar Myrdal as the "American dilemma."[18] Two centuries earlier, Thomas Jefferson (who owned slaves while opposing slavery) had referred to it as justice in conflict with avarice and oppression.[19]

[18]Gunnar Myrdal, *An American Dilemma*, Harper and Row, New York, 1944.
[19]Ulrich B. Philips, *American Negro Slavery*, Louisiana State University Press, Baton Rouge, 1969, p. 122.

Population Changes

At the time of the first census in 1790, blacks made up 19 percent of the total population. In spite of a high rate of natural increase, the proportion of blacks in the population declined during the nineteenth century because of substantial European immigration. European immigration was restricted by the immigration laws of the 1920s; thus, since 1930, blacks have been increasing as a proportion of the population. They currently constitute 12 percent of the population.

The black population was—until this century—overwhelmingly rural and southern. Despite the Civil War and the extensive political and social upheavals of Reconstruction, there was but slight change in this pattern. As recently as 1910, nine out of ten blacks still lived in the south, and 73 percent of blacks were rural. Today only half (52 percent) live in the south, and 85 percent live in urban areas (compared to 71 percent of whites). According to the 1980 census there are now fifteen cities with populations over 50,000 that have black majorities. This is up substantially from 1970, when there were only seven such cities.

Slavery in Cities

Slavery was basically a rural institution, founded upon the plantation economy, but by 1820 about 20 percent of the people in the major southern cities were slaves.[20] Slavery in southern cities differed fundamentally from slavery on the plantations, so much so that plantation owners vigorously opposed the use of slaves in urban manufacturing, fearing that it would undermine the south's "peculiar institution." As a consequence, slavery drastically declined in the large cities by 1860. (Richmond's iron works were an exception.) The reason for the decline was not economic but social.

On the plantation, slaves were totally dependent upon the white overseer and could, if necessary, be controlled through fear of repression. Some might try to run away, but pursuit by specially trained tracking dogs and professional slave hunters made successful escapes difficult. In urban areas, on the other hand, slaveholders had far less mastery:

> While plantation slaves were typically field hands or house servants, urban slaves engaged in a wide variety of occupations, skilled as well as unskilled, in addition to those who worked as domestic servants for their owners. A very large number of slaves were hired out to work for others, the arrangement being made either by the slave owners or the slaves themselves.[21]

The system of slaves being "hired out" or hiring themselves to others and sharing the income with their owners meant that the slave was, in Frederick Douglass's words, "almost a free citizen."[22] In effect, the slave and owner entered into an informal contract in which the slave, through the sharing of

---

[20]Richard C. Wade, *Slavery in the Cities: The South 1820–1860.* Oxford University Press, New York, 1964.
[21]Thomas Sowell, *Race and Economics,* David McKay Company, New York, 1975, p. 12.
[22]Wade, op. cit.

his or her earnings, "purchased" some degree of freedom. Escaping from slavery was far easier and more common in the cities; therefore, to prevent the loss of large capital investments, urban slaveholders had to rule with a lighter hand.

The fact that urbanism undermined the traditional slave-master relationship did not escape plantation owners. Therefore, they were constantly making new restrictions and laws to govern urban slavery. Many nineteenth-century southerners saw city life as a direct threat to the southern way of life, and they were right.

"Free Persons of Color"

Nor were all urban blacks slaves. By the eve of the Civil War, roughly one out of eight blacks was a "free Negro," and most of these lived in cities—usually in border states. This growing population of "free persons of color" created serious problems for the slave states, for although most "free persons" faired poorly in economic terms, they were still free men and women, and thus a threat to the system. A handful of the southern antebellum free blacks were wealthy slave owners themselves. For example, William Ellison of South Carolina owned more slaves than all but the richest white southerners and lived in the former home of a governor of South Carolina.[23]

Until fairly recently the descendants of those who were not slaves at the time of the Civil War dominated leadership roles in the black urban community. While Booker T. Washington was indeed "up from slavery," few other leaders were. W.E.B. DuBois and most other founders of the NAACP, for example, had never been slaves.

> Only in the post-World War II period did black students descended from the masses of those freed by the Civil War predominate in black colleges, and their arrival forced wholesale changes in the general character of these institutions. Descendants of the ante-bellum free persons of color similarly dominated Negro leadership at the local and national level a generation ago.[24]

Jim Crow Laws

It should be noted that segregation of public facilities was not characteristic of the pre-Civil War urban south. Jim Crow laws, which established separate railway cars, dining areas, rest rooms, and even doorways for blacks, were largely a product of the years between 1890 and 1910.[25] Grandfather clauses, literacy tests, and poll taxes disenfranchised blacks, while segregation laws were passed to separate the races in schools and public facilities. Crucial to segregation was the 1896 case of *Plessy v. Ferguson,* in which the Supreme

---

[23]Michael P. Johnson and James L. Roark, *Black Masters: A Free Family of Color in the Old South,* Norton, New York, 1984.

[24]Sowell, op. cit., p. 41.

[25]C. Van Woodward. *The Strange Career of Jim Crow,* Oxford University Press, New York, 1966.

Blacks were evicted from houses in white areas after the Chicago race riot of 1919. (Jun Fujita/Chicago Historical Society)

Court ruled that separate racial facilities were legal if they were equal. The pernicious doctrine of "separate but equal" was not finally eliminated until the famous 1954 case of *Brown v. Board of Education of Topeka,* in which the Supreme Court ruled that "separate educational facilities are inherently unequal."

Movement North

Significant migration of blacks out of the south began with World War I. When the war cut off the tide of European immigrant labor and flooded industries with war orders, a new source of labor had to be found. Soon labor recruiters were scouring the south, encouraging blacks to migrate north to "the promised land." In some cases, one-way railroad tickets were even provided. Recruiters

Leavin' the South

". . . When I drove into town that next Saturday after I quit at Bonds, I ran into this fella's son, Henry Bonds. He was a big stout guy—wanted to know why I left his dad. I told him, "I can get more money." He said, "If you don't come back to Dad by Monday, we'll do away with you."

I knew what that meant. He and his brothers were gonna get me if I drove for Asa Lever on Monday. I didn't dare argue with him, cause maybe he'd got me right then.

Quite a few left to come into Tennessee. From there they'd go to St. Louis, Murphysboro, some to Detroit, in fact all over the East. None went as fast as I did though.

I was in danger of my life when I left Macon. It seemed like it was a period when white folks was angry. The Negroes were leaving out, and they were leaving out by numbers. They were comin' north because jobs were open. They may not have been the best, but they were far better than we had there.

They were rough in that period. They beat up a lot of our people, left 'em out on the road. The flies got in some of 'em before the people found 'em. Just because they were trying to better their condition. It was awful rough in that time.

When they began to leave, if you owed these fellas a quarter, you daren't talk about leavin'. They'd say, "You owe me money." And they'd make it whatever they want to, and you dare not leave. So, I beat the rap by gettin' out of there that Sunday night."*

*Interview by Clem Imhoff with Reverend D. W. Johnson, "The Recruiter," *Southern Exposure*, 4:83–87, 1976.

"stirring up the negroes" were unwelcome guests in southern communities. A licensing regulation in Macon, Georgia, required each labor agent to pay a $25,000 fee and obtain recommendations from ten local ministers, ten manufacturers, and twenty-five merchants. Elsewhere, methods were more direct and recruiters were shot or tarred and feathered.

The pull of northern industrial jobs, combined with the boll weevil's destruction of cotton and the mechanization of agriculture, encouraged migration. Cotton production was shifting out of the old south to the west and southwest, and field-hand labor was no longer so necessary. Between 1910 and 1920 the five states of the deep south—South Carolina, Georgia, Alabama, Mississippi, and Louisiana—lost 400,000 blacks through out-migration. (Whites were also out-migrating at this time.)

There were three major migratory streams. The first was from the Carolinas, Georgia, and Florida up the east coast to key locations such as Washington, Philadelphia, New York, and Boston. The second was from Mississippi, Arkansas, and part of Alabama into the midwestern cities of St. Louis, Detroit, Chicago, and Milwaukee. The third stream was from Texas and part of Louisiana to Los Angeles and the west coast.

The depression of the 1930s cut off employment opportunities in the north and stemmed the flow of in-migrants to the cities. But the resurgence of industry during World War II again accelerated the pace of migration, and it continued into the 1950s and 1960s. Mississippi's black population declined more than 100,000 during the decade 1960–1970, and there were also losses (in spite of high birthrates) in Alabama and South Carolina.

This was an extremely substantial migration, but it should be kept in perspective—particularly since there is a tendency to exaggerate it. Between 1910 and 1960 somewhat under 5 million blacks left the south, largely for the big cities of the north. This is a great number of people but hardly compares with the waves of European immigrants that inundated American shores during the first years of this century. For example, a total of 8.8 million European immigrants entered the United States between 1901 and 1911 alone. Even today in urban areas there are far more foreign immigrants than blacks in-migrating. In fact, there are not enough rural southern blacks left to have all that great an impact, even if they all migrated out. Foreign immigrants, on the other hand, continue to flow into the United States at a pace of approximately 400,000 a year. (On top of this there are perhaps 1 million illegal immigrants—largely from Mexico—each year.) Thus in-migration of southern blacks to the cities should be kept in perspective.

As a result of the great northern migration, Chicago houses more blacks than all of Mississippi, and the New York metropolitan area has more blacks than any state of the old south.[26]

[26]Thomas F. Pettigrew, *Racially Separate or Together?*, McGraw-Hill, New York, 1971, p. 3.

End of Mass Migration

The period of mass migration from the south is now history. This movement contained the seeds of its own destruction, for as blacks moved to the cities, there were fewer persons left behind to become migrants in the future. Today most black movement is from one urban area to another. Increasingly, urban blacks are second- and third-generation urban residents. The image of the black as a southern rural sharecropper migrating to the big city is a picture out of another age and time. Today, while just over half of all blacks still live in the south, blacks are now one of the most urban segments of the total population. Blacks are more concentrated in the large cities and MSAs than whites. Over half of all blacks (55 percent) now live in central cities of metropolitan areas (this is down from 59 percent in 1970), and one of five (19 percent) resides in suburbs.[27] As of 1985 the major cities of Philadelphia, Atlanta, Chicago, and Los Angeles, as well as numerous smaller cities, had black mayors.

Moving South

For the first time since the Civil War, there now are more blacks leaving than entering northern central cities. According to Bureau of the Census figures, between 1975 and 1980 some 195,000 more blacks moved into the south than moved out.[28] Most of this movement is from northern cities to southern urban areas, not rural areas. Blacks, like whites, are now more likely to be moving south and west than moving north. Black migration patterns in the late 1980s increasingly resemble white migration patterns.

Urban Segregation Patterns

Amount of Segregation. Segregation of racial and ethnic groups into ghettos is not new to American life. Anti-immigrant and anti-Catholic political movements, from the Know-Nothing Party of the nineteenth century to the Ku Klux Klan of the 1920s, attempted to keep newcomers "in their place" socially and physically. Their "place" was the old and overcrowded housing in the central area near the factories. As members of ethnic groups prospered, they often moved out of the ghetto into outlying neighborhoods with better-quality housing, and so residential segregation decreased.[29] Blacks also started in the poorest central-city ghetto neighborhoods, but to a far greater degree, they remained restricted to such "black belts."[30] For blacks, until very recently,

---

[27]U.S. Bureau of the Census, "Social and Economic Characteristics of Metropolitan and Nonmetropolitan Population: 1977 and 1970," *Current Population Reports,* series P-23, no. 75, Washington, D.C., November, 1978, table F.

[28]U.S. Bureau of the Census, "Geographical Mobility of the Population of the United States: March 1975 to March 1980," *Current Population Reports,* series P-20, no. 368, 1981, table 42.

[29]Lieberson, op. cit.,; and Gireot and Weed, op. cit.

[30]For an excellent study of ghetto life during the 1930s, see St. Clair Drake and Horace Cayton, *Black Metropolis,* Harcourt, Brace, New York, 1945.

race automatically overrode economics. (For details on housing programs see Chapter 11, Housing Programs and Urban Change.)

The landmark study of changing patterns of racial segregation was that of Karl and Alma Taeuber, in which they compared segregation indexes for American cities for 1940, 1950, and 1960.[31] Later studies have updated the findings for 1970 and 1980. Their segregation index, called the "index of dissimilarity," used the computer to analyze census data for blacks and gave an index figure representing the proportion of nonwhites that would have to move to another block in order to have a complete balance of the races. For example, in a city where 10 percent of the population is black, the index would have a value of zero if one-tenth of the households on each block were black and a value of 100 if there was total segregation. Thus, the index has a theoretical range of 0 to 100, with 100 representing complete segregation.

The average segregation index of 207 of the largest cities in the United States was 86.2 in 1960. This means that 86 percent of all nonwhites would have had to change the block on which they live in order to produce an unsegregated pattern. Of the 207 cities in the sample, each having a population of 50,000 or more, the value of the segregation index ranged from a high of 98.1 in Fort Lauderdale to a low of 60.4 in San Jose. Thus, they found that a high incidence of segregation was virtually universal.

Extensive segregation of southern cities is a modern rather than a long-standing trend. In the south of days gone by, social segregation was so rigid that spatial segregation was unnecessary. Especially in the older southern cities, whites frequently lived in the big house on the street while blacks lived in the smaller house in the alley behind. Black servants lived on the premises. As of 1940, the *least* spatially segregated city of the 109 cities for which data are available was Charleston, South Carolina, the "birthplace of Confederacy." By 1960 the segregation index of Charleston had increased almost 20 points, to 79.5. Spacial distance was being substituted for social distance.

As a rough generalization one could say that in the south it was acceptable for blacks to live close to whites but not to rise to the levels of white social classes. In the north, on the contrary, it was all right to move up but not to move next door. As the old folk saying went, "Down South, it's Nigger, you can live close but don't move up'; while up North, it's Nigger, you can move up, but don't get too close.'"

Research based on samples of 109 and 237 cities for 1970 indicated decreasing segregation in all regions of the country including the south.[32] Slow declines in segregation continued to be the pattern for 1980.[33]

[31]Karl E. Taeuber and Alma F. Taeuber, *Negroes in Cities: Residential Segregation and Neighborhood Change,* Aldine, Chicago, 1965.

[32]Annemette Sorenson, Karl E. Taeuber, and Leslie J. Hollingsworth, Jr., "Indexes of Racial Residential Segregation for 109 Cities in the United States, 1940 to 1970," *Sociological Focus,* April, 1975, pp. 125–142; and Thomas Van Valey, Wade Clark Roof, and Jerome E. Wilcox, "Trends in Residential Segregation: 1960–1970," *American Journal of Sociology,* **82**:826–844, January, 1977.

[33]Karl E. Taeuber, "Racial Residential Segregation in 28 Cities, 1970–1980," Center for Demography and Ecology, University of Wisconsin Working Paper 83–12, 1983.

Racial Turnover. The fact that racial segregation in cities is decreasing is now established. The question is whether this reflects changes in racial attitudes or reflects only the period of integration occurring between the in-migration of the first black and the out-migration of the last white to the suburbs. White flight and black suburbanization are discussed extensively in Chapter 8, Patterns of Suburbanization, and so that material is not repeated here. Suffice it to say that the data indicate that whites were and are moving more *toward* perceived suburban advantages than *from* problems created by minorities, and black suburbanization increased more dramatically during the 1970s and 1980s than were expected.

Note that racial turnover of central-city areas does not require massive flight by white residents. Approximately one out of every five American households changes location each year; and even without panic by out-migration, an area will change from white to black if all or most of the newcomers are black. Harvey Molotch examined the process of racial transition in Chicago's South Shore neighborhood, where he found that in spite of attempts to create an integrated area, the neighborhood became resegregated as an all-black area.[34] This was not because of whites fleeing, but rather because the dwelling units within the area, as they became vacant, were less likely to be filled by whites. The area thus turned over not because of white flight but because of a lack of white in-migration.

On the other hand, a study done in Cleveland suggested that "white flight was a factor in household turnover in a few neighborhoods."[35] Also, an examination of Detroit suburbs by Reynolds Farley indicated that white preference for all-white areas strongly contributes to residential segregation.[36] Farley's research suggested that blacks are willing to enter mixed areas, but whites are not. Thus, there is a "ratchet effect"—the more blacks there are in a neighborhood, the less likely it is that whites will move in. Building on this idea, Bud Wurdork has further suggested that data from the Detroit Area study indicated that the blacker a neighborhood becomes, the more likely it is that whites will move out for racial reasons.[37] It is hypothesized that once a threshold of "blackness" is reached, the "ratchet" process of whites moving out and blacks moving in begins. Most experts say this tip point is somewhere about 20 percent.

However, an unanswered question is whether the Detroit area is typical of metropolitan patterns nationwide. The data presented in Chapter 8 seems to suggest that white flight is less significant nationally. What is clear is that while legally enforced segregation is a thing of the past, most blacks, by choice

[34]Harvey Molotch. *Managed Integration,* University of California Press, Berkeley, 1972.

[35]Avery A. Guest and James J. Zuiches, "Another Look at Residential Turnover in Urban Neighborhoods," *American Journal of Sociology,* 77:457–467, November, 1971.

[36]Reynolds Farley, Howard Schuman, Susanne Bianchi, Diane Colansanto, and Shirley Hatchett, "Chocolate City, Vanilla Suburbs," a paper presented at the August 1977 meeting of the American Sociological Association, Chicago.

[37]Bud Wurdock, "The Role of White Flight in Neighborhood Racial Transition," a paper delivered at the April 1978 meeting of the Midwest Sociological Society.

or necessity, continue to reside in predominately black areas. The major cause of such segregation is racial rather than economic differences. As Karl Taeuber bluntly says, "I have concluded from my own research and a review of the work of others that the prime cause of residential segregation by race has been discrimination both public and private."[38] (For a discussion of governmental real estate practices see Chapter 11, Housing Programs and Urban Change.)

Social-Class Distribution. As regards spatial distribution by social class, blacks tend to follow the same pattern as whites. The larger and older cities of the north are much more likely to have status differentials favoring suburban over central-city residence.[39] Within cities, there is commonly an increase in the level of socioeconomic status for blacks with distance from the city center.

Middle-class blacks live in areas which are far more mixed in terms of socioeconomic composition than those inhabited by middle-class whites. A study done in Chicago indicates that the black middle class may be isolated from public housing, but middle- and upper-class black people live, on the average, closer to lower-class blacks than middle-class whites live to lower-class whites.[40]

HISPANIC POPULATION

Hispanic Americans constitute the most rapidly growing segment of the urban population. The nation's 14.6 million persons of Hispanic origin account for 6.4 percent of the national population, and this figure largely excludes the estimated 3.5 to 5 million illegal aliens. If present immigration—legal and illegal—continues, the Spanish-origin population may outnumber blacks within a score of years. Half the Hispanic population of the United States is clustered in two states: California and Texas. Hispanics in Houston will outnumber both blacks and whites by 2000 A.D. Spanish-origin population is more concentrated in metropolitan areas than either the whites or blacks, with 84 percent living in such areas. Within metropolitan areas the Spanish-speaking population is more evenly distributed than the black population. Some 41 percent of metropolitan-area Hispanics reside in suburbs (35 percent of all Spanish-speaking Americans live in suburbs).[41]

The Spanish-speaking population is now quite diverse, including 6.5 million Mexican Americans and 1.7 million Puerto Ricans, plus Cubans, Dominicans,

[38]Karl E. Taeuber, "Racial Segregation: The American Dilemma." *The Annals of the American Academy of Political and Social Science,* **422**:91, November, 1975.

[39]J. John Palen and Leo Schnore, "Color Composition and City-Suburban Status Differences," *Land Economnics,* **41**:87–91, February, 1965.

[40]Brigitte Mach Erbe, "Race and Socioeconomic Segregation," *American Sociological Review,* **40**:801–812, December, 1975.

[41]U.S. Bureau of the Census, "Population Profile of the United States: 1981," *Current Population Reports,* series P-20, no. 374, pp. 15–18; and U.S. Bureau of the Census, "Social and Economic Characteristics of the Metropolitan and Nonmetropolitan Population: 1977 and 1970," *Current Population Reports,* Special Studies, series P-23, no. 75, Washington, D.C., November 1978, pp. 5, 7.

TABLE 9-3
States with Largest Hispanic Populations, 1970 and 1980

	1980			1970		
	Rank	Number	Percent distribution	Rank	Number	Percent distribution
United States	—	14,608,673	100.0%	—	9,072,602	100.0%
California	1	4,544,331	31.1	1	2,369,292	26.1
Texas	2	2,985,824	20.4	2	1,840,648	20.3
New York	3	1,659,300	11.4	3	1,351,982	14.9
Florida	4	858,158	5.9	4	405,036	4.5
Illinois	5	635,602	4.4	5	393,204	4.3
New Jersey	6	491,883	3.4	7	288,488	3.2
New Mexico	7	477,222	3.3	6	308,340	3.4
Arizona	8	440,701	3.0	8	264,770	2.9
Colorado	9	339,717	2.3	9	225,506	2.5
Michigan	10	162,440	1.1	10	151,070	1.7
Pennsylvania	11	153,961	1.1	13	106,893	1.2
Massachusetts	12	141,043	1.0	15	66,146	0.7
Connecticut	13	124,499	0.9	16	65,458	0.7
Washington	14	120,016	0.8	19	57,358	0.6
Ohio	15	119,883	0.8	11	129,995	1.4
Total	—	13,254,580	90.7	—	8,026,186	88.5

Source: U.S. Bureau of the Census.

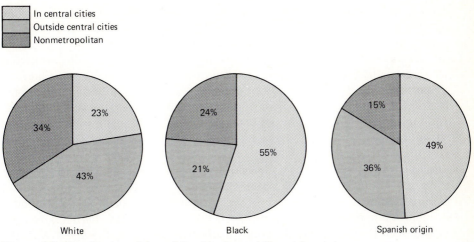

In central cities
Outside central cities
Nonmetropolitan

White
23%
34%
43%

Black
24%
21%
55%

Spanish origin
15%
36%
49%

Figure 9-2. Distribution of the white, black, and Spanish-origin populations, by metropolitan and nonmetropolitan residence, 1980. (*From Bureau of the Census.*)

and other Latin Americans. Mexican Americans and Puerto Ricans—the two largest groups—are discussed below.

Mexican Americans

Today 60 percent of all Hispanics are Mexican Americans.[42] The stereotype of Mexican Americans as agricultural workers—an image strengthened by Cesar Chavez's successful struggle to organize California farm workers—is quite erroneous. Ninety percent of California's 4.5 million persons of Mexican descent are urban residents. Los Angeles today has 2.1 million Mexican Americans, without fully counting the "undocumented aliens" in the Spanish-speaking East Los Angeles area. There are now more Hispanics than blacks in Los Angeles.

Housing Patterns. The crowded *barrios* of California and Texas are where new arrivals are most likely to settle. Poverty is common in the urban *barrios*, or ghettos, and Chicano gangs remain a serious problem. Gang-related drug use and crime are a way of life in the *barrios*.[43] Los Angeles County is estimated to have 13,000 gang members and scores of gang murders yearly.

For Mexican Americans, unlike blacks, there are wide variations in patterns of physical segregation. Outside of the border states, economics plays

---

[42]There is no generally accepted term used by Americans of Mexican ancestry to describe the ethnic group. "Mexican American," "Spanish American," "Latino," and, among younger activists, "Chicano," are all used, and the preferred term differs from place to place. For convenience, we will generally use the term "Mexican American."

[43]For a study of Chicano gangs and the role of drugs, see Joan W. Moore, *Homeboys: Gangs, Drugs and Prison in the Barrios of Los Angeles*, Temple University Press, Philadelphia, 1978.

a larger part than discrimination in determining residential patterns. In the southwest there is a long history of prejudice against Mexican Americans, but elsewhere in the country (excepting cities such as Chicago) there is a general unawareness of Mexican Americans as a group—a situation with positive as well as negative aspects. There is a failure to know of, and appreciate, the richness of Mexican culture, but at the same time, there are no long-accepted patterns of discrimination against and segregation of Mexican Americans. Although segregation and discrimination do occur, they are not institutionalized to the extent that they are in the relationships between blacks and whites.

Immigration. The majority of the present Mexican American population are fairly recent immigrants. The immigrants came north because there was a lack of economic opportunities in the labor-heavy Mexican economy and a demand for temporary farm workers in the United States. Particularly after World War II, the economic boom in the United States, coupled with the inability of the Mexican industrial economy to absorb all of its workers, led both legal ("green-carders") and illegal immigrants northward to supply the shortage in American agricultural labor. During World War II some 300,000 to 500,000 Mexican Americans served in the armed forces, and others left the farms for the booming war industries of southern California. Few returned to the farms after the war. Today the agribusiness enterprises in California and Texas are replacing human workers with machines, a process that is likely to accelerate. The recent financial crisis in Mexico has increased the influx.

Currently, a substantial portion of Mexican Americans in the United States are illegal immigrants. Just about every aspect of the immigration question is embroiled in emotional dispute. The Immigration and Naturalization Service tabulated over 1.4 million arrests of incoming aliens in 1984. Estimates of how many undocumented aliens are in the United States run from 2 to 12 million, but the Bureau of the Census's more conservative estimate is between 3.5 to 6 million persons. Sober estimates say that this number is being increased by 500,000 illegals each year.[44] Roughly nine out of ten undocumented immigrants in the United States are Mexicans, and the torrent shows no sign of decreasing along the 2,000 miles of Mexican-American border. All signs, in fact, point toward considerable increase in such migration.

The fact that immigration reform means a great deal of Mexican Americans but little to Puerto Ricans, all of whom already are citizens, reflects their different experiences.[45]

Socioeconomic Position

Economically, the Spanish-speaking population is as a whole better off than blacks. While one-third (32 percent) of blacks are below the poverty level, this is true of only one-quarter (26 percent) of Hispanics.[46] This general comparison,

---

[44]Charles B. Keely, "Illegal Immigration," *Scientific American,* March, 1982, p. 41.
[45]William A. Diaz, *Hispanics: Challenges and Opportunities,* Ford Foundation, New York, 1984.
[46]U.S. Bureau of the Census, "Population Profile," op. cit., p. 56.

Hispanics are today a major population group in larger U.S. cities.
(Eric A. Roth/The Picture Cube)

however, masks wide variations among those of different Spanish-speaking backgrounds. Puerto Ricans earn slightly less than blacks, Mexican Americans earn slightly more, and Cuban Americans—many of whom as refugees from Fidel Castro's rule left Cuba with marketable skills—earn considerably more.

In spite of the considerable diversity among the Mexican American population, it is often negatively stereotyped by other Americans as poor, complacent, fatalistic, not goal-oriented, emotional, superstitious, and traditional. "Anglo" (non-Mexican) society tends to assume, erroneously because there are so many lower-class Mexican immigrants, that all persons of Mexican descent are poor.

Contributing to the low economic position of Mexican Americans are generally low levels of education. As of the beginning of the decade, among adults only one-third had completed high school and only four percent were college graduates. Since in the United States lack of a high school diploma means virtual exclusion from much of contemporary industrial life, many Mexican Americans are employed in the so-called secondary labor market of marginal jobs and illegal enterprises.

Problems of Adjustment. Unfortunately, inferior social status and economic position have sometimes led Mexican Americans to internalize some of the negative stereotypes of the majority culture. Surveys of San Antonio, Los Angeles, and Albuquerque indicate that Mexicans often accept the self-deprecatory stereotypes as well as the more positive ones: e.g., laziness and volatility as well as a special warmth for life.[47]

Mexican Americans have, in fact, had serious problems with the formal education systems of North America. In all states, Mexican Americans have lower median levels of education than blacks. American schools have been ill-equipped to deal with students who are not fluent in English, and have frequently shunted them aside as if they were poor learners or deficient in intelligence. Bilingual education programs still have difficulty becoming accepted. Frequent moving of families also disrupts some children's education. The comparatively lower value placed on education in the traditional lower-class Mexican family is also a factor, particularly as regards the education of women.

Movement to Cities. The problem of adequate schooling and other problems of adjusting to the larger Anglo society have become more acute with the rapid urbanization of the Mexican American population during the last two decades. Traditional isolated towns and villages in New Mexico and other southwestern states have been losing population, while the Mexican American population of cities such as Albuquerque, San Antonio, and Los Angeles has been increasing.

Today Los Angeles has more people of Mexican ancestry than any other

[47]Joan W. Moore, *Mexican Americans*, Prentice-Hall, Englewood Cliffs, N.J., 1976, p. 8.

city in the Americas, except Mexico City and Guadalajara. Clearly, the Mexican American's future is an urban future. The geographical movement out of the southwest is not only migration out of a region; it is a symbol of the inevitable change from rural to urban residence and rural to urban ways of life.

Mexican Americans have as a group attracted less attention to themselves than have other minorities such as blacks. The relative quiet of Mexican American city dwellers can be partially attributed to the fact that despite low-level income, housing, and services, cities in the United States are still infinitely superior to the destitute *barrios* of the Mexican *municipios*. The United States offers relative opulence compared with the poverty of the suburban squatter *barrios* of Ciudad Juárez—the latter sometimes without electricity or water. And even in these Mexican border slums, the per capita income is two or three times higher than in other regions of Mexico.[48] Moreover, a substantial portion of those of Mexican ancestry in the United States are undocumented immigrants and thus do not seek attention in any way.

Differences between Mexican Americans and Anglos. Mexican Americans, as a rule, put heavier emphasis on familism than Anglo society does—although the difference in the cities is lessening. Women are still expected to fill traditional roles as wives and mothers. It is, however, easy to exaggerate the extent and depth of the Mexican American traditionalism. The overwhelming majority of Mexican Americans identify themselves as Roman Catholic, for instance, but at the same time as increasing proportion of Mexican American women use means of birth control disapproved of by the Catholic church. Of course, some differences do persist. Fertility rates among Mexican Americans are still extremely high, with an average family of four children in 1980. Only American Indians, another poor minority, have larger families. Increasing urbanization and urbanism, plus socioeconomic mobility, should bring fertility rates of Mexican Americans more in line with those of the larger society over the next decade.

Today the Mexican American population is a young population. High fertility rates and the large number of young immigrants have resulted in a population much younger than the national population. The median age of the Mexican-origin population is 20.8 years, well below the median age of 29.9 years for Americans as a whole.

Internal Diversity. A previously noted, the Mexican American population is remarkably diverse. Traditionally, Mexicans (and Anglos) made a broad distinction between the upper-class "Spanish" of "pure blood" and the lower-class "Mexicans." "Spanish" ancestry has traditionally been considered more prestigious than "Mexican" ancestry, and "Indian" ancestry is at the bottom. This attitude is not a reaction to the racial situation in the United States, but

---

[48]Ellwyn R. Stoddard, *Mexican Americans,* Random House, New York, 1973, p. 31.

rather has roots deep in the early colonial history of Mexico under the Spanish Crown. (The Spanish colonial social system is discussed further in Chapter 17, Urbanization in Latin America.)

The gracious Spanish grandee on his California rancho typifies the first stereotype. Mexicans, by contrast, were stereotyped as lazy and cowardly. The lesson of the Alamo was clear: "One Texan was worth ten Mexicans." Particularly disparaged are the most recent Mexican immigrants. Often residing in the country as undocumented aliens and serving in menial jobs, they constitute one of the poorest-educated and least skilled segments of the population. This division into "Spanish" and "Mexican" serves the sociological function of allowing the former to be accepted into the businesses, homes, and even families of Anglo society, while discrimination and exploitation of lower-class Chicanos continues.

Mexican Americans are still underrepresented in the halls of political power. As of 1985 San Antonio and Denver were the only major cities to have Hispanic mayors. In spite of their numbers, there is only one Mexican American on the Los Angeles city council and the Los Angeles County board of supervisors. (By contrast, Mayor Bradley is black.) Signs point to increased political activity among Mexican Americans. Mexican Americans today are torn between viewing themselves as a distinct minority group or as individual Americans who share the speaking of Spanish. Chicanos often look to black groups as an example of how they should organize, while assimilated middle-class Mexican Americans resist the minority-group label. ("Chicano" is a contraction and corruption of "Mexicano"; it originally was a term of derision for one who was unsophisticated, but now means one who has soul.) Overall, political awareness is increasing and class division and rhetoric are more muted than a decade ago. While economically successful Mexican Americans are moving out of the *barrios,* their places are being taken by ever more newcomers attracted by the promise of life in urban America.

Regional differences among Hispanics are considerable. For example, while Mexicans as a group voted for Walter Mondale in 1984, Hispanics in the south and Florida, where Cubans dominate, voted for Ronald Reagan. Hispanics in the south are generally also more upscale in income and more likely to perceive themselves in the mainstream of American life.[49]

Puerto Ricans

General Characteristics and Conditions. Puerto Ricans constitute the second-largest Hispanic minority in the United States. Puerto Ricans differ from other Spanish-speaking Americans in several significant respects. First, Puerto Ricans have been American citizens since 1917. Thus, there is no question regarding their legal right to live on the mainland. Second, many Puerto Ricans are first-generation migrants, the bulk of Puerto Rican migration having occurred

---

[49]Cheryl Russell, "The News About Hispanics," *American Demographics,* March, 1983, p. 20.

Chicago's Street Gangs

Mention Hispanic street gangs and many people immediately think of *West Side Story* or, if they are middle-aged, the youth gangs of the 1950s. In Chicago, though, gangs are not something out of a past era. Nor are they the stuff of musicals. Groups such as the Latin Kings and the Insane Unknowns account for over two dozen murders a year—a fact the newspapers play down to avoid encouraging even greater violence.

Today, Chicago's gang violence is concentrated in the Hispanic and black slum and project areas of the North Side and West Side. (Gang activity is far more subdued in the older black ghettos of the South Side, partially because the leaders of the Blackstone Rangers who were powerful there a decade ago are now almost all either dead or in prison.) Blacks in the massive Cabrini-Green housing project and Hispanics in the surrounding neighborhoods join the gangs as "peewees" (ages nine to eleven) and then graduate to "juniors" (age twelve to sixteen or so) and eventually "seniors." Girls form auxiliaries and also wear the gang colors. Gang members join for a variety of reasons including protection or even boredom, but the major reason is self-respect. As put by a gang member who has been in and out of jail since he was twelve:

> I was a little gang-banger. That means like a rumble—we call it gang-banging though. We used to fight with bricks and sticks and chains, now they use bats and guns. But when I was little I used to fight the other groups, and go to parties and get drunk and get high, get away from my house, go to jail.
>
> I don't really know how I got into all that. I just grew up with it, you know, it was in my neighborhood and I grew up into it. . . . I am tired of being a nobody.
>
> On the other hand, once you put on a sweater with the gang colors, you become somebody. You are a person of status—a King, an Unknown, a Lord.
>
> A sweater represents the gang you're in. You feel like you've got power wearing that sweater. You say yes, these are my colors and I've got all these guys behind me, and they're backing me up 100 percent.
>
> I never did no real big gang-bang except take away sweaters, that's what I like to do, you know, I thought it was fun and games. It was just like playing a sport. They got a sweater, you try to take it away from them. We've got sweaters and they try to take it away from us. To see who could hang on to your sweater, you know.
>
> It was just a game—until they started to shoot. Then I said wait a minute, this ain't no game. This is for keeps. This is for your life.*

*BUILD descriptive material, Chicago, updated.

Today avenging a slight comes not through rumbles (gang fights) as in the 1950s, but through hit squads being sent out to open up on rivals from a moving car. Sometimes contracts are even put out. The murderers are often only fourteen or fifteen, since it is believed—with justification—that if caught they will be treated only as delinquent juveniles. Police crackdowns have had little except publicity value; they only alienate the community. Police have shown little sensitivity to the community, or ability to distinguish between hard-core gang leaders and people just hanging around a corner.

Because of this difficulty, traditional community organizations such as the YMCA and Boys Clubs have dropped out of youth gang work. Gang members often don't go to school or work—the gang is their whole life. As put by Hank Bach, one of the co-founders of BUILD, the only organization actively working with gang members in the streets:

> We're talking about young people who are very easily frustrated. We're dealing with the kids that have the poorest attitudes, the kids whose behavior is very violent and very aggressive in many instances. The problem so often is the time that they've got to spend on the street corner without anything else going on. That's part of the problem—just the whole concept of time. If you occupy time, then you're minimizing the things they'll be getting into. We're talking about active young people, and we're saying, "What are the most active kinds of ways of getting them involved?" So we use the athletic situation and we use the social recreational situation to develop money in the bank. We're establishing a relationship based on those short-term objective activities, and that relationship can then help carry the kids into other more demanding programs which have greater long-range benefits. Education and employment—the type of programs that the kids might back away from.†

BUILD workers, most of whom live within the community, stay on the street with the gangs. Many are former members or dropouts who are now back in school working part-time with the organization. Particular attention is given to gang leaders, since members will usually follow where they are led. BUILD offers help to dropouts in completing high school and provides guidance, training, placement, and advice on how to get and hold a job. Many of the gang youth have few skills for legitimate employment. Most, until they are taught, cannot even fill in the standard employment application properly.

In all cases the emphasis is on dealing with the youth realistically. No one is promised a free ride. Because they are

†Ibid.

former dropouts who are now making it, the street workers provide successful noncriminal role models. As such they are more likely to be listened to than formally trained social workers. Generally BUILD has been reasonably successful. While it has not eliminated the gangs—and it cannot change the massive unemployment and drug use that underlies so much of the communities' problems—it can and does provide these youths an alternative to gang warfare. It shows them how to achieve status as individuals outside the gang structure—by itself a considerable achievement.

since World War II. Third, Puerto Ricans are almost totally urban. Some 96 percent of mainland Puerto Ricans reside in metropolitan areas. Finally, as noted earlier, Puerto Rican family income is the lowest of that of Hispanic groups, with four out of ten (39 percent) of Puerto Rican families living in poverty.[50] Puerto Ricans, thus, are even more hard pressed than blacks.

As with blacks, but not other Hispanics, there is a high proportion of female-headed families. Four out of ten (41 percent) of all Puerto Rican families are headed by a woman without a husband present. Compared with Mexican women, Puerto Rican women are relatively independent. Single or divorced women find life far more liberating in New York than in Puerto Rico. The New York area houses approximately half (49 percent) of mainland Puerto Ricans. This is down from 64 percent in 1970.

Mainland Puerto Ricans have a very young age structure, with half the population under twenty. Educational levels are the lowest among the Spanish-origin population. As of the 1970 census, only 2 percent had finished college.[51] In 1980 college graduates totaled only 3 percent.

Drastic upgrading of educational levels is essential if Puerto Ricans are to move ahead. New York's former deputy mayor for education. Herman Badillo, himself a Puerto Rican, is not optimistic about the schools' accomplishments with Puerto Rican youngsters. He estimated the dropout rate at 85 percent. "We have plenty of jobs in skyscrapers of midtown Manhattan," he says, "The problem is that kids can't spell."[52]

Central cities such as New York are losing the entry-level blue-color jobs filled by immigrants. Newcomer Puerto Ricans can't sell their muscles the way the earlier Germans and Italians did. Today economic advancement strongly favors those having white-collar skills and levels of education. For Puerto Ricans, political involvement tends to be low compared with that of previous immigrant groups. In part, this is due to the availability of flights back to Puerto Rico. If things get difficult, it is sometimes easier just to return to the island.

The New Generation. The picture just sketched overwhelmingly reflects experiences of first-generation mainland Puerto Ricans.[53] Thus it may be unduly pessimistic for younger generations. The median age of Puerto Ricans born in the mainland United States is only ten years; the second generation is just beginning to make its impact. Indications are that the educational and occupational levels of young Puerto Ricans will be far higher than those of their parents (although still below the average for all whites). Family patterns are also changing. First-generation Puerto Ricans have larger-sized families than

---

[50]U.S. Bureau of the Census, "Persons of Spanish Origin in the United States," *Current Population Reports,* series P-20, no. 329, Washington, D.C., figs. 7 and 8.

[51]Jose Hernandez et al., *Social Factors in Educational Attainment among Puerto Ricans in U.S. Metropolitan Areas,* Aspira, New York, 1979, pp. 1–2.

[52]Quoted in *Time,* October 16, 1978.

[53]U.S. Commission on Civil Rights, "Puerto Ricans in the United States: An Uncertain Future," Washington, D.C., 1976, p. 36.

the national average, while second-generation Puerto Ricans born in the United States have fewer children than the national average.[54] Thus, while the first generation is among the nation's poorest citizens, the fate of the mainland-born may be far brighter.

AMERICAN INDIANS

By omission, we have in essence denied that the American Indian has a heritage other than that portrayed in old John Wayne movies on late-night television.[55] Only recently have there been popular books telling history from the Indian's side, such as *Bury My Heart at Wounded Knee*.[56] Such works have helped to restore our perspective, but valuable as they are, they do not confront one basic problem: our tendency always to refer to Indians in the past tense, as if they had disappeared with the buffalo and the frontier. They didn't disappear: they were simply ignored and forgotten.

As noted in Chapter 3, The Rise of Urban America, the first colonists saw Indians as part of the environment, to be mastered and tamed like the forests and wild animals. The Indians' antiurban orientation—they lived in nomadic bands or small villages—left them particularly vulnerable to exploitation. Indians were systematically exterminated by Indian wars, destruction of the buffalo, and epidemics of European diseases against which they had no immunity. By 1890, when the first federal census of Indians was taken, their population had been reduced to 250,000, most barely surviving on government reservations. Today Native Americans number 1.4 million—six-tenths of a percent of the national population.

Chances in Life. Indians were our first minority, and despite dramatic recent improvements, they remain our most deprived. Infant mortality, for example, is still about 20 percent higher among Indians than among other Americans.[57] Two decades ago, it was 44 percent above the national average.[58] Life expectancy for the average Native American is now six years below the national average but far better than the shockingly poor life expectancy of only two decades ago, which was forty-six years.

In spite of higher mortality, the extremely high birthrate of American Indians indicates that the "vanishing red man" is vanishing no more. A birthrate almost double that of the whole population ensures continued growth.

---

[54]Ibid.

[55]American Indians—from Cherokee to Sioux to Algonquin—are heterogeneous in patterns of social organization and in their world view. The only justification for subsuming such diversity under the generic term "Indian" is that the white society has consistently done this for several centuries and has responded similarly to all groups it has labeled "Indian." Only in this sense can we speak of Indians as a unitary group.

[56]Wounded Knee was the final episode of the Indian wars. Here 300 Sioux were massacred by the army in 1890. It was also the site of an unsuccessful militant political occupation by Indians in 1973. See Dee Alexander Brown, *Bury My Heart at Wounded Knee,* Holt, Rinehart, and Winston, New York, 1971.

[57]Population Reference Bureau, *Interchange,* 4:2, November, 1975.

[58]*Indian Health Trends and Services,* Program Analysis and Statistics Branch of the Indian Health Service, Dept. of H. E. W., Washington, D.C., 1969.

These Navajo children are being taught to read in their native
language before they learn in English. (Paul Conklin/Monkmeyer)

Rural Indians have an average of five children per family—the highest fertility
rate in the country. The Indian population doubled between 1960 and 1970 and
then increased 72 percent between the 1970 and 1980 census. Part of this
increase was due not to a growth of the Indian population, but to changes in
how Indians were enumerated.

Roughly one-third of Native Americans live in poverty. Educational
attainment among Native Americans is also poor—particularly on reservations.

The educational levels are rising, but a special Bureau of the Census survey showed a low 61 percent of Indians being high school graduates.[59] At present, almost all Indian children are attending school, but the quality of the education, particularly in reservation schools, is suspect.[60]

Movement to Cities. Indians are increasingly deserting the reservations for the cities, since most reservations offer only a future of illiteracy, poverty, and alcoholism, all too frequently terminated by an early death. The Bureau of Indian Affairs has been urging Indians to leave their reservations and resettle in urban areas. Today, only one-third of American Indians live on reservation lands.

Between 1930 and 1980, the minority group that experienced the greatest degree of urbanization was not, as is commonly thought, blacks but rather American Indians. As of 1930, only 10 percent of the Indian population lived in metropolitan areas, and as recently as 1960, seven out of ten Indians were estimated to be rural. Today, over half of the Native American population is urban.[61] Indians have been moving to cities in general rather than to any one city. A dozen cities in the country have more than 10,000 Indians each, but in no large city do Indians account for more than 5 percent of the population. The largest urban Indian populations are found in Los Angeles, Chicago, Minneapolis, Milwaukee, Phoenix, Albuquerque, and Oklahoma City.

The common pattern of shuttling between city and reservation hinders effective urban organization. Tribal differences and lack of stable urban Indian populations have worked against the creation of tight ethnic social communities such as those of European immigrants. Shuttling back and forth also interferes with holding stable city jobs. In the words of a sympathetic writer, the reservation is still necessary, since it "functions as an outpost and haven from the urban scene where the adult battle for survival really takes place.[62]

Life in the city may not be grand, but it is superior to the cycle of acute poverty that is the lot of Indians on the reservation.

Urban Native Americans generally live in poorer central-city neighborhoods, much as European immigrants did. However, not all Native Americans live in such areas. Persons whose ancestry is Indian but who have been assimilated into middle-class America may not identify themselves as Indians except under particular circumstances, such as the distribution of funds from selling tribal estates. These people have Indian ancestry, but in their behavior, attitudes, and daily life, they are indistinguishable from their neighbors of European ancestry. These culturally assimilated Indians are sometimes referred to by other Indians as "apples"—"red on the outside and white on the inside." More than one-third of Indians now marry non-Indians.

[59]U.S. Bureau of the Census, "Ancestry and Language in the United States," series P-23, no. 16, Washington, D.C., 1982, p. 11.
[60]Report of the U.S. Commission on Civil Rights, *The Navajo Nation: An American Colony*, Washington,D.C., 1975, p. 60.
[61]Ancestry and Language, op. cit., p. 11.
[62]Jeanne Guilhemin, *Urban Renegades*, Columbia University Press, New York, 1975, p. 150.

TABLE 9-4
Japanese Immigrants to Mainland United States, 1861–1940*

Period	Number	Percent of all immigrants
1861–1870	218	0.01
1871–1880	149	0.02
1881–1890	2,270	0.04
1891–1900	27,982	0.77
1901–1907	108,163	1.74
1908–1914	74,478	1.11
1915–1924	85,197	2.16
1925–1940	6,156	0.03

* Not including migrants from Hawaii after its annexation. The use of the term "immigrant" is not clear even in official statistics. The above table is for "immigrants" who intended to settle permanently as opposed to "nonimmigrants" who did not.
Source: William Petersen, *Japanese Americans*, Random House, New York, 1971, p. 15. Calculated from U.S. Bureau of the Census, *Historical Statistics of the United States*, U.S. Government Printing Office, Washington, D.C., 1960, Series C-88. C-104; Yamato Ichihashi, *Japanese Immigration: Its Status in California*, Marshall Press, San Francisco, 1915, p. 9.

Urban ways can produce culture shock for Native Americans. Most (but not all) Indian cultures stress cooperation and noncompetitiveness over competition and achievement. Indian heritages are thus often at variance with the larger American culture, with its emphasis on hard work and economic success. Militant Native Americans are caught in a dilemma: they want educational and employment opportunities and at the same time want to live according to Indian ways that make it difficult to take advantage of such opportunities.[63]

The problem of being pulled between two cultures is, of course, not unique to groups new to the American city. The antiurban orientation of most Native American cultures, however, gives special sharpness to the issue of cultural separateness versus assimilation. Policy makers in Washington have also vacillated: they seem unable to decide whether Indians should be encouraged to remain tribal nations, with separate cultures, or whether Indians are better served by detribalization and urban relocation. The Reagan administration stressed the latter.

A NOTE ON JAPANESE AMERICANS

Whenever one starts making generalizations about minorities, one is brought up short by the example of the Japanese Americans. For the Japanese

[63]Bruce Chadwick and Joseph Strauss, "The Assimilation of American Indians into Urban Society, The Seattle Case," paper presented at the meeting of the American Sociological Association, San Francisco, August 1975, pp. 33–34.

Household and personal goods of Japanese Americans being interned in Salinas, California in May, 1942. (Russell Lee/Library of Congress)

Americans, who only four decades ago were possibly our most hated minority, are now accepted, successful, and prosperous citizens.[64]

Japanese Americans have been notably successful in adapting to the values, behaviors, and expectations of the American system. Harry Kitano suggests that the statement "Scratch a Japanese American and find a white Anglo-Saxon Protestant" is generally accurate.[65] What makes this all the more remarkable is that Japanese Americans have had to overcome severe discrimination—discrimination which included being forcibly driven from their homes and businesses during World War II and being incarcerated behind barbed wire in "relocation camps."

The Internment Camps

The entry of the United States into World War II on December 7, 1941, resulted in anti-Japanese hysteria. It was popularly believed that a Japanese fifth column existed, conducting sabotage on orders from Tokyo. Interestingly, considering their later political development, such well-known liberals as Earl Warren and Walter Lippmann were among the most vocal against the Japanese, while one of the few public officials to denounce the rumors of sabotage as "racist hysteria" was J. Edgar Hoover, the director of the FBI.

[64]William Petersen, "Success Story: Japanese-American Style," *The New York Times Magazine*, January 9, 1966.
[65]Harry H. L. Kitano, *Japanese Americans: The Evolution of a Subculture*, Prentice-Hall, Englewood Cliffs, N.J., 1976. p. 3.

The public clamor for action was met in February 1942, when President Roosevelt, on the recommendation of advisors, signed Executive Order 9066. The order designated military areas from which military commanders could exclude persons because of national security. The order also authorized the construction of inland "relocation centers." It was quickly implemented. On March 2, 1942, General De Witt, commander of the Western Defense Area, ordered all persons of Japanese ancestry to be evacuated from the three western coastal states and part of Arizona. He summed up his feelings with the statement, "Once a Jap, always a Jap." The evacuation order included children with as little as one-eighth Japanese ancestry. Two-thirds of those ordered to leave their homes were citizens of the United States. They were each allowed to take one suitcase with them as they were herded by army troops into assembly centers and then shipped to one of ten inland relocation camps. More than 110,000 of the 126,000 Japanese in this country were put in these camps—regardless of their citizenship.

No such action was taken against those of German and Italian ancestry on the east coast, nor was any action taken against the Japanese on the strategic islands of Hawaii, where the Japanese made up a full 37 percent of the population. Long after the war, it was officially admitted that no Japanese American had committed a single subversive act anywhere within the United States. But for as long as three years many Japanese Americans lived in dismal tar-paper shacks in deserted, inhospitable areas of California, Arizona, Idaho, Wyoming, Utah, and Arkansas, surrounded by barbed wire and machine guns. The inmates were let out only on "seasonal leaves"—which was an euphemistic way of saying that they were used as cheap labor on local farms. Jobs in the camps paid from $16 to $19 a month. In 1942 the Federal Reserve Bank of San Francisco estimated the Japanese Americans' financial loss—abandoned or cheaply sold stores, farms, and businesses—at $400 million. The United States government eventually paid settlement claims at the rate of 5 to 10 cents on the dollar. In 1986 the courts recognized the right of interned Japanese Americans to compensation.

Life in the camps radically changed the structure of Japanese American society. The second-generation, or Nisei, who spoke English and were citizens, quickly filled most of the local leadership positions, displacing the older Issei or first-generation. Ironically, the Nisei could fill a host of leadership positions which anti-Japanese discrimination on the west coast would have made unavailable to them on the outside. After the war many Nisei chose to move east, where their skills and abilities had a better chance of recognition, rather than back to the more ghettoized west coast.

One of the many paradoxes of this period was that the 442d Regimental Combat Team—the most-decorated American unit in World War II—was composed of Japanese Americans. More than 1,000 of the men in the 442d had enlisted directly from the internment camps to fight for the country that had forcibly removed them from their homes and livelihood. The 442d's war cry, "Go for Broke," is a part of American history. Less well known is the fact that the average IQ of the unit was the highest (119) for a combat group and that the 442d had more college graduates than any other comparable unit in the armed forces. The Nisei earned, in blood, the grudging respect of other GIs. In action in Italy and France, the unit suffered 9,486 casualties—or over 300 percent of its original infantry strength.

Japanese Americans Today

After the war and the internment camps, the second-generation Nisei had an unparalleled record of upward mobility. In 1940 over a quarter of all Japanese Americans were laborers; by the 1980s this figure was down to only an insignificant number. Among all nonwhite groups the Japanese rank first in income and education. The "Sansei," or third generation, born since World War II, has become almost totally acculturated.

Compared with other Americans, Japanese Americans, particularly on the west coast, still live largely in ethnic communities with a strong sense of group responsibility and group "image." The sense of group identity is reflected in the low delinquency and crime rates—rates that are rising as "American" behavior patterns replace those of the once tightly bound ethnic community.

Soon after arrival, Japanese Americans stopped teaching their children the Japanese language, and over the years many Japanese customs have been abandoned in favor of American models. Another sign of change has been the number of marriages outside the group. Marriage of Sansei out of the ethnic community has become common, particularly away from the more traditional ethnic communities in California.

The breakdown of distinctive ways of life is a mixed blessing. On the positive side, Japanese Americans now participate fully in all aspects of national life. However, it would be sad and more than a little ironic if in an urban world that is seeking a sense of community the Japanese Americans, who prospered because of their strong community and their cohesive family system, would now allow their distinctive culture to be eroded or abandoned.

SOUTHEAST ASIANS: A SUCCESS STORY

"The Boat People" was the name given to the waves of refugees leaving southeast Asia in the late 1970s and in the early 1980s, following the total U.S. pull out from Vietnam. Unlike earlier refugees from Vietnam the boat people had little education and few resources or transferable skills. Most were farmers, fishermen, or laborers. Those picked up adrift at sea were packed into refugee camps. Most of those refugees reaching America arrived at a time of economic recession during the early 1980s. Few spoke any English. Their prognosis seemed one of long-term economic dependency and social problems.

The reality, however, has been one of remarkable progress against stiff odds. Research on 1,400 refugee households in Houston, Chicago, Boston, Seattle, and Orange Country California—major resettlement areas—found that the families are rapidly moving from bleak poverty to economic self-sufficiency. Most families are still below the federally defined poverty level, but according to the researcher Nathan Caplan, "a stunning proportion of these families are climbing out of deep poverty—largely through an impressive demonstration of hard work and initiative."[66]

The refugees had a long way to climb. Only one-quarter of the refugees has completed high school and only one in a hundred spoke fluent English when arriving in America. Moreover, resettlement programs were of only limited use to the refugees. Sixty percent of those employed found jobs not through employment programs but exclusively through friends and relatives. Caplan found that three years after arrival, nine out of ten refugee households reported at least one family member employed, usually at low-status, low-income jobs. Three-quarters of the refugees were taking classes in English.

In a separate, related study of 350 school-aged children it was found that the children were making even more remarkable progress. Although most spoke no English on arrival in the United States, after an average of just three years in the country they were outperforming their school-age peers in terms of grade point averages. They remain somewhat below the national average in English, but 27 percent score in the ninetieth percentile on math achievement—almost three times the national average.[67] The highest-achieving children came from cohesive families with traditional Confucian values and a strong respect for education.

Overall, Southeast Asian refugee families remain generally poor and in marginal jobs. But in only a handful of years they have already made noticeable progress. For the southeast Asian "Boat People" the American dream of hard work and success appears to be an emerging reality.

[66]Nathan Caplan, "Southeast Asian Refugees: Achieving Independence in America," ISR *Newsletter,* Institute for Social Research, University of Michigan, Spring/Summer, 1985, p. 7.
[67]Ibid., p. 4.

PART FOUR

URBAN PROBLEMS AND PLANNING

CHAPTER

10

URBAN CRISIS OR URBAN REBIRTH

The decline of Rome was the natural and inevitable effect of immoderate greatness—as soon as time or accidents had removed the artificial supports, the stupendous fabric yielded to the pressure of its own weight.

Edward Gibbon, 1737–1794

THE URBAN CRISIS?

As recently as 1930 a planner could describe Los Angeles as "a federation of communities coordinated into a metropolis of sunlight and air."[1] No one makes such claims today. It is an accepted cliché that we live in an age of urban crisis. Crime, violence, pollution, ugliness, congestion, and alienation are all attributed in one degree or another to urban life. Certainly there is no lack of prophets to passionately catalog our urban ills. As Lewis Mumford says:

> Nobody can be satisfied with the form of the city today. Neither as a working mechanism, as a social medium, nor as a work of art does the city fulfill the high hopes that modern civilization has called forth—or even met our reasonable demands.[2]

Are cities, particularly large cities, doomed? During the 1970s voices were raised everywhere proclaiming the inevitable decline, if not death, of the city. Over and over we heard of the doleful state of the city.[3] A conference of large-city mayors in 1977 proclaimed that what was at stake was not only "the survival of our cities" but the survival of the American way of life as we have known it. The chairman of the New York Real Estate Board stated: "American cities are collapsing. This peril to the nation, and in consequence to over 200 years of experiment in democracy, is no overstatement."[4]

Philip Hauser contends that "the stark facts indicate that the worst still lies ahead. The urban crisis will grow worse before it grows better.[5] Similarly, George Sternlieb has pessimistically suggested that "the Newarks of America are forecasts of things to come, and if we want to understand the probable future that faces many of our older cities, then we will first have to get clear on what is happening—has happened—in places like Newark,"[6] Sternlieb contends that the older cities have lost their economic function, particularly as areas of entry for newcomers, and have become simply "sandboxes." People in the sandbox occasionally get new toys (federal programs), but these don't allow the underclass to move into the larger world—they just keep the people in the sandbox from being bothersome to the rest of society.

In this view, cities are having their vital signs maintained by external life-support systems, with the federal government making the judgment about whether to pull the plug. To those holding such views, shrinkage in city size is inevitable.[7] Not surprisingly, such discussions regarding the future of urban

---

[1]R. M. Fogelson, *The Fragmented Metropolis: Los Angeles 1850–1930,* Harvard University Press, Cambridge, Mass. 1967, p. 163.

[2]Lewis Mumford, *The Urban Prospect,* Harcourt Brace Jovanovich, New York, 1968, p. 108.

[3]See *U.S. News and World Report,* April 5, 1976, pp. 49–64.

[4]Seymour B. Durant, "Laetrile for the Urban Crisis: Planned Shrinkage' and Other Dangerous Nostrums," *Journal of the Institute for Socioeconomic Studies,* 4:68, Summer, 1979.

[5]Philip M. Hauser, "Chicago—Urban Crisis Exemplar," in J. John Palen (ed.), *City Scenes,* Little, Brown, Boston, 1977, pp. 15–25.

[6]George Sternlieb, "The City as Sandbox," *The Public Interest,* 4:(25):14, Fall, 1971.

[7]Roger Starr, "Making New York Smaller," *New York Times Magazine,* November 19, 1976, pp. 32–33, 99–106.

areas have focused not on what will occur, but rather on questions of the degree and timing of the collapse.

THE CITY RESURRECTED?

Now other voices are proclaiming with no less authority that the crisis is past and that a new urban renaissance is dawning. That some cities will inevitably continue to falter economically as well as demographically is generally acknowledged, but in many cities the last few years have witnessed a rebirth of hope. The media discovered that the city was not only alive but healthy.[8] Only a few industrial midwestern cities are said still to show signs of fiscal stress, and the employment gap between cities and suburbs is closing. Particularly in the south and west cities are "now generating new jobs twice as fast as the nearer suburban centers."[9] Suddenly we hear that the "urban crisis" has left town, and the slumming of the suburbs is the new problem.[10] Meanwhile, the central cities have bottomed out and are now experiencing an urban renaissance. Revitalized downtowns are showing economic vigor, while affluent whites are rediscovering the city as a place of residence and are rehabilitating inner-city areas. (This is discussed in detail in Chapter 11, Housing Programs and Urban Change.)

What is the case? Readers, understandably, may be confused by the contradictory claims. Just as they have come to accept the urban crisis as part of American life, they are told, "Never mind; the crisis is over." This section attempts to evaluate the various claims and counterclaims; but as you read the material, keep in mind that these are the judgments of this author, and others might draw different conclusions. Also, you might want to review the material on invasion and succession of land usages in Chapter 4, Ecology and Structure of American Cities.

Central Business Districts

In evaluating what is occurring in cities, it is helpful to distinguish between what is occurring in the economic heart of the city—the central business district (CBD)—and what is happening in residential neighborhoods.

Discussions of the decline of downtowns often focus on the weakening position of the CBD as a center of retail trade. As shopping centers, downtowns have been declining both in absolute terms and in terms of a percentage of metropolitan-area sales. Aging downtown stores have not been able to compete effectively with suburban shopping malls.

On the other hand, the CBD has been far more successful in retaining business and government administrative offices. Economically, the downtowns

---

[8]Horace Sutton, "America Falls in Love with Its Cities—Again," *Saturday Review,* August, 1978, pp. 16–21; and "A City Revival," *Newsweek,* January 15, 1979,

[9]T. D. Allman, "The Urban Crisis Leaves Town," *Harpers,* December, 1978, p. 5.

[10]Ibid., pp. 41–56.

A Marxist View

One cannot discuss the urban crisis without the perspective provided by the new Marxist urban sociology.* Marxist sociologists hold that cities cannot be examined separately from the political, historical, and, particularly, economic system of which they are a part. Manuel Costells argues, for example, that not only is the crisis of the cities real, but the decay of the central cities, their fiscal insolvency, and flight to the suburbs are inevitable and necessary consequences of a capitalistic economic system.† He says that the quest for ever-greater profits by large monopolistic companies led to government policies such as government-insured mortgages and subsidies for expressways. The corporations—and their wealthy managers—thus could move to the suburbs, where land costs and taxes were lower, while still maintaining the economic benefits of being near the central city. The fiscal crises of cities such as New York were not the consequence of excessive services, public service jobs, and welfare, as the elites argue. Rather, New York's near "bankruptcy" was the result of the corporations' rejection of increased taxes to pay for these social services. The result is the abandonment—and destruction—of largely poor areas of the city, while corporations concentrate on issues important to themselves such as downtown redevelopment. Social movements by the poor are either repressed or bought off. The consequence is said to be a future where the urban crisis is sharpened and mass repression and control become inevitable adjuncts of an exploitative metropolitan model.‡

Similarly, Marxists analyze gentrification as a conscious product of land-based interest groups able to control the real estate market.§ According to this view investment capital was systematically moved out of inner cities and into suburbs because suburban profit rates were higher. The subsequent deterioration of inner-city neighborhoods led to the development of a rent gap, which in turn made it possible for capital to return to the central city seeking profits. The ownership class benefits from these decisions, while the costs of gentrification fall upon the urban poor in the form of displacement.

*See, for example, Manuel Costells, *The Urban Question: A Marxist Approach*, Alan Sheridan (trans.), M.I.T. Press, Cambridge, Mass., 1977.
†Manuel Costells, "The Wild City," *Kapital State*, **4–5**:2–30, Summer, 1976.
‡Ibid.
§Neil Smith and Michele LeFaiure, "A Class Analysis of Gentrification," in J. John Palen and Bruce London (eds.), *Gentrification, Displacement and Neighborhood Revitalization*, State University of New York Press, Albany, N.Y., 1984.

San Antonio has converted its once-dull riverfront into a major tourist attraction. (San Antonio Convention & Visitors Bureau)

of most large cities are experiencing new business construction. New office towers and high-rise apartment buildings are sprouting on Manhattan streets; Houston doubled its office space during the last decade; downtown Los Angeles is undergoing a building boom, Chicago has over $1 billion in new skyscrapers planned or under construction, and New York is experiencing a major influx of foreign capital—including reinvested oil money.

Between 1960 and 1979 a remarkable 142 new buildings were completed in midtown Manhattan containing 77 million square feet of space.[11] This is more than all of the office space in Houston and Dallas together. Moreover, thirty new buildings have been added since 1979. More office space was built in the first five years of this decade than during all of the 1970s (one consequence of all this office building is high city, and even higher suburban, vacancy rates for office space.)

Downtown shopping malls such as Harbor Place in Baltimore are again drawing people. Throughout the country new downtown convention facilities, cultural centers, hotels, and office buildings are sprouting. This is occurring in Atlanta, Denver, San Antonio, Portland, and a host of other cities. Thus, for CBDs the worst may be over. The presuburban era of downtown total

[11]Paul Goldberger, "The Limits of Urban Growth," *New York Times Magazine,* November 14, 1982, p. 47.

The South Bronx has become symbolic of urban decay and abandonment. (© Sepp Seitz/Woodfin Camp & Assoc.)

dominance will not return, but most cities' CBDs are in the process of stabilizing at a moderate but reasonable level of economic activity.

Overall, downtown stores will never again have the unchallenged control of retail trade they exhibited during the centralizing era of the streetcar and subway; but so long as the downtown is a major white-collar employment center, the CBD will be a solidly profitable location for retail sales. Moreover, downtown remains the location of choice of insurance firms, financial and legal services, government, and administrative headquarters of all sorts. One visible consequence of CBDs' change from retail trade to office space is that the crowded CBD of working hours often becomes a virtual wasteland after 5:00 P.M., when offices close.

However, there is a catch to this development of the CBD. Central-city offices provide new jobs—but only for those possessing specific white-collar skills. City factories and manufacturing plants continue to move to the suburbs— or beyond. For example, from 1960 to 1970, cities experienced a 13 percent reduction in blue-collar jobs but a concurrent 7 percent increase in white-collar jobs.[12] This pattern accelerated during the 1970s and 1980s.

[12]John Kasarda, "The Changing Occupational Structure of the American Metropolis," in Barry Schwartz (ed.), *The Changing Face of Suburbs,* University of Chicago Press, Chicago, 1976, p. 122.

The result often is a mismatch between people and jobs. Stagnant or declining central-city manufacturing and factory sectors offer scant employment opportunities for those with limited educational backgrounds and job experience. Poor minority-group members have not been able to follow manufacturing jobs to the suburbs. The consequence is that cities often have high unemployment and welfare rolls at the same time that white-collar opportunities are expanding. Depending on where the emphasis is placed, one can make a case that things are either much better or much worse.

Fiscal Crisis and Federal Support

During the 1970s it was common for cities to be in grave financial trouble. The middle class with its tax dollars was flowing to the suburbs while central-city expenses were skyrocketing. Particularly in the frost belt cities, declining populations meant greater costs to those who remained. As middle-class taxpayers departed, municipal payrolls and public assistance expenditures usually increased rather than declined. Growing numbers of poor residents needing services raised costs while depressing revenues. Cities were becoming polarized between affluent and poor. (As of 1985 the income of one of four New Yorkers was below the poverty line.) Aging city properties also required more fire and police protection, and older street, lighting, and sewer systems required more maintenance.

Today the poor remain, but there is less talk of the fiscal crisis of the cities. Most cities are meeting their day-to-day expenses. According to a major financial study, only four of sixty-six cities studied suffered serious financial stress.[13] Terry Clark et al. have similarly showed that cities vary dramatically in their fiscal health.[14] In their study, New York City's debt crisis was an extreme case of high expenditures and poor financial management. Today New York has a budget surplus.

A major reason for the improved municipal fiscal picture was direct and indirect federal aid to cities. However, the fact that cities can meet their payrolls does not mean that they are in robust financial health. Federal revenue sharing provided temporary relief but did not resolve long-term problems. Cities are still squeezed between growing expenditures and a declining tax base. The larger the city, the greater the financial burden. Per capita debt is more than twice as high in cities of over 1 million as in smaller cities.[15]

Most citizens are unaware of the extent to which cities are dependent on federal and state aid to balance their budgets. During Lyndon Johnson's Great Society programs (1967), direct federal aid to St. Louis was only 1 percent,

---

[13]"Urban Fiscal Stress," a report by Touche Ross and Co. and the First National Bank of Boston, 1978. This report is challenged by the Department of Housing and Urban Development in "The Urban Fiscal Crisis: Fact or Fantasy?" Office of Policy Development and Research, Washington, D.C., March, 1979.

[14]Terry N. Clark, Irene Sharp Rubin, Lynne C. Pettler, and Erwin Zimmerman, *How Many New Yorks? Comparative Study of Community Decision-Making*, Research Report no. 72, University of Chicago, Chicago, 1976.

[15]*U.S. News and World Report*, April 6, 1976, p. 51.

Baltimore 3.8 percent, and Los Angeles 0.7 percent.[16] A decade later (1979) direct federal grants totaled 19.1 percent of St. Louis's budget. The figures for Baltimore and Los Angeles were 25.7 percent and 21.1 percent.[17] State funds for these cities provided respectively 12.2, 21.7, and 14.8 percent of the budgets. These are fairly typical cases.

Today the belief in local economic independence has major elements of myth. A local mayor's performance is measured in part by the federal monies he or she can obtain from Washington. Cities may talk of local decision making and self-sufficiency, but the reality is that American cities all have become to some degree the clients of Washington. The price of solvency may be the loss of some local autonomy. However, a sharp reversal of the process would be disastrous for urban places since many crucial services such as police and fire protection as of the mid 1980s were partially funded by revenue sharing.

General Revenue Sharing

President Reagan in his 1986 budget proposed the total elimination of the $4.6 billion general revenue sharing that had been going to 39,281 local governments.[18] Not surprisingly, both Republican and Democratic mayors united to lobby against what they viewed as a massive threat to the health and solvency of local areas. Without revenue sharing, either local taxes have to escalate sharply or local services such as police be drastically reduced. At a time when there is great citizen concern over crime, the prospect of far fewer police has little citizen support. Cost cutting does not always cut costs. Cutbacks in fire services, for example, not only brings higher risks, but also higher insurance rates.

Generally overlooked by most observers is the problem of infrastructure deterioration. In the 1980s deterioration of the cities' physical infrastructure is actually a far more serious problem than potential default. In New York, bursting water mains and collapsing streets have become commonplace, yet little is being done. At the present level of construction, it would take over 200 years to replace New York City's streets and water mains and 300 years to replace its sewers.[19] Nor is New York alone; Philadelphia's sewers are falling apart, while Boston and Houston are plagued by hemorrhaging water mains.

Quo Vadis?

The overall future of the cities remains clouded. On the positive side, cities have not defaulted. The state of the cities is fiscally and—perhaps more important—psychologically healthier than a decade ago. Bright new office buildings and refurbished shopping malls are a sign of hope. There are also clear if limited signs of middle-class movement into older city neighborhoods.

[16]T. D. Allman, "The Urban Crisis Leaves Town," in J. John Palen (ed.), *City Scenes* (2d ed.), 1981, p. 29.
[17]*Newsweek*, May 4, 1981, p. 29.
[18]*Washington Post*, February 4, 1985, p. A5.
[19]"City Fiscal Time Bomb—Decaying Facilities." *New York Times*, January 29, 1979.

On the debit side, the long-term indicators are still grim. There is still an outflow of tax dollars; older cities continue to lose manufacturing jobs; and the cost of services is rising. Physically some neighborhoods are experiencing regeneration, but deterioration of the physical infrastructure (e.g., water mains and sewers) remains an expensive if often unseen problem. The political climate favors tax cutbacks rather than new urban programs.

Not all cities are going to experience similar situations. Declines in size may reflect deterioration or may spur the development of new roles as cultural and service centers. Cities such as Newark and Cleveland may well continue their declines regardless of valiant efforts to reverse the process. Old cities such as Boston and Baltimore, on the other hand, are undergoing an urban renaissance. Others such as Denver, Dallas, Seattle, and Phoenix show signs of increasing problems but also retain considerable vigor and attractiveness. Ironically, there is widespread public acceptance of the thesis of inevitable and irreversible urban decay, just as the data indicate renewed urban vitality and regeneration.

NEIGHBORHOOD REVIVAL

For decades there has been talk of a "back to the city" movement, but the talk has not been followed up by actual movement.[20] As Chapter 8, Patterns of Suburbanization, documents, the movement has long been outbound rather than directed toward the central city. The assumption has been that those having the choice (i.e., white middle-class home buyers) would shun the central city for the suburbs. As noted in Chapter 6, City Life-styles, Gallup polls supported the view of suburban preference, with only 13 percent of those interviewed preferring city residence to residence in suburbia or a small town.

However, there is now a limited but symbolic countermovement toward residence in the central city. Ironically, the movement is not to leveled and rebuilt urban renewal areas, but to older neighborhoods that are recycling from a period of decay. Middle-income and upper-middle-income whites (and some blacks) are buying and restoring old homes and new houses—a process commonly known as "neighborhood regeneration" or "gentrification."[21]

"Gentrification" is a recent phenomenon, with the majority of activity occurring since 1975. Also, revitalization is not occurring in all city neighborhoods, but is thus far limited largely to areas having substantial residences with historic or architectural merit. While the homes in these neighborhoods may be in disrepair when purchased by the "urban pioneer," they were originally constructed to standards generally unavailable in new suburban houses. Revitalizing areas are also generally well located in terms of accessibility, transportation routes, and overall physical location.

---

[20]The purpose of the urban renewal programs of the 1950s and 1960s was to rebuild the cities' inner cores in order to encourage middle-class residency in such areas. As we will see in Chapter 11, the effort was largely unsuccessful.

[21]J. John Palen and Bruce London (eds.), *Gentrification, Displacement and Neighborhood Revitalization*, State University of New York Press, New York, 1984.

Middle-class in-movement to older central-city neighborhoods challenges traditional theories of growth. According to the classical Burgess model (discussed in Chapter 5, Metropolitan, Nonmetropolitan, and Sun Belt Growth) or the filtered-down economic model, this in-movement should not be occurring. Rather, older central-city residences should be abandoned to the economically marginal. Also, according to the original Burgess model, central-city residential property is vacated for commercial or industrial usage. Today, the pattern is more often the reverse; in some cities, formerly commercial buildings such as warehouses are being rehabilitated as residences. The SoHo section of New York, for instance, contains numerous older commercial structures which have been transformed into homes.[22] Other cities provide similar examples. Commercial-to-residential transformations may become more common during the next decade, but most of the regeneration is occurring in older residential neighborhoods. Neighborhoods such as Ansley Park in Atlanta, the Fan in Richmond, New Town in Chicago, Five Points in Denver, Montrose in Houston, the Mission District in San Francisco, and Capitol Hill in Washington, D.C., are physically more robust than they were a decade ago.

Role of Government

Urban regeneration has not occurred as a consequence of federal, state, or municipally funded programs. To date, urban regeneration has been funded almost entirely by the private sector. Nonetheless, government, particularly municipal government, has played a role in urban regeneration—a role different from what one might imagine. Municipal governments have unintentionally been influential in serving as a catalyst to bring neighbors together. Whether it is failure to enforce building codes, inadequate police protection, poor garbage collection and sanitation, nonmaintenance of parks, streets, and sidewalks, or just general neglect of the area, residents are often brought together in opposition to city hall. The common cry is, "They can't do that to us." It will be interesting to see whether communities can maintain the same level of commitment after winning their battles with city hall.

Who Is Moving In?

Descriptive accounts suggesting that renovators are disillusioned suburbanites returning to the city from the suburbs are simply in error. Although one commonly hears the phrase "return to the city," most in-movers actually come from other areas of the city.[23] Thus they are perhaps better described as "urban stayers" than "urban in-movers."

While it is a misconception to suggest that those moving into or staying in the city are largely childless professionals, it is true that young adults have

[22]James R. Hudson, "SoHo, A Study of Residential Invasion of a Commercial and Industrial Area," *Urban Affairs Quarterly*, **20**:46–63, September, 1984.

[23]Denis Gale, *Neighborhood Revitalization and the Postindustrial City*, Lexington Books, Lexington, Mass, 1984.

DOONESBURY   by Garry Trudeau

been in the vanguard of the return to older neighborhoods. Donald Bradley in his study of the Virginia-Highlands area of Atlanta found that newcomers were generally young, childless, married adults, white, urban-bred, well-educated, employed in professional or managerial positions, and earning middle-class to upper-middle-class incomes.[24] Other studies support the view of renovators being relatively affluent.[25] Newcomers also are portrayed as socially active, with an intense commitment to "their" neighborhood, although some research suggests that older community residents may have higher levels of community participation.[26]

WHY IS GENTRIFICATION OR REVITALIZATION TAKING PLACE?

Changes in three areas help to explain the surge of urban revitalization. Revitalization is a consequence of major changes in the demographic, economic, and life-style factors impacting on the U.S. population.

Demographic Changes

Probably the most predictable indicators are the demographic variables. The 1980 census clearly documented the continuing decline in the number of young children per family, while the young adult and elderly populations grew rapidly.[27] This changing population composition of urban households, with more of both the young adults and elderly living in separate households, means

---

[24]Donald J. Bradley, "Neighborhood Transition: Middle-Class Home Buying in an Inner-City, Deteriorating Community," paper presented at the annual meeting of the American Sociological Association, Chicago, September, 1977.

[25]Daphne Spain and Shirley Laska, "Renovators Two Years Later: New Orleans," in J. John Palen and Bruce London, op. cit., p. 108.

[26]J. John Palen and Chava Nachmias, "Revitalization in a Working-Class Neighborhood," in J. John Palen and Bruce London, op. cit., pp. 128–139.

[27]U.S. Bureau of the Census, "Household and Family Characteristics," *Current Population Reports,* series. P-20, Washington, D.C., 1981.

Older housing in some central city neighborhoods has come back into vogue. This renovation is being done in Boston. (© Phyllis Graber Jensen/Stock, Boston)

increasing demand for housing. This demand is compounded by the fact that the baby boom generation of 1946–1964 is now in the home-buying ages. As a consequence, between the censuses of 1970 and 1980 the U.S. population increased 9 percent, but the number of households increased 25 percent.

Several other demographic factors are also important. Among well-documented recent demographic changes are: the rising age at first marriage, declining fertility rates, nontraditional living arrangements, later birth of the first child, increasing entry of both single and married women into the labor force, and the rising number of dual-wage-earner families. These factors are not only reciprocally related, but taken together, they represent a decline of the sort of "familism" that played such an important part in the post-war flight to the suburbs. The post-World War II American ideal of a suburban home, your own backyard, good schools, and so on, neatly met the needs of many new families with children. However, this option has far less appeal for contemporary two-career families without children.

Relatively affluent, young, childfree couples, not having to worry about the quality of inner-city schools and the shortage of playspace, are more likely than their parents' generation to choose to live in the city, close to places of work and recreation. To the extent that aggregate demographic changes are producing more nontraditional family units of this type than ever before, we have another partial explanation of urban revitalization of central-city neighborhoods.

Economic Changes

Economic factors also favor increased gentrification. Economic considerations, particularly for single persons or two-income households, are now likely to encourage central-city location more than in the past. This is a major change. For most of the years following World War II, both the cost of new housing and the availability of mortgage money clearly favored the suburbs. It was easiest for new homeowners to obtain minimum-down-payment, low-interest loans on suburban housing. In spite of critics of surburbia, suburban housing met the needs of families with young children (see Chapter 8, Patterns of Suburbanization). And if a suburban move necessitated a long commute to work, the cost of gasoline prior to 1974 was under 40 cents a gallon.

Today the situation is altered. Commuting costs, which were judged prior to 1974 almost solely in terms of time, have increased. Suburban home heating and cooling expenses also can be expensive. Couples are rediscovering what their grandparents knew: heating and/or cooling a two-story townhouse with buildings on either side is more efficient than heating and/or cooling a single-story, freestanding ranch-style home. Higher energy and maintenance costs are particularly onerous when both partners work, leaving the home empty during large portions of the work week.

Revitalizing existing city housing is often less expensive than new construction on the suburban periphery. This is especially the case if the new urban homeowners are willing to put in sweat equity by doing rehabilitation and upgrading work themselves. Most important, mortgage funds for city properties are now available. Changes in government loan policies mean government-insured mortgages are now available in the city. Lending institutions are also increasingly realizing that revitalizing areas are good investment risks.

Changes in living patterns, increasing numbers of persons of home-buying ages, and fewer new housing starts have increased pressure on the available housing stock. Compared to earlier decades, young adults are more often living independently, and there are high rates of separation and divorce. Where in the past there would be one household of several people, today there is often a fragmentation into several households, each containing fewer people. As noted earlier, over a decade these and other factors resulted in a 9 percent increase in persons but a 25 percent increase in number of households.

Housing construction, however, has clearly not been keeping pace with demands. The year 1982, for example, witnessed the lowest number of new housing starts in two decades. Limited new suburban housing starts has in turn meant greater interest in existing residences. Some of the increased demand for existing city housing would thus have occurred even without any changes of life-style considerations favoring city residence, since there is often an inverse relationship between the level of new housing construction and the rate of investment in older city housing.

Life-style Changes

Many of the new central-city households are not "typical," two-children families. Young couples are postponing, and sometimes sidestepping, matrimony. Childbearing, likewise, is being postponed in favor of dual incomes and freer life-styles. Inner-city living tends to have a disproportionate appeal to such nontraditional households. The potential quality of the housing units, the greater convenience to central-city work, and the availability of adult amenities associated with the central city dovetail well with the needs of the increasingly numerous, smaller sized, adult-oriented households.

One of the most serious liabilities of central-city neighborhoods—the low quality of city schools—does not weigh as heavily on such urbanites. The availability of cultural and social activities and shorter commuter time are more important. This is particularly the case for urban subpopulations such as the gay community. Establishments and activities that low-density suburban areas tend to ban, such as late-night bars, restaurants, and grocery stores, are just the things that give high-density urban areas their vitality. A growing number of middle-class urbanites are in effect voting for sticking with their image of good city life.

There also seems to be a growing change in esthetic values. After postwar decades in which newer homes were more or less automatically judged better, there appears to be a reversal of values among some buyers. Older restorable houses are often considered more desirable. Residences in regenerating neighborhoods frequently have design and construction features that appeal to young, upwardly mobile adults, a group whose tastes outrun their pocketbooks. Where else but in older U.S. neighborhoods can one obtain a first home possessing hardwood floors and trim, fireplaces built with tile or marble, lath-and-plaster walls, leaded glass windows, and oak doors with solid brass trim? True, much of this charm may be under several coats of paint at the time the house is purchased, but the basic quality is present. To central-city aficionados, the ones to be pitied are those suburbanites who remain trapped in outlying postwar suburban housing developments.

DISPLACEMENT OF THE POOR

Finally, let us discuss the question of displacement, since physical regeneration can have social costs. While there is widespread agreement that it is desirable for neighborhoods to improve and upgrade themselves, there is less agreement as to how to evaluate this change if it also causes displacement of incumbent residents. The National Urban Coalition fears that the poor will become "urban nomads," priced or pushed out of their neighborhoods.[28]

---

[28]National Urban Coalition, *Displacement: City Neighborhoods in Transition,* Washington, D.C., 1978.

There are very real problems of displacement, particularly for lower-income and elderly households.[29] Displacement, however, has to be placed in perspective. The impression is sometimes given that prior to the onset of revitalization both the neighborhood and its population were stable and secure. The implied suggestion is that, were it not for revitalization, the area would again return to stability. Both these assumptions are usually inaccurate. While displacement of long-term residents does occur, the media portrait—such as portrayed by *Sixty Minutes*[30]—of typical potential displacees having lived in the area for years is usually inaccurate.

Potential displacees are most often poorer renters, and poorer renters as a group have high mobility. For example, according to census data nearly 40 percent of all renters move at least once a year. For the poor, who rent from month to month rather than under long-term leases, the moves are far more frequent. Areas undergoing revitalization thus are likely to have had high levels of residential mobility prior to renewal activity. Such areas frequently also have high levels of displacement due to eviction and building abandonment.

Fortunately, research indicates displacement may not be as serious a problem as originally thought.[31] While displacement has high emotional costs for some displacees, others find moving has long-term benefits. Research findings (as opposed to public statements) usually indicate that the majority of displacees move to nearby housing of comparable or better quality, but they pay more after moving.[32]

Hand-wringing over too-rapid upgrading has a bit of an "Alice in Wonderland" quality to it. Many of the people who are most vocal about the consequences of middle-class return to the city have also been the most eager to condemn middle-class flight from the city. It seems ironic that some now are complaining that housing is being upgraded and the property tax base being augmented too fast. The conflict of varied political-interest groups creates a situation in which someone is always unhappy.

Gentrification is still a relatively new urban phenomenon and as yet encompasses only a few neighborhoods in any one city. Its importance lies not so much in its size but in its reversing long-term patterns and in its potential for shaping future trends.

[29]Barre T. Lee and David Hodge, "Social Differentials and Metropolitan Residential Displacement," and Jeffrey Henig, "Gentrification and Displacement of the Elderly," in J. John Palen and Bruce London, op. cit., pp. 140–169 and 170–184.

[30]CBS, November 29, 1981.

[31]George Grier and Eunice Grier, "Urban Displacement: A Reconnaissance," in Shirley Laska and Daphne Spain (eds.), *Back to the City*, Pergamon, New York, 1980, pp. 252–268. and Michael H. Schill and Richard P. Nathan, *Revitalizing America's Cities: Neighborhood Reinvestment and Displacement*, State University of New York Press, 1983.

[32]U.S. Dept. of Housing and Urban Development, "Residential Displacement: An Update," Office of Policy Management and Research, Washington, D.C., 1981; and Michael Schill and Richard Nathan, *Revitalizing America's Cities: Neighborhood Reinvestment and Displacement*, State University of New York Press, Albany, 1983.

CHAPTER

11

HOUSING PROGRAMS AND URBAN CHANGE

Through me the way into the doleful city,
Through me the way into eternal grief,
Through me a people forsaken.
                    Inscription over the gate of hell in Dante's *Inferno*

STATUS AS OF THE 1980s

Before talking about specific government programs let us outline the overall housing situation in the United States. The 1980 census recorded one of the most dramatic increases of housing units in the nation's history—an increase of nearly 29 percent.[1] This represents a net increase of almost 20 million housing units, or more than the entire housing stock of Canada, the United Kingdom, or France. During the decade the United States added nearly one new unit for every person added to the population. Some two-thirds (68 percent) of the housing increase occurred in the sun belt, with the three states of California, Florida, and Texas alone accounting for some 6 million additional units. Eight out of ten new homes are located in the suburbs or nonmetropolitan territory.

The median age (half older–half younger) of houses in the United States is 23 years, and the median overall quality is relatively high. Ninety-seven percent of year-round homes have complete private plumbing. Living space has also increased, with 97 percent of the units having less than one person per room. This is a great improvement over the more crowded post-World War II period. Almost 98 percent of all housing units have complete kitchens, and 93 percent have telephones.

A full 80 percent of married couples are homeowners—up from 70 percent in 1970. Renters now constitute only one-third of all households, and—significantly—about 40 percent of all rental units have a female head of household. Two-thirds (68 percent) of all white households live in their own homes, but only 44 percent of blacks and Hispanics do so. For blacks and whites, but not Hispanics, this represents a 3 percent increase since 1970. Contrary to what many people think, we are not becoming more mobile as a people. The rate of moving from residence to residence has been declining since the 1960s. About 20 percent of the population moved in 1960, compared with 16 percent in 1983.[2]

EARLY FEDERAL PROGRAMS

The United States government's official housing policy was formulated in 1949. It states that it is the aim of the government to:

1. Eliminate substandard and other inadequate housing through clearance of slums and blighted areas.
2. Stimulate housing production and community developments sufficient to remedy the housing shortage.
3. Realize the goal of a decent home and a suitable living environment for every American family.

[1]Arthur F. Young and F. John Devaney, "What the 1980 Census Shows About Housing," *American Demographics,* 5:17, January, 1983.
[2]U.S. Bureau of the Census, "Geographical Mobility: March 1982 to March 1983," *Current Population Reports,* series P-20, no. 393, Washington, D.C., 1984, p. 1.

However, in the almost four decades that this has been official policy, no administration has taken these to be guidelines for clear and decisive action; rather, they have been viewed as goals or objectives to be sought. Today, as when the policy was written into law, safe, decent, and sanitary housing at affordable prices within a suitable living environment remains but a dream for all too many Americans.

Housing in America has traditionally been considered a private rather than a public concern, and the whole concept of involvement by the federal government in the housing of its citizens is fairly recent in the United States. The concept of government support for housing is far from universally accepted in the United States—a situation unlike that in European countries, for example. The Reagan administration attempted to substantially limit or eliminate existing programs.

It took the massive economic collapse of the great depression of the 1930s to involve the government permanently in the question of housing. During the depression, residential construction dropped by 90 percent and downtown skyscrapers stood vacant. Even the prestigious Empire State Building in New York City was unable to fill its many offices. Franklin D. Roosevelt's administration came into office committed to reviving the economy through federal intervention, a new and radical approach at that date. In order to get a sick housing industry on its feet and encourage "builders to build and lenders to lend" the government engaged in extensive "pump-priming" in the housing area.

The Housing Act of 1937, for example, established a slum-clearance program and created the United States Housing Authority, which built some 114,000 low-rent public housing units before the program was ended during World War II. However, it was never clear whether the goal of the programs of the 1930s was to put people to work or to provide new housing for those lacking "standard" dwellings. Whatever the purpose, the result was that several deteriorating slums were cleared, and every substandard unit of housing that was cleared was replaced with a standard unit.

The program of the 1930s differed from later efforts in at least two respects: first, only public housing was built on the cleared land, not shopping centers or office buildings; second, the housing projects were by and large successful— many of them are still well maintained today. Their success can be attributed both to their design (few were over four stories high, giving the buildings the atmosphere of family apartment buildings where people knew each other) and to the fact that residents initially were largely workers and artisans on WPA or other jobs. Projects at this time did not house the very poor on welfare.

FEDERAL HOUSING ADMINISTRATION (FHA) SUBSIDIES

In order to get bankers to invest in mortgages during the depression, the government, through the Housing Act of 1934, created the Federal Housing Administration to insure home loans. After World War II, the Veterans

Administration also made loans (VA loans) guaranteed by the government to veterans. Under such schemes, private lending institutions still decide who will get loans—the FHA or VA in effect insures the bank against loss if the buyer defaults. The theory is that this system encourages lending institutions to make loans to buyers whom they would otherwise reject.

After World War II, the FHA and the VA became active in issuing mortgages to working-class and lower-middle-class families who wanted to buy homes. The consequence was the urban exodus to the new subdivisions discussed in Chapter 8, Patterns of Suburbanization. During the 1950s a young couple could move into a new suburban home with a $500 down payment. The FHA program encouraged and subsidized white suburbanization. At the same time the urban renewal program, which will be discussed presently, was designed to hold these same middle-class white families in the central city. The government was thus simultaneously trying to hold the middle class in cities while subsidizing them to leave.

After World War II suburbs (with FHA encouragement) used restrictive covenants to exclude blacks and other "undesirables" who might lower property values and threaten the FHA's investment. Until 1950 FHA regulations expressly forbade issuing loans that would permit or encourage racial integration.

> From 1935 to 1950, the federal government insisted upon discriminatory practices as a prerequisite to government housing aid. The Federal Housing Administration's official manuals cautioned against "infiltration of inharmonious racial and national groups," "a lower class of inhabitants," or "the presence of incompatible racial elements" in the new neighborhood. . . . Zoning was advocated as a device for exclusion, and the use was urged of a racial covenant (prepared by FHA itself) with a space left blank for the prohibited races and religions, to be filled in by the builder as occasion required.[3]

Government policy thus directly encouraged "white-only" suburbs and held blacks in the inner city. Restrictive racial covenants were declared illegal by the 1968 Fair Housing Act. Civil rights legislation and policies since the 1960s have placed the federal government in the forefront of attempts to eliminate remaining de facto housing discrimination.

In the United States today we have anything but a laissez-faire housing policy. Almost all financing for new houses or apartments involves the federal government in one way or another. The federal government pours over $20 billion a year into direct and indirect subsidies of the housing market. Included in this figure are appropriations for urban renewal, public housing, interest on mortgage loans, and subsidy programs. Included in the indirect subsidies are the funds provided by the FHA and VA mortgage-guarantee programs. Until the 1980s about half the outstanding mortgage debt on single-family homes was insured by either the FHA or the VA.[4] Most of the balance is financed

---

[3]Charles Abrams, *The City in the Frontier,* Harper and Row, New York, 1965, p. 61.
[4]Bernard Weissbroud, "Satellite Communities," *Urban Land,* **31**:6, October, 1972.

Discrimination in Housing

For years it has been assumed that blacks are discriminated against in the sale and rental of housing. The extent is documented by a major national study done by the National Committee Against Discrimination in Housing under contract for HUD.* Forty metropolitan areas were randomly selected from 117 MSAs having large central cities and large central-city black populations. During the spring of 1977 approximately 300 whites and 300 blacks in matched pairs shopped for the same housing units advertised in local metropolitan newspapers.

The housing to be audited was selected by random sample. In five areas selected for "in-depth" study—Atlanta, Boston, Dallas, Milwaukee, and Sacramento—some 80 real estate and 120 rental visits were conducted by each pair of couples. In the thirty-five other sites, thirty to fifty visits each were conducted. In all, some 3,264 real estate agencies and apartment-rental complexes were visited by both couples.

With regard to an index of housing availability—the most important of the measures of discrimination—27 percent of the rental agents and 15 percent of the sales agents discriminated. Discrimination treatment as measured by other indexes exhibited smaller but still significant differences. Rental housing discrimination was uniformly high in the midwest, southern, and western regions, while incidents of discrimination in housing purchases were approximately three times higher in the midwest region than in the northeast, south, and west.

Not surprisingly, these estimates of discrimination have been challenged by the housing industry as being too high and by civil rights groups as being too low. Nonetheless, the study has generally become the landmark against which further progress can be judged. Overall, it indicates that efforts to combat racial discrimination have had some success. Potential black purchasers are in the great majority of cases treated no differently from potential white purchasers.

*Ronald E. Wienk, Clifford E. Reid, John C. Simonson, and Frederick J. Eggers. *Measuring Racial Discrimination in American Housing Markets: The Housing Market Practice Survey*, Office of Policy Development and Research, Department of Housing and Urban Development, Washington, D.C., 1979.

through savings and loan associations or banks whose deposits are insured and whose investments are regulated by federal laws. Additionally, the American tax system (unlike that of Canada) provides for tax reductions on money paid for interest on mortgages.

URBAN RENEWAL

Since World War II a variety of programs has been implemented to upgrade cities in general and improve housing stock in particular. After the war it was widely recognized that cities were headed for trouble if the federal government didn't intervene. Housing was in poor shape, and downtowns were showing age and wear. Problems were particularly acute on the deteriorating fringe areas of CBDs. Land was being used only for warehouses or slum housing, but was nonetheless extremely expensive. Compared with costs on the city's edge, the expense of buying, tearing down, and rebuilding in the inner city was not economically feasible for private developers.

Liberals and conservatives in Congress had radically different ideas of what government should do. The eventual result was a classic American compromise, the Housing Act of 1949. The act contained both a public housing section, which the liberals had lobbied for, and an urban development section, which conservatives and businesspeople had sought.

Commercial and financial interests in the central cities supported urban renewal because they saw the renewal areas as providing the downtown area with a buffer or *cordon sanitaire* against encroachment by slums. Moreover, the occupants of the urban renewal housing were expected to be families with substantial purchasing power and thus able to help stimulate retail trade. Urban renewal was seen as being both good for business and good for the city. The purpose of urban renewal was not to rebuild the area for the old residents but rather to *change* land-use patterns.

The urban redevelopment section of the Urban Renewal Act was a radical break with past housing policies in that it provided for the use of public funds to buy, clear, and improve the renewal site, after which the ownership of the land would revert to the private sector. When the renewal area was approved, the authorities were given the power of buy properties at market prices and, in cases where the owner refused to sell, to have the property condemned and compensation paid through the government's right of eminent domain. The Supreme Court ruled five to four that this exercise of the right of eminent domain was constitutional.

Once the city acquired all the land in the renewal area, the existing buildings were destroyed (or rehabilitated under later modifications of the act) and the land was cleared. New streets, lights, and public facilities were then installed, and finally the land was sold to a private developer who agreed to build in accordance with an approved development plan.

The developer paid about 30 percent of what it had cost the local government to purchase, clear, and improve the land. This so-called "write-down'' was the difference between what the land had cost the public and what it was sold for to the private developer. Two-thirds of the city's loss was made up in a direct cash subsidy from the federal government. Thus, the control of the program was basically local, while most of the funds were federal.

Rehabilitation

The Housing Act was revised in 1954 to provide a more workable program. In order to qualify, an area could be "blighted," that is, be a potential slum. The act also allowed funds to be used for projects that were not predominantly residential.

Rehabilitation of existing structures theoretically made it possible for at least some of the original residents to remain in a renewal area. In practice it usually worked differently. Poor families had little financial flexibility. They were not able to invest additional funds in their homes to bring them up to the rigorous standards required by the redevelopment agency, even when loans for improvements could be obtained at low interest. The end result was that the house was sold to a middle-class or upper-middle-class person who could better afford the cost of rehabilitating the property. Thus, though the houses remained, the tenants frequently changed.

Since the purpose of urban redevelopment is to change patterns of land use for the benefit of the city as a whole, there is no requirement that housing which is destroyed has to be replaced with housing for people with a similar income level. Most of the housing built in renewal areas has been high-income or upper-middle-income apartments rather than apartments with low or moderate rent. This has been done with the intent of holding in the city, or luring back into the city, upper-middle-class whites, with their spendable—and taxable—incomes. In fact, once the dwelling units within the renewal area have been demolished and cleared, the land can be used for a shopping center, a park, or an office building. When urban renewal ended in the 1970s, over one-third of the federal funds were being used for largely nonresidential projects.

Relocation and New Housing

The most glaring weakness of urban renewal programs was the displacement of large numbers of low-income families without adequate provision for their relocation. Until criticism built up to a point where it could no longer be ignored, little had been done to rehouse those who were forced to move from a renewal area. It is generally agreed that during the first years of the urban renewal program, residents were dispossessed and ejected from their homes in a fashion that can only be characterized as ruthless. The residents of the West End of Boston, for example, found themselves bulldozed out of their old Italian community virtually before they knew what was happening. Far from being encouraged to participate in planning for the area, local residents were actively discouraged, since it had already been decided that the existing

Public housing projects generally are conceded to be a failed housing policy. (Peter Southwick/Stock, Boston)

low-rent area would be far more valuable to the city as an area of expensive high-rise apartments.[5] The result was essentially similar when removal was for the purpose of construction of expressways.

In early urban renewal projects relocation programs were given the very lowest priority. As one housing authority put it: "There was a tendency to give families a few dollars and tell them to get lost."[6] Certainly, funds were not lavished on those who had to move. For instance, in the West End of Boston each family received $100 for moving expenses. Between 1949 and 1964 only 0.5 percent of all federal expenditures for urban renewal went to families and individuals; and this figure increases to only 2 percent if businesses are included.[7]

From 1949 to 1965 a total of 311,197 dwelling units were demolished on urban renewal sites, with only 166,288 units built or planned to take their place.[8] Federal law required that priority be given in any low-rent units to be constructed to those who were displaced. There was, however, no requirement that low-income housing be provided on the renewal site. In practice, the implicit goal of renewal was to move the old residents out so that they could be replaced by middle-class or upper-middle-class groups.

[5]Herbert J. Gans, *The Urban Villagers,* Free Press, New York, 1962.
[6]Jeanne R. Lowe, *Cities in a Race with Time,* Random House, New York, 1967, p. 206.
[7]Herbert J. Gans, *People and Plans,* Basic Books, New York, 1968, p. 263.
[8]Lowe, op. cit., chap. 6.

Critique

Scott Greer contends that much of the confusion and downright contradiction in urban renewal programs were a result of the mixture of three different goals. These were increasing low-cost housing while eliminating slums, revitalizing the central city, and (this last is the most recent goal) creating planned cities through community renewal programs.[9] There is no question that urban renewal has done little to increase low-income housing. As Greer put it: "At a cost of three billion dollars the Urban Renewal Agency (URA) has succeeded in materially reducing the supply of low-cost housing in American cities."[10]

Finally, it is only fair to say that the urban renewal program has had some notable successes, such as the comprehensive renewal effort in New Haven, the Southwest Project in Washington, D.C., the Western Addition in San Francisco, and Society Hill in Philadelphia. Also, very few of the renewal sites were originally attractive communities; the majority were blighted, dilapidated, filthy slums which no one wants to bring back. Even critics of urban renewal concede that the grossest mistakes were made by the earliest projects and that as the program matured, it profited from earlier errors.

PUBLIC HOUSING

Public housing was originally designed to provide standard-quality housing for those who could not afford decent, safe housing on the private market. One of the basic unwritten assumptions of the program was that by changing a family's residence you could also change the way they lived and the way they behaved.

Advocates of social planning originally supported public housing as a means of social uplift and betterment. The tearing down of slum housing was seen as a way of destroying the crime, delinquency, drunkenness, and lax morals that were considered to be associated with the slum housing. Once again, technology was going to solve social problems—a naive belief of long standing in America. This can be characterized as a "salvation by bricks and mortar" or "architectural determinism" approach.

Public housing erected during the 1930s was built as much to give workers jobs as to eliminate slums. Projects were filled mainly with lower-middle-class families who were there because, owing to the depression, family heads could not get regular work and could not find adequate housing elsewhere. After World War II, with other housing becoming more plentiful, those who were working their way into the middle class sought new housing. As these families moved out, the projects gradually lost their sound working-class image.

By the 1960 public housing was beset by massive problems. Families living in projects were often minority, female headed, on welfare, and without any reasonable expectation of moving into the middle class. The lack of

[9]Scott Greer, *Urban Renewal and American Cities*, Bobbs-Merrill, Indianapolis, Ind., 1965, p. 165.
[10]Ibid., p. 3.

education and training of the newer project residents, coupled with regulations that placed low limits on how much a family could earn and still qualify for public housing, meant that those who could be upwardly mobile moved on, while those who were not mobile stayed. The policy of evicting the successful also has meant that in the largest projects successful adult role models are virtually nonexistent. This has had disastrous results for children, who have few images of successful adults who are not dealing in drugs, gambling, or prostitution.

Public housing is concentrated in relatively few, usually minority neighborhoods. This is because "aldermanic courtesy" traditionally allowed aldermen and women to veto public housing in their own wards. Attempts to disperse public housing to suburban locations met with intense opposition from suburbanites.

The consequence is that many inner-city projects have today become the residence of last resort for the permanently poor. The public has become disillusioned with the whole concept of public housing, since it obviously isn't remaking the present-day poor into middle-class citizens. Once professionals thought that if they could get problem families out of the slums, then fathers would stop drinking, mothers would stop fooling around, and kids would stop doping and stealing. It didn't work; as caustically expressed by one professional in urban affairs, "they're the same bunch of bastards they always were."[11]

Public housing, in its present form, has few supporters, liberal or conservative, black or white, well-to-do or poor. Without conscious intent, we designed a public housing program that almost ensures its own failure.

Recent Programs

With it apparent that public housing projects were not providing safe, clean, and well-maintained housing for the poor, an answer was thought to be to provide subsidies so that the poor could become homeowners. Thus they would have a stake in both the upkeep of their own homes and the quality of the neighborhood in general. The 1968 Housing and Urban Redevelopment Act thus provided direct subsidies for low-income families so that they could purchase homes under the so-called "Title 235" program; a companion "Title 236" program provided for rent subsidies enabling the poor to afford to rent apartments rather than go into public housing.

However, bureaucratic sloppiness in the way the program was administered permitted criminal collusion between real estate speculators and FHA and VA employees. The act directed the Department of Housing and Urban Development (HUD) to relax standards so that low-income buyers could obtain mortgages. In practice, in cities such as Detroit and Chicago it provided a massive ripoff opportunity for real estate speculators. Huge profits were made by selling at big mark-ups supposedly rehabilitated properties that in fact had

---

[11]Michael Stegman, "The New Mythology of Housing," *Trans-Action*, 7:55, January, 1970.

Pruitt-Igoe: Profile of Failure

In 1951, *Architectural Forum* featured an article entitled "Slum Surgery in St. Louis" which described a public housing project "of 11 story apartment houses, which even unbuilt have already begun to change the public housing pattern." The complex of twenty-six or more buildings was to be laid out on a fully landscaped site incorporating the latest principles of design, which would "save not only people, but money."* The project, known as Pruitt-Igoe, was supposed to pave the way for a bright new era in public housing.

Pruitt-Igoe was completed in 1955, with thirty-three buildings of eleven stories each. A few changes had been made. The plan to mix some townhouses in with the high-density units was rejected on the basis of a cost-benefit analysis done by the Public Housing Authority. There were also other economies, such as eliminating the landscaping, not painting the cinder-block galleries and other public areas, eliminating public washrooms on the ground floor, leaving steam pipes uninsulated, and not providing screens for the gallery windows. Although the project won an award in 1958 for architectural design, very serious problems were beginning to emerge. The economies listed above had some unexpected consequences: children urinated in hallways, burned themselves on exposed pipes, and fell out of gallery windows.

The project had been designed for a racially mixed population—one-third white and two-thirds black—but a heavy influx of hard-core poor families with numerous social problems soon drove out all who could escape. The project soon became inhabited mainly by black households headed by women with a large number of children—five to twelve per household—and on welfare. Of the 10,736 people living in Pruitt-Igoe in 1965, there were only 900 men—many of them elderly—but over 7,000 children, of whom 70 percent were under twelve years of age.

During the 1970s, Pruitt-Igoe became a symbol of all that is wrong with public housing projects, with elevators battered and out of order, stairwells with lighting fixtures ripped out, galleries unused and unsafe, and laundry rooms that invited robbery and rape. Laundry rooms, stairwells, and halls in Pruitt-Igoe were used by adolescents for sex. Making many "conquests" was one of the few ways for a boy there to achieve status with his peer group, and the girls viewed sex as a way of achieving popularity and maturity. The mean age for becoming sexually active was thirteen, and half the girls in

---

*"Slum Surgery in St. Louis," *Architectural Forum*, April, 1951, pp. 128–135.

the project became pregnant at least once before age eighteen.† Mothers found it practically impossible to supervise children. They feared to go out of their apartments; and this was a reasonable fear: a survey of residents disclosed that 41 percent of the adults had been robbed, 20 percent physically assaulted, and 39 percent insulted by teenagers.‡ The absence of resident men and the physically unsafe design features, such as skip-stop elevators and open galleries, resulted in a constant threat of mugging or rape for female inhabitants.

One by one, the buildings were simply abandoned by their tenants. Even the most down-and-out welfare recipients were unwilling to tolerate the degradation and the constant threat of personal danger. Rehabilitating the buildings to make them fit for human habitation, it was estimated, would cost more than $40 million, and then there was no guarantee that addicts and vandals would not destroy and terrorize the buildings again.

In the fall of 1972, with occupancy down to only 2,788 persons, the Housing Authority took the drastic action of blowing up the two worst buildings and began dynamiting the top seven stories off others in order to convert them into more manageable four-story buildings. It was hoped that the resulting low-rises would be easier for the tenants to control against outsiders and would provide some sense of defensible space and physical security. This effort was not successful, and in 1973 the Housing Authority began to demolish the remainder of the buildings. Today Pruitt-Igoe is a wasteland.

If there is a lesson to be learned from Pruitt-Igoe and similar abandoned projects across the country, such as the Columbus housing project in Newark, it is that public housing all too frequently removes "nonhuman" problems such as leaking roofs, faulty electricity, and rats at the cost of isolating the residents from the rest of society and increasing the human problems. Designs based on low-rise buildings or townhouses provide greater defensible space and make possible surveillance by adults, which can reduce crime rates and give residents an important sense of territory. However, architecture can never solve the basic problem of an economic system that creates an underclass and effectively isolates it from the rest of society. Until this is changed, we are merely attacking symptoms rather than the disease. The ultimate problem is not housing but poverty.

†Lee Rainwater, *Behind Ghetto Walls*, Aldine, Chicago, 1970, p. 309.
‡Ibid., p. 103.

only cosmetic improvements. As expressed by the director of HUD's Chicago office: "Every unethical, unscrupulous real estate broker and lender, many of them so slimy they crawled out from under a rock, looked at this program and said, What a gold mine out there."'[12]

The poor, as always, were the victims. The scheme worked like this: A real estate speculator bought a run-down, inner-city home at a low price and then put in at most cosmetic repairs such as a new coat of paint. A qualified low-income buyer was then found, and the appraiser was bribed to considerably overvalue the house. The FHA or VA then insured the mortgage at the higher price, and the speculator made a fast profit, minus the bribe.

William Keye, for example, thought he was getting a good deal when he bought a house for $22,500 from Conteco in Chicago and financed it with a loan insured by the Veterans Administration.[13] He soon discovered that the furnace was totally inoperable, the house needed a new roof, and the indoor-outdoor carpeting in the kitchen covered a large hole rotted through the floor. Research revealed that Conteco had purchased the home for $12,000. Another home purchased from HUD for $500 was later sold for $19,000. Not surprisingly, most such properties are eventually abandoned by the low-income homeowners. The mortgage is then foreclosed by the bank, which gets its money, and the government finds itself owning another house that no one wants, in an area where no one will buy. Thus the federal government in effect finances the creation of urban blight.

The ideal buyer from the speculators' viewpoint was one who was so economically marginal that he or she would default so that the bank could foreclose and get its guaranteed money from the FHA or VA. Even those on welfare could purchase such homes. The program was designed to save the cities, but it was exploited in some cities to encourage neighborhood turmoil and abandonment while providing windfall profits for speculators. The fact that several hundred persons have been convicted of fraud will not help the poor who bought decaying homes. Nor will it bring back the abandoned neighborhoods. Callous greed seriously undermined what potentially was a good program.

By 1975 the federal government was stuck with over 100,000 abandoned properties. Today the program is dead, but the U.S. government still retains thousands of homes, making HUD the nation's largest slumlord. As of the 1980s, attempts to sell off rundown properties remain plagued by mismanagement and scandal.[14]

Experimental Housing Allowance Program

The concept of direct housing assistance to tenants (rather than through landlords) has been debated for years, but until the Experimental Housing

---

[12]Quoted in *Milwaukee Journal*, December 15, 1976.
[13]*United Press International*, September 19, 1976.
[14]"Excess U.S. Housing Said Mismanaged," *Washington Post*, October 12, 1984.

Allowance Program (EHAP) began in the early 1970s under the direction of HUD, there was little data on what would occur.[15]

The EHAP experiments were extremely elaborate, involving a ten-year study of providing vouchers to 30,000 households in 12 cities at a cost of $160 million.[16] The study covered numerous cities and the comparison of different types of payments. For example, some received assistance payments limited to use for housing payments, some received assistance payments not limited to use for housing, and control groups received no assistance (they received $10 a month for providing monthly information). In Pittsburgh and Phoenix, some 1,250 renter households received aid in each city while 550 similar but unassisted families served as controls.

Findings indicated that about one-half of the eligible renters and two-thirds of the eligible homeowners chose not to participate in receiving housing assistance. If assistance is not specifically designated for housing, 90 percent of those eligible will participate. However, only about 10 percent of that assistance will go for housing.

The allowances did cost less than other forms of subsidy. However the program did little to increase the supply of low-cost housing, promote reinvestment, or reduce segregation. Contrary to expectations, neither housing assistance nor unconstrained assistance seemed to affect rates of mobility. Those receiving assistance did not move any more often than those not receiving assistance. It was also assumed that housing assistance would increase demand for acceptable housing units, and thus rents would inflate, with landlords being the major beneficiaries. This did not occur; rents were not inflated by the program.

The EHAP housing assistance programs thus did not have as large an impact on the housing of lower-income participants as was expected. Where the program did have unexpected impact was in boosting the rate of family dissolution among participants. The reasons for the increased divorce rates are not known with certainty, but what is certain is that this plus the equivocal housing results cooled support for the program. Few members of Congress want to be on record as voting for a program that appears to encourage family dissolution.

ABANDONMENT OF BUILDINGS

Nationally there are 150,000 housing units abandoned a year. In New York City, abandonments have reached 40,000 units a year (housing starts, by comparison, have averaged only 6,000 units annually for the last five years). The city brought foreclosure actions for nonpayment of taxes against 33,000

[15]*A Summary Report of Current Findings from the Experimental Housing Allowance Programs,* Office of Policy Development and Research, U.S. Department of Housing and Urban Development, Washington, D.C., April, 1978.

[16]Katherine Bradbury and Anthony Downs (eds.), *Do Housing Allowances Work?*, Brookings, Washington, D.C., 1981.

properties in 1978, and as of that date owned over 35,000 apartments, half of them walk-up tenements 60 to 100 years old.[17] Moreover, these figures do not include the larger number of buildings that have been razed.[18]

How is it that usable buildings are being abandoned? The answer lies in the economics of the private housing market. Being a slumlord traditionally was a lucrative business, but by the late 1960s things had begun to change. Tenants, often urged on by community organizers, began militantly to demand improvements in their buildings. Sometimes these demands were accompanied by rent strikes. At about the same time, some cities began to actually enforce housing codes and even order that illegally converted units be returned to original occupancy (that is, increase the number of rooms per apartment and decrease the number of paying renters). The interest of absentee landlords declined dramatically further with the urban riots of the late 1960s, increasing vandalism, and the rapidly escalating heating costs of the 1970s. Slumlords simply found that housing the poor was no longer a paying proposition, particularly in cities with rent controls. The cost of owning buildings was rising faster than rental income.

When landlords saw no long-term economic potential in their property, improvements and even necessary maintenance were allowed to slip. As a last type of profit taking, the landlord invariably stopped paying property taxes. (Cities traditionally did not begin foreclosure action until there were three years of tax arrears. Some states such as New York have now shortened the period to one year.) An area with a sharp spurt in tax delinquencies is almost always on the verge of abandonment.

Finally, when landlords see no more economic potential, they default on their mortgages and simply abandon their buildings. Under the law action can be taken by the city to take possession of the property, but no action can be brought against the slumlords themselves. Once the landlord abandons a building, services are cut off and the tenants move to other housing. Vandals and professional looters strip the building of anything of value. They pull up with trucks and rip out plumbing and heating systems and whatever else can be sold. Fires set by vandals or others are common in such abandoned buildings.

BURNING FOR PROFIT

Arson for profit is a common phenomenon in the older cores of central cities. Exact figures are difficult to determine, partially because a good arsonist destroys the evidence and partially because there are an inadequate number of fire investigators to officially categorize suspicious blazes as arson. In the

---

[17]Seymour B. Durant, "Laetrile for the Urban Crisis," *Journal of the Institute of Socioeconomic Studies,* **4:**72, Summer, 1979.

[18]Some conservative scholars argue that abandonment can occur because there is a housing surplus in some cities. See William Gorham and Nathan Glazer, *The Urban Predicament,* The Urban Institute, Washington, D.C., 1976, pp. 129–130.

United States as a whole, it is estimated that the arson rate has tripled in the last fifteen years to roughly 15,000 cases annually.[19] Detroit had more than 200 cases of arson on the nights before Halloween in 1985. The chief of operations of the New York City Fire Department estimates that 25 to 40 percent of the building fires in that city are deliberately set.

Many of these fires are set by slumlords or businesspeople who burn their buildings for the insurance money. Some are entrepreneurs who buy decrepit buildings in order to set profitable fires. Others are "building strippers" who "torch" old buildings in order to gain access and strip the building of plumbing and other items that can be sold for scrap. In New York, slum residents have been known to ignite their own apartments to get the relocation allowance of up to $2,000. Those who are burned out also obtain a higher priority for public housing vacancies. There are also youngsters who, even if they are not paid to torch a building by the owner, will do it for the sheer excitement.

New York State is trying to take some of the profit out of arson by permitting the city to deduct unpaid taxes and other payments from landlords' insurance settlements. There also have been sporadic attempts in New York and elsewhere to indict persons for arson fraud, but so long as urban decay and building abandonments continue in inner cities, arson will also be an urban problem.

OTHER DEVELOPMENTS

Conversion to Condominiums

Across the country rental apartments are being converted to condominium units where the occupant of an apartment owns the unit. New buildings are also being constructed for condominium occupancy. Currently there is an annual conversion of an estimated 100,000 to 200,000 existing units.

While gentrification (discussed in Chapter 10, Urban Crisis or Urban Rebirth) primarily displaces low-income families, condominium conversion impacts mainly on middle-class renters. After conversion the monthly cost in mortgage, taxes, and maintenance fees is well above the previous rent. The apartment shortage and increased rental costs are also a real problem to "young mobiles" who are not yet prepared to make a commitment on a house. However, if the trend continues, those who will suffer most are the working poor who are unable to qualify for public housing or subsidies and also unable to compete with the more affluent for scarce apartments. If condo conversion remains a nationwide pattern, working-class families will increasingly find themselves priced out of the apartment market, as they already have been out of the market for new single-family homes. On the other hand, those able to obtain financing for condominium purchases gain the advantages of property appreciation as well as the tax advantages that come with home ownership.

[19]Joseph P. Fried, "Arson, A Devastating Big-City Crime," *New York Times,* August 14, 1977.

Urban homesteading often demands "sweat equity" from those rehabilitating the property. (Courtesy of the Baltimore Department of
Housing & Community Development)

Urban Homesteading

How can government, particularly the federal government, aid cities in housing
their populations? Public housing is bankrupt; today few people argue for more
projects. Urban renewal and programs making the poor homeowners similarly
have few remaining backers. One idea of the 1970s that has caught on, though,
is "urban homesteading." Homesteading programs turn over abandoned and
foreclosed homes to those who agree to stay for at least three years and bring
the homes up to code standards within eighteen months.

Urban homesteading programs conjure up the image of the handy
pioneers, who, under the 1862 Homestead Act signed by President Lincoln,
were given 160 acres of western land if they could stick it out for five years.

Urban homesteaders, on the other hand, are not supposed to build on the land but to rebuild inner-city neighborhoods.[20] The first urban homesteading program (and still one of the most active) began in Wilmington, Delaware, in 1973. As expressed by Wilmington's mayor, who pushed the program, "We are not trying to provide housing for people. We are trying to provide people for (abandoned) housing."[21] Offering homes at nominal fees such as $100, urban homesteading programs implicitly recognize that by definition there is no market for abandoned property. Thus it is given away to those who agree to improve and use it. The Housing and Community Development Act of 1974 got the federal government into the business of transferring residential properties to local governments for homesteading.

So far, the record of urban homesteading has been mixed. While the concept sounds ideal, there are some major limitations.

First, it is only a relatively small program. The program to date is, indeed, only a drop in the bucket, with 60,000 homes having been rehabilitated by the homesteading mechanism. (By comparison, 150,000 inner-city homes and apartments are abandoned annually.)

Second, and perhaps most serious, by the time government action is taken, most abandoned properties are beyond the point of economic rehabilitation. As noted earlier, professional and amateur looters strip homes to the shell, and vandals deface what isn't taken. Fires are also common, and no one wants to rehabilitate a burned-out hulk. Unlike gentrification, urban homesteading often occurs in less desirable areas without historic distinction.

Third, there is the cost factor. Title to the property may come cheap, but rehabilitation costs big money. Even when owners use "sweat equity" (i.e., their own labor), rehabilitation loans commonly run from $25,000 to $80,000. Thus urban homesteading is definitely not the answer for the urban poor.

Fourth, as a home rehabilitation program, urban homesteading does not affect multifamily apartments, where the bulk of the poor are housed.

Fifth, for loans, of course, lenders are necessary, and thus far financial institutions have been reluctant to invest in rehabilitating abandoned slum properties. Thus low-interest municipal loans or loans guaranteed by the municipality appear to be essential. Also necessary are changes in municipal tax policies. While cities invariably say that they are in favor of urban homesteading, most are unwilling to change policies that raise taxes when improvements are made. Without some form of tax moratorium, those who upgrade abandoned buildings are rewarded by the municipality with higher taxes.

Finally, there is no point in rehabilitation of one home if the remainder of the neighborhood consists of vandalized burned-out buildings. There has to be an overall change in the neighborhood, with a substantial number of homes being simultaneously redone and reasonable public services and police protec-

[20]Ann Clark and Zelma Rivin, *Homesteading in Urban U.S.A.*, Praeger, New York, 1977.
[21]Quoted in Wiltram G. Conway, "People Fire in the Ghetto Ashes," *Saturday Review*, July 23, 1977, p. 15.

Death of Poletown

Today, the razing of central-city neighborhoods for public purposes, expressways, or urban renewal projects is largely history. Public outcry over the destruction of residential neighborhoods and changing program priorities have stopped the bulldozers. However, the new threat to older neighborhoods in some cities is that homes will be taken by eminent domain, not so that the land can be put to public use, but so that it can be turned over to a private company. This is what happened to the Poletown neighborhood in Detroit, a long-standing neighborhood that involuntarily vanished in less then a year. During 1981 the entire neighborhood of Poletown—1,362 homes and apartments, 143 businesses and stores, 16 churches, 2 schools, and 1 hospital—was torn down.

The land, which was condemned and razed at a cost of over $200 million in local, state, and federal tax money, was then sold to General Motors at a price of $8 million. The reason that all of this took place was economics and employment. Mayor Coleman Young had seen many industries leave Detroit, and felt that everything had to be done to keep the new GM plant and its promised 6,000 jobs in the city. It was felt downtown that Detroit needed the jobs more than it needed an aging neighborhood. It was also believed that GM, by building a new-generation assembly plant in the city, would give a much-needed psychological lift to a city that had lost 800,000 people and much of its economic energy since its heyday in the 1950s. The sharp bitterness and anger of those Poletown residents who saw their homes, businesses, and churches torn down was felt to be the unfortunate price an industrial heartland city with an aging infrastructure and tax base had to pay in order to keep GM in Detroit.

Poletown was leveled because GM made it clear that it would build its new assembly plant outside Detroit unless the city cleared and gave the corporation the 465.5 acre area. The world's third largest corporation also demanded and received a 50 percent tax concession from the city administration as the price for not leaving the city. What is more, the United Auto Workers Union, the city council, the Archdiocese of Detroit, and both the Carter and Reagan administrations supported the deal. Even the Michigan Supreme Court, in a controversial decision, ruled that Detroit had the right to condemn and clear Poletown and sell the site to General Motors.* Almost everyone was in favor of the new plant except

*"Legal Report," *Planning*, June, 1982, p. 10.

the residents of Poletown, who saw their homes and businesses leveled.

By 1982, Poletown had been cleared to the ground. The *Detroit Free Press*, in a special sixty-page section on the Poletown controversy, commented that

> . . . What stands between now and that day when the first 1985 Seville, Eldorado, Toronado or Riviera eases out of the New General Motors Assembly Division Detroit-Hamtrack plant is, in relative terms, a matter of details. For the city of Detroit, the hard part is over.†

All that remains is the bitterness.

†Gary Blonston, "Poletown: The Profits, the Loss," *Detroit* (special issue), *Detroit Free Press*, November 22, 1981, p. 8.

tion provided. Homesteading, therefore, is likely to be most successful in areas where only a few homes have been abandoned.

Nonetheless, urban homesteading has had a psychological as well as physical impact on cities ranging from Baltimore to Pittsburgh to Oakland. However, urban homesteading remains to be transformed from a catchy slogan to a substantial program. A start in this direction was taken by HUD in 1979, when pilot projects were begun to repair and sell some 100 houses in the Roseland neighborhood of Chicago and 75 homes in the Buckeye-Woodland and Union-Miles areas of Cleveland. Urban homesteading is still a limited contributor to the upgrading of neighborhoods. An additional "nonlegal" form of homesteading is "walk-in homesteading," or urban squatting. This is a politically important movement in European countries such as Holland, Germany, and Sweden.

Tax Credits

In order to encourage the private rehabilitation of older central-city areas, the Reagan administration encouraged Congress to pass a rehabilitation tax credit program in 1981. Under the program investors who renovate old structures can qualify for tax credits of up to 25 percent of their investment. The amount of the credit depends on the age and the historical or architectural significance of the structure. This program has been a boon to older cities. Under the program central city office buildings have been restored, hotels revitalized to their nineteenth century glory, and factories converted into rental apartments or commercial space. As of 1986, it is uncertain how tax revisions before Congress will affect the tax credit program.

CHAPTER
12
PLANNING IN EUROPE:
With Discussion of New Towns

Let there be one man who has a city obedient to his will,
and he might bring into existence the ideal polity about
which the world is so incredulous.

Plato
The Republic

INTRODUCTION: HISTORICAL BACKGROUND

The Bible, in Genesis 11:4, tells of one of the earliest attempts at urban planning:

> It came to pass as they journeyed to the East that they found a plain in the land of Shinar and they dwelt there, . . . And they said, "Come let us build us a city, and the tower the top of which may reach unto heaven; and let us make ourselves a name, lest we be scattered upon the face of the whole earth. . . .

As we all know, the Tower of Babel was not noticeably successful as a form of urban planning in spite of the fact that it did have full citizen participation. The hope is that some of our more modest attempts will be more successful.

Ancient Greece and Rome

Ancient cities, as was indicated in Chapter 2, Emergence of Cities, were rarely based on a plan or even a general concept of what the city should be. The Greeks, who appreciated organization and structure in other aspects of their lives, gave little attention to the physical arrangement of the communities in which they lived. In classical Greek cities the main thoroughfares were generally planned as processional avenues, but residential development was undisciplined and chaotic. Rhodes, with its avenues radiating from a center, was something of an exception. What planning did take place was limited to the central municipal area, containing the principal monuments, temples, and stately edifices.

Aristotle tells us that Hippodamus of Miletus, who lived in the fifth century B.C., was an early city planner. According to Aristotle,

> Hippodamus, son of Euryphon, a native of Miletus, invented the art of planning and laid out the street plan of Piraeus. . . . He planned a city with a population of 10,000 divided into three parts, one of the skilled workers, one of farmers, and one to defend the state. The land was divided into three parts: sacred, public, and private supporting in turn the worship of the gods, the defense of the state, and the farm owners. . . .[1]

Note that provision was made for farming within the city walls, a most necessary consideration during periods when the city was under siege.

The Romans were somewhat more successful than the Greeks at planning their towns. Rome itself showed limited evidence of planning, but provincial Roman towns, with their central square and gridiron pattern of residences, established a model that can be seen in most American communities today. The provincial cities of western Europe were modeled after the pattern of encampment developed by the Roman legions. Since the provincial towns were initially military outposts, civilian buildings followed the pattern of the military camp, particularly since much of the planning was done by military engineers. It has been said that these outpost towns were so similar that if a

---

[1]Aristotle, *Politics, Book VII, ii, 8*, B. Jowett (trans.), 1932 ed.

TURRIS BABEL

The Tower of Babel provides biblical example of how urban planning can go awry. (Bettmann Archive)

Roman centurion was dropped in the middle of any one of them, he could not tell which town he was in. The largest of the planned Roman cities was Constantinople, the "Rome of the East," which the emperor Constantine built to glorify his reign and escape the fate of previous emperors at the hands of the Roman Senate and street mobs.

Medieval and Later Developments

The fall of the Roman empire in the west meant the death of urban planning for virtually a millennium. However, even during the Middle Ages, when gradual organic growth was most likely to be the rule, some of the newly reviving towns built by French, Italian, and German princes followed the planned pattern of the earlier Roman colonial settlements—a grid layout and a central square with a market.[2]

The Renaissance revived cities and thinking about cities, but few of the planners' conceptions for total communities ever became more than academic exercises. Since these conceptions were rather fanciful and artificial, and bore virtually no relationship to the haphazard but vital cities then in existence, it is perhaps just as well that they were rarely executed. Star-shaped cities were especially popular; Vicenzo Scamozzi designed a utopian city shaped as a twelve-pointed star and actually built a small city, Palma Nova, in the shape of a nine-pointed star in 1593. The star shape was not entirely fanciful, however, since in the age of cannons and gunpowder the points of a star could serve as bastions for directing the defenders' enfilading fire.

Planners often designed unrealistic static communities that completely ignored the needs of the inhabitants, as well as basic considerations such as topography. Stylized form rather than naturalness was the goal. The epitome of the insistence on symmetrical perfection was Versailles, the magnificent home of the French kings, whose gardens, palaces, and town were planned as a unit.[3]

The English also made their own attempts, largely unsuccessfully, at town planning. In 1580 Queen Elizabeth proclaimed restrictions on London's growth that were designed to give the city a green belt of open land and thus prevent crowding and poverty.[4] This policy—which foreshadowed the twentieth-century green-belt towns discussed later in this chapter—failed, although it was backed by royal statute. Probably the most noteworthy master plan was that designed by Christopher Wren for the rebuilding of London after the disastrous fire of 1666. His plan was, unfortunately, not adopted in the rush to rebuild the city.

During the nineteenth century, the changes in the physical organization of Paris must be listed among the more successful attempts at planning. Contemporary Paris, with its broad avenues and magnificent squares, is the

---

[2]Howard Saalman, *Medieval Cities,* Braziller, New York, 1968, p. 114.
[3]Ralph Thomlinson, *Urban Structure,* Random House, New York, 1969, p. 205.
[4]Daniel R. Mendelker, *Green Belts and Urban Growth,* University of Wisconsin Press, Madison, 1962, p. 27.

Planned Capitals

Twentieth-century planned capital cities have been mixtures of success and failure. Canberra, Australia, which was begun in 1918, is pleasing to the eye; but it is difficult to go anywhere in Canberra without using a car, owing to the strict segregation of the city into governmental, residential, and commercial areas. Canberra is sometimes referred to as the world's most inconvenient suburb.

Brasilia, the capital of Brazil, located 600 miles inland from Rio de Janeiro, has a different problem. Brasilia, begun in 1957 and inaugurated as the capital in 1960, did not just grow; rather, it was designed from the ground up, primarily by Lucio Costa. The city was designed for the age of the automobile, and it is characterized by massive superblocks of concrete and glass.

Brasilia is grand and impressive, but the visitor finds it hard to escape the feeling that is not really meant to be lived in. Separate centers for government, commerce, and recreation are clustered along one axis of the city, while housing occupies the other main axis (creating monumental twice-daily traffic jams). Although Brasilia is proving successful in encouraging the economic development of the center of the country and infusing national spirit, it is less successful in generating that perhaps indefinable human response we experience in the great cities of the world. Brazilian government officials and bureaucrats resist being transferred to Brasilia, and those who are assigned there fly back to the far more lively Rio de Janeiro as often as they can afford to. Brasilia lacks Rio's human warmth and livability. While the design is unquestionably bold and creative, it is also somewhat stark and abstract. The city is a remarkable monument, but monuments are not always comfortable places in which to live.

An unanticipated problem has been the continuing influx of poor workers into the so-called "satellite cities" and the favelas (unplanned peripheral slums) at a rate of over 10 percent a year. The superblocks of the central—city known as the "plano piloto" (pilot plan)—house the upper and middle classes, while the slum settlements are mostly hidden from view miles from the center of the city.

Too much may have been expected of the utopian city. As the designer, Costa, replies to critics:

Things are done differently here. You have to accept the country for what it is. Of course, half the people in Brasilia live in favelas. Brasilia was not designed to solve the problems of Brazil, it was bound to reflect them.*

Perhaps the Brazilian spirit will, with the passage of time, convert Brasilia if not into another Rio, at least into a more comfortable and livable city.

*"Brazil's Dream City Has Flaws," *United Press International*, August 19, 1973.

result of seventeen years of rebuilding directed by Baron Haussmann under the sponsorship of Napoleon III (1852–1870). The beauty of Paris today is not accidental but the result of Haussmann's genius. Boulevards were cut through festering slums, and the city was planned for separate industrial and residential areas. However, the rationale for the changes was not solely aesthetic; the broad boulevards provided excellent fields of fire for cannon and divided the city into districts which could be more easily controlled and isolated in times of civil insurrection.

Unfortunately, under more recent French governments the skyline of Paris has been disfigured by some of the worst-designed skyscrapers in Europe. The controversial skyscraper complex of La Defense is an example: its insurance company building blots out the view of the Arc de Triomphe.

URBAN PLANNING IN WESTERN EUROPE

Europe has a tradition of urban planning for the community welfare that goes back many years. Europeans, lacking the land resources of the United States, have been more concerned with conserving their resources and preventing unlimited growth. The tendency toward compactness and public ownership also means that the desires of the individual builder are more subject to the criteria of the public welfare.

The United States, by contrast, has yet to formulate a national or even regional land-use policy.[5] In the United States, plans concentrate on the local level. (Ironically, those who most oppose national land-use controls as "socialistic" are often the strongest supporters of stringent local controls in their suburbs. Some opponents of a national land-use policy live in suburbs that regulate matters such as lot sizes, home sizes, placement of fences, and even whether residents can park a trailer in the driveway.)

In North America, urban rebuilding almost invariably meant the tearing down of older buildings and rebuilding using modern architectural designs and materials. In Europe, rebuilding has sometimes had quite a different effect. Much of the rebuilding of German cities after World War II has consciously attempted to return the destroyed areas to the same appearance that they had before the war. Urban renewal need not mean changing existing patterns: this decision is one for us to make. Poland, after considerable thought and debate, rejected a modern glass-and-concrete design for rebuilding the center of Warsaw after its total destruction. The Poles consciously reproduced the appearance of this section of Warsaw during the period of its medieval glory. Brick by brick, the medieval section has been replicated. The fact that in North America renewal has taken place in one direction does not mean that there are not other alternatives.

---

[5]William K. Reilly (ed.), *The Use of Land: A Citizen's Guide to Urban Growth*, Rockefeller Brothers Fund, Thomas Crowell, New York, 1973.

Control of Land

One advantage enjoyed by some European communities is control over their own municipal lands. Stockholm began buying land in 1904 outside the city limits, with the goal of providing both green space and room for future garden suburbs. Most of this land has since been annexed to the city, so that Stockholm is now in the position of owning about 75 percent of the land within its administrative boundaries. The city rarely sells its land; instead, it leases the land on sixty-year renewable leases to both public and private developers. The money earned from the leases pays off the cost of the loan used to buy the land; and the municipality has the additional advantage of profiting directly from increases in land values. The public, rather than private land speculators, thus profits from the increased value of the land. If the city wants the land after the sixty-year lease is up, it must go to court and prove that the land is needed for the public interest, and then pay the leaseholder the value of any buildings on the property. Such a system would clearly not be politically or economically acceptable in the United States, with its value of private profit making.

Since World War II, the city-owned land in Stockholm has been used to develop a system of subcenters or "mini-cities," built one after another along rapid-transit lines extending in five directions from the old city center. Each subcenter contains between 10,000 and 20,000 inhabitants and is served by its own community services, schools, and shops. Unlike the British new towns, these subcenters emphasize easy access to the center city. Blocks of flats, frequently high-rises, are built 550 yards from the transit station; detached and terrace-style housing is built beyond up to about 1,000 yards from the station. Cars are routed through green areas surrounding the living areas.

Along each string of subcenters, "main centers" are built at appropriate intervals. Each main center, with a larger shopping mall, theaters, and a major transit station, has a supporting population of between 50,000 and 100,000 persons within ten minutes by automobile or public transit.

Housing Changes

The chronic post-World War II western European housing shortage largely came to an end during the 1970s. Recent attention has thus been shifting from massive building programs to a greater emphasis on the quality of the urban environment. During the postwar period there was heavy emphasis on clearance of slums and war-damaged central areas, and on the building of new towns on the urban periphery. Outside of England, these new towns were often high-rise in nature. A welfare state approach also led to the construction of largely rent-controlled and rent-subsidized units.[6] In Great Britain, council housing— that is, public housing—accounts for a third of the entire housing stock. In

---

[6]Wynn Martin (ed.), *Housing in Europe,* St. Martin's Press, New York, 1984.

Sweden only 35 percent of all housing built since World War II has been constructed by the private sector.

Now greater affluence and interest in upgrading older central-city housing is leading to more owner-occupied housing and to the rehabilitation and revitalization of older inner-city housing stock. Middle-class populations have less interest in the massive high-rise housing projects of twenty years ago and greater interest in gentrification of older neighborhoods. More conservative governments have led to greater emphasis on private-market housing, although this is often subsidized to an extent unknown in the United States.

Most new residential building in Europe is subsidized in one way or another in order to hold down costs and maintain quality. Germany and the Netherlands have elaborate programs for loans to nonprofit housing organizations, Great Britain has rent rebates, and Sweden has an annual housing allowance for all families with two or more children.

Rents in most countries take less than 20 percent of family income because of subsidies. This is excellent by American standards. In the Netherlands and Germany, rents frequently do not exceed 15 percent of family income. The extreme is found in the Soviet Union, where the rent for a small apartment for a family of four absorbs only 3.5 percent of the average monthly income of an industrial worker. Utilities cost another 3.5 percent on the average. The drawback in the Soviet Union is that owing to a severe housing shortage the current amount of living space is just below the government set "housing norm" of 9 square meters (approximately 97 square feet) per person.[7] That is very tight living.

Transportation

Cars are relied on extensively in comparatively low-density American cities, with their commitment to housing patterns of dispersed single-family houses on private land. On the other hand, in more densely populated European cities, where most people reside in apartment buildings (typically of three or four stories), public transit is the norm. Even in affluent Sweden, which has a higher per capita income than the United States, only 7 percent of the households have two cars; and 45 percent do not own an auto.[8] Sixty percent of the trips to or from work in Stockholm are made by public transit and 20 percent by foot. In spite of their high auto taxes Swedes can afford automobiles. Many do not buy cars because they do not need them; there is excellent, public subsidized subway and ground transportation.

In many European cities with narrow streets and few garages the convenience of driving is outweighed by the problem of where to park the car. In cities such as Rome or Paris cars are often parked on sidewalks as well as streets. An average European city may have only half the autos of its American

---

[7]Henry M. Morton, "The Soviet Quest for Better Housing—An Impossible Dream?," *Soviet Economy in a Time of Change*, Joint Economic Committee of Congress, Washington, D.C., October, 1979, p. 795.
[8]David Popenoe, *Private Pleasure, Public Plight*, Transaction, New Brunswick, N.J., 1985, p. 43.

In spite of too many autos, Montmartre in Paris retains much of its vitality. (Hugh Rogers/Monkmeyer)

counterpart, but these cars can cause immense congestion and parking problems, as an American tourist driving there can attest. Fortunately, mass transit in London, Paris, or anywhere in Holland, Germany, or Scandinavia is remarkably fast and efficient.

Urban Growth Policies

While the United States does not have a national land-use or growth policy, several European countries have explicit growth policies. Great Britain, France, Italy, the Netherlands, Sweden, and the Soviet Union are all seeking to disperse national population and stem migration to the largest centers. While the measures haven't been entirely successful, they have slowed the movement from smaller to larger places.

In Britain the goal has been to stem the so-called "drift to the south"— out of Scotland and Wales and into the area centering on London. In France the goal has been to lessen the domination of Paris; in Italy, to develop the economy of the depressed south, or Mezzogiorno; in the Netherlands, to save the remaining green areas; and in Sweden, to halt the flow out of more northern jareas into Stockholm and the south. (As noted in Chapter 5, Metropolitan, Nonmetropolitan, and Sun Belt Growth, less than 3 percent of U.S. land area is defined as urban.)

The basic tool has been to provide manufacturers with economic incentives to invest in depressed areas needing growth. Subsidies in terms of capital grants are provided by the national government. In addition, controls are increasingly imposed upon adding factories or offices to places where growth isn't wanted. For example, to build a factory or office building in the London area, the developer must show that the enterprise cannot be developed elsewhere. The Netherlands also puts higher taxes on buildings in the cities of Amsterdam, Rotterdam, and The Hague. Another policy is to relocate government offices to areas where growth is desired. Sweden is relocating one-quarter of its government offices outside of Stockholm—a policy that definitely does not appeal to the government bureaucrats who have to move. In the Soviet Union, hard-to-get residence permits (*propiska*) are necessary before one may move into large cities. Long waiting lists have slowed population concentration.

It is difficult to see any urban growth and redistribution policy being implemented in the United States. There is no clamor for a program administered out of Washington, and programs by individual states are unlikely to be effective. If one state imposed sanctions, a company could—and probably would—simply up and move to another state that did not. Thus, while European programs for dispersion of growth have been reasonably successful, they are unlikely to be copied in North America, with our stronger opposition to decision making by the central government. Our decentralized system also has a flexibility lacking elsewhere.

The Dutch Approach

Americans who fear that certain regions of the United States are turning into unrelenting megalopolises should find it instructive to see how the Dutch are coping with similar problems. The Netherlands is a small country with a population of 14 million and a population density of over 410 persons per square kilometer. If the United States had this population density, it would have a population of over 4.8 billion, or roughly the present population of the world. The problem in the Netherlands is aggravated by the fact that the majority of the Dutch population is found in a megalopolis about 100 miles in diameter, including Amsterdam, Rotterdam, and The Hague. This conurbation is known as the *randstad,* or "rim city." Thus, because of necessity the Dutch have had to make planning choices not addressed by the land-abundant United States.

Nonetheless, in spite of the population in the Netherlands, it is possible to reach the open countryside in half an hour's time from the center of any of the cities in the *randstad.* In spite of considerable population growth and a housing shortage following World War II, the Dutch lead remarkably uncluttered lives. Urban sprawl such as that found in the United States is virtually unknown. The line between town and country is sharply drawn. When a city such as Amsterdam stops, it stops abruptly. It is quite common at the city's edge to see massive blocks of high-rise apartments overlooking cows peacefully grazing in totally open fields. By building upward rather than outward, the Dutch have kept their towns compact; and valuable woods, lakes, and fields are kept as a reserve for the use of all.

The Dutch have been able to save much of their environment, and at the same time provide for an ever-expanding demand for housing, by building tall, multiple-unit residential buildings. The use of high-rises is dictated by the shortage of land and the necessity to keep down costs of land. Almost without exception, single-family houses are built in rows.[9] Many families in the Netherlands, particularly those with small children, prefer single-family houses; and the privately financed dwellings now being built are substantially of this type. However, only the more affluent segment of the population can afford the high building costs. Because of limited land the Dutch cannot afford American-style suburban sprawl.

The government in effect subsidizes both rents and building costs for those not able to carry the full cost. The Dutch feel that every family, regardless of income level, is entitled to reasonable housing. As a result, rents are low by comparison with those in the United States. After deduction for taxes and social insurance, the average Dutch family pays under 15 percent of its income for rent.[10] This is a result of the government's policy of rental subsidies and loans for building new dwellings. The average rent of a new dwelling financed with a state loan is roughly 15 or 16 percent of the average gross income of an industrial worker.[11] Subsidies and rent supplements are periodically readjusted so that the poor and the working classes will not be priced out of the housing market. All this requires high taxes, but the government has chosen this over lower human services.

The Dutch also believe in public ownership of urban land; about 70 percent of Amsterdam is now owned by the city. In The Hague the policy is somewhat different: only about 20 percent of the land is owned by the city, but it is strategically located so that it can be used to set the pattern of real estate

---

[9]*The Netherlands: Current Trends and Policies in the Field of Housing, Building, and Planning During the Year 1968,* Ministry of Housing and Physical Planning. The Hague, 1970, p. 18.
[10]Ibid., p. 14.
[11]Ibid.

Bicycles in Amsterdam have their own traffic lanes. (Richard Wood/ Taurus Photos)

prices for the city. The third major city of the Netherlands, Rotterdam, saw its downtown area reduced to rubble by Nazi dive bombers in 1940. Rotterdam began to reconstruct after the war, with the core of the city as a commercial, cultural, and administrative center. Dutch officials now concede that it was a mistake to rigidly segregate commercial and residential areas. The Lijnbaan, the downtown shopping mall which has received much praise, contains fine shops, sidewalk cafes, and several apartment buildings without vacancies. Rotterdam's land policy is somewhere between that of Sweden and that of the United States. The city retains ownership of industrial and commercial land, with the land being leased and rents reviewed every three to five years. Land to be used for housing, on the other hand, is sold outright after it has been determined that the land use is in conformity with the overall development plan for the city.

Rotterdam also has what is credited to be the most successful housing revitalization program in Europe, a program that allows low-income residents to remain in their neighborhoods.[12] The city has avoided the problem of other European and American cities where gentrification has meant the displacement of existing residents. Neighborhood project groups of residents are used to involve existing residents in the whole range of local decisions. Public monies

[12]J. van der Ploeg, "The Rotterdam Model: Renewal without Gentrification," *Urban Innovation Abroad*, **6**:4, April, 1982.

are used for acquisition and upgrading of existing structures, whether small-scale or wall-to-wall renovations. Only when the local project group cannot agree on what should be done is the matter referred to the Town Urban Renewal Committee for resolution.

Throughout Holland a system of local, regional, and—finally—national controls prevents unwanted urban sprawl. New buildings cannot be constructed unless they conform to the detailed development plan prepared by each municipality. Plans for development are drawn up by the city, but they must be approved by provincial authorities, who have certain limited powers of review and veto. If a local development is in conflict with the regional plan, and if the differences cannot be resolved at that level, the question then goes to the national level for a decision. There is no national plan, as such; rather, there are national guidelines which influence the regional plans and the detailed city development plans. An attempt is made to avoid rigidity, and plans are constantly being modified—within the national guidelines—to meet new situation and needs. Without some controls, the remaining green space between The Hague, Rotterdam, and Amsterdam would soon be filled, and a megalopolis would become inevitable.

German Urban Renewal

As in the United States there has been a movement of the German population toward more suburban areas, although city centers remain active economically and socially. Current national urban policy is directed toward encouraging movement into cities.[13] Emphasis is being put on increasing the livability of cities through changes such as pedestrian malls even if they interfere with efficiency and rapid transportation. Housing and other facilities are deliberately intermixed. The German new town program has been stopped largely because of residents' feelings that the peripheral new towns lacked a sense of urban feeling and vitality.

Within German cities there are extensive subsidy programs that would make U.S. planners green with envy. Emphasis has gone from urban renewal (clearing away old buildings and rebuilding) to urban revitalization in which internal work goes from minimal to complete rebuilding. Much of the rebuilding and renovation has been "social flats," or what would be called public housing in the United States. Social housing constitutes 30 percent of the postwar housing in Frankfurt and 80 percent of that in West Berlin. However, unlike the public housing in the United States, social housing is built to the same standards as other housing.

Social housing is occupied not only by the poor. In Germany getting a social flat depends on your income at time of application. You can stay even if your income increases. Thus, there is a rush by young people to get social

---

[13]Data in this section are based in part on a 1982 study of German cities arranged by the Federal Republic of Germany.

housing before their income goes up. Over time social housing, like private units, shows a wide range of income levels among occupants.

Rehabilitation. Rehabilitation of middle-class dwellings is also subsidized by the state. Additional subsidies are available to all homeowners in historic reconstruction districts. However, of the private owners rehabilitating their properties, only a small minority actually accept government subsidies since acceptance limits whom they can rent to and means subjugation to strict rent controls.

The rehabilitation program in German cities is running into problems, the most serious being renewal costs. Unlike cities in the United States, which pay for much of their activities from local property taxes, German cities receive the bulk of their funds from state and federal programs. The cost to the federal government in high. The average cost of revitalizing each family flat in an urban renewal area of Frankfurt during the late 1970s was $25,000 (approximately $45,000 in 1986 dollars). As costs have gone up the amount of internal modernization (all new bathroom fixtures, for example) has declined in favor of minimal structural changes.

Pollution. German cities also suffer from increasingly severe air pollution problems. Cologne's world-famous cathedral is literally crumbling away because of air pollution. Autos built before 1988 do not have to use lead-free gasoline, nor do they have the advanced pollution control devices mandated in places such as the United States and Japan. Germany's forests are dying because of auto pollution. Moreover, in the cities coal is still the major heating source, either through central heating or individual room stoves. German cities are only reluctantly coming to the application of pollution controls; controls that have been routine in the United States for over a decade.

East Berlin. To most observers the communist showcase city of East Berlin, when compared to West Berlin, seems affected by considerable dullness. Most buildings are drab and in need of repair while the transit system looks like New York subways—minus the grafitti but with even more age, disrepair, and grime. While public buildings have been magnificently restored, new and old housing flats are often ill maintained. The grand boulevards of East Berlin have only limited auto traffic, and there is little of the bustling crowds that overflow the stores and cafes of the major arteries of West Berlin.

EASTERN EUROPEAN PATTERNS

The Soviet Union

Any discussion of socialist cities should begin with the Soviet Union, which has set the pattern for eastern Europe. In contrast to western Europe or the United States, the Soviet Union is still undergoing rapid urbanization. Fifty years ago, it had only two cities of over 1 million (Moscow and Leningrad) and no cities between 500,000 and 1 million. The Soviet Union remained a predominantly rural country until 1960. As of 1980 the USSR was 63 percent urban.[14] There are thirteen cities of over 1 million and twenty-nine cities of between 500,000 and 1 million. Regionally, the rate of urbanization is highest in the European areas of the nation and lowest in the Central Asian republics, with their Muslim populations.

Cities. Contemporary Soviet cities are the product of a number of distinctive forces, of which the most influential have been (1) the unprecedented destruction of housing stock during World War II, (2) the rigidity and massiveness of "socialist realist" architecture of the Stalin era, (3) national emphasis on developing heavy industry rather than housing, and (4) the attempts to build a "socialist city."

Land Use. Under the Soviet system the use of land is determined not by market values (the underpinning of the tradition of the Chicago school discussed in Chapter 4) but by government policy. According to Szelenyi, socialist urban developments were expected to look different from western cities because (1) the western mechanisms of land values couldn't prevail, (2) most urban housing is built by the state, and rents are highly subsidized, thus replacing the housing market by a redistribution of national income through the housing system, and (3) state-owned enterprises have a virtual monopoly in the construction industry, trade, and servicing.[15]

Housing. Housing its people remains the most critical urban problem faced by the Soviet Union. (This is a problem on which only limited data were available in the west until recently.) Under the tsars much of the population was ill-housed, and conditions did not improve after the communist revolution. Stalin followed a policy of "industry first; cities be damned" which has been difficult for leaders coming from that era to break.[16] Nonetheless, in recent decades great efforts have been made. Since the 1950s the Soviet Union has built 2.2 million housing units a year.[17] Most of these units are in huge, identical slablike complexes, and the units fall far short of western standards in quality and size. Less than half the urban dwellers have the official housing norm of 97 square feet of living area. Some Soviet families still share kitchens, bathrooms, or whole apartments with another family. The Minister of Housing reported in 1981 that 20 percent of urban families still share their apartment

[14]Murray Feshback, "The Soviet Union: Population Trends and Dilemmas," *Population Bulletin,* Population Reference Bureau, Washington, D.C., August, 1982, p. 37.

[15]Ivan Szelenyi, "Urban Sociology and Community Studies in Eastern Eruope," *Comparative Urban Research,* 4(213):11–20, 1977.

[16]William Taubman, *Governing Soviet Cities: Bureaucratic Politics and Urban Development in the USSR,* Praeger, New York, 1973, p. 18.

[17]Henry W. Morton, "Who Gets What, When and How? Housing in the Soviet Union," *Soviet Studies,* **32**:235–259, April, 1980; and Dmitri Shalin, "Housing in the Soviet Union," *Environmental Sociology,* **43**:7–13, Fall, 1985.

The Soviet government builds almost all of its new housing using preformed sections which are assembled at the construction site. (Tass/Sovfoto)

with another family. The problem is not that nothing is being done, but that after half a century during which housing needs were virtually ignored, the housing problem has become so massive that only exceptional measures can reduce the deficit. The result is that many young couples must of necessity live with their parents for many years. This, plus limited availability of child care for working wives, virtually insures continuing low urban birthrates.

City governance. Actual city governance in the Soviet Union is only partially in the hands of local officials. Mayors and city officials, particularly outside the largest cities or the state capitals, have far more responsibilities than authority to carry them out. Managers of large factories often have direct responsibility for municipal services such as housing, electricity, water supply, or even running the streetcars. But factory managers are judged by their superiors on how well they meet production quotas, not on how they maintain city services. As a consequence, the need for services is often indifferently met. William Taubman suggests that it is the local Communist Party officials who often lobby for increased services and environmental improvements such as reducing industrial pollution.[18] Factory directors, by contrast, are more likely to oppose change, since improvement in city services and amenities will in effect by an added "cost" of production. Ironically, business directors and factory managers in the Soviet Union often have more direct control over local affairs than their counterparts in capitalistic systems do.

Social-Class Distribution in Socialist Countries

Theoretically, socialist countries have largely abolished social segregation. Low, state-subsidized rents mean that the upper class can't outpurchase other groups. Housing is allocated on the basis of need, family size, and the possession of key job skills. Nonetheless, while a free market in which the upper class can get the best housing by paying higher rents does not exist, the upper strata still get the best housing. Rather than a market system, a system of social rewards applies. Political, military, scientific, academic, and cultural elites receive special consideration *before* those on the allocation list. They go to the head of the line. With consumer goods limited, housing is the major symbol of social status.

The elites receive priority for the newest and largest housing. "Thus the group that are most advantaged become the beneficiaries of redistributed social wealth by living in units that are the most highly subsidized by the state.[19]

> All the available data from Poland, Czechoslovakia and the G.D.R. (German Democratic Republic) suggest that the inhabitants of heavily subsidized state rental housing are of higher social status than the owners of the less subsidized family-built dwellings. Workers with lower qualifications build their own houses, workers with higher qualifications and professionals receive new state housing.[20]

Thus, in eastern European socialist countries housing inequalities resulting from market inequalities have been replaced with housing inequalities as a consequence of the systems of social rewards. East or west, the upper strata still get the best. Or as in commonly put, "them that has, gets."

There are, however, some real differences between socialist countries and other countries. For example, the pattern of cities and suburbs found in North America is largely reversed in the Soviet Union and eastern European countries. With city housing in extremely short supply, and permits to move to the city difficult to obtain without influence, poor workers often must live in the country while working in the city. The "suburban" commuter from Moscow, Warsaw, or Budapest is most likely to be a blue-collar worker living in a

[18]Taubman, op. cit.
[19]See Henry Morton, op. cit., and Ivan Szelenyi, *Urban Inequalities under State Socialism,* Oxford University Press, London, 1983.
[20]Szelenyi, op. cit., 1977, p. 19.

peripheral slum community. In Hungary, for example, 70 percent of the cities' unskilled workers and half the industrial workers commute into the cities.[21] Thus, in direct contrast to the cities of the developing world (discussed in Part Five, Worldwide Urbanization), eastern European cities have more employment and industry than housing for workers.

The best housing areas are often the new housing developments located on the near edges of the city. Since in socialist countries the price of land isn't taken into account, there is no economic incentive for renewal of inner-city areas for occupancy by the upper class. The consequence is that in socialist countries the location of newer state housing rather than market price affects the social status of areas. Government planning thus plays a direct—if unintentional—role in socially segregating the city into upper-, middle-, and lower-class areas.

NEW TOWNS

Throughout the centuries, humans have had visions of creating new towns free from the fads and foibles of older cities. The term "utopia" originated as the title of a book (1516) by Thomas More which gave his version of how a new land of towns should be organized. Here the emphasis is on new towns that have actually been built, beginning with the world-renowned English new towns program and then discussing other European alternatives. The chapter concludes with a discussion of experiences in the United States.

British New Towns

The British new town movement owes its origins to Ebenezer Howard (1850–1928), an English court stenographer who proposed the building of whole new communities. His idea appeared in a book called *To-morrow, A Peaceful Path to Real Reform* (1898), which was soon reissued under the title *Garden Cities of To-morrow* (1902). Howard's new towns, which were called "garden cities," were not to be simply another version of suburbs. Rather, they were to be self-contained communities of 30,000 inhabitants which would have within their boundaries ample opportunities not only for residence but also for employment, education, and recreation. The towns were to be completely planned, with all land held in public ownership to prevent speculation.

Howard's garden cities were essentially a reaction against the urban abuses of the industrial revolution in England. His new towns were not to be extensions of the morally and socially polluted city but self-sufficient towns with all necessary amenities, where one could enjoy the benefits of a healthful country life. In Howard's words:

> There are in reality not only, as is so constantly assumed, two alternatives—town life and country life—but a third alternative in which all the advantages of the

---

[21]Ibid., p. 15.

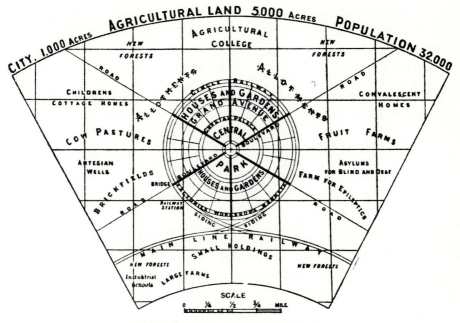

GARDEN CITY AND RURAL BELT

Howard's Garden Cities were designed to be self-sufficient and self-contained communities. Note that the railroads were not to enter the city proper, but would remain within the manufacturing belt on the town periphery.

most energetic and active town life, with all the beauty and delight of the country, may be secured in perfect combination.[22]

This combination would in turn spur "the spontaneous movement of the people from our crowded cities to the bosom of our kindly mother earth, at once the source of life, of happiness, of wealth, and of power." Thus the garden city was fundamentally antiurban in its basic conception. It was to solve the problem of the great cities largely by abandoning them and starting over with a fresh environment.

Frederick Osborn, one of the major proponents of new towns, described them as follows:

Howard's Garden City is to be industrial and commercial with a balanced mixture of all social groups and levels of income. Areas are worked out for the zones: public buildings and places of entertainment are placed centrally, shops intermediately, factories on the edge with the railway and sidings. Houses are of different sizes, but all have gardens and all are within easy range of factories, shops, schools, cultural centers, and the open country. Of special interest is the central park and

[22]Ebenezer Howard, *Garden Cities of To-morrow,* Faber and Faber, London, 1902, pp. 45–46.

the inner Green Belt or Ring Park, 420 feet wide, containing the main schools with large playgrounds and such buildings as churches.[23]

However, the most distinctive feature of the garden cities was that beyond the city itself there was an encircling "green belt" of natural fields and woodlands which were owned by the town and could never be sold. This green belt could not be encroached upon for housing, business, industry, or even farming—although it could be used for pasturage. Because of this feature, garden cities are also known as green-belt cities. The green belt not only provided a way for the residents to enjoy nature, it also was intended to prevent the city from growing beyond its planned limit of 30,000 inhabitants.

Nor was the internal design of the garden city left to chance. The whole town, including its pattern of roads, was planned with both the quality and the basic design of buildings controlled. The central 5 or 6 acres were to contain civic buildings, a library, lecture halls, and theaters. Stores and shops were nearby. This core was surrounded by rings of houses, each with its own yard. Neighborhood schools and churches were scattered throughout the city, and small parks connected the various neighborhoods. The outermost ring of the city was to contain industries and warehouses with direct access to rail lines. The rail lines did not penetrate the center of the city proper.

The town was totally planned, and strict zoning was central to Howard's basic scheme. The residential city was divided into five neighborhoods or wards, each with approximately 5,000 residents. Each was to have its own centrally located school and community subcenter, and every attempt was to be made to keep all houses within walking distance of factories, schools, churches, shops, and, of course, the open country.[24]

The whole site, including agricultural land, was to be under quasi-public or trust ownership to ensure planning control through leasehold covenants. When the population outgrew the prescribed size and area, another new town was to be created with its own sacrosanct green belt. As with the ancient Greeks, problems of growth were to be handled by colonization rather than by extending city boundaries.

First Towns. The concept of garden cities would have gone the way of other utopian plans had Howard not been an activist as well as a visionary. In 1902, with the aid of the newly formed Garden City Association, he established the first garden city at Letchworth, some 30 miles north of London.[25]

This initial venture was plagued by many difficulties, the principal one being that the site selected was poor. Another problem was the difficulty of finding investors for a project that limited dividends to a maximum of 5 percent

---

[23]Frederick J. Osborn, *Green-Belt Cities,* Schocken, New York, 1969, p. 28.
[24]For a detailed discussion of the community's organization, see Osborn, op. cit. For a detailed description of the history of new towns, see E.R. Scoffham, *The Shape of British Housing,* George Godwin, London, 1984.
[25]Frank Schaffer, *The New Town Story,* MacGibbon and Kee, London, 1970, p. 4.

per year. In fact, it was twenty years before the shareholders received any dividends at all.[26]

The understandable reluctance of industry to move out to the new town meant that residents became commuters to London—a situation directly opposed to Howard's conception of a town that would provide its own employment. Howard was emphatically against the green-belt towns' becoming commuter suburbs.

Despite these problems, while the first garden city was still not out of the financial woods, land for a second, Welwyn Garden City, was secured in 1920. Howard did this without consulting his board of directors since he knew they would not approve. Welwyn Garden City suffered financial crises for many years, but it eventually surmounted them. Today it is a pleasant and prosperous community of 44,000 residents about twenty-five minutes by rail from London.

Government Involvement. Were it not for World War II, Howard's garden cities would probably have remained a quaint experiment. However, World War II, with its extensive destruction in the heart of London, led Patrick Abercrombie to publish a Greater London Plan of 1944, with decentralization as one of its major aims.

The new towns were to be one part of a four-part policy. The policy included: (1) a green belt around London to halt continuous metropolitan growth, (2) new towns to house the expanding urban population, (3) redevelopment of inner-city areas, conforming to higher standards than had existed previously, and (4) an attempt to control the location of employment and to prevent everyone from building in London.[27]

The British government became directly involved in the building of new towns through the New Towns Act of 1946. Advocates of new towns had long argued that they would provide a healthier, cleaner, safer, and more democratic environment. In the back of everyone's mind was also the fact that London had suffered grievously from bombing during the war and that new towns would disperse both population and industry at numerous smaller nodes rather than create one massive target in London. Furthermore, it was considered undesirable to rebuild badly damaged areas of London, such as the East End, at the old unsatisfactory population densities; new towns would help to absorb the surplus population. Government involvement in new towns meant that building on a grand scale was now possible, as a result of government financing. Compulsory purchase of land from private owners for building the town was also available.

The involvement of the British government, however, meant that the new towns would differ in significant ways from Howard's original scheme. First, the development corporation was appointed by and answerable to the central

---

[26]Lloyd Rodwin, *The British New Towns Policy*, Harvard University Press, Cambridge, Mass., 1956, pp. 12–13.

[27]Wyndham Thomas, "Implementation: New Towns," in Derek Senior (ed.), *The Regional City*, Aldine, Chicago, 1966, pp. 19–20.

government, not to the town. Second, the size range was pushed upward—first to 60,000; and some towns plan for ultimate populations of up to 250,000 in cluster cities. This is far from Howard's limit of 30,000. Third, no provision was made for nearby land to be used only for agriculture. "As far as access to the countryside is concerned the new towns do not differ from most other settlements in Britain."[28] Finally, the concept of a city providing all its own employment was also abandoned, in practice if not in theory, although the new towns are certainly not designed to be commuter suburbs. They are basically manufacturing centers, with approximately half the population in industry and the other half in trade, the services, and the professions.

The first of the English government-sponsored new towns, Stevenage, was begun in 1947. Among other innovations, it had the first pedestrian shopping mall in Britain and neighborhoods designed to separate pedestrian walkways from contact with automobile and truck traffic. Today Stevenage is a pleasant and economically self-supporting community of 66,000.

Houses and apartments built by the local new towns development corporations are not distributed on a first-come, first-served basis. Rather, priority is determined by a number of criteria, including employment by local or incoming industries and previous residence in one of the more crowded inner-city areas of London. Originally, following Howard's plan, almost all dwellings were rented, but successive British governments have been moving toward increasing the number of owner-occupied homes. As a means of encouraging home ownership, the conservative government offered renters the option of purchasing the property in which they lived for 20 percent below the market value.

As of 1980, thirty-three new towns had been completed in Great Britain, with a total investment of over $5 billion. It should be pointed out that only 5 percent of Britain's housing construction after World War II has taken place in new towns. Still, the British are well pleased with their new towns program. By the end of the 1980s, they expect to have nearly 4 million persons living in new towns.

New Towns in Western and Eastern Europe

Not only England but other European countries, including Sweden, Finland, the Netherlands, and the Soviet Union, built new towns after World War II. The Soviet Union has probably founded more new towns than any other nation. About one-third of these were established in totally undeveloped areas. The Soviets' development of new towns has been generally explained as part of broad schemes for national development and the decentralization of industry. Many of their earlier new towns were connected with hydroelectric power projects and then expanded into manufacturing centers.[29]

In the Soviet Union, as in England, the new towns were planned to be separate from existing urban centers although related to them. Local industry

[28]Ray Thomas and Peter Cresswell, *The New Town Idea*, Open University Press, England, 1973, p. 24.
[29]J. Clapp, *New Towns and Urban Policy—Planning Metropolitan Growth*, Dunellen, New York, 1971, p. 28.

The Swedish new town of Täby is located on a subway/elevated line and has rapid access to the center to Stockholm. (Swedish Information Service)

was to provide sufficient employment so that few, if any, residents would be required to commute to the large city. Generally, these communities were originally designed to house a maximum of 60,000 to 100,000 people. These new communities were not a consequence of the garden city concept, as were the British new towns. Rather, they were closer to company towns. The goal was not to build more humane environments but to provide housing for the workers in the factories.

In Sweden and the Netherlands, the new communities were designed to be closely tied to the central city, and to serve as residential—not employment— areas. Scandinavian new towns such as Vallingby, Farsta, and Taby are basically residential and shopping areas. Unlike the British new towns, they are constructed along rapid-transit lines so that they will be an integral part of the city's life; they are not designed to be independent and self-contained employment units.[30] It is expected that most residents will work in the central

[30]For a description of urban planning in Sweden, see Goran Sidenbladh, "Stockholm: A Planned City," in *Cities: A Scientific American Book*, Knopf, New York, 1965.

city; consequently, rapid transit to the core of the central city is a basic feature of the design of these towns. Zoetermeer, a Dutch new town of 100,000 inhabitants 7 miles from The Hague, speeds its residents to the center of The Hague in less than twenty minutes. Such new towns are really extensions of the older city into the countryside rather than attempts to create new rural or suburban utopian communities.

All European new towns have in common the fact that they were initiated, planned, and financed by the government. While there has occasionally been some financing from cooperatives, unions, or even private sources, the land and the facilities built on it have been owned either directly by the local government or by quasi-public corporations chartered by the national government to build and administer the town. Dutch planners also have the advantage that, since much of the land for new towns was drained from marshes, there is little dispute as to how the land is to be used.

Throughout Europe high-rise apartment buildings are generally used, not only because land costs are high but also to avoid suburban sprawl and to provide open spaces for recreation and enjoyment of the natural environment. In Sweden, Finland, and the Netherlands over 80 percent of the units are in blocks of flats. English new towns, on the other hand, have over 80 percent single-family homes.[31]

Some of the concentration of high-rise units in Sweden has less to do with planning ideology than with economic considerations. Owners of large stores in the main towns demanded a high density of residents in close proximity to the shopping malls as a condition for opening department stores or supermarkets.

Everywhere automobiles remain a problem. Britain, for example, has proportionately only half the autos of the United States but higher densities, fewer garages, and narrow streets in older cities, creating considerable congestion.[32] Every attempt is made to put parking lots underground or otherwise out of sight to preserve the environment. The increasing number of cars, however, seems to constantly outrun the planners' ideas about where to put them all. Still, by building compactly the planners ensure that much open space is left for woods, sports areas, and lawns.

Generally there is satisfaction with the new towns, although they lack the excitement of the central city. Residents of Vallingby, a suburb of Stockholm, report that both sexes have more time to devote to recreation and other leisure activities than do American suburbanites. This is because residents of Vallingby as apartment dwellers do not have to spend weekends on home maintenance and repair.[33]

Since the housing in new towns is constructed first and amenities follow, there is a problem, particularly in the early years, of boredom and its consequences. Not everyone can adjust to the absence of night life and city

---

[31]Pierre Merlin, *New Towns*, Methuen, London, 1971, p. 250.
[32]David Popenoe, op. cit., p. 51.
[33]David Popenoe, *The Suburban Environment*, University of Chicago Press, Chicago, 1977, especially chap. 9.

excitement. Sweden's planned communities, for example, have had problems with alcohol and drugs—although these problems are hardly unique to new towns. Germany, as noted earlier, has stopped building new towns.

Although Swedish new towns such as Vallingby and Farsta were constructed in the 1950s to deliberately high densities (only 8 percent of the former and 13 percent of the latter are single-family homes), the communities have an oppenness and closeness to nature that residents find appealing. While there are no private yards as in the North American model, there are many walkways, trees, and common open spaces.

More recently built Swedish new towns have a far more negative image among Swedes.[34] The brick-sided walk-up apartments characteristic of Vallingby have been largely replaced with six- to eight-story concrete-slab buildings—many more than a block long. Such slab cities have been criticized as "inhuman environments" and social disaster areas. Built in parallel rows, they present a very sterile and uninviting appearance. Only the color of the buildings distinguishes one group from another. (After dark all the colors look alike, a fact I once discovered when I got lost trying to locate the building where I was staying.)

The relative lack of popularity of such buildings has resulted in their having a high concentration of younger persons with lower incomes and being identified in the popular mind with social problems—drug addiction, alcoholism, and crime. Some of the newest housing areas also have high concentration (25 percent or more) of foreign workers such as Turks—groups often poorly integrated into Swedish society. German new towns have had similar problems.

These social problems—and the high cost of new towns—resulted in European nations' ending or drastically curtailing new town building during the economic belt-tightening years of the 1980s.

[34]Ibid., chaps. 3 and 4.

CHAPTER

13

PLANNING IN THE UNITED STATES

Make no little plans, they have no magic to stir men's blood.

Daniel Burnham

City planning in the United States is usually regarded as a twentieth-century development, but as early as 1672 Lord Ashley Cooper instructed that Charles Town be laid out "into regular streets for be the buildings never so mean and thin at first, yet as the town increases in riches and people, the void places will be filled up and the buildings will grow more beautiful." The town was designed to form a narrow trapezoid four squares long by two squares wide, fronting on the Cooper River. Philadelphia was also laid out according to the gridiron pattern. Today, the area surrounding Independence Hall once again shows the original pattern as William Penn intended. North American colonial cities as disparate as Quebec in the north and James Oglethorpe's Savannah in the south began their existence as planned enterprises.

However, as is indicated in Chapter 17, Urbanization in Latin America, planning was developed furthest in the Spanish colonies. The sixteenth-century Laws of the Indies, promulgated by the Spanish Crown, clearly specified how the conquistadores should construct their cities. Every new town was to have a wide central plaza (the *plaza mayor*) bordered by the major religious and administrative buildings, which were to radiate outward from the *plaza mayor* according to a gridiron plan. Better residences were located near the center of the city; the poor lived on the periphery. The effect of the Spanish town-planning can be seen to this day in Latin America. The patterns are almost the reverse of Burgess's pattern, which was by and large typical in the development and growth of North American cities.

EIGHTEENTH AND NINETEENTH CENTURIES

Washington, D.C.

There is little that can be said for North American town planning during the eighteenth and nineteenth centuries. Pierre L'Enfant's plan for Washington, D.C., is one of the few bright spots in the picture of urban planning after the Revolutionary War. L'Enfant's original design, produced in 1791, called for broad, sweeping diagonal boulevards overlying a basic gridiron pattern with major avenues. Economic realities soon forced the effective abandonment of L'Enfant's overall plan, and L'Enfant himself was removed in 1792, after numerous disputes. His contention that his plan was "most unmercifully spoiled and altered" is largely accurate. For example, he planned a broad boulevard along the river to be lined with gardens; these have never been seen except on his own detailed maps. He even had a plan to divert the river, making it flow toward the Capitol, whence it would be routed over a 40-foot waterfall and then back to its original course.[1] It was probably fortunate, however, that this particular feature was never constructed.

For much of the nineteenth century Washington remained, in Charles

---

[1]Charles N. Glaab and A. Theodore Brown, *A History of Urban America,* Macmillan, New York, 1967, p. 253.

Salt Lake City's streets were planned to be wide enough for a team of oxen to be turned around. (National Archives)

Dickens's words, "a city of magnificent intentions." Washington's oppressively hot, unhealthful summers did not encourage year-round residence. At the time that Lincoln assumed the presidency, Washington was still a half-finished quagmire, packed with members of Congress, lobbyists, job seekers, prostitutes, gamblers, and hangers-on while Congress was in session, and deserted when it was not. Only near the end of the century did a revival of interest in L'Enfant's original plans give us the neoclassical style of government buildings found in the capital today.

One of the city's most notable legacies from L'Enfant is the numerous traffic circles. Any tourist who has ever had the folly of drive into the city is not likely to forget the traffic circles, which disorient even the most experienced drivers.

Nineteenth-Century American Towns

During the nineteenth century little creative energy went into the design of the rapidly multiplying new towns. New western settlements merely replicated older urban traditions. Communities were built as if God had intended that streets be laid out in a grid, at right angles to each other. This was in fact a fairly useful model in the midwest and on the prairie, but it was applied even when it was inappropriate. If hills got in the way, for example, as in San Francisco, streets were simply cut up one side and down the other rather than following the natural contour of the land.

The gridiron pattern, in which plots could easily be divided, was well suited to the feverish speculation that accompanied the nation's early growth; most promoters of sites were speculators whose major interest in the new communities was quick profit. The Federal Land Ordinance of 1785 also encouraged the gridiron pattern, since it divided all lands west of the Appalachians in the public domain into units of 1 square mile to facilitate their sale to settlers.[2] A gridiron pattern was also good for fire protection.

[2]Edmund K. Faltermayor, *Redoing America,* Harper and Row, New York, 1968, p. 17.

Roads and the way they divide land are another strong influence on the pattern of development of a city. A circular pattern, with roads leading from the center like the spokes of a wheel, focuses attention on the center of the city. It is a system "beloved by chieftains, emperors, priests, and popes."[3] Washington, D.C., and Detroit, Michigan, were both designed on modified circular patterns. The gridiron system, with its square lots, has always facilitated subdivision and thus is the model used in industrial and other economically oriented cities in the United States and elsewhere (Johannesburg is an example outside the United States). According to Christopher Tunnard, "the open lot and speculation have always gone hand in hand."[4] This was certainly true of the development of North American cities.

It is interesting to note that by the early twentieth century the rectangular grid, although also used for newer additions to European cities, had come to be identified with the American city.

> It is in America that the persistence of uniform right-angled streets has been most marked. Here the universality of the plan's adoption, and the rigidity of adherence to it, has been such that Europeans, forgetting the long history of rectangular street planning refer to it now as the American method.[5]

In the new frontier towns, housing was as predictable as the pattern of streets. The same American businesspeople who prided themselves on their originality and inventiveness in business created towns that were dull and drab.

Planned Communities

Totally planned communities fared little better. Lowell, Massachusetts, for all its early promise as an idealistic, paternalistic community, quickly deteriorated into just another New England mill town. Pullman, Illinois, was designed in the 1880s as an experiment in both well-managed labor relations and town planning. In the words of its founder and sole owner, George Pullman, "With such surroundings and such human regard for the needs of the body as well as the soul the disturbing conditions of strikes and other troubles that periodically convulse the world of labor would not be found here." George Pullman proved to be a poor prophet. Pullman is today best known because of a bitter strike which took place there in 1894 and was finally put down by the National Guard.[6] Today the Pullman community is legally part of the city of Chicago and is undergoing urban revitalization efforts.

Planned urban communities tended quickly to become satellites and then suburbs of the nearest central city, since, on their own, they lacked both the economic and the social diversity necessary to keep them viable. Of the new communities organized around religious or political-philosophical doctrines—

[3]Christopher Tunnard, *The City of Man,* Scribner, New York, 1953, p. 121.
[4]Ibid., p. 77.
[5]C. M. Robinson, *City Planning,* Putnam, New York, 1916, p. 16.
[6]Stanley Buder, *Pullman,* Oxford University Press, New York, 1967, p. vii.

New Harmony and Oneida, for example—only Salt Lake City has grown and prospered, possibly because it had, under Brigham Young, a very tight social organization, plus an excellent environmental location along the trail to the California gold fields. Utopian socialist communities such as Alice Austin's turn-of-the-century feminist new town of Llano del Rio, California had less success in remaining financially viable.[7]

Parks

One of the brightest aspects in the rather discouraging story of nineteenth-century urban planning is the work of Frederick Law Olmstead. In 1857, after much controversy, he began the building of Central Park on 843 acres of wasteland on the outskirts of New York City. The site was hardly promising, for, as Olmstead described it, much of it was a swamp "seeped in the overflow and mush of pigsties, slaughterhouses, and boneboiling works, and the stench was sickening." Central Park not only served the function of providing "lungs" for the city, but it inspired other cities to copy New York's successful plan. Parks were built across the country, and some of them, such as the park systems of Kansas City, Milwaukee, Chicago, Philadelphia, and San Francisco, have become invaluable assets of their cities. There also was a pronounced profit motive in creating parks since adjacent property greatly increased in value. Thus, major real estate developers favored the construction of parks and parkways.

The City Beautiful

The movement that had the most pronounced effect on the design of American cities was the "city beautiful" movement that more or less emerged from the Chicago Columbian World Exhibition of 1893. The Columbian exhibition gave Chicago a chance to show the world that it was no longer a ramshackle town surrounding stockyards, but a booming modern metropolis; and the city leaders were determined to make a good impression.

Daniel Burnham was placed in charge of assembling the nation's leading architects and landscape designers to create for the exposition the famous White City. In order to produce an impression of magnificence, a uniform cornice line was set. All the buildings—with the exception of the Transportation Building, designed by the great architect Louis Sullivan—were classical in style. The classical buildings of White City, combined with harmoniously planned lagoons and grounds, created an overwhelming impact even to the architecturally sophisticated.

The classical ancestry and majestic size of such buildings neatly meshed with the optimistic and expansionist mood of the country at the turn of the century. Strong, powerful buildings were a way of expressing the fever of imperialism and material success then sweeping the land. The United States

---

[7]Dolores Hayden, "Two Utopian Feminists and Their Campaigns for Kitchenless Houses," *Signs,* 4:283–286, winter, 1978.

The World Columbian Exposition of 1893 impressed all who saw it.
Its emphasis on monumental grandeur influenced American public
architecture for decades. (Culver Pictures)

had easily humiliated Spain in a short war and was (it believed) blessed by
God with a "manifest destiny" to rule.

White City, with its magnificence and grandeur, started a trend; it became
customary to design all government buildings in neoclassical or pseudoclassical
style. As a result of the city beautiful movement, there is not a city in the
nation without at least one building—a city hall, court, or library—designed
to resemble a Greek temple.

The influence of this movement on the architecture of the federal government has been even more pronounced. For fifty years after the Colombian
exposition, almost every large post office was designed as a Greco-Roman
temple. Many of these buildings were poor imitations of the classical style,
but among the better products of the neoclassical revival are the famous civic
center in San Francisco and the Benjamin Franklin Parkway in Philadelphia.
The latter terminates at a majestic neoclassical art museum. It must be pointed
out that the city beautiful movement paid attention almost exclusively to city
centers; there was little concern for housing or neighborhoods.

Parks, which have already been discussed briefly, were related to—though
not an integral part of—the city beautiful movement. A number of elaborate
parks systems, tied together by attractive boulevards, were developed to
further beautify the city. The excellent parks of Chicago, Kansas City, and
Washington are largely a result of the early-twentieth-century trend for planned
public, if not yet private, development.

The model for the ideal city beautiful plan was Daniel Burnham's Chicago

Plan. At the request of Chicago's businesspeople, Daniel Burnham drew up in 1909 a master plan for that city which included a massive civic building program; a central feature of this plan was an extensive network of city parks tied together by a system of grand, tree-shaded boulevards. It is noteworthy that pressure for planning came from business and civic leaders rather than city hall. Burnham captured the mood of the age when he ordered his staff to "make no little plans." The nation's capital also profited from the new emphasis on planning. L'Enfant's long-neglected design for Washington, D.C., was revived, and the appearance of the Capitol was greatly improved by the removal of the Pennsylvania Railroad tracks from the Mall in front of it. Burnham and other architects prepared plans for the beautification of Washington from which have been developed the present-day "federal triangle" group of government buildings and the Mall between the Capitol and the Lincoln Memorial.

The city beautiful movement may of course be criticized on aesthetic grounds, but it did have a concept of the city as an integrated whole and a vision of what it could be. It was a solid, conscious, and sincere attempt to improve the urban environment. Perhaps the greatest weakness of the city beautiful movement was that it almost totally ignored the problem of housing, particularly that of the slums.

Tenement Laws

The end of the nineteenth century saw a movement by social reformers such as Jane Addams to improve the quality of life in inner-city slums. This meant enforcing building codes and passing model tenement laws to correct some of the worse abuses of the design and construction of older tenements. To reformers such as Jacob Riis, the slum was the enemy of the home and of basic American virtues. To quote Riis:

> Put it this way: You cannot let men live like pigs when you need their votes as freemen; it is not safe. You cannot rob a child of its childhood, of its home, its play, its freedom from toil and care, and expect to appeal to the grown-up voter's manhood. The children are out to-morrow, and as we mould them to-day so will they deal with us then. Therefore that is not safe. Unsafest of all is any thing or deed that strikes at the home, for from the people's home proceeds citizen virtue, and nowhere else does it live. The slum is the enemy of the home. Because of this the chief city of our land [New York] came long ago to be called "The Homeless City." When this people comes to be truly called a nation without homes there will no longer be any nation.[8]

The answer at that time appeared clear: Destroy the slum and you will destroy the breeding ground of social problems. Symptoms of social disorganization such as alcoholism, delinquency, divorce, desertion, and mental illness were to be cured, or at least greatly reduced, through the provision of better

---

[8]Jacob Riis, *The Children of the Poor*, Scribner, New York, 1892.

housing and more open spaces for the young. This belief in salvation by bricks and mortar fit in neatly with the American belief in the unlimited potential of technology.

Many greatly needed improvements in housing were made as a result of the campaigns of the turn-of-the-century reformers; but crime, violence, and alcoholism were not banished as a result. The relationship between housing and social behavior is complex and unfortunately not amenable to simplistic solutions.

TWENTIETH CENTURY

The City Efficient

The golden age of concern with, and reform of, urban social life, esthetics, and politics died with the entry of the United States into World War I. Holistic visions of the city's future such as had been provided by the city beautiful movement did not fare well in the post-war laissez-faire atmosphere of the 1920s. As a result, the emphasis was gradually shifted from the city beautiful to the city efficient, and urban planning was replaced by city engineering. During the 1920s, the city was viewed as an engineering problem, and planners became technicians concerned with traffic patterns, traffic lights, and sewer systems. The city was viewed as a machine, and the goal was to keep the machine running smoothly. To this end planning and land use regulation became accepted functions of local government.

Zoning

The concept of the city as an evolving organic unit was also overshadowed by the development of a new planning tool, zoning. Zoning, which became a force in the United States with the New York City Zoning Resolution of 1916, was originally seen as a device to "lessen congestion in the streets" and to "prevent the intrusion of improper uses into homogeneous areas."[9] "Improper" use of land meant not only industrial and commercial establishments, but also lower-class housing. It was an attempt, largely successful, to segregate land use and freeze "noncompatible" uses out of upper-middle-class neighborhoods.

The effect of the first weak zoning laws was mainly negative—that is, to keep unwanted types of buildings from being constructed. Zoning laws had little retroactive effect. (Zone boundaries in many cases recognized the existence of "natural areas" described by the early human ecologists, and then went a step farther and tried to prevent further change in these areas.) The 1921 Standard State Zoning Enabling Act, which was issued by the federal government, advised state legislatures to grant the following power to the cities:

---

[9]Dennis O'Harow, "Zoning, What's the Good of It?" in Wentworth Eldridge (ed.), *Taming Megalopolis*, Doubleday (Anchor), Garden City, New York, 1967, p. 762.

> For the purpose of promoting health, safety, morals, and the general welfare of the community, the legislative body of cities and incorporated villages is hereby empowered to regulate and restrict the height, number of stories, and size of the buildings, and other structures, the percentage of the lot that may be occupied, the size of the yards, courts, and other open spaces, the density of the population, and the location and use of buildings, structures, and land for trade, industry, residence, or other purpose.[10]

After World War II, subdivision regulations often became the main control device in new suburban areas.

Today Houston, Texas, is the only major city in the country without zoning laws. Houston does not look noticeably different from other cities because the market mechanism allocates the downtown land to business and commercial usage while outlying land is used for residential purposes. It is not economically feasible to deviate from the normative pattern of land use. Deed restrictions on land use are a de facto functional equivalent of zoning in many cases. More than 10,000 deed restrictions cover over two-thirds of the city although they are most often enforced in wealthy neighborhoods along Memorial Drive and in River Oaks.[11]

Master Plans

The idea of the city efficient was also evidenced in the general or master plans for city development that became the hallmarks of the city-planning agencies from the 1920s to the 1960s. The purpose of the master plan was to coordinate and regulate all phases of city development; but in practice the preparation of the plan frequently became an end in itself, since the planners rarely had any real authority over the nature and direction of urban development. The plan, even if formally adopted by the city council, was not legally binding unless backed up by specific zoning and other laws.

In defining neighborhoods physical criteria were used almost exclusively. In the words of Herbert Gans:

> The ends underlying the planners' physical approach reflected their Protestant middle-class view of city life. As a result, the master plan tried to eliminate as "blighting influences" many of the land uses and institutions of lower class and ethnic groups. Most of the plans either made no provision of tenements, rooming houses, second hand stores, and marginal loft industry, or located them in catch-all zones of "nuisance uses," in which all land uses were permitted. Popular facilities that they considered morally or culturally undesirable were also excluded. The plans called for many parks and playgrounds but left out the movie theater, the neighborhood tavern, and the clubroom; they proposed churches and museums, but no night clubs and hot dog stands.[12]

---

[10]Newman F. Baker, *Legal Aspects of Zoning*, University of Chicago Press, Chicago, 1927, p. 24.

[11]Richard F. Babcock, "Houston: Unzoned, Unfettered, and Mostly Unrepentent," *Planning*, **48**:21–23, March, 1982.

[12]Herbert J. Gans, "Planning, Social: II, Regional and Urban Planning," in David Sills (ed.), *International Encyclopedia of the Social Sciences*, Crowell Collier and Macmillan, New York, 1968, vol. 2, p. 130.

The Approach of Jane Jacobs

Among the critics of urban planning practices, Jane Jacobs is the best known. More than two decades after publication, *Death and Life of Great American Cities* remains the classic critique of zoning and other planning tools as commonly applied.*

Using as an example her own beloved area of Greenwich Village in New York City (she now lives in Toronto), Jacobs argued that the mixed housing and commercial usages and the resulting congestion—factors which orthodox planners are said to deplore—are the very reason why the area has retained its buoyancy and unique character over time. Cities, she suggested, are natural economic generators of diversity and incubators of new enterprises, and attempts by planners to zone various activities into distinct areas only work toward dullness and eventual stagnation both economically and socially.†

Jacobs said that four conditions are indispensable if diversity and liveliness are to be generated in a city:

1. The district, and indeed as many of its internal parts as possible, must serve more than one primary function; preferably more than two. These must insure the presence of people who go outdoors on different schedules and are in the place for different reasons.
2. Most blocks should be short; that is, streets and opportunities to turn corners must be frequent.
3. The district must mingle buildings that vary in age and condition, including a good proportion of old ones so that they vary in the economic yield they must produce. This mingling must be fairly closegrained.
4. There must be a sufficiently dense concentration of people, for whatever purposes they may be there. This includes dense concentration in the case of people who are there because of residence.‡

Thus she saw the physical environment of the city directly affecting city life, and argued for a mix of social activities and a heterogeneous population to increase neighborhoods'

---

*For a retrospective analysis of Jacobs's views, see Harvey M. Choldin, "Retrospective Review Essay: Neighborhood Life and Urban Environment," *American Journal of Sociology,* **48**:457–463, September, 1978.

†Jane Jacobs, *The Death and Life of Great American Cities,* Random House, New York, 1961.

‡Ibid., pp. 150–151.

vitality. By advocating mixed populations and land usages she directly challenged one of the basic tenets of city planning. Jacobs argued that by providing a mixture of functions—residence, work, place of entertainment—a district ensures that eyes are constantly on its streets, maintaining safety. This diversity of use further means that uniquely urban specialty shops can operate profitably, since there is considerable traffic past their doors. Short city blocks provide for alternative routes and use of different streets—with the result that a cross section of the public passes the doors of the smaller specialty operations. Old buildings are needed, since, as Jacobs puts it, "Old ideas can sometimes use new buildings. New ideas must use old buildings." New buildings are limited to enterprises that can support the high costs of construction and rent. Old buildings not only provide space for new enterprises; they also break the visual monotony, and they can house cozy stores that provide gossip and a place to leave your keys as well as merely selling goods. Finally, the dense concentration of people in an area contributes to its vitality and liveliness, Jacobs suggests that it is not accidental that the district in San Francisco with the highest dwelling density is the popular North Beach-Telegraph Hill section. High building density does not, of course, necessarily mean crowding. Medium-density areas fail to provide liveliness and safety, and they have none of the advantages of low-density, semisuburban areas.

In Jacobs's view, the population and environmental characteristics of a neighborhood shape its social character:

> Great cities are not like towns, only larger. They are not like suburbs, only denser. They differ from towns and suburbs in basic ways, and one of those is that cities are, by definition full of strangers. . . . Even residents who live near each other are strangers, and must be, because of the sheer number of people in small geographical compass. The bedrock attribute of a successful city district is that a person must feel safe and secure among all these strangers. He must not feel automatically menaced by them. A city district that fails in this respect also does badly in other ways and lays up for itself, and for its city at large, mountains on mountains of trouble.§

A valid criticism of Jacobs is that her preoccupation with street safety makes her oblivious to other urban problems and values. She views the city as a place where people will do violence to one another unless restrained. One of her most knowledgeable critics, Louis Mumford, suggests that Jacobs puts so much emphasis on the necessity for continued street

§Ibid., p. 300.

life because her ideal city is mainly an organization for the prevention of crime.

Mumford points out that according to Jacobs's view, "the best way to overcome criminal violence is to create a mixture of economic and social activities such that at every hour of the day the streets will never be empty of pedestrains and that each shopkeeper, each householder, compelled to find both his main occupations and his recreations on the street, will serve as watchman and policeman, each knowing who is to be trusted and who not. . . ." **Mumford points out that London of the eighteenth century, violent and crime-ridden, met these prescriptions. Furthermore, the benefits of high density, pedestrian-filled streets, cross-lines of circulation, and a mixture of primary economic activities can be found in Harlem—where they do not reduce street or other crime. On the other hand, a dispassionate observer would have to concede that whatever else Harlem is, it is certainly not dull.

Mumford also argues that the emphasis on safety blinds Jacobs to other values in an urban environment. Convenience, beauty, the absence of the noise of trucks crowding the street, the minimizing of the effects of pollution—all these factors are made subservient to safety.

Jacobs can also be criticized for not dealing with the question of racial change in the city. Nonetheless, the importance of her work should not be underemphasized. Partially because of her influence, the planners of today are far more conscious of the social impact of design and planning decisions. The message that cities are for people is finally affecting urban policies.

**Lewis Mumford, "Home Remedies for Urban Cancer," in Louis K. Loewenstein (ed.), *Urban Studies*, Free Press, New York, 1971, pp. 392–393.

Reston, Virginia has become one of the more successful privately
built American new towns. (Jim Kirby, courtesy of the Reston Land
Corp.)

    Case studies of the actual planning process indicate that planners often
made their recommendations on the basis of arbitrary considerations without
fully examining or understanding the consequences.[13] The death blow for many
a general plan was the upsurge of urban renewal and other development plans
after World War II. These development schemes were frequently put forward

[13]Martin Meyerson and Edward C. Banfield, *Politics, Planning, and the Public Interest*, Free Press, Chicago,
1955.

by interest groups in business or government that had no concern for the general plan as such. Conflicts between the static general plan and specific development proposals with available funding were almost always resolved in favor of the specific proposals. The social upheavals of the 1960s and advocacy planning has led to more socially responsive planning.[14] Today planners themselves are questioning the utility of creating citywide plans, unless the plans are directly related to, and can have influence on the future development of the city. Neighborhood-level plans are often more useful.

American New Towns

Government-Built New Towns. Today, when European governments have directly taken the responsibility for planning and financing new towns, it is almost forgotten that during the 1920s Radburn, New Jersey was the archetype of the planned community. Also, during the 1930s the United States government designed, financed, built, and for a decade managed three of the world's first planned new towns surrounded by areas of open land. The United States however, has never had a national program for developing new towns as such. The building of these towns reflected specific measures that were being taken to combat the depression of the 1930s. The government had three main objectives in building new towns:

1. To demonstrate a new kind of suburban community planning which would combine the advantages of city and country life
2. To provide good housing at reasonable rents for moderate-income families
3. To give jobs to thousands of unemployed workers which would result in lasting economic and social benefits to the community in which the work was undertaken.

The three American green-belt towns were Greenbelt, Maryland, outside of Washington, D.C.: Green Hills, Ohio, near Cincinnati; and Greendale, Wisconsin, just south of Milwaukee. They were basically experimental or demonstration projects. (An interesting sidelight is that bureaucrats in Washington somehow mixed up the blueprints so the homes with basements designed for wintery Wisconsin were authorized for Cincinnatti, while the cement-slab homes designed for Cincinnati were built outside Milwaukee.) Plans called for the towns to be composed of neighborhood units and to have their own industry, as in the British model. But first a shortage of funds and then World War II kept them basically commuter suburbs. After World War II, the private housing industry was able to convince Congress that having the government involved in the building and renting of low-rent homes was socialistic and dangerous to the free-enterprise system. As a result of Public Law 65 of 1949,

---

[14]Allan Heskin, "Crisis and Response: A Historical View on Advocacy Planning," *Journal of the American Planning Association,* **46**:50–63, January, 1980.

all the homes built by the government were sold. The green belts surrounding the towns—which with the expansion of the central cities had become valuable land—were converted to other uses. Much of Greendale's green belt, for example, is now occupied by privately developed housing tracts and a large shopping center.

Privately Built New Towns. Although the business of building cities is the largest single industry in the United States, we still construct our cities on a largely ad hoc basis. Thousands of small enterprises build our towns and cities, with little planning and even less research.

Privately built new towns were a phenomenon of the years after World War II. Among the best known and most successful of the American new towns are Reston, Virginia, just west of Washington, D.C., and Columbia, Maryland, near Baltimore on the way to Washington, D.C. Both Reston and Columbia are financed privately rather than by the government.

Reston, which was the brainchild of the developer Robert E. Simon, was taken over by Gulf Oil Corporation in 1967 and later by Mobil because the town was not returning a profit. Economically, the town is now healthy and has a large number of corporate offices and other "clean" industries. Reston, like other privately financed new towns, and unlike the earlier ventures by the government, has from the first had a distinctly upper-middle-class character. Studies revealed that the average buyer in Reston was between thirty and forty years old, was the head of a family with two children, and had an annual income over one-third higher than the national average. Reston, however, does have several hundred units of federally subsidized housing. Architecturally, Reston represents some of the best in contemporary design. Although Robert Simon had attempted to integrate the community economically by placing middle-income and more expensive houses side by side, this was abandoned as not being economically sound. Mixed-income housing is desirable for social reasons, but it is a drain on profits, and Reston is a profit-making enterprise.

Columbia, Maryland, the second new town, 20 miles from Washington, D.C., was developed by James Rouse, perhaps the nation's most respected builder. Architecturally, Columbia is less successful than Reston. Columbia resembles an ideal supersuburb. It covers 15,600 acres and will eventually house 110,000 people. As of 1986, it had some 60,000 residents living in eight "villages." It represents an investment of over $2.5 billion. Builders of Columbia's various sections were given a relatively free hand and built a mixture of their best-selling models. For example, a buyer could choose a standard interior and then decide whether the facade was to be Cape Cod, Nordic, or Georgian colonial. Columbia is, however, a pleasant and well-planned community. Wooded areas and pathways run throughout the town. Like most new towns, it is organized into neighborhoods. Each neighborhood has some 900 houses, and each has its own elementary school and recreational facilities, including a swimming pool, a neighborhood center, and a convenience store. Four neighborhoods are combined to form a "village" of about 3,500 units, which has an intermediate or middle school, a meeting hall, and larger and more varied shops plus a supermarket. These are all designed to cluster around a small plaza with benches and a fountain. There is also a larger shopping center for the whole community in the downtown city center, which contains office buildings and larger department stores. Other innovations include a community college and a comprehensive full-care medical program in conjunction with the Johns Hopkins Medical School.

Socially, Columbia has made a conscious effort to be a racially integrated community: one-fifth of the residents are black. Income integration has generally not been as successful. Subsidized units have not been as clustered as in Reston, but are spread over five different sites to avoid the creation of a low-income ghetto. Nonetheless, when a ten-speed bicycle is stolen, it is the low-income residents who are usually blamed. Within the community, use of automobiles is discouraged by providing walkways and bicycle paths that are both more direct and not in physical contact with the highways. Nonetheless, cars are as numerous as in other suburbs, the parking lots of the shopping centers are generally filled, and the corporation has had to discontinue the minibus service within the city because it did not attract enough customers.

All in all, residents seem pleased with new towns, although they are not significantly more satisfied than residents of other suburban communities. Raymond Burby and Shirely Weiss compared responses of 7,000 residents in fifteen new towns and fifteen conventional suburbs of similar location age, size, and income level.[15] Ninety percent of the respondents from the new towns thought their community a good place to live—but then so did 86 percent of those in conventional suburbs. New towns per se had little effect on social behavior or perceptions.

Federal Experiences

Enthusiastic about the idea of new communities free from urban blight or suburban sprawl, Congress during 1968 and 1970 passed legislation to spur the development of new towns. The legislation offered federal funds and technical aid to developers and—most important—guaranteed up to $50 million worth of each developer's bonds plus the interest on the bonds. This was done because a new town is an inherently risky financial venture and requires front-end outlays for land purchase and infrastructure well before the first house is built or sold. The Nixon administration, however, opposed the program and withheld all funds for planning grants and technical assistance. The processing of applications was deliberately ensnarled in red tape.[16]

By 1974, twelve projects had issued bonds for a total of $252 million in federally guaranteed debentures. At this critical point the program was hit with the energy crisis and a depressed housing market, and developers found themselves caught between expensive front-end costs (one developer spent

---

[15]Raymond J. Burby III, et al., *New Communities U.S.A.*, Lexington Books, Lexington, Mass., 1976.

[16]Helen V. Synookler, "Administrative Hari Kari: Implementation of the Urban Growth and New Community Development Act," *Annals of the American Academy of Political and Social Science*, **422**:131–132, November, 1975.

$13,000 a day just for interest and taxes) and no customers. While established towns such as Reston and Columbia were able to weather the crisis, brand-new towns still in the infrastructure-building stage were not. At that point (1975) the Ford administration announced that the new towns would be cut loose to sink or swim. They didn't make it. The last to go under was Soul City, North Carolina, the dream of the civil rights activitist, Floyd McKissick. The Department of Housing and Urban Development assumed ownership of Soul City in 1980.

As of 1985 the federal government had acquired nine of the thirteen new towns by foreclosure, and had sold the assets of every town but one at a total loss of $570 million. Critics charge that much of this loss was the government's own doing, since it deliberately underfunded the towns and then pulled back at a critical juncture. By contrast, the British do not anticipate that their government-built new towns will be self-supporting for the first decade and a half. There is at present no sign that the United States government is willing to make such a commitment. Economically, new towns, except for the affluent, cannot be expected to stand alone financially in their early years.

Limits to Growth

One of the newer planning concerns in rapidly growing communities is the question of limiting growth. For years it was part of the American creed that bigger is better. City boosters, as a matter of course, bragged that their town or city was growing faster than neighboring places. Now that is changing, and rapidly growing communities from St. Petersburg, Florida, to Boulder, Colorado, to San Diego are seeking ways of limiting growth. A few years ago, Governor Ariyoshi of Hawaii stirred up considerable controversy by seeking to slow down Hawaii's exploding population by limiting in-migration from the other forty-nine states.

Those favoring control, such as the Sierra Club, generally argue that uncontrolled sprawl has destroyed the physical and cultural environment, and believe that indiscriminate gobbling up of land by developers has to be controlled. Opponents of control, such as the National Association of Home Builders and the National Association for the Advancement of Colored People, on the other hand, say that the real question is whether those already in the area can infringe on what they see as a constitutional right to settle where one chooses. They deplore a "pull up the gangplank" approach on the part of established communities that resist change in their way of life or level of amenities. Not all opponents have similar reasons for opposition. The home-building industry is concerned about the effect of building restrictions on the profits of developers; the NAACP, on the other hand, is concerned that settling minimum lot sizes and imposing environmental protections (e.g., requirements for municipal sewers and water hookups rather than septic systems and wells) will drive up prices and exclude blacks.

While the debate goes on, the legal issue has been resolved for the moment by a case involving the farming center of Petaluma, a city of some 35,000 roughly 35 miles north of San Francisco. A new freeway allowed commuters to discover Petaluma, and by the early 1970s growth had reached 18 percent a year, schools were in double session, and the water and sewage systems were strained to the maximum. It was clear that in a few years the entire pleasant valley would be covered with wall-to-wall subdivisions of look-alike homes. In desperation, the city instituted a plan limiting development to 500 new dwellings units a year. Developers and builders challenged the limits in court. In 1976, the Supreme Court, by refusing to hear the case, let stand the decision by the Court of Appeals that the traditional responsibility of local communities for public welfare was sufficiently broad to allow Petaluma to preserve its small-town character and open spaces. The court of appeals rejected the developers' argument that limits to growth unconstitutionally restricted people's right to travel and live where they please.

Now Petaluma is dealing developers another blow. Forced with the limitations on property taxes set by Proposition 13, the city is charging developers a fee to pay for the public services needed by new homes. The fee is largely passed on to home buyers. The idea is that new residences should not be a financial burden to existing taxpayers.

To date, only a limited number of communities, usually in areas in the south and west which are environmentally attractive, have actually tried to put lids on growth. However, decisions by the courts seem to indicate that while a town can't simply ban all growth, it can control its future.

The Use of Space

As noted in Chapter 6, City Life-styles, and Chapter 7, Social Environment of the City: Strangers, Neighbors, Crowding, and Crime, physical space often has different meanings to different groups. Understanding the symbolic uses of space can certainly be of practical use to architects and planners who want to use sociological information to increase the adequacy of their designs.

Public housing projects in particular can be designed to minimize rather than maximize feelings of deprivation and isolation from the community at large. Traditional high-rise projects too often are designed to be not only dull and monotonous but also dangerous to the inhabitants. Large open areas outside the projects frequently become "no man's lands" after dark, while within the buildings the corridors, washing rooms, and even elevators are unsafe. Residents are helpless to prevent muggings and rapes and feel that the only area they can control, and thus feel safe in, is the space within their own apartments. (See the section on unstable slums in Chapter 6 and Chapter 11, Housing Programs and Urban Change.)

Architectural design can do a great deal to increase the security and livability of projects. One of the simplest changes is to build low-rise buildings (six stories at most) where no more than a dozen families share the same stairwell and thus know who should or should not be present. Oscar Newman suggests that some other elements which can help in providing security are:

1. The territorial definition of space in developments reflecting the areas of influence of the inhabitants. This works by subdividing the residential

environment into zones toward which adjacent residents easily adopt proprietory attitudes.

2. The positioning of apartment windows to allow residents to naturally survey the exterior and interior public areas of their living environment.
3. The adoption of building forms that avoid the stigma of peculiarity that allows others to perceive the vulnerability and isolation of the inhabitants.
4. The enhancement of safety by locating residential developments in functionally sympathetic urban areas immediately adjacent to activities that do not provide continued threat.[17]

The effect of proper planning can be seen in a comparison of the Brownsville and Van Dyke housing projects in New York, which are separated only by a street (see Table 13-1). The low-rise Brownsville buildings, although older, have significantly fewer problems of crime and maintenance than the high-rise Van Dyke buildings. This is in spite of the fact that the average density per acre of the two projects is virtually idential. The difference appears to be that the Brownsville projects, with their six-story buildings and three-story wings, are humanly manageable and controllable to a far greater degree than the thirteen- and fourteen-story Van Dyke projects across the street.

Internal space can also be designed to decrease alienation. Architects define spaces inside apartments usually in terms of the functions they serve: kitchens for cooking, bedrooms for sleeping, dining rooms for eating, and windows for letting in light and air. Urban residents, however, often have their own ideas of the functions of space. Windows, for example, are not only for air and light but also for observing and communicating with the street; living rooms may not be viewed as an area for entertainment but as sacred space to be used for formal family occasions.

In one experiment, Puerto Rican residents of tenement buildings in East Harlem, a local community group, and an architect jointly redesigned apartments according to the needs of the residents.[18] On the basis of what they learned from interviewing the residents and from their own observations, they designed the apartments to avoid the large areas of undifferentiated space so desired by middle-class whites. The residents wanted a design where the apartment entrance would not open directly into the sacred space of the living room and where the kitchen, contrary to middle-class preference, could be closed off from the rest of the house by a solid wall with a door. This is what the families themselves wanted in their homes.

Unfortunately, this experiment was a rare occurrence. Working-class and lower-class people are seldom asked what they want in housing. Perhaps some of the worse mistakes would have been avoided if those designing the housing had spoken with those for whom the apartments were being designed. Since this is unlikely to occur—because architects deal not with occupants but with city officials and bureaucrats—a more realistic improvement would be to

[17]Oscar Newman, *Defensible Space,* Macmillan, New York, 1972, p. 9.
[18]John Zeisel, "Symbolic Meaning of Space and the Physical Dimension of Social Relations," in John Walton and Donald E. Carns (eds.), *Cities in Change,* Allyn and Bacon, Boston, 1973, pp. 252–263.

TABLE 13-1
Van Dyke and Brownsville: Some Comparisons

Comparison of crime incidents

Crime incidents	Van Dyke	Brownsville
Total incidents	1,189	790
Total felonies, misdemeanors and offenses	432	264
Number of robberies	92	24
Number of malicious mischief	52	28

Source: New York Housing Authority Police Records, 1968.

Comparison of maintenance

Maintenance	Van Dyke (constructed 1955)	Brownsville (constructed 1947)
Number of maintenance jobs of any sort (work tickets) 4/70	3,301	2,376
Number of maintenance jobs, excluding glass repair	2,643	1,651
Number of nonglass jobs per unit	1.47	1.16
Number of full-time maintenance staff	9	7
Number of elevator breakdowns per month	280	110

Source: New York City Housing Authority Project Managers' Bookkeeping records.

A comparison of physical design and population density

Physical measure	Van Dyke	Brownsville
Total size	22.35 acres	19.16 acres
Number of buildings	23	27
Building height	13–14 story 9–3 story	6 story with some 3 story wings
Coverage	16.6	23.0
Floor area ratio	1.49	1.39
Average number of rooms per apartment	4.62	4.69
Density	288 persons/acre	287 persons/acre
Year completed	1955 (one building added in 1964)	1947

Source: New York City Housing Authority Project Physical Design Statistics.

Source: Oscar Newman, *Defensible Space*, Macmillan. New York. 1972 pp. 46–48, tables 5, 6, and 7.

involve directly in the design process sociologists who are aware of cultural and social preference.[19]

Finally, it is well to keep in mind that even the best-designed cities and housing cannot solve social and economic problems. Unemployment, low educational levels, drug usage, and crime cannot be expected to vanish simply because of redesigned buildings. Making cities more attractive and livable is a noble goal in and of itself.

[19]John Zeisel, *Sociology and Architectural Design*, Russell Sage, New York, 1975.

PART FIVE

WORLDWIDE
URBANIZATION

CHAPTER

14

LESS DEVELOPED COUNTRIES:

Overview and Common Problems

He that will not apply new remedies must expect new evils; for time is the greatest innovator.

Sir Francis Bacon

THE URBAN EXPLOSION

Each year the world's population increases by 93 million persons, and 90 percent of them are born in less developed countries (LDCs). Three-quarters of this growth is concentrated in LDC cities. The population of developing countries is doubling every twenty-five to thirty years, but the population of their large cities is doubling every ten to fifteen years. The number of persons in urban shanty towns is doubling at an even faster five to seven years. As recently as 1950 there were only two cities in developing countries with populations of over 5 million. Today there are twenty-six LDC cities that large or larger, and by the year 2000, forty-six of the sixty cities of over 5 million will be in less developed nations. What this means is that the so-called population explosion is in actuality an urban population explosion.

By the turn of the century, the world will for the first time in history be more urban than rural. More important, most of the growth will be in the third world mega-cities.[1] Mexico City, which reached 1 million population only in 1930, is projected to have between 26 and 31 million people by 2000. And it will not be alone. Using low estimates São Paulo is projected at 24 million, Bombay and Calcutta may reach 16–17 million each, and Seoul and Jakarta 14 million each. To ignore or give only glancing attention to these major urban developments would be the height of ethnocentrism.

Cities of less developed countries will add some 1.3 billion additional urban inhabitants between 1975 and 2000.[2] Already there are 118 cities of over 1 million in LDCs, and by the year 2000, the United Nations projects there will be 284 such large cities in LDCs.[3] How many of us could name more than a score of these cities? It is difficult to keep up either mentally or emotionally with the spectacular nature of these changes, and while this text devotes more attention than others do to third world urban changes, we obviously cannot look at every city. What this and the following chapters can do is give the reader some feeling and understanding of the patterns of urban change.

Plan of Organization

The chapters in Part Five, because of limited space, necessarily focus on what is common to third world cities rather than on their unique differences. Readers should keep in mind, though, that particular cities may differ from the general pattern. Instructors who are familiar with specific cities or cultures may wish to expand on the influence of particular historical, cultural, geographic, religious, or economic factors.

---

[1]For elaboration on the impact of growth on third world cities see J. John Palen, *Cities and the Future: The Urban Explosion,* United Nations report, New York, 1985.

[2]U.S. Bureau of the Census, "Illustrative Projections of World Population to the Twenty-first Century," *Current Population Reports,* series P-23, no. 79, Washington, D.C., 1979.

[3]United Nations Population Division, "Trends and Prospects in the Population of Urban Agglomerations 1950–2000, United Nations, New York, 1985.

TABLE 14-1
Ten Largest Cities in the World, 1950, 1985, 2000

1950	Population (in millions)	1985	Population (in millions)	2000	Population (in millions)
1. New York-N.E. New Jersey	12.3	1. Mexico City	18.1	1. Mexico City	26.3
2. London	10.4	2. Tokyo-Yokohama	17.2	2. São Paulo	24.0
3. Rhine-Ruhr	6.9	3. São Paulo	15.9	3. Tokyo-Yokohama	17.1
4. Tokyo-Yokohama	6.7	4. New York-N.E. New Jersey	15.3	4. Calcutta	16.6
5. Shanghai	5.8	5. Shanghai	11.8	5. Greater Bombay	16.0
6. Paris	5.5	6. Calcutta	11.0	6. New York-N.E. New Jersey	15.5
7. Greater Buenos Aires	5.3	7. Greater Buenos Aires	10.9	7. Seoul	13.5
8. Chicago-N.W. Indiana	4.9	8. Rio de Janeiro	10.4	8. Shanghai	13.5
9. Moscow	4.8	9. Seoul	10.2	9. Rio de Janeiro	13.3
10. Calcutta	4.6	10. Greater Bombay	10.1	10. Delhi	13.3

Source: United Nations, Department of International Economic and Social Affairs, 1985.

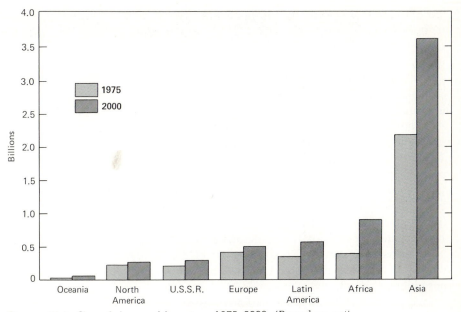

Figure 14-1. Growth by world region: 1975–2000. (*Based on estimates by the Population Reference Bureau.*)

Common or Divergent Paths?

Large-scale urbanization in Europe and North America was a process that spanned more than a century and involved massive economic and social change. Industrialization spurred in-migration from rural hinterlands. As documented in Chapter 2, Emergence of Cities, urban places in Europe and America, with their high death rates, were able to grow only because of massive inflows of rural population.

The context of contemporary urbanization in less developed countries differs from that of North America and western Europe in several respects. First, the extent—and rapidity—of the urban increase in LDCs is outpacing anything that occurred in the west. Between 1920 and 1980 the population in LDC cities of over 1 million increased fiftyfold.[4] While western cities grew rapidly during the nineteenth and even the twentieth centuries, the absolute numbers of urbanites were not anywhere as large as the numbers found today in Cairo, Manila, or São Paulo.

Second, industrialization, rather than providing a spur for urbanization, often trails far behind the rate of urban growth. In the nineteenth century the western, industrializing cities needed workers. Often the jobs were low paying, physically exhausting, and emotionally unsatisfying, but they were available. The cities of the industrial revolution were magnets drawing peasants off the

[4]Phillip Hauser and Robert Gardiner, "Urban Future: Trends and Prospects," in Phillip Hauser et al., *Population and the Urban Future*, State University of New York Press, Albany, 1982, p. 6.

land. Today by contrast, people flood into the cities in spite of high urban unemployment because of a push from overpopulated rural areas. In India today, for example, there is only one acre of arable land for each peasant farmer. With 15 million Indians being added each year it is almost invariable that surplus population gravitates toward the cities.

Third, cities in LDCs differ from the western model in having continued high rates of growth by natural increase as well as migration. Until a century or so ago, western cities lost more inhabitants through disease and illness than they gained through births. By contrast, between 54 and 60 percent of current LDC city growth comes from natural increase. Modern public health and vaccination programs mean that contemporary third world cities are not the "graveyards of countrymen" as developing western cities were. Cities in developing countries may appear unhealthful by contemporary western stand-ards, but they are, nonetheless, often more healthful than the rural alternatives. The consequence often is traumatic urban growth.

Fourth, LDC cities of today are part of the legacy of colonialism. As is detailed in the next chapters, LDC cities were most often founded not as a consequence of internal economic development but rather because of the colonial powers' need for trade and administrative centers.

LDC INCREASES

By the year 2000 almost two-thirds of the world's urban population of 3.1 billion will live in developing countries. As noted earlier, the United Nations estimates that two-thirds of the world's cities of over 5 million will be in less developed regions.[5] The impact of this urban explosion on cities of the developing world is difficult to overexaggerate. Some cities in less developed countries already top 10 million; with current growth rates, they will double their population in a decade (London or Tokyo, by contrast, will grow less than 1 percent). While each city is in some ways unique, they generally share problems of unemployment, poverty, and crowding in slums and squatter settlements.

Recently publicity has been given to the fact that the worldwide rate of population increase has begun to show declines. Today's growth rate of 1.7 percent is likely to continue falling during this decade and may reach 1.5 percent by the year 2000. This, however, emphatically does not mean that world population will be declining, since today's growth rates are being applied to a base population of 4.8 billion. This translates into nearly 200,000 persons being added to the world's population each day; and even with declines in fertility another 1 billion will be added during the 1990s.

[5]George J. Beier, "Can Third World Cities Cope?" *Population Bulletin*, 31:3, December, 1976.

Problems of Growth

Increases of this magnitude are certain to create almost unbearable pressures for food, better living conditions, more education, and more employment. Zero population growth may be a reality in Europe and Japan; but it is still only a slogan in the developing world, where the combined population of the various countries is currently increasing by more than 50 million a year. This means an additional 50 million persons a year who must be fed, clothed, housed, and otherwise provided for before the developing countries can even begin to improve the quality of life for those already present.

Much of the present population explosion, with its yearly national population increases of 2.5 and even 3.5 percent (2 percent doubles a population in only thirty-five years; 3.5 percent, in less than twenty years) can be traced to the importation of modern sanitation, public health, and medicine. After World War II, death rates were reduced drastically and at little cost, but were often only slowly accompanied by other changes in the social or economic fabric of the societies. Malaria, for example, was largely eradicated in Sri Lanka (Ceylon) by the decision of a handful of officials in government ministries to spray DDT from airplanes. This achieved declines in the death rates that took half a century in the west. The result was a population explosion. In contrast to reducing death rates, the decision to restrict the number of births must be made by millions of individual couples. Even when a society favors small families, there is a time lag in implementation.

The resulting population increases greatly exacerbate already serious problems, including problems of economic development. Funds that should be devoted to economic development are instead consumed in providing minimal subsistence and service to an ever-increasing number of people. Rather than investing capital, some developing nations are forced to spend it in order to meet, even marginally, the needs of their growing populations. Less developed countries have 35 to 50 percent of their population under age fifteen, as contrasted with a maximum of 25 percent in the industrialized countries. The consequence is that the cities of LDCs are filled with dependent children and young people who must be fed, clothed, housed, educated and otherwise provided for. The problem is not just that there are more people, but that LDCs have an age structure in which much of the population consists of dependents who have yet to make any contribution to the economic well-being of their families or nation.

In addition to the economic demands put on developing countries by new mouths to feed, there are also increasing demands from those already present. This "revolution of rising expectations" occurs because increasing numbers of people in developing countries—and particularly in the cities—became aware that their condition of poverty is not the immutable natural order of life everywhere. Developments in communication technology—first radio and now even television—have exposed the urban underclasses to the existence of higher standards of living. The urban populations, with their greater exposure to alternatives and their greater awareness of nontraditional ways of life, have

Plants and flowers symbolize the residents' efforts to improve a squatter settlement in Mexico City. (Beryl Goldberg)

expectations for themselves and their children; and governments that ignore these expectations do so at their own risk.

The Case of Mexico City

Urban change can be grasped more easily by looking at the impact on an individual city. Mexico City had one-quarter of New York's population in 1950 (2.9 million compared with 12.3 million). Currently Mexico City has 18 million inhabitants, and it will have 31.6 million by the year 2000 if the city's current growth rate of 4.4 percent continues.[6] The most recent estimates (Table 14-1) project Mexico's population in the year 2000 at 26 million. This will give Mexico City the world's largest urban population—2.5 times as large as London or Paris.

Mexico City may be an extreme case but the pattern and problems it represents are, unfortunately, not unique. Mexico City, even after the deadly 1985 earthquake that killed 10,000 persons, still attracts newcomers seeking employment in its 300,000 factories.[7] These factories, plus millions of autos without pollution controls, result in *six thousand tons* of gas and soot pollution falling on the city daily. In practical terms, this means simply living in the city

---

[6]Hauser and Gardiner, op. cit., p. 6.
[7]Based on material in J. John Palen, op. cit.

gives every man, woman, and child the equivalent health damage of smoking two packs of cigarettes a day.

Keep in mind when demographers make projections about future population size, there is nothing inevitable or sacred about these projections. Mexico City, for example, does not *have* to contain 31 million persons at the beginning of the twenty-first century. However, while it is not certain that Mexico City will have 31 million persons, or even 26 million, it is a sure bet that the populations of Mexico City and other LDC metropolitan areas are going to continue to increase for the next several decades. To a resident of Mexico City, it is probably academic whether the urban area will have 26 million or 31 million persons in less than a score of years.

No matter what the figure is, the infrastructure is not up to handling double the present population. Even without natural disasters such as earthquakes, transportation systems, sewers, and school plants will not be able to cope. Already two million Mexico City children do not have access to a school. Unless a miracle occurs, there is no way that services such as garbage collection, schooling, and medical services can be adequately provided for 26 million people. Badly strained systems simply cannot handle double and triple the present load—not in Mexico City, and not elsewhere.

RICH COUNTRIES AND POOR COUNTRIES: SOME DEFINITIONS AND EXPLANATIONS

Less developed countries vary in their rates of development, but they all suffer in varying degrees from common problems such as low industrial output, low rates of savings, inadequate housing, poor roads and communication, a high proportion of the labor force engaged in agriculture, insufficient medical services, inadequate school systems, high rates of illiteracy, poor diets, and sometimes malnutrition. The developing countries contain two out of three of the world's people, but they account for only one-sixth of the world's income, one-third of the food production, and one-tenth of the industrial output.

It is this quite clear that the term "developing country" is a euphemism. Various other terms, such as "modernizing country," "third world country," and "noncommitted country," have been used, and they sometimes reflect ideological differences, but essentially they are all polite ways of saying "poor country." The current preferred term is "less developed countries." While the differences between the developed and the underdeveloped countries is usually phrased less harshly, the major distinction is that one category includes the "haves" and the other the "have-nots."

This rich-poor classification cuts across conflicting ideological systems. Developed nations, whether capitalistic or communistic, whether in Europe, Asia, or the western hemisphere, all have urban-industrial economies. The level of urbanism is not tied to any ideology such as capitalism or socialism.[8]

---

[8]Jack P. Gibbs and Walter T. Martin, "Urbanization Technology, and the Division of Labor: International Patterns," *American Sociological Review,* 27:677, 1962.

Less developed countries are so named because of their relationship to the economic power of the developed countries, which are used as the standard of comparison. "Development" is thus a relative rather than an absolute state. Newly developing countries are underdeveloped in the context of an economic comparison with Europe, the United States, or the Soviet Union. Whether the indigenous economic organization of a developing country is simple or complex—and in many cases it is extremely complex—it is invariably not a modern industrialized urban economy.

Economically, the developing nations of Asia, Africa, and Latin America find themselves locked into a system where prices for the raw products they produce remain relatively stable while the cost of imported goods skyrockets. Such nations are seeking to achieve industrial development while the marketplace in which they must operate is largely controlled by the developed nations. The major exception to this statement, of course, are Arab countries of the Organization of Petroleum Exporting Countries (OPEC), which, largely for historical reasons, are often, classified as developing countries. In actuality, they should be classified as rich nations, or at least newly developed nations.

Much of the underdevelopment of third world countries, then, is due not to traditionalism or internal problems but to a worldwide system of structural dependency and unequal exchange. Increased oil prices during the past decades have increased this dependency. Data indicate that for many developing nations the status of "underdevelopment" may become relatively permanent; while the poor nations are not getting poorer—as a whole—the rich nations are certainly getting richer. As a result, the gap between the developed and developing nations is increasing rather than decreasing. A survey of 150 nations by the Department of Social and Economic Affaris of the United Nations shows that in the decade 1960–1970 the per capital output of the developed countries rose 43 percent, compared with an increase of only 27 percent in the less developed countries.

The 1970s and 1980s saw some LDCs make major strides while others—particularly in Africa—fell even farther behind. Singapore, for example, has clearly moved into the newly developed category, while, just as clearly, Chad has not. Sometimes the distinction between countries that are developing and countries that are not is expressed in terms of the third world and the "fourth world." The following chapters detail some of the differences between LDCs; here the emphasis is on their general similarities.

CHARACTERISTICS OF THIRD-WORLD CITIES

Youthful Age Structure

While each city, like each person, is distinct and in some ways unique, there are certain characteristics that are more or less general to cities of the developing world. The first of these is the youthful population age structure. An almost certain comment of tourists upon first encountering third world cities is that "children and young people are everywhere." This is not an illusion but an observation of demographic reality. It is estimated that as of 1985, some 39 percent of the inhabitants of LDCs were under fifteen years of age. This compared to 23 percent under fifteen in economically developed nations.[9]

Thus, compared with the developed nations, the poorer countries have age structures that are heavily loaded with dependent young people. This dependency is particularly so in cities, where often almost half of all city residents are youngsters. LDC cities, thus, not only have more people vis-à-vis resources than do the richer cities, they also have far more persons who are dependent young—people who have yet to make any contribution to the cities' economy or well-being. One does not have to be an expert to figure out that these large numbers of dependent young are a heavy drain on limited resources. Even if more schools are built and new jobs created, there is no gain if these advances merely keep pace with growth of young people.

National figures underline the problem: Kenya, Togo, Rwanda, Zimbabwe, and Jordan all have half their populations under age fifteen. Other nations such as Mali and Nicaragua have only marginally lower degrees of 48 percent. By comparison, the percentage of dependent young is at most only half as high in developed nations. Sweden, Denmark, West Germany, Luxemburg, and Switzerland, for example, have only 20 percent or less of their populations under age fifteen.[10]

The consequence of these differences is that the cities of LDCs are getting hit twice. First, they have less resources. Second, the lower resource base must be stretched to cover double the proportion of young dependents. Of course, it goes without saying that this leaves precious little for either personal or national investment purposes. And the United Nations projects that by 2025 83 percent of the world population will live in less developed regions.[11]

Employment and Industrialization

Of all the common problems faced by the cities in developing countries, the problem of providing employment is, next to that of population growth, the most severe. The situation is quite different from that faced by the economically advanced western countries during their earlier periods of urban-industrial expansion. In the era of western industrialization during the nineteenth century, farmers and peasants were drawn to the city because of the economic opportunities it offered. Entry-level jobs, both in manufacturing and in services, were generally available; and there was a solid demand for unskilled, if low-paid, workers. This was true both in Europe and in North America.

The experience of the developing countries has been quite different.

[9]Population Reference Bureau, "1985 World Population Data Sheet," Washington, D.C., 1985.
[10]Ibid.
[11]United Nations, "World Population Prospects as Assessed in 1980," *Population Studies,* No. 78, United Nations, New York, p. 6.

Workers flood into the cities not because of the availability of jobs but because of the lack of opportunity in the rural areas and small villages. Data for twenty-seven Asian and Latin American nations show that high agricultural density and plantation-type agriculture spur urbanization regardless of the rate of economic development.[12] The consequence is "subsistence urbanization," in which the ordinary citizen has only the bare necessities for urban survival.[13] Urban unemployment rates commonly exceed one-quarter of the work force.

Many, if not most, urban workers in less developed countries are employed in the informal sector of the economy—that is, small enterprises without access to credit, banks, or formally trained personnel. Nonetheless, the informal sector commonly provides most of the consumable food products and much of the services, trade, transportation, and construction.[14]

In the vast majority of developing countries, the modern or formal sector of the economy is only a small portion of the whole. In spite of some gains in industrial productivity and some increases in the gross national income, the rate of unemployment remains high. Industrialization starting from the low base found in the developing world may have only a marginal effect on employment even when the *rate* of industrialization is relatively high.[15] Modern industrialization, unlike that in the United States during the latter part of the nineteenth century, does not require tremendous number of unskilled laborers.

Nor do public works necessarily benefit those most in need. Public funds also tend to be invested in projects such as airports or multilane highways for the automobiles of the rich and universities for their offspring, while slums still have mud roads and the poor receive only minimal schooling.

Squatter Settlements

The population growth of virtually all cities in LDCs has outrun the capacity of municipalities to house them.[16] Decaying central-city slums and new squatter settlements house one-third of the entire urban poupulation in developing countries. The present squatter population of Mexico City exceeds 4 million, and squatters in both Seoul and Calcutta number over 2 million. With shantytowns mushrooming at 15 percent a year (doubling their size in six years), the squatter population of poorer cities is certain to increase.[17]

Squatter of peripheral settlements are called *barriedas, favelas, bustees, kampongs,* or *bidonvilles* in various countries; but everywhere their function is the same—to house those who have the least resources and nowhere else

---

[12]Glenn Firebaugh, "Structural Determinants of Urbanization in Asia and Latin America, 1950–1970," *American Sociological Review,* **44**:195–215, April, 1979.

[13]Gerald Breese, *Urbanization in Newly Developing Countries,* Prentice-Hall, Englewood Cliffs, N.J., 1966, p. 5.

[14]S. V. Sethuraman, "The Informal Urban Sector in Developing Countries: Some Policy Implications," in Alfred de Souza (ed.), *The Indian City,* South Asia Books, New Delhi, India, 1978, pp. 1–15; and Johannes F. Linn, *Cities in the Developing World,* World Book Publications, Oxford University Press, New York, 1983.

[15]Gunnar Myrdal, *Asian Drama,* vol. 2, Pantheon, New York, 1968, pp. 1174–1175.

[16]For information on third world housing patterns with emphasis on Delhi, see Geoffrey K. Payne, *Urban Housing in the Third World,* Routledge & Kegan Paul, Boston, 1977; Linn, op. cit.; and Palen, op. cit.

[17]Estimate by the United Nations.

to go. In the squatter settlements shanties and shacks are built in random fashion out of whatever refuse material the builder can salvage. Old packing crates, loose lumber, and odd pieces of metal are somehow patched together to provide a shelter. Since shantytowns almost by definition are "illegally" occupying the land on which they are built, they cannot demand city services. Streets, police, and fire protection, and—most important—sanitary services are usually nonexistent. Water almost always has to be carried from the nearest public tap. Schools are rare. Electricity is the most commonly found utility, since wires can easily be strung from shack to shack.

Public services such as running water and schools are first provided to those with economic clout. Shanty dwellers in Lima, for instance, pay ten times as much for water carried on private trucks as the middle class pays for plumbing in its homes. Health problems are exacerbated by the crowding, by the lack of proper disposal for sewage and refuse, and by the fact that the settlements are frequently built on the least desirable terrain, such as city dumps, marshlands, or hillsides.

Attempts by the government to remove squatters are invariably unsuccessful: if one slum is destroyed, another is built overnight with the refuse from the earlier settlement. When no other city housing is available, there is little alternative. As one authority confesses, "We have learned that we cannot hope to provide 'standard' housing for all, or even most of the urban poor in the developing countries in this century, almost no matter how one defines 'standard.'"[18]

Demolishing settlements and relocating the urban poor in new fringe settlements is sometimes disastrous for the poor. It often impoverishes families who not only lose what they have invested in the demolished squatter shack, but also are faced with increased transportation costs. Women in particular tend to become unemployed because of the increased distance to their traditional places of work. The poor who were forcibly removed from squatter settlements in Delhi during the 1970s and moved to outlying areas now spend one-fifth of an unskilled worker's daily wage on bus transportation to the city. For the very poor a location near work is more important than the quality of the shelter. The same was true of the nineteenth-century American poor, who crowded into tenements near central-city factories.

Primate Cities

A characteristic common to most developing countries is the "primate" city. A primate city is a principal city overwhelmingly large in comparison with all other cities in the country. In many countries, the primate city is frequently the only city of note.[19] Commonly, within developing countries there is no

[18]Maurice Kilbridge, "Some Generalizations on Urbanization and Housing in Developing Countries," *Urban Planning, Policy Analysis, and Administration,* Policy Note P. 76–1. Harvard University Press, Cambridge, Mass., 1976, p. 13.

[19]Mark Jefferson, "The Law of the Primate Cities," *Geographical Review,* **29**:226–232, April, 1939.

hierarchy of cities of various sizes such as that found in developed nations. Ethiopia, for example, is 95 percent rural and has few towns; but its capital city, Addis Ababa, has over 1.5 million inhabitants. Bangkok, with over 3 million people, is the most extreme case.[20] Bangkok is over 30 times larger than Thailand's second largest city, Chang Mai.

Most primate cities owe their origin and development to European colonialism. Cities such as Accra, Nairobi, Saigon, Hanoi, Singapore, and Hong Kong do not have long histories as urban places but rather were created consciously by colonial powers in order to establish bases from which they could exercise administrative and commercial control. They were established as little "Europes-in-Asia" or "Europes-in-Africa." Thus, they were usually located along the coasts in order to facilitate communication with, and transportation of raw material to, the mother country. From the very first, the orientation of the primate city was toward other cities in the developed countries rather than toward its own hinterland, and this pattern of commerce and culture coming from the outside has largely endured to this day. Government elites, particularly in Africa and Asia, may also be more oriented to the outside than to their own hinterland or "bush."

The concentration of population and economic activity in primate cities presents some typical features throughout the developing world:

1. In the earlier stages, the economies of such cities were primarily export-oriented, and the cities also specialized in political and administrative activities. Today, manufacturing and services are the primary economic activities.
2. Economic advantages result from the concentration of industry. Thus, income from peripheral areas finds its way to the metropolitan area. The higher rate of return attracts more capital: and this in turn leads to more enterprises, particularly services.
3. The concentration of industrial activities—and above all the accompanying services—increases employment. Skilled workers are attracted from peripheral locations. Thus, the city represents an advantage in terms of quality as well as quantity.
4. Concentration of population and economic activities goes hand in hand with the centralization of administrative activity. The decision-making power of the primate city increases, while that of outlying cities and towns decreases. The center thus receives the lion's share of the available investment funds.
5. The basic infrastructure of the nation is heavily determined by the requirements of the major city. This in turn encourages further concentration.[21]

The rate of growth of large LDC primate cities invariably outpaces that

---

[20]Ralph Thomlinson, "Bankok: Beau Ideal of a Primate City," *Population Review*, 16:32–38, January–December, 1972.

[21]Based on information in "Some Regional Development Problems in Latin America Linked to Metropolitanization," *Economic Bulletin for Latin America*, United Nations, New York, 17:58–62, 1972.

of the country as a whole. The largest city grows the fastest. This is often in spite of government policies to encourage more regional growth. The cities of Mexico City, Bogotá, and Santiago continue to grow faster than their national populations even though the governments of Mexico, Columbia, and Chile all seek a more balanced growth. Latin America has one-fifth (21 percent) of its urban population in very large cities of over 5 million persons.

Primate cities dominate the rest of the nation economically, educationally, politically, and socially. They control the lion's share of the manufacturing, administrative, investment, and service activities of the country. Government, education, and commerce all are concentrated in the primate city, and skilled workers are attracted from outlying regions. The city thus has a qualitative as well as a quantitative advantage. Growth and concentration, as noted above, lead to further concentration of resources, which, in turn, leads to greater growth. The decision-making power of the city increases while that of outlying towns decreases. Urban-bred civil servants, teachers, or employees are, perhaps understandably, most reluctant to give up the activity and excitement of city life for the underdevelopment of the more backward hinterland.

However, given the above it does not necessarily follow that such places are parasitic on the countryside. While regional balance is a desirable goal of planners, many smaller developing nations simply cannot support more than one major city at this point. In time, intermediate-size cities may emerge, but meanwhile there frequently is no realistic alternative to the primate city.

Whatever their faults, primate cities grew in part because the residents were—and still are—open to economic and social change. Most of the movements for independence were nurtured in the cities, and those who currently set policy and govern are invariably urban dwellers. The city remains an incubator of change.

Overurbanization

Closely related to the concept of primate cities is the concept of "overurbanization." The term overurbanization suggests that there is too large a proportion of the nation's population residing in cities for the nation's level of economic development. Overurbanization is defined as "a level of urbanization higher than that which can 'normally' be attained given the level of industrialization."[22] Given the level of national economic development, there are too many urban residents for the available jobs, housing, schooling, and other services. Egypt, for instance, is far more urbanized than its degree of economic development would lead one to expect: indeed, it is more urbanized than France or Sweden, both industrial nations. Some urbanists refer to Egypt, therefore, as being overurbanized.[23]

---

[22]Manuel Castells, *The Urban Question,* Alan Sheridan (trans.), MIT Press, Cambridge, Mass., 1977, pp. 41–43.

[23]See, for example, Kingsley Davis and Hilda Hertz Golden, "Urbanization and the Development of Pre-Industrial America," *Economic Development and Cultural Change,* 3:6–26, October, 1954.

Cairo has a much-overworked bus system; riders hang on the bus
roofs or from windows. (Bettmann Newsphotos)

   While there has been some attempt to keep the term "overurbanization"
free of any connotation of values, the concept usually does have negative
connotations: it suggests that overurbanization is both artificial and harmful
to economic growth. As one United Nations publication expressed it:

> Thus the recent rapid rate of urbanization visible in Asian countries does not
> bespeak of a corresponding growth of industry but of a shift of people from low
> productive agricultural employment to yet another section marked by low produc-
> tivity employment, namely handicraft production, retail trading, domestic servics
> in urban areas.[24]

   However, the whole picture is not as glum as the term "overurbanization"
suggests, for the productivity of the rural in-migrants is higher in the city than
in the rural areas, and per capita incomes of rural immigrants to cities are
almost universally higher than in rural areas.[25] If the concept of overurbanization
is meant to suggest the undesirability of rapid urbanization in developing
countries, the argument is difficult to prove. Certainly the data do not support
the belief that rapid urbanization slows or impedes economic development.

[24]*Urbanization in Asia and the Far East,* Proceedings of the Joint UN/UNESCO Seminar held in Bangkok,
   August 8–18, 1956, UNESCO, Calcutta, 1957, p. 133.
[25]N. V. Sovani, "The Analysis of Over-Urbanization," *Economic Development and Cultural Change,* **12**:113–
   122, January, 1964.

Life may be difficult in the city, but unfortunately, it is not better in the countryside; and in the city there is at least always hope and the possibility of something better.

It can be argued that the rapid growth of cities is a positive sign of the social and economic development of an area.[26] The city is not only the first area to reflect change, but also in a source of change. City growth is correlated with the change from agriculturalism to industrialism, with economic rationality, with lower birthrates and death rates, with increased literacy and education—in short, with the whole process of modernization. Insofar as urbanization is associated with the development of a modernized mode of life, the problem in much of the developing world, one could argue, is not overurbanization but underurbanization. As expressed by one expert, "The continued growth of a metropolis is evidence that, on balance, the positive aspects continue to outweigh the negative."[27]

CONCLUSION: THE FUTURE

This chapter concludes with a number of observations regarding the most likely patterns for the remainder of this century. The reader should keep in mind, though, that what follows are this author's views; the opinion of others may differ.

First, cities in the developing world are going to continue to grow, and to grow at a rapid rate. Growth will occur in spite of government policies to the contrary. For example, Jakarta was unsuccessful in becoming a "closed city," and China has been unable to halt city growth. India's new policies of directing growth to smaller places will be equally unsuccessful. Natural increase as well as in-migration will spur city growth.

Second, given such growth, squatter settlements, which currently hold one-third of the urban population, are unavoidable. Official disapproval will not make them go away. Thus, it is best to accept and legalize them, and provide at least minimal community services.

Third, urban infrastructure will inevitably remain inadequate. For example, attempts to provide "standard housing" are probably doomed to failure, though countries experiencing new wealth (as from oil), or highly organized states such as Singapore, will be an exception. Western-style industrialization will lag behind population growth and thus will not provide necessary jobs. A secondary informal labor market will remain a fact of life.

---

[26]See, for example, Kingsley Davis and Anna Casis, "Urbanization in Latin America," *Milbank Memorial Fund Quarterly,* **24**:186, April, 1946.

[27]Slaneslaw H. Wellisz, "Economic Development and Urbanization," in Jacobson and Prakash (eds.), *Urbanization and National Development,* Sage Publications, Beverly Hills, Calif., 1971, p. 42. Not all agree that "overurbanization" and primate cities are not a problem. See, for example, Antony J. La Greca, "Urbanization: A Worldwide Perspective," in Kent P. Schwirian (ed.), *Contemporary Topics in Urban Sociology,* General Learning Press, Morristown, N.J., 1977. One of the strongest arguments for the negative impact of overurbanization is in Joseph Gugler, "Overurbanization Reconsidered," *Economic Development and Cultural Change,* **31**:173–189, October, 1982.

Convergence and Modernization Approaches versus Dependency Theory

A crucial question regarding cities in less developed countries is whether such cities will in rough fashion repeat the North American socioecological patterns of growth (as detailed in Chapter 4, Ecology and Structure of American Cities, and Chapter 5, Metropolitan, Nonmetropolitan, and Sun Belt Growth), or whether developments in the third world will follow entirely different paths. If there is a rough evolutionary process based on an ecological model which is in turn based on land values and competition for scarce space, urban planning can predict what will occur. The belief that such patterns exist is sometimes referred to as "convergence theory."

If, on the contrary, there are divergent paths, because of fundamentally different processes, cultures, and historical and religious factors, making plans and policies on the basis of what has occurred in the west could be disastrous. Brian Berry argues for such different growth patterns. To date there is no consensus about the pattern of the future; some believe that third world cities will converge toward the western model, and some believe that there will be divergent paths of development.

Convergence theory makes two assumptions. The first is that all nations, although their starting points differ, are headed for the same general goals of economic development and modernizing societies. The second assumption is that eventual success is assured in spite of limited resources, ethnic diversity, a corrupt political leadership, and remaining noncolonial dependency.* Although the second of these assumptions has in particular been challenged, convergence theory and its derivative, "modernization theory" (which deals with developing countries' adopting the western, rational-industrial model), have been the common model for two decades. Modernization theory suggests that with the adoption of western technology and thought processes economic development will eventually—if sometimes painfully—follow. Thus, what happened in the West can be repeated elsewhere. With the acceptance of "economic development," people come to accept "modern" attitudes and values. Modernization of

*Wilbert E. Moore, *World Modernization: The Limits of Convergence*, Elsevier, New York, 1979, p. 26.

attitudes includes openness to innovation, planning for the future, faith in science and technology, and an emphasis on technical skills.† Modernization thus can be defined as the "process of rationalization of social behavior and social organization."‡ It is "all those social and political changes" accompanying western industrialization.§ South Korea, Taiwan, and Singapore are sometimes cited as examples of how modernization theory works. Modernization theory suggests that for LDCs the major factor bringing about change is time.¶

Dependency theory, on the other hand, reflects a radical rejection of the long-held orthodoxy of modernization theory. Instead of looking within a society for blockages to economic development, dependency theory looks to the external world order. Dependency theory views the relative economic stagnation of some LDCs as a direct consequence of the process of capitalistic expansion.** The industrial growth of the West is seen as occurring because of an unbalanced economic relationship in which western nations control the world market prices. Raw materials are extracted through the exploitation and subordination of the third world.†

So the development of some cities and nations is seen as a direct consequence of the underdevelopment of others. While the models for modernization theory are often Asian nations, the models for dependency theory are usually African or, most often, Latin American. Much of the writing on dependency theory focuses on the replacement of political colonialism with an economic neocolonialism that is said to lock LDCs into a permanently subordinate position.‡ Moreover, economic dependence is said to generate increased levels of overurbanization in dependent countries.§

Reconciling modernization and dependency theories is not easy. Modernization theory has been criticized by leftists for

†Alex Inkeles, "Making Men Modern: On the Causes and Consequences of Change in Six Countries," *American Journal of Sociology*, **75**:208–225, September, 1969.

‡Moore, op. cit., p. 29.

§Richard Bendix, *Nation Building and Citizenship*, University of California Press, Berkeley, 1964, p. 413.

¶Walt Rostow, *The World Economy: History and Prospect*, University of Texas Press, Austin, 1978.

Alejandro Portes, "On the Sociology of National Development: Theories and Issues," *American Journal of Sociology*, **82:55–85, July, 1976.

†Immanuel Wallerstein, *The Modern World System—Capitalist Agriculture and the European Economy in the Sixteenth Century*, Academic Press, New York, 1974.

‡Ronald H. Chilote, "Dependency: A Critical Synthesis of the Literature," in Janet Abu-Lughod and Richard Hay, Jr., (eds.), *Third World Urbanization*, Marqufa Press, Chicago, 1977.

§Jeffrey Kentor, "Structural Determinants of Peripheral Urbanization: The Effects of International Dependence," *American Sociological Review*, **46**:201–211, April, 1981; and Alan Gilbert and Josef Gugler, *Cities, Poverty and Development: Urbanization in the Third World*, Oxford University Press, New York, 1982.

being outdated, while dependency theory is criticized for being a sloppy catchall for excusing everything that is wrong with LDCs. The modernization/dependency debate often degenerates into a capitalist/socialist debate. Both models need less theoretical debate and more empirical and historical testing using individual nation states.

Fourth, the factors just noted suggest that political instability will be a serious problem in some countries. Rising expectations, widespread problems, and the availability of mass media will enable charismatic leaders to exploit anger and frustrations. (Iran is not a unique case but rather an example of the conflicts accompanying industrialization.)

Urban growth and urban industrialization are transforming traditional societies throughout the world, upsetting traditional attitudes, beliefs, customs, and behaviors. Scholars and politicians can debate whether these changes are for the better, but it is certain that urban industrial growth means change—a great deal of change.

CHAPTER
15
ASIAN URBAN PATTERNS

The whole city is arranged in squares just like a chessboard, and disposed in a manner so perfect and masterly that it is impossible to give a description that should do it justice.

Marco Polo, writing on Beijing

INTRODUCTION: ASIAN CITIES

Of all the world's regions, it is Asia about which one must be most careful when attempting to make generalizations. Patterns of urbanization in China, Japan, India, and southeast Asia all have different historical roots and have developed in dissimilar cultures. These areas do, of course, have some things in common; but generalizations must be applied with some care to individual cities.

What can be said is that Asia has a great tradition of city life and numerous cities whose histories go back many centuries. In fact, until 200 years ago Asia contained more city dwellers than the rest of the world combined.[1] And if present demographic trends continue, by the year 2000 Asia will again have more city dwellers than any other continent. Asia's population is projected to jump 40 percent to 3.64 billion by the century's end. By that time Asia will contain 58 percent of the world's population. And of this number, perhaps half will reside in urban areas. Already, Asia has more large cities and a larger number of people—but not a larger *percentage* of people—in cities than either Europe or America.

Despite this, the majority of Asia's population still consists of village-based agrarians; only a minority live in true urban places. Overall, some 31 percent of the population of Asia is urban.[2] This low level of overall urbanization places Asia just above Africa as regards the percentage of the population that is urbanized. While Asia is still predominantly rural, it has some of the world's largest cities. Tokyo has between 9 and 23 million people, depending upon whether one uses the most restrictive definition of the historic twenty-three wards of the city or the broad definition of the Tokyo agglomeration. The Asian cities of Shanghai, Beijing (Peking), Calcutta, and Bombay also number among the world's largest.

It has been suggested that less developed Asian nations are in the position of being "overurbanized" while at the same time their momentum of urbanization is increasing. "Overurbanization," however (as suggested in Chapter 14, Less Developed Countries: Overview and Common Problems), is a loaded term.

Indigenous Cities

Asian cities other than those founded and developed by westerners display a spatial organization having much in common with the preindustrial city (discussed in Chapter 2, The Emergence of Cities). Indigenous Asian cities of the past were predominantly political and cultural centers and only secondarily economic centers. The function of these traditional capital cities was to serve as a symbol of the authority, legitimacy, and power of the national government. Administrative functions were everywhere more important than commercial or industrial functions.

[1]Rhoads Murphey, "Urbanization in Asia," *Ekistics,* 21:8, January, 1966.
[2]Population Reference Bureau, *1986 World Population Data Sheet,* Washington, D.C., 1986.

Such cities were located inland, near the centers of their empires, except in Japan and parts of southeast Asia, where this was not practical. Such inland cities were centers physically as well as socially and were also far safer from attack than coastal cities. Beijing, Old Delhi, and Ankor are classic examples: they served as symbols of legitimate authority and were planned with monumental architecture, such as temples and palaces, that would emphasize this role. Beijing is famous for its Forbidden City Palace, Old Delhi for its magnificent Red Fort, and Ankor, until their recent destruction, for its many fine temples. In China and sometimes in India the city was walled; in southeast Asia it usually was not; and in Japan walls rarely existed.

Colonial Cities

The history of western-type cities is quite different from that of indigenous cities. Western-type cities were imported to the east by Europeans seeking trade. These cities, in contrast to the traditional preindustrial cities, were primarily oriented toward exportation and commerce and thus were located along seacoasts in order to facilitate trade and communication with the mother country. Originally small trading sites, perhaps with a small fort for protection, these cities are now among the largest in the world. Hong Kong, Singapore, Shanghai, Calcutta, and Bombay all developed as foreign-dominated port cities.

INDIA

India is only 23 percent urban, but that accounts for 171 million city dwellers. The Indian colonial city was the location of the rich and powerful. As such it not only reflected western organization and values, but also housed the upper-class "sahibs." British "civil lines" contained civil administrative headquarters and the homes of the British in the Indian civil service, while "cantonments"—military reservations—graciously housed the British officers (the troops themselves fared far worse).

In contrast to the model typical in the United States, the military reservations occupied central land rather than being peripherally located. Much of the city of Poona, for instance, is still occupied by military cantonments reflecting that city's heritage as a headquarters for the British and then the Indian army. Even within New Delhi, military bases continue to occupy much prime land. Attempts to persuade the military to move to outlying areas have been notably unsuccessful.

The spacious houses of the colonial city, graciously separated by large lawns and trees, to a lesser degree also reflect the nineteenth century's lack of knowledge about causes of disease. Malaria was thought to be caused by bad air *(mala aria),* and so the British constructed their residential areas with ample space for circulation of air between homes.

Density figures clearly document the difference between the old and new areas. The gross density is 13.2 persons per acre in New Delhi, but 213.3

persons per acre in Old Delhi.[3] The high figure for Old Delhi, moreover, is not for an area of apartment buildings but for an area of one- and two-story buildings. (In parts of Old Delhi the density rises to 600-700 persons per acre, while in Calcutta the average density is 45,000 people per square kilometer.)[4]

Old Delhi, with its stores and homes right on the edges of its always crowded streets and lanes, is a world apart from New Delhi, with its lawns and boulevards. Old Delhi is also a remarkably lively and interesting place. Its largely Muslim population successfully fought Indira Ghandi's plans to raze some of the area and resettle its inhabitants elsewhere. It is important to keep in mind that while indigenous cities often lack modern amenities, this may be more than compensated for in the eyes of residents by the areas' vitality and activity.

In the following pages we will focus on the nations' two largest cities—the economically developing city of Bombay and the more economically stagnant city of Calcutta.

Bombay

Bombay, India's traditional gateway to the west, is perhaps that nation's most dynamic city.[5] It is the heart of India's financial and industrial life and the center of the nation's large and colorful film industry. Greater Bombay, with 10 million residents, provides a full third of India's income taxes and 30 percent of India's gross national product.

Yet Bombay is showing signs of coming apart at the seams. The reason isn't difficult to understand. Bombay, built on a peninsula, can extend only northward along a narrow corridor of two rail lines; but it contains more people than it can reasonably service—and the situation is getting worse. Bombay gains 10,000 residents every day, and few cities anywhere could keep up with such an influx. Most come seeking not better employment, but any employment.[6] Sewage systems, housing, educational systems, and transportation systems are overwhelmed. For example, only one-fifth of the sewage now receives treatment, and the once-beautiful beaches along the bay are badly polluted. Likewise, the air is seriously polluted.

Many of the poor commute by rail from the suburbs on the once-excellent but now alarmingly overused and overextended commuter railroads. Not only are the rail cars full, but riders hang on to the exterior of windows and even crowd the roofs. Not surprisingly, there are frequent accidents and approximately a dozen deaths on the commuter lines each day.[7] Inside the city

[3]Gerald Breese, *Urbanization in Newly Developing Countries,* Prentice Hall, Englewood Cliffs, N.J., 1966, p. 62.
[4]Alfred de Souza (ed.), *The Indian City,* South Asia Books, Columbia, Mo., 1978, p. xiv.
[5]This section is partially based upon discussions with officials of the Bombay Metropolitan Region Development Authority and the City of Bombay Industrial Development Corporation. The opinions are, of course, the author's.
[6]P. Ramachandran, *Pavement Dwellers in Bombay City,* Tata Institute of Social Sciences, Bombay, India, 1972, p. 18.
[7]*Poona Herald,* February 23, 1979, p. 2.

Until 1911, Calcutta was the colonial capital of British India. (Mary Evans Picture Library/Photo Researchers)

overloaded derelict trucks, crowded buses, cars, and bicycles all congest the jammed streets.

Bombay, like other great cities, has always had its wealthy and its poor, but it is becoming more and more a city of sharp and painful contrasts. It is increasingly difficult to ignore the disparity between the conspicuous display of wealth by the rich residing in the high-rise apartments lining the bay and the quarter million desperately poor "pathway dwellers" or "pavement people" who must sleep, eat, work, and raise their families while living in hovels on the edges of the roads. For Bombay's pavement people, the city streets are not paved with gold. Rather, they are the last refuge of a swelling tide of humanity.

To stress the point made originally, Bombay is better off than many LDC cities. Bombay is also fortunate to have a trained civil service to administer the city. However, planners and city administrators openly concede they are losing the battle. Those who love the city admit sadly that it has physically declined over the last decade. Given Bombay's population growth, urban decline is likely to continue.

Bombay is a city that could handle 5 million people reasonably well and, possibly, even cope with 8 million—but it has 10 million. And the 10 million are straining the municipality beyond its limits. Officials keep reassuring everyone that Bombay is not another Calcutta. The fear now increasingly expressed is whether, with a projected population of 16 million in a decade and a half, Bombay will still be able to make such a claim.

A new satellite town, New Bombay, is being built across the bay, and it is intended eventually to house over 1 million residents. Thus far, however, New Bombay is more a hope than an actual community, owing to bureaucratic delays and the reluctance of industries and government offices to resettle there. The city contained fewer than 50,000 persons as of 1985. Few people want to leave the central city, with its excitement and vitality, for resettlement across the bay.

Calcutta

Calcutta is on the opposite side of India from Bombay, both geographically and emotionally. If Bombay is entrepreneurial, Calcutta is fatalistic. Until 1910 Calcutta was the proud seat of the British Raj and a major financial center, landscaped with Victorian parks and monuments. Today, Calcutta's international image is one of decay, misery, and disaster; Calcutta's very name suggests the nadir of urban life. As of 1985 more than 70 percent of Calcutta's population lived below the poverty level, which is calculated at a low $8 a month.

Calcutta's overall metropolitan-area population of 11 million is not growing as rapidly as that of Bombay or New Delhi, but neither is its aging industrial economy. Calcutta is losing its economic base. The once-active machine-shop industry, for example, is now too antiquated to compete with more advanced operations elsewhere in India. The important jute industry is also affected by a fluctuating market and obsolescence.[8] Nor has the national government been eager to invest its interest and funds in Calcutta—partially, perhaps, because the municipal officials are Marxists.

The city also has problems with a unique land-tenure system which virtually ensures nonmaintenance of slum properties. In the *bustee* one person owns the land, another then builds a hut upon it, and a third serves a tenant, paying a monthly rent without any claim to either the land or the hut. Under this system no one has any incentive to maintain the property. *Bustee* residents technically are not squatters but tenants. Since landlords can't legally raise the rent without the tenants' permission, buildings are literally left to rot until they tumble into the street.

Attempts by the Municipal Development Authority to upgrade the slums, and by the Municipal Corporation to maintain them (a major problem), are hampered by lack of funds. Meanwhile, people and the sacred cattle coexist in the *bustees*. As a form of recycling, cattle dung is collected by women and children and formed into circular patties that serve as fuel when dried.

Physically, there is no question that Calcutta is decaying. Forty percent of the city's buildings are more than seventy-five years old. Twenty percent

[8]Harold Cubell, *Urban Development and Employment: The Prospects for Calcutta,* International Labour Office, Geneva, 1974.

Rickshaw pullers remain a common form of transportation in Calcutta. (Photograph by author)

of the buildings are classified as unsafe. A series of development plans to arrest further deterioration have not been successful in reversing the damage done by decades of infrastructure collapse. For instance, drainage and sewer networks, all of which were laid in the central city prior to 1910, are in a serious state of disrepair. The last main sewer was laid in 1896. Currently, most of the sewer system is either inoperative or badly clogged. However, this is not the only problem, for were the sewers cleared the old treatment plant would be overwhelmed. All this is of little consequence to the majority of municipal area residents living in *bustees* or in outlying squatter settlements since most of their dwellings are without private toilets or sewers.

Water, electricity, and telephone systems are also overloaded and in need of both major repairs and extensive upgrading. Power blackouts are a regular evening feature, and telephones often do not work. Water supplies are, however, getting better, with two-thirds of Calcutta's residents now having some access to piped drinking water—frequently from a street standpipe. In Calcutta physical labor often is substituted for technology. Some 40,000 barefoot rickshaw pullers still transport goods and people. This is long after rickshaws have been banned elsewhere in India.

Within the city, groups occupy geographical wards largely on the basis of religion (Hindu or Muslim), caste, and ethnic region of origin.[9] Occupations are also ethnically segregated. For example, Bengalis traditionally prefer white-

[9]Nirmal Kumar Bose, *Calcutta 1964: A Social Survey*, Larani, Bombay, India, 1968. See also Brian J. Berry and John D. Kasarda, *Contemporary Urban Ecology*, Macmillan, New York, 1977, pp. 134–157.

collar jobs and avoid heavy labor, while the rickshaw pullers are mostly Bihari. Taxi drivers used to be largely Punjabi, but now also include some Bengalis.

Three-quarters of the population of Calcutta is housed in crowded tenements and *bustee* huts.[10] These *bustee* dwellers are in some ways fortunate, for between half a million and 1 million pathway dwellers—no one knows the exact figure—have no housing of any type. They work, eat, sleep, breed, and die on the streets without the benefit of any shelter.

Nonetheless, Calcutta, even with all its social and physical problems, remains one of the world's more vital cities. It is the active center of Bengali poetry and theater, and few Bengali intellectuals would trade the city's excitement for all the fine neighborhoods and homes of New Delhi.

Calcutta is also remarkably free of street crime. Residents fatalistically may accept power outages, poor housing, malaria, cohlera, antiquated transportation, and constant strikes that close down municipal services, but they do not tolerate street crime against women. Any violator risks the wrath of the ever-present street crowds. Indian women in Calcutta can walk even at night with a degree of safety unknown in New Delhi, London, or New York. Physically the city is in decay; socially it retains a vigor of life and pride that other cities might envy.

Programs to alleviate Calcutta's problems have been proposed by the United Nations, the Ford Foundation, and the Indian government. Unfortunately, the aid that Calcutta has received has not always met its real needs. For example, to solve the city's transportation problems, the national government is now building an expensive subway system. The system is being built in a city where all buses are ancient and constantly in disrepair, where the last new streetcar was purchased before World War II, and where rickshaw pullers still provide transportation for people and goods. Despite this, despite periodic floods, and despite the certainty that subway stations inevitably will become a home for pavement people, it was decided for political reasons to build a subway to provide employment. The protests of state and municipal officials on the scene have been of no avail.

In a perverse fashion the very excesses of Calcutta's problems are acting to slow the city's growth. Such problems are accomplishing what urban planning and policy could not. The shrinking industrial base and difficult living conditions have made the city less attractive to rural in-migrants. Improvements in rural living have also reduced the pressures to abandon the countryside for Calcutta. Calcutta thus may be going through a self-correction cycle.

Government Intervention

National Programs for Housing the Poor. India is currently engaged in various programs to build low-cost self-help homes on the urban periphery for the poor. Very basic homes to be furnished by the occupant are being built

---

[10]K. C. Sivaramakrishnan, "The Slum Improvement Programme in Calcutta: The Role of the CMDA," in de Souza, op. cit., p. 134.

Entire families living on the pavements have become an unfortunate feature of contemporary Bombay. (Jehangir Gazdar/Woodfin
Camp & Assoc.)

by development authorities for as little as $300. However, even this price is
well beyond the reach of most squatters and pavement people. In relatively
prosperous New Delhi, for instance, half the people in the lowest-status
"economically weaker section" have a monthly income under $50. Another
quarter (23 percent) earn between $50 and $90 a month.[11] Elsewhere the
monthly incomes are generally lower.

[11]Delhi Development Authority figures, March, 1979.

Increasing attention is thus being given to "site and service" projects, in which a housing site is provided with basic sewerage facilities and a shared water pump. Construction of the house over time is the responsibility of the resident. While some Indian planners are still put off by the disorderly nature of the site and service areas, there is no reasonable alternative. Government-built public housing projects on the western model are too expensive and have been beset by massive maintenance and other problems.

The major problem with site and service projects is that they are often far from the city centers where the poor must seek employment. For the poor, a location near employment is more important than housing quality. Working women with families are particularly dependent on location.

Government Policy on Urban Places. Despite the pleas of urban officials and planners, India's national government has yet to develop an effective policy for urban growth. (Responsibility for urban development technically rests with each state.) The legacy of Gandhi—an emphasis on rural and village India—still prevails in policy making. Politicians are largely of rural origin themselves and depend upon rural support to stay in office. City dwellers, because they constitute but one-fifth of the population, remain politically underrepresented.

Current national policy is attempting to slow the growth of the larger cities and disperse their population. This is being done through consciously limiting economic expansion in the largest cities. However, attempts to divert the flow of migration toward smaller cities have not been successful. To date, prohibiting new industrial enterprises has not really had a deterrent affect on in-migration. On the other hand, limiting economic expansion in the cities will further accelerate problems of jobs, housing, transportation, sewage, and schooling. Short of draconian measures—which no one is even suggesting—India's great cities will continue to grow with or without government approval.

Prognosis

Overshadowing all other Indian problems is that of how to cope with population growth. Since the 1981 edition of this book India's population has grown by over 85 million.

India now has some 780 million people and will top 1 billion by the year 2000.[12] To put it in more understandable terms, each year India is adding 15 million persons, or the total population of Australia.

The eradication of smallpox, the partial eradication of malaria, and control of cholera have reduced infant mortality drastically. As a consequence, 43 percent of the population is under fifteen years of age. When these young people come of age, it will be difficult to provide the necessary educational opportunities, jobs, and housing. India for decades has had various birth control programs, but the population is already so large that even a moderate growth rate has a tremendous numerical impact. (India, with a 2.3 percent

[12]Population Reference Bureau, op. cit.

yearly increase, will double its population in less than 35 years.) India feeds itself, and there are also very substantial nonagricultural resources. Economic growth, though, tends to benefit the elite and the middle class more than the masses. (Nationally over half of the urban families must survive on monthly incomes of between $15 and $50.) Also, as a result of continual population growth, development is distorted: attention must be constantly focused on increasing the amount of foodstuffs available. Other problems such as education and housing necessarily receive lower priority. Questions of improving the quality of life and saving the environment receive much less attention.

CHINA

The 1982 Chinese census revealed that China had some one billion people. Most demographers believe that even this figure is a bit of an undercount. To put China's population in terms most westerners would understand: China *alone* is roughly equal to the combined populations of all the twenty-one nations of western Europe, all the thirty-six nations of Latin America and the Caribbean, plus the populations of the United States and Canada.

Today one of every four infants born is Chinese, and China yearly adds *22 million* persons to its population. This is in spite of China's having a 1.5 percent rate of natural increase, which is well below the 2.4 percent a year for all other LDCs. China's 1.5 percent rate of natural increase is, nonetheless, twice as high as the United States' rate of 0.7 percent. China's goal is to hold its population to 1.2 billion by the end of the century.

China's billion-plus population is still four-fifths rural, but the urban population is already the world's largest population of urban dwellers. Moreover, this has not been primarily due to rural-to-urban movement. Two-thirds of the urban growth since 1949 has come from natural increase of urban births over deaths.[13]

The People's Republic of China has an area of about 3.8 million square miles, with 96 percent of the population living on 40 percent of the land area. The population of China is concentrated in the southern and eastern sections of the country. The greatest density is found in the Yangtze valley, where there are 2,000 to 2,500 persons per square mile.

Background

The first modern manufacturing and industrial cities of China were the western-dominated treaty ports. During the nineteenth and twentieth centuries the ports of Chinese coastal cities were at various times physically controlled and occupied by European, and later Japanese, administrators and troops.

The European powers forced the weak and ineffectual Manchu, or Qing, dynasty to give foreigners substantial control over the economic life of the

---

[13]H. Yuan Tien, "China: Demographic Billionaire," *Population Bulletin,* Population Reference Bureau, Washington, D.C., April, 1983, p. 29.

major Chinese cities. Europeans lived in separate, newer sections of the cities. The foreign concessions of Shanghai were even policed by European troops; nor could foreigners be tried for crimes in Chinese courts. In Shanghai, the largest and most prosperous of the treaty ports, the park along the "Bund," or riverfront had signs stating "No Dogs or Chinese Allowed." Even the capital of Peking had its "legation quarter" for foreigners, near the central Imperial City. However, the number of foreign residents was never particularly large. In Canton, China's major southern city, foreigners at their most numerous were only 894 out of a city population of over 1 million.[14]

The Nationalist government, which replaced the Qing dynasty in 1911, was made up of an urban military and upper-class elite which continued the traditional practices of taxing and coercing the peasants to support the urban-based government. Landowners, many of whom lived in the cities, had little sympathy for the declining quality of life in rural China. The government continued to serve the landowners and disregard the plight of the peasants; land reform was ignored.

The communists also initially ignored the peasants and attempted to organize in the cities, but having failed at that, Mao Tse-tung redirected attention to the peasants. After decades of internal struggle and the civil war of 1947–1949, the communists achieved national dominance.

Urbanization Policies

China currently has an urban population of 320 million. This would mean that China—although still seven tenths rural—has the world's largest national population of urban dwellers.

China's policy under Mao was resolutely antiurban. This was in part a reaction to the treaty port cities' being seen (correctly) as the centers of western thought and influence. "The foreign presence (in China) was almost exclusively urban."[15] (Inland cities such as Tsinan were more successful in resisting foreign intervention.[16] The initial failures of the communist cause in the cities further separated the cities from the original communist leadership. However, in spite of the discouraging of urban growth, between 1949 and 1956 some 20 million Chinese migrated from rural areas into the cities.

Rustication. In 1963, following the economic crisis brought on by the failure of the "great leap forward" campaign, the government decided to stabilize the urban population at 110 million, which was considered a manageable figure.[17] In order to so this, it was decided to "rusticate," or return to the countryside, urban school graduates; this would lessen the pressure on the

[14]Ezra Vogel, *Canton Under Communism,* Harvard University Press, Cambridge, Mass., 1969.

[15]Rhoads Murphey, "The Treaty Ports and China's Modernization," in Mark Elvin and G. William Skinner (eds.), *The Chinese City between Two Worlds,* Stanford University Press, Stanford, Calif., 1974, p. 67.

[16]David D. Buck, *Urban Change in China,* University of Wisconsin Press, Madison, 1978.

[17]Pi-chao Chen, "Overurbanization, Rustication of Urban-Educated Youths, and Politics of Rural Transformation," *Comparative Politics,* April, 1972, p. 374.

urban economy and help promote agriculture and indigenous industry in rural areas. During the "cultural revolution" of 1966–1976, the government tried to reverse the flow to the cities and send surplus urban population into the countryside. A combination of social coercion and ideological conviction was used to persuade at least 15 million urban Chinese youths to "volunteer" to resettle permanently in rural villages.[18] Some estimates suggest that as many as 25 million urban young adults were resettled in this manner. Many of these migrants made a poor adjustment to their new surroundings.

The present government's "responsibility system" stresses modernization and economic development and has abandoned the rural resettlement of urban youth. The majority of those resettled during the Maoist era have now legally or illegally returned to the cities.

While the rustication campaigns of the 1960s and 1970s did slow the pace of urbanization, there was only limited success in slowing the growth of the largest cities. While for three decades ideology emphasized the stabilization or reduction of urban growth, antiurban ideology ran up against economic reality. Shanghai, for example, has an extended urban-area population of over 12 million people and is the dominant industrial center of the nation. With more than 1.5 million workers employed in industries such as steel, shipbuilding, machine tools, chemicals, and motor vehicles, it is all but impossible to disperse this industrial population to outlying sites. At least, it cannot be done without severe economic repercussions. China's opening to the west is already intensifying Shanghai's role as a major port and industrial center.

Urban Control and Rural Relocation

Nonetheless, China is making a major effort to relocate industries to outlying areas in order to stem the potential flood of rural-to-urban migrants. Currently, Chinese officials estimate that some 25 to 30 percent of the rural labor force is unemployed or underemployed. Moreover, Chinese demographers estimate that mechanization of farming will eventually displace a total of 300 to 500 million peasants, of whom 100 million will be displaced between now and the turn of the century.[19] Planners hope to relocate displaced peasants in small cities and towns scattered across the countryside. The size of large cities is to be strictly controlled. Thus far, rural-to-urban migration has been held in check by a very strictly enforced policy of household registration which does not legally permit those without urban jobs to remain in the cities.

One consequence of China's approach is that there are no shantytowns housing masses of unemployed workers. When government controls who may stay in the cities, all workers who are legally in the city theoretically have a job. Technically, there are no unemployed persons, only those working or those temporarily awaiting assignment. An indirect consequence of this policy of job and housing control has been proliferation of marginal jobs outside the

---

[18]Ibid., p. 235.
[19]H. Yuan Tien, op. cit.

Bicycle parking lots of this sort can be found throughout Beijing.
(Bruce Rosenblum/The Picture Cube)

formal structure, such as free-enterprise markets and food stalls—places where those not supposed to be in the city sometimes can find work.

Shanghai

Shanghai, China's largest city, grew as a treaty port built on western commercial enterprise. It was largely imposed upon the existing civilization.[20] Within a decade of its opening to foreign trade in 1843, Shanghai's manufacturing sector had become a physical and economic embodiment of nineteenth-century European thought. In nineteenth-century Shanghai, with its extraterritoriality (foreigners having their own laws, police, and courts), foreign concessions, and foreign gunboats, the modern industrial world of European rationality came face to face with the traditional seclusionist ways of the Chinese Empire.

Today Shanghai, with an urban area population of over 12 million, is one of the world's largest cities. For Chinese planners, the physical development of Shanghai has been complicated by several factors. For example, the Chinese have had to overcome the effects of the previous pattern of mixed foreign domination. Each of the foreign settlements had not only its own administration and police but also its own pattern and width of streets, water pipes, and sewers. Developing a uniform citywide street pattern has required widening

---

[20]For a description of Shanghai before communism, see Rhoads Murphey, *Shanghai—Key to Modern China*, Harvard University Press, Cambridge, Mass., 1953.

existing streets as well as extending others by tearing down buildings and houses. The total length of city streets increased more than ten times—from 200 miles to over 2,000 miles—over the period from 1949 to 1972.[21]

With the mass of industrial activity located within the city proper, there is considerable pollution and transportation congestion. Most of the city's factories and utilities burn heavily polluting soft coal for energy. The pollution and congestion from automobiles is minimal, however, since there are no private automobiles on the streets. The absence of private automobiles also limits the distance one can live from one's workplace. In order to get to work, the populace uses a crowded bus system and bicycles. Recent prosperity has led to an explosion in the number of bicycles: there are perhaps 4 million in the city.

At the time of the revolution, Shanghai, like other Chinese cities, was faced with a massive housing problem. Years of war and turmoil had left the poor to exist in shacks and straw huts along the streets and the riverbank. These hovels are now gone, and some ninety-five residential villages have been constructed. Housing, like other sectors, is only now recovering from the ravages of the 1966–1976 cultural revolution. For over a decade virtually no new urban building, repairs, or even painting was done anywhere in China. For example, the prestigious Singapore Conservatory of Music saw not only its once-fine buildings decay but most of its instruments destroyed and historically invaluable sheet music sold as scrap paper.

Now housing is being repaired and new buildings constructed. One's place of work usually not only provides a job, but also manages the housing where one lives. Serious crowding remains a problem, but the rent is low; the average working family pays only 4 to 8 percent of its income for monthly rent.[22] Within the city virtually every family has electricity and indoor cold water service.

Beijing

Beijing was first made the capital of China in the Yuan Dynasty in 1292. The old walled city was expanded during the Ming and Qing dynasties into the political and cultural center of the nation. At the time of the 1982 census the municipality had 9.2 million residents.[23] This is not an accurate reflection of the actual city population, for the Beijing municipality covers a huge, 16,800-square-kilometer territory (roughly four-fifths the size of New Jersey) and 3.7 million of the inhabitants of the municipality are rural residents.[24] These agricultural workers worked collectively prior to the abolishment of communes in 1984. Now, under the free-enterprise-type "responsibility system," they represent a highly prosperous category of largely independent farmers who

---

[21]Hung-Mao Tien, "Shanghai: China's Huge Model City,'" *Milawukee Journal,* December 16, 1973.
[22]Ibid.
[23]*Beijing Review,* **26**:24, January 1, 1983.
[24]David Buck, "New Municipal Plan for Beijing," *Urbanism Past and Present,* **8**:14, summer/fall, 1983.

help feed the capital city. Beijing's urban residents are the most economically favored in China. The average annual salary of a Beijing workers in 1982 was $1,200, compared with the far lower national urban average of $250.[25] This reflects Beijing's role as the home of China's political leaders and top bureaucrats. It is the chief center of political, administrative, industrial, educational, and cultural activity.

During the 1950s, when Soviet influence was still important, the city was divided into functional zones for different activities following the Moscow model. Factory sectors were concentrated in the eastern and southern suburbs, while the northwest sector was primarily for higher education and research. Since the prevailing winds are from the northwest, this also helps to keep down pollution levels.

Beijing has very serious pollution problems, particularly in the winter, when soft coal is the fuel used by virtually all businesss and families for heating. On some cloudless days the sun is not visible until afternoon because of the heavy pollution. Contributing to the problem of windblown particulate matter is Beijing's location on an almost treeless plain south of the Gobi Desert. Also, during the cultural revolution, it was decreed for health reasons that all birds in the city be killed. This led to a proliferation of insects, so the municipal government then decreed that all grass be torn up. This was done, with the result of substantially increased dust in the air.

In 1983 an overall plan for the future development of Beijing was revealed.[26] The plan envisions placing the entire former central Imperial City under special protection to preserve historic buildings and prohibit any more houses taller than two stories in that area. Older neighborhoods are to be renovated, polluting factories are to be moved away from the city, parks and woodlands are to be greatly expanded, and streets are to be improved. However, shutting down major industrial polluters has already proven to be a difficult task.[27]

All of this comes none too soon since, while Beijing still has only 250,000 motor vehicles, it now has over 5 million bicycles, and their number is increasing by 9 percent a year. Beijing's empty streets of a decade ago are now wall-to-wall bicycles at morning and evening rush hours.

In spite of considerable building of high-rise flats, crowded housing still remains a major problem in the capital. The 1966–1976 cultural revolution did not cause the physical suffering in Beijing that was found in other cities, but there was a gap in housing construction which will take current programs many years to fill. Still, Beijing is clearly moving forward, and if it meets most of its modernization plans it will indeed be a first-rank metropolis by the end of the century.

---

[25]Ibid. By 1985 the average annual wage for urban workers throughout China had increased to $394, according to China's State Statistical Bureau.
[26]"Beijing to Be Turned into a Metropolis," *Hong Kong Standard,* August 3, 1983.
[27]"Beijing Achieves Good Progress," *Beijing Review,* **26**:10, April 18, 1983.

Hong Kong intensely uses all available space. Even the streetcars are double-deckers. (Derek Lepper/Black Star)

A Note on Hong Kong

The British Crown Colony of Hong Kong, although on the Chinese mainland, is most noted for its extremely laissez-faire economic structure. Hong Kong, including the New Territories, will revert back to mainland Chinese ownership in 1997. Much of Hong Kong's 404 square miles are so steep and mountainous as to be incapable of development or are on scattered islands where development would be uneconomical. This, plus the strong desire of newcomers to remain in the city proper, means that Hong Kong's population is heavily concentrated in a narrow ring around the harbor. As a consequence densities in Hong Kong reach 6,500 persons *per acre,* the highest in the world.[28] The continued influx of refugees into this already overcrowded environment further strains the city's resources.

In an attempt to provide public housing for all who need it, Hong Kong is developing several new towns. Tsuen Won, which was begun in 1973, already holds over 800,000 persons and eventually will have over 1 million. (Obviously the new towns are far larger than Ebenezer Howard's vision of self-contained communities of only 30,000.) Hong Kong's new towns (or cities) are being developed as self-sufficient entities, but in fact cannot yet meet their own educational, retail trade, and entertainment needs, much less provide their own employment base.

Hong Kong is noted for its vitality and for having produced an economic miracle. What it has not produced is a means of equitably sharing that miracle. One reason new towns can be constructed rapidly is that construction workers labor ten hours a day, seven days a week. The only break in the workers' routine occurs at the Chinese New Year holidays. Nonetheless, for its residents, Hong Kong represents living standards and opportunities unavailable on the mainland. The city now boasts a substantial middle class. This population is particularly nervous about the consequences of Hong Kong's transfer from British to mainland Chinese control in 1997.

JAPAN

Any discussion of Asian urban patterns must include Japan, the region's most urbanized large nation. Japan is not an urban newcomer; it has an urban tradition even longer than that of India as regards the role of the city in regional and national life. Japan's urban tradition goes back at least to the fifteenth century. The so-called "castletowns" formed a basic urban stratum upon which later cities were built. Edo, as Tokyo was then called, may have had 1 million people in 1700, while Osaka, the great trade center, and Kyoto, the ancient capital, both had several hundred thousand inhabitants.[29]

The Extent of Urbanization

The forced opening of Japan to western influences in the nineteenth century led to a boom in city building. Cities such as Tokyo, Nagoya, and Osaka grew, first as trading centers, and later as manufacturing and commercial cities. Industrialization and urbanization took place so completely that today Japan

[28]Murray MacLehose, "Modern Urban Development in Hong Kong," paper delivered by the Governor to the Commonwealth Society, Hong Kong, November 28, 1977.
[29]Edwin O. Reishauer, *The Japanese,* Belknap Press, Cambridge, Mass., 1978, p. 25.

Density and Economic Development

It should be noted that there is no clear relationship between density per se and the level or rate of economic development. High agricultural density is usually seen as a sign of underdevelopment, but high urban densities may or may not be desirable, depending on the level of economic development.

High densities of rural, and particularly agricultural, labor indicate inefficient agricultural production and a surplus of personnel which is either unemployed or underemployed. In closed extractive economies—such as farming, lumbering, and mining—the employment of a high proportion of the labor force in such pursuits means smaller average holdings. India, for example, employs about 70 percent of its labor force in agriculture, with an average holding of about 2 acres for every person of working age (fifteen to sixty-five years of age). In Asia over 83 percent of the available acreage is already under cultivation; thus increases in rural population will necessarily mean less land per person. Rural out-migration thus will continue to be a major force into the foreseeable future.

In developed countries, where nonextractive industries dominate and a large volume of trade is possible, density is frequently an advantage rather than a liability. The industrial ring cities of the Netherlands and the Rhine River urban complex of Germany both have extremely high densities and high standards of living. Hong Kong provides an even more extreme example. Hong Kong has a population of over 4 million crowded on a land area of 398 square miles: this comes out to over 10,000 persons per square mile. Nonetheless, Hong Kong has for years managed to increase its GNP at a rate far in excess of the rest of the world. Hong Kong has practically no natural resources, but it is blessed with a literate, energetic, and trained labor force. Its extremely high population density has not prevented Hong Kong from achieving one of the highest levels of per capita income in Asia, although much exploitation of workers remains.

This in no way suggests, of course, that high densities automatically result in high income levels and economic expansion. However, high density can be an advantage to a highly organized and heavily industrialized economy. The city concentrates large numbers of people in one place and thus minimizes what has been called "the friction of space." Production can be concentrated in one place; the city itself is a massive factory. Technological breakthroughs in transportation and communication also are means of overcoming the friction of space, and allow the city to export both to its rural hinterland and to other urban areas.

In the noneconomic sphere, population concentration also permits and encourages specialized educational, cultural, and scientific organizations. Accumulations of personal and capital resources necessary for the emergence of such organizations can be found only in the city. The requirements of urban living also produce new problems, such as housing, sanitation, and the prevention of crime; and the necessity of dealing with these problems can lead to an emphasis on innovation and rational problem solving.

The requirements of contemporary urban life and those of industrialization complement one another. Both emphasize the importance of adapting to changing conditions. Urbanization and industrialization are not the same thing, but it is not surprising that industrialism in the third world is directly associated with the growth of urban areas and the spread of urban ideas.

equals and in some cases surpasses western levels in these two areas. Today Japan is three-quarters urban (76 percent), a figure which is essentially the same as that for the United States.[30] Moreover, the urban population of Japan is remarkably concentrated, with an overall national density of over 300 persons per square kilometer and 45 percent of the total population occupying only 1 percent of the land area.

Current Patterns

In discussing contemporary Japanese urbanization it is important to remember that while Japan is an Asian country, its levels of urbanization and industrialization are far closer to those of Europe and North America than to those of the rest of Asia. The strengths and problems of Japanese cities are largely those of developed western metropolises. Japan, along with the small enclaves of Hong Kong and Singapore, has both a level and a pattern of urbanization atypical of Asia in general.

Many current urban problems in Japan are a result of the decision of the Japanese after World War II to concentrate all their efforts on industrial production for export. Only minimal attention and resources were devoted to ''social overhead'' such as sewage systems, water systems, housing, pollution control, and urban transportation. The result is that today Japan has a massive backlog of demands for urban services. Japan spends less on urban infrastructure than other industrial nations.

The picture, however, is not as grim as these considerations alone would indicate, for while Japan has large problems, it also has great resources. Japan has the technology, the skilled personnel, and the financial resources to rebuild and remake its cities. What it now requires is the will to make the commitment. The problem is one of social policy rather than technology or resources.

Tokyo

Tokyo-Yokohama, the world's most populous city (or second most populous depending on definition), is to the western observer a series of contradictions.[31] Signs of prosperity are everywhere, from the streets clogged with new automobiles to futuristic new office buildings to luxury department stores unmatched in Paris, London, or New York. A shabbily dressed person is difficult to find. Few would disagree with the contention of President Isomura of Tokyo University that Japanese women are, as a group, better and more expensively dressed than women anywhere in Europe or the United States.

Yet Japan, in spite of its affluence, has not been able or willing to house its population properly and provide urban amenities taken for granted in other developed countries. Japan's cities reflect the emphasis on production for export rather than an attempt to upgrade the urban infrastructure. For example,

---

[30]Population Reference Bureau, *1986 World Population Data Sheet,* Washington, D.C., 1986.
[31]Material in this section is based largely on my own observations and conversations with Japanese planning officials.

housing conditions are extremely cramped and excessively expensive by American standards. Land prices are estimated to be ten times as high as in New York.[32] This means that a small plot of land within commuting distance that would cost the average American worker 45 days' wages to purchase would cost the average Tokyo worker 6.5 years' wages.[33] Again and again one hears that young people spend money on consumer goods and holidays, since, without major parental assistance, they are unable to purchase homes.

Housing. Exorbitant land costs have also resulted in structures being built wall to wall up to the lot lines. Unfortunately, within the Tokyo-Yokohama agglomeration, the traditional Japanese gardens exist only in memory or on the estates of the wealthy. Zoning regulations are minimal, and even they are frequently flouted. This absence of control over construction is notable in such a structured society.

There is also a lack of public services. Within the area of the Tokyo metropolitan government (the old city of twenty-three wards and the immediate surrounding suburbs with a population of 11.5 million), a decade ago half the population still had no flush toilets.[34] Today, it is one fifth of the housing units. Ironically, at the same time 98 percent of the homes in Tokyo have color television.

The Japanese economic miracle has thus far failed to provide the average family with a standard of housing commensurate with the nation's wealth. Three-quarters (77 percent) of those in Japan's urban areas live in homes or apartments of less than 60 square yards of floor space. Central-city housing is prohibitively expensive, and as a result most Japanese are forced to commute long distances between their offices and cheaper residential accommodations in satellite towns on the outskirts of Tokyo.

Pollution and Transportation. Tokyo-Yokohama is not only the world's largest metropolitan area; it is also among the world's most congested and polluted. Air pollution is so severe that it directly causes scores of deaths each year. Workers in some industries automatically use face masks. The level of water pollution was graphically demonstrated when a Tokyo newspaper printed on its front page a photograph that had been developed solely by dipping the negative in a chemically polluted river.

In the area of transportation, Tokyo has a remarkably clean and efficient subway system, but during rush hours it and commuter rail lines must employ an army of 700 pushers whose job it is to force additional passengers into the overcrowded cars. The record was set by the Chico line, which in 1972 carried 260 percent of its supposed capacity. Above ground, the roads are continually packed with wall-to-wall vehicles. Because space is at a premium, express

---

[32]Peter Hall, *World Cities,* McGraw-Hill, New York, 1977, p. 227.
[33]Ibid.
[34]Ibid., p. 228.

The Japanese commuter lines employ uniformed pushers to shove additional people into already overcrowded cars. (Richard Kalvar/ Magnum)

roads are usually built above existing roadways, but they also are commonly clogged. The system is simply not adequate for a city half Tokyo's size.

For many Japanese the bicycle, not the auto, is the most efficient means of transportation. The nation has some 55 million bicycles, and at least 5.6 million of these are in Tokyo, which represents an increase of 25 percent between 1980 and 1985.[35] Since a third of all Tokyo office workers spend between two and four hours a day commuting, a bicycle stored during the day at the suburban railway station may help people cut ten or fifteen minutes off this total in the morning and evening. It also leads to unbelievable seas of bicycles outside railway stations and stores. Periodically police confiscate illegally parked bicycles (200,000 in Tokyo in 1983), but it seems to have little impact.

Planning. During the final years of World War II much of Tokyo was leveled— the city lost 56 percent of its housing stock—and Tokyo had the opportunity to rebuild itself with widened streets, open spaces, parks, and reasonable lot sizes. The fact that this was not even seriously considered is still seen as more of a tragedy by outsiders than by the business elites of Tokyo. These elites continue Japan's extremely successful emphasis on foreign exports and trade surpluses, while strongly resisting any meaningful national or municipal government spending on infrastructure. Thus far urban planning and development have taken a distinct back seat to export-oriented economic growth.

Planned Towns

There are, of course, some major exceptions. For example, Suma New Town, near Kobe, currently with a population exceeding 100,000, was built on reclaimed land. To provide land the tops of hills were literally blasted and bulldozed off, and the rock was then carried underground for miles to the sea on huge conveyer belts. The fill was then used to construct the artificial port and Rokko Islands in Kobe harbor. The inland project, which was officially dedicated in 1980, is estimated to have cost $2.5 billion.

Public housing, in new towns or elsewhere, is built for middle-class rather than low-income groups. The public Japan Housing Corporation, for example, is required by law to break even financially on the projects it constructs, and so rents are usually far more than the poor can afford. Limited public housing for low-income groups is built by the Metropolitan Housing Supply Corporation.

Suburbanization

Suburbanization has been a factor in Japan ever since the massive earthquake of 1923, which encouraged decentralization and until the last decade limited multistory dwellings to a height of 102 feet. The Japanese have a tradition of city living; and before World War II, the poor lived outside the municipal

---

[35]Clyde Haberman, "For Cramped Japan, 55 Million Bicycles Is a Glut," *New York Times,* March 4, 1985.

boundaries, particularly in marshy areas. A long commute to work in that era was a penalty of poverty rather than a perogative of affluence as in the United States.

More recently, high land costs have resulted in heavy middle-class and even upper-class suburbanization. Since commuting to and from suburbs is done largely by rail, the greatest suburban development has been along the very profitable suburban rail lines. (The average commute is 1.5 hours each way.) As land prices rise, the center of Tokyo is more and more given over to shops and commercial and business activities. The resident central-city population can be expected to decline further while suburban growth—some of it quite distant—accelerates.

SOUTHEAST ASIA

General Patterns

Most cities of southeast Asia—except in Thailand—are a product of European colonial expansion, Chinese enterprise, or a combination of the two.[36] This is somewhat of an exaggeration, but generally the pattern holds true. Cities in southeast Asia are relatively new. Few date back more than a century or so. Primate cities, particularly ports, are common. Most of the cities were clearly divided into western and nonwestern districts. Ho Chi Minh city, formerly Saigon, provides an example.

Saigon's urban history began in 1859, when the French captured a village of native huts, none of them permanent structures. On this site the French built Saigon as an administrative capital, laying out the streets in the grid pattern. The Chinese quarter and marketplace, known as Cholon, developed simultaneously with Saigon. Thus Saigon became the French colonial capital for Cochin China, later named Vietnam, while Cholon was the Chinese city. Early growth in Saigon was orderly, while Cholon grew haphazardly. The two areas were merged by the French in 1932 for administrative purposes.

Before World War II, the largest population group in Saigon-Cholon was Chinese.[37] From about 300,000 inhabitants in 1940, the population increased to an estimated 1,400,000 by 1953.[38] Roughly 60 percent of Cholon, and 30 percent of the entire city, was Chinese at this time. More recently the government of Vietnam has been expelling the Chinese, fearing that they dominate the economy and constitute a potential "fifth column" loyal to China. The majority of the early so-called Vietnamese "boat people" fleeing Vietnam were in fact ethnic Chinese.

[36]Norton S. Ginsburg, "Urban Geography and 'Non-Western' Areas," in Philip M. Hauser and Leo F. Schnore (eds.), *The Study of Urbanization,*Wiley, New York, 1965, p. 332.

[37]Norton S. Ginsburg, "The Great City in Southeast Asia," *American Journal of Sociology,* **60**:459, March, 1955.

[38]D. W. Fryer, "The Million City in Southeast Asia," *Geographical Review,* **43**:477, October, 1953.

Singapore

The modern island Republic of Singapore is quite atypical of southeast Asia.[39] Whether this is good or bad depends on the perspective of the observer. Economically there is no question that, in spite of the total absence of natural resources (Singapore even has to import sand for building), the country is prosperous. Singapore has some 2.4 million persons in an area of only 225 square miles (584 square kilometers), making it one of the most densely crowded areas on the globe. Singapore has roughly ten times the density of Holland, which is the most densely populated western country. Officially Singapore is 100 percent urban, although some semirural areas remain.

What makes Singapore unique, though, is its strategy for control and development. Since independence in 1965 the government has been involved in an ambitious program to replace virtually all of Singapore's previous housing with high-rise apartment buildings. Slums and squatter settlements have been eradicated, sometimes by the use of draconian measures. The old Chinese neighborhoods of street vendors and dilapidated overcrowded buildings so dear to the hearts of travelers and the Malay *kampongs* (villages) have been replaced almost entirely by government-sponsored high-rise estates and new office buildings and hotels. Currently, over three-quarters of the population reside in government-built high-rise housing estates. By 1995 some 85 percent of the population will live in government-built housing. Singapore is also rapidly building several new towns—also of high-rises—the largest of which is Woodlands New Town, with a population of 290,000.

The rapid transformation of Singapore into an ultramodern city, however, is not without its critics. Some charge that too much of the traditional culture has been sacrificed to the god of efficiency. For example, once government planners decide to rebuild a district, the land is compulsorily acquired; and although compensation is paid, neither litigation by owners nor public protests by residents will stop redevelopment. If an ancient temple sits on land desired for redevelopment, the temple is either moved or rebuilt elsewhere.

Singapore's sharp break with the past has both advantages and disadvantages. While the high-rise structures are not as effective as the old *kampongs* and squatter settlements in fostering community ties and close human relationships, they do provide better housing and living facilities for the majority of the population.[40] Compared with high-rise housing projects in the United States, the buildings are well maintained. Perhaps this is because, as a result of government policy, more residents own than rent their flats.

Under the government's "home ownership for the people" scheme, residents can draw upon their mandatory social security payments for the down payment and even monthly payments for their flats. Two-thirds (64 percent) of those living in the government-built housing estates are engaged in purchasing their apartments. Most apartments are still relatively small, but it

---

[39] The author was a visiting professor at the National University of Singapore in 1983–1984.

[40] Peter S. J. Chen and Tai Ching Ling: *Social Ecology of Singapore,* Federal Publications, Singapore, 1977.

is not uncommon for a family to spend a considerable amount upgrading and redecorating its flat. The Housing and Development Board has "thinned out" some of the earlier projects by tearing down every second building. At the same time it is phasing out one-room flats by converting them to two-room units. Singapore is thus in the unique positon of having solved in two decades its physical housing problems, insofar as government-built housing of standard quality is available to most residents.

Whether the high-rise projects can meet the social and community needs of the populace remains to be seen. Singaporeans enjoy one of the highest standards of living in Asia, with a per capita income second only to that of Japan.[41] Economic prosperity has resulted in so many automobiles that to control congestion and pollution, cars not having an expensive entry permit are banned from the center of the city during working hours. The city is also engaged in a major program of beautification by planting trees and bushes along the roadways. (Because Singapore is near the equator, newly planted trees grow rapidly along the streets and around the housing projects.)

Overall, Singaporeans live in a tightly controlled society where efficiency ranks well ahead of participation by citizens in making decisions. Regulations, even on littering (a $225 fine), are enforced. Today Singapore is a modern commercial city. If it isn't as quaint, colorful, and interesting as in the old days, that is a price most residents seem willing to pay.

CONCLUSION

Everywhere in Asia urbanization and urbanism are increasing rapidly, if not spectacularly. Even in China, where government policies strongly encourage birth control, the cities are inevitably going to grow, since the Chinese government is also encouraging industrial development and trade.

Individual cities are frequently immense, but the overall level of urbanization is still relatively low. This is certain to change. Looking at Asia as a whole, it is quite possible to assume that by the year 2000 as many as half of all Asians will be city dwellers. Asian cities will be booming well into the next century.

Generalizing beyond this point for the entire region is impossible, since the outstanding characteristic of the area is its diversity. Many of the urban problems may be similar, but the solutions to date have differed widely both in content and degree of success.

Japan is by far the most urbanized of the large nations of Asia and has the greatest resources, both technical and economic, that can be brought to bear on specific problems such as housing, sanitation, and transportation. China has immense human resources but a far more limited technical base. Thus far it has managed potential urban problems by controlling urban

---

[41]Thai-Ker Lin, "Housing Policies and Life Style," paper presented at High Rise, High Density Housing Conference, Singapore, September 5–9, 1983.

population growth. Indian cities, by contrast, come closer to the old "teeming masses of Asia" stereotype. Rapid population growth has severly strained the physical capabilities of the cities to house, educate, and employ their residents. Indian cities, though, possess vitality, color, and even safety that other nations might envy.

It has to be kept in mind that everywhere in Asia the cities, even with all their very real problems, are not places of defeat and despair but of hope and life. Clichés such as the "death of the city" have little meaning in the Asian context.

CHAPTER
16

AFRICAN AND MIDDLE EASTERN URBANIZATION

There is always something new out of Africa.

Pliny the Younger (A.D. 62–113)

AFRICA

Africa is currently the least urbanized of the continents. As of 1985, 31 percent of its inhabitants lived in urban places. At the same time, however, Africa is the continent with the highest rate of increase in urban population (4.8 percent).[1] In 1950 there were only three sub-Saharan African cities of more than half a million; today there are twenty-nine. The population of the continent as a whole is estimated to be 551 million.[2]

The United Nations estimated the mid-1984 population of sub-Saharan Africa's forty-two nations at 434 million, with an annual growth rate of 3.1 percent—up from 2.5 percent in the 1960s—and rising. Birthrates are collectively the world's highest at 48 per 1000. Death rates average 17 per 1000, and are falling. (Comparable U.S. birthrates and death rates are fifteen and nine.) sub-Saharan cities are growing by an average of almost 6 percent a year—an astounding rate. Sub-Saharan population is projected to more than triple to 1.4 billion in the next 40 years. This is a key factor in the food crises that have been wracking sub-Saharan Africa.

Population control is still not recognized by most governments as a major factor in economic development. Indeed, a few African nations still have official policies encouraging more rapid population growth. At the same time, per capital agricultural productivity is lower than it was in 1970, and as of 1985 some 150 million people in twenty-two countries were facing hunger and malnourishment. Per capita income in 1984 in Sub-Saharan Africa was 4 percent lower than it was in 1970.[3]

Although nearly self-sufficient in food in 1970, sub-Saharan Africa had to import one-fifth of its grain requirements by 1984. As a consequence, when drought strikes, its effects are far more severe than might otherwise be the case.

Regional Variations

Africa has some fifty separate nations, and African cities vary greatly; the major regional distinction is between the cities of north Africa and those of sub-Saharan Africa. North Africa is the most urbanized of the African regions. All the countries bordering the Mediterranean Sea have between two-fifths and three-fifths of their population in places of 20,000 or more inhabitants. This is not at all surprising when one considers the great civilizations this region has produced and its superior location for the development of trade centers. Also, away from the coast much of the land of north Africa is either mountainous or arid desert and hardly suited for urban growth (the Nile Valley

---

[1]Philip Hauser and Robert Gardiner, "Urban Future: Trends and Prospects," in Philip Hauser et al. (eds.), *Population and the Urban Future*, State University of New York, Albany, 1982, p. 8.

[2]Population Reference Bureau, "1985 World Population Data Sheet," Washington, D.C., 1985.

[3]World Bank, "Toward Development in Sub-Saharan Africa: A Joint Program of Action," Washington, D.C., 1984, p. 1.

Nairobi is the expanding capitol of Kenya, the nation with the highest birthrate on earth. (© Georg Gerster/Photo Researchers)

being the obvious exception). Thus the population is highly concentrated in a limited area.

West and central Africa lie in the middle range of African urbanization—ranging between 8 percent in Burkina Faso (Upper Volta) to 60 percent in Equatorial Guinea.[4]

The larger cities are located along, or within easy access to, the coast. Their founding and development can almost always be tied to their role as colonial entrepôt cities. Of the west African countries, oil-rich Nigeria, with 92 million inhabitants, is the largest and has by far the most cities. The World Bank projects that Nigeria's population could increase to 618 million a century from now.[5]

East Africa is the least urbanized part of the continent.[6] It does not have a tradition of cities: only Zimbabwe and Zambia have as much as one-sixth of their populations in cities over 20,000. Tanzania, for example, has roughly 14 percent of its population in cities.

It should be noted that virtually none of what can be said regarding the rest of sub-Saharan Africa applies to white-ruled southern Africa. The Republic of South Africa is easily the most industrialized nation on the continent, with

[4]Population Reference Bureau, op. cit.

[5]Thomas J. Goliber, "Sub-Saharan Africa: Population Pressures and Development," *Population Bulletin*, **40**(1):3, 1985.

[6]Edward Soja, "Spatial Inequality in Africa," *Comparative Urbanization Studies*, University of California School of Architecture and Urban Planning, Los Angeles, 1976.

half (53 percent) of its population in urban places. In terms of economic position South Africa, with its gold reserves and industrial base, is a world economic power. In South African cities the government policy of *apartheid,* or forced racial segregation, has resulted in a conscious division of the major cities into African, European, Indian, and "Coloured" (mixed-race) areas.[7] Each of the populations is allotted specific areas in which, and only in which, they can purchase property. For South Africa, race overrides all other criteria in determining the spatial development of the city.

Early Cities

One sometimes hears considerable nonsense about African cities before the nineteenth-century colonial period. Until a decade or two ago, a reading of the literature gave the impression that there were few, if any, indigenous African cities south of the Sahara. This was due partially to a colonial mentality which did not admit the possibility that "backward natives" were capable of building cities, and partially due to a lack of serious research on African history.

Scholars from Muslim Africa also have been prone to minimize the contributions of black Africa. For instance, one writer suggests that "historic (or ancient) capitals are confined to Arab Africa" and "Native" (or Medieval) capitals are in fact a transition between the historical and colonial capitals. . . . "Culturally, they are universally associated in one way or another with intrusive, alien influences, mainly Arab and generally Asian."[8]

More recently, the pendulum swung in the opposite direction. Trading centers such as Timbuktu (whose current population is approximately 6,000 poverty-stricken inhabitants) were elevated to the status of major metropolises, a position they occupied for only relatively short periods of time, if at all. On the other hand the region did produce cities, some of which had considerable importance, especially during the Ghana, Mali, and Songhay empires of west Africa (roughly the eleventh to late sixteenth centuries).

Of all African cities, those of north Africa have the longest urban traditions. Alexandria was founded by its namesake, Alexander the Great, in 332 B.C., but settlements on that location go back at least another 1,000 years. The north African city of Carthage, until it was destroyed, was the greatest rival of Rome. During the height of the Roman Empire, north Africa was dotted with important cities, some of which may have contained as much as 25 percent of the population of their regions.[9] With the decline of the Roman Empire these cities suffered the same fate as Roman cities in Europe. Over time, most of them disappeared—although, again as in Europe, newer cities now sometimes sit over the ancient ruins.

Elsewhere in Africa, many cities were first built during the peak of Muslim

---

[7]Lutz Holzner, "Urbanism in Southern Africa," *Geogorum,* **4:**75–90, 1970.

[8]G. Hamdan, "Capitals of the New Africa," *Economic Geography,* **40:**239–241, July, 1964.

[9]William A. Hance, *Population, Migration, and Urbanization in Africa,* Columbia University Press, New York, 1970, p. 211.

power. The revival of trade in the tenth century benefited not only north African cities such as Fez and Algiers but also sub-Saharan towns, including Kano in northern Nigeria. The Yoruba towns of southwest Nigeria also emerged at about this time, as did caravan centers such as Timbuktu. During the following centuries a number of west African kingdoms created capitals, but most of these capitals had short histories. Segou in Mali, Labe in Guinea, Zinder in Niger, and Kumasi in Ghana all rose and fell. These cities served their kingdoms primarily as market and trade centers.

Then, as now, east African cities were less numerous, with only a few Muslim towns, found generally along the coast of the Indian Ocean. Present cities such as Mogadishu in Somalia and Mombasa in Kenya prospered as Muslim trading centers. These towns served almost until the present century as centers for the trading in goods, and slaves from the interior, for shipment to Arabia.

The Colonial Period

European Influence. During the sixteenth century, the Portuguese founded the first European settlements. These were little more than fortified trading posts where goods from the interior could be collected and stored for shipment to Europe. Attempts by the Portuguese to extend their influence inland were unsuccessful. Their early successes in Ethiopia, for example, were short-lived, and Portuguese missionaries and traders were later expelled from that country.

Until the late nineteenth century, Europeans showed little interest in colonization. Cape Town in the Republic of South Africa, for example, was established by the Dutch East India Company only as a station to provide meat, fresh produce, and water to the Dutch ships on the way to the Indies.[10]

The seizure of land in black Africa by Europeans rapidly accelerated during the last quarter of the nineteenth century. Britain, France, Germany, Belgium, and Portugal all rushed in to carve up the continent into colonies. Important African cities of the present are largely the products of this colonialism, since each colony had to have an administrative capital. Major cities, founded during the colonial period, with the dates of their founding, are: Accra, Ghana (1876); Abidjan, Ivory Coast (1903); Port Harcourt, Nigeria (1912); Brazzaville, Congo (1883); Kinshasa, Zaire (formerly Leopoldville, Belgian Congo) (1881); Yaoundé, Cameron (1889); Kampala, Uganda (1890); Nairobi, Kenya (1899); and Johannesburg, South Africa (1886). Of the major new towns founded during this period, only Addis Ababa in Ethiopia (1886) and Omdurman in Sudan (1885) were indigenous creations.

Most of the cities of Africa are in actuality far newer than the dates mentioned above would indicate, for rapid increases in the populations of sub-Saharan African cities did not begin until somewhat over thirty years ago. Until World War II, most African cities were relatively small. Nairobi, one of

---

[10]H. M. Robertson, *South Africa,* Cambridge University Press, London, 1957, pp. 3–4.

the most pleasant of all African cities, had a population of only 20,000 in 1920 and only 33,000 in 1930. The population jumped to 200,000 in the 1950s, and today it is in excess of 1 million. The pattern is similar, and in many cases even more spectacular, in other African cities. Kinshasa, for example, has tripled its population in the last two decades. In spite of these increases, Africa still remains—as has been noted—the least urbanized of the world's major regions.

Colonial Cities. The colonial cities founded by Europeans did not grow out of the local culture. Rather, the layout of the city, its social and political organization, and even its architectural styles came from Europe. The government housing in Accra, Ghana, with its wide lawns and large single-family houses, looks like nothing so much as Victorian England. The centers of colonial cities were for the use and residence of Europeans. Nighttime curfews frequently prevented the entry of Africans into the European sections and the entry of Europeans into the African sections.

The colonial city was organized around the central district, which in addition to stores and other business offices also included the administrative offices of the colonial government. Streets were usually wide and crossed at right angles in a grid pattern. A description of Stanleyville (now Kisangani) is typical:

> The physical layout of the town could be seen as both an expression and a symbol of the relations between Africans and Europeans. European residential areas were situated close to, and tended to run into, the area of administrative offices, hotels, shops, and other service establishments, while African residential areas were strictly demarcated and well removed from the town centre.[11]

Spatial location thus reflected social power within colonial society.[12] Without significant industrialization, central residence was preferred. Africans who worked in the European center were in effect commuters from suburban locations—although, in this case, the suburbs were high-density indigenous communities. This is, of course, the complete reverse of the pattern in American industrial cities.

Indigenous Cities. Indigenous cities often were located next to colonial developments, but in other cases they were almost completely separate developments. In west Africa the most noted cities of strictly African origin are the Yoruba cities of Nigeria. Many of these cities have fairly large populations, although there is a continuing scholarly debate about whether these were and are true cities or extremely large agglomerations of basically agricultural villages. These are referred to in the literature as "rural cities," "city villages," or "agrotowns." In any case, the Yoruba cities had the largest

[11]V. G. Pons, cited by A. L. Epstein, "Urbanization and Social Change in Africa," *Current Anthropology,* 8:(4)277, 1967.
[12]Goeffrey K. Payne, *Urban Housing in the Third World,* Routledge & Kegan Paul, Boston, 1977, p. 53.

populations in sub-Saharan Africa before the colonial period. Ibidan as of 1850 had roughly 70,000 inhabitants. In east Africa many of the functions of towns, such as markets, took place at permanent sites—although residence was not one of the functions.[13]

Ecologically indigenous cities are not as sharply differentiated as western cities. In the indigenous city the main focus was and is the central market, which is commonly quite large and frequently out of doors rather than housed in buildings. Nearby are the quarters of the chief or ruling prince. The main mosque is also centrally located in Muslim cities. Historically, surrounding this central core were the quarters of the lesser chiefs and nobles. These areas contained not only the nobles but also their retainers, soldiers, followers, and servants. Each quarter was a self-contained city within the larger city. Much of this legacy persists today in cities such as Addis Ababa.

Frequently, quarters were divided on the basis of tribal or religious affiliation. Walls and gates sometimes separated the quarters from one another. Within a quarter, there was no overall plan or scheme. Streets wind in an irregular pattern and are suitable only for walking or animal traffic, since the lanes are narrow and buildings come right up to the passageway. Structures are rarely more than two stories high and are constructed of local materials. Congestion is common.

As these indigenous towns came under the control of colonial powers, a new administrative area on the European style was frequently appended to the periphery of the old city, and a major road or two would be cut through the old city to connect its center with the offices of the colonial administrators. Rarely did the indigenous city and the colonial city blend. Each was a separate entity; and though existing side by side, they frequently even followed different laws, with western legal systems applying only in the European quarters. In time, the European quarters expanded to include modern commercial and business districts. In a few cases, the modern city came completely to surround the old city. The Casbah in Algiers, for example, has long been completely enclosed by a modern city largely created by the French.

Contemporary Patterns

Primate Cities. The term "primate city" is clearly appropriate to the pattern of urbanization found in the independent black nations of sub-Saharan Africa. For example, as of 1980 57 percent of Kenya's urban population was found in Nairobi; 83 percent of Mozambique's, in Maputo; and half of Tanzania's, in Dar es Salaam; and half of Zimbabwe's, in Harare. Moreover, this urban primacy is increasing. As earlier noted, between 1970 and 1984 urban populations in sub-Saharan Africa grew at a rate of almost 6 percent annually.[14]

Cities—and most particularly the capital cities—are the dominant economic

[13]D. R. F. Taylor, "The Concept of Invisible Towns and Spatial Organization in East Africa," *Comparative Urban Research,* **5:**44–70, 1978.
[14]Population Reference Bureau, "The Food Crisis in sub-Saharan Africa," *Interchange,* **14:**2, March, 1985.

force, the seats of government, the cultural centers, and the hubs of transportation and communication networks. The primate city is the manufacturing center, the break-of-bulk transportation node, the major market, and the financial center.

The dominance of the primate cities is easy to document. Dakar, for example, which has only 16 percent of the population of Senegal, consumes 95 percent of all the electricity in the country and accounts for three-quarters of its commercial and manufacturing workers and over half its employees in transportation, administration, and other services.

The importance of the primate cities is heightened by the economic separation of the major city from the surrounding countryside. Africa is noted for a sharp break between the modernizing city and the tribal "bush." Urban influences are concentrated in the cities themselves. There is little of the American pattern, in which the city gradually tapers off and becomes the countryside. Going a few miles into the bush can take someone not only away from built-up areas but also away from the major influence of modernization.

The physical size and structure of the primate city is the most visible sign of its dominance, but its social role as the breaker of the cake of custom is even more significant. The primate cities "are not merely the focal points where the break with tradition can be seen most clearly, but also the centers in which a major restructuring of African society as a whole is taking place."[15] Just how deep into the countryside major restructuring has penetrated is, of course, open to some dispute. But that change is taking place in the cities is accepted by all.

The association between the growth of cities and the rise of African independence movements has been commented upon by many observers. In Africa the city is the incubator of social change. More than on any other continent, the city not only towers over the countryside but controls it economically, educationally, politically, and socially.

Squatter Slums. *Bidonvilles* ("tin-can cities") or squatter settlements are a standard part of the "suburban" landscape of every growing African city. They house up to one-third of the total urban population. The rapid population growth of recent years, along with the push from the land, has resulted in an explosive expansion of the urban population without a proportionate increase in city housing.

As a result, *bidonvilles* are a fact of city life, from Casablanca in the north (180,000 residents in shantytowns) to Lusaka in the south (100,000 in shantytowns). Most governments simply do not have the resources to engage in massive housing programs. Even a relatively affluent country such as the Ivory Coast has not been able to begin to meet the housing demand. Improvements in central-city housing act as magnets drawing ever more rural newcomers.

---

[15]Peter C. Gutkind, "The African Urban Milieu: A Force for Rapid Change," *Civilizations,* **12:**185, 1962.

A Case Study of One Indigenous City

Indigenous cities are most common in north and west Africa. In east Africa the most notable indigenous city is Addis Ababa, Ethiopia. Although founded in 1886 at the height of European colonial expansion, the city was an authentically African creation.*

Addis Ababa (the name means "new flower") was not originally intended to be a permanent city. Rather, it was founded by Emperor Menelik II as a temporary capital. Having no urban tradition, the Ethiopian emperors moved their capital from time to time as military factors, weather, or exhaustion of local resources (food and firewood) dictated. Addis Ababa— which was Menelik's eighth capital—was laid out as an armed camp. The emperor chose for his *guebi*, or palace, a hill above the northern thermal springs and then allotted various surrounding quarters, known as *sefers*, to his leading nobles. Social organization was strongly feudalistic. Each *sefer*— literally, "camp"—included the residence of an important noble plus all the noble's warriors, troops, retainers, and slaves and their families. No distinctly upper- or lower-class areas were initially developed, as was the case in cities founded by Europeans. The effect of this original organization as an armed camp can still be clearly seen in the city's social, economic, and ethnic arrangements.

Early visitors to Addis Ababa universally commented that it resembled a large straggling village more than a city.† Further contributing to this impression of a large floating camp were fluctuations in the city's population. The normal population around 1910 was roughly 60,000; during the rainy season, it sometimes dropped to as low as 40,000‡ When important chiefs came to the capital, they brought their entire armies and households with them. There are reports of chiefs who brought 100,000 to 150,000 people with them, and even as late as 1915 it was not unusual for a governor to bring 30,000 to 50,000 people along as a personal guarantee of safety.

As the city grew, its eastern side surrounding the palace gradually developed into the administrative center, while the

---

*J. John Palen, "Urbanization and Migration in an Indigenous City: The Case of Addis Ababa," in Anthony Richmond and Daniel Kubat (eds.), *Internal Migration*, Sage Publications, London, 1976.

†Docteur Merab, *Impressions d'Ethiopie*, vol. 2, Leroux, Paris, 1921–1923, p. 11.

‡Richard Pankhurst, "Notes on the Demographic History of Ethiopian Towns and Villages," *The Ethiopian Observer*, 9:71, 1965.

western zone surrounding the old marketplace, or *mercado*, became the commercial center. Because the ruling Amhara tribe despised any type of commercial activity or trade, business activities were relegated to subordinate tribes. The Amhara concentrated their attentions on ruling, farming, and mounting expeditions to the south to capture more slaves.

Haile Selassie I ruled the country, first as regent and then as emperor, from 1916 to 1973. Since then, Ethiopia has been a Marxist state. Haile Selassie officially decreed the end of slavery in the early 1920s, but this was not observed to any large degree inside the city and virtually not at all outside. It is estimated that 25,000 of the 60,000 inhabitants of the city were slaves in 1910. Today slavery in the true sense is gone. However, the descendants of slaves—the Shanquellas, Sidamo, Gurages, and some of the darker-skinned Gallas— still are at the bottom of the social ladder; the men serve largely as *zabanias* (guards for houses and walled compounds) and the women as domestic maids or *mamitas* (children's nurses).

The Italians occupied Ethiopia from 1936 to 1941. They envisioned Addis Ababa as the capital of their sub-Saharan African empire and engaged heavily in building, constructing the country's first road network—five roads radiating outward from the capital. These roads, which still make up the basic road network, ensured that Addis Ababa would become the transportation and administration center of the country. The Italians also constructed a new market area, known as the Piazza, east of the traditional market, and built a road from this new market to the small railway station at the southern end of the city. The southern end of the city, which is somewhat lower in altitude and thus warmer, was set aside as the Italian residential area. A southward movement has been characteristic of the city since this time. Most of the newer European-style villas and high-rise apartments are in the southern area.

Today the radius of the city is about four to five miles, with the most heavily built-up area roughly in the center. Although its present population is over 1 million, Addis Ababa still essentially retains its nonurban character. Most of the housing units are still constructed of *chica*—a mixture of earth, straw, and water plastered around eucalyptus poles. The ever-present and fast-growing eucalyptus trees also serve to give the city a small-town appearance by masking the houses. The trees do a yeoman service, since they provide firewood for all heating and cooking, lumber for building, and wood for furniture. Even the leaves are used in baking the Ethiopian bread, called *injera*.

The rural feeling of the city is also partially due to the fact that Addis Ababa is a city of rural migrants. Three-quarters of the inhabitants were not born in the city, and the continuing warfare with Somalia and the Eritrean Liberation Front has encouraged greater movement to the city, as of course have the disastrous famines of 1984 and 1985.

In terms of its functional base, Addis Ababa is still primarily a political and administrative center. All major Ethiopian government agencies, all foreign embassies, the United Nations Economic Commission for Africa, and the Organization of African Unity are located in the capital. Recently there have been noticeable increases in several sectors: transportation, communications, manufacturing, and education. Industrialization is growing but is still, relatively speaking, in its infancy, with all capital goods being imported. Retail trade is also growing, but is oriented largely to Addis Ababa itself. Tradition, which gives low status to those working with their hands, has inhibited the development of handicraft industries. Weavers, for example, are still believed by some to possess the evil eye.

Transportation to and from the city is still primitive, particularly for goods. With the sole narrow-gage railroad connecting Addis Ababa and the port of Djibouti often closed because of warfare, goods from the outside must come by air. The large continent of Cuban troops used to support the government in power is brought in and supplied mostly by air. Each day thousands of donkeys also bring wood, hay, and produce into the city from surrounding areas, but they are being supplanted by large, overloaded trucks.

Addis Ababa is both a feudal city and a modern city. It is an overgrown village and the headquarters of the United Nations Economic Commission for Africa. It has high-rise apartments, but still no sanitary sewers. For better or worse, it represents the future.

Compounding the problem is the inability of the increasing urban population to pay even the minimal rents that government-built housing would require. Food and clothing generally absorb from two-thirds to nine-tenths of a newcomer's income.[16] That doesn't leave much for extras such as decent housing. Shantytowns with homes of packing crates, scrap metal, or mud and wattle thus will be part of the urban scene for years to come.

Lagos: An Example of Urban Growing Pains. Lagos, the capital of Nigeria, provides an example of the difficulties facing even relatively affluent metropolises. Lagos has grown from a city of just over a million residents in 1963 to a metropolis of over 4.5 million today. Because of oil revenues, Lagos is far better off than many growing cities, but it is nonetheless unable to keep up with its need for roadways, sewers, housing, and efficient government.

Some of the problems stem from the city's location. Lagos was originally founded on a narrow island close to the coast. This made considerable sense when the concern was defending a trading post; but today the island is the crowded center of the city, and the lagoon separating it from the mainland is a foul-smelling, polluted sewer. There are currently only two bridges connecting the island with the mainland. At peak traffic hours, it can take forty-five minutes just to get over the bridge. Urban problems apparently can be exported to developing countries more rapidly than urban solutions.

Population growth by in-migration is about 10 percent per annum, and the many local state and federal governments and agencies often seem to work at cross purposes.[17] While new, expensive, high-rise buildings were constructed during the last decade, the open street drains continue to overflow, refuse collection is erratic, and big, overloaded trucks continue to tear up colonial-era roads.

If comparatively economically affluent cities such as Lagos in Nigeria or Abidjan in the Ivory Coast are having growth pains, the problems of poorer countries are far more severe. Dar es Salaam in Tanzania, for instance, is quite visibly decaying. The run-down buildings emphasize the country's status as one of the world's twenty-five poorest. Unlike other countries, Tanzania's socialist government has virtually ignored its capital while emphasizing the total resettlement of the agricultural population in new communal agricultural villages.

The Economic Picture

Colonialism may be dead, but the economic effects of exploitation linger on. Overdependence on a single crop or mineral resource leaves many countries vulnerable to fluctuations in world market prices. Ghana was set back by two decades of depressed cocoa prices; Ethiopia is affected by fluctuations in the

[16]Hance, op. cit., p. 286.
[17]Rasheed Gbadamosi, "Growing Pains in Lagos," *Draper World Population Fund Report*, Spring, 1976, pp. 15–17.

price of coffee; Liberia is subject to fluctuations in the price of crude rubber; Zambia depends on the price of copper. It is difficult to plan a development budget under such circumstances.

Economically, sub-Saharan Africa is in serious trouble. Over two dozen countries have a negative rate of economic growth, while the total foreign debt mounts alarmingly. The Organization of African Unity (OAU) in 1985 adopted a declaration that most of the continent's countries are near "economic collapse."[18] The infrastructure of roads, buildings, and sewers has been allowed to deteriorate (the Ivory Coast is an exception). Poor planning, political instability, and widespread corruption have contributed to the deteriorating economic picture.

Agriculture. Problems are particularly severe in the crucial agricultural sector. As of late 1984, the U.N. Food and Agriculture Organization reported that nineteen sub-Saharan countries containing 190 million people required massive food aid to avert famine.[19] The immediate cause was drought, but the long-range cause was twenty-five years of declining per capita food production.[20] The result, as mentioned earlier, is that while sub-Saharan Africa was agriculturally self-sufficient in 1960, it now imports one-fifth of its grain needs.

Stagnation in this crucial area is generally attributed to inefficient methods of farming and, most important, government policies that have deliberately depressed agricultural prices to benefit urban dwellers at the farmers' expense. As a result, nations whose economies are based on agriculture find themselves in the unfortunate position of importing foodstuffs.

In a report on Africa's economic development the OAU acknowledged that "Africa in particular is unable to point to any significant growth rate or satisfactory index of general well-being" in almost two decades of independence.[21] It was noted that per capita income in Africa is still the world's lowest, and infant mortality rates are among the world's highest.

The proposed solutions were the avoidance of the "narrow nationalism" that hinders regional development, and the establishment of an African common market to pool strength and avoid uneconomic duplication. However, given the political and economic realities, these are not likely developments. While it would be pleasant to predict a better future for all the developing African countries, the economic facts of life indicate that this is unrealistic. Developing countries that have few natural or other resources are almost certain to see the gap between themselves and the developed world widen rather than close unless the present pattern and rate of investment and aid are radically increased.

---

[18]"Africa Near 'Economic Collapse,' OAU Says," *New York Times*, July 21, 1985.

[19]U.N. Food and Agriculture Organization, "Brief on the 1984–85 Cereal Import and Food Aid Needs for 21 African Countries," Rome, December 5, 1984.

[20]World Book, op. cit.

[21]Quoted in Leon Dash, "African Leaders Have Seen the Future and It Looks Bleak," *Washington Post Service*, July 29, 1979.

When men migrate to the cities seeking employment, women are often left to till the soil. (Beryl Goldberg)

Urban Growth. Regardless of the extent of economic growth, continued urban growth is clearly the pattern for as far into the future as anyone cares to project. There really is little alternative. Many semiarid agricultural and grazing areas are already overused. Remaining in the area of one's birth, and further raising the density of the area, is not a reasonable alternative for those who hope to better their way of life. The opening up of new lands not previously used for settlement requires costs far out of proportion to the possible returns. The cost of providing necessary services—water, roads, schools, housing— would be extremely high. In east Africa it would also involve a political decision to destroy many of the remaining game parks and wildlife refuges, since there is little other land that is not already being used.[22]

The following description of the situation in Tanzania a score of years ago could be applied equally well today to the social, political, and economic situation in other African countries.

> Almost 45 percent of the population is under sixteen, and raises immediate political issues. The economy will have to expand in the industrial and cash-crop sectors if these people are not to be either unemployed workers in the cities or subsistence farmers. Many youths are migrating to the towns, producing a severe strain on the social services. Unemployed or semi-employed youth, loitering in the streets or

[22]For a discussion of some of the problems in Kenya, see Dick Oloo (ed.), *Urbanization: Its Social Problems and Consequences,* Kenya National Council of Social Service, Nairobi, 1969.

waiting around TANU offices for small jobs, begin to be a political problem. Party leaders are aware of them; but haranguing against loiters, telling unemployed youth to go and farm, and even restricting people's freedom to come to Dar es Salaam has not dissuaded youth from accumulating in the towns.[23]

Finding employment for the masses in the cities is an increasingly serious problem. Urbanization is clearly the wave of the African future, but whether it will mean economic development is still problematic. Another pressing problem in African cities is housing. Kenya, for example, will require 3 million new housing units to accommodate the projected increase in urban dwellers between 1980 and 2010.[24] This is roughly equivalent to constructing fifteen new Nairobis in thirty years.

Some west African governments have tried to stem the migrant tide by passing legislation providing for the repatriation of unwanted new workers back to their villages and setting stiff prison terms for those who return to the city. Repatriation has not proved successful: Workers either drift back to the city or are replaced by others. Other governments have tried to increase the attractiveness of rural villages and to settle unemployed urban populations in new, self-contained communal villages. Both of these approaches are expensive, and as a result seldom move beyond the planning or pilot-project stage. Such schemes have difficulty competing for scarce govermental funds. Moreover, the pressures driving younger people to the cities are social as well as economic and are not likely to be solved by such government programs as can be presently implemented.

The construction of low-cost houses or flats cannot come near to meeting the need for new housing. Abidjan in the Ivory Coast is doing better than most; it constructs roughly 1,200 government units annually, but the need is for between 6,000 and 8,000 units annually. As a result, governments are coming more and more to accept the idea of aiding in the construction of reasonably planned slums which at least have minimal urban amenities such as an available water supply, roads, and group sanitary facilities for the disposal of human waste.

Zambia adopted a "site and service" scheme, by which a township is laid out and a prospective builder is given a plot and a loan of $50 to buy necessary building materials, such as cement for the floor or a corrugated iron roof. After that, the builders are for all intents and purposes on their own. The rationale underlying this approach is that the goal of the government should not be to build housing but to raise the standard of living. Slum dwellers don't need more prodding to improve their living conditions; what they need is more money. As shanty dwellers get decent jobs and begin to make some money, they begin to improve their housing on their own.

---

[23]Henry Bienen, *Tanzania: Party Transformation and Economic Development,* Princeton University Press, Princeton, N.J., 1970, p. 265. Reprinted by permission of Princeton University Press.
[24]Goliber, op. cit.

Social Composition of Contemporary African Cities. The recent explosive growth of urban areas means that the majority of the adults in the cities were not born there but are in-migrants. The African city is a city of newcomers. In Abidjan, only 7 percent of those over twenty years of age were actually born in the city. Research by the author shows that over three-quarters of the inhabitants of Addis Ababa over fifteen years of age were born outside the city and are thus migrants.

The sociologist Louis Wirth's view of the city as a place where social relations are dominated by the labor market and contacts with others are superficial, impersonal, and transitory is only partially accurate as a description of African urbanism. There is no question that some of the disorganizing aspects of urbanism posited by Wirth can be found in any large African city. Family life sometimes breaks down, and prostitution is common. The latter situation is partially due to urban sex ratios, which are typified by disproportionate numbers of males. The situation is reasonable in west Africa, where in the cities there is a ratio of roughly 95 females to every 100 urban males. However, in middle Africa there are only about 85 females per 100 males, and in parts of east Africa there are only 55 to 75 females per 100 urban males. The situation is most extreme in South Africa, where government policy prevents workers from bringing their wives to the cities. The resulting abnormal family situations encourage drunkenness, gambling, prostitution, and violent crime. The situation is not unlike that found in the towns of the American west before the arrival of the homesteaders with their families.

Problems of psychological maladjustment appear as a rule to be far rarer than Wirth's thesis would suggest. The town may be a new experience, but since a major proportion of the townspeople were once migrants themselves, almost all newcomers know someone in the city who will take them in and who will help them adjust to urban life. Family ties and wider kinship ties are surprisingly strong and resilient to urban pressures. Relatives are expected to take the newcomers in and provide for their basic needs until they can get on their feet. A migrant who does get a job is then expected to contribute to providing for the family.

In the cities tradition and modern ways often blend. An example of such blending is the use of both courts and traditional agents to resolve conflicts.[25] Outside observers are struck by the ebullience, gusto, and camaraderie found in African towns, particularly in west Africa. A description of Dar es Salaam fits other African cities equally well:

> It would be difficult to find a single African who arrived in Dar-es-Salaam knowing not a soul. . . . Almost every African who decides to come comes to a known address, where lives a known relation; this relation will meet him, take him in and

---

[25]Michael J. Lowy, "Me Ko Court: The Impact of Urbanization on Conflict Resolution in a Ghanaian Town," in George Foster and Robert Kemper (eds.), *Anthropologists in Cities,* Little, Brown, Boston, 1974, pp. 153–177.

feed him and show him the ropes, help him seek a job . . . until he considers himself able to launch out for himself and take a room of his own.[26]

It is well to keep in mind that the pull of the town is not uniform for all groups. The Masai of Kenya, although pressured by the Kenyan government to rationalize their agriculture and adopt modern ways, have consistently rejected town life in favor of their traditional rural culture. The Ila of Zambia have also rejected urbanization and modernization. Both tribes seem to be an embarrassment to their national governments because they don't want to "modernize." The Kenyan government plans to divide up the Masai communal lands and give each family individual plots. A similar program was tried by the United States government to modernize the American Indians, with the result that many Indians lost their lands. There are indications that the same fate awaits the Masai. It is quite possible that by the year 2000 the self-reliant virtues and warrior strengths of the Masai will be praised in every local Kenyan schoolbook but that by then the independent Masai culture may have been effectively destroyed.

Tribal and Ethnic Bonds. Urbanization is supposed to weaken traditional bonds, but it can be argued that urbanization in Africa has strengthened rather than weakened tribal identification.[27] The immigrant, rather than being "de-tribalized," is "supertribalized" as a result of coming into contact, for perhaps the first time, with people from other cultures. Tribal origin usually replaces kinship as a symbol of belonging. This is an expansion of identity from the parochial to the more general.

The role played by cultural or tribal subsystems in modernizing societies is analogous to that played by immigrant enclaves in the American city of several decades ago. Cultural, ethnic, tribal, class, or occupational groupings perform a number of functions not only for the newcomer but for the society at large. First, the tribal, ethnic, or other group introduces newcomers to others in the city and indoctrinates them into the ways of the city. Information on such matters as where to live, how to get a job, and how to avoid the police is transmitted to migrants in order to aid their adaptation to the city. Second, the subgroup, being originally itself a part of the rural culture, maintains within the city many rural customs and traditions. While learning the new ways, migrants will still have some contact with their past. Third, because migrants return to rural areas for periods of time, and because there is a pattern of visiting between rural villages and the city, the customs and ways of the city (urbanism) are spread to villages—so that patterns of urbanism are gradually being diffused throughout rural areas.[28]

Kinship and tribal affiliation provide bridges by which the migrant crosses

---

[26]J. A. K. Leslie, *A Social Survey of Dar es Salaam,* Oxford University Press—The East African Institute, London, 1963, p. 33.

[27]William John Hanna and Judith Lynne Hanna, *Urban Dynamics in Black Africa,* Aldine-Atherton, Chicago, 1971, p. 107.

[28]Gideon Sjoberg, "Cities in Developing and in Industrial Societies: A Cross-Cultural Analysis," in Philip M. Hauser and Leo F. Schnore (eds.), *The Study of Urbanization,* Wiley, New York, 1965, pp. 226–227.

into the urban arena. Being a member of a tribe gives a newcomer an immediate identification that is recognized by everyone. It tells the newcomer how to behave, and it provides a more or less ready-made group of associates, friends, and even drinking partners. While tribalism may have negative effects in a country seeking to develop national rather than tribal loyalties, on the individual level one's tribal membership eases the adjustment to city life.

Status of Women. It is difficult to make generalizations about the position of women in Africa, since this varies from country to country and from one tribal and cultural group to another. Stilll, several overall statements can be made. It is generally safe to say that norms, attitudes, and values in Africa have a long history of strongly favoring male dominance. It is also clear that, regardless of other factors, cities are far more equalitarian in practice than the countryside. Urban populations are young, new to urban life, and more flexible than their rural counterparts.

In Ghana "mammy wagons" (small buses) dominate local transportation. Ghanaian women are noted throughout the continent for their organizing skills. Ninety percent of the retailing of food and other goods is controlled and operated by women. Even in north African Muslim cultures, where the status of females has been traditionally inferior, changes are taking place in the education of women and participation by women in national life—Libya, with its strongly traditionalist internal policies, being the major exception.

Nonetheless, while the overall situation is improving, women have yet to attain equal status with men. Among the elites, western ideology—particularly Christian missions, with their doctrine of equality of marriage partners and schools open to both sexes—generally fostered equality.[29] However, no African nation at the time of this writing has a woman head of government or any women in the very top policymaking positions. Women are also underrepresented in the education system, with roughly two boys at school for every girl in most countries.[30]

In the bush and in rural villages, the position of women is set by custom; but in the city, with its new occupations and skills, the occupational structure is more flexible. Urban occupations may be so new that they are not yet sex-defined. Skills and professional training of all sorts are usually in short supply, so that the woman who has had the benefit of education and training can generally use her training. On the other hand, women (or men, for that matter) without specific skills or abilities are likely to remain locked into poverty. While it is true that trained women participate in the social and economic life of the city to an extent unknown in the countryside, it is also true that for lower-class women without husbands there frequently is little alternative to prostitution and other marginal economic enterprises.

Further clouding the situation is the problem of distinguishing between

[29]Ester Boserup, *Women's Role in Economic Development*, St. Martin's Press, New York, 1970.
[30]Josef Gugler and William G. Flanagan, *Urbanization and Social Change in West Africa*, Cambridge University Press, London, 1978, p. 136–137.

Women play a major role in the market economy of West Africa.
This market is in Abidjan, Ivory Coast. (Marc & Evelyne Bernheim/
Woodfin Camp & Assoc.)

the normative beliefs regarding the position of women and the actual practice
in the cities. Laws based on western models may specify equality in the civil
code while customary marriage practices continue.[31] On the other hand, in
Muslim countries, where the position of women may be legally inferior, the
actual practice, for economic and social reasons, may be more equal.

Differences from the Western Pattern. The geographer William Hance has
assembled a number of characteristics differentiating between urban growth
in Africa and urban growth in the west during the nineteenth century. These
differences highlight certain aspects of African urbanization that differ from
the western experience. The points of difference Hance notes are as follows:

1. The rates of growth, particularly of the major cities, are much more rapid
   in Africa. Some have achieved their present position in one-fifth to one-
   tenth the time required in western Europe.
2. There is less correlation—association—between the cities' rate of growth
   and the measures of economic growth in their countries.

[31]Alain A. Levasseur, "The Modernization of Law in Africa with Particular Reference to Family Law in the
Ivory Coast," in Philip Foster and Aristotle R. Zolberg (eds.), *Ghana and the Ivory Coast: Perspectives on
Modernization,* University of Chicago Press, Chicago, 1971, pp. 151–168.

3. The growth of urbanization is often not paralleled by a comparable revolution in the rural areas.

4. A less favorable ratio of population to resources in rural areas means that the push factor is more important than it was in Europe. That is, people pour into the cities not because the city needs workers, but because the countryside is overpopulated.

5. The linkage of some cities with their domestic hinterlands is less developed, while the ties of these cities to the outside world and their dependence on it remain striking.

6. There is relatively less specialization in the African cities. The division of labor is less developed.

7. There are generally higher rates of unemployment. Here the European cities had the advantage of being able to drain off large numbers of people who might have become redundant to the new world. The African cities have no such convenient safety valve.

8. Differences in outlook and values may slow the adjustment to the city and reduce the tempo of its economic life, as, for example, the reliance on the extended family for support and the absence of the Protestant Ethic with its emphasis on hard work, achievement, and success.

9. There is a dual tribal and western structure in many African cities.

10. Migrants to the town differ in several important respects: almost all are unskilled, their level of educational achievement is relatively lower though above average as far as the source areas are concerned, and almost all arrive without capital resources.

11. Heavier responsibility is placed on governments, local and national, to provide for the urban residents. In the west, private enterprise normally met the needs for new housing, while local governments had a tax base adequate to provide the public services. Not so in Africa, where the demands on government are far more onerous, and almost none are capable of meeting them.[32]

The reference to a "dual structure" in point 9 has to do with the simultaneous existence of tribal customs and westernized ways of life. Generally, western ways tend to dominate in the economic sphere, while in the social and family sphere traditional customs relate their old strength. For instance, a man who has graduated from college may choose his job, but his father may strongly influence his choice of a wife.

The Future

Discouraging overall figures regarding population growth, rural poverty, and economic stagnation must be applied with discretion. While urban growth is occurring virtually everywhere, some nations are coping with the transformation more adequately than others. In sub-Saharan Africa, Nigeria, Kenya, and the

[32]Hance, op. cit., pp. 293–294.

Ivory Coast appear to be on the road to national economic development, while other nations just as clearly appear to be mired in internal strife and economic regression. For the remainder of this century Africa will remain the world's least urbanized continent even while its major cities continue to mushroom.

THE MIDDLE EAST

The middle east is in many respects more a political than a geographical concept. Technically, most of what we call the "middle east" is in Asia Minor, with some overlap into north Africa (for example, Egypt). However, in terms of history, culture, and development, the middle east is a relatively distinct area.

The middle east is sometimes referred to as the "cradle of civilizations." This is not entirely an exaggeration, for the great ancient civilizations of Mesopotamia, Egypt, and the Levant all developed in this relatively small geographic area. The early development of this area was discussed briefly in Chapter 2, Emergence of Cities. In this chapter, the emphasis is on the cities of the middle east from the Islamic period to the present, for the social and spatial organization of present cities in the area is directly related to their preindustrial past. In terms of economic development as well as geography, the middle east occupies a position somewhere between the countries of western Europe and those of Asia and Africa, with some OPEC nations developing as economic forces.

Scholars agree that Islamic civilization has been predominantly an urban civilization.[33] In the words of Lapidus, "From the beginning of recorded history Middle Eastern cities and civilization have been one and the same."[34] The city was the center of political, social, and cultural activities. This was true in spite of the fact that many of the countries still are not unified and tribal factors are important.

Middle eastern cities differed in significant respects from the medieval corporate city and the autonomous city-state of the classical world. The medieval European city with which we are most familiar grew out of a feudal, land-based system; its charter defined its rights vis-à-vis the rural manors which were the real centers of power. European medieval cities initially were only on the fringes of power and were forced to develop their own political structure because they did not fit into the dominant, agriculturally based system. They had to evolve their own laws and customs, often in opposition to those of the countryside.

Islamic cities, by contrast, did not have distinct legal privileges of a charter—criteria which Max Weber, using the legally autonomous European model, has suggested were necessary for a true city.[35] Under Islamic law all

---

[33]S. M. Stern: "The Constitution of the Islamic City," in A. H. Hourani and S. M. Stein (eds.), *The Islamic City*, Bruno Cassirer, Oxford, 1970, p. 25.

[34]Ira M. Lapidus, *Middle Eastern Cities*, University of California Press, Berkeley, 1969, p. v.

[35]Max Weber, *The City*, D. Martindale and G. Neuwirth (trans.), Free Press, New York, 1959, p. 88.

believers, whether in the city or the countryside, were equal. The laws of the city were those of the entire territory. Since laws were written in the cities, there was no need for autonomous laws and regulations for cities—and thus no independent group which could legally challenge the caliphate as the western middle class challenged its rulers by developing constitutional law. The caliphs, like the earlier Roman emperors, lived in the cities, not the countryside with its fortified rural castles. The city was not viewed as a rival of the hinterland: the city was superior and dominant. City authorities enforced the laws and collected the taxes. Thus there was no need for independent municipal governments of the type developed in western Europe. Rather, the middle eastern cities resembled Asian cities in that they lacked independent formal organizations.[36]

In the middle east, the peasants—many of whom actually lived within the protection of the city walls and cultivated adjacent lands—needed the technical skills, such as the canalizing and storing of water, and the military security, particularly from roaming nomads, provided by an urban population. Some cities, like Damascus, had agriculturalists living within the city and working the fields outside.[37] This is directly opposite to the American pattern of people living outside the city and working within it.

Traditional Islamic Cities

Roughly four-fifths of the middle east is either desert or arid mountains, and this basic environmental fact greatly influenced the location of cities. In addition to the limitations of the environment, political and military considerations influenced the location of Islamic cities. During the Roman Empire and earlier, the great cities were almost always seaports—Alexandria, Antioch, and Carthage are examples. The Muslims did not follow this ancient pattern: they shunned the sea and instead built an inland empire. This was partly from choice—the origins of Islam were in the interior rather than on the more sophisticated coast—but also partly from military necessity. Arab armies were successful on land, but the Mediterranean Sea was controlled by others—first by the hostile Byzantine Empire and later by the equally dangerous Italian city-states.

As a result, the Muslims built an interior empire, and previously great cities such as Alexandria shrank to the status of frontier outposts. The great Muslim cities, such as Damascus, Baghdad, Cairo, Tehran, Jerusalem, Mecca, and Medina, were all inland. Some, such as Kairouan and Fustat, were originally Arab camps at the edge of the desert; others, such as Damascus and Yazd, had been handling desert traffic for centuries; still others, such as Samarra, Baghdad, and Cairo, had once served as royal cities; and a few, such as Jerusalem and Mecca, were religious centers.

---

[36]J. Gernet, "*Note sur les villes chinoises au moment de l'apogee islamique,*" in Hourani and Stern, op. cit., pp. 77–85.

[37]Charles Issawi, *The Economic History of the Middle East,* University of Chicago Press, Chicago, 1966, p. 216.

One of the stations of the cross in the old Arab section of Jerusalem.
Note the narrow, enclosed street suitable for only pedestrian or
animal traffic. (Mary Doody)

The holy city of Mecca in Saudi Arabia illustrates how social organization
can sometimes override environmental conditions. Mecca is 40 miles from the
Red Sea along a series of *wadis,* or gullies, flanked by steep granite hills.
Summer temperatures reach 105°F, and there is an almost total lack of greenery
and cultivation. Nonetheless, as the focus of prayer and pilgrimage for Muslims
throughout the world—non-Muslims are forbidden to enter the holy city—
Mecca has prospered.

The traditional Islamic cities had a number of physical features in common.
First, located in the most dominant natural defense position within the city
would be the citadel. This was the military heart of the city, the place where,
if necessary, a last-stand defense could be made.

Second, all cities had a central mosque which served as the focus of urban
life. Around the mosque—which contained the religious school—could generally be found the main religious, civic, social, cultural, and even economic
activities.

Third, there was the palace of the local ruler. Sometimes this was located
in the very heart of the city, and sometimes on virgin land; but wherever it
was placed, it invariably grew and absorbed surrounding properties. The
compound contained not only the palace, treasury, and other directly related

operations; it also was the center for all administrative offices. In addition, there were barracks for the house guards and personal troops whose loyalty could be counted on in times of revolt or attempted coup.

Finally, there was the central market area or bazaar. The citadel and palace are now tourist sights, but the grand bazaars continue to serve an important commercial function. Various sections of the bazaar are devoted to specific goods or products; all the spice markets are found in one section, another section specializes in shoes, another in clothing, and another in copper or brass metalwork. Silversmiths and goldsmiths also have their own special locations. The fabled Khanel Khalili bazaar of Cairo covers over a square mile of the city center.

Internally, Islamic cities have traditionally been divided into quarters that resemble village communities. Damascus in the sixteenth century had some seventy quarters.[38] Most of one's daily life would be lived within a quarter; there were relatively few institutional ties cutting across district lines to bind various quarters together. Guilds, merchant associations, and professional organizations, which were so important in medieval European cities, were all extremely weak.[39] What little organization that did cross the boundaries of quarters was created by the *ulma,* the learned religious elite that later came to exercise political and social power as well. The schools of law of the *ulma* were socially, religiously, and physically central.

Within the various quarters there were wide differences in social, economic, and political power. There were no specifically upper-class districts. Residence in quarters was based on adherence to particular religious or political positions. Ethnic minorities, specialized crafts, and even foreign merchants might have their own quarters. Some of the more suburban quarters were composed largely of people of recent village or nomadic origin—again, a contrast to the North American pattern.

Contemporary Urban Trends

Urbanization in Arab countries today is so diverse that generalizations are no longer realistic.[40] Most cities are growing at a rapid rate, with many doubling their population in a decade. Accurate figures are difficult to come by, since censuses are often viewed as political instruments. Saudi Arabia, for instance, will probably never release the results of its last census because it would document that at most 10 million Saudis live in an oil-rich country three times the size of Texas.[41]

---

[38]Ira M. Lapidus, *Muslim Cities in the Later Middle Ages,* Harvard University Press, Cambridge, Mass., 1967, p. 86.

[39]Lapidus, *Middle Eastern Cities,* op. cit., p. v.

[40]Janet Abu-Lughod, "Culture, Modes of Production, and the Changing Nature of Cities in the Arab World," in J. Agnew, J. Mercer and D. Sopher (eds.), *The City in Cultural Context,* Allen and Unwin, Boston, 1984.

[41]According to a story that may be true or apocryphal, former King Saud commissioned a national sample during World War II. In making his report to the king, the western demographer confidently said that the monarch had some 3 million subjects. The king, with some upset, replied that he had at least 7 million subjects. The expert countered that there might be 4 million. The king demanded 6 million; the expert said that perhaps there might be 5 million. "So be it," the king declared.

In oil-wealthy OPEC countries such as Kuwait old sections have been virtually obliterated by new building. Air-conditioned steel, cement, and glass office buildings tower over streets clogged with automobile traffic. Residential neighborhoods are filled with new villas and apartments, while garages are filled with Mercedes automobiles. Elsewhere on the Arabian peninsula traces of the previous traditional—and often poverty-stricken—cities remain.

The world city of Cairo is a place of extremes. Over the past three decades Cairo's population has grown from 2.5 million to over 8 million. Another 6 million are massed in the greater metropolitan area. For twenty years there was virtually no meaningful maintenance or repair of the city's streets, sewers, telephones, or housing. Even today building codes are not enforced. The city is notorious for its power outages, garbage-strewn porches and streets, and out-of-commission telephones. Egyptian residents, with endless patience and tolerance, respond with an Arabic expression: *Molish* ("Never mind").

The housing crisis is so severe that landlords can charge $4,000 a month for an unheated apartment where the water may or may not run. The poor among Cairo's residents fare much worse. Building space is so scarce that several hundred thousand Cairo residents live in rooftop shanty shacks where residents raise food and even goats, as well as children. Another unique response is that half a million people live in the mausoleums of Cairo's cemetery, the famous City of the Dead. Squatters have returned the City of the Dead to life. However, even with all its problems, Cairo has a magic allure for newcomers, and remains one of the world's great cities.

There is no pattern of economic and social change common to all middle eastern cities. Tel Aviv, for example, differs enormously from Baghdad, Damascus, or even Jerusalem. The development of Tel Aviv as a primate city can be explained in great part by the emergence of Israel as a nation-state. Founded in 1909 as a Jewish "garden city" separated from the Arab city of Jaffa, Tel Aviv grew rapidly, particularly after World War II. Its reservoir of trained professional and managerial talent aided its transformation into a major industrial commercial center. Tel Aviv has expanded its metropolitan area until now it encompasses numerous formerly independent surrounding towns. After Jerusalem came under Israeli administration as a result of the Six-Day War in 1967, Tel Aviv was no longer the only Israeli city, but its economic primacy remains.

Comparisons and Conclusions

In making comparisons with other regions of the world, and particularly with North America, certain differences should be remembered. First, middle eastern cities are not industrialized centers in the western sense. The cities are commercially oriented, but the way of life is far less bureaucratic than in industrialized states. Contacts count for more than formal rules. For example, *baksheesh* (the giving of bribes or gifts) is often an accepted way of doing business in the middle east.

In the middle east, cafes have long served for males as both business settings and social clubs. (Carl Frank/Photo Researchers)

Second, theories of urban ecological organization developed in America have little relevance to the middle east. If one looks at the ecology of Cairo, it is apparent that Burgess's concentric-zone theory has little utility there.[42] Contrary to the American pattern, in Cairo the areas of high social status are centrally located, and close to both the old and the new central business districts. Housing patterns still largely follow the traditional preindustrial model rather than the industrial model.

[42]See, for example, S. S. Hassan, "The Ecology and Characteristics of Employed Females in Cairo City," paper presented at the Seminar on Demographic Factors in Manpower Planning in Arab Countries held at the Cairo Demographic Center, November, 1971; and Janet Abu-Lughod, "Testing the Theory of Social Area Analysis: The Ecology of Cairo, Egypt," *American Sociological Review,* **34:**198–212, April, 1969.

Third, because they are in-migrants, many city dwellers exhibit characteristics and behavior patterns that reflect their rural or village background. Families ties, kinship, ethnic groups, and primary groups still have a great deal to do with determining the nature of the life one will lead. In Cairo, more than one-third of the residents were born outside the city. Migrants do not simply pick up urban ways; they also, in effect, ruralize the cities. Many city dwellers are still tied to rural customs and culture, and migrants shape the city as much as the city shapes them. Overall, evidence indicates that migrants do not suffer from social disorientation on the scale experienced by America's immigrants.[43]

Fourth, formal institutions, such as civic associations, labor unions, and charitable organizations, rarely play more than a minor role in adjusting the migrant to the city. Informal organizations or subsystems based on tribal, cultural, or ethnic identification are far more important. For instance, the role of the coffee shop is often central. Men conduct much of their social and business lives from the coffee shop. Frequently it is a place where news of the village can be exchanged and assistance can be given to newcomers. As such the coffee shop is more of a social than an economic institution.[44]

Finally, the existence of large cities should in no way be confused with the existence of a secular urban culture. Secular ways have not replaced traditional ways, even within the oil-rich cities which are physically most modern. External signs of western influence such as high-rise buildings, western automobiles, and western clothing styles do not signify abandonment of traditional beliefs. Even in supposedly secular states the statements of traditional Islamic religious leaders can produce civil disorder and even bring down governments. The power of religious leaders in expressly religiously oriented states such as Saudi Arabia and Iran is even greater. The urbanites of the middle east often remain more traditional than those of Asia, Europe, or the Americas.

[43]V. V. Costello, *Urbanization in the Middle East,* Cambridge University Press, Cambridge, 1977, chap. 5.
[44]For a description of this pattern in Cairo, see Janet Abu-Lughod, "Migrant Adjustment to City Life: The Egyptian Case," *American Journal of Sociology,* **67**:22–32, July, 1961.

CHAPTER 17

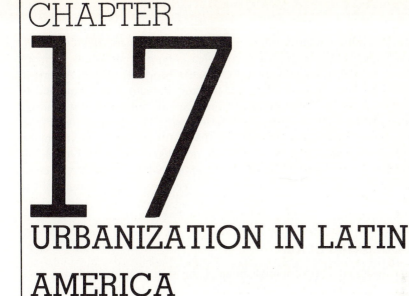

URBANIZATION IN LATIN AMERICA

Gazing on such wonderful sights, we did not know what to say or whether what appeared before us was real, for on one side in the land there were great cities and in the lake ever so many more, and the lake itself was crowded with canoes, and in the causeway there were many bridges at intervals, and in front of us stood the great City of Mexico, and we . . . we did not even number four hundred soldiers.

Bernal Díaz del Castillo,
The True History of the Conquest of New Spain, 1568

Many people still think of Latin America as an overwhelmingly rural continent, but the facts suggest otherwise. Latin America is 66 percent urban, or more urban than the USSR (which is 64 percent urban).[1] Moreover, Latin American cities, unlike most of those of Asia and Africa, are not a consequence of European colonial expansion during the late nineteenth century. Latin America already had grand cities at the time the Pilgrims were beginning to learn from the Indians how to raise corn. In fact, all the Latin American metropolitan areas that had more than 1 million inhabitants in 1960—except Montevideo— were founded in the sixteenth century.[2] However, while many of the cities have ancient roots, the bulk of their growth is very recent, a product of the last forty years.

SPANISH COLONIAL CITIES

The Spanish designed their colonial cities to be remarkably similar in both ecological plan and functional purpose. Growth and development over the centuries have blunted many of the original similarities, but elements of the first cities still remain. The purpose of the cities was to serve as administrative centers and garrison posts for the Spanish military forces.

Spanish colonial cities did not enjoy the virtual independence of most of the early English towns in North America. Administrative decrees were promulgated from Spain. The city was the center from which the mining or agricultural hinterland was to be controlled and the funnel through which wealth was to flow to the mother country. The Spanish Crown discouraged commercial or manufacturing activities that would make the colonial city any less dependent on Spain.

Socially and commercially, the city looked toward Spain rather than toward its own hinterland. Cities were placed on the land; they did not grow out of it. Unlike the North American colonies, the Latin American cities did not develop into commercial or manufacturing centers. The limited manufacturing and processing that did exist, such as the production of syrup and molasses and the spinning and weaving of cotton and woolen cloth, took place on the *haciendas* and other large landed estates.

The decrees governing the colonies were written in Spain by the Council of the Indies; home rule was unknown. These policies had two objectives, "(1) to make the colonies into producers of gold, silver, and precious stones; and (2) to limit their consumption of manufactured goods strictly to those produced in Spain, shipped in convoys from Spanish ports, and destined for a few strongly fortified seaports, of which the principal ones were Vera Cruz, Cartagena, and Callao."[3] The effect of all this was a throttling of trade and

[1]Population Reference Bureau, 1985 World Population Data Sheet, Washington, D.C., 1985.
[2]Jorge E. Hardoy, *Urbanization in Latin America: Approaches and Issues,* Doubleday (Anchor), Garden City, New York, 1975, p. viii.
[3]T. Lynn Smith, "The Changing Functions of Latin American Cities," *The Americas,* **25**:74, July, 1968.

Traditionally the central plaza, as the Plaza de los Armos in Lima, Peru, was dominated by the cathedral. (Alain Keler/Art Resource)

commerce as a basis for urban life in Latin American cities under Spanish domination. The merchant, who enjoyed such a prominent position in the social structure of New England, did not have influence in the Spanish colonies. The seaports were heavily fortified entrepôts for receiving the manufactures of Spain in the annual convoys and assembling the treasure that was to be shipped to Spain on the return voyage. The impact of this pattern can be seen today; only in Mexico and Colombia are metropolitan areas of over 1 million found other than on the coastline.[4]

Physical Structure

Regulations of Charles V and Philip II, eventually codified into the famous laws of the Indies, specified how cities were to be organized. For example, cities were to follow a rectangular plan and be founded near rivers in a manner permitting expansion. However, as Hardoy points out, "legislation only formalized a situation already perfected defined in practice."[5] The existence of indigenous cities, of course, modified the plans, as did various practical considerations such as topography.

Nonetheless, most Spanish settlements adhered to the classical model of a central *plaza mayor*. Around the central plaza was the cathedral and major

---

[4]The planned city of Brasilia is also an exception to the rule.
[5]Hardoy, op. cit., p. 30.

government buildings. The *solares,* or house lots, were of uniform shape, and the city was laid out in a grid with intersections at right angles. Houses and grounds were to be surrounded by walls, and because of this the early cities frequently appeared to be more heavily inhabited than was actually the case. Since the cities were to serve as fortified strong points performing administrative functions for the surrounding hinterland, they were not always ideally located from the standpoint of transportation; Mexico City was located on an island in the middle of a lake. Political rather than economic considerations often weighed heavily in the location of cities. Even the legal rank of a city was a matter decided in Spain rather than in the new world.

The Spanish government did everything possible to retain a rigid class system. One edict even reserved all the top administrative, religious, and political positions for *peninsulares,* or those born in Spain. Those born in the colonies, regardless of their wealth or family position, were relegated to a secondary status—a factor that directly motivated local leaders to instigate the rebellion against Spain.

Fortunately, the grid layout of the cities offered considerable flexibility; the boundaries could be expanded as more room was needed. Additional grids were easily added by extending the straight streets and adding more identical blocks. The focus on the central plaza meant that there were no markets, walls, or storehouses at the periphery of the city to impede expansion.[6] The large lots (which the law required be enclosed by walls) initially resulted in a relatively low population density. Later, subdivision of lots occurred, and this—and the cutting of new streets midway between existing streets—allowed the city to increase its density with relative ease.

Brazilian cities differed considerably from the model just described in that they were not built to any standard plan such as that provided by the Laws of the Indies. Cities in Brazil were few and with little influence, since the Portuguese, unlike the Spaniards, preferred to live a semifeudal existence on their estates in the country. Portuguese policy also kept towns such as Santos, Bahia, and Recife relatively small. Their splendid natural ports were open only to ships from Portugal, and this trade was not sufficient to turn these towns into real cities. By the nineteenth century Rio de Janeiro was the undisputed political, economic, and cultural center of Brazil.

Policy and Traditions

The differences in ecological patterns between the North American and South American cities are frequently attributed to Spanish colonial policy as typified by the Laws of the Indies.[7] However, Leo Schnore suggests that factors more powerful than "Iberian values" were at work: "The fact of the matter is that

---

[6]Ralph A. Gakenheimer, "The Peruvian City of the Sixteenth Century," in Glen H. Beyer (ed.), *The Urban Explosion in Latin America,* Cornell University Press, Ithaca, N.Y., 1967, p. 50.

[7]See George A. Theodorson (ed.), *Studies in Human Ecology,* Row, Peterson, Evanston, Ill., 1961, pp. 326–327.

the traditional Latin American pattern' could be observed in cities of the New World prior to the Spanish conquest."[8] He cites historical and archeological evidence that among the pre-Colombian Aztec and Maya civilizations the elites tended to live in the centers of the great cities. According to Bishop Landa's account, first published in 1566,

> The fundamental unit of the town settlement, with its core of civic and religious buildings, is dominant in all periods and in all but the most remote and inaccessible localities. Landa's classic description of the town of Yucatán can be applied with only minor variations to most of the known archeological history within the areas of high culture in Meso-America: "Before the Spaniards had conquered that country, the natives lived together in towns in a very civilized fashion. . . . In the middle of the towns were their temples with beautiful plazas, and all around the temples stood the houses of the lords and the priests, and those of the most important people. Thus came the houses of the richest and of those who were held in the highest estimation next to these, and at the outskirts of the town were the houses of the lower class."[9]

Thus, the pattern of spatial distribution by social class was set well before the Spaniards arrived. The pattern conforms to that suggested by Gideon Sjoberg for all preindustrial cities.[10] (See Chapter 2, Emergence of Cities.)

EVOLVING PATTERNS

Before the introduction of modern transportation technology, and before industrialization contaminated central areas with its noise, noxious fumes, and congestion, the central area of the city was the most pleasant and the most convenient area. This is where the elite built their homes, frequently with extensive grounds and almost always behind high walls that effectively isolated the home from the confusion of the streets and markets outside.

The pattern of high socioeconomic status in the center has also been found in North American cities before industrialization, particularly in the old south. Heberle gives a clear account of the development of these cities:

> It seems to be characteristic for the older, smaller cities in the South that the homes of the socially prominent families were to be found just outside the central—and only—business districts. . . . As the city grew and as wealth increased, the "old" families tended to move toward the periphery—following the general fashion of our age. . . . The old homes are then converted into rooming houses and "tourist homes."[11]

---

[8]Leo F. Schnore, "On the Spatial Structure of Cities in the Two Americas," in Philip Hauser and Leo Schnore (eds.), *The Study of Urbanization,* Wiley, New York, 1965, p. 369.

[9]Quoted in Edwin M. Shook and Tatiana Proskouriakoff, "Settlement Patterns in Meso-America and the Sequency in the Guatemalan Highlands," in Gordon R. Wiley (ed.), *Prehistoric Settlement Patterns in the New World,* Wenner-Gren Foundation for Anthropological Research, New York, 1956, pp. 93–100.

[10]Gideon Sjoberg, *The Preindustrial City: Past and Present,* Free Press, New York, 1960, pp. 96–98.

[11]Rudolph Heberle, "Social Consequences of the Industrialization of Southern Cities," *Social Forces,* October, 1948, pp. 34–35.

The "traditional" model, with its central plaza and with groups of higher socioeconomic status occupying the center rather than the suburbs, is true of all but the newest cities of Latin America.[12] According to Leo Schnore, the data suggest that the residential structure of cities evolves in a predictable direction and that this pattern is observable both in North America and, more recently, in Latin America:

> Given growth and expansion of the center, and given appropriate improvements in transportation and communication, the upper strata might be expected to shift from central to peripheral residence, and the lower classes might increasingly take up occupancy in the central area abandoned by the elite. Despite mounting land values occasioned by the competition of alternative (nonresidential) land uses, the lower strata may occupy valuable central land in tenements, subdivided dwellings originally intended for single families, and other high-density "slum" housing arrangements.[13]

POET

The previously discussed ecological complex of *population, organization, environment,* and *technology* (POET) helps us understand these changes. Technology has done much in recent times to change the configuration of cities. As was indicated earlier, railroads and steam power did much to produce the nineteenth-century American city. Since the 1920s the automobile has permitted a form of population dispersion that was impossible earlier. The telephone and other advances in communication technology have meant that interrelated functions can be spatially separated without loss of contact and control. In Latin American cities, the elite preempted the more central areas for their residences, since these were the most accessible sites in an era of primitive transportation technology. Technological changes—automobiles, good roads, extension of power and sewage lines—have drastically reduced the attractiveness of the central city as a place of residence. Upper-class suburbanization is now found in Latin America on the pattern of North America.

Early Social and Economic Structure

As previously noted, in colonial Latin America the pattern was one of creating deliberate dependency. Political independence from Spain and Portugal in the early nineteenth-century did not end economic dependency. Independence, if anything, increased the dependence of the new republics upon European powers and the United States.[14] Cities remained tied to external markets while virtually ignoring their hinterlands. Until this century geography also set limits on penetration of the interior and fostered a pattern of external dependence.

---

[12]Schnore, op. cit., p. 366.
[13]Ibid., pp. 373–374.
[14]Hardoy, op. cit., p. viii.

The absence of a substantial entrepreneurial middle class also stunted the economic growth of the cities. Merchants and businesspeople were looked down upon socially; for membership in the elite, one's income was expected to come from land holdings rather than manufacture or trade. As a result, the Latin American city—in contrast to cities in North America—was a political rather than an economic center:

> Political considerations and motivations, rather than economic or social, have historically controlled urbanization in Latin America. The city has, therefore, often emerged as an imposition, an appendage, tucked onto a relatively underdeveloped agricultural countryside—the military centers of the Aztecs, the political centers of the Incas, the political towns of the Spaniards, the political capitals of the nineteenth century republican cities of Latin America. Not only has the city not grown out of the economic needs or in relation to the socioeconomic development of its surrounding area; it has until very recently been divorced from the national reality.[15]

The growth of the middle class in the nineteenth century, when it did occur, was due in large part to the technological changes in transportation and to immigration. The railroad and later the highway opened up new territories— territories that could be developed with the newly emerging agricultural technology. Also, in the latter years of the nineteenth century, waves of European immigrants brought about the formation of new urban institutions. Simultaneously, a new professional middle class and an urban bureaucracy began to develop.

However, this middle class, the most important group in economic growth and industrial development, usually weakened its possible influence by allying itself with the upper classes and against the urban proletariat. Upper-middle-class professional groups often became so involved with the establishment that they ceased to be a force for political change. The urban middle class, which so dominates political life in North America and Europe, still has limited influence on national policy in many Latin American nations. The "ruling families" are still a fact of life in many Latin American countries.

RECENT DEVELOPMENTS

Urban Growth

The Latin American cities of today are far from the sleepy towns of the turn of the century. Urbanization in Latin America is currently proceeding at a phenomenal rate. As recently as 1950, 39 percent of the population lived in places of 20,000 or more, but this figure had risen to 50 percent in 1960. Currently Latin America is 66 percent urban.[16]

---

[15]James Scobie, quoted in Beyer, op. cit., p. 63.
[16]Population Reference Bureau, op. cit.

Mexico City today is well on its way to becoming the world's largest city. (Rene Burri/Magnum)

The world's largest urban place (Mexico City), third largest (São Paulo), and seventh and eighth largest (Greater Buenos Aires and Rio de Janeiro) are all found in Latin America. By contrast, among the ten largest urban places there are no European cities, and only one North American city: New York (fourth).[17]

Latin American cities are growing at an annual rate of 3.6 percent a year, compared with a much slower rural growth rate of only 0.8 percent a year. Every year between 1985 and the year 2000 over 11 million new persons will live in Latin American cities, if present trends continue.[18]

To put it another way, in 1930 Latin America had only one city of over 1 million persons (Mexico City); as of 1980 the number was twenty-six. The greatest growth has been in the very largest cities. Latin America is a continent of primate cities, with half (49 percent) of its population in cities of over 100,000 inhabitants.[19]

Within the period of a lifetime, Latin America is being transformed from a rural, agriculturally oriented continent to one that is predominantly urbanized and urban-oriented. The process of urbanization, which took over a century in North America, is being compressed into decades.

[17]United Nations, Department of International Economic and Social Affairs, 1985.

[18]Jorge E. Hardoy, "Urbanization in Latin America," in J. John Palen (ed.), *City Scenes*, Little, Brown, Boston, 1981, p. 266.

[19]Philip M. Hauser and Robert W. Gardner, "Urban Future: Trends and Prospects," in Philip Hauser et al. (eds.), *Population and the Urban Future*, State University of New York Press, Albany, 1982, table 1.6.

Figures for the entire continent, of course, cloud variations among nations. The range of urbanization in Latin American countries is great. Haiti has 26 percent of its population in urban places, while Argentina (82 percent), Chile (81 percent), and Uruguay (84 percent) are among the most urbanized nations in the world. Half of Uruguay's population lives in the capital city of Montevideo.

Taken as a whole, Latin America is considerably more urbanized than other third world regions. It is far more urbanized than Asia and Africa. The rate of growth is now higher in African cities, but the urban population explosion in Latin America continues. Latin American cities, and particularly the largest primate cities, are growing at a rate that considerably outpaces their ability to provide urban services and employment.

During the remainder of this century Latin America's rural-to-urban migration is expected to slow considerably. As a consequence, the growth of the cities will come increasingly from the natural increase of births over deaths. Latin American cities already generally have low death rates owing to reasonably adequate programs of public health, vaccination, and sanitation. Birthrates, on the other hand, are two and sometimes three times as high as European levels. The inevitable consequence of such a high rate of natural increase is an urban population explosion.

The annual increase in the rural populations of Latin America is such that each year jobs on the land should be found for over half a million new workers.[20] The chance of finding employment for so many workers in the already overloaded agricultural sector is, however, minimal. There is already a considerable surplus in the rural labor force. According to one expert:

> Under-employment in Latin American agriculture is so evident to anyone with first-hand knowledge of the agrarian situation that it is difficult to take seriously the academic debates about whether or not it exists. The CIDA studies showed that, by any common-sense definition of under-employment, from one-fifth to over one-third of the workers in Latin American agriculture are practically surplus.[21]

Economically, while agriculture needs to be made more productive it probably does not make sense to try to hold the peasants in the country or in small towns. It is sometimes argued that if rural life can be made more attractive, people will be less likely to abandon rural areas for the opportunities and advantages of the city. However, the costs of modernizing the rural sector are high, particularly when the cities also need modernization. Rural electrification, for example, is far more expensive than providing electricity for urban slum dwellers. The same amount of money often can do more for more people if it is spent in the city than if it is spent in the country. Because funds are limited, "community development" often is more effectively directed toward

[20]*Estudio Económico para América Latina,* ECLA, United Nations, 1966, pp. 41–51.

[21]Solon L. Barraclough, "Rural Development and Employment Prospects in Latin America," in Arthur J. Field (ed.), *City and Country in the Third World,* Schenkman, Cambridge, Mass., 1970, p. 106.

urban populations, who by their very presence in the city have already indicated a willingness to make changes.

For the majority of ruralites, the move to the city is a wise decision. Even low urban standards are likely to represent an improvement in quality of life. On the other hand, what is good for them personally is often a disaster for the city itself when viewed from a national perspective. The in-migration of ever more peasants simply compounds already severe urban problems.[22]

Characteristics of Urban Inhabitants

Latin America is typical of the third world in that half or more of the inhabitants of its largest cities are migrants from elsewhere. In Latin America, migration to cities for years has been more permanent and less seasonal than in other developing regions.[23] The city-bound migrants, like those elsewhere in the world, tend to be mostly young adults. Older people are less prone to leave villages or rural areas for the opportunities and bright lights of the city.

This heavy migration of young persons, plus the population explosion—which, of course, adds only young people to the population—means that there are proportionately few people of working age in the urban population. The impression of outsiders that "everyone seems so young" is borne out by the empirical data: some 39 percent of the Latin American population is under fifteen years of age. (The figure for Europe and North America is 22 percent.)

The cities of most developing countries have more males than females; Latin America, on the contrary, has more females than males. In this respect, it is more similar to economically developed western areas. While there is general agreement that there are more females, there is no agreement about why this is the case. Perhaps the greater degree of urbanization and economic development in Latin America, compared with developing countries elsewhere in the world, accounts for the difference.

Shantytowns

In addition to central-core slums, squatter settlements ring all the great cities of Latin America, but there is no universally accepted view of this phenomenon. Some observers emphasize the squalor and disorganization of the squatter settlements; some argue that these shantytown settlements are in effect evolving into reasonable low-income suburban housing areas. Frequently, it seems that what a writer describes is not shaped as much by what he or she sees as by the writer's philosophy and political beliefs. There is no unanimity, as the next pages show.

What is agreed upon is that the peripheral slums grow like mushrooms (in Chile they are called *poblaciones callampas,* which means "mushroom towns"). They grow because of the population explosion and the migration of peasants

---

[22]Aprodicio A. Laquian, "Issues and Instruments in Metropolitan Planning," in Hauser, op. cit., p. 68.
[23]"Some Regional Development Problems in Latin America Linked to Metropolitanization," *Economic Bulletin for Latin America,* United Nations, New York, 1972, p. 70.

These squatters in Rio de Janeiro at least are compensated by a
magnificent view of the city and mountains behind. (Hans Mann/
Monkmeyer)

from the countryside in search of a better life. For instance, the number of
squatters in São Paulo is estimated to be between 500,000 and 1.5 million.
One-quarter of Lima's population lives in *barriadas*. In Caracas, the capital
of Venezuela, over 35 percent of the total metropolitan population is living in
squatter settlements, while in Bogotá, Colombia, more than half the population
lives in neighborhoods still considered clandestine by officials. (In Bogotá,
unlike elsewhere, the illegal occupants are not really squatters since they
technically own the land upon which their illegal "pirate developments" have

been built.) Over one-third of Mexico City's inhabitants live in slums and squatter settlments, many in the aptly named "lost cities" surrounding Mexico City. Mexico City's Netahualcoyotl houses some 3 million persons. Twenty years ago it was a dry lake bed.

In spite of sporadic resettlement programs, it is clear that shantytown squatter settlements will be part of the Latin American urban scene for the foreseeable future. As long as the urban population continues to increase because of high birthrates and migration to the cities, the cities will continue to add more people than they can house. The Peruvian government has been more candid than most in admitting that it is unable to reduce the urban housing deficit because public investment must be directed toward developing national objectives, but the situation elsewhere is similar.

Social upheavals and mob violence may become more common in marginal settlements. Clashes between squatters and police often occur in places such as Mexico City when landlords, as land prices escalate, attempt to evict squatters who previously were ignored. Leftist attempts to organize the vast but largely still silent urban proletariat have had some limited success. But in-migrant squatters and slum dwellers, in contrast to better-off university students, are generally more interested in day-to-day survival than Marxist theory. For the future, an undercurrent of resentment and the seeds of social conflict are being sown by governments whose policies continue to favor the "haves" over the "have-nots."

Settlements as Squalor. A description of daily life in squatter shantytowns is provided by the supposed diary of a dweller in a *favela* outside São Paulo, Brazil. The following are excerpts from her diary for one day in July:

> July 16 I got up. . . . I went to get the water. I made coffee. I told the children that I didn't have any bread, that they would have to drink their coffee plain and eat meat with *farinha*. I was feeling ill and decided to cure myself. I stuck my finger down my throat twice, vomited, and knew I was under the evil eye. The upset feeling left and I went to Senor Manuel, carrying some cans to sell. Everything that I find in the garbage I sell. He gave me 13 cruzeiros. I kept thinking that I had to buy bread, soap, and milk for Vera Eunice. The 13 cruzeiros wouldn't make it. I returned home, or rather to my shack, nervous and exhausted. I thought of the worrisome life that I led. Carrying paper, washing clothes for the children, staying in the street all day long. Yet I'm always lacking things.[24]

The picture conjured up by such accounts is one of fecund, festering slums filled with dirty shacks and having no sanitary facilities, no garbage collection, and no hope of improvement. Typically, squatter settlements are built without planning or organization on undesirable land such as hillsides, marsh lands, or even dumps. Building materials are often whatever the squatter

---

[24]From the book *Child of the Dark: The Diary of Carolina María de Jesús,* David St. Clair (trans.), p. 18. Copyright © 1962 by E. P. Dutton & Co., Inc., and Souvenir Press, Ltd. Published by E. P. Dutton & Co., Inc., and used with their permission. There is some question about the diary's authenticity.

can salvage. One graphic account describes the notorious *barridas* of Lima as:

> . . . so bestial, so filthy, so congested, so empty of light, fun, color, health, or comfort, so littered with excrement and garbage, so swarming with barefoot children, so reeking of pitiful squalor that just the breath of it makes you retch.[25]

A former official of the United Nations has described squatter settlements as a "spreading malady" and "plague" of "excessive squalor, filth, and poverty, fostering mounting social disorder and tension."[26]

Squatter Settlements as Transitional Settlements. On the other hand, others suggest that while there is some truth in the conventional image, and while some inhabitants of squatter settlements are indeed wretchedly poor, there are "many squatter settlements that are socially developing and physically self-improving suburbs rather than slums.[27] William Mangin's description of the same areas surrounding Lima, described above as "bestial" and "filthy" is far more optimistic.

> At worst a *barriada* is a crowded, helter-skelter hodge-podge of inadequate straw houses with no water supply and no provision for sewage disposal; parts of many are like this. Most do have a rough plan, and most inhabitants convert their original houses to more substantial structures as soon as they can. Construction activity usually involving family, neighbors, and friends is a constant feature of *barriada* life and, although water and sewage usually remain critical problems, a livable situation is reached with respect to them.
>
> For most of the migrants the *barriada* represents a definite improvement in terms of housing and general income, and Lima represents an improvement over the semi-feudal life of the Indian, *cholo,* or lower-class mestizo.[28]

In generalizing it has to be remembered that squatter settlements differ markedly not only in their physical appearance and services available but in the social composition of the groups inhabiting them. Usually, the newest settlements are most disorganized and ramshackle; others that have existed longer are highly organized "slums of hope." Some squatter settlements have well-built homes.

Contrary to conventional assumptions, not all squatters own their own houses. As areas become more settled, the proportion of squatter renters often increases. There are several distinct squatter types.[29]

[25]James Jorris, *Cities,* Harcourt Brace Jovanovich, New York, 1964, p. 227.

[26]Morris Juppenlaty, *Cities in Transformation: The Urban Squatter Problem in the Developing World,* University of Queensland Press, Australia, 1970.

[27]John F. C. Turner, "Squatter Settlements in Developing Countries," in Daniel P. Moynihan (ed.), *Toward a National Urban Policy,* Basic Books, New York, 1970, pp. 256–257.

[28]William P. Mangin, "Mental Health and Migration to Cities: A Peruvian Case," *Annals of New York Academy of Sciences,* **84:**911–917, 1960.

[29]Charles Abrams, "Squatting and Squatters," in Janet Abu-Lughod and Richard Hay, Jr. (eds.), *Third World Urbanization,* Maaroufa Press, Chicago, 1977, pp. 297–298.

1. *Owner squatters* are the "typical" squatters who own their own shack, but not the land on which it stands.
2. *Squatter tenants* are new in-migrants who pay rent to another squatter. Landlord's profits are often considerable, since landlords pay no taxes or upkeep.
3. *Speculator squatters* are holding property as a way to make a profit. They view squatting as a sound business venture, expecting eventually to obtain title to the land.
4. *Store or business squatters* open businesses, catering to the needs of other squatters. They often live on the premises. Most are marginal operators; but some, in the absence of rents or taxes, make substantial profits.
5. *Semisquatters* build their huts on private land but eventually come to some sort of terms with the owner. Strictly speaking, semisquatters are perhaps better classified as tenants.

A casual observer, however, is unlikely to be conscious of these differences. While most settlements are terribly poor and without municipal amenities, it has to be remembered that they differ in condition, services, and social composition. Some are self-upgrading communities; many are horrendous.

The Myth of Marginality. Authorities differ when discussing the lives lived by the inhabitants of shantytowns. One view is that these inhabitants are set apart from the other city residents not only by their poverty but by their marginality and traditional rural orientation. Their rural backgrounds and continued rural ties mean that they remain essentially peasants, but peasants who by force of circumstance live in what is defined as an "urban" area. They are in but not of the city. The implicit, if not explicit, assumption here is that the problem is how to integrate these nonurban people into a complex modern economic system.

The view of the city as a disorganizing force is part of an intellectual tradition going back to the "Chicago school" of sociology and its concern with problems of assimilating immigrants into the inner-city slums of North America. Louis Wirth—as you recall from Chapter 6, City Life-styles—defines "urbanism" as the mode of life of people who live in cities and are subject to their influences. These influences, it is said, act to destroy primary groups, weaken family ties, loosen the bonds of kinship, and lessen neighborliness. The result was said to be impersonality, superficiality, anonymity in personal relations, and the substitution of large secondary organizations for the declining role played by kith and kin. Disruption of family life, rejection of traditional religion, delinquency and alienation among the young, and a generally fragmented social world were some of the consequences associated with life in the slums of North American industrial cities.

A second position is that the rural character of the immigrants is considerably overemphasized, and that problems of adjustment are far less severe than is commonly supposed.

The largest study of an LDC city—sponsored by the World Bank and called The City Study—covers 3,000 householders in Bogotá. It indicates that the behavior of city dwellers in developed and developing countries is much more similar than was once believed.[30] In-migrants to Bogotá, for example, are not worse off than the rest of the population. In fact, they earn higher wages than nonmigrants in all income categories.[31] Moreover, informal sector jobs, such as domestic service, showed wage rates as high or higher than formal-sector factory worker jobs. There was, however, great disparity in income levels between the well off and the poor, with the lowest 40 percent of the population earning less than 12 percent of total income.[32]

The most important finding of The City Study was that even the very poor newcomers to the city showed economic rationality.[33] There was little support for the widely held belief that the poor had a distinctly short-term orientation or culture of poverty that made them unable to defer gratification or plan for the future.[34] The City Study showed the poor, like others, acting to maximize utility. That the poor are rational does not, however, necessarily mean that they will be economically successful.

Other empirical study has also tended to discredit the so-called myth of marginality.[35] That is the widespread belief that squatter settlers have behaviors and attitudes supposedly associated with marginal groups. What sets squatters apart is not their different values or aspirations, but their lack of opportunity.

There is little question that the move from the country to the city has a considerable impact upon the migrant's way of life. However, what strikes many observers living in developing countries is not the difficulty of the adjustment to urban life, but rather the speed and facility with which the rural migrant becomes a city slicker. It is easy to forget that the urban dwellers with whom we are comparing the new migrant were quite likely migrants themselves. Half the population of many Latin American cities were originally migrants. Within a few months of his or her arrival, it is often very difficult to tell the migrant from someone who has spent years in the city.

An unanswered question is how the squatter or slum dweller, after the initial period of adjustment, will respond to his or her relative deprivation, compared with affluent city dwellers. Will the slum dweller accept semipermanent poverty? News reports from El Salvador, Nicaragua, and Chile suggest not.

[30]R. Mohan and N. Hartline, "The Poor of Bogotá: Who They Are, What They Do, and Where They Live," World Bank Staff Working Paper no. 635, 1984.

[31]Ibid.

[32]World Bank, "Anatomy of a Third World City," *Urban Edge*, **8**(8):4, 1984.

[33]Ibid., p. 3.

[34]See, for example, Oscar Lewis, "The Culture of Poverty," *Scientific American*, **215**(4):19–25, 1966.

[35]Janice E. Perlman, *The Myth of Marginality*, University of California Press, Berkeley and Los Angeles, 1976.

PART SIX

CONCLUSION

CHAPTER

18

TOWARD THE URBAN FUTURE

We will ever strive for the ideals and sacred things of the city, both alone and with many; we will unceasingly seek to quicken the sense of public duty; we will revere and obey the city's laws; we will transmit this city not only not less, but greater, better and more beautiful than it was transmitted to us.

Oath of the Athenian city-state

A RECAPITULATION

This book—through its examination of the concept of the interaction of population, organization, environment, and technology (POET)—has illustrated the evolution of the first cities. Such initial urban places were severely limited in size by the fertility of the environment and the limited agricultural technology. As the nineteenth century began only 3 percent of the world's population lived in places of 5,000 or more. Then, spurred by inventions in agriculture, manufacturing, and transportation, nineteenth century city populations in Europe and North America began to mushroom. A classic example is Chicago. The city that had only 4,100 people when incorporated in 1833 had some 2 million residents only three-quarters of a century later. The development of railway technology in the mid-nineteenth century made it possible to locate commercial and industrial cities inland.

The nineteenth century and early twentieth century fostered a period of concentration. From the Civil War to World War II population, power, manufacturing, finance, and fashion concentrated in urban areas. Technological developments in transportation and communication during the first half of this century both reinforced the importance of the core and extended its dominance to the end of the paved road and telephone lines. As Part Five, Worldwide Urbanization, demonstrated, urban economic, political, and population concentration remains the dominant third world pattern.

Deconcentration

Now, however, communication and—to a lesser degree—transportation technologies no longer automatically favor centralization. Urban deconcentration and dispersion has increasingly become the western European as well as the American pattern.[1] Technology has overcome spatial barriers. Today, goods as well as information can move from one coast to another with unprecedented speed. Many companies guarantee overnight delivery of packages; door-to-door pick up and delivery of a letter by facsimile mail takes under two hours. Computer-to-computer hookups are, of course, faster.

The degree to which technology can become a substitute for propinquity is still not fully grasped. We are only beginning to understand, for example, that Nissan's building its first American automobile manufacturing plant in semirural Tennessee reflects more than a desire to escape Detroit's unions and wage scales. While the late-nineteenth-century industrial city demanded concentration, the late-twentieth-century city does not. Changed transportation and communication technologies have outmoded the necessity to locate factories in urban centers. Today, the once-proud, industrial-based, railway-built cities of the industrial midwest are among the nation's most economically depressed. The growth cities are service-based.

---

[1]Daniel R. Vining et al., "Population Dispersal from Core Regions: A Description and Tentative Explanations of Patterns in 21 Countries," in Donald A. Hicks and Norman J. Glickman (eds.), *Transition to the 21st Century*, JAI Press, Greenwich, Conn., 1983, pp. 81–111.

Given the declining importance of propinquity, the much-heralded recent population growth of nonmetropolitan areas discussed in Chapter 5 (Metropolitan, Nonmetropolitan, and Sun Belt Growth) should not have surprised demographers and sociologists (including this author) as much as it did. What we had failed fully to recognize was that spatially uncoupling from the metropolitan area by moving out no longer means leaving behind urbanism as a way of life. Socially, the urban and rural behavioral characteristics that played such an important part in the late-nineteenth- and early-twentieth-century social theories discussed in Chapter 1, The Urban World, have largely lost their explanatory force. At the end of World War II substantive distinctions could still be made between metropolitan and nonmetropolitan ways of life. Today with the nation having almost 350 Metropolitan Statistical Areas, and with the boundaries of existing areas progressively expanding, it becomes increasingly difficult to distinguish between metropolitan and nonmetropolitan areas. Satellite TV discs, VCRs, and PCs are today an integral part of nonmetropolitan growth. Increasingly, urban-nonurban differences are differences that have ceased to make a difference.

Urban Services: An Example

To illustrate how technology can become a substitute for propinquity let us briefly examine what is occurring with health care.[2] Throughout the twentieth century, medical services and facilities have centralized and specialized. The family physician bringing health care directly to the home was replaced by the large-scale hospital medical center or clinic. Treatment, particularly specialized diagnosis and treatment, has increasingly become the prerogative of urban-based and urban-organized health care systems. Those living in nonurban areas journey to the city for medical care.

The attempts to decentralize medical and health services have been based in part on the ideological belief in the virtues of simpler family practice medicine. They have not been very successful. Arguments that what is wrong with contemporary health care is that there are too many specialists, too much technology, too much treatment, and too much surgery have not had noticeable success in changing health care delivery.[3] In spite of the emphasis on general practice, the best and brightest of health practitioners still choose to specialize in the city with its research hospitals and extensive medical community.

However, the future may well see the current pattern of urban concentration of health services supplanted by a more dispersed pattern. Where subsidies and exhortations failed to break the metropolitan areas' near monopoly of medical services a radical expansion and transformation of our communication

---

[2]Material in this section is based on J. John Palen and Daniel M. Johnson, "Urbanization and Health Status," in Ann L. Greer and Scott Greer (eds.), *Cities and Sickness,* Sage Publications, Beverly Hills, Cal., 1983, pp. 25–54.
[3]Ann L. Greer, "Health Care Policy: Disillusion and Confusion," in J. Blair and D. Nachmias (eds.), *Urban Policies in Transition,* Sage Publishers, Beverly Hills, Cal., 1979.

capabilities may do so. Contemporary communication technologies have the potential to break the cities' monopoly on skills and equipment. For example, advances in interactive communication technology can now make the most complex medical diagnostic procedures, and even treatment, available to geographically remote areas of the country.

A rural physician whose clinic is wired for conference communications could consult simultaneously with specialists in diverse cities. A closed-circuit cable medical channel would also allow distant diagnosticians actually to see and speak with the patient. A physician who prefers a rural life-style could even, by means of a closed-circuit medical educational channel, attend medical lectures or hospital rounds. Although its capabilities have yet to be grasped, technology has once again made it possible for the physician to come to the patient rather than requiring the patient to come to the physician.

The crucial questions today regarding the adoption of these options are not technological but social. Technically we can do it. However, social changes have yet to be accepted. Will these possible communication technologies actually be utilized? It is one thing to discuss how spatial barriers can be overcome; it is another to say that they will be overcome, particularly in a socially conservative area such as health care. Militating against adoption is the well-documented fact that physicians are noted for their conservative social and political orientation. This has historically been true of practitioners, particularly those in small towns or small cities. Will nonurban physicians be interested in plugging into high-tech medical access systems?

The evidence of the past decade suggests that it will be difficult for health professionals—whatever their personal desires—to avoid the consequences of living in what is increasingly becoming a "wired" society. Nor will health professionals be able to ignore the fact that after two centuries of concentration the nation is now dispersing its residents, industries, and services. With this diminishing need for propinquity, and the resulting dispersal of population, will come a dispersal of health and medical services—both physically and through communication technology. It is reasonable to predict that the general practitioner's famous black bag will increasingly be supplanted by the health practitioner's interactive computer's black box.

Of course, huge central-city medical complexes will not suddenly fade away; downtown department stores did not close once widespread auto ownership made outlying shopping more convenient. Downtown medical complexes, like downtown department stores, will continue to have a substantial, if diminished, clientele. However, the master trend for the remainder of this century will be dispersal rather than concentration.

None of this should be taken as suggesting that America's existing urban places are in danger of becoming ghost towns. They aren't. The "death of the city" clichés of the last decade have turned out to be poor prophecy. Within many older cities both central business districts (CBDs) and residential neighborhoods have arrested the pattern of decline and are showing evidence of stability or even growth. What is clear is that American urban places and patterns are undergoing profound changes. It appears that the future will be both more complex and more interesting than previously projected.

MAJOR ISSUES AND QUESTIONS

Urban Funding

Until the Reagan Administration of the 1980s, the major disputes in Washington, D.C. over urban programs were where to target the money and how much to budget. There was a consensus among both Democrats and Republicans that programs and funding were needed; they fought over specific programs. President Nixon, it should be recalled, initiated the program of Federal Revenue Sharing.

Now that broad consensus regarding at least partial responsibility for urban places has been shattered. President Reagan's second-term agenda envisioned not just the trimming back, but the total elimination of virtually all federal aid to cities. Although that has not occurred as of this writing (1985), it appears that the next half-decade will witness a period of declining federal support for cities. The consequence of the closing of the federal coffers may return older central cities to the patterns of economic insolvency common in the 1970s. However, to date that has not occurred. Current tax policies, as distinguished from specific programs, favor central-city investment. The investment tax discussed in Chapter 11, Housing Programs and Urban Change, is a case in point.

People versus Places

Beyond the question of amount of funds is disagreement as to how the limited urban funds should be spent. The policy dispute goes to the heart of existing programs. Should the federal government continue efforts to revitalize the economies of older central cities? The orthodox response for the approximately four decades since the Housing Act of 1949 has been to funnel funds into the renewal and rebuilding of the economic and housing bases of the neediest older cities. Although there has been a mishmash of various programs, policies designed during the 1950s, 1960s, and 1970s, had at least the implicit goal of halting or at least slowing the middle-class exodus to the suburbs. More recently this implied goal has been enlarged to include arresting the drift of jobs and population from older frost belt cities to the sun belt.

However, some urban sociologists and other urbanologists argue that trying to restore older industrial cities is a mistake.[4] Those holding this position say that present policies place the needs of places ahead of those of people. They maintain that rather than propping up obsolete industries or declining

---

[4]See John D. Kasarda, "The Implications of Contemporary Redistribution Trends for National Urban Policy," *Social Science Quarterly* **61**:373–400, 1980; and Gerald D. Suttles, "Changing Priorities for the Urban Heartland," in J. John Palen (ed.), *City Scenes: Problems and Prospects,* Little, Brown, Boston, 1981.

Ghirardelli Square in San Francisco was the first project demonstrating how abandoned buildings could be transformed into vibrant shopping and restaurant areas. (Fred Kaplan/Black Star)

places, urban policies should be redesigned to help the poor and the unemployed to migrate to places where job opportunities are still expanding. The current focus on saving the cities, they argue, results simply in warehousing the poor in cities, to no one's advantage.

According to a proponent of this view, John Kasarda, "It would be an expensive mistake to attempt to draw (by tax incentives or other means) larger production facilities back to the metropolitan cores or continuously to prop up declining urban industries that are no longer nationally or internationally competitive."[5] Obsolete areas should be allowed to shrink to a size where they are economically viable.

In practicing this would mean, for example, that the declining steel manufacturing city of Gary, Indiana, which received one of the nation's highest per capita infusions of federal money during the 1970s, should not have received such massive urban renewal, redevelopment, and retraining funds. Rather than pumping in funds in a futile attempt to save a dying industrial city, the federal government should have encouraged and aided Gary's residents to move from an area with a minimal future to regions where jobs were available. Not surprisingly, central-city mayors take especially strong exception to this view. They say that not attempting to save older cities seriously undermines both the places and the people who live in them.

Changing Population Distribution

For two hundred years cities had a growth rate far in excess of that of the countryside because of the combination of heavy migration from abroad and internal movement from farm to city. Now that period has ended.

Without substantial numbers of new arrivals, central-city populations generally can be expected to remain fairly stable for the next decade. The exceptions to this pattern are the growing cities of the sun belt, particularly those of Texas, California, and Florida. These three states accounted for half of the total U.S. population gain between 1980 and 1985. All three experienced substantial in-migration from other states plus immigration of Spanish speaking population. Population losses have been most severe in the old industrtial cities of the midwest. This shift also means a shift of political power from the industrial cities and farm belt to the growing areas of the south and west. After reapportionment based on the 1980 census the midwest and northeast lost seventeen seats in the House of Representatives.

However, the hemorrhaging population losses that affected older U.S. cities during the 1970s appear to have ended. The sharp population declines during the 1970s that cost New York and Chicago 10 percent of their residents have moderated. As of 1985 Detroit, Cleveland, Baltimore, Philadelphia, Boston, Seattle, and Milwaukee were still losing population, but at a declining rate. Elsewhere urban populations generally were remaining stable or even showing minor increases.

Migration in North America today is increasingly between one metropolitan area and another. Poorer migrants most commonly go from central city to central city. The more affluent move from the suburbs of one metropolitan area to the suburbs of another metropolitan area without touching the cities themselves. Aggregate movement in the United States is toward the south and the west, particularly the southwest. Population movement also is toward deep

[5]Kasarda, op. cit., p. 395.

water: the Atlantic and Pacific oceans, the Gulf of Mexico, or the Great Lakes. Today more than two out of five Americans live in a metropolitan area abutting deep water. The effects of such concentration are already all too visible in parts of California and Florida.

Continued suburban and exurban sprawl has been constrained not by government fiat or planning, but by escalating costs. For some new young homebuyers a housing alternative may be purchasing a home in a revitalizing central-city neighborhood. Changing life-styles and priorities combined with commuting costs (time and money) have made residence in peripheral locations less attractive for some. For young urban professionals and perhaps even the elderly, the option of living in a restored central-city neighborhood may well become incresingly attractive. However, as indicated in Chapter 11, Housing Programs and Urban Change, such a location does not appeal to all house-holders. Most intra- or internal Metropolitan Statistical Area (MSA) movement is still toward the periphery rather than toward the central city.

Suburban Developments

Suburbanism is destined to remain the American way of life for the balance of this century. As noted in Chapter 8, Patterns of Suburbanization, and Chapter 13, Planning in the United States, survey after survey indicates that suburban living is a life-style that appeals to most Americans. Equally important, an immense investment has already been made in existing suburban homes, office complexes, shopping centers, and industrial parks. Since most suburbanites not only live but also work in suburban areas, these suburbanites have little incentive to move back to the city for reasons of employment. Moreover, there is a tendency to exaggerate the distance people commute to work. The median distance from home to work, according to Bureau of the Census data, is 7.6 miles.[6] In Philadelphia it is only 4.4 miles, in Chicago 6.6 miles, and in Dallas 6.2 miles. Even in the Los Angeles area, where one hears stories of 75-mile commuter trips, the average distance is under 9 miles.

Racially, suburban areas continue to maintain their image as all-white enclaves, but black suburbanization—particularly black middle-class suburbanization—is accelerating. Currently one out of every five blacks lives in a suburb, and the proportion is increasing. Suburbanization, of course, does not necessarily indicate integration. To the extent that black suburbanization is disproportionately concentrated in the older and generally less affluent inner ring of suburbs, it may only reflect black neighborhoods moving across city-suburban legal boundaries.

However, regardless of the amount of black migration to suburbs, as long as blacks constitute only one-eighth of the population and whites continue to move to or remain in the suburbs, it is demographically impossible for suburbia as a whole to develop a black majority.

[6]U.S. Bureau of the Census, "Selected Characteristics of Travel to Work in 20 Metropolitan Areas: 1976," *Current Population Reports,* series P-23, no. 72, Washington, D.C., 1978.

Suburbia is no longer just families with children living in free-standing homes. (Ellis Herwig/The Picture Cube)

PLANNING FOR THE FUTURE CITY

To many people, urban planning almost automatically means physical planning: but physical planning is never free from social implications—the two are always intertwined. Moreover, our view of the future influences our contemporary behavior. As Scott Greer has expressed it:

> It is my assumption that images of the future determine present actions. They may or may not determine the nature of the future—that depends on a much more

complex set of circumstances. But willy-nilly much of our behavior is postulated upon images of a possible and/or desirable future.[7]

Ebenezer Howard's "garden cities" have already been discussed in Chapter 12, Planning Europe: with Discussion of New Towns. Howard advocated a system of compact, self-contained cities of limited size that were designed to attract residents away from large cities such as London. Other planners have had different visions of utopia. Frank Lloyd Wright's model (1934) of a decentralized garden city called "Broadacres" was more explicitly antiurban than Howard's. Wright proposed that each individual in his "urban" model be allotted at least 1 acre, which he or she would be expected to farm. Significantly, his book *The Living City* ends with material excerpted from Ralph Waldo Emerson's "Essay on Farming."[8]

A different type of "city of tomorrow," and one that has had far more influence on American planners, is Le Corbusier's "radiant city." This was to be composed of a center of towering skyscrapers surrounded by parks and open spaces. Residences, similarly, would be tall, thin apartment superblocks surrounded by greenery.[9] Much of the high-rise urban renewal of the 1960s was affected by Le Corbusier's vision of the city of the future.

Brasilia, the new capital of Brazil, although not designed by Le Corbusier, followed his general plan: it has a unified high-rise center and residential superblocks united by a radial system of freeways. However, as was indicated earlier, Brasilia, while striking, is too uncomfortably monumental for most people, who prefer the chaos of a Rio de Janiero.

Sometimes physical planning for the future takes on a fanciful, "brave new world" character. The vision of Buckminster Fuller is an example: It cuts our ties to the physical earth and to mundane things such as water mains and sewers by means of recycling packs that we could wear on our backs like the astronauts' life-support systems. The urban architectual critic Wolf von Eckardt has a more earthbound view of such a future:

> The box regenerates our wastes and water and even reconditions our air and provides us with light and heat. If only we strap those little boxes to our backs, he says, we can all disperse over the world's mountains and deserts, telecommunicate with each other, and dispense with crowded settlements. Fuller, needless to say, did not acquire his astounding, sophisticated knowledge from video screens on lonely mountaintops. He acquired it in the lively bustle, the intellectual interchange, and the accumulation of wisdom that crowded human settlements stand for.[10]

The visionary and planner Constantinos A. Doxiadis's prescription for planning an organized community likewise is radically removed from the

---

[7]Scott Greer, *The Urbane View,* Oxford University Press, New York, 1972, p. 322.

[8]Frank Lloyd Wright, *The Living City,* Mentor-Horizon, New York, 1958.

[9]Le Corbusier, *The Radiant City,* part I, Pamela Knight (trans.), parts II and VI, Eleanor Levieux (trans.), parts III, IV, V, VII, and VIII, Derek Coltman (trans.), Grossman-Orion, New York, 1967; this is a translation of the French version, *La Ville Radieuse, 1933.*

[10]Wolf von Eckardt, "Urban Design," in Moynihan, op. cit., chap. 9, p. 113.

situation in contemporary cities. Doxiadis proposes a city of 2 million, organized into communities of 30,000 to 50,000—each within an area of 2,000 yards by 2,000 yards. Services, schools, stores, businesses, and parks would all be organized so that residents could walk to them; public transit and highways would be around the communities. Movement from community to community within the city would be by means of "deepways"—underground highways.[11]

Another fanciful model for future cities is architect Paolo Soleri's "arcology," a compact three-dimensioned city. Soleri places heavy emphasis on building a city vertically, or layer on layer, and on using "miniaturization," or a more compact form, which he believes is the rule of evolutionary development.[12] Instead of urban sprawl Soleri would have cities confined to a few square miles, with buildings 300 stories high. Soleri and volunteers attempted to build in Arizona a 3,000-person, twenty-five story prototype of the future named Acrosanti. However, by the 1980s work on Acrosanti had been virtually abandoned. Today Acrosanti contains only eight low-rise auxiliary buildings, some in a half-completed state. Acrosanti at this point resembles a ghost town more than a visionary city.

Dantzig and Saaty take this idea of vertical compactness a step further and propose a compact vertical city that makes round-the-clock use of all facilities.[13] Such a city, though, would require constant services. Strikes by municipal workers would paralyze such a compact high-rise city, and thus would have to be prohibited. It is easy to foresee such a city turning into a tightly monitored totalitarian state.

Planned utopias may challenge the imagination, but they also frequently appear rather sterile and lifeless. They often seem better suited to guided tours than day-in, day-out habitation. To theorize about the future is one thing; to want to live in it is another. For example, plastic domes, similar to that covering the Houston Astrodome, can now be constructed, permitting a controlled climate and environment. Cities covered by domes could theoretically be built in otherwise hostile environments such as desert regions or even the smog-filled Los Angeles basin. Inside the domes, artificial light, controlled heating and cooling, and even synthetic grass could be provided. The question is whether we really want to live with synthetic lawns.

On the other hand, viewing the future as a lineal multiplication of the past is not only far less interesting but over the long run almost certain to be inaccurate. It would be rather depressing if our only dream for the future of the metropolitan area was of an endless growth of subdivisions and shopping malls. The choice for the future is not between planning and no planning—we will plan, even if it is only low-level planning of individual pieces of property or individual buildings. The question thus is not whether planning should be done, but rather on what level it should be done.

[11]C. A. Doxiadis, *Ekistics,* Hutchinson, London, 1968.

[12]Paolo Soleri, *Arcology, The City in the Image of Man,* M.I.T. Press, Cambridge, Mass., 1969.

[13]George B. Dantzig and Thomas L. Saaty, *Compact City: A Plan for a Liveable Urban Environment,* Freeman, San Francisco, 1973.

Planning for City Dwellers

Planners and social critics often seem caught in all-or-nothing approaches by which we exercise our imaginations either in grand fantasies or not at all. The trick is to find the line between speculative fancy and unimaginative extension of the past. This is another of those things which are far simpler in theory than in practice, for novel and innovative schemes are all too often considered unrealistic and dismissed out of hand. As Machiavelli accurately observed centuries ago, "There is nothing more difficult to carry out, nor more doubtful of success, nor more dangerous to handle than a new order of things."[14]

It is crucial to remember that whatever our formal plans for the city of the future, much of what will actually happen is the result of untold numbers of diverse decisions made by different individuals. As stated by Jane Jacobs:

> . . . most city diversity is the creation of incredible numbers of different people and different private organizations with vastly differing ideas and purposes, planning and contributing outside the formal framework of public action. The main responsibility of city planning and design should be to develop—insofar as public policy and action can do so—cities that are congenial places for this great range of unofficial plans, ideas and opportunities to flourish, along with the flourishing of the public enterprises.[15]

We need far more ideas and schemes of the middle range. An interesting architectural innovation in housing design, for example, was Moshe Safdie's "Habitat," erected for Expo '67 in Montreal. Safdie's design of modular boxes piled irregularly upon one another was originally hailed by some observers as the answer to the urban housing problem. The modular units were prefabricated and shipped to the construction site; the irregular placement of the units provided not only for variety but also for balconies and private space. The result was a rare combination of both privacy and a sense of community. Unlike most modern apartment buildings, Habitat gave the immediate impression of being concerned with human needs and designing buildings to meet these needs rather than simply stuffing people into space. Unfortunately, "Habitats" have turned out to be both more expensive and less practical than was hoped. In addition to the financial difficulties, there is also a less clearly expressed but nevertheless deep reluctance to try anything as different from conventional apartment buildings as Habitat.

One transportation alternative proposed by the author—and having little chance of adoption—is his "borrow a bike" plan. This plan was actually proposed in Amsterdam but rejected by the officials. The idea is quite simple: The city would put up numerous clearly marked municipal bicycle racks and fill them with city-owned bicycles. Anyone could use any bike from any rack, the only requirement being that he or she eventually return it to one of the racks. The bikes would be simple, straightforward, one-speed models painted a distinctive common color. There would be little point in stealing them, since

[14]Niccolo Machiavelli, *The Prince*, W. K. Marriot (trans.), J. M. Dent, London, 1958, p. 29.
[15]Jane Jacobs, *The Death and Life of Great American Cities*, Vintage-Random House, New York, 1961, p. 241.

in any event they would be freely available as transportation to anyone who wanted them. Some people would undoubtedly lock their "own" bikes, but if enough bikes were available, this would not be an important problem. Certainly some riders would move on to purchase their own more elaborate models, so that the scheme would probably increase rather than decrease sales by private dealers—just as Henry Ford's cheap Model T spurred the purchase of more elaborate automobiles. Bicycles could be manufactured and assembled at little cost by the city itself, employing persons on public assistance who want jobs but have only minimal skills.

Such a scheme would reduce pollution, reduce gasoline consumption, ease traffic, and increase the physical—and probably emotional—health of the population. Increasing public awareness of the importance of regular exercise should contribute to the plan's success. The concept would have even greater appeal in certain types of communities, such as university towns and sun belt retirement villages. The possible disadvantages would be the initial cost of the bicycles (although lower costs of repairing streets should more than compensate for this over the long run) and the fact that in some cities the bikes would probably not be used much through the winter months. Also, even if the plan saved the city money, some residents would no doubt complain that it was socialistic nonsense and that the city had no business giving people bicycles.

The "borrow a bike" plan is simply one example of how, without massive rebuilding or expense, we can make our cities more healthy and livable. If American city dwellers used bicycles as much as the residents of Amsterdam, or Beijing there would be fewer problems with pollution and with energy crunches.

Planning Metropolitan Political Systems

Organizationally, metropolitan areas appear in a state of confusion and disorganization. Present home rule provides for local control at a substantial price. The political system itself becomes a major obstacle to effective planning. A multiplicity of city, suburban, county, township, regional, state, and federal bureaucracies all must intermesh if the metropolitan area is to be serviced effectively and at minimum cost, and this rarely works as well in practice as in theory. The interminable squabbling between city mayors and suburban political officials is one index of the ineffectiveness of the present system. The New York conurbation (admittedly an extreme example) includes people from three different states and some 1,400 different jurisdictions of one sort or another.

One alternative would be to abandon most local jurisdictions and move in the direction of one metropolitan-area government such as those found in Dade County, Florida (Miami) or Nashville, Tennessee. However, in spite of the generally favorable reports on these consolidations, there is little real agitation or political pressure in major American urban areas for adoption of this system.

Another approach is a two-level, system which would move certain decision-making powers and organization to the level of a county or MSA while other functions would be handled by dividing the entire area—including the central city—into political units the size of suburbs, which would handle local problems. Toronto, Canada, is a successful example of the two-tiered approach.

> What is necessary, therefore, is to move in two directions. One is to create the kind of urban governmental mechanism that is capable of handling the major maintenance functions of a metropolitan aggregation, playing the coordinating role essential to a specialized and large-scale community, and guaranteeing the "openness" of the opportunity structure. The other is to establish local governmental units of such size that the individual will have meaningful opportunity to participate in and control those public activities which directly and immediately affect his neighborhood and his life style. The first objective will require the creation of a metropolitan or regional government with territorial jurisdiction over the entire urbanized area; the second will necessitate the division of the central city into smaller political units of 100,000 to 150,000 population, each with governmental structures and power similar to those of the suburban municipalities. Under this plan, the counties and all special districts within the urban region would be abolished as governmental entities; the other local units—the suburban municipalities and suburban school districts—would continue in existence as at present, although some industrial concentrations, because of their importance to the total community, would be placed under the jurisdiction of the larger government. Elections to the regional council would be by district, with the chief executive selected at large.[16]

Under the larger metropolitan unit would be placed functions common to the urban system as a whole, such as water supply, waste disposal, expressways and streets, control of air and water pollution, museums, public hospitals, and major recreational facilities. On the other hand, local matters such as education, enforcement of housing codes, and recreation would be left to the local community. As for education, there is no reason why local central-city areas should not have their own school boards and school policies, just as suburbs currently do. Given the present low quality of many central-city schools, more localized control could probably only improve the situation.

Police departments could also be organized on a local basis—with a common radio network and other specialized facilities—while fire protection should be provided on a metropolitan basis. It makes little sense for suburban fire departments to duplicate expensive equipment; furthermore, the area that a fire station services should be determined by the needs of a population rather than by political boundaries. Police officers, on the other hand, have a day-to-day contact with the community that firefighters do not. Small, locally administered departments such as those found in suburbs today are most likely to provide a setting in which the police and the community can come to know

---

[16]Henry J. Schmandt, "Solutions for the City as a Social Crisis," in J. John Palen and Karl H. Flaming (eds.), *Urban America*, Holt, Rinehart and Winston, New York, 1972, p. 363.

and respect one another. Large bureaucratic departments in which police are shifted from district to district seldom are able to establish rapport with citizens. This is especially true of many black inner-city areas, where the police are objects of overt hostility and are viewed by the residents as an occupying army. In such a situation, the police generally respond in kind. What would happen to the extremely high crime rates in these areas if locally controlled police forces replaced the present system? A new system would certainly be worth trying, in selected cities and as a closely monitored experiment.

However, dissatisfaction with past policies and practices has yet to create sufficient pressures for change. There is little chance that such new approaches will receive serious consideration by policy makers, particularly since some politicians would see their control diminish. City mayors have little interest in transferring authority to council officials. For the immediate future we can only hope that voluntary cooperation among the various governmental units within metropolitan areas will increase.

Social Planning

Three Approaches to Social Planning. Approaches to social planning and problem solving range from the use of existing social mechanisms in conventional ways to attempts to radically restructure the entire system. Three general assumptions regarding problem solving and the resulting approaches to planning can be delineated: (1) conventional approaches, which assume that problems can be solved by existing mechanisms, (2) reformist approaches, which assume that the system needs some major modification, and (3) radical approaches, which assume that problems cannot be solved by the existing social system (see Table 18-1).

Conventional approaches to planning and problem solving assume that the system itself is not in question. Inadequacies are attributed to the failings of individuals. The appropriate traditional response thus is to replace the offending personnel with new faces. Reassessment of priorities is also an essentially conventional response. Here, the emphasis is upon the allocation of resources and weighting of priorities within the system rather than upon structural modification of the system itself.

Reformist responses, as outlined in Table 18-1, are characterized by ideological commitment to the goals and ideals of the society but not by attempts to achieve them through conventional means. Reformers are more likely to see the system itself as the source of the problem and to have little faith in correcting it by traditional means. They accept quasi-legal methods falling outside the traditional system, as did some members of the civil rights movement and the environmental movement. Legislation such as the Clean Air Act reflect reformist pressure.

Radical approaches differ from the conventional and reformist positions by rejecting, at least implicitly, the goals of the society as well as the means used to implement them. The existing system is judged to be so corrupt and

TABLE 18-1
Strategies for Planning and Problem Solving

Assumptions regarding problem solving	General approach to planning	Resulting action taken
Most, if not all, problems can be solved by existing mechanisms	Conventional approaches (System needs minor modifications, fine tuning, or both)	New leadership, better administration, shift in priorities, new legislation
Some problems cannot be solved by existing mechanisms	Reformist approaches (System needs some major modification; likely to see system itself as source of problems)	Mobilization of power bases outside existing party structures, quasi-legal protests, civil disobedience
Most, if not all, problems cannot be solved by existing mechanisms	Radical approaches (System needs major revision or replacement)	Rejection of societal goals, extreme countercultural movements, revolution, planned violence.

Source: Based on J. John Palen and Karl H. Flaming. *Urban America*, Holt, Rinehart and Winston, New York, 1972, p. 335.

repressive that the response is to destroy it and start over. Radical responses (Marxist approaches, for example) are almost always overtly ideological in their vision of the new utopia.

Social Planning and Technology. One point upon which urbanists, including conservatives, generally agree is that the core problems of the city are social problems. The difficulty is that we are frequently unwilling to admit the existence of social problems, until they reach serious proportions, and even then we seek solutions through other than social reforms in the naive belief that "technology saves." Public housing projects and freeways are perhaps the two best-known examples of how we have, with disastrous results for the cities, attempted to provide engineering solutions for social problems. For example, the technology exists for building mile-high apartment buildings. The real question should not be "Is it possible?" but rather "Is it desirable?" Still, the faith in the ultimate technical solution persists. As Jeb Magruder, at one time a technology consultant for the Nixon administration, expressed it:

> The cities have no place else to turn except to technical solutions. There is no political or social solution to providing more adequate energy, or waste disposal, or drug abuse. I want to see something better and technology can do it if we work at it.[17]

---

[17]*The New York Times*, July 29, 1972.

The answers even to questions about energy are, of course, far more social and political than technical. America's social orientation toward automobiles, its values concerning the environment, and even its political policies toward the oil monopolies determine whether the nation has an "energy crisis" far more than technology alone. The decision of an oil company not to build a needed refinery may be an economic or a political decision, or both, but it is not a technological decision. Of course, if one expects technology to solve all problems, even including drug abuse, there really isn't any need to even consider modifying or changing the social, economic, or political system.

THE "POSTCITY" AGE

Superterritoriality

Some futurists see us as inevitably moving toward immensely larger metropolises. Doxiadis, for example, viewed population increases resulting in a world where urban settlements covered an area not just seven to ten times larger than they now do, but as much as thirty, forty, or even fifty times as large. Moreover, he predicted that it is probable that all settlements will become interconnected to form a continuous system covering the inhabitable earth. In Doxiadis's opinion, there is no possibility of halting or changing the growth of this ultimate megalopolis he calls "Ecumenopolis." He felt that stopping the trend toward Ecumenopolis is impossible for two reasons:

1. These are trends of population growth determined by many biological and social forces which we do not even understand properly, let alone dare countermand.
2. The great forces shaping the Ecumenopolis—economic, commercial, social, political, technological, and cultural—are already being deployed, and it is too late to reverse them.[18]

He further believed that the eventual creation of Ecumenopolis should be considered "an inevitability which we must accept." The challenge as he saw it is "to make the Ecumenopolis fit for Man."[19]

Fortunately, this prediction has little contact with empirical reality. Population growth is far from inevitable; and biological and social forces do not operate in response to mysterious and mystical "forces" beyond our knowledge. Whatever our urban areas become, they will be the result of our present and future actions—wise or unwise—not the result of unchangeable forces.

---

[18]Doxiadis, op. cit., p. 430.
[19]Ibid.

Our visions of the urban future are sometimes less than accurate. This is the City of the Future as predicted by General Motors at the 1939 New York World's Fair. (Norman Bel Geddes Collection, Theatre Arts Library, Harry Ransom Humanities Research Center, The University of Texas at Austin; by permission of Edith Lutyens Bel Geddes, executrix.)

Nonterritoriality

Others see the traditional city as passing away. In recent years, we have come to think less in terms of the city versus the country and more in terms of a larger urban-dominated community that often includes rural sectors. This new unit, commonly called the "metropolitan community," has evolved rapidly in the United States during the past half century. Now some scholars believe that we are moving from metropolitan communities to a new "postcity" age. As Melvin Webber states this position, "We are passing through a revolution that is unhitching the social processes of urbanization from the locationally fixed city and region."[20] Webber maintains:

> A new kind of large-scale urban society is emerging that is increasingly independent of the city. In turn, the problems of the city place generated by early industrialization are being supplanted by a new array different in kind. With but a few remaining exceptions (the new air pollution is a notable one), the recent difficulties are not place-type problems at all. Rather, they are the transitional problems of a rapidly developing society-economy-and-polity whose turf is the nation. Paradoxically, just at the time in history when policy-makers and the world press are discovering the city, "the age of the city seems to be at an end."[21]

He suggests that we have failed to draw up a simple conceptual definition distinguishing between the spatially defined urban area and the social systems that are localized there. Because our cities have historically been spatially structured, we don't have the concepts or language to deal with the new situation. The resulting problems, Webber says, are serious ones, for we seek local solutions to problems that transcend local boundaries and are not susceptible to municipal treatment. Problems of poverty, crime, unemployment, and even transportation transcend any city or even cities in general.

Webber suggests that the future pattern can be discerned in the life-styles of the new cosmopolites who through frequent use of airlines and telephones have established new spatially dispersed networks of specialized knowledge. These cosmopolites are the producers of the information and new ideas that are transforming societies.

Like much of the "Chicago school" of sociology of half a century earlier, Webber assumes that movement from localized primary-group relationships to territorially unbounded secondary-group relationships is inevitable and irreversible. He states:

> At one extreme are the intellectual and business elites, whose habitat is the planet; at the other are the lower-class residents of city and farm who live in spatially and cognitively constrained worlds. Most of the rest of us, who comprise the large middle class, lie somewhere in-between, but in some facets of our lives we all

[20]Melvin M. Webber, "The Postcity Age," Daedalus, 97(4):1092, Fall, 1968.
[21]Webber, Ibid., pp. 1092–1093. Reprinted by permission of Daedalus, Journal of the American Academy of Arts and Sciences, Boston, Mass., Fall, 1968, The Conscience of the City.

seem to be moving from our ancestral localism toward the unbounded realms of the cosmopolites.[22]

This is far from certain. It *may* be true for segments of the upper middle class; but, as we have seen in earlier chapters, upper-middle-class professionals tend to consistently underrate both the strength and the utility of territorially bounded urban life-styles.

The Passing of the City?

Another reworking of the concept of the passing of the city is provided by John Seeley, who suggests that the western nations have reached their highest point of development and institutional practices. He goes on to say: "If the view is correct, there is something tragicomic about sitting around planning' to secure, extend, and improve what is to be shortly swept away. . . ."[23] In his view, the city as we know it will pass, to be replaced by a new and as yet undefined form:

> Very little will need planning—just enough control over the spread of cities and their ways to permit the conscience of the city to find itself chiefly outside these centers, to spread through the society which, by then, may be ready, having reached its fevered climax, to abandon its delirium and search out a new way. That new way, I am confident, will not be, cannot be, in content, organization, aim, or spirit, anything like a continuation or culmination of what we have hitherto nurtured and known.[24]

Most urban sociologists, on the other hand, are extremely dubious as to whether this prophecy of the passage of the city will come to be. To paraphrase Mark Twain's famous remark on being told that he had been reported dead, the reports of the death of the city have been greatly exaggerated. Today urbanism is *the* American way of life.

---

[22]Webber, op. cit., p. 1095. Reprinted by permission of *Daedalus*, Journal of the American Academy of Arts and Sciences, Boston, Mass., Fall, 1968, *The Conscience of the City*.

[23]John R. Seeley, "Remaking the Urban Scene: New Youth in an Old Environment," *Daedalus*, **97**(4):1125, Fall, 1968.

[24]Ibid., p. 1139. Reprinted by permission of *Daedalus*, Journal of the American Academy of Arts and Sciences, Boston, Mass., Fall, 1968, *The Conscience of the City*.

BIBLIOGRAPHY

CHAPTER 1

Berry, Brian J. L.: "The Counterurbanization Process: Urban America Since 1970," in *Urbanization and Counterurbanization,* Vol. II, *Urban Affairs Annual Reviews,* Sage Publications, Beverly Hills, Cal., 1976.

Chandler, Tertius, and Gerald Fox: *3000 Years of Urban Growth,* Academic Press, New York, 1974.

Davis, Kingsley: *World Urbanization 1950–1970, Volume II, Analysis of Trends, Relationships, and Development,* University of California, Berkeley, 1972.

Demographic Handbook for Africa: United Nations Economic Commission for Africa, Addis Ababa, 1968.

Durkheim, Emile: *The Division of Labor in Society,* George Simpson (trans.), The Free Press, Glencoe, Ill., 1960.

Eldridge, Hope Tisdale: "The Process of Urbanization," in J. J. Spengler and O. D. Duncan (eds.), *Demographic Analysis,* The Free Press, Glencoe, Ill., 1956.

Fischer, Claude S.: "Urban Malaise," *Social Forces,* vol. 52, December 1973.

Hauser, Philip, and Robert Gardner: "Urban Future: Trends and Prospects," in Philip Hauser et al., *Population and the Urban Future,* U. N. Fund for Population Activities, SUNY Press, Albany, N. Y., 1982, pp. 10–11.

Hauser, Philip and Leo Schnore: *The Study of Urbanization,* Wiley, New York, 1965.

Hawley, Amos H.: *Human Ecology: A Theory of Community Structure,* Ronald Press, New York, 1950.

Lofland, Lyn H.: "Understanding Urban Life: The Chicago Legacy," *Urban Life,* **11:**491–511, 1983.

Macura, Milos: "The Influence of the Definition of Urban Place on the Size of Urban Population," in Jack Gibbs (ed.), *Urban Research Methods,* Van Nostrand, New York, 1961.

Marx, Karl, and Friedrich Engels: *The German Ideology,* R. Pascal (trans.), International Publishers Company, New York, 1947.

Meadows, Paul, and Ephraim Mizruchi (eds): *Urbanism Urbanization, and Change: Comparative Perspectives,* Addison-Wesley, Reading, Mass., 1969.

Palen, J. John, and Daniel Johnson: "Urbanization and Health Status," in Ann and Scott Greer (eds.), *Cities and Sickness,* Sage Publications, Beverly Hills, 1983, Chapter 2, pp.25–54.

Park, Robert E.: "The City: Suggestions for the Investigation of Human Behavior in the Urban Environment," in Robert E. Park, E. W. Burgess, and Roderick D. McKenzie (eds.), *The City,* University of Chicago Press, Chicago, 1925.

Redfield, Robert: "The Folk Society," *American Journal of Sociology,* vol. 52, 1947.

Schnore, Leo: "Urbanization and Economic Development: The Demographic Contribution," *American Journal of Economics and Sociology,* vol. 23, 1964.

Shaw, Clifford R.: *The Jack Roller,* University of Chicago Press, Chicago, 1930.

Simmel, Georg: "The Metropolis and Mental Life," in Kurt Wolff (trans.), *The Sociology of Georg Simmel,* New York, 1964.

Srole, Leo: "Mental Health in New York," *The Sciences,* **20**:16–29, 1980.

Stein, Maurice R.: *The Eclipse of Community,* Princeton University Press, Princeton, N.J., 1961.

Thomas, William I., and Florian Znaniecki: *The Polish Peasant in Europe and America,* 5 vols., University of Chicago Press, Chicago, 1918–1920.

Tönnies, Ferdinand: *Community and Society,* Charles P. Loomis (trans.), Harper and Row, New York, 1963.

United Nations: *The State of World Population, 1978,* New York , 1978.

———: *Urbanization in the Second United Nations Development Decade,* New York, 1970.

Vidich, Arthur, and Joseph Bensman: *Small Town in Mass Society,* Princeton University Press, Princeton, N.J., 1958.

Weber, Adna Ferrin: *The Growth of Cities in the Nineteenth Century,* Cornell University Press, Ithaca, N.Y., 1899.

Weber, Max: *Essays in Sociology,* C. Wright Mills and H. H. Gerth (ed. and trans.), Oxford University Press, New York, 1966.

Wirth, Louis: *The Ghetto,* University of Chicago Press, Chicago, 1928.

———: "Urbanism as a Way of Life," *American Journal of Sociology,* Vol. 44, July 1938.

Zorbaugh, Harvey W.: *The Gold Coast and the Slum,* University of Chicago Press, Chicago, 1929.

CHAPTER 2

Adams, Robert McC: "The Origins of Cities," *Scientific American,* September 1960.

Aristotle: Book VII, *Politics,* B. Jowett (trans.), 1932 ed.

Braidwood, Robert J.: "The Agricultural Revolution," *Scientific American,* September 1960.

Braudel, Ferdinand: *The Mediterranean and the Mediterranean World in the Age of Phillip II* Sian Reynolds (trans.), Harper and Row, New York, 1972.

Carcopino, Jerome: *Daily Life in Ancient Rome,* Yale University Press, New Haven, Conn., 1940.

Castells, Manuel: *The Urban Question,* MIT Press, Cambridge, Mass., 1977.

Chandler, Tertius, and Gerald Fox: *3000 Years of Urban Growth,* Academic Press, New York, 1974.

Childe, Gordon: "The Urban Revolution," *Town Planning Review,* vol. 21, 1950.

———: *What Happened in History,* Penguin Books, London, 1946.

Creel, H. G.: *The Birth of China,* Reynal and Hitchcock, New York, 1937.

Coulanges, Fustel de: *The Ancient City,* Doubleday, Garden City, N.Y., 1956.

Curwin, E. Cecil, and Gudmund Hart: *Plough and Pasture,* Collier Books, New York, 1961.

Davis, Kingsley: "The Origin and Growth of Urbanization in the World," *American Journal of Sociology,* March 1955.

Deauz, George: *The Black Death,* Weybright and Talley, New York, 1969.

Duncan, Otis Dudley: "From Social System to Ecosystem," *Sociological Inquiry,* vol. 31, 1961.

Engels, Friedrich: *The Condition of the Working Class in England in 1844,* Progress Publishers, Moscow, 1973.

Flannery, Kent J.: "The Origins of Agriculture," *Annual Review of Anthropology,* 2:271–310, 1973.

George, Dorothy: *London Life in the Eighteenth Century,* Harper Torchbooks, New York, 1964.

Gibbon, Edward: *The Decline and Fall of the Roman Empire,* Dell, New York, 1879 (first published 1776).

Glotz, Gustave: *Ancient Greece at Work,* Norton, New York, 1967, pp. 291–293.

Hammond, Mason: *The City in Ancient World,* Harvard University Press, Cambridge, Mass., 1972.

Hawley, Amos H.: *Urban Society,* Ronald Press, New York, 1971.

Hiorns, Frederick: *Town Building in History,* Harap, London, 1956.

Hoselitz, Burt F.: "The Role of Cities in the Economic Growth of Underdeveloped Countries," *Journal of Political Economy,* **61,** 1953.

Jacobs, Jane: *The Economy of Cities:* Random House, New York, 1969.

July, Robert W: *A History of the African People,* Charles Scribner's Sons, New York, 1970.

Kenyon, Kathleen: *Archeology in the Holy Land,* Praeger, New York, 1970.

Lampara, Eric: "The Urbanizing World," in H. J. Dyds and Michael Wolfe (eds.), *The Victorian World,* Routledge and Kegan Paul, London, 1976.

Langer, William L.: "The Black Death," in Scientific American's *Cities: The Origin, Growth, and Human Impact,* W. H. Freeman, San Francisco, 1973.

Lee, Rose Hum: *The City,* Lippincott, Chicago, 1955.

Lenski, Gerhard: *Human Society,* McGraw-Hill, New York, 1970.

Mumford, Lewis: *The City in History,* Harcourt, Brace and World, New York, 1961.

Mundy, John H., and Peter Reisenberg: *The Medieval Town,* Van Nostrand, New York, 1958.

Petersen, William: *Population,* Macmillan, New York, 1969.

Piggot, Sturat: "The Role of the City in Ancient Civilization," in E. M. Fisher (ed.), *The Metropolis and Modern Life,* Doubleday, Garden City, N.Y., 1955.

Pirenne, Henri: *Economic and Social History of Medieval Europe,* Harcourt, New York, 1936.

———: *Medieval Cities,* Princeton University Press, Princeton, N.J., 1939.

Plato: *The Laws,* Book V, B. Jowett (trans.), 1926 ed.

Rice, Lee R.: *Man's Nature and Nature's Man: The Ecology of Human Communities,* University of Michigan Press, Ann Arbor, 1955

Rorig, Fritz: *The Medieval Town,* University of California Press, Berkeley, 1967.

Saalman, Howard: *Medieval Cities,* Braziller, New York, 1968.

Siegfried, Andre: *Routes of Contagion,* Harcourt, Brace and World, New York, 1965.

Sjoberg, Gideon: "The Preindustrial City," *American Journal of Sociology,* vol. 60, March, 1955.

Trigger, Bruce: "Determinants of Urban Growth in Pre-Industrial Societies," in Peter Ucko, Ruth Tringham, and G. W. Dimbleby (eds.), *Man, Settlement, and Urbanism,* Schenkman, Cambridge, Mass., 1972.

Weber, Max: *The City,* D. Martendale and G. Neuwirth (trans.), The Free Press, New York, 1958.

Wirth, Louis: "Urbanism as a Way of Life," *American Journal of Sociology, vol. 44, July, 1938.*

CHAPTER 3

Blake, Nelson M.: *A History of American Life and Thought,* McGraw-Hill, New York, 1963.

Bogue, Donald J.: *The Population of the United States,* Free Press, Glencoe, Ill, 1969, p. 178.

Bridenbaugh, Carl: *Cities in the Wilderness,* Capricorn Books, New York, 1964.

Brown, Theodore, and Lyle W. Dorset: *K. C.: A History of Kansas City Missouri,* Pruett, Boulder, Colo., 1978.

Bryce, James: *The American Commonwealth,* Putnam, New York, 1959. (First Edition 1888.)

———: *Forum,* vol. X, 1890, p. 25.

Cassedy, James H.: *Demography in Early America,* Harvard University Press, Cambridge, Mass., 1969.

Chudacoff, Howard P.: *The Evolution of American Urban Society,* Prentice-Hall, Englewood Cliffs, N.J., 1975.

Cressey, Paul F.: "Population Succession in Chicago: 1898–1930," *American Journal of Sociology,* vol. 44, 1938.

Davis, William T. (ed.): *Bradford's History of Plymouth Plantation,* Charles Scribner's Sons, New York, 1908.

De Tocqueville, Alexis: *Democracy in America,* Henry Reeve (trans.), New York, 1839.

Ford, P. L.: *The Works of Thomas Jefferson,* Putnam, New York, 1904, pp. 503–504.

Frame, Richard: "A Short Description of Pennsylvania in 1692," in Albert Cook Myers (ed.), *Narratives of Early Pennsylvania, West New Jersey, and Delaware,* Charles Scribner's Sons, New York, 1912. Reprinted in Ruth E. Sutter, *The Next Place You Come To,* Prentice-Hall, Englewood Cliffs, N.J., 1973.

Gallup poll, *Los Angeles Times,* March 24, 1985.

Glaab, Charles N.: *The American City,* Dorsey Press, Homewood, Ill., 1963.

Glaab, Charles N., and A. Theodore Brown: *A History of Urban America,* Macmillan, New York, 1967.

Glazier, Willard: *Peculiarities of American Cities,* Hubbard Brothers, Philadelphia, 1884.

Green, Constance McLaughlin: *The Rise of Urban America,* Harper and Row, New York, 1965.

Hofstadter, Richard: *The Age of Reform,* Knopf, New York, 1955.

Hurd, Richard: *Principles of City Land Values,* The Record and Guide, New York, 1903.

Jackson, Kenneth T., and Stanley K. Schutty (eds.): *Cities in American History,* Knopf, New York, 1972.

Lipscomb, Andrew A., and Albert E. Bergh (eds.): *The Writings of Thomas Jefferson,* vol. X, the Thomas Jefferson Memorial Association, Washington, D.C., 1904.

McKelveg, Blake: *The Urbanization of America 1860–1915,* Rutgers University Press, New Brunswick, N.J. 1963.

Merton, Robert K.: *Social Theory and Social Structure,* The Free Press, Glencoe, Ill., 1957.

Mumford, Lewis: *Sticks and Stones,* Horace Liveright, New York, 1924.

Petersen, William: *Population,* Macmillan, New York, 1961.

Riis, Jacob A.: *How the Other Half Lives,* Charles Scribner's Sons, New York, 1890.

Sandberg, Carl: *Chicago Poems,* Holt, New York, 1916.

Schlesinger, Arthur M: "The City in American History," *Mississippi Valley Historical Review,* vol. 27, June 1940.

————: *Path to the Present,* Macmilan, New York, 1949, p. 60.

Smith, John: *The General Historie of Virginia, New England, and the Summer Isles,* University Microfilms, Ann Harbor, Mich. (First published in London, 1624.)

Steffens, Lincoln: *The Autobiography of Lincoln Steffens,* Harcourt Brace, New York, 1931.

Strong, Josiah: *Our Country: Its Possible Future and Its Present Crisis,* Baker and Taylor, New York, 1885.

Tunnard, Christopher, and Henry Hope Reed: *American Skyline: The Growth and Form of Our Cities and Towns,* New American Library, New York, 1956.

U.S. Bureau of the Census: *Historical Statistics of the United States, Colonial Times to 1957,* Washington, D.C., 1960.

Warner, Sam Bass, Jr.: *Streetcar Suburbs,* Harvard and MIT Presses, Cambridge, Mass., 1962.

————: *The Private City: Philadelphia In Three Periods of Its Growth,* University of Pennsylvania Press, Philadelphia, 1972.

————: *The Urban Wilderness,* Harper and Row, New York, 1972.

White, Morton and Lucia White: *The Intellectual Versus the City,* MIT Press and Harvard University Press, Cambridge, Mass., 1962.

Wink, Harold: *City Bosses in the United States,* Duke University Press, Durham, N.C., 1930.

CHAPTER 4

Abbott, Walter F.: "Moscow in 1897 as a Preindustrial City: A Test of the Inverse Burgess Zonal Hypothesis," *American Sociological Review,* vol. 39, August, 1974.

Alihan, Milla A.: *Social Ecology,* Columbia University Press, New York, 1938.

Alonso, William: " A Theory of Urban Land Market," in Larry Bourne (ed.), *Internal Structure of the City,* Oxford University Press, New York, 1971, pp. 154–159.

Anderson, Theodore R., and Lee L. Bean: The Shevksy-Bell Social Areas: Confirmation of Results and Reinterpretation," *Social Forces,* **40:**119–124, December, 1961.

Bell, Wendell, and Scott Greer: "Social Area Analysis and Its Critiques," *Pacific Sociological Review,* vol. 5, 1962.

Burgess, Ernest W.: "The Growth of the City: An Introduction to a Research Project," *Publications of the American Sociology Society,* vol. 18, 1924.

————: "Residential Segregation in American Cities," *The Annals of the American Academy of Political and Social Science,* vol. 140, November, 1928.

Caplow, Theodore: "The Social Ecology of Guatemala City," *Social Forces,* vol. 28, 1949.

Davie, Maurice R.: "The Pattern of Urban Growth," in George Murdock (ed.), *Studies in the Science of Society,* Yale University Press, New Haven, Conn., 1937.

Duncan, Otis Dudley, and Beverly Duncan: "Residential Distribution and Occupational Stratification," *American Journal of Sociology,* vol. 60, March, 1955.

Eachman, Donald, and Melvin Marcus: "The Geologic and Topographic Setting of Cities," in Thomas Detwyler and Melvin Marcus (eds.), *Urbanization and Environment,* Buxbury Press, Belmont, Cal., 1972.

Firey, Walter: "Sentiment and Symbolism as Ecological Variables," *American Sociological Review,* vol. 10, 1945.

Gettys, Warner E.: "Human Ecology and Social Theory," in George A. Theodorson (ed.), *Studies in Human Ecology,* Row Peterson, Evanston, Ill., 1961.

Gist, Noel: "The Ecology of Bangalore India," *Social Forces,* vol. 35, May, 1957.

Haggerty, Lee J.: "Another Look at the Burgess Hypothesis: Time as an Important Variable," *American Journal of Sociology,* May, 1971.

Harris, Chauncy, and Edward Ullman: "The Nature of Cities," *The Annals of the American Academy of Political and Social Science,* vol. 252, 1945.

Hauser, Francis L.: "Ecological Patterns of European Cities," in Sylvia F. Fava (ed.), *Urbanism in World Perspective,* Crowell, New York, 1968.

Haynes, Norman: "Mexico City—Its Growth and Configuration," *American Journal of Sociology,* 50:295–304, January, 1945.

Hoyt, Homer: "The Structure and Growth of Residential Neighborhoods in American Cities," U.S. Federal Housing Administration, Government Printing Office, Washington, D.C., 1939.

Hunter, Alfred E.: "Factorial Ecology: A Critique and Some Suggestions," *Demography,* vol. 9, February, 1972.

Kafes, Robert, Ian Burton, and Gilbert F. White: *The Environment as Hazard,* Oxford University Press, New York, 1978.

Janson, Carl A. Gunnar: "Factorial Social Ecology," in Alex Inkeles (ed.), *Annual Review of Sociology,* 6:433–456, 1980.

Johnston, R. J.: "Residential Characteristics in Cities," in D. T. Herbert and R. J. Johnston (eds.), *Social Areas in Cities,* Wiley, New York, 1976, pp. 193–235.

Marston, Wilfred G.: "Socioeconomic Differentiation within Negro Areas of American Cities," *Social Factors,* 48:165–176, December, 1969.

McKenzie, Roderick: *The Metropolitan Community,* McGraw-Hill, New York and London, 1933.

Mehta, Surinder: "Patterns of Residence in Poona by Name, Education, and Income," *American Journal of Sociology,* vol. 73, March, 1968.

Michelson, William H.: *Man and His Urban Environment,* Addison-Wesley, Reading, Mass., 1970.

Palen, J. John, and Leo F. Schnore: "Color Composition and City-Suburban Status Differences," *Land Economics,* vol. 41, February, 1965.

Park, Robert: *Human Communities,* The Free Press, New York, 1952.

Pinkerton, James R.: "The Changing Class Composition of Cities and Suburbs," *Land Economics,* vol. 49, November, 1973.

Reckless, Walter C.: "The Distribution of Commercialized Vice in the City: A Sociological Analysis," *Publications of the American Sociological Society,* vol. 20, 1926.

Rees, Phillip H.: *Residential Patterns in American Cities: 1960,* Department of Geography, University of Chicago, Chicago, 1979.

Schnore, Leo: "The Myth of Human Ecology," *Sociological Inquiry,* vol. 31, 1961.

———: "The Socioeconomic Status of Cities and Suburbs," *American Sociological Review,* vol. 28, February, 1963.

———: *Class and Race in Cities and Suburbs,* Markham, Chicago, 1972.

Schnore, Leo, and Joy K. O. Jones: "The Evolution of City-Suburban Types in the Course of a Decade," *Urban Affairs Quarterly,* June, 1969.

Schwirian, Kent, and Marc D. Matre: "The Ecological Structure of Canadian Cities," in Kent P. Schwirian (ed.), *Comparative Urban Structure,* D. C. Heath, Lexington, Mass., 1974.

Shevky, Eshref, and Wendell Bell: *Social Area Analysis,* Stanford University Press, Palo Alto, Cal., 1955.

Simkus, Albert: "Residential Segregation by Occupation and Race in Ten Urbanized Areas 1950–1970, *American Sociological Review,* vol. 43, February, 1978.

Sjoberg, Gideon: *The Preindustrial City,* The Free Press, New York, 1960.

————: "Cities in Developing and in Industrial Societies: A Cross-cultural Analysis," in Philip M. Hauser and Leo F. Schnore (eds.), *The Study of Urbanization,* Wiley, New York, 1965.

Sweetser, F. L.: "Neighborhood Typologies and Social Ecological Theory," paper presented at the ninth World Congress of Sociology, Uppsala, Sweden, August, 1978.

Thomlinson, Ralph: *Urban Structure,* Random House, New York, 1969.

Ullman, Edward: "The Presidential Address, the Nature of Cities Reconsidered," *The Regional Science Association Papers and Proceedings,* vol. 9, 1962.

Van Arsdol, Maurice Jr., Santo F. Camileri, and Calvin F. Schmid, "The Generality of Urban Social Area Indexes," *American Sociological Review,* **23:**277–284, 1958.

Wirth, Louis: *The Ghetto,* University of Chicago Press, Chicago, 1928.

————: "Urbanism as a Way of Life," *American Journal of Sociology,* vol. 44, July, 1938.

Zorbaugh, Harvey W.: *The Gold Coast and the Slum,* University of Chicago Press, Chicago, 1929.

CHAPTER 5

Bernard, Richard M. and Bradley R. Rice (eds.): *Sunbelt Cities: Politics and Growth Since World War II,* University of Texas Press, Austin, 1983.

Birch, David: quoted in *Richmond Times-Dispatch,* October 11, 1984.

Garreau, Joel: *The Nine Nations in North America,* Houghton Mifflin, Boston, 1981.

Guterbock, Thomas A.: "Suburbanization of American Cities of the Twentieth Century: A New Index and Another Look," paper presented at meeting of the American Sociological Association, Toronto, 1982.

Hawley, Amos H.: *Urban Society: An Ecological Approach,* Ronald Press, New York, 1971.

————: "Urbanization as Process," in David Street (ed.), *Handbook of Contemporary Urban Life,* Jossey-Bass, San Francisco, 1978.

Hawley, Amos H., and Vincent P. Rock (eds.), *Metropolitan America in Contemporary Perspective,* Holsted Press, New York, 1975.

Humphrey, Craig, and Ralph Sell: "The Impact of Controlled Access Highways on Population Growth in Pennsylvania and Non-Metropolitan Communities, 1940–1970," *Rural Sociology,* vol. 40, 1975.

Jusenius, C. L., and L. C. Ledebur: *A Myth in the Making: The Southern Economic Challenge and Northern Economic Decline,* Economic Development Administration, Department of Commerce, Washington, D.C., November, 1976.

Kasarda, John D.: "The Implication of Contemporary Redistribution Trends for National Urban Policy," *Social Science Quarterly*, **61**:389, December, 1980.

LaGory, Mark, and James Nelson: "An Ecological Analysis of Growth Between 1900 and 1940," *Sociological Quarterly*, **19**:590–603, 1978.

Long, Larry H.: "Population Redistribution in the U.S.: Issues for the 1980's," *Population Reference Bureau*, Washington, D.C., 1983.

Manners, Gerald: "The Office in the Metropolis: An Opportunity for Shaping Metropolitan America," *Economic Geography*, vol. 50, 1974.

McKenzie, Roderic: *The Metropolitan Community*, McGraw-Hill, New York, 1933.

Mollenkopt, John H.: *The Congested City*, Princeton University Press, Princeton, New Jersey, 1983.

National Resources Committee: *Technological Trends and National Policy*, Government Printing Office, Washington, D.C., 1937.

Perry, David D., and Alfred J. Watkins (eds.): *The Rise of the Sunbelt Cities*, Sage, Beverly Hills, 1977.

Sale, Kirkpatrick: *Power Shift: The Rise of the Southern Rim and Its Challenge to the Eastern Establishment*, Random House, New York, 1975.

Sawers, Larry and William K. Tabb (eds.): *Sunbelt/Snowbelt*, Oxford University Press, New York, 1984.

Schnore, Leo F.: "Satellites and Suburbs," *Social Forces*, vol. 36, December, 1957.

———: *Urban Society: An Ecological Approach*, Ronald Press, New York, 1971.

———: "Urbanization as Process," in David Street (ed.), *Handbook of Contemporary Urban Life*, Jossey-Bass, San Francisco, 1978.

Schnore, Leo F., and Vincent P. Rock (eds.), *Metropolitan America in Contemporary Pespective*, Holsted Press, New York, 1975.

U.S. Bureau of the Census, U.S. Department of Commerce and Agriculture, "Farm Population of the United States: 1977," *Current Population Reports*, series P-27, no. 51, Washington, D.C., November, 1978.

U.S. Bureau of the Census, U.S. Department of Commerce, "Population Profile of the U.S.: 1981," *Current Population Reports*, series P-20, no. 374, Washington, D.C., September, 1982, p. 7.

———: 1980 Census of Population, *Metropolitan Statistical Areas*, PC80-51-18, Washington, D.C., January, 1985.

U.S. Department of Commerce News, Social and Economic Statistics Adminstration, Washington, D.C., April 21, 1982.

Zuiches, James: "Residential Preferences and Rural Population Growth," paper prepared for Farmers Home Administration, U.S. Department of Agriculture, Washington, D.C., 1980.

CHAPTER 6

Bell, Wendell: "The City, the Suburb, and a Theory of Social Choice," in Scott Greer, et al. (eds.), *The New Urbanization*, St. Martin's Press, New York, 1969.

Bott, Elizabeth: *Family and Social Network*, Tavistock, London, 1957.

Boulding, Kenneth E.: "The Death of the City: A Frightened Look at Postcivilization," in *Modernization, Urbanization and the Urban Crisis*, Gino Germani (ed.), Boston: Little, Brown, 1973, p. 265.

Drabeck, Thomas, et al.: "The Impact of Disaster on Kin Relationships," *Journal of Marriage and Family*, **37**(3):481–484, August, 1975.

Drabeck, Thomas and William Key: *Conquering Disaster: Family Recovery and Long Term Consequences,* Irvington Publishers, New York, 1874.

Fischer, Claude: "Toward a Subcultural Theory of Urbanism," *American Journal of Sociology* **80:**1319–1341, 1975.

————: *To Dwell Among Friends: Personal Networks in Town and City,* University of Chicago Press, Chicago 1982.

Gans, Herbert J.:*The Urban Villagers,* Free Press, Glencoe, Ill., 1962.

————: "Urbanism and Suburbanism as Ways of Life: A Re-evaluation of Definitions," in J. John Palen and Karl H. Flaming (eds.), *Urban America,* Holt, Rinehart and Winston, New York, 1972.

Kornblum, William: *Blue Collar Community,* University of Chicago Press, Chicago, 1974, p. 80.

LeMesters, E. E.: *Blue Collar Aristocrats,* University of Wisconsin Press, Madison, 1975.

Liebow, Elliot: *Tally's Corner,* Little Brown, Boston, Mass., 1967.

Matza, David: "The Disreputable Poor," in Neil J. Smelser and Seymour M. Lipset (eds.), *Social Structure and Mobility in Economic Development,* Aldine, Chicago, 1966.

Milgram, Stanley: "The Experience of Living in Cities," *Science,* vol. 167, March 13, 1970.

Munro, William B.: "City," *Encyclopedia of the Social Sciences,* Macmillan, New York, 1930.

Poplin, Dennis E.: *Communities,* 2nd ed., Macmillan, New York, 1979.

Rainwater, Lee: "Fear and the House as Haven in the Lower Class," in J. J. John Palen and Karl H. Flaming (eds.), *Urban America,* Holt, Rinehart, and Winston, New York, 1972.

Sennett, Richard and Jonathan Cobb: *The Hidden Injuries of Class,* Vintage Books, New York, 1973.

Simmel, Georg: *The Sociology of Georg Simmel,* Kurt H. Wolff (trans.), The Free Press, Glencoe, Ill., 1950.

Starr, Joyce R., and Donald E. Carns: "Singles and the City: Notes on Urban Adaptation," in John Walton and Donald E. Cans (eds.), *Cities in Change,* Allyn and Bacon, Boston, Mass., 1973.

Taeuber, Irine: "The Changing Distribution of the Population of the United States," in S. M. Mazie (ed.), *Population, Distribution, and Policy,* vol. 5, U.S. Commission on Population Growth and the American Future, Government Printing Office, Washington, D.C., 1972.

Toffler, Alvin: *Future Shock,* Random House, New York, 1970.

U.S. Bureau of the Census: "Consumer Income: 1981," p. 60, no. 138, March, 1983.

————: "Marital Status and Living Arrangements: March, 1983," *Current Population Reports,* series p-20, no. 389, 1984.

CHAPTER 7

Bahr, Howard M.: *Skid Row,* Oxford University Press, New York, 1973.

Biderman, A. D., M. Lauria, and J. Bacchus: *Historical Incidents of Extreme Overcrowding,* Bureau of Social Science Research, Washington, D.C., 1963.

Blacks, Donald J.: "Production of Crime Rates," *American Sociological Review,* **35:**753, August 1970.

Bogue, Donald J.: *Skid Row in American Cities,* University of Chicago, Community and Family Study Center, Chicago, 1963. p. 2.

Buckout, Robert: "Pollution and the Psychologist: A Call to Action," in Joachim F. Wohlwill and Daniel H. Carson (eds.), *Environment and the Social Sciences,* American Psychological Association, Washington, D. C., 1972.

Calhoun, John B.: "Population Density and Social Pathology," *Scientific American,* vol. 206, February, 1960.

Caplow, Theodore: "Changing Patterns of Inequality in Middletown," *1978 Annual Meeting of the American Sociological Association,* San Francisco, California.

Chadwick, Bruce: "Convergence of Diverging Life Styles of Working and Business Class Families in Middletown, 1920–1977," *1978 Annual Meeting of the American Sociological Association,* San Francisco, California.

Choldin, Harvey M., and Dennis Rancek: "Density, Population Potential and Pathology: A Block Level Analysis," *Public Data Use,* vol. 4, July, 1974.

Department of Juctice, F.B.I.: *Uniform Crime Reports* (1983), Washington, D.C., table 2, 1984.

Dickens, Charles: *The Adventures of Oliver Twist,* Chapman S. Hall, Ltd., London, pp. 42–43.

Ennis, P. H.: *Criminal Victimization in the United States: A Report of a National Survey,* U.S. Government Printing Office, Washington, D.C., 1967.

Fischer, Claude S.: *The Urban Experience,* Harcourt Brace Jovanovich, New York, 1976.

Fischer, Claude S., Mark Baldassare, and Richard Ofshe: "Crowding Studies and Urban Life: A Critical Review," *Journal of the American Institute of Planners,* vol. 41, November 1975.

Freedman, Jonathan: *Crowding and Behavior,* Viking, New York, 1975.

Galle, O. R., and Walter R. Grove: "Crowding and Behavior in Chicago, 1940–1970," in J. R. Aiello and A. Blaum (eds.), *Residential Crowding and Design,* Plenum, New York, 1979.

Gallup Poll: Field Enterprises, July 28, 1975.

Goffman, Erving: *Relations in Public,* Basic Books, New York, 1971.

Green, Edward: "Race, Social Status and Criminal Arrest," *American Sociological Review,* **35**:476–490, June, 1970.

Hartley, Shirley Foster: *Population Quantity vs. Quality,* Prentice-Hall, Englewood Cliffs, N.J., 1972.

Hillery, G. A.: "Definitions of Community: Areas of Agreement," *Rural Sociology,* vol. 20, 1955.

Hunter, Albert J.: *Symbolic Communities: Persistence and Change in Chicago's Local Communities,* University of Chicago Press, Chicago, 1974.

Janowitz, Morris: *The Community Press in an Urban Setting,* University of Chicago Press, Chicago, 1952.

Kasarda, John D., and Morris Janowitz, "Community Attachment in Mass Society," *American Sociological Review,* **39**:328–339, June, 1974.

Keller, Suzanne: *The Urban Neighborhood,* Random House, New York, 1968.

Kornblum, William: *Blue Collar Community,* University of Chicago Press, Chicago, 1974.

Latane, B., and J. M. Darley: *The Unresponsive Bystander: Why Doesn't He Help?,* Appleton-Century-Crofts, New York, 1970.

Leigh, Geoffrey K.: "Family Life Cycle and Kinship Interaction," *1978 Annual Meeting of the American Sociological Association,* San Francisco, California.

Lofland, Lyn: *A World of Strangers,* Basic Books, New York, 1973.

Lupo, Alan, Frank Colcord, and Edmond P. Fowler: *Rites of Way,* Little, Brown, Boston, 1971.

Lynd, Robert, and Helen Merrell Lynd: *Middletown,* Harcourt, Brace, New York, 1929.

———: *Middletown in Transition,* Harcourt, Brace, New York, 1937.

MacLeod, Celeste: "Street People: The New Migrants," *The Nation,* **217**::395–397, October 22, 1973.

Poplin, Dennis E.: *Communities,* 2d ed., Macmillan, New York, 1979.

Redfield, Robert, and Milton Singer: "The Cultural Role of Cities," *Economic Development and Cultural Change,* vol. 3, 1954.

Shaw, Clifford R., and Henry McKay: *Juvenile Delinquency in Urban Areas,* University of Chicago Press, Chicago, 1942.

Suttles, Gerald: *The Social Construction of Communities,* University of Chicago Press, Chicago, 1978.

Swan, James A.: "Public Responses to Air Pollution," in Joachim F. Wohlwil and Daniel H. Carson, *Environment and the Social Sciences,* American Psychological Association, Washington, D.C., 1972.

Thernstrom, Stephen: "Yankee City Revisited: The Perils of Historical Naivete," *American Sociological Review,* vol. 30, April, 1965.

U.S. Bureau of the Census: "Consumer Income," *Current Population Reports,* series P-23, October, 1971.

Warner W. Lloyd (ed.): *Yankee City,* Yale University Press, New Haven, Conn., 1963.

Warren, Roland L.: *Perspective on the American Community,* Rand McNally, Chicago, 1966.

Washington Post: November 15, 1984, p. C7.

Wellman, Barry: "The Community Question: The Intimate Networks of East Yorkers," *American Sociological Review,* **84**:1201–1231, March, 1979.

Wilson, James Q.: "The Urban Unease," *Public Interest,* vol. 12, 1968.

Wirth, Louis: "Urbanism as a Way of Life," *American Journal of Sociology,* vol. 44, July, 1938.

Young, Michael, and Peter Willmott: *Family and Kinship in East London,* Penguin Books, Baltimore, 1962.

CHAPTER 8

Bell, Wendell: "The City, the Suburb, and a Theory of Social Choice," in Scott Greer, Dennis L. McElrath, David W. Minar and Peter Orleans (eds.), *The New Urbanization,* St. Martin's Press, New York, 1968.

Berger, Bennett M.: *Working Class Suburbs,* University of California Press, Berkeley, Cal., 1960.

———: "The Myth of Suburbia," *Journal of Social Issues,*, vol. 17, 1971.

Clark, S. D.: *The Suburban Society,* University of Toronto Press, Toronto, 1966.

Choldin, Harvey, Claudine Hanson, and Robert Bohrer: "Suburban Status Instability," *American Sociological Review,* **45**:972–983, 1980.

Cohen, Albert, and Harold M. Hodges, Jr.: "Characteristics of the Lower Blue-Collar Class," *Social Problems,* **10**:307, spring, 1983.

Donaldson, S.: *The Suburban Myth,* Columbia University Press, New York, 1969.

Fischer, Claude S., and Robert Max Jackson: "Suburbs, Networks, and Attitudes," in Barry Schwartz (ed.), *The Changing Face of the Suburbs,* University of Chicago Press, Chicago, 1976.

Gans, Herbert J.: "Urbanism and Suburbanism as Ways of Life: A Re-evaluation of Definitions," in Arnold Rose (ed.), *Human Behavior,* Houghton Mifflin, Boston, Mass., 1962.

———: *The Levittowners,* Vintage Books, New York, 1967.

Glaab, Charles N.: "North Chicago: Its Advantages, Resources and Probable Future," reprinted in *The American City,* Homewood, Ill., 1963.

Greer, Scott: *The Urbane View,* Oxford University Press, New York, 1972.

Hawley, Amos H., and Basil Zimmer: *The Metropolitan Community: Its People and Government,* Sage, Beverly Hills, Cal., 1970.

Kasarda, John D., and George Redfearn: "Differential Patterns of Urban and Suburban Growth in the United States," *Journal of Urban History,* vol. 2, 1975.

Lineberry, Robert L.: "Suburbia and Metropolitan Turf," *The Annals of the American Academy of Political and Social Science,* vol. 422, 1975.

Lineberry, Robert L. and Ira Sharkansky: *Urban Politics and Public Policy,* Harper and Row, New York, 1971.

Logan, John R., and Mark Schneider: "Stratification of Metropolitan Suburbs, 1960–1970," *American Sociological Review,* **46:**175–186, 1981.

Long, Larry, and Diana De Are: "The Suburbanization of Blacks," *American Demographics,* **3:**16–21, 44, September, 1981.

Spectorsky, A. C.: *The Exurbanites,* Berkeley, New York, 1958.

Spinrad, William: "Blue-Collar Workers as City and Suburban Residents—Effect of Union Membership," in A. Shoslak and W. Gomberg (eds.), *Blue-Collar World,* Prentice-Hall, Englewood Cliffs, N. J., 1964.

Sternlieb, George, and Robert W. Lake: "Aging Suburbs and Black Homeownership," *The Annals of the American Academy of Political and Social Science,* vol. 422, 1975.

Tauber, Conrad: "Population Trends in the 1960's," *Science,* vol. 176, 1972.

U.S. Bureau of the Census, Dept. of Commerce, "Black Movers to the Suburbs: Are They Moving to White Neighborhoods," *Special Demographic Analyses,* CDS-80.4, Washington, D.C., December, 1981, p. 21.

———: "Population Profile of the United States: 1981," *Current Population Reports,* series P-20, no. 374. Washington, D.C., September, 1982, table 3-6.

Warner, Sam B., Jr.: *Streetcar Suburbs,* Harvard University and MIT Presses, Cambridge, Mass., 1962.

Weber, Adna Ferrin: *The Growth of Cities in the Nineteenth Century,* Macmillan, New York, 1899.

Whyte, William H.: *The Organization Man,* Doubleday (Anchor), Garden City, N. Y., 1956.

Zelan, Joseph: "Does Suburbia Make a Difference?," in Sylvia F. Fava (ed.), *Urbanism in World Perspective,* Oxford University Press, New York, 1968.

CHAPTER 9

Alba, Richard D.: "Social Assimilation among American Catholic National-Origin Groups," *American Sociological Review,* vol. 41, December, 1976.

Caplan, Nathan: "Southeast Asian Refugees: Achieving Independence in America," *ISR Newsletter,* Institute for Social Research, University of Michigan, spring/summer, 1985 p. 7.

Chadwick Bruce, and Joseph Strauss, "The Assimilation of American Indians into Urban Society, The Seattle Case," paper presented at the meeting of the American Sociological Association, San Francisco, August, 1975.

Díaz, William A.: *Hispanics: Challenges and Opportunities,* Ford Foundation, New York, 1984.

Drake, St. Clair, and Horace Cayton: *Black Metropolis,* Harcourt Brace, New York, 1945.

Ellis, David et al.: *A Short History of New York State,* Cornell University Press, Ithaca, N. Y., 1957.

Erbe, Brigitte Mach: "Race and Socioeconomic Segregation," *American Sociological Review,* vol. 40, December, 1975.

Farley, Reynolds, et al.: "Chocolate City, Vanilla Suburbs," paper presented at the August, 1977 meeting of the American Sociological Association, Chicago, 1977.

Gireot, Avery M., and James A. Weed: "Ethnic Residential Segregation: Patterns of Change," *American Journal of Sociology,* vol. 81, March, 1986.

Glazer, Nathan, and Daniel Patrick Moynihan: *Beyond the Melting Pot,* MIT Press, Cambridge, Mass., 1963.

Gordon, Milton M.: *Assimilation in American Life,* Oxford University Press, New York, 1964.

Grant, Madison: *The Passing of the Great Race,* Charles Scribner's Sons, New York, 1921.

Greer, Scott: "The Faces of Ethnicity," in J. John Palen (ed.), *City Scenes,* Little Brown, Boston, Mass., 1977.

Guest, Avery A., and James J. Zuiches: "Another Look at the Residential Turnover in Urban Neighborhoods," *American Journal of Sociology,* vol. 77, November, 1971.

Guilhemin, Jeanne: *Urban Renegades,* Columbia University Press, New York, 1975, p. 150.

Hernandez, José: *Social Factors in Educational Attainment among Puerto Ricans in U.S. Metropolitan Areas,* Aspira, New York, 1979.

Higham, John: *Strangers in the Land,* Atheneum, New York, 1977.

Howe, Irving: *World of Our Fathers,* Touchstone Books, New York, 1976.

Interchange, Population Reference Bureau, **4:**2, November, 1975.

Johnson, Michael P., and James L. Roark, *Black Masters: A Free Family of Color in the Old South,* Norton, New York, 1984.

Keely, Charles B.: "Illegal Immigration," *Scientific American,* March, 1982.

Kitano, Harry H. L.: *Japanese Americans: The Evolution of a Subculture,* Prentice-Hall, Englewood Cliffs, N.J., 1976.

Lieberson, Stanley: *Ethnic Patterns in American Cities,* The Free Press, New York, 1963.

Molotch, Harvey: *Managed Integration,* University of California Press, Berkeley, Cal., 1972.

Moore, Joan W.: *Mexican Americans,* Prentice-Hall, Englewood Cliffs, N.J., 1976.

———: *Homeboys: Gangs, Drugs and Prison in the Barrios of Los Angeles,* Temple University Press, Philadelphia, 1978.

Myrdal, Gunnar: *An American Dilemma,* Harper and Row, New York, 1944.

Olmstead, Frederick Law: *The Cotton Kingdom,* Modern Library, New York, 1969.

Palen, J. John, and Leo F. Schnore: "Color Composition and City Suburban Status Differences," *Land Economics,* vol. 41, February, 1965.

Petersen, William: "Success Story: Japanese-American Styles," *New York Times Magazine,* January 9, 1966.

Pettigrew, Thomas F.: *Racially Separate or Together,* McGraw-Hill, New York, 1971.

Phillips, Ulrich B.: *American Negro Slavery*, Louisana State Press, Baton Rouge, 1969.

President's Commission on Immigration and Naturalization, *Who Shall We Welcome?*, U.S. Government Printing Office, Washington, D.C., 1953.

Ross, E. A.: *The Old World in the New*, Century, New York, 1941.

Russell, Cheryl: "The News about Hispanics," *American Demographs*, March, 1983, p 20.

Sorenson, Annemette, Karl E. Taeuber, and Leslie J. Hollingsworth, Jr.: "Indexes of Racial Residential Segregation for 109 Cities in the United States, 1940 to 1970," *Sociological Focus*, April, 1975.

Sowell, Thomas: *Race and Economics*, David McKay, New York, 1975.

Stoddard, Ellwyn R.: *Mexican Americans*, Random House, New York, 1973.

Strong, Josiah: *Our Country*, Baker and Taylor, New York, 1891.

Taeuber, Karl E.: "Racial Segregation: The American Dilemma," *Annals of the American Academy of Political and Social Science*, vol. 422, November, 1975.

Taeuber, Karl E., and Alma F. Taeuber: *Negroes in Cities: Residential Segregation and Neighborhood Change*, Aldine, Chicago, 1965.

U.S. Bureau of the Census: "Persons of Spanish Origin in the U.S.," *Current Population Reports*, series P-20, no. 329, Washington, D.C., 1978.

———: "Social and Economic Characteristics of Metropolitan and Non-Metropolitan Population: 1977 and 1970," *Current Population Reports*, Washington, D.C., November 1978.

———: "Population Profile of the United States, 1981," *Current Population Reports*, series P-20, no. 374, Washington, D.C., 1982.

———: "Geographical Mobility of the Population of the United States: March 1975 to March 1980," *Current Population Reports*, series P-20, no. 368, Washington, D.C., 1981.

———: "Ancestry and Language in the United States," series P-23, no 16, Washington, D.C., 1982.

U.S. Commission on Civil Rights: *The Navajo Nation: An American Colony*, Washington, D.C., 1975.

U.S. Department of Health, Education and Welfare: *Indian Health Trends and Services*, Program Analysis and Statistics Branch of the Indian Health Services, Washington, D.C., 1969.

Van Valey, Thomas, Wade Clark Roof, and Jerome E. Wilcox: "Trends in Residential Segregation: 1960–1970," *American Journal of Sociology*, vol. 82, January, 1977.

Van Woodward, C.: *The Strange Career of Jim Crow*, Oxford University Press, New York, 1966.

Wade, Richard C: *Slavery in the Cities: The South 1820–1860*, Oxford University Press, New York, 1964.

Webber, Melvin M.: "The Post-City Age," in J. John Palen (ed.), *City Scenes*, Little, Brown, Boston, Mass., 1977.

Whyte, William F.: *Street Corner Society*, University of Chicago Press, Chicago, 1943.

Wurdock, Bud: "The Role of White Flight in Neighborhood Racial Transition," paper delivered at the April, 1978 meetings of the Midwest Sociological Society, 1978.

CHAPTER 10

Allman, T. D.: "The Urban Crisis Leaves Town," *Harpers*, December, 1978.

Bradley, Donald J.: "Neighborhood Transition: Middle Class Home Buying in an Inner-

City Deteriorating Community,'' paper presented at the annual meeting of the American Sociological Association, Chicago, September, 1977.

C.B.S.: "Sixty Minutes," November, 29, 1981.

Clark, Terry N., et al.: *How Many New Yorks?*, Research Report 72, University of Chicago, 1976.

Costells, Manuel: *The Urban Question: A Marxist Approach*, Alan Sheridan (trans.), MIT Press, Cambridge, Mass., 1977.

————: "The Wild City," *Kapital State*, vol. 4–5, 1976.

Durant, Seymour B.: "Laetrile for the Urban Crisis: Planned Shrinkage and Other Dangerous Nostrums," *Journal of the Institute for Socioeconomic Studies*, vol. 4, 1979.

Fogelson, R.M.: The Fragmented Metropolis: Los Angeles 1850–1930, Harvard University Press, Cambridge, Mass., 1967.

Gale, Dennis: "The Back to the City Movement Revisited: A Survey of Recent Homebuyers in the Capital Hill Neighborhood of Washington, D.C.," George Washington University, Department of Urban and Regional Planning, 1977.

Goldberger, Paul: "The Limits of Urban Growth," *New York Times Magazine*, November 14, 1982.

Grier, George, and Eunice Grier: "Urban Displacement: A Reconnaissance," in Shirley Laska and Daphne Spain (eds.), *Back to the City*, Pergamon, New York, 1980.

Hauser, Philip M: "Chicago—Urban Crisis Examplar," in J. John Palen (ed.), *City Scenes*, Little, Brown, Boston, Mass., 1977.

Henig, Jeffrey: "Gentrification and Displacement of the Elderly," in J. John Palen and Bruce London (eds.), *Gentrification, Displacement and Neighborhood Revitalization*, SUNY Press, Albany, N.Y., 1984.

Hudson, James R.: "SoHo, A Study of Residential Invasion of a Commercial and Industrial Area," *Urban Affairs Quarterly*, **20**:46–63, September, 1984.

Kasarda, John: *The Changing Face of Suburbs*, University of Chicago Press, Chicago, 1976.

Lee, Barrett, and David Hodge: "Social Differentials and Metropolitan Residential Displacement," in J. John Palen and Bruce London, *Gentrification, Displacement and Neighborhood Revitalization*, SUNY Press, Albany, N.Y., 1984, pp. 140–169.

Mumford, Lewis: *The Urban Prospect*, Harcourt Brace, Jovanovich, New York, 1968.

National Urban Coalition: *Displacement: City Neighborhoods in Transition*, Washington, D.C., 1978.

Palen, J. John, and Bruce London (eds.): *Gentrification, Displacement and Neighborhood Revitalization*, SUNY Press, New York, 1984.

Palen J. John, and Chava Nachmias, "Revitalization in a Working-Class Neighborhood," in J. John Palen and Bruce London, *Gentrification, Displacement and Neighborhood Revitalization*, SUNY Press, Albany, N.Y., 1984.

Smith, Neil, and Michele Le Faivre: "A Class Analysis of Gentrification," in J. John Palen and Bruce London (eds.), *Gentrification, Displacement and Neighborhood Revitalization*, SUNY Press, Albany, N.Y., 1984.

Spain, Daphne, and Shirley Laska: "Renovations Two Years Later: New Orleans," in J. John Palen and Bruce London, *Gentrification, Displacement and Neighborhood Revitalization*, SUNY Press, Albany, N.Y., 1984.

Stars, Roger: "Making New York Smaller," *New York Times Magazine*, November 19, 1976, pp. 32–33, 99–106.

Sternlieb, George: "The City as Sandbox," *The Public Interest*, 1971.

Sutton, Horace: "America Falls in Love with Its Cities—Again," *Saturday Review,* August, 1978.

U.S. Bureau of the Census: "Household and Family Characteristics," *Current Population Reports,* series P-20, Washington, D.C., 1981.

CHAPTER 11

Abrams, Charles: *The City Is the Frontier,* Harper and Row, New York, 1965.

Blonston, Gary: "Poletown: The Profits, the Loss," *Detroit* (special issue), Detroit Free Press, November 22, 1981.

Bradbury, Katherine and Anthony Downs (eds.): *Do Housing Allowances Work?,* Brookings, Washington, D.C., 1981.

"Chicago Suburbs to Pay Landlords to Integrate," *New York Times,* November 11, 1984, p. 24.

Clark, Ann, and Zelma Rivin: *Homesteading in Urban U.S.A.,* Praeger, New York, 1977.

Conway, Wiltram G.: "People Fire in the Ghetto Ashes," *Saturday Review,* July 23, 1977.

Durant, Seymour B.: "Laetrile for the Urban Crisis," *Journal of the Institute of Socioeconomic Studies,* **4:**72, summer, 1979.

"Excess U.S. Housing Said Mismanaged," *Washington Post,* October 12, 1984.

Fried, Joseph P.: "Arson, A Devastating Big-City Crime," *New York Times,* August 14, 1977.

Gans, Herbert J.: *The Urban Villagers,* The Free Press, New York, 1962.

————: *People and Plans,* Basic Books, New York, 1968.

Gorham, William, and Nathan Glazer: *The Urban Predicament,* The Urban Institute, Washington, D.C., 1976, pp. 129–130.

Greer, Scott: *Urban Renewal and American Cities,* Bobbs-Merrill, Indianapolis, Ind., 1965.

"Legal Report,": *Planning,* June, 1982.

Lowe, Jeanne R.: *Cities in a Race with Time,* Random House, New York, 1967.

Milwaukee Journal, December 15, 1976.

Rainwater, Lee: *Behind Ghetto Walls,* Aldine, Chicago, 1970.

Reinhold, Robert: "Nation Watching Outcome of Racial Puzzle in Illinois," *New York Times Service,* April 15, 1979.

"Slum Surgery in St. Louis," *Architectural Forum,* April, 1951.

Stegman, Michael: "The New Mythology of Housing," *Trans-Action,* vol. 7, January, 1970.

United Press International, September 19, 1976.

U.S. Bureau of the Census: "Geographical Mobility: March 1982 to March 1983," *Current Population Reports,* series P-20, no. 393, Washington, D.C., 1984, p. 1.

U.S. Department of Housing and Urban Development, Office of Policy Development and Research: *A Summary Report of Current Findings from the Experimental Housing Allowance Program,* Washington, D.C., April, 1978.

Weissbroud, Bernard: "Satellite Communities," *Urban Land,* vol. 31, October, 1972.

Wienk, Ronald E. et al.: *Measuring Racial Discrimination in American Housing Markets: The Housing Market Practice Survey,* Office of Policy Development and Research, Department of Housing and Urban Development, Washington, D.C., 1979.

Young, Arthur F. and F. John Devaney: "What the 1980 Census Shows About Housing," *American Demographics,* **5:**17, January, 1983.

CHAPTER 12

Aristotle: Book VII, *Politics,* B. Jowett (trans.), 1932.

Burby, Raymond J., III et al.: *New Communities U.S.A.,* Lexington Books, Lexington, Mass., 1976.

Clapp, J.: *New Towns and Urban Policy—Planning Metropolitan Growth,* Dunellen, New York, 1971.

Di Maio, Alfred John, Jr.: *Soviet Urban Housing Problems and Policies,* Praeger, New York, 1974.

Feshback, Murray: "The Soviet Union: Population Trends and Dilemmas," *Population Bulletin,* Population Reference Bureau, Washington, D.C., August, 1982, p. 37.

Howard, Ebenezer: *Garden Cities of Tomorrow,* Faber and Faber, London, 1902.

Martin, Wynn (ed.): *Housing in Europe,* St. Martin's Press, New York, 1984.

Mendelker, Daniel R.: *Green Belts and Urban Growth,* University of Wisconsin Press, Madison, Wisc., 1962.

Merlin, Pierre: *New Towns,* Methuen, London, 1971.

Morton, Henry M.: "The Soviet Quest for Better Housing—An Impossible Dream?" *Soviet Economy in a Time of Change,* Joint Economic Committee of Congress, Washington, D.C., October, 1979.

———: "Who Gets What and How? Housing in the Soviet Union," *Soviet Studies,* **32:**235, April, 1980.

The Netherlands: Current Trends and Policies in the Field of Housing, Building, and Planning During the Year 1968, Ministry of Housing and Physical Planning, The Hague, 1970.

Osborn, Frederick J.: *Green Belt Cities,* Schocken, New York, 1969.

Popenoe, David: *The Suburban Environment,* University of Chicago Press, Chicago, 1977.

———: *Private Pleasure, Public Plight,* Transaction, New Brunswick, N.J., 1985.

Reilly, William E. (ed.): *The Use of Land: A Citizen's Guide to Urban Growth,* The Rockefeller Brothers Fund, Thomas Crowell, New York, 1973.

Rodwin, Lloyd: *The British New Towns Policy,* Harvard University Press, Cambridge, Mass., 1956.

Saalman, Howard: *Medieval Cities,* Braziller, New York, 1968.

Schaffer, Frank: *The New Town Story,* MacGibbon and Kee, London, 1970.

Scoffham, E. R.: *The Shape of British Housing,* George Godwin, London, 1984.

Sidenbladh, Goran: "Stockholm: A Planned City," in *Cities: A Scientific American Book,* Knopf, New York, 1965.

Synookler, Helen V.: "Administrative Hari Kari: Implementation of the Urban Growth and New Community Development Act," *Annals of the American Academy of Political and Social Science,* **422:**131–132, November, 1975.

Szelenyi, Ivan: "Urban Sociology and Community Studies in Eastern Europe," *Comparative Urban Research,* vol. 4, 1977.

———: *Urban Inequalities Under State Socialism,* Oxford University Press, London, 1983.

Taubman, William: *Governing Soviet Cities: Bureaucratic Politics and Urban Development in the USSR*, Praeger, New York, 1973.

Thomas, Ray, and Peter Cresswell: *The New Town Idea*, The Open University Press, England, 1973.

Thomas, Wyndham: "Implementation: New Towns," in Derek Senior (ed.), *The Regional City*, Aldine, Chicago, 1966.

Thomlinson, Ralph: *Urban Structure*, Random House, New York, 1969.

United Press International: "Brazil's Dream City Has Flaws," August, 19, 1973.

van der Ploeg, J.: "The Rotterdam Model: Renewal Without Gentrification," *Urban Innovation Abroad*, **6**:4, April, 1982.

CHAPTER 13

Babcock, Richard F.: "Houston: Unzoned, Unfettered, and Mostly Unrepentent," *Planning*, **48**:21–23, March, 1982.

Baker, Newman F.: *Legal Aspects of Zoning*, University of Chicago Press, Chicago, 1927.

Buder, Stanley: *Pullman*, Oxford University Press, New York, 1967.

Choldin, Harvey M.: "Retrospective Review Essay: Neighborhood Life and Urban Environment," *American Journal of Sociology*, vol. 48, September 1978.

Faltermayor, Edmund K.: *Redoing America*, Harper and Row, New York, 1968.

Gans, Herbert J. "Planning, Social: II, Regional and Urban Planning," in David Sills (ed.), *International Encyclopedia of the Social Sciences*, Crowell Collier and Macmillan, New York, 1968.

Glaab, Charles N., and A. Theodore Brown: *History of Urban America*, Macmillan, New York, 1967.

Hayden, Dolores: "Two Utopian Feminists and Their Campaigns for Kitchenless Houses," *Signs*, **4**:283–286, winter, 1978.

Heskin, Allan: "Crisis and Responses: A Historical View on Advocacy Planning," *Journal of the American Planning Association*, **46**:50–63, January, 1980.

Jacobs, Jane: *The Death and Life of Great American Cities*, Random House, New York, 1961.

Meyerson, Martin, and Edward C. Banfield: *Politics, Planning and the Public Interest*, The Free Press, Glencoe, Ill., 1955.

Mumford, Lewis: "Home Remedies for Urban Cancer," in Louis K. Loewenstein (ed.), *Urban Studies*, The Free Press, New York, 1971.

Newman, Oscar: *Defensible Space*, Macmillan, New York, 1972.

O'Harrow, Dennis: "Zoning: What's the Good of It?," in Wentworth Eldridge (ed.), *Taming Megalopolis*, Doubleday (Anchor), Garden City, New York, 1967.

Riis, Jacob: *The Children of the Poor*, Scribner, New York, 1892.

Robinson, C. M.: *City Planning*, Putnam, New York, 1916.

Tunnard, Christopher: *The City of Man*, Scribner, New York, 1953.

Zeisel, John: "Symbolic Meaning of Space and the Physical Dimension of Social Relations," in John Walton and Donald E. Carns (eds.), *Cities in Change*, Allyn and Bacon, Boston Press, Mass., 1973.

———: *Sociology and Architectural Design*, Russell Sage, New York, 1975.

CHAPTER 14

Beier, George J.: "Can Third World Cities Cope?," *Population Bulletin,* vol. 31, December, 1976.

Bendix, Richard: *Nation Building and Citizenship,* University of California Press, Berkeley, 1964, p 413.

Breese, Gerald: *Urbanization in Newly Developing Countries,* Prentice-Hall, Englewood Cliffs, N.J., 1966.

Castells, Manuel: *The Urban Question,* Alan Sheridan (trans.), MIT Press, Cambridge, Mass., 1977, pp. 41–43.

Chilcote, Ronald H.: "Dependency: A Critical Synthesis of the Literature," in Janet Abu-Lughod and Richard Hay, Jr., *Third World Urbanization,* Maaroufa Press, Chicago, 1977.

Davis, Kingsley, and Anna Casis: "Urbanization in Latin America," *The Milbank Memorial Fund Quarterly,* vol. 24, April 1946.

Davis, Kingsley, and Hilda Hertz Golden: "Urbanization and the Development of Pre-Industrial Areas," *Economic Development and Cultural Change,* vol. 3, October, 1954.

Firebaugh, Glenn: "Structural Determinants of Urbanization in Asia and Latin America, 1950–1970," *American Sociological Review,* vol. 44, April, 1979.

Gibbs, Jack P., and Walter T. Martin: "Urbanization, Technology, and the Division of Labor: International Patterns," *American Sociological Review,* vol. 27, 1962.

Gilbert, Alan, and Josef Gugler: *Cities, Poverty and Development: Urbanization in the Third World,* Oxford University Press, New York, 1982.

Gugler, Joseph: "Overurbanization Reconsidered," *Economic Development and Cultural Change,* **31:**173–189, October, 1982.

Hauser, Phillip, and Robert Gardiner: "Urban Future: Trends and Prospects," in Hauser et al., *Population and the Urban Future,* SUNY Press, Albany, 1982, p. 6.

Inkeles, Alex: "Making Men Modern: On The Causes and Consequences of Individual Change in Six Countries," *American Journal of Sociology,* vol. 75, September, 1969.

Jefferson, Mark: "The Law of the Primate Cities," *Geographical Review,* vol. 29, April, 1939.

Kentor, Jeffrey: "Structural Determinants of Peripheral Urbanization: The Effects of International Dependence," *American Sociological Review,* **46:**201–211, April, 1981.

Kilbridge, Maurice: "Some Generalizations on Urbanization in Developing Countries," *Urban Planning Policy Analysis and Administration,* Harvard University Press, Cambridge, Mass., 1976.

LaGreca, Anthony J.: "Urbanization: A Worldwide Perspective," in Kent P. Schwirian (ed.), *Contemporary Topics in Urban Sociology,* General Learning Press, Morristown, N.J., 1977.

Linn, Johannes F.: *Cities in the Developing World,* World Book Publications, Oxford University Press, New York, 1983.

Moore, Wilbert E.: *World Modernization: The Limits of Convergence,* Elsevier, New York, 1979.

Myrdal, Gunnar: *Asian Drama,* Pantheon, New York, vol. 2, 1968.

Palen, J. John: *Cities and the Future: The Urban Explosion,* United Nations, New York, 1985.

Payne, Geoffrey K.: *Urban Housing in the Third World,* Routledge and Kegan Paul, Boston, Mass., 1977.

Population Reference Bureau: "1985 World Population Data Sheet," Washington, D.C., 1985.

Portes, Alejandre: "On the Sociology of National Development: Theories and Issues," *American Journal of Sociology,* vol. 82, July, 1976.

Rostow, Walt: *The World Economy: History and Prospect,* University of Texas Press, Austin, 1978.

Sethuraman, S. V.: "The Informal Urban Sector in Developing Countries: Some Policy Implications," in Alfred De Sousal (ed.), *The Indian City,* South Asia Books, New Delhi, 1978.

"Some Regional Development Problems in Latin America Linked to Metropolitanization," *Economic Bulletin for Latin America,* United Nations, New York, vol. 17, 1972.

Sovani, N. V.: "The Analysis of Over-Urbanization," *Economic Development and Cultural Change,* vol. 12, January, 1964.

Thomlinson, Ralph: "Bangkok; Beau Ideal of a Primate City," *Population Review,* vol. 16, January-December, 1972.

United Nations: "World Population Prospects as Assessed in 1980," *Population Studies,* no. 78, United Nations, New York.

United Nations Population Division: "Trends and Prospects in the Population of Urban Agglomerations 1950–2000, as Assessed in 1973–75," United Nations, New York, November, 1975.

Urbanization in Asia and the Far East: Proceedings of the Joint UN/UNESCO Seminar held in Bangkok, August 8–18, 1956, UNESCO, Calcutta, 1957.

U.S. Bureau of the Census: "Illustrative Projections of World Population to the 21st Century," *Current Population Reports,* series P-23, Washington, D.C., 1979.

Wallerstein, Immanuel: *The Modern World System—Capitalist Agriculture and the European Economy in the Sixteenth Century,* Academic Press, New York, 1974.

Wellisz, Staneslaw H. "Economic Development and Urbanization," in Jacobson and Prakash (eds.), *Urbanization and National Development,* Sage, Beverly Hills, Cal., 1971.

CHAPTER 15

"Beijing Achieves Good Progress": *Beijing Review* **26:**10, April 18, 1983.

Beijing Review: **26:**24, January 1, 1983.

Bose, Nirmal Kumar: *Calcutta 1964: A Social Survey,* Lakuani, Bombay, 1968.

Breese, Gerald: *Urbanization in Newly Developing Countries,* Prentice-Hall, Englewood Cliffs, N.J., 1966.

Buck, David D.: *Urban Change in China,* University of Wisconsin Press, Madison, Wisc., 1978.

———: "New Municipal Plan for Beijing," *Urbanism Past and Present,* **8:**14, summer/fall, 1983.

Chen, Peter S. J. and Tai Ching Ling: *Social Ecology of Singapore,* Federal Publications, Singapore, 1977.

Chen, Pi-chao: "Overurbanization, Rustication of Urban-Educated Youths, and Politics of Rural Tranformation," *Comparative Politics,* April, 1972.

Cubell, Harold: *Urban Development and Employment: The Prospects for Calcutta,* Internation Labour Office, Geneva, 1974.

Delhi Development Authority: March, 1979.

De Souza, Alfred (ed.): *The Indian City,* South Asia Books, New Delhi, 1978.

Fryer, D. W.:"The Million City in Southeast Asia," *Geographical Review,* vol. 43, October, 1953.

Ginsburg, Norton S.: "The Great City in Southeast Asia," *American Journal of Sociology,* vol. 60, March, 1955.

————: "Urban Geography and 'Non-Western' Areas," in Philip M. Hauser and Leo F. Schnore, *The Study of Urbanization,* Wiley, New York, 1965.

Haberman, Clyde: "For Cramped Japan, 55 Million Bicycles Is a Glut," *New York Times,* March 4, 1985.

Hall, Peter: *World Cities,* McGraw-Hill, New York, 1977.

Hauser, Philip M., and Leo F. Schnore: *The Study of Urbanization,* Wiley, New York, 1965.

Hong Kong Standard, "Beijing to Be Turned into a Metropolis," August 3, 1983.

Lin, Thai-Ker: "Housing Policies and Life Style," paper presented at High Rise, High Density Housing Conference, Singapore, September 5–9, 1983.

MacLehose, Murray: "Modern Urban Development in Hong Kong," a paper by the Governor to the Commonwealth Society, Hong Kong, November 28, 1977.

Murphey, Rhoads: *Shanghai—Key to Modern China,* Harvard University Press, Cambridge, Mass., 1953.

————: "Urbanization in Asia," *Ekistics,* vol. 21, January, 1966.

————: "The Treaty Ports and China's Modernization," in Mark Elvin and G. William Skinner (eds.), *The Chinese City Between Two Worlds,* Stanford University Press, Stanford, Cal., 1974.

Poona Herald: February 23, 1979, p. 2.

Population Reference Bureau: "1980 World Population Data Sheet," Washington, D.C., 1979.

Ramachandran, P.: *Pavement Dwellers in Bombay City,* Tata Institute of Social Sciences, Bombay, 1972.

Reishauer, Edwin O.: *The Japanese,* Belknap Press of Harvard, Cambridge, Mass., 1978.

Sivaramakrishnan, K. C.: "The Slum Improvement Programme in Calcutta: The Role of the CMDA," in de Souza, *The Indian City,* South Asia Books, Columbia, Mo., 1978.

Tien, Hung-Mao: "Shanghai: China's Huge 'Model City'," *Milwaukee Journal,* December 16, 1973.

Tien H. Yuan: "China: Demographic Billionaire," *Population Bulletin,* Population Reference Bureau, Washington, D.C., April, 1983.

Vogel, Ezra: *Canton Under Communism,* Harvard University Press, Cambridge Mass., 1969.

CHAPTER 16

Abu-Lughod, Janet: "Migrant Adjustment to City Life: The Egyptian Case," *American Journal of Sociology,* vol. 67, July, 1961.

————: "Testing the Theory of Social Area Analysis: The Ecology of Cairo, Egypt," *American Sociological Review,* vol. 34, April, 1969.

————: "Culture, Modes of Production, and the Changing Nature of Cities in the Arab

World," in J. Agnew, J. Mercer, and D. Sopher (eds.), *The City in Cultural Context*, Allen and Unwin, Boston, 1984.

"Africa Near Economic Collapse," *New York Times*, July 21, 1985.

Bienen, Henry: *Tanzania: Party Transformation and Economic Development*, Princeton University Press, Princeton, N.J., 1970.

Boserup, Ester: *Women's Role in Economic Development*, St. Martin's Press, New York, 1979.

Costello, V. V.: *Urbanization in the Middle East*, Cambridge Univerity Press, Cambridge, Mass., 1977.

Dash, Leon: "African Leaders Have Seen the Future and It Looks Bleak," *Washington Post Service*, July 19, 1979.

Gbadamosi, Rasheed: "Growing Pains in Lagos," *Draper World Population Fund Report*, 1976.

Gernet, J.: "Notes sur les villes chinoises au moment de l'apogée islamique," in A. H. Hourani and S. M. Stern (eds.), *The Islamic City*, Bruno Cassirer, Oxford, 1970.

Goliber, Thomas J.: "Sub-Saharan Africa: Population Pressures and Development," *Population Bulletin*, **40**(1):3, 1985.

Gugler, Josef, and William G. Flanagan: *Urbanization and Social Change in West Africa*, Cambridge University Press, London, 1978.

Gutkind, Peter C: "The African Urban Milieu: A Force for Rapid Change," *Civilization*, vol. 12, 1982.

Hamdan, G: "Capitals of the New Africa," *Economic Geography*, vol. 40, July, 1984.

Hance, William A.: *Population Migration and Urbanization in Africa*, Columbia University Press, New York, 1970.

Hanna, William John, and Judith Lynne Hanna, *Urban Dynamics in Black Africa*, Aldine-Atherton, Chicago, 1971, p. 107.

Hassan S. S.: "The Ecology and Characteristics of Employed Females in Cairo City" a paper presented at the Seminar on Demographic Factors in Manpower Planning in Arab Countries held at the Cairo Demographic Center, November, 1971.

Hauser, Philip, and Robert Gardiner: "Urban Future: Trends and Prospects," in Philip Hauser et al. (eds.), *Population and the Urban Future*, State University of New York, Albany, 1982, p. 8.

Holzer, Lutz: "Urbanism in Southern Africa," *Geoforum*, vol. 4, 1970.

Issawi, Charles: *The Economic History of the Middle East*, University of Chicago Press, Chicago, 1966.

Lapidus, Ira M.: *Muslim Cities in the Later Middle Ages*, Harvard University Press, Cambridge, Mass., 1967.

————: *Middle Eastern Cities*, University of California Press, Berkeley, Cal., 1969.

Leslie, J. A. K.: *A Social Survey of Dar es Salaam*, Oxford University Press, Cambridge, Mass., 1967.

Levasseur, Alain A.: "The Modernization of Law in Africa with Particular Reference to Family Law in the Ivory Coast," in Philip Foster and Aristide R. Zolberg (eds.), *Ghana and the Ivory Coast: Perspectives on Modernization*, University of Chicago Press, Chicago, 1971.

Lowy, Michael J.: "Me Ko Court: The Impact of Urbanization on Conflict Resolution in a Ghanaian Town," in George Foster and Robert Kemper (eds.), *Anthropologists in Cities*, Little, Brown, Boston, Mass., 1974.

Merab, Docteru: *Impressions d'Ethiopie*, Leroux, Paris, vol. 2, 1921–1923.

Oloo, Dick (ed.): *Urbanization: Its Social Problems and Consequences,* Kenya National Council of Social Service, Nairobi, 1969.

Palen, J. John: "Urbanization and Migration in an Indigenous City: The Case of Addis Ababa," in Anthony Richmond and Donial Kubat (eds.), *International Migration,* Sage, London, 1976.

Pankhurst, Richard: "Notes on the Demographic History of Ethiopian Towns and Villages," *The Ethiopian Observer,* vol. 9, 1965.

Payne, Geoffrey K.: *Urban Housing in the Third World,* Routledge & Kegan Paul, Boston, 1977, p. 53.

Pons, V. G. as cited by A. L. Epstein: "Urbanization and Social Change in Africa," *Current Anthropology,* vol. 8, 1967.

Population Reference Bureau: *1985 World Population Data Sheet,* Washington, D.C., 1985.

————: "The Food Crisis in Sub-Saharan Africa," *Interchange,* **14:**2, March, 1985.

Robertson, H. N.: *South Africa,* Cambridge University Press, London, 1957.

Sjoberg, Gideon: "Cities in Developing and in Industrial Societies: A Cross-Cultural Analysis," in Philip M. Hauser and Leo F. Schnore, *The Study of Urbanization,* Wiley, New York, 1965.

Soja, Edward: "Spatial Inequality in Africa," *Comparative Urbanization Studies,* University of California School of Architecture and Urban Planning, Los Angeles, Cal., 1976.

Stern, S. M.: "The Constitution of the Islamic City," in A. H. Hourani and S. M. Stern (eds.), *Islamic City,* Bruno Cassirer, Oxford, 1970.

Taylor, D. R. F.: "The Concept of Invisible Towns and Spatial Organization in East Africa," *Comparative Urban Research,* vol. 5, 1978.

United Nations Food and Agriculture Organization, "Brief on the 1984–85 Cereal Import and Food Aid Needs for 21 African Countries," Rome, December 5, 1984.

Weber, Max: *The City,* D. Martindale and G. Neuwirth (trans.), The Free Press, New York, 1958.

World Bank, "Toward Development in Sub-Saharan Africa: A Joint Program of Action," Washington, D.C., 1984.

CHAPTER 17

Abrams, Charles: "Squatting and Squatters," in Janet Abu-Lughod and Richard Hay, Jr. (eds.), *Third World Urbanization,* Maaroufa Press, Chicago, 1977.

"Anatomy of a Third World City," *Urban Edge,* **8**(8):4, 1984.

Barraclough, Solon L.: "Rural Development and Employment Prospects in Latin America," in Arthur J. Field (ed.), *City and Country in the Third World,* Schenkman, Cambridge, Mass., 1970.

Estudia Económico par América Latina: ECLA, United Nations, 1960.

Gakenheimer, Ralph A.: "The Peruvian City of the Sixteenth Century," in Glenn H. Beyer (ed.), *The Urban Explosion in Latin America,* Cornell University Press, Ithaca, New York, 1967.

Hauser, Philip M. (ed.): *Urbanization in Latin America,* UNESCO, Paris, 1961.

Hauser, Philip M., and Robert W. Gardiner: "Urban Future: Trends and Prospects," in Philip Hauser et al. (eds.), *Population and the Urban Future,* State University of New York Press, 1982, p. 8.

Herberle, Rudolf: "Social Consequences of the Industrialization of Southern Cities," *Social Forces,* October, 1948.

Hordoy, Jorge E. *Urbanization in Latin America: Approaches and Issues,* Doubleday (Anchor), Garden City, New York, 1975.

Juppenalty, Morris: *Cities in Transformation: The Urban Squatter Problem in the Developing World,* University of Queensland Press, Australia, 1970.

Laquian, Aprodicio A.: "Issues and Instruments in Metropolitan Planning," in Philip M. Hauser, *Population and the Urban Future,* State University of New York Press, 1982, p. 68.

Lewis, Oscar: "The Culture of Poverty,"*Scientific American,* vol. 215, 1966.

Mangin, William P.: "Mental Health and Migration to Cities: A Peruvian Case," *The Annals of New York Academy of Sciences,* vol. 84, 1960.

Mohan, R., and N. Hartline: "The Poor of Bogotá: Who They Are, What They Do, and Where They Live," World Bank Staff Working Paper, no. 635, 1984.

Morris, James: *Cities,* Harcourt Brace Jovanovich, New York, 1964.

Perlman, Janice E.: *The Myth of Marginality,* University of California Press, Berkeley, Cal., 1976.

Population Reference Bureau: "1985 World Population Data Sheet," Washington, D.C., 1985.

Schnore, Leo F.: "On the Spatial Structure of Cities in Two Americas," in Philip Hauser and Leo Schnore (eds.), *The Study of Urbanization,* Wiley, New York, 1965.

Scobie, James: quoted in Glenn H. Beyer (ed.), *The Urban Explosion in Latin America,* Cornell University Press, Ithaca, New York, 1967.

Shook, Edwin M., and Tatiana Proskouriakoff: "Settlement Patterns in Meso-America and the Sequency in the Guatemalan Highlands," in Gordon R. Willey (ed.), *Prehistoric Settlement Patterns in the New World,* Wenner-Gren Foundation for Anthropological Research, New York, 1956.

Sjoberg, Gideon: *The Preindustrial City: Past and Present,* The Free Press, Glencoe, Ill., 1960.

Smith, T. Lynn: "The Changing Functions of Latin American Cities," *The Americans,* vol. 25, July, 1968.

"Some Regional Development Problems in Latin America Linked to Metropolitanization," *Economic Bulletin for Latin America,* United Nations, New York, 1972.

St. Clair, David (trans.): *Child of the Dark: The Diary of Carolina Mariá De Jesús,* E. P. Dutton, New York, 1962.

Theodorson, George A. (ed.): *Studies in Human Ecology,* Row Peterson, Evanston, Ill., 1961.

Turner, John F. C.: "Squatter Settlements in Developing Countries," in Daniel P. Moynihan (ed.), *Toward a National Urban Policy,* Basic Books, New York, 1970.

CHAPTER 18

Dantzig, George B., and Thomas L. Saatz: *Compact City: A Plan for a Liveable Urban Environment,* W. H. Freeman, San Francisco, 1973.

Doxiadis, C. A.: *Ekistics,* Hutchinson, London, 1968.

Greer, Ann L.: "Health Care Policy: Disillusion and Confusion," in J. Blair and D. Nachmias (eds.), *Urban Policies in Transition,* Sage, Beverly Hills, Cal., 1979.

Greer, Scott: *The Urbane View,* Oxford University Press, New York, 1972.

Jacobs, Jane: *The Death and Life of Great American Cities,* Vintage-Random House, New York, 1961.

Kasarda, John D.: "The Implications of Contemporary Redistribution Trends for National Urban Policy," *Social Science Quarterly,* **69:**373–400, 1980.

Le Corbusier: *The Radiant City,* Grossman-Orion, New York, 1967.

Machiavelli, Niccolo: *The Prince,* J. M. Dent, London, 1958.

Palen, J. John, and Daniel M. Johnson: "Urbanization and Health Status," in Ann L. Greer and Scott Greer (eds.), *Cities and Sickness,* Sage Publications, Beverly Hills, Cal., 1983, pp. 25–59.

Schmandt, Henry J.: "Solutions for the City as a Social Crisis," in J. John Palen and Karl H. Flaming (eds.), *Urban America,* Holt, Rinehart and Winston, New York, 1972.

Seeley, John R.: "Remaking the Urban Scene: New Youth in an Old Environment," *Daedalus,* vol. 97, 1968.

Soleri, Paolo: *Arcology, The City in the Image of Man,* MIT Press, Cambridge, Mass., 1969.

Suttles, Gerald D.: "Changing Priorities for the Urban Heartland," in J. John Palen (ed.), *City Scenes: Problems and Prospects,* Little, Brown, Boston, 1981.

Tilly, Charles: "Migration to American Cities," in Daniel P. Moynihan (ed.), *Toward a National Urban Policy,* Basic Books, New York, 1970.

U.S. Bureau of the Census: "Selected Characteristics of Travel to Work in 20 Metropolitan Areas, 1976," *Current Population Reports,* series P-23, Washington, D.C., 1978.

Vining, Daniel R. et al.: "Population Dispersal from Core Regions: A Description and Tentative Explanation of Patterns in 21 Countries," in Donald A. Hicks and Norman J. Glickman (eds.), *Transition to the 21st Century,* JAI Press, Greenwich, Conn., 1983.

Von Eckardt, Wolf: "Urban Design," in Daniel P. Moynihan (ed.), *Toward a National Urban Policy,* Basic Books, New York, 1970.

Webber, Melvin W.: "The Post-City Age," *Daedalus,* vol. 97, 1968.

Wright, Frank Lloyd: *The Living City,* Mentor-Horizon, New York, 1958.

INDEXES

NAME INDEX

SUBJECT INDEX